Brian Howard
Portrait of a Failure

Brian Howard
Portrait of a Failure

Edited by Marie-Jaqueline Lancaster
with an Introduction by D. J. Taylor

TIMEWELL PRESS

First published in the UK in 2005 by
Timewell Press Limited
10 Porchester Terrace, London W2 3TL

A catalogue record for this title is available from the
British Library.

ISBN 1 85725 211 X

Typeset by TW Typesetting, Plymouth, Devon
Printed and bound in the UK by Biddles Ltd, King's Lynn

Contents

Illustrations

Foreword

by Marie-Jaqueline Lancaster

This note is for the many people whose lives have been more tranquil, but the poorer, for never having known Brian Howard. He was a man of great attraction to both men and women, of considerable talents, who grew up with the usual 'advantages', that euphemistic term for a bullying father, spoiling mother, the rigours of public school life, and his family's conviction that he was going to be a *great* man. But instead of being the expected success, aesthetically or commercially, he turned into a charismatic failure. He was an intractable homosexual, became an alcoholic, later took to drugs, and finally committed suicide. Simultaneously he was a prolific minor poet with a few really fine poems to his name; an admired literary critic; and an impassioned anti-Nazi from the earliest days. He invites comparison with the very best and then somehow fails the test of equality. He was famous for his extempore mastery of words, and it is his unique tone of voice, with his inimitable turn of phrase, that is most elusive to catch in print. He was not exactly a catalyst, more a cross-fertiliser of persons against whom he loved to polish his wit and malice until he set off sparks, sometimes of pleasure—more often than not of pain.

He was tall, dark and handsome, mad, bad, and dangerous to know. He was everything the young are warned against, and yet he was immeasurably kind and loyal to his few great friends, devoted—on the face of it—to his mother, regretful in later life of his estrangement from his father, and above all *true to himself.* He had pity and compassion for all human suffering, he loved the beauties of nature, literature and the arts, and a certain type of young man ... He had a magic quality, perhaps delicately striated in black more than lines of innocent white, a built-in Machiavellian streak; quasi-sadistic mentally, quasi-masochistic physically. His lethal weapons were words, but in defeat he preferred a knock-out punch for himself.

'He was born to success. It was written on his forehead. He assumed it himself, and so did everyone else. Good looks, and a famous name ...' That was Malcolm Muggeridge on Randolph Churchill, but it could have been about Brian.[1] 'Worldly success has no surprises, and supreme success is always supremely commonplace ... Failure, on the other hand, is incalculable, and therefore entertaining,' Mr. Muggeridge continued. Why, then, did Brian court failure? He would have agreed with the 'commonplace' gibe, and he was certainly 'entertaining', but *despite* not *because* of his failure. He had neither the impetus of desire to make money, nor a great urge to walk alone; he was cocooned by misplaced benevolence (twisted into family malevolence), seemingly unable to break through the net, and paralysed by his Holy Grail of Absolute Integrity.

---

[1] In Brian Howard's world in the early 'twenties his father's assumed choice of surname was taken to infer some claim to kinship with the Duke, Earls or Barons whose family name was Howard.

This precluded working to order, 'It is because I am obsessed, night and day, by images of perfection, that I cannot earn' (1931). To give birth to the second best would have been the ultimate betrayal of self.

Admittedly he was self-obsessed, self-deluding, self-analysing (in his unpublished writing) to the point of no return, but who, subconsciously at least, is not? Day after day, year after year, he used his conscience in the Attlee-approved way, as a persistently 'still, small voice rather than a loud-speaker', but he wrote rather than spoke out. At the age of forty-five he was consumed by self-awareness, 'And the dreadful guilt that walks quietly behind one, through the day, into the dream, and back into the day, like some huge, friendly dog. This dog is the gift that life gives to those who are selfish, know it and hate it.'

But to whom goes the blame for a selfish child? Is he born, or made, and should the son's sins be attributed—at least in part—to the parents? Reared in an Anglo-American social-Bohemian atmosphere in the early 1920s, he became a precocious poet-aesthete at Eton, and went on to shock the older generations first as a Bright Young People leader, and later as an unwelcome political doomster.

He fell in love, romantically, with Daphne Vivian in the mid-twenties, but had marriage been remotely encouraged it is most unlikely that he would have buckled down to earning the sort of income, let alone living the kind of life, required for that estate. Unlike most normal young men he did not consider that earning money could almost be turned into a pleasurable necessity heralding the joys of wife and family to come.

There is no doubt he became hugely promiscuous, and remained so for several years, but this must be accepted as part of the homosexual context, the eternal chase of fresh conquests being irresistible. He did not feel himself to be practising immorality, but to be extending the frontiers of morality, and at the same time fighting those who equated homosexuality with free love and libertinage. (That much of his time *was* taken up with free love and libertinage somewhat weakens his case, but fundamentally he was at one with the Quakers in striving towards a higher standard of *loving*.)

Brian's character was so highly overlaid with sensitive, sensuous and sensual emotions that it is small wonder he never got down to real work. Even Dylan Thomas, having more to cope with in life than Brian was ever to have, knew that it was *work* that counted, 'genius so often being an infinite capacity for "aching pains" '. For a decade or more, up till 1940, Brian lived mainly abroad, sight-seeing, toying with drugs, drinking to excess, gastronomising (however narrowly), devouring books, surveying the *jeunesse dorée* as well as keeping a penniless German boy friend (permanently devoid of occupation through lack of work permits, let alone natural capacity), yet he still hoped, and was expected, to produce a literary opus on the side.

While 'Muzzy' held the purse-strings, enforcing her 'Baba' to beg (successfully, nevertheless) for money week in, week out, the need to work was faint indeed. The sheer volume of his letters to her during his lifetime is overwhelming. She was his sounding board, for better or for worse. Descriptive vignettes abound, interspersed with the threnetic litany of requests for money already spent in anticipation, so that the supply and demand merge into a meretricious circle.

Throughout his years of waste, especially in the 'thirties, he harped on his lack of identity, being still in search of his unknown Grandfather Gassaway as late as 1936. But had he known the back roots that might or might not have contributed to his creative genius, plus or minus his latent addictions, would it really have helped? He suffered from his belief in the divine right of self-acclaimed geniuses to live—and be let live—without benefit from paid labours. 'Failure has its successes,' he wrote with alcoholic bravado to his mother in 1937, 'you don't see them. By this, I mean myself.'

The poet, Wystan Auden, in declining to contribute his reminiscences gives the sad, finishing touch to this portrait foreword: 'I was extremely fond of Brian and also full of compassion for him because he was, inside, I think the most desperately unhappy person I have ever known. I would be completely incapable of writing about him because, particularly during the last years, there is so little factually to *describe* except the paranoid scenes, so that readers who never met him would see that he was tiresome (which he often was) but not that he was lovable.'

So many questions are posed and attitudes attacked, but who can supply the answers? I can but leave to each and every reader his own interpretation.

Introduction

By D. J. Taylor

> You can't just go and *have* children, you know, and then sit back and watch
> them become Chancellors and members of White's. Sometimes they turn
> out odd . . .
>
> Brian Howard—letter to his mother

Not long before his death, in the spring of 1966, Evelyn Waugh could be found
doubtfully enquiring of Nancy Mitford if she knew of 'a Mrs Lancaster, who
gives you as reference in soliciting help in writing a treatise on Brian Howard'.
Intrigued by the project ('I can't believe he will be subject of many biographies'),
Waugh was also anxious that a man with whom he had enjoyed deeply equivocal
relations should be given his due. 'It would be a pity' he pronounced, 'if some
hack who didn't know him or see his point should take him in hand.' Calmed
by his friend's assurances, Waugh suggested to Mrs Lancaster that she make use
of the brief details supplied in his own recently published autobiography. *Portrait
of a Failure*, first published in 1968, and a compendium by many hands rather
than a treatise, consequently reproduces *A Little Learning*'s lapidary judgment: 'At
the age of nineteen he had dash and insolence, a gift of invective and repartee
far more brilliant than Robert's [Byron] . . . Mad, bad and dangerous to know.'

Brian Howard's was a chaotic, frustrating and in the end, for all its
high-octane attachments, rather solitary life. Lived out for the most part in that
exotic never-never land where the Ritz Bar meets the out-of-season continental
resort, it was also hedged about with a disappointment of which its subject
remained defiantly aware. Launched into the world as a precocious teenage poet,
his only lasting achievement was the co-editorship of a glorified school
magazine. Expected, not least by himself, to write novels that would out-Firbank
Firbank in their orchidaceous subtleties, he ended up as tragic-comic turn in
works by other people. The success was eternally deferred, the glory all
second-hand, and the piece of writing that most accurately perpetuates his
memory is a pastiche by Cyril Connolly ('Where Engels Fears to Tread') that,
however indulgent its tone, holds nearly everything he did or believed in up to
ridicule.

At the heart of this thirty-year chronicle of waste and dereliction lay what his
Eton contemporary Anthony Powell would certainly have diagnosed as a
question of upbringing. He was born in 1905, into an almost Jamesian world of
mid-Atlantic shades and splendours. Howard senior was a freewheeling
international art-dealer who enjoyed setting his cap at the famous people who
patronised his exhibitions. His mother Lura, the daughter of a US Civil War
veteran, apparently discovered the existence of 'the other woman' mid-way
through her honeymoon. There was plenty of money—at one stage the Howards
maintained an establishment in Bryanston Square and a sixteen bedroom country

house in Sussex—and some exalted family connections (Brian's godparents included Prince Christian of Schleswig Holstein and George Meredith), but also a sense of something having gone wrong, of dramatic frets and fractures beneath the surface, disagreeable roots imperfectly covered up. Even the family surname was a fraud. The original patronym turned out to be 'Gassaway', and one of the last poems Howard ever published was an evocation of his lost American grandfather.

To obscure origins and Francis Howard's intermittently roving eye could be added the problem of Brian himself. Ever perceptive where his own inadequacies were concerned, he defined his claustrophobic relationship with Lura Howard as 'an absolutely *boringly* classical text book case—sissy son, Oedipus and everything'. Exasperated by his son's homosexuality, Howard senior eventually ordered his wife to choose between the two of them. Unhappily, her choice of Brian made things worse. Doting, obstinate about money, at times practically vampiric in her attentions, Lura still managed to convey a faint impression that her real affection lay elsewhere. As well as leaving Brian, as one friend put it, 'on the outside of his own family', these maternal shacklings also drove him into a kind of emotional cul-de-sac. Deep into middle age, he noted shrewdly that 'If I *make a success* I leave her. If I continue as a failure, I naturally remain.'

None of this, though, gives a proper idea of the person Brian Howard was, the kind of career he led, or failed to lead, and the curious mixture of frivolity and idealism that characterised his rackety progress through life. At Eton he combined a jaw-dropping precocity in the arts ('Who is this Proust? Huxley was talking about him. Perhaps I ought to read him') with a complete determination to please himself. 'It has seldom been my lot, in many years of work amongst boys, to come upon one so entirely self-centred and egotistical' a housemaster wrote anxiously back to Bryanston Square; 'as far as his moral nature is concerned I cannot find what standards he has other than those of pure selfishness.' Still in sight of his sixteenth birthday, he had a poem accepted by Orage's *New Age* and was 'discovered' by Edith Sitwell ('I see more remarkable talent and promise in your work than of any other poet under twenty with the exception of my brother Sacheverell') who published his 'Barouches Noires', a ninety-ish fantasia about drowned lovers, in *Wheels*.

Not everyone was convinced by the displays of intellectual fireworks. Anthony Powell, among several early detractors, 'never liked him, nor thought, even at Eton, that he had a vestige of real talent in any of the arts. All he seemed to me interested in was self-advertisement and forms of exhibitionism that brought him into disrepute.' It is the eternal anti-dandy complaint about showing off, but even Powell had to admit that without Howard's administrative zeal the *Eton Candle*, co-edited with Harold Acton, would have perished on the drawing-board. Published in the spring of 1922, priced half a crown, dedicated to 'the illustrious memory of Algernon Charles Swinburne' and, with the exception of an Old Etonian supplement, mostly written by the editors, the *Candle* whipped up a terrific storm, despite the refusal of the Poet Laureate, Robert Bridges, to contribute. 'Amazing how some people will throw away their opportunities, isn't it?' Howard remarked to Acton on receiving the letter.

His own contributions included 'The New Poetry', a spirited defence of Eliot-era *vers libre,* and a poetic salute to 'The Young Writers and Artists Killed in the War'. Already, though, there were indications that his talent, if that was what it was, had passed its sell-by date. Having scraped into Oxford ('a sort of passionate party all the time—one rushes from one amusement to another until all one's sense of proportion and self-control gradually vanishes ...') where harder-headed contemporaries like Acton were already forging careers for themselves, he spent his time in well-bred socialising. Maurice Bowra remembered a dinner party of such blue-blooded exclusivity that Howard was able to address the throng—a meaningful glance at Bowra, who sat beside him—as 'My lords and gentleman.' Coming down from the university without a degree, he progressed by easy stages into the role of impresario to the party-going Bright Young People of the late 1920s. As 'Johnnie Hoop' he wanders through *Vile Bodies,* devising elaborate costumes for fancy-dress balls and designing outsize party invitations: 'These had two columns of close print: in one was a list of all the things Johnnie hated, and in the other all the things he thought he liked. Most of the parties which Miss Mouse financed had invitations written by Johnnie Hoop.'

The cameo appearances in Waugh's novels continued for another twenty years: as late as 1950 a letter sped forth from Piers Court, Stinchcombe, to assure Nancy Mitford that the Wandering Jew in *Helena* was 'B. Howard again'. Meanwhile, there were livings to be earned, or rather to be contemplated and held fastidiously at bay. 'It is no *good* trying to make me a journalist' Lura Howard was briskly informed in a letter of 1930, 'I would rather kill myself'. If it performs no other function, *Portrait of a Failure* offers a cautionary tale from twentieth-century literature's crowded ante-room, a spectacular warning to every promising young man or woman who has ever gazed out of a college window and thought that it might be nice to 'write'. Howard's post-Oxford papers fairly seethe with phantom projects: a symposium entitled *Values,* to be co-edited with Robert Byron and containing, among other highlights, a drawing by Waugh of 'God', consisting entirely of abstract form 'yet in some measure coherent and having perhaps some slight relation to the Revelations of St John the Divine'; an anthology of new poetry for Leonard Woolf at the Hogarth Press; a collaboration with Auden; a novel to be written at a rate of four thousand words a day 'until it is done'. In the end the 'genius' that its possessor 'preferred to let mature slowly' realised only a solitary collection of verse, *God Save The King* (1931), privately printed by his friend Nancy Cunard, a few contributions to Connolly's *Horizon* and a sheaf of *New Statesman* reviews.

By this time, in any case, the stream of personal destiny had been muddied by politics. According to Howard's account the laughter which greeted an incautious remark about Hitler, made at a lunch-party of Thomas Mann's in Munich in 1931, persuaded him to study the German situation. These were early days for the pansy pinks of Orwell's demonising (although Orwell seems never to have met Howard in the flesh, there are good grounds for suspecting that he knew all about him.) Of all the twenties aesthetes who 'went Left' in the era of Jarrow, Spain and re-armament, he was, if not the first, then certainly one of the noisiest: interviewing the Nazi press chief Dr Hanfstaengl (Hitler eluded him, after a quarrel with the potential conduit, Unity Mitford), helping Nancy Cunard to assemble her combative pamphlet *Writers Take Sides on Spain* and contributing one of his best poems, 'For Those With Investments in Spain 1937' to the series *Les Poètes du monde defendent le peuple espagnol.*

This transition from Bright Young Person to Serious Left Wing Figure required a degree of harmonisation that—see Connolly again—was occasionally rather beyond him. Some of the juxtapositions of his diary jottings from Sanary in the South of France where he lingered in 1939 trying to extricate his German boyfriend Toni from the displaced persons camps must have seemed incongruous even to their author (*24th August—war almost inevitable; 25th August—end of everything for us; 31st August—back from party 3.30 A.M.*) There was a similar moment in the early part of the war when, sequestered with his MI5 colleague Guy Burgess in a Soho nightclub, loud hammerings on the door advertised a police raid. Asked for his name and address, Howard produced the legendary reply: 'I live in Mayfair. No doubt you come from some dreary suburb.' Discharged from the secret services, apparently for an inability to keep his mouth shut, he volunteered—quixotically for a man of thirty-seven in poor health—for the RAF, eventually coming to rest as a clerk in the Public Relations department at Bomber Command.

The war supplied characteristic glimpses of Howard, as it were, in action: weaving alcoholically towards a group of army officers in the Gargoyle Club just after Dunkirk with a murmur of 'Hmm. Members of a rather unsuccessful profession, my dears', bringing in the elevenses tray at Bomber Command with a cry of 'Delicious Teazle!', getting his mother to intercede with the squadron leader over a uniform left behind in a pub toilet. Thereafter the path ran steadily downhill: post-war wanderings in Europe with Toni's successor Sam; TB cures; an addiction to, amongst other narcotics, synthetic morphine. Of his 'memoirs', confidently announced in a letter to Connolly, there was, predictably, no sign. The domestic stability promised by Lura's purchase of a house for the three of them to share near Nice was quickly cancelled out by Sam's accidental death in early January 1958. Four days later, Howard killed himself. He was fifty-two.

The obituarists waxed surprisingly lyrical. 'It was part of Brian's tragedy that he should have been so like Baudelaire' (Connolly); 'a kind of ferocity of elegance that belonged to the romantic era of a century before our own' (Waugh); 'a dangerous, brilliant and seminal nuisance' (V. S. Pritchett). The temptation to write off the extraordinary *reclame* that Howard possessed among his contemporaries as a kind of gentlemanly plot got up by a band of literary-minded Old Etonians is sometimes rather difficult to resist. 'Today the gentlemen are on the defensive, but there are still reasons for being miffed about (to take a small instance) the seriousness with which a book about the talentless Brian Howard, talented perhaps but amusing, and *one of us*, was recently treated' Julian Symons protested, not long after *Portrait of a Failure*'s appearance. To a Symons or a John Carey, whose shrieks of rage over his exploits may be easily imagined, the Howard cult is simply an exercise in bogus values, the kind of seigneurial tampering with literature that Q. D. Leavis complained about in her review of *Enemies of Promise*: 'Those who get the jobs are the most fashionable boys in the school, or those with feline charm, or a sensual mouth and long eyelashes'—a complaint made yet more pointed by the fact that Mrs Leavis is silently reproducing Connolly's description of Howard in his Etonian pomp.

As for salvaging anything from Howard's microscopic *œuvre*, there is hardly anything to salvage; although a poem like 'Gone to Report' published in the May 1940 number of *Horizon* ('For twenty-one years he remained, faithful and lounging/There, under the last tree, at the end of the charming evening street . . . And he wasn't at all what he said he was. Mr Pleasure') could hold down a place in any war-era verse anthology. The terrible fascination of *Portrait of a Failure,* on the other hand, lies in what *didn't* get written; the creative stasis that overwhelmed each new idea and good intention, and the bitter determinism that ran beneath it. For all the surface deceptions ('Fortunately I am the kind of writer who will make money') Howard knew very well the kind of life he was leading, where he would end up, what would come of it all. There is, consequently, something altogether dreadful about the oscillations of his letters to his mother, the flights of self-delusion ('When my book is finished and when I begin to make a little . . . *Success will come* . . . I shall marry some day . . .') forever brought to ground by an awareness of what really lies ahead ('I'm nearly thirty and you've done just about all anyone could . . . I love you so much and I am such a frightful disappointment to you . . . Will has left me, and the capacity truthfully to imagine—vision—is leaving. I consider myself damned'). In strict literary terms, Howard is an example of a rather typical twentieth-century phenomenon, the aesthete whose political career is fatally compromised by a reluctance to discard social and artistic baggage picked up along the way. All this, though, is to ignore the human cost of a life lived out of suitcases, where each morning's post brings either a bill or a letter from one's mother, and from beneath the canopy of the writing desk, undeflowered sheets of paper stare up in permanent reproach.

1905–1927
Seeds of Promise

1. In search of a Grandfather

'I was born at Winkworth, Hascombe, Surrey in 1905 and have been brought up in England as an Englishman, although by blood I am an American, my father coming from Washington D.C. and my mother from Louisville, Kentucky.

'My father, Francis Gassaway Howard, was founder, with Whistler, of the International Society of Sculptors, Painters and Gravers. My mother is Lura Chess, daughter of William Chess of Louisville, Kentucky. He was a Captain of Artillery on the Northern side during the Civil War, and was one of the most admirable men I have ever known.

'My memories of the United States, from childhood visits, are very few but very vivid. I remember the peculiar scent of a certain little red grape my grandfather grew on his estate over the Ohio—the fox grape, I think—and his rows of giant, tasselled corn. The taste of spearmint gum, of wintergreen, of a breakfast food called "Force", and of certain pink and white striped sweets like miniature barbers' poles are all most nostalgic, also. That part of the country outside Louisville where my grandfather lived remains with me as a sort of heaven, with golden escarpments reaching up to vast white-marble clouds and gentian-blue skies. I still catch something of it in the illustrations of that terrible artist whom I love so much, Maxfield Parrish.

'Words first struck me, so to speak, because of George Moore, who used to come to tea with us in London. At the age of about six I was playing with my guinea-pig under the piano when he said that he thought our housemaid looked like a "wizened tangerine". He noted my laughter, and said that henceforth words would fascinate me. He was right.

'I treasure, greatly, the memory of my paternal grandmother, Elizabeth Paschal, of Houston, Texas, who became Mrs. T. P. O'Connor. He, "Tay Pay", was at one time what was called the "Father of the House of Commons". The memory of my godfather, George Meredith, I treasure not at all. His letters of advice to my mother as to how to bring me up were supercilious and sadistic.

'About poetry, I must at once confess that I began writing it far too soon, was too successful—undeservedly—and stopped writing it too soon, too. At fourteen, I read an appalling poem about crows wheeling above the Thames to my English literature master at Eton, who was Aldous Huxley. It is painful to think of how I must have bored him. In return, he gave me such encouragement as I have never forgotten, and implanted in me the impulse to become a writer. I find that as regards poetry, help, inspiration, influences etc., have come much more from living people than authors I have read, or the classics.

'At sixteen, when still at Eton, I edited, with the help of Harold Acton, a magazine, the *Eton Candle*, which was unusual in that a number of established writers, old Etonians, contributed to it, such as the Sitwell brothers, Maurice Baring, Aldous Huxley etc. Gosse gave me an unpublished Swinburne poem for it. I myself wrote the opening article which was the rashest possible paean of praise for free verse and the Imagists, Amy Lowell, Pound etc., and occupied pages with imitations of them by myself. Eton was an extraordinary school. I remember being allowed, in the class for poetry recitation, to learn and recite my own work. On one occasion a large section of my poem, which was about a Victorian summer-house in the rain, consisted of the word "Plop!", repeated slowly, with pauses.[1] No other school would have stood such a thing for a moment.

'Edith Sitwell came down to lecture at my invitation, and encouraged me more than anyone. I had already had poems printed by Orage in the *New Age*, the leading *avant-garde* weekly of the early 'twenties, and she included another in her anthology *Wheels* (1921) which was the great poetic excitement of the day. She was also extremely kind about me in an article and continued to encourage my literary efforts at Oxford, and in London. Alas, this rather turned my head, and my poems became increasingly affected, cerebral, self-confident and poor.

'At Oxford I wasted my time almost completely. I hunted (which terrified me), gave luncheons for peers; wrote very badly; neglected my work; failed to take a degree, and sowed the seeds of what became, till quite lately, a lifetime's laziness.

'Later, in London, the friendship of Edward Gathorne-Hardy made me realise that, in fact, I hardly understood English literature at all. In 1930 I read a poem by Tennyson about a swan, and quite suddenly I began to grow up, from a literary standpoint. This did not prevent my first book of poems, called ironically *God Save the King*[2] and published in Paris by Nancy Cunard in 1931, from being of little consequence. (There are not many of them I should care to re-print now.) In the same year I began reviewing for the *New Statesman* and went to Bavaria. There I became influenced by the (Thomas) Mann family's loathing of Hitler, and I devoted myself to writing anti-Hitler articles in the English press. I had the gratification of being personally threatened with reprisals by the German Embassy in London but politics were not my vocation. I managed to get inside the Brown House, where I had a polite quarrel with Hanfstaengl, Hitler's press chief, but I am grateful, today, that Miss Unity Mitford prevented my meeting Hitler himself. I should certainly have tried to convert him to a more reasonable point of view. How absurd that seems, now. And how unwise, in every way, it would have been!

'I continued to go to Bavaria every summer, until 1933, by which time most of my German friends had left for Austria, or America. When the Anschluss put an end to my visits to Austria I began going to the South of France. I was in Sanary in September 1939, and decided to stay on in order to be of assistance to certain anti-Nazi Germans whom the French had put in concentration camps. Shortly afterwards, in June 1940, I decided to leave myself . . .'

Thus Brian opens his own biography with an unbiased resumé written some time after the war, probably as background information for *Harper's*, the American magazine that published some of his poetry.

---

[1] Published in the *Eton Candle* as *Grotesque—Mabelle of the waving hands.*
[2] Published as *First Poems*, by the Hours Press, 1930–1931.

Brian was an only son, born to American parents, destined to be neither wholly British nor all American, and to live most of his life in Europe. To understand him he must be seen in the context of his family background, always proud, somewhat grand in a rich, Southern States American sense, and slightly obscure on his father's side. He was at heart all American, which would explain his 'snobbishness' in early life and his unnecessarily aggressive 'English' behaviour at other times. That he had Jewish blood was an accepted fact. He frequently told friends that he was partly Jewish, and everyone assumed that this came through his unknown paternal grandfather whose surname was reputedly Gassaway—not Howard. It was only when this book was nearly completed that I heard from Brian's surviving first cousin (on his mother's side) that she had just discovered her great grandfather's name to have been Chesser, not Chess, so that it could be the Jewish strain came from that side, or again from Brian's paternal grandmother's Paschal or Duval Huguenot ancestors, but the well-documented Duval family history only shows one cousin to have married a French Jewess.

All through his life until after the 1939–1945 war Brian worried and wondered about this grandfather Gassaway/Howard. In the 'thirties he wrote to his mother: 'I may be English, but pretty soon someone really must confide in me about my paternal grandfather ... Heaven knows who Daddy *really* is, still less his father ... he triumphed over me, come to think of it, quite successfully from the day I was born, in presenting me with an obviously false and pretentious name—not even adding the slight support of deed of poll.'

It was a rough typescript of a poem (written in 1948) that showed Brian had at last identified him to some degree. This poem was about his *two* grandfathers, the Artillery Captain (Chess), and the young Washington poet, and in it he quoted some verse by the latter called *The Dandy Fifth*.

There was a minor Civil War poet called Frank H. Gassaway, and according to Brian's father's entry in *Who's Who* this Gassaway parent (referred to as Francis Gassaway *Howard*) claimed Benjamin Franklin as great grandfather. Professor Labaree, in charge of the monumental volumes on *The Papers of Benjamin Franklin* at Yale University Library, can find no trace of any connection, however indirect, between a Gassaway or a Howard—and Benjamin Franklin. The mystery is not helped by finding that Brian's grandmother, although ostensibly a young widow called Elizabeth *Howard*, signed the register at her (officially second) marriage, to T. P. O'Connor, as 'Elizabeth Paschal *Wright*—a widow'. Why no mention of Gassaway or Howard at this most legal of moments? And as for Wright, that name has never appeared in any other papers or letters of family references that I have seen, nor does it substantiate the Franklin connection.

'Bessie' O'Connor, as his grandmother was best known in London, was born in Texas, the daughter of a famous divorce lawyer, later Supreme Court Justice, George W. Paschal, but she was proud of her Virginian ancestors on her mother's side, the Duvals, who originally came from Rouen. She could also claim kinship with George Washington, through her great grandmother Ann Duval, *née* Pope, who shared a grandmother with Washington. This Ann Duval's son, William Pope Duval, was the inspiration for 'Ralph Ringwood' in Washington

Irving's *Wolfert's Roost*. There were Claibornes and Christians in the Duval family tree as well as Howards, so if fanciful it is not altogether surprising to find that her grandson was christened Brian Christian de Claiborne Howard. Strength to this was added by one of his godfathers being Prince Christian of Schleswig-Holstein, described by Bessie O'Connor in her autobiography[3] as, 'one's ideal of a Prince, always courteous, always kind, perfectly simple and unassuming—a really grand old gentleman'; the other being the unloved George Meredith.

Brian's father, Francis (known as Toodie, later Tudie), was born on New Year's Day 1874, within a year or so of his parent's marriage, and Bessie adored him right from the start. But her husband soon deserted her and she had to earn her own living in order to support their young son. Having apparently made an impression on the then President of the United States, General Grant, at a White House reception, she asked him to give her employment. He did not let her down, and she was allowed to help sort and index War Office archives from her home, as he considered her too young to go to an office! She then became quite a successful staff reporter on the *New York World*, and later a publisher's reader for Harper's.

According to a Duval family tree, penned in 1927, Elizabeth ('Betty') Paschal first married a Frank Harrison *Gassaway*, their child being Francis Howard *Gassaway* (Tudie), and his child being noted as 'Brian Howard' *Gassaway*. So it seems that in America as late as 1927 Brian's rightful surname was considered to be Gassaway. There is, however, a valid explanation for this use of Howard as a surname, for after her first marriage to 'Gassaway, of the Virginia family' was dissolved Brian's grandmother got attached to a young army officer 'of fine record'—named Howard—who unfortunately shot himself within a year of their marriage. She told her cousin, Helen Beall,[4] that she had not been married three months before she realised he was insane. It was because of this connection that her young son (Brian's father) came to be known as Tudie *Howard*, not Gassaway.

To confuse the issue even more, Bessie O'Connor published a novel in 1913 called *Little Thank You*.[5] It was dedicated to her grandson, 'My Own Little Thank You—Brian Howard', and the story was obviously based on her life with young Tudie in America (even repeating some episodes included in her earlier autobiography), but the child had been merged into her grandson, Brian.

Her meeting with T. P. O'Connor was characteristically romantic. She had been very ill with peritonitis in America and after many weeks in bed went to Ireland for a convalescent vacation, and thence to London for a few days in the winter of 1884–1885. The American Vice-Consul offered to take her to the House of Commons one evening to meet Justin M'Carthy, to whom she had a letter of introduction. He had left by the time they got there but a policeman on duty, seeing how disappointed she was, suggested that Mr. T. P. O'Connor (then Liberal M.P. for Scotland Division, Liverpool) 'who was always most polite to Americans' might do the honours instead. T. P. was indeed enchanted to show this pretty young American round.

---

[3] *I Myself*, published by Methuen, 1910.
[4] Later Mrs. David Houston, from whose unpublished memoirs I have drawn.
[5] Published by Putnam, 1913.

They were married within a few months and lived in Chelsea, where they entertained politicians and journalists, artists and actors, literary lions and the more Bohemian socialites, but after twenty years they separated. According to her cousin, 'T. P. was much enamoured of a certain lady and, while she was tolerant, 'Cousin Betty' said she could not stand the strain of two sets of creditors sitting on the doorstep trying to collect the bills . . . If she could have written as she talked, her fortune would have been made. Witty, spontaneous, interesting as she was, something seemed to get between her and her pen, and the wise woman of the world turned into a sentimentalist.'

Of her grandson Brian ('Boysey') Mrs. T. P. wrote in her autobiography:

Now I have an adorable little love (who) one day told me he wanted a picture of me, and I said, 'Oh, no, Damma is too old and ugly,' whereupon his eyes flashed and he said, 'Damma is *not* ugly, *not a single bit of her is ugly*,'—and I determined then and there always to look my best in those young, beautiful, and star-like eyes. No one who has seen can ever forget them—even George Meredith, his godfather, was impressed by their singular beauty.

Tudie is often said to have been a social-climbing snob. Could it be that intellectual snobbishness sits easier on the shoulders of a pretty American woman such as his mother than a capitalising young art dealer—such as Tudie was—and that it was only when he discovered that 'titles' and tycoons were worth cultivating for his business interests that the label was deserved? At the turn of the century Tudie, already a fluent French and German linguist (from his schooling in Roman Catholic colleges in Paris, Geneva and Germany), was becoming quite a successful artist, art critic, and exhibition-organising entrepreneur. He met and fell in love with Lura Chess, a very pretty young American from Louisville, Kentucky whom he married a few years later. During this three-year courtship he had unfortuitously fallen even more in love with another woman in England, by whom he was alleged to have had a child just before his marriage. This does in part explain his ambivalent attitude to Brian, the first-born and yet not. His wife, Lura, was one of two 'cultured and intellectual daughters of a charming man—William E. Chess, ex-Civil War (Northern) Artillery Captain'. Her mother had died when Lura was in her early teens, and she had virtually become her father's hostess at this early age.

The Chess family money originally came from oil, but after a business disagreement with his rich partner, Brian's grandfather sold out and started making whiskey barrels as he had a great knowledge of wood. He invented the manner of charring the insides of the barrels over slow charcoal fires, which helped to mature and colour the whiskey. The Chess home in Chatauqua, N.Y. became a cultural centre for 'talks', with eminent speakers of the time. Thomas Edison was one of their close friends and neighbours, young Edison being Brian's aunt's first beau.

Tudie and Lura (who were married in America in 1904) first lived at Claridges and then found a house in Warwick Square. Although they may have been happy at the start, it appears that Lura discovered the truth about 'another woman' on her honeymoon, never forgave Tudie, and suffered this knowledge all the time she was carrying Brian, who was born in March 1905, Added to this, Tudie's alleged other son, only a year older than Brian, was his double in looks and they always feared that the two boys might meet somewhere and recognise each other as blood brothers. In effect this son was said to have committed suicide before he was twenty, discouraged because of his less privileged life, and the dissatisfaction of 'sharing' a father.

There is no doubt that jealousy of Tudie's lady friends coloured Lura's whole life. She was American and possessive, expecting her husband to idolise her. Had she been less dominant she might have held him for longer. As it was he flitted in and out of their several homes, quarrelling over Brian's upbringing and behaviour, obviously a demanding husband from the social point of view, and for a long time, he preferred to be financially dependent on Lura even though he soon began to make money by picture-dealing. He later sent most of his capital to America to be invested (profitably) by his brother-in-law, Avery Robinson.

Tudie had an eye for the main chance and never stopped organising 'International' exhibitions, and it was this activity that enabled him to write to famous people, crowned heads, exiled royalty—celebrities of all ranks, asking for their patronage by way of pictures, money, or just their presence at the various private views and charity benefit occasions. His family albums overflowed with autographs of the great, always accepting or declining with grace whatever it was he had called upon them to do. Even as early as 1920 he perceived artistic talent in Winston Churchill, then at the War Office, who sent him this courteous refusal to exhibit:

Dear Mr. Francis Howard, I am much complimented by your kindness in suggesting that I should exhibit a couple of pictures at the Grafton Galleries. But I am quite sure that none of them are worth showing, and I have made up my mind not to exhibit under my own name until I have succeeded in being selected on merits and under an assumed name. Perhaps you will give me the pleasure in the Spring of next year, when Parliament assembles, of coming and looking at some of my things. I should greatly value your criticism and advice. Yours sincerely, Winston S. Churchill.

His other cherished record of Churchillian contact was over twenty years later, in 1942, when Tudie, representing the Committee of the International Society, sent Churchill a drawing, to which he replied, 'It is with much pleasure that I accept the Dulac cartoon, though I agree with you that it is not too complimentary to either of us! . . .'

In 1912 Tudie was Managing Director of the Grosvenor Gallery for Knoedler and Colnaghi, moving to the Grafton Galleries in 1921, about which there was acrimonious correspondence in *The Times*. Amongst his greatest friends were the artists Harrington Mann and McEvoy (both of whom painted interesting portraits of Lura and Brian). He promoted their pictures with zeal, and Mr. Mann's daughter Mona (now Mrs. Macdonnell) remained one of the Howards' most loyal friends, finally becoming Lura's executor. Tudie made enemies in the art world as he was probably infinitely more go-getting in a business sense than most people working in and on the periphery of that world were used to. He became a great friend of the Benjamin Guinnesses, who gave him a flat in their Carlton House Terrace home, which was his address for many years. He became art advisor to Mrs. Guinness and much of his success must be owed to their friendship and patronage.

Tudie died in October 1954, having severed all links with Lura by the early 'thirties. Sir Gerald Kelly, then P.R.A., added a long, candid but affectionate tribute to the official obituary in *The Times*, ending with 'What a beautiful figure, a bitter enemy, a warm friend'.

Looking back on Brian and his father it seems they had many points of similarity, however much Brian would like to deny it. Tudie was the luckier in that despite the lack of a 'father' in the home until he was eleven, his devoted mother managed to bring him up without the worst results of spoiling, whereas Lura and Brian endured for over half a century, one of the most disastrous of love-hate mother-and-son relationships.

2. The boy, Brian

Lura Howard had a younger sister of considerable charm, Grace Chess, who married a Mr. Avery Robinson, their daughter Carley being Brian's nearest surviving relation. Carley (now Mrs. Dawson) writes from America candidly and without sentimentality:

> To me, even as a child (he was four years older than I) I found Brian infinitely pathetic. I was 'observing' him from ten years old on: why he did what he did—whatever it may have been—and what accounted for the reasons behind it.
>
> The fact that my aunt discovered Tudie with his mistress on their (Tudie's and Lura's) honeymoon was a blow and a shock which undoubtedly sowed the seed for her future relationship with Brian. For Lura, thereafter, and at all costs, Tudie was never to have a chance with his son—if she could help it. Either for domination, or for love. Brian from that moment on, I'm sure, was to be all hers.
>
> Lura made her own life by *always* wanting *her* way, to the total exclusion of any thought of how other people might live, their way. Of course, like many Southern women, what appeared to be velvet outside was steel within, but one has to learn this by degrees. This is why the Southern belles were so resolute through the Civil War; they're very, very tough. The 'belle' is sugar-coating. To have been truly loving of Brian, Lura would have fitted him for life better; at least with discipline. Sound and justified discipline makes for security in the child. Brian was given in to always. Lura thought to bind him to her this way. She did, by making him so weak as far as managing his finances were concerned, that he was always dependent on her. But I think he must have loathed this.
>
> When Brian was barely able to walk my mother told me that he would be brought downstairs at tea-time, in the habitual nursery pattern, to be admired. He was then dressed in the short dresses babies of that time wore, and Tudie would invariably jeer at him, 'Oh, look at the little girl!' While the baby Brian couldn't understand what the words were, or what they meant, he *could* understand a tone of voice, and usually went out in tears. As he grew, Lura vacillated in her attitude towards Brian, always threatening—but never carrying out—punishment.

Yet according to a diary Lura Howard kept of Brian's babyhood (in which she proudly listed his first words as being 'Dada' ... 'pretty' ... and 'all gone!'), as a small boy he was very fond of his father, and although Lura and Tudie were largely estranged during his childhood there were many occasions when they could, and did, enjoy family life. Tudie used to recount a typical story of how

Brian, being warned not to touch a big, ferocious looking dog, quickly said, 'Oh, I'll be *gentle* with him'. Lura found Brian to be fearless, affectionate, observant, and extraordinarily retentive of episodes during his family visits to America in 1906 and 1907. His critical faculties were sharpening early in life—he was not yet four years old when he said to an unpopular French governess who insisted on wearing an ugly big black hat when taking him to parties, 'Well if you have to wear that horrible hat walk back of me so I can't see it!'

Following the usual pattern Brian was sent to day school in London when he was just six, the choice being Gibbs, and his first report found him 'a good little boy, with drawing a strong point'. Lura took him off on another visit to her family in America in the autumn of 1911, and the following letter from Tudie—addressed to *Brian de C. Howard Esq.*—surely did not emanate from a disillusioned father:

Dearest Baby Boy, It is more than twenty days since you went away but I have not yet had a letter from you—I don't think, if you write, you can have put 'hurry' on the envelope—please put it on whenever you write again.

The other day I was whistling in the bath thinking how *very* sad I was you couldn't answer it, when that little spotted cat came in and looked at me as if to say, 'Will I do?' I think he had been in the nursery looking for you. The other day when I went to lunch with Mrs. Tata who lives at Twickenham in the French King's house where Queen Anne was born, she asked me to ask you if you would give her a photograph of yourself. She has heard so much about you she thought that she would like to take a picture of you with her to India, where she is going for a long time.

Mrs. (Harrington) Mann has offered to give me their fox terrier dog [his head is sketched here] but he is so quarrelsome I don't think I shall like him, and the spotted cat says he thinks I am quite right. What do you think?

With all his love to his baby boy, Your Daddy.

In the autumn of 1913 Brian was sent away to preparatory school. His cousin Carley fills in here:

The fact that when Brian first went to preparatory school he was apparently seduced by one of the masters was possibly too late to change a pattern which was already superimposed, but once again it didn't help. (Years later, when I was thinking of sending my own son to that same school, Brian said to me 'If you ever send your son there I shall never forgive you. It was there that my life was ruined . . .'). After this incident Tudie insisted that Brian be removed from the school, but Lura, I imagine just to be perverse, wouldn't hear of it.

Writing to his mother during the period 1914 to 1917 Brian showed he could be as bloodthirsty, and homesick, as any other little boy: The following brief quotes are representative of his schoolboy correspondence:

... I want to go and shoot Von Klucke and Von Möltke and the Kaiser, and go into Antwerp and kill German spies. Please let me go as a drummer-boy and you come too and Daddy ... I'm so sorry about poor old Lord Roberts, arnt you?

... Do you think the Zepps will come and blow you up? I read that Indian book and is it true that by exposing oneself to the forest you can be holy? Mummy I'd like to know I should think you could. If you can by setting still and praying, wouldn't you? ... I love you so please Mummy if you can will you come down a little bit earlyer than in three week. I want you ... Three aeroplanes came over our cricket ground. It was exciting, lots of people, including me think one was a German.

... I have been ill again—also homesick. I really don't know what is the matter. I'm in the sort of mood when I appreciate Macaulay's essays and lays. I am constantly having fits of moodiness ... and I take a frightful aversion to all the noise and shouting, that of course, must go on amongst a lot of boys. I am very unhappy about my work, and I don't know what to do about it, and the result is I think and read in quiet corners, wanting you or somebody sympathetic to talk to ... I have beaten three boys this week ...

Just before Christmas 1917 Brian wrote to his cousin Carley, who was in America:

It's very funny in London now, I came up from my school in the country and see that lots of motors go about driven by coal gas, with great balloons full of this gas on top of them. Also you often see long queus of women waiting for their butter or sugar or tea rations—I hope it wont come to that in your 'Land of Plenty' ... On the day I came to London we have an air-raid, and we all bundled down into the cellar, at least it was the pantry really, and had dinner there. And two days afterwards I saw the place where an incendiary bomb had fallen, and, luckily, having my walking stick I pulled out the bottom of the bomb from its inside, and took it home ...

During these years at preparatory school Brian's reports were of the usual mixture: 1913—'Brian shows every sign of being a success both in work and in dealing with others. He has wit, and his share of 'grit'.' 1914—'still very original and amusing and I think he will make a man quite out of the common.' 1915—'Brian won't think at all, but writes down absurd things ... he can no longer be regarded as a baby ... I like the boy very much: he has a delightful and original nature—but that won't get him through exams.' 1916—'developing well ... but he is a funny child who works for those whom he likes better than for others. In a small boy this is quite intelligible but he will have to get credit and work for work's sake and not the teacher's when he goes to a public school.'

There was some discussion as to whether Brian should try for Winchester or Eton. The Headmaster, of his prep school wrote at the end of 1917 (when Brian had only one more term to go) that he thought he would do better at Winchester: 'It is easier to 'slack' at Eton, and the greater intellectual activity at

12

Winchester will be good for him. He is quite a clever boy in some ways . . . some of his Bible exam paper was thoughtful and well expressed beyond his years . . . but he is too ready to give in to disinclination to work at some subjects, which at this stage of his existence are necessary. He sings very well, I consider, for a small boy, with taste and feeling. All this you will say is off the point—but not quite: it shows that the boy has brains and will show it in some way at school or later—and I think that Winchester will give him a better chance. Further, I fancy that he would have greater temptation to develop a taste for luxury and dressiness at Eton. There is not the same suspicion of swelldom in the air at Winchester.'

Lura Howard, however, favoured Eton, and after making great efforts to improve his work Brian was accepted for Eton the second half (term) of 1918.

3. Eton by candle-light

1918–1922

Preparatory school may have left its mark on Brian, but it was Brian who contrived to leave his mark on Eton. The next few years were probably the most formative of his life; whether they acted as a power for his good or to the contrary is a debatable point.

The man who was Brian's first fag master at Booker's remembers with clarity his arrival:

> He was quite the best turned out boy I'd ever seen, very neat and clean—not like the usual type of scruffy new boy at all. He had tremendous self-confidence and did not scuttle off down corridors at the sight of us Senior boys or anything like that. One day he saw me arranging my scrap book (I used to paste in headlines from the newspapers about great events of the day with decorations to form a sort of collage). Brian offered to paint a frontispiece for me, which he did in the Bakst manner, and I still have it in the front of this album.

Sandy Baird, who was to become a great friend of Brian's later on, remembers the first time he saw him at Eton: 'It was raining. And there Brian was, immaculately dressed, holding up his trousers between thumb and finger (as Irish jig-dancers do), and picking his way through the puddles . . .'

That first year Brian wrote regularly to his mother, who not only wrote back several times a week but also visited him frequently as well She kept a scrappy collection of his Eton letters but the following extracts give an idea of his reaction to the freedom and restrictions that combine to give Eton its almost university quality.

Letters to his mother, from Eton (Summer 1918):

> I find Mr. Booker [his Housemaster] the fullest of fun person I have ever seen, always laughing. The Lower boys strike me as being *remarkably* silly here. I work all day long, I don't know why they say Etonians don't work! . . . Yesterday at early school I let my attention slip for a moment, and Mr. Slater, finding that I could not answer the question, gave me a 'ticket' (to Mr. Booker). I was very upset as the punishment was almost entirely unjust and I went to his rooms and spoke to him about it, but he remained obdurate and even laughed . . . I am top of my mathematical division and second in my French which is good, isn't it? I feel that a change is coming over me as regards my work and my religious interest. It is coming very slowly and I am not yet sure if it is a fraudulent imagination or not—I don't think it is. I seem to be unable so far to attain a consciousness of God, a holy and calm atmosphere that is necessary for meditation.

14

Last night I sat on the floor (Indian position) to try and meditate and I succeeded in banishing all thought from my mind but nothing came instead. In the book, *A visit to a Gnani*, it says the muscles must be tense—but I find that that combined with the Indian position is so uncomfortable that I can't get settled so to speak—no calmness comes. Please tell me how to meditate successfully. I want to *know* about religion now.

P.S. Hadn't you better get tickets and arrange about Lord's [the annual Eton and Harrow cricket match], and don't forget the Russian Ballet in the evening! . . ., I am coxing for two boys in the Second House boat for the races . . .

[November 1918] On the Monday of the Armistice at 10.40 a.m. the Headmaster announced that it was to be a half holiday and a *non dies* (that is no work at all) on the morrow. Then a riot commenced, all the school rushed up and down the streets yelling and screaming, one person was beating a bathtub, another a tea tray, and you never *heard* such a noise, then for two or three days cheering and singing and fireworks continued and I nearly burnt the house down, then Mr. Booker gave a banquet, with fruit salad and chicken and pheasant and cider (I had two and a quarter glasses—big glasses—of cider) and then we carried a maid up and down the house and sang songs till nearly 10 o'clock. Japanese lanterns were hung outside the houses, and the place is covered in Flags. I have a Union Jack out of my window and a Belgian Flag inside the room. Oh, it was great fun, but I'm afraid I spent a good deal. I am feeling much calmer now. I have started writing for the Press to get some money. I wish I could be with you in this time of great rejoicing.

> Quickly they gathered at the Call
> Brave Hearts that stood the test
> Though they knew that they would fall
> They fought for what is Best
> They answered England with a nod
> Smiled in the face of the Hun
> Fighting for Country and for God
> With Bravery and a gun.

I did these lines spontaneously (I hope my spelling is alright) isn't it *splendid*, to think that they stood firm and *died* right 'in the face of the foe'. I think the English are a glorious people—what happened in London, I *would* like to have seen it?

Jim Knapp-Fisher, who was at Eton with Brian, recalls Armistice Day vividly even now. He says Brian's description of it is true in parts, but the letter itself sounds most unlike Brian and as if he had written it because he thought it would please his mother.

Records for 1919 are sparse, even the reports from Brian's Housemaster being missing. I believe he was both working and behaving badly, so the leaning towards religion, however contemplative, was something of a smoke-screen between him and his mother (who was to remain a follower of Hindu philosophy all her life).

Letters to his mother, from Eton (1919):

... It is a wonderful thing that you can always tell if I don't do my best. Last week, I am sorry to say, I didn't and you knew it. Next holiday I shall become a disciple and you shall be the guru (until I become at last a sannyasin). It's very hard to carry out the doctrine of self-abnegation, isn't it? ... You know I said that I wouldn't use my candles for amusement, well, I did just for ten minutes last night—to finish copying some poems and make up half another one. I'm sorry ...

Brian's private diary for 1920 is intact, and I have selected entries from it to show the variety of his activities and interests which were by no means confined to writing *avant-garde* poetry and listening to classical records, although references to these activities predominated.

Private diary extracts (1920):

Memoranda: To keep this diary. To read Hindu philosophy regularly. To work for Mummy's sake. To write five times a week. To, keep as calm and peaceful an attitude of mind, as possible, and atmosphere to the room. To complete all work before play (reading etc).

[January–March] *New Age* accepts my poem *Balloons*.[1] Start article *The Advance of the Moderns*. Buy crème de Menthe—bad! *The New New* accepted by *New Age*. Great intrigues—everyone against everyone else. House Sports: I jump 13 foot 10 inches and am in finals for long jump and junior hundred yards. Food improving through complaint. 12th in form out of 32. Promise to rally myself. Play racquets. Play golf. Shoot in evening. Mr. Kindersley complains of me. Extensive epidemic of measles. Disease rapidly gaining. Trained nurse since about four days ago. Cultivate (Athole) Hay's acquaintance, and find him very amusing and interesting. He writes decidedly well.

13th March—My Birthday. Mummy and Daddy come down. Lovely, lovely day. From today EFFORT. Originate a magazine to be produced at Lord's. Hay and I to do the *whole* thing. Boxing, fencing, Giu-Gitsu in the evening. New Eton Art Club idea. Must work for Trials.

Continuing letters to his mother, from Eton (January–March 1920):

... Mr. Butterwick has sent mine and another boy's holiday task up to be judged for the best in the block, the same as last time. He privately told me *mine was the best* out of 32 boys. If I gain the prize it will make my fourth. [He did.] He said my paper was 'admirable in parts' (which is effusive for Eton) ...

---

[1] See Appendix I.

I am getting on with my work but what I am going to say doesn't sound—perhaps—like it. That is, I enclose two poems, one good and one bad. You see, I love writing, and—I just do it in my spare time. I intend to publish under the name of 'Jasper Proude' and I can begin with the *New Age* thing ... I have just received your letter with Daddy's infringement of copyright. There's something extraordinarily good about Daddy's copy of my poem. I think it's better than the original. But he mustn't do it in public on account of endangering my tremendously far-reaching reputation for flawless *vers-libre*. There's also a suspicion of horridness about it—you see the poem was meant to be serious—I think he'd better go and make fun of Shelley or somebody. But it's very good; he ought to make a little money.

P.S. Tell Daddy that if he insults my art any more I'll slang him and McEvoy and Titian in the *New Age*. I'm just writing an article on Realism for the *N.A.* now—he'd better be careful.

... Yesterday I burnished up the clubs and played with them. Excellenza! I love golf. Mumsey, I do not want to be put off doing this magazine with Hay. It will *not* interfere with my work. The enjoyment I will get out of concocting the magazine, all the tremendous enjoyment of settling the cover, posters, printing, size, shape, and finish will simply be nice for me, and there is *no* reason to stop it. Hay will most certainly—and enthusiastically—do his share, and together we will make it a great, great success. It will be my triumph, Mummy. *Why* should you spoil it all, it worries me greatly. It will be called *The Wing* ...

Continuing private diary extracts (1920):

[May–July] Remember resolutions. Elected permanently for Second House boat. Acton comes with a note, wishing to conciliate. Become friendly with Harold Acton after one year's silence. Remember for *mother's* sake *to renounce* pleasure. Do your *duty*. It is for your father and mother. FIGHT. My *Procession* appearing in *Eton Review*.[2]

3rd and 4th of June—lovely days with Mummy and Daddy. Mummy sets me alright again. Fall into the water in novice sculling. Bottom in Greek. Excellent sermon from Headmaster. Lose ten shillings racing. STOP IT NOW.

[According to his diary he was continually betting on horses.] Go on a surreptitious bicycle ride with Digby and Rice to Maidenhead. Tea at Skindle's. 440 lines. Read Buddhist Catechism ... An utterly miserable day at Henley in a punt. How I hate this place ... 220 lines for putting feet up in Chapel. More chastisement from 'Library'[3] for being late for bath. Meet Mr. (Ernest) Thesiger—charming man. Mr. Thesiger consents to be an honourable member of the Eton Dramatic Society if we can get it up ... Tremendous outburst of unpopularity. My flowers mauled about on a silly

---

[2] Published by Spottiswoode, Ballantyne for the Eton Political Society. The June 1920 issue contained the first part of an unlikely one-act play by Brian, *Procession*, which was a truly dreadful moral tale.

[3] Committee of Senior boys who administer punishment and help the Housemaster to keep order.

pretext. *Everyone* except (Lord) Pelham (that is to say) all the Lower boys and Uppers up to Talbot-Rice seem to hate me. Unpopularity is *so* depressing.

Mr. A. R. Orage, editor of *New Age*, the weekly review of politics, literature and art, wrote to Brian concerning his article *The New New* (which he published in July): 'I shall be quite amused to publish your *New New* in the 'Pastiche' page before very long. As an attempt to express the chaos of the modern mind it is very good; and I hope I am correct in reading it partly as a parody of James Joyce and his school. Later on, however, I hope that you will write about something you really like; since *only* cleverness comes of writing about one's hates and contempts.'

THE NEW NEW by 'Jasper Proude'

It's a fight . . . a fight, against a gamut of gawks and *grisâtres*. We wonder if it is, really, a rebellion of the Right People against the Wrong People. Of all the hundreds of new movements there's Wyndham Lewis . . . suffering from a paucity of ideas. He's got a movement. (An art critic . . . cowed by it all . . . enthuses.) There is an exhibition at the Adelphi Galleries of some chaotics. A cohort of Oxfordesques say those things about charlatans and little minds . . . on the other side there's the 'group' . . . grouping.

The New Era is coming, and all inanities in trashy architecture like St. Thomas's Hospital will go . . . all the wretched inmates being presumably foisted upon Bart's . . . or Dr. Barnardo's.

But there's terror abroad—who, *who* ever saw such inundations . . . there's a new *Wheels*. And Mr. Huxley has written an insult to the Catholics (it's not in *Wheels*, and the title is the insult), dissecting our premier public school with ululant yowls. (Mr. Huxley has been getting ready to do so ever since he became one of its *ci-devant* teachers—assistant masters.)

Then there's the new *Wheels* . . . *remplissage, remplissage.* It's the fourth (bi) cycle *rechauffée*, and I wonder if Edith Sitwell has dreadful dreams . . . re, Scarabombazons. The worst of it *is*—this passion for houseling.

What is the future going to be? And not only that, but even that's getting so previous!

              *   *   *

Visions of juniper-trees exuberating down Queen Anne's Gate. And M. Poiret in Paris . . . are we going to be draped like Shushans . . . in orange and lake; gamboge primroses like a parcel of glistering Omega workshops? Are we? We are!

And what about the (*Times Literary Supplement*) Dada Movement . . . my God! that *with* Poiret . . . does one expect others to essay speech—does one expect oneself to essay speech like 'ouaih, aouih, aoiuh, uaoih . . . boum, boum, boum' . . . that's Dada . . . Adda, Adad, Daad, Aadd, Ddaa . . . one feels the nauseous lethargies creeping up . . . ouaih, uaoih.

              *   *   *

What are the 1947 Vorticist houses going to be? (Snivellings from the 'group leaders'.) Why the devil should I live in a Wyndo-ferro-concrete gun-emplacement? Why should I, swounding and pallid, exist amongst

thicknesses and (savage) plainnesses! All these b—— NEW movements—
pah! . . .

'The Caliph's Design' . . . pish!

But where is one to turn?

Not to the National Gall.—the walls (the retired 'dazzle artist' with
theatrical aspirations who has done the backgrounds has caught on to the
craze for vivid 'décor') have got the spotted measles—salmon pink and
ohld-gohld . . . and . . . Whistler looks like—Barribal.

But—in the swirls of derivative symbolism . . . there is one place to turn
(before one is chased to Battersea Park Road), where our Ozzies and
Sacheys and Ezras cannot follow with bombilatory pursuance . . . The
LONDON MERCURY.

O! how I love Derain and Roberts . . . *there's* colour without any of your
Café Royal Edmund X. Kapp's portrait of Very Windy Lewis-esque
atmosphere . . . Such tone . . . and Van Gogh and Cézanne . . .

But there goes the art critic of the *Spectator* again . . . still vamping toshily
about 'clichés'.

How catching it all is!

Continuing private diary extracts (1920):

[September–December] New house and room. Mr. Blakiston instead of Mr.
Booker [who had retired]. Work hard. Play racquets. Join Corps. Play
football. Shoot. Rows with people. Unpleasant day. Am afraid Mr.
Blakiston is going to adopt the 'Schoolmaster' attitude towards me, and *not*
be sympathetic with my type of mind, as Mr. Booker predicted he would
be. Alas! . . . *Rencontre* with Mr. Blakiston re my hair! Do a pastel. Lovely
M. Hambourg concert (*Jeux d'eau*—Ravel). Write thing for colliery paper
for Mr. Blakiston. Exciting field day with the Corps . . . Compose
Night-Piece (for piano). 'Pass out' of Corps. Get eyeglass. Get black spats.
Reply from Orage saying he will 'pour' my *Rain-drops* poem into the *N.A.*
[It appeared as *Nausea*.] . . . Daddy sees Drawing Exhibition—likes my
things (three exhibits). Motor to lunch with him at Sunninghill, where Mrs.
(Benjamin) Guinness asks me to write a play for Tanis, Méraud and Loel.

NAUSEA (an extract)
>The dark light and the grey half-light . . .
>The wet, beaded inside of the water-jug glinting
>   diamond and elusive grey-white,
>And the irregular spots of moisture.
>The meat is sodden (so is the bread) and unattractive;
>The greens are colding and give one the vertigo,
>   Or ever the dull spoon digs at them . . .

(First published in the *New Age*, 1921, reprinted in the *Eton Candle*, 1922.)

From an early age Brian took an avuncular interest in his young cousin Carley,
and in 1920 wrote to his aunt, Grace Robinson, from Eton in the hope of
dissuading her from sending Carley away to boarding school:

Well, I have a friend here who tells me that his sister went to school at Heathfield and left it because she detested it so. This boy himself is quite an ordinary boy, and his sister, I should think, would be an ordinary girl, and consequently since an English girl has left the school purely from dislike of the place, it seems rather inadvisable to me to send Carley there.

. . . I, at present, have a very real knowledge of a schoolboy's existence, and I really shudder to think of Carley being sent to a school with crowds of all types of girls, some of whom are bound to possess undesirable ideas. Carley, to me, seems to possess an indefinable sweetness of character; a certain innocence and lovableness which I *know* will be spoilt and effaced if she is sent away to school . . . What *is* the good of sending her away from you—just after she has come from a different country, and is gradually assimilating English ideas? She will be plunged among strange girls of an entirely different type, *and she may become like them.* Dear Aunty Grace, don't you see what I mean? Carley *has* her own little ideas, her own charming little personality. As soon as she goes to school—I have this at first-hand experience—an entirely new and thoroughly undesirable world opens before her. You may smile at the earnestness with which I beg you not to send her away, but then I *know* and *feel* that it is almost a criminal thing to send a girl of her type to an English girl's school. She isn't the type that would profit by it.

Carley writes about this period in retrospect:

When we, the Robinsons, and my grandfather Chess came to England in 1920 for several years, my grandfather (having lived with my mother all her married life) tactfully but unwillingly went to live with Lura, of whom he was not as fond. Tudie, many faults though he might have had, was the soul of courtesy to the old man. Every night without fail he would play several games of draughts with him, and then go to 'the cinema', or, far more likely, a lady friend! During the summers, when Lura took a country house, Tudie would play endless games of croquet. It simply was not possible to be anything but pleasant to my grandfather because he was such a gentle person, and unfailingly kind . . .

I remember this first summer we all shared a large house, Little Bognor in Sussex. One day Lura and Tudie got into a flaming row over Brian. I think he had been in some trouble at Eton, or perhaps his marks were not good. In any event, Lura's and Tudie's voices became so loud that even from behind a closed door one could hear everything. Brian realised that something was afoot, and left off playing with me to go put his ear against the drawing-room door. Tudie was expressing himself on the subject of Brian in no uncertain terms, and Brian began to cry, but wouldn't leave. I tried to pull him away, without success, and then ran upstairs to my grandfather and mother, telling them what was going on, and begging them to get Brian away from hearing such shattering things about himself. But it was too late. At fifteen, he knew how his father felt about him. He finally ran upstairs and shut himself into his room, where he cried, alone and

20

without food, for the better part of two days and nights, not opening the door to anyone.

Despite family rows the following letter from Brian to his mother in December 1920 indicates that Tudie was not yet totally anti-Brian:

On Saturday I went to Sunninghill [to the Benjamin Guinnesses] with Daddy. He really is brilliant! The subtle, *subtle* methods he is using to un-Chess me and re-Howard me! The reflections on Uncle Avery! And you! It's almost too serious to be taken seriously! It's rather entertaining. I have discovered that I *like* the Guinnesses. I had *great* fun. It was a grey, windy day and we went in a yellow punt on a grey lake under grey clouds, and got whirled about. Daddy says he doesn't know what he is doing as regards the family. He says I'm the only one who hasn't gone mad—he said that at table. Awful. He was saying that I ought to be a barrister, and I said I wouldn't be any good at defending people I knew were wrong. He said, oh yes I would—I'd been doing it all my life!!! What is all this going to end in—hey? Oodles of Love from Baba—

1921 was to prove a memorable year for Brian. He was discovered by Edith Sitwell (who published his first poem in her magazine *Wheels*), he visited Algeria, and started planning that unique publication, the *Eton Candle*. His diary entries continue to be revealing:

[January–February 1921] ... Have my first boxing lesson (it is just bearable). The man says I am 'shaping very well!' Mr. Rayner-Wood complimented me on my 'Sunday Questions'. (An essay on *Pacifism* did it.) ... In the evening Mr. Blakiston had a long talk with me about my future. I wonder—should I go to Oxford? Buy *Cock and Harlequin* by Cocteau. Polish off some Dadaïste poems and send them to Edith Sitwell ... Received a *wonderful* letter from Edith Sitwell. She compliments me tremendously and writes four pages advising me, and asking for more and other poems. I *am* so encouraged.

Edith Sitwell wrote from her Pembridge Mansions flat on 14th February:

Dear Mr. Howard, I am going to do a thing that I have never done before,—I am going to write you detailed criticism and advice about your poems. I get a very great many manuscripts sent to me, and I invariably return them with a short note of regret. But in your case it is different. You have quite obviously very real gifts, and I hope to publish some work of yours in *Wheels*—perhaps this year, perhaps next. It depends on you.

You may be angry at first at what I am going to say; but your promise is far too real for me to risk your future by publishing these poems of yours *in their present state*. In ultra-modern work it is absolutely necessary to have someone who will give, both destructive and constructive criticism. Now, I have had all this myself. If I had not, I should have ruined my career by publishing too soon. I have great experience in the criticising of poems; I see nearly all the poems of the newest school in an unfinished state; and if you like to send me your work from time to time, I shall be very pleased to do anything I can to help you.

With regard to the poems you have sent me. You have got great perceptions, and feel and notice the relations between things. But I don't think you go far enough in these relations. What I mean is,—roughly, this. You write a *Mind Expression of the Sea*[4] and it is in a way admirable . . . but why don't you tell us something about the way it reacts on other minds? You should, I think, humanise your poetry a little.

Again, it is an admirable idea of yours to put *To be shouted to the accompaniment of breaking glass*; that gives one the texture of the air, the sound and colour of the sea. But *why* spoil it by writing *Tah—h—h—h—Bloom* etc. It only holds up the action of the poem, and gives, at once, a feeling of insincerity. You spoil all your poems in the same way.

In your *Musical Marvels*; nobody but a writer of real talent could have written . . . *Exquisite little chopped up canary wings. Falling down in jerks and bursts and jangles out of a blue-gilt sky.* That is simply *admirable* (though I think Lord Berners is a goose). But then off you go again, and spoil it. And you don't tell us half enough. The one sentence by itself won't convey anything to anybody excepting a writer.

Now if these poems were mine, this is what I should do with them. I should call the whole lot of them *The Café by the Sea*, I should melt *the first* sentence of the *Still life by Picasso* (the towel-horse description would be marvellous as a description of the sea)[5] the first *Musical Marvel* the *Expression of Still Life*—(admirable, the part about the omelette and the water lilies;[6] it shows most remarkable talent), and the *Mind Expression of the Sea*,—I should melt all these together, leaving out the *Tah—h—h—Bloom* sounds that occur in each poem.

Will you consent to try this. And will you not try some conventional verse-forms. Control of that kind is very salutary in ultra-modern verse.

Work hard and with a stinging conscience. Never be satisfied, and you will become a very fine writer. You will indeed.

Wheels will go to press in May. Will you not re-write these poems, and send me some others? I shall do nothing to risk your career, if it means sending your poems back to you a hundred times; but I hope to print some poems of yours, as soon as they have taken on their final shape.

Forgive me for my plain speaking; I write to you like this because you have real gifts. I shall expect to see some more poems of yours very soon.

---

[4] See third version in Appendix I.
[5] 'a towel horse,—painted in half . . . a rounded upsurging of brown
                                     with a green fringe.
ferrules of the towel horse made sideways . . . a biscuit . . . a bottle of
                                     tin and glass high lights . . .'
[6] 'EGG. they all belong to Partlet.—omelettes aux fines herbes—
GRANULAR. like unpleasant dough or Monet water lilies. hard. gritty.
                                     you swallow them by mistake . . .'

Believe me, with very real interest, Yours sincerely, Edith Sitwell.

Continuing private diary extracts (1921):

[February] I send eight (more) poems to Edith Sitwell, and also a letter with the amalgamation of the four poems that I previously sent her. I am caught going ten feet down Peascod Street (out of bounds) by a French master (I was going to a typewriting agency to have my poems done for Edith Sitwell as Spottiswoode's were shut) and reported to Mr. Blakiston, but he merely cautioned me—like the charming man he is—and all is well . . . I am top of my classical division! Mummy writes me about 41 Bryanston Square, which we HAVE BOUGHT. An end to our house-hunting troubles at last. In the evening I have an awful row with Blakiston about not coming down to breakfast. I have a long, tearful conversation, and then we arrange to forget about it. I get a second complimentary letter from Edith Sitwell, really enthusiastic and encouraging (dated 18th February):

Dear Mr. Howard, There can be not the slightest doubt that your gifts and promise are exceedingly remarkable. You are undoubtedly what is known as a 'born writer'. 'Born writers' are subject to one great danger—they are apt to grow careless, and to be too easily satisfied; but I do not think this is a temptation to you. If it is, guard against it. In any case, you will have me on your track pretty quick if I see any traces of it. I will tell you something; I see more remarkable talent and promise in your work than in that of any other poet under twenty I have seen, excepting that of my brother Sacheverell, who also displayed great gifts early (his book *The People's Palace* was published when he was still nineteen).

There is an immense improvement in *Mind Expression of the Sea*. You have pulled the thing together, given it force, and it is extremely good. But there are one or two places where something has gone wrong. *I* know what is wrong, but I think it better for you to find out for yourself. If you can't, then I will tell you. But I have marked the lines, and I want you to put the poem away and not look at it for two months. Then take it up again, see if you can find what spoils those particular lines, and send the poem back to me. It is, all the same, *really* remarkable, and I expect great things of you. *Diversion Sentimentale* is also really beautiful. Will you look at that poem too, and see if you would like to alter it, and send the two poems back to me in May. At the moment, I am going to leave the question of when you are to come into *Wheels* vague. *Because* your future is of the greatest interest to me, and will have to come before anything else, and to this end, I wish to spur you on to work hard, as hard as you can (though *never* when you are tired or disinclined) and because at all costs your head must be kept screwed on the right way.

I once knew a young poet who rushed into print before he was used to being called a poet, and to knowing himself to be one; and the praise he got ruined him, as fatally as discouragement could have done,—indeed, more fatally. Let me tell you that I want, badly to print these poems at once; but before I make up my mind, I shall have to get to know you as a person, better. Because, you see, I am perfectly determined that you are to become an extremely distinguished writer, and I must not spoil your gifts. Send the poems back to me in May, and we will see.

Be careful about the arrangement of your lines. They want managing.

Never invoke the aid of a painter's name when visualising scenery; it is too easy, it disturbs one's vision, and it is a mistake ever to make statements of an obvious kind . . . you should suggest. Everything you say should be a door.

Remember that when you describe scenery (as in *Night Sea* and *London Night-Piece*)[7] it is only the prelude to, or study for, an achievement. It cannot be, as in painting, the achievement itself.

That is why *Illusion* is a poem of promise. It shows that you see states of mind and of heart beyond the exteriors. And that, again, is why *Diversion Sentimentale* and *Mind Expression of the Sea* are so really remarkable. One must feel, you know, as well as see. But never never, pretend to yourself that you are *feeling* something when you are not. One must be rigorous with oneself too, as to expression. One must allow no insincerity to escape one, ever. The least touch of insincerity, or striving to startle, will ruin a whole poem.

The *Seaside Impressionist Symphony* is very good, though not quite as good as the other poems. The *Circular Triptych* interests me very much; but then again it is not quite cohesive; and you state too much. Put it aside for two months, and then look at it again.

Do you live in London, when you are not at Eton? Or, if you do not live in London, do you ever pass through? If so, let me know, and come and spend the afternoon with me. We would work at your poems together before tea, and after tea we would talk about books, pictures, and music.

Meanwhile, you might write and tell me what books you like reading; and also send me your other poems, no matter if you do think them not quite satisfactory.

Send me everything you write. I will do everything in my power to help you, and will print you when it is the moment to print you.

With all good wishes, believe me, Yours sincerely, Edith Sitwell.

P.S. 'Monet water lilies'[8] is excellent; but it was better as describing an omelette.

The *Seaside Impressionist Symphony* is admirable, better than I thought it was, even. Give it more meaning.

Continuing private diary extracts (1921):

[February–March] I win the Junior Long Jump. I play a few records and think a great deal. [According to his diary he also *bought* a multiplicity of records.] Letter from Daddy in Cannes which he says is a mixture of one of his private views and Wimbledon tennis championships. Visit Chaundy on long leave—it is the finest bookshop I have ever seen. Mummy arranges

---

[7] First published in *Wheels*, reprinted in the *Eton Candle*, see Appendix I.
[8] '. . . THE WHOLE SEASIDE IS MADE OF BITS OF APPLE. like unpleasant dough, or Monet water lilies. hard. gritty. you swallow them by mistake . . .'

for me to lunch with Ewan Cox (whose shop it is) and J. C. Squire of the *London Mercury*.

Go to Mr. Evans' [Eton Art master] exhibition of Professor Cizek's Austrian children's drawings. They are perfectly marvellous—with a freshness of conception and mastery of treatment which is amazing. Wonderful! . . . Draw up some prospectuses for my magazine, the *New Etonian*. At the Loder Prize I fail miserably in consequence of getting confused in the middle of my speech. Extremely annoying . . . Do cover designs for the *New Etonian*. I wonder when I'll be able to publish it? My £5 worth of books come that I bid for from Hodgsons catalogue— *Intentions* first edition (Wilde), *The Queen who Flew* in vellum, signed copy—one of twenty-five in this edition (by Ford Hueffer), etc. etc.

A long weary, exciting 'Field day'. Harold Acton takes me to see Mr. Oakley—a peculiar artist—and we have tea. He is a polite, nice man, but the atmosphere of the house; the terrible atmosphere of lustre pots and stuffs and bad stencillings and sweepings from Heal's and woolly tassels drives me mad . . . A long day of escape and intrigue. Engage in a fracas with the enemy, retreat gracefully into the house of a clergyman acquaintance. I hit Clonmore [now Earl of Wicklow] on the *chapeau* with an apple.

Easter Day: In the afternoon go to Dorney to tea with Mr. Bartlett. Am given some chocolate that tastes like weak cocoa and soda. Disgusting! Mr. Bartlett was kind to think of it though. (He says New York is unbearable—I always suspected it.) . . . Handel's music is perfectly dreadful. (*Alleluia Chorus* sounds like the unconscious burblings of some religious fanatic.) . . . My reports seem bad and yet good. Mr. Blakiston still uncomfortably gruff. I pass in Trials entirely.

There are no records of what Brian's original housemaster, Mr. Booker, felt about his pupil but his successor, Mr. Blakiston, wrote in no uncertain terms to Lura Howard in March:

Dear Mrs. Howard, . . . I feel, now that I have had six months experience of him, and the novelty has worn off for both of us, that I must express strongly my opinion of him as a boy, and as a member of a great community like Eton. To take his character first. It has seldom been my lot, in many years of work amongst boys, to come upon one so entirely self-centred and egotistical. Mentally he has some equipment—not in the ordinary school subjects because they are naturally cut and dried and lack romance: and, incidentally, call for moral effort. But he undoubtedly has some taste both literary and artistic. However mental qualities do not go towards character building: and so far as his moral nature is concerned I cannot find what standards he has other than those of pure selfishness. 'I will do this, because I like it. I will not do that, because it doesn't appeal to me.' In this code there seems no room for principles outside himself, such as duty and truth.

As a member of a great school, he is subject to discipline—which to most boys becomes so much a matter of routine that they hardly notice it except when they accidentally break a rule. But, in his case, rules as such do not seem to appear to him to matter, and if he can find a loophole for evasion or excuse, he thinks he has scored a point: and in some cases he has definitely broken or evaded rules because he thinks his own case superior to them. I have still to recover from the surprise with which I found him proposing to make a habit of shirking prayers and breakfast on Sundays, and even suggesting to my servants to allow him to do so: I have had him reported to me for walking in forbidden parts of Windsor, and he is prepared to argue his 'right' to walk elsewhere at will: he has disobeyed my plain directions as to the observance of rules as to visiting other houses after 'lock-up', and he disgraced himself and me by behaviour on Easter Sunday which caused disturbance to scores of boys in Chapel.[9]

All these little failings—none of them serious in themselves—mount up to a serious indictment in the mass. As a Housemaster I must needs be jealous of the reputation of my house, and insist on implicit obedience to myself: any tampering with my clearly expressed wishes—and I made them clear at the outset last September and have tried to do so since—is disloyalty as well as disobedience: and a boy who wishes to be a law to himself is a danger which I cannot over estimate. I have many boys here already and due to come to me, from homes which I know, from whom I shall expect complete loyalty and confidence: and I do not wish a bad example set up to them by any already in the house.

Perhaps this reads as though I had taken a dislike to the boy. This is not the case—it is my business to do the best I can for those under my care, and I can safely say I have gone out of my way to be kind to him, to make allowances for him, and even to give him special leave or privilege when it seemed advisable to do so. I have tried to see his point of view and to help him: but he is so convinced always of his own rectitude that he is not open to argument.

I feel that he is not doing any good to others, and am not sure he is doing much good to himself at Eton: his choice of friends is not all that I could wish, outside the house, and I am never quite sure how he spends his leisure hours.

If he does not alter his attitude towards school life and discipline, I should strongly advise that he should leave Eton early and find some other form of education. I shall take him back next half and hope he will try to do better, but shall be glad if you would consider seriously the advisability of removing him after the summer . . . Yours very truly, C. H. Blakiston.

This bombshell must have arrived when Brian was at Camp, as in the following letter to his mother he was sublimely unaware of his equivocal situation:

. . . I shall arrive home—all in my nice smart uniform covered in vegetables, tobacco, and dirt. I'll tell you a secret—a *real* secret ON THE WHOLE I

---

[9] Brian's diary entry for Easter Day made no mention of any misbehaviour, but Lura Howard wrote to me in 1964: 'He was so naughty at Eton as the very strict laws irritated him. He took a little toy engine to Chapel and I had a time getting Mr. Blakiston to keep him.'

HAVE ENJOYED CAMP IMMENSELY. But it has been a revelation in discomfort, dirt, dirty language, bad food etc. etc. I have been behaving like a young barbarian—using the most dreadful language and doing all sorts of schoolboy things. Jessel and Bridgeman and my artistic friends are amazed at my happy sprightliness. I have become QUITE PECULIAR—I actually go to rag-time sing-songs and enjoy myself immensely. I'm still 'young', I'm afraid . . . Since I told you about my great lapse over a certain subject, the 'subject' has never entered my head. Or when it did I thought of you, and that came to the same thing. I think that if ever I was on the point of doing some really terrible thing I'd only have to think of you to save myself. I am so sorry for your sake that I am not the kind of person to whom wicked things never occur—it is so much simpler, isn't it? However, I think one misses a certain quite valuable (anyway valuable from a writer's point of view) side of life if one has never probed the darker paths . . . Why doesn't Papa return my spontaneous spasm of good nature? I thought of such a good simile today: 'he had a moustache like a gothic Cathedral' . . .

So he returned to Eton for the summer half and after his mother had been down to talk to Mr. Blakiston found even him 'moderately pleasant . . . and everything will be all right if I keep in touch with her'. Lura Howard may have charmed Mr. Blakiston into keeping Brian on at Eton, but she obviously felt the strain when she wrote the following letter, with its implications of sexual misbehaviour:

Dearest, I am writing because I was afraid you'd worry—because I was weeping. Without your knowing the reason. There were two—I am very, very tired, not sleeping and such a tiring day. And the second I *hate* your being unhappy, so I try to make you happy and as you grow older it's no good. And now I'm worrying for fear someone comes in tonight that you won't want to turn out . . . Baba don't take any risks—and one reason which I don't think you quite realise is Mummy's health. You must do your best for that reason too. This is not lightly said.

Remember, Baba, that little things *do* matter—bricks make a house. The hardest thing I have to do *is* to take the other side in a case like this, but it is the *only* way I can help you dearest dear. No one can take our love for each other away—nor our appreciation of lovely things, so God *is* in his Heaven—Muv.

A further letter, more concerned with Brian's *avant-garde* aestheticism than his adolescent failings, gives an idea of the strength, and weakness, of their relationship:

Dearest, dear, Something you said made me realise that I wasn't making myself understood and that is so dangerous between mother and son. All your faults are on the *surface*—the surface is what people see—that is why manner is so vitally important. I often wish I had more pleasing manners and a more joyful manner. It comes of having no mother. Now I think you do not realise that the greatest joy I have on earth is your character ... the fact you are *truthful* is to me a source of real thanksgiving ... Books are a *snare*—they are only someone else's ideas of life ... you are luckier than most for you have the gifts of telling what you see. I want you to use your eyes for the story in man's eyes and lives—not for the printed word always. I do not want you to yell forth complaints to the *New Age* and shriek criticisms. The key to life is love of it—and any hatred in our heart is a well for our egoism to wallow in ... Lonely—of course, *in a way*—only no one need know it. To be lonely is really to have *no one's* love. We have each other, and we have the *whole world*—the trees, the stars, the flowers, the loving mothers and fathers and little children—the books, the beauty of it all—and it's a good part to be a stepping stone for others to mount by—for most of us are dumb in our appreciation— have no way to pass it on. Keep your pieces for helpfulness and joy—let them never be dipped into the shadows that lurk in the best of frail humanity.

Ramakrishna became every religion to know it. Don't say to yourself, 'I am a type'—be open to it all ... meet people on *their* platform, not your own—then it is a thousand times more interesting ... It is hard not to try and force experience on to youth—and patience is a great virtue of which I have not enough! Remember companionship is absolutely essential to proper development—because insight into men's minds is not learned otherwise. Always your Muv.

In theory Brian turned over a new leaf but his diary entries were much the same as before; he bought records—from Wagner to jazz—books and pictures both old and new, serious and frivolous. There is also evidence of his expensive habit of backing horses. He noted that Edith Sitwell accepted some of his poems, including *Barouches Noires*,[10] for *Wheels* (her 'enthusiastic' letter is missing), and had a brush about baths with Mr. Blakiston 'so unreasonable—am severely beaten by the "Library" *and* Jessel *and* Rice ...'

In retrospect Lord Jessel says of Brian:

Although he was not a typical Etonian, too independent and obviously artistic, don't imagine that he was lonely. He was really quite popular, always amusing, had a good sense of humour and was quite a warm person. Like us all, he played football and rowed. He dressed rather more aesthetically, scented a bit more, but was certainly not namby-pamby at all. He could even become quite hearty, as at Camp.

(Sir Maurice) Bridgeman and I were terribly successful as Etonians— both in Pop—I was in the Field football team and Bridgeman was in the Cricket Eleven, Fives, became Captain of the Oppidans. We were the big boys then and we liked Brian, and he liked being liked by us.

---

[10] See Appendix I.

I knew his family, and his mother had originally asked me to look after him at Eton. Of course he never got on with his father although I think he admired him for his knowledge of pictures. If you went to their house in London the father was never there. I remember Brian could be in very up and down moods sometimes; he had a streak of melancholia in him, even at Eton.

In this his fourth year at Eton Brian was supposed to be studying for School Certificate, but when did he find time to work? On the '4th of June' 1921 he deserted the usual celebrations for more sophisticated spheres, and described the occasion in his diary as:

ONE OF MY VERY FINEST DAYS—I go up to London. In the morning I go over 41 Bryanston Square, our new home. It's going to be wonderful. Then I go to Max Beerbohm exibition—good ones of G. Phillips, John, Shaw, Sassoon etc. Then I lunch at home. After lunch go to the Private View of the New English, and am introduced to Mr. and Mrs. A. E. (Augustus) John, also Dodd and Lowinsky. Then *marrons* and a cinema—then the Royal Academy, Orpen and Philpot—then the best tea I have ever had at Rumpelmeyers. Then Queen's to see Daddy play tennis. Then a lovely dinner at home.

[His diary continued] ... Decide to call myself Charles Orange in *Wheels* ... Mr. Blakiston distinctly unpleasant about my coming back. The time has certainly come when I must turn about and fight for strength of character. It is my last chance. Pray for courage and steadfastness of purpose ... A good self-control day—but there's a *soupçon* of danger in the air. For God's sake be careful! Win £5 sweepstake. Celebrate winnings by eating a lot of ice cream. *I give way in the evening.* NOT SO GOOD.

Haven't done any extra work as I have been *plagued* with people. Oliver Messel comes to my room and eats up all my cake. Order white spats. Really too hot for any additional study. Order lovely tie, new patent leather shoes—lovely new suit ... Mr. Blakiston didn't think my 'order card' was *at all bad.* I'm going up hill!

At last *Wheels* (1921) was due to come out and Edith Sitwell, who edited it, wrote yet again to Brian in November:

My dear Charles Orange, *Please* forgive me for not answering your letter and thanking you for the *Fanfare*, before this. The truth is I have been very overworked, worried, and unwell.

Owing to the persistent attacks made on us by various people, the publisher refused *Wheels*, and I have had to find a fresh publisher, get the book out within a month (much reduced in size and price)—and the way has been really hilly. I have had to leave out the *entire* work of three contributors, and leave out innumerable poems both by myself and other people. Owing to the fact that I regard you as one of my most promising people, you are represented in the book (though it has meant leaving out the work of former contributors). But alas, only *one* poem of yours has been able to go in. It is your best—*Barouches Moires*. I had had all your poems put up in type, but the publisher put too large a print, and it has thrown the whole book out of gear. I am keeping your poems in type for next year; meanwhile, I have taken charge of them, and will try to place them with editors. So you must *please* forgive me for what is really not my fault—i.e. the delay in their appearance in book form. As I have told you, I really believe in you. Therefore, you have been given precedence: of other contributors.

I'll see what I can do with editors. The book will be sent to you tomorrow. Will you by any chance be in London on the evening of December 15th? If so, will you come with me to a meeting of the Anglo-French Poetry Society,—I am one of the Committee,—and hear William Davies read his poems, Mrs. Arnold Bennett recite, and meet them both? I hope you will be able to. Believe me, always your admirer, Edith Sitwell.

P.S. You should not send poems to Leigh Henry. He is an ignoramus and a fool.

This P.S. referred to a ruthless letter from Leigh Henry, the editor of *Fanfare* (rejecting two of Brian's poems, *Bagatelle* and *I am being carried, screaming off . . .*) who even went so far as to type in red on the envelope: *If carried off, please follow up: traceable by screams.*

The only review in Brian's cuttings book of this edition of *Wheels* was from the *Athenaeum* (January 1922):

. . . In *Wheels* the unicorn shows his circus paces, and it is perhaps not inappropriate that the title has been pasted upside down. Mr. Osbert Sitwell's Mexican songs ('Up flames the flamingo over the fandango') bleed a rich crimson; Mr. Aldous Huxley is at his liveliest grimaces, and concludes with an arsenical benediction; Mr. Barber frisks divertingly in Piccadilly; Mr. Charles Orange [Brian Howard] jazzes with the macabre (the ghosts of the lovers drowned in the lake change hats in the old barouches); Mr. Sacheverell Sitwell indulges now a sombre, now a quaint fancy; Miss Edith Sitwell's very special fruit (pomegranates) falls into her mouth in rhyming the fall of the Countess of Desmond from an apple-tree at the age of one hundred and forty; Mr. Paul Selver has a Panurgeical Pantoum on the folly of fame, and Mr. Augustine Rivers a savage, rather ill-natured, but very shrewdly mordant satire on a certain autocratic literary group in our midst. It's a queer game, but it has its points, even though we have nothing more to say of it at the end than Holy Cockatrices, and Boot-buttons . . .

To be reviewed in this *galère* was not bad going for a sixteen-year-old, but far from it turning his head he had gone to some pains to disguise the connection, hence the 'Charles Orange' pseudonym. What he gained on the *avant-garde* wheels he could lose on his family's roundabouts, and the pressure was already being put upon him to forego the aesthetic for the hearty life if, and when, he ever got to university. This did not deter him from going ahead with his plans of well over a year to produce a literary magazine at Eton. *The Wing* and the *New Etonian* had been tentative titles, but he finally settled on the *Eton Candle*, the magazine to be produced with the help of his great friend and rival, Harold Acton. It was to have a section devoted to contributions from Old Etonians, and Brian managed to write off requesting some of these before he left for a visit to Algeria with his mother and grandfather just after Christmas 1921. He wrote to Harold from Algiers:

> ... I saw Trefilova dancing in London—God! She is superb! The Domergue 'Venetian' ballet was really exquisite—practically as good as Bakst. The Bakst ballet was monstrous! Dreadful! I can't believe he did it. (They introduced an imitation of Charlie Chaplin into it!!!) ... I hope that you and William [Harold Acton's younger brother] are writing and painting like the very devil. Remember that the *Eton Candle* is our challenge—our first fruits—the first trumpet call of our movement—it is OURSELVES ... In Marseille I bought *A Rebours* by Huysmans. I have been reading it (yes—I admit—with difficulty). If you haven't read it—read it at once—now—immediately. It is the supreme masterpiece of decadence—it is a chef d'oeuvre in OUR atmosphere. Wilde suffers dreadfully from being less intellectual. Huysmans equals Wilde in passages like the dinner in mourning—and surpasses him elsewhere ... How I love the warm, pungent luxuriance of the south! Algiers is a delightful combination of the East and West. Everything is smothered in Moorish tiles and arches—sometimes it gets dangerously like Harrods' rug department.[11]

In a state of euphoria he addressed one envelope to: *Harold Acton 'who lives in discreet distinction, not unfavoured with a certain elusive gayety, at—La Pietra, Firenze, Italia*:

> I have such a stupendous piece of news ... [Gerald] Kelly advised me to approach Edmund Gosse for something (as yet unpublished) of Swinburne's, for the *Eton Candle*. I have got a letter from Gosse 'offering' me an as yet unpublished sonnet—a sonnet of Swinburne's. We will be reviewed all over England, and our success is certain. Oh—my friend, my friend Harold, aren't you glad!

Returning to Eton after his Algerian trip letters awaited Brian from contacts and potential contributors to the *Eton Candle*. Arthur Clutton-Brock, the art critic and father of his fellow Etonian, Alan, agreed to contribute although he felt most things written on pure aesthetics or modern art were dull. He also suggested Brian try Robert Bridges, the Poet Laureate. The reply to this attempt was short and to the point on a postcard: 'I am afraid I must ask you not to try and inveigle me into contributing to your Magger. With every wish for its

---

[11] His 'Algerian Journal' was too long to reproduce here.

success.' Brian's comment to Harold on this was, 'amazing how some people will throw away their opportunities, isn't it?' Sir Shane Leslie, the author, enclosed a poem written on Breakspear, the only English Pope, 'written while waiting for the Papal Election'. Sir Osbert Sitwell must have been asked for alternatives, for he wrote, 'Alas! The long poems are long for you—and also I like having a secret hoard of long poems. So if you can put up with the other two, or one, I'll be pleased.' It was Ernest Newman, the music critic, who took up a charming discussion by letter:

Dear Mr. Howard, What does it matter whether you are right or wrong? People will agree or disagree with you in either case, according to their lights and their livers. If you are looking for readers who will all agree with everything you say you had better keep a few trained dogs for the purpose. I shouldn't myself say that the Luigini is better music than the average Mozart symphony: but if *you* think so, why not say so? I am sure I should have agreed with you about the singer and about lots of other things. I fully appreciate your summing-up of the singer's voice as more of an accident than a voice. I know that sort. The trouble with accidents is that they *will* happen, whereas voices so rarely do.

Wishing you all success, Yours, sincerely, Ernest Newman.

Producing the *Eton Candle* did not consume all of Brian's attention. He found time to promote ideas for various clubs and debates with a literary or artistic bias. He suggested an Eton master, Mr. Gow, as Treasurer of 'The Parnassian', which was to serve as 'a very useful hot-house for that exquisite flower—"The Cremorne"—to thrive in'. The manifesto and rules of the Gremorne were listed, together with its exclusive quartet of members: Brian, Harold and William Acton, Roger Spence: *Life is an Art, and to be encountered with a button-hole of flowers. Members of the Cremorne Club must believe in the interpretation and appreciation of Life as evolved in* 1890, *and must courageously oppose and denounce the modern tendency of hysterical revolution—speed and efficiency, in modern Art and Life.* The list of 'honorary' members was impressive: Whistler, Beardsley, Swinburne, Mallarmé, Samain, Savage, Wilde, Symons, Verlaine, Gautier, Ricketts, Pryde, Housman, Herbert Beerbohm Tree, Max Beerbohm, George Meredith. Still on the subject of clubs Brian wrote to Harold:

The first meeting of the 'Candle Club' is the day after tomorrow. Since you seem so thunderstruck at the prospect of attacking Post-Impressionism, you may make a speech supporting it instead, and *I* will attack it for you. This means—alas—that I have to make the opening speech, which gives you a catastrophic advantage which I was hoarding up for myself.

Harold Acton thinks that neither the Parnassian nor the Cremorne Club ever materialised. 'Brian was wont to discuss other clubs *ad infinitum*.' At the Candle Club meeting he remembers supporting Cézanne and the Post-Impressionists while Robert Byron attacked them with extreme virulence in favour of Ruskin and the Dutch school. Gow was famous as 'Gow on the Plough', a great authority on ancient Greek ploughshares, and a friend of A. E. Housman, about whom he wrote a memoir. '*Au fond*, we liked him, though he mocked us with his sarcasms.'

In early 1922 Brian wrote to his mother, who was still in Algeria:

I get fits of dreadful depression, and yet I'm understanding and actually *loving* this place—in patches ... How I hate this constant struggle against sloth. I'm just 'wrong' somehow. Life is hell for people who don't do the right thing always.

Well! I made my first debate speech last night and very successful it was too. Immediately after I sat down Jessel got up and congratulated me on a fine speech, and then the President Bromley-Martin complimented me in his speech. The subject was, 'Whether cinemas are bad for public morals'. I said that on the whole they were—in 'exsquisite' English ... I enclose the critique (from the *Eton College Chronicle*) of my acting. *Most* satisfactory! Daddy objected to my taking the part of a girl in the play. Poor Daddy!

MR. BLAKISTON'S HOUSE DRAMATIC SOCIETY

... the second and longer piece was entitled *My Lord in Livery* in which the humour rests chiefly upon a mistaken identity between a noble lord, who for reasons of his own impersonates a footman, and the real article. Bridgeman, as the real footman, was extremely convincing. He seemed to enjoy his part, and certainly made the most of it. Jessel was very heroic as the hero, and Pelham was a success as the page in a very tight-fitting suit. Mr. Blakiston, as Spiggot, the old family butler, was admirable, and provoked storms of merriment from the audience, and he kept the action of the play from flagging. Of the ladies, Howard as Sybil Camberley showed real dramatic power, and made a very excellent leading lady. (A. Niall T.) Rankin and (Athelstan G.) Neville as her two friends each had their bright moments but they were undoubtedly carried through by Howard ...'

Mother, I'm desolately sorry, but I simply can't send you the proofs of the *Candle* in time to get them back—anyway I give you my word it's all passed the censors and is all right. Eton is *at last* paying me the attention I—perhaps?—deserve ... I have founded a society here called the Eton Society of Arts, which is a great success.

Even so, life had its ups and downs, as that very same week he fell foul of Colonel Sheepshanks, the Corps Commanding Officer, at a Field Day at Aldershot, and had to call on his father to support his resignation from the Corps. Neville, Pelham and Brian had been caught playing 'catch', 'we were treated in the way that vaudeville Prussian officers treat vaudeville Prussian privates'. For once Brian was not entirely in the wrong as Mr. Blakiston wrote an extenuating letter about the incident to Tudie Howard, 'to force Brian to stay in the Corps would make him a bit of a martyr—whilst to let him resign would be no great loss either to him or to the Corps and would not be sufficiently unusual to make him conspicuous.' Tudie told Brian that resignation was always a mark of defeat and advised him not to.

While waiting for his *Eton Candle* to appear Brian got distinctly cold feet, writing again to his mother in Algeria:

I'm worried to death about the magazine. I have written a long article on Modern Poetry advocating *vers libre* and praising everyone—that is to say, criticising no one—except J. G. Squire, whom I have attacked—properly. Perfectly civilly, of course. It's a good article—a *very* good article. I praised the Sitwells (I said Edith was a genius—so she is). I can only shout and yell with sorrow if I *have* made a mistake, anywhere . . . I don't think I have. I said Squire's clique were mediocre—so they are: his criticisms of modern poetry were imbecile—so they are. I'm sorry if it isn't the right tone or something, but you have no *right* to be way off in Algeria when I am doing such important things. I've tried to do my best—but I shrink a little about that article. A little healthy, well expressed criticism *can't* do any harm. Only I know you always hate it so. I am arranging to have the damned thing sold in Cannes . . . Oh—I'm *not* 'up a by road'. Youth *has* to have its transient interests. They make the world go round . . . Edith Sitwell has invited me to go and see her next holidays and—with your leave—I'm going. I fail to see why I shouldn't have my little youthful literary excitements. Seventeen is the age to have them. I can't sit around reading Carlyle and James Russell Lowell. I *can't* do it. I've *got* to have my cubist posters—my dances—my visits to the Sitwells. Just because I go and see Edith who admires me, and discuss poetry with her I don't SEE why you should think I'm ruining my literary sense and being petty and ephemeral, and mixing myself up with worthless people. Let me smell green carnations while I am still of an appropriate age.

4. A great Ephemeral: the *Eton Candle*

1922

A great ephemeral—that is how Cyril Connolly described the *Eton Candle* in his retrospective review for a 1963 St. Andrew's Day 'ephemeral' (the generic name bestowed on all Eton College magazines) called *Porcupine:*

> *The Eton Candle*, like the *Savoy* or *Blast* or *Verve* or the *Minotaure* is one of the few magazines one takes as much care of as a book. It had only one number, about the size of a local telephone directory, bound in stiff covers of shocking-pink with gold lettering: *The Eton Candle. Volume I. Half a crown* and on the enormous title page *edited by Brian Howard*. It was printed in March 1922,[1] and *This, the first volume is dedicated to the illustrious memory of Algernon Charles Swinburne*. It was almost entirely the work of two precocious Anglo-Americans: Brian Howard and Harold Acton, who has described its inauguration in his *Memoirs of an Aesthete*, 'It was to have a solid binding, good paper and spacious margins; the print was to emulate that of Max Beerbohm's early works.'
>
> The margins seemed large enough to ride a tricycle round and were part of that calculated impertinence which was the characteristic of Brian Howard throughout his tormented life. Many a parent must have felt his half-crown (the equivalent of about seven pounds today) was flung away on these white open 'spaces one of which bore a clerihew by Maurice Baring in microscopic type. The *Eton Candle*, which our enemies called the 'Eton Scandal', was sold out on the day of publication. 'Nothing like it has ever before been done at Eton. Those who think Howard is a charlatan, or the *Eton Candle* a great joke, are, we are certain, quite wrong,' wrote the *Eton College Chronicle*, and Harold Acton also tells us that the business manager, Roger Spence, collected enough advertisements to pay for the number in advance. These advertisements are the only things that date—it is the motor bicycles and biplanes, the 'Barker enclosed cabriolet', and the 'holiday instruction for young shooters' which remind one it is forty years old. 'In those days,' Acton goes on, 'literary activity at school was still regarded with disfavour. Even Cyril Connolly hung back. Robert Byron submitted a parody of the *vers libre* in vogue . . .' I wrote a parody of Acton myself but I do not remember being asked to contribute. I think I would

---

[1] By Spottiswoode, Ballantyne, at the Savile Press, 1922.

have been too shy; for the *Eton Candle* represented the only element in the school which was *avant-garde*, and most of us had not yet caught up with Brooke or Flecker.

When I looked at the *Candle* the other day I read Brian Howard's essay on *The New Poetry* and I saw that it might have saved me because it would have brought me Ezra Pound as an influence. Pound's poetry formed a bridge by which one could have crossed over from the classics like Catullus and the early French and Provençal poetry which I loved into the modern idiom instead of remaining bogged down in Flecker and Housman. In 1922 very few senior magazines bothered about Pound and Howard's flair was remarkable; for his essay is a plea for the Imagists, for F. S. Flint, H. D. [Hilda Doolittle] and for *Wheels* and the Sitwells. He had himself appeared in *Wheels* under his pseudonym of Charles Orange and in this essay he acclaims *Façade* and also the poetry of the Sitwell brothers and that *brilliant young genius Aldous Huxley*, whose *Leda* contained, *really subtle cynicisms, real command of language, real poetry*. But his highest praise was for Pound, *the greatest living writer of vers libre . . . one feels that he has been in England very badly treated, not that he cares two hoots, probably . . . here is another great writer whose recognition will probably come twenty years late and a master of this clean white spirit of disinfection—this modern irony . . .*

The indignation behind Brian's criticism flared up in his own poetry (not at that time memorable).

> You were a great Young Generation . . .
> And then you went out and got murdered—magnificently—
> Went out and got murdered . . . because a parcel of damned
>   old men
> Wanted some fun or some power of something.
> Oh, we will fight for your ideals—we, who were too young to
>   be murdered with you . . .
> And—we haven't forgotten you! we haven't forgotten!

One need only be unable to get on with one's father to have all the glorious dead on one's side . . . Aggressive aestheticism was the weapon (of which Robert Byron and William Acton were the local masters) and the Sitwells were the most distinguished exponents. Eliot was still unknown except possibly to Harold Acton—

> I often wish to cut my veins,
> inside a comfortable bath;
> I'm sure it would be worth the pains
> of summoning celestial wrath
> to see the crimson spirals rise . . .

A wish which the future historian has fortunately denied himself.

What makes the *Eton Candle* so dynamic is the alliance between the poetry and rather gritty ninetyish prose-poems or sinister anecdotes and the old Etonian section, headed by Huxley and the Sitwells. The names of Stravinsky, Ravel, Cézanne, Epstein, Rodin are found with translations from Rimbaud and Mallarmé.

1922 was a good moment; the *annus mirabilis* of the modern movement, with *Ulysses* and *The Waste Land* just round the corner, and the piping days of Huxley, Firbank, Waley and the Sitwells, of the Diaghilev ballet and Stulik in his pride at the Eiffel Tower.

The elegant shocking-pink volume—*Eton Candle*—with its bright yellow end papers ran to over a hundred pages and the contents list (with my brief descriptions) will give an idea of its scope:

The New Poetry by Brian, an introduction in praise of *vers libre* (reprinted here).

Defeat by Alan Clutton-Brock, a short prose essay 'in defeat' of a layer of ghosts.

Nature Morte by William Acton, reproduction of a much high-lighted still life.

Poems by Harold Acton: *Fireworks, Bal Saturnien, Town Typing Office, Still Life by Cézanne, Disquietude, Coiffeur Chorégraphique* (to Edith Sitwell), *La Belle au Bois Dormant* (dedicated to Léon Bakst), *My House, Hommage à Maurice Ravel, Pastorale.*

The Baroness Ada by Charles Orange (Brian), the story of a macabre encounter (reprinted here).

OLD ETONIAN SUPPLEMENT

Love by Algernon Charles Swinburne, an unpublished 'lyric'.

Adrian the Fourth's Tomb by Shane Leslie, a poem.

Portrait and *A Lady* by Gerald Kelly, two paintings.

Art and First Principles by A. Clutton-Brock (father of Alan C-B), a plea for 'design' in all the arts.

Portrait of a Harlequin by Sacheverell Sitwell, a poem.

The Fall of the Tower of Babel and *Helen of Troy* by Thomas Lowinsky, two paintings.

Siesta Thoughts and *Jonah, Evening Party* and *Merry-go-Round* by Aldous Huxley, two poems and two pieces of *avant-garde* prose.

Sir John Simon by Maurice Baring, a clerihew (see footnote page 54).

The Fur Hat by The Hon. Neville Lytton, a painting.

Landscape by Sir G. J. Holmes, a painting.

Aux Bords de la Mer and *The Jealous Goddess* by Osbert Sitwell, two poems.

Old McLatchie, Mary Hamilton and Mrs. Tait and *Pipers of the Scots Guards* by William Ranken, two paintings.

END OF OLD ETONIAN SUPPLEMENT

White and White by Brian Howard, a Manet-inspired concoction.

For a Lacquer and *Mattchiche Funèbre* by 'Simon Badaron', two poems.

Colonel Caesar Cannonbrains of the Black Hussars by Anthony Powell, an illustration.

A Note on Jean Arthur Rimbaud, and three of his Poems done into English by Harold Acton.

Poems by Brian Howard, *The Lotus of Hue-Lih*—cadence poem (to my cousin Carley), *To the Young Writers and Artists killed in the War:* 1914–18 (see Appendix I), *Nausea* (see extract, page 19), *L'Oiseau de Feu, Two German Waterscapes, Grotesque—Mabelle of the Waving Hands, The Coming* (see Appendix I), *Two Decorations* (dedicated to Aldous Huxley), *The Water Fall, London Might-Piece* (see Appendix I), *Symbole, Algerian.*

Divine Disappointment and *The Coffee Pot* by Alan Clutton-Brock, a satirical prose essay and a still life painting.

Hansom Cab No. 213 bis by Harold Acton (dedicated to Brian Howard), the first chapter of a planned novel about a young man whose whole life was 'a meticulous study of harmonies, cadences, blatancies, senses, discords . . .'

THE NEW POETRY by Brian Howard

The opposite of poetry is not prose, but science; the opposite of prose is not poetry, but verse.

True poetry is recognisable in any garment.

In 1872 Rimbaud was writing *vers libre* (*Mouvement* and *Marine*), and since then there has been a renascence of poetry as it was known before the Moors of Cordova and Granada swamped the world with rhyme, which they invented: since then Walt Whitman, Henley, Verhaeren, Fort, Gustave Kahn, H. de Régnier, Apollinair and Buzzi have been writing in free verse, and in 1913 there appeared in Paris an *Anthologie de Poètes Nouveaux*, in which eight poets—among them Marinetti (who had been writing free verse since 1905 in the *Poesia*)—were writing *vers libre*. And then, later, came Edgar Lee Masters, the Imagists, Amy Lowell, *Wheels*, and Ezra Pound. Yet *still* the average person treats it as a personal insult, as Edgar Saltus would say, when asked to read or even contemplate reading poetry that does not rhyme or scan.

For some reason or other people are under the astounding delusion that rhyme and scansion are necessities—are part of the body of poetry. *They are nothing of the sort.* They are external and unnecessary additions. Of course the combination of scansion and rhyme in themselves has a great beauty; but it is a specialised beauty; it is an appeal to the senses more than to the intelligence. Rhyme and metre are the overcoats of rhythm, and it is rhythm that really matters to poetry. Moreover, it is a physical impossibility to express thought to the truest, and therefore best, advantage in rhyme and scansion: the words, the phrasing, the expressions *have* to be modified—modified *away* from their purity of conception—to fit the metre and the rhyme. It is like trying to dance with the feet and the hands chained. A beautiful effect can be obtained, but the liberty, the exactitude of expression must suffer. It is restricted . . .

Swinburne did all that could be done with conventional verse. His was the supreme beauty of that particular *genre* of poetry. Great geniuses like him, Shelley and Keats, are able to express themselves in metre and rhyme so well that one no longer feels cheated by the restriction. In Swinburne's case his whole art was moulded on, and subservient to, metre—metre was his principal aesthetic. But to pretend for a moment that the greatest poet in the world is capable of expressing beauty as truthfully in rhyme and metre as in free verse is absurd. Geniuses achieve sublime, brilliant effects with it. . . but the chains are always there. It is a significant fact that Shakespeare was more and more prone to substitute conversation for blank verse in his later plays: he understood the subtle cramp of metre.

In the Preface to his book of poems, *Other-world*, F. S. Flint writes: '. . . that poetry is a quality of all artistic writing, independent of form; that rhyme and metre are artificial and external additions to poetry and that, as the various changes that could be rung upon them have been worked out, they grew more and more insipid, until they have become contemptible and encumbering . . .' Every word of this is absolutely true. Rhyme and metre can *only* be justified on the grounds of rhythm, and there is quite as much of that in the work of Flint or of Amy Lowell as in Robert Bridges or Austin Dobson: rhyme and metre should be recognised at once, everywhere, as a purely literary 'style'—a thing apart, in itself—like poker-work—and something which is perilously near developing into a vast *cliché*.

Figure to yourself an attempt to transpose the corresponding aesthetic values of a picture by Gaugin, Whistler, or Augustus John; a piece of music by Chopin, Debussy, or Stravinsky; a bust by Epstein or Rodin, into the constrictions of scanned and rhymed verse. At once the grotesque impossibility of such a transposition is apparent. It is not possible to encompass the delicacies, the *nuances* of such work in verse. Verse requires a definite attitue of mind—a sort of dim emotionalism . . . the subtleties of Art are not here, unless they be subtleties of verse craftsmanship. Now such poets as Aldous Huxley, Ezra Pound, Hilda Doolittle, and Amy Lowell, *can*, and do, accomplish corresponding aesthetic values to the forementioned painters, composers and sculptors.

An instance of my argument is discovered in Swinburne's poem *Before the Mirror*, written about Whistler's Little White Girl. It is an exquisite, exquisite poem—but. . . an improvisation, an embroidery. It is by no means the *poème juste* for the picture. No poem in verse could be.

It is amazing to think that this appallingly stupid opposition to *vers libre* is practically confined to England. To quote Mr. Ford Madox Hueffer (one of the very few critics worth listening to on contemporary poetry), the English cannot understand that 'prose is a form as well adapted for the utterance of poetry as verse' (the prose of W. H. Hudson), and that 'only in Anglo-Saxondom is poetry something silly, impracticable, and rhymed' . . . (Mr. Hueffer then proceeds to prove the 'case' for free verse by means of diagrams). For instance, gentlemen like Mr. J. C. Squire are fond of periodically launching attacks upon the free verse movement: they say, firstly, that it is so 'easy' to write it. This is as shallow as it is untrue. Mr.

Squire made a ridiculous attempt to write free verse among his other and excellent parodies; the result was rather more insignificant than irritating. Secondly, they say that the practitioners of free verse always choose such unpleasant and unpoetical subjects. This also is simply a mendacity; and even supposing it *were* true, it is probably a preferable state of affairs when one is unpleasant than when one is as mediocre as most of the living writers of verse.

In a newspaper article I discovered the following. Mr. Squire wrote it . . . 'It may be significant that the positive achievements of the propagandist school (Mr. Squire forgets that every living writer of *vers libre* is automatically a propagandist) of free verse writers are almost negligible . . . What is wrong with most of the free verse writers is not that they write free verse, but that they lack the qualities which make good poets . . . the best of them are in some instances honest and intelligent, but devoid of passion and of ear, unacquainted with the emotions that have always produced what men have agreed to call (?) poetry . . . it is not even enough to keep the eye on the subject if there is nothing behind the eye.'

I have no wish to appear immoderate or ill-mannered, but I genuinely doubt if those last two sentences of Mr. Squire's can be equalled in the whole of literary criticism for sheer imbecility. They are typical of the smug short-sightedness of the modern Academic: they typify a kind of disease of the perceptions—they are essentially the production of the tribe which William Lyon Phelps, the American critic, labels 'crystallized'.

Connected with the Squire group are the 'Georgians', amongst whom there are sereral very fine poets indeed, all being habitual writers of verse. Of these the first and best group, W. H. Davies, Ralph Hodgson, J. Drinkwater, W. de la Mare, Wilfrid Wilson Gibson, Siegfried Sassoon; in the second group F. B. Young, H. Monro, R. Graves and R. Nichols. The quality of poetry, of beauty, in any of these poets is completely divorced from their rhyme and metre. Their worth is in their words and their thoughts. (One does—perhaps—gain a pleasure from the treatment of verse by the two great poets among them, W. H. Davies and W. de la Mare.)

In artistic opposition to these we find the Imagists, the *Wheels* group, and one or two separate literary personalities, all of whom I shall attempt to deal with.

For these people—as Harold Monro says—'the test of the intellect is more important than the tests of prosody, or of tradition'.

Thank Heaven . . .

The Imagists' first *Anthology* appeared the same year as the *Spoon River Anthology* of E. L. Masters (1915) and was received with a tempest of abuse. People didn't like so much truth . . .

The Imagists have, roughly, six tenets, (i) to use the exact word (they raged at that in the 'nineties), (ii) to create new rhythms, (iii) freedom in choice of subject, (iv) to present an image, (v) to produce poetry that is hard and clear, (vi) to study concentration.

Of these I shall take firstly Amy Lowell.

Amy Lowell is one of the very most considerable characters in the poetry of today, and of poetry in general. She was one of the first pioneers of the rediscovery of free verse, and besides being what Mr. Squire would call 'honest and intelligent' she is one of the most conscientious, capable writers living, and has a marvellous technique and vocabulary. Also, she is an instance, in common—if the truth be known—with practically all free verse writers, of a *vers libriste* who writes excellent conventional verse. It is well known that she devoted years of study to the Art of Poetry, and emerged an advocate of free verse, and a superb poet. It is she who wrote *The Captured Goddess*, which I must not try to praise as it should be praised, lest I fail, or become redundant.

> Over the housetops,
> Above the rotating chimney-pots,
> I have seen a shiver of amethyst,
> And blue and cinnamon have flickered,
> A moment,
> At the far end of a dusty street.

That is poetry. The use of the word 'shiver' is so ... so perfect.

How is it possible to thus quintessentialize (and all poetry should be quintessential) in rhyme? I agree with Henley—it is not. Amy Lowell shows this same wonderful quality in such poems as *The Pike* and *Music* ('And the round notes flutter and tap about the room').

Secondly among the Imagists I will take H.D. (Hilda Doolittle), whose poems are as sunlit, as crisp, and as exquisite as her favourite violets. Here is one, called *Song*.

> You are as gold
> as the half ripe grain
> that merges to gold again,
> as white as the white rain
> that beats through
> the half-opened flowers
> of the great flower-tufts
> thick on the black limbs
> of an Illyrian apple bough.
> Can honey distil such fragrance
> as your bright hair—
> for your face is as fair as rain,
> yet as rain that lies clear
> on white honey-comb
> lends radiance to the white wax,
> so your hair on your brow
> casts light for shadow.

In H.D.'s poems is found that same bright clarity of expression, that amazing use of lovely metaphors that are at the same time exact and 'right'.

F. S. Flint is an Imagist of depth, and of beauty of thought. His long poem *Other-world* is a poem which is not obvious; one re-reads it . . . in it there are glimpses of something spiritual; it reminds one of the mental splendour of Maeterlinck. One finds clear beauty joined to insight into life. It is like a flower . . .

> Therefore, as I sit here, dreaming and writing of that other me
> Whom I have chosen from the myriad men who bear my nature,
> He is sitting beneath a cherry tree in bloom,
> Watching the afterglow of the sunset and the evening stars. . . .

It is men like Flint who are the real poets—the real lights in all this dreary expanse of tinkling commonplaces. *The Swan* is another of his poems.

> O Swan
> My eyes watch you through the sallows,
> Wounded by your cruel beauty . . .
> O white splendour,
> You have hurt me.

The remainder of the poem is like a delicate picture carved in crystal.

The poem *Lunch* is almost overpowering in its supreme brilliancy and exquisiteness.

> Frail beauty,
> Green, gold, and incandescent whiteness,
> Narcissi, daffodils,
> You have brought me spring and longing,
> Wistfulness,
> In your irradiance.
>
> Therefore, I sit here
> Among the people
> Dreaming,
> And my heart aches
> With all the hawthorn blossom,
> The bees humming,
> The light wind upon the poplars,
> And your warmth and your love,
> And your eyes . . .
> They smile and know me.

The fragile loveliness of this seems to me marvellous . . . I admire Mr. Flint very much indeed.

Of the other Imagists there is Richard Aldington, who among other excellent poems wrote *Whitechapel,* and John Gould Fletcher, the poet of *The Unquiet Street, Mexican Quarter* and *The Skaters* . . .

> And the grinding click of their skates as they
> impinge upon the surface,
> Is like the brushing together of wing tips of
> silver . . .

The *Wheels* movement of 1916 is rather more a *bouleversement* of subject than of treatment, for many of the contributors are verse writers, as, indeed, is Edith Sitwell herself, but all the same it may be included in the free verse movement both on account of its large proportion of free verse, and its courageous introduction into England of the purely modern in literary *décor* and subject; its championship of the grotesque inherited from the French *Symbolistes.*

Edith Sitwell, the leader of the movement, uses rhyme for the same purpose as Verlaine used it—for the accentuation of an essentially artificial, cultivatedly personal outlook. With her, rhymes suit the staccato pungency of the poetry. Her poetry is one of the rare, rare instances where rhyme and metre serve to enhance, and not to coop up, expression. This is only possible, however, in the most highly specialised poetry of a particular kind.

In the following poem it is clear how the rhyme is *used* to help the effect. *Pedagogues* . . .

> The air is like a jarring bell
> That jangles words it cannot spell,
> And black as fate the iron trees
> Stretch thirstily to catch the breeze.
>
> The fat leaves pat the shrinking air;
> The hot sun's patronising stare.
> .   .   .   .   .
> Beneath the terrace shines the green
> Metallic strip of sea, and sheen
> Of sands, where folk flaunt parrot-bright
> With rags and tags of noisy light.

There rhyme is used as it should be used, and hardly ever is. Used to accentuate . . . with a realization and understanding of its limitations.

Edith Sitwell also wrote this—*The Doll* . . .

> If cold grew visible again,
> We should see bell-flowers on the plain,
> With shivering stalks as white as kings,
> In trembling ermine. Each one rings
> A little tune for vespers, matins

> Beneath the polar sky's red satins
> (The cold is but the shivering
> Of the white bell-flowers as they ring).

This wonderful poem, which I have not quoted in full, and all the rest of the poems in the volume *Façade*, and *Two Country Suck-a-Thumbs*, are among the best things Edith Sitwell has written. She is a genius, and the greatest poet of the *grotesquerie de cauchemar* that has ever existed (that poem *The Doll* is ideal of its most admirable type).

Osbert Sitwell in *Who killed Cock Robin?* has invented a delicious name for the contemporary academic critic. It is the 'Mammon of Righteousness' ... In this book he points out some writers who were heaped with invective by the 'Mammons' of their times. He mentions Marlowe, Swinburne, D'Annunzio, Byron, and Keats. The criticism of Keats' poems is indistinguishable from the criticisms of *Wheels*. Just the same genteel superiority. To these five I will add some others—all of whom have been criticised in the same way, simply and solely because they had the courage to innovate: the writers of free verse are being criticised for the same reason. The following writers were all hooted and booed at (some of them still are ...) All the Parnassians, George Moore, Mallarmé, Baudelaire, Ibsen, George Egerton, Arthur Symons, Wilde, and even Pinero ... and then of course artists like Whistler, Beardsley, Rossetti, Ford Madox Brown, and all the Pre-Raphaelites, Monet and Manet, and all the Impressionists, Turner, etc. ... everyone ... everyone. It becomes almost a guarantee of worth to be attacked by Academics: and it is so interesting to consider that identically the same criticisms are levelled at the free verse writer of today as were levelled at the new writers and painters of the 'eighties and 'nineties. 'Oh, they are only trying to 'create a sensation'—or 'be original'—or 'be different from other people'—or 'be morbid'' ... the same old jargon, the same old stupidity ... the Mammon of Righteousness. They say it is easy to write free verse. Is it not equally easy to write verse? Is it not as difficult to write good free verse as good verse? But then ... what do the 'crystallized critics' matter? It has always been the same, and always will be. It is the instinct of self-preservation in the decrepit against the new, vital impulses of the vigorous. The desperate, leech-like adhesion to precedent and tradition ...

To return to Osbert Sitwell. As a poet he may be said to be one of the most interesting literary personalities in England. His poetry has an invariably excellent level. In such poems as *Fountains* and *Cornucopia* he attains a very rare beauty, and in the poems *Sunday Afternoon* and the brilliant *Church Parade* he is a master of the flashing imagery, and that particular modernist irony which *Wheels* introduced into England. *Cornucopia* ...

> Now music fills the night with moving shades;
> In velvet darkness, veined like a grape,
> Obscures and falls round many a subtle shape
> —Figures that steal through cool tall colonnades,

Vast minotaurian corridors of sleep;
Rhythmic they pass us, splashed by red cascades
Of wine, fierce-flashing fountains whose proud waves
Shimmer awhile; plunge, foaming, over steep
Age polished rocks, into the dim cold caves,
Of starlit dusk below—then merge with night,
Softly as children sinking into sleep. . . .

Sacheverell Sitwell is difficult for the reader of normal culture to understand, and that I think is the only criticism that might be made against him. But, however obscure he may be, he is obscure for a definite purpose—for a definite literary purpose. Such titles as *Laughing Lions will come* most certainly have their value. At the same time Sacheverell Sitwell is, in my opinion, a poet of the few.

Sherard Vines has a most interesting present—(such poems as *Design for a Printed Calico*)—and an even more interesting future.

Aldous Huxley is a brilliant young genius for whom one also anticipates a future, but, in his case, one of the great careers in English poetry. Already he has produced astoundingly fine work—work that has placed him, with Edith Sitwell, at the head of the new movement in English poetry, and his prose (*Crome Yellow*) is one of the most significant literary portents for the last thirty years; it is condensed, full of subtle irony and penetrating vision, powerful and original. *Leda*, his book of poems, contains—besides the title poem, the technique and verbiage of which is magnificent—among others *A Melody by Scarlatti*—a poem of ravishing delicacy, *Frascati's, Morning Scene, Variations on a Theme*. These contain really subtle cynicisms, real command of language, real poetry. Huxley, already a leader in what will be known as one of the principle movements in the literature of the modern world (at the present moment this new spirit in creative work has outstripped that of 1890 in importance and influence), has a future that, by virtue of his accomplishments in the past, is by far the most interesting in English letters.

His poems *Picture by Goya* and *Nero in the Circus* (both in *Wheels*, 1921) are masterpieces of free verse.

Disassociated from any particular movement is Ezra Pound, the greatest living writer of *vers libre*. This genius is deplorably ill read, and having been practically hounded into those refuges of good writers, the American journals, one feels that he has been, in England, very badly treated; not that he cares two hoots—probably. However, I do wish he would write for English papers some of the articles one gathers in those excellent periodicals of New York, *The Little Review* and *The Dial*. But then, of course he writes *vers libre* . . .

Ezra Pound has an amazing erudition, an unsurpassable technique, and poetic vision of the first order. Just because he is violently interested in the pre-Renaissance literature of Latin Europe there is no need to murmur things about his being an obscurantist. Nonsense!

It is very upsetting when one realises that here is *another* great writer whose recognition will probably come twenty years late. More Mammon of

Righteousness . . . It is the same thing, of course, with that most deserving of poets—Ford Madox Hueffer.

Pound is another master of this clean, white spirit of disinfection—this modernist irony. His *Ancora* is an instance . . .

> Good God! they say you are *risqué*,
> O canzonetti!
> We who went out into the 4 a.m. of the world
> Composing our albas,
> We who shook off our dew with the rabbits,
> We who have seen Artemis a-binding her sandals,
> Have we ever heard the like?
> O Mountains of Hellas!!

And to *Formianus' Young Lady Friend* . . . Let us quote some more—*Fish and the Shadow* . . .

> The salmon-trout drifts in the stream,
> The soul of the salmon-trout floats over the stream
> Like a little wafer of light.
>   .   .   .   .
> Light as the shadow of the fish
> That falls through the pale green water.

And that superb piece of *vers libre*, *The Return* . . .

> See, they return; ah, see the tentative
>   Movements, and the slow feet,
>   The trouble in the pace and the uncertain
> Wavering!

I wish there was room to quote the rest.

And now, as an example to the average *London Mercury* poet, with his Varsity *naïveté*, here is a really fresh, charming poem of the ingenuously picturesque type. It is by Pound. *An Immorality* . . .

> Sing we for love and idleness,
> Naught else is worth the having.
> Though I have been in many a land,
> There is naught else in living,
> And I would rather have my sweet,
> Though rose leaves die of grieving,
> Than do high deeds in Hungary,
> To pass all men's believing.

Space prohibits me from quoting *Further Instructions* and *Deux Mouvements*, but for an end I will rehearse Pound's encouragement to the fighters against Mammons. *The Rest* . . .

> O helpless few in my country,
> O remnant enslaved!
> .   .   .   .
> You of the finer sense,
> Broken against false knowledge,
> You who can know at first hand,
> Hated, shut in, mistrusted.
> Take thought:
> I have weathered the storm,
> I have beaten out my exile.

What enrages me is that he should have been compelled to beat it out . . .

The other solitary and also thoroughly misused free verse poet of note is F. M. Hueffer, the leader of the *vers libristes* in England. The way he is ignored is grotesque: it could only happen in England. If he were a Frenchman or an American he would be accounted a great poet. As it is, isolated people like myself are observed making small disturbances about (people like) him . . . here and there . . . No one pays any attention, of course. Why should they? when they vastly prefer the *Morning Post* to even 'Tennyson, who wrote *real* poetry'.

Ford Madox Hueffer is wrong, I think, in saying that free verse is not appreciated in Anglo-Saxondom, for presumably this includes America, which is no longer Anglo-Saxon, and is the home and retreat of *vers libristes*. No wonder all the writers and artists in England seem to be migrating to America: there they are listened to and respected. Apparently it is a sort of paradise for that enormous legion in Art of the deserving unappreciated.

Here are the first nine lines of *To all the Dead*, by Hueffer:

> A Chinese Queen on a lacquered throne,
> With a dragon as big as the side of a house,
> All golden, and silent and sitting alone
> In an empty house.
> With the shadows above and the shadows behind,
> And the Queen with a paper white, rice white face,
> As still as a partridge, as still as a mouse,
> With slanting eyes you would say were blind—
> In a dead white face.

From *The Great View* . . . an historical piece of free verse . . .

> Up here, where the air's very clear,
> And the hills slope away nigh down to the bay,
> It is very like Heaven . . .
> For the sea's wine-purple and lies half asleep
> In the sickle of the shore and, serene in the west,
> Lion-like purple and brooding in the even,
> Low hills lure the sun to rest.

Very like Heaven ... For the vast marsh dozes,
And waving plough-lands and willowy closes
Creep and creep up the soft south steep;
In the pallid North the grey and ghostly downs do
    fold away.
And, spinning spider-threadlets down the sea, the
    sea-lights dance
And shake out a wavering radiance.

When Hueffer first published his poems he received wonderful reviews. I believe the public purchased fourteen copies ... well ... what can one say when confronted with such things? It is a tragedy. Here one has one of the precious few—who *know*. He is utterly ignored. *The Rest* of Ezra Pound, you see ...

.   .   .   .   .

Of course there are charlatans now practising their charlatanry by means of *vers libre*. With the public intelligence in its present state it is easy to do so. But hasn't *every* movement had its attendant scum since the beginning of the world? Always they are there at the first, taking advantage of the novelty of the genuine work. Soon the novelty wears away, and so do they. But to condemn a whole living, working movement because it looks easy, or doesn't imitate Keats, or contains dots, or is new ... is wicked, and only excusable in the elderly-minded. And Free Verse, after all, is the poetry of Humanity ...

ENVOI.

I have tried—in a stumbling way—to state my beliefs about the New Poetry. I have tried to explain why I firmly and fervently believe in it as a medium of Art. And I have a wild hope that I may have done a little something for what is at once the most misprized and the worthiest of literary causes.

THE BARONESS ADA by Charles Orange [Brian Howard]

I had been walking a long, long way, trying not to be depressed by the grey, uninteresting sky—the clinker built fences—the black, shiny tar road—the brown telegraph poles—all the 'English' atmosphere of an English Sunday road in the Aldershot district after a rainy morning, when I suddenly decided—irrevocably—that I would march up to the next front door I found and ask if they would consider it a great impertinence if I came in to tea. It was nearly five o'clock.

For some time I was obliged to walk on ... past a stretch of damp larches, between black iron fencing ... over a flat 'common' of burnt heather covered with putty coloured sandpits ... a mauvish horizon of wooded hillocks, occasionally showing a pink roof ... On and on I trudged, desperately, passionately longing for California, Italy, the Riviera, the Sahara ...

It was when I had passed as unsuitable a hospital, that I found the elaborate Victorian metal gates of Abbeyfield. Abbeyfield ... written in

Gothic calligraphy in white on a dark green background. Taking off my gloves I opened the wet gates and shut them again, and resolutely walked up a well-kept yellow gravel drive towards the house. The drive wound in a rather unnecessarily ambitious way through carefully placed groupings of shrubbery, and at length stopped—after a final twirl round a tall monkey tree—at the front door. The façade of the house, like the monkey tree opposite to it, was tall and thin . . . it was covered in an old, weather-stained cement, cracked here and there, and quite innocent of ivy or architecture. The woodwork, such as the window frames and the carved overmantel to the small porch on either side of the front door, was painted a hot brown, and each of the windows had its hot brown Venetian curtains—pulled up with two wide strings of rough tape. Standing on the geometrically tesselated pavement of the porch I pulled a brightly burnished brass bell . . . 'Visitors' . . .

I rang again.

Almost immediately after the second tug someone trotted to the door and, after slipping back innumerable bolts and chains, admitted me. I discovered myself in a long dark hall. Vaguely I made out vast bunches of pampas plumes . . . walls of thickly varnished wood . . . somewhere, I remember, a Zulu calf-hide shield and a stuffed badger. And what an atmosphere!—heavy, gloomy and close.

Suddenly, from behind, a voice: 'Your name, please?'

'Oh, I'm a stranger here, and I came to ask you—I do hope you won't think it very rude of me—for a cup of tea. I've had such a long walk . . .' As I said this I examined my companion, who apparently was of a status above a servant, as she was wearing a black crêpe dress, ruched over the chest, a thin gold necklace, and a bunch of keys at the waist. She was a stout woman . . . and short.

When I had finished she rapidly wreathed her pale face into a smile, and replied: 'Ah . . . yes . . . I'm the governess, you know . . . Miss Bradlaugh's the name—yes, I'm sure—now my employer—the Baroness—will give you tea—you know—I'm busy now. I'll take you up to the drawing-room—follow me—you know (chuckle) it's a darkish hall—ours—I'm the secretary—Miss Bradley's the name—I have the use of the governess cart—come along! upsy daisy—here we are . . . mind the step, dearie (chuckle). Lawks—the elastic has snapped on my slipper—never mind. In there! That door—(louder) Ada! visitor!' I heard her trot away, still chattering . . .

Just as I had laid my hand on the black china knob, the brown varnished door flew open, and I was confronted by a very striking figure of a woman, festooned in a caped dressing gown of scarlet flannel. Her hair was grey and thin, except over her wrinkled fore-head, where it hung in a thick, polished bang. Her face was more or less the same tint as her hair, and had the high, protruding cheek-bones and side-long almond eyes of a Malay. The dressing gown was loosely corded round a wasp-like waist and, slipping away from the shoulders, folded over her thighs in the manner of panniers . . . above was a satinette whatnot . . .

'Enter, my dear sir—at once. Charmed to see you. To what am I indebted for this unexpected but altogether delightful visit?'

'Madam,' I said, as she enveloped her upper part in a red Paisley quilt, 'I am tired; a stranger; and I came to ask—impertinent as is my nature—for a cup of strong tea . . .'

'Camomile or green?'

'Indian, madam.'

We both smiled at our little piece of mutual facetiousness.

'Well, sir, you're welcome, you're welcome. You shall have your tea at once.'

Meanwhile I had been observing the room, and it seemed to me to be so fascinating that I intend to describe it in detail. There were two windows, draped with thick curtains of faded pink and 'champagne' brocatelle, with ball fringes. Between these windows was a plain deal dressing table, ornamented with dusty bows of pink silk, on which were multitudes of boxes and bottles—of wood, tin and glass—pincushions of every conceivable shape and colour, hand mirrors, combs, brushes, and other toilet accessories. In the opposite corner of the room, against the wall, was an enormous rococo gilt four-poster bed, the pillows and sheets of which looked as if they had assisted in a nightmare. The walls of the room were glossily papered in a green and brown design of tulips. The carpet was worn, and patterned in dull red and green. Against the walls, in various parts of the room, were numerous wardrobes—all of wood of contrasting shades of brown. Dotted about the floor were a quantity of chairs, some wicker-work, made comfortable by faded red cushions; some stiff and straight—cane-seated; some 'easy' chairs loosely covered with stuffy looking cretonnes. At the foot of the bed was a narrow blue rep settee with a switchback outline. In a far corner were piles of cardboard boxes propped up by a broken towel-horse. The windows were shut and misty at the cracks . . . There was a worrying aroma of white rose and camphor . . .

The Baroness rang a bell, and presently a dumb waiter creaked up to a standstill in an aperture in the wall over the pillow on the bed. She approached it and, breathing stentorously, hoisted out a tarnished silver tray, on which reposed a huge green teapot painted with red roses, and a solitary glass . . .

'Thank you,' I murmured, as she placed the tray on a bamboo table by my side. 'Thank you.'

'Now,' she said brightly, beaming at me in a way that reminded me curiously of the governess, 'I suppose Ruby let you in—she's my secretary; magnificent at figures, she is . . . I live a very sedentary life, you know—quite apart, quite apart . . . Oh, I forget, I must apologise for my *négligée*. You see—you see, me and Ruby don't mind, and one gets used to one's comfort. . .'

Here she picked up a steel comb and began to run it through her bang, ruminatively.

'I'm writing a monograph, you know (smiling dis-quietingly). I couldn't tell you what on—simply couldn't! . . . However, tell me about yourself, do.'

During this I noticed an amazing tendency in her voice to lower by octaves during a long speech. When she got to '*négligée*' she rolled like a bassoon. Then I discovered that the person who had made my tea had forgotten the tea, and consequently I had to content myself with hot water.

'Gracious goodness me!' exclaimed the Baroness, suddenly noticing that I had not been supplied with any eatables. 'Ruby must have forgotten the digestive biscuits . . . I believe I have some somewhere . . .' She rummaged in the folds of a parasol that she produced from under the mattress and drew forth an oblong box of Burmese brasswork, which she handed to me. 'Here they are—you'll find they sit very lightly on the stomach . . . very . . . I'm afraid it's nearing the time for my cold bath . . . I wonder what I did with my violet kimono.' (I had opened, with difficulty, the brass box, and disclosed three and a half uninviting looking biscuits. I bit at one and found it gritty and old.) 'Cripes, it's dark, isn't it? Let's light the gas.' (Does so.) 'I'm so glad you like the biscuits . . . I'm not allowed to eat them myself. My doctor says they produce eczema in sensitive people . . .' I thought it was time I assisted the conversation, so I put in: 'Dear, dear . . . what luck I'm not sensitive! How curious, madam, that you should be an author. So am I. I write stories.' 'Do you reely,' she replied, 'how interesting of you . . . But ah! you have a kind face' (smiling vaguely), 'a nice kind face . . .'

Advancing to the dressing table she picked up a large ivorine bowl of powder and proceeded to apply it with deft motions all over her face, accompanied by dips in the cold cream pot. 'The rouge comes *after* my shower bath!' she remarked.

'You have a delightfully decorated bedroom,' I murmured.

However, my hostess did not seem to hear, or, rather, did not pay me attention. Her eyes began to rove filmily over the room—ever and again stopping at the dumb waiter.

'Well,' I added a trifle louder, 'I must be getting on now; It's been most char——'

She interrupted quietly: 'Wait a little, please. Just a little while.' Half out of my chair, I sank back. Silence . . ., 'I've something to show you . . . so interesting . . .' Suddenly, with a somewhat disagreeable shock, I heard the dumb waiter creaking down to the next floor. It stopped. Faintly I heard the echoings of someone's hearty laughter. Then came scrapes and thuds, as if someone was settling down into something. Renewed creakings . . . coming nearer . . .

'Yes,' I said tentatively, 'you have something to show me?' 'I *have*,' she growled in a changed tone, with startling emphasis. 'You see these?' She opened, rapidly, all the doors of all the wardrobes. The interiors were tightly packed with hundreds and hundreds of costumes, dresses, coats, capes, shirt-waists, petticoats, jerseys.

I felt a nauseous panic creeping over me. I replied in a lamentably weak fashion, with a badly managed pleasant expression: 'Are they all yours, madam? What a lot, aren't they?'

She did not answer me, but stood by a further cupboard with a fixed expression—a face pregnant with malignity.

51

The dumb waiter stopped with a crack behind me. Some instinct made me whirl round. I had an unforgettable vision of the governess-secretary leaping towards me out of the hole in the wall—her gold tooth gleaming in the gaslight. At my back I heard the quick patter of the Baroness's carpet slippers. As Ruby rushed forward, pawing at my face, I felt two small muscular hands clutch me in the small of the back and propel me toward the bed. I fell across it—screaming. Out of the corner of one eye I saw Ruby tearing out armfuls of clothes from the wardrobes: suddenly she ran towards me, and a deluge of dresses descended all over me. I attempted to rise, but the Baroness beat me down again. All the time I sensed the fall of piles of clothes on my prostrate form: soon I was unable to move and hardly able to breathe . . . more clothes . . . thud . . . thud . . . like a whisper the shrill, excited voices of the women came to me . . . 'There! there! My summer suits for 1909!' . . . Thud . . . 'My blue wool coat' I couldn't breathe any more . . . the terrible, intimate odour of the bedclothes . . . oh . . . I couldn't . . . breathe . . . any more . . .

Brian's other story in the *Eton Candle*, *White and White* was sub-titled 'Dans le bois de Viroflay' and dedicated to Harold Acton. It was an imaginative essay concocted round Manet's picture, *Déjeuner sur l'herbe*. The time is 1880 and the hero, Herbert, is having a gay picnic party in the woods with his friends, Adele, Adolphe, Zizi and Rose, when they are joined by the famous artist 'Monsieur Manet' who asks if he can sketch them. *Ten years later*—Herbert, with his depressingly suburban wife Edna, revisits the same wood—wherein she finds no magic. Herbert drifts on by himself and suddenly glimpses his old friends as if time had stood still, and they greet him without surprise, showing him Manet's sketch of them all. *Ten years later*—Herbert is taking his dull son 'who has leanings towards engineering' round the Impressionist pictures at the Louvre. In front of Manet's 1880 chef d'oeuvre the son stops, 'Here! Dad! I say, you know, don't you call this mad? Nothing like real. Putrid rot, I think . . . With a shock Herbert recognised himself, and Rose, and Zizi, and Adèle, and Adolphe . . .'

Unfortunately there is not space enough to reprint further extracts from the *Eton Candle* here, but four of the poems are included in Philip Toynbee's selection of Brian's verse.

Harold Acton had matriculated and left Eton by Easter 1922, but was sent to an Oxford crammer to polish up his Latin for Responsions. Brian wrote to him there about the *Eton Candle* reviews:

The Times is, as you say, merely unappreciative—and I thought, a shade stupid. That commonplace little idiot Clutton-Brock (*père*) wrote the article . . . if I had known that the man was so entirely devoid of all aesthetic instincts as by this article he has proved himself to be I should never have had him contribute to the *Candle*. There is a kind of patronising, fatherly stupidity about the man which riles me. The *Morning Post* review was better. As I know the *Daily Express* critic we are going to have a good review there, and Edith Sitwell herself is going to review it for the *Sackbut*. Also there are going to be reviews in the *Observer*, and the *Sunday Times*.[2]

Clutton-Brock (boy) is going to review the *Candle* in the *Eton College Chronicle*. Of course it doesn't really matter a damn what the *Chronicle* says—but it is *so* annoying to have that little shrimp, who thoroughly misunderstands the whole thing, and who is inartistic to a degree review *our* paper. *So* like Eton. MERRY HELL.

For a 'school magazine' the *Eton Candle* received unprecedented review coverage, Edith Sitwell (as 'E.S.') in the *Sackbut* of June 1922 being the most illuminating:

This is a very interesting and promising book, and augurs well for the next generation of English writers. Here we find none of the wrong ideals of false simplicity which disfigure a certain section of the older generation, and very little of the 'eighteen-ninety' taint of affectedness which is so often to be found in young writers.

The book opens with the editor's essay on *The New Poetry*, which shows the writer's wide reading. I am not always in agreement with him, as he tends to exaggerate the importance of certain free-verse writers, simply because they write in free verse (though he is certainly unconscious that this is the reason). But his views are all in the right direction in spite of this minor defect. Mr. Howard is an extremely gifted young writer; I have watched his work with great interest for over a year, and though I find nothing in this volume which quite equals his *Barouches Noires* (a really remarkable poem which appeared in the 1921 *Wheels*, under the pseudonym of 'Charles Orange'), yet his work is always interesting. His poetry and his prose are both alive and arresting, he has a great gift for phrases, and the harder he works the better he will become. One must remember that free verse is a very difficult medium (a fact of which a good many people are unconscious), and to be a good writer in free verse, a transcendental technique, a virtuosity like that possessed by Mr. T. S. Eliot, is necessary. Mr. Howard has a real sense of form: he is what is known as a born writer—which all writers should be, but, alas! are not—and if he does not succumb to his own natural facility, he has a very distinguished career ahead of him. That is my convinced opinion. I should like to see him writing hard, knuckly, dramatic poems, with tight, taut rhyme-schemes for a while, because of the practice that they would give him. *The Baroness Ada* is an admirable piece of work, clearly imagined and well constructed.

Another young poet of promise is Harold Acton. I like the lines in his *Coiffeur Chorégraphique* which run—

Till down upon my head Niagara Falls
Descend with all the heat of music halls.

---

[2] I could not trace all these reviews in the British Museum Library editions.

But his prose seems to me to show even more achievement than his verse. *In the summer, during the long hot mornings when the sunshine spots would dance little gavottes* . . . Is not that charming? . . .

Apart from national reviews Brian also received many congratulatory letters (which he kept in a special folder for the rest of his life). Sir C. J. Holmes, the artist and museum director, wrote: '. . . May your *Candle* be like Ridley and Latimer's.[3] It is really a wonderful publication and augurs an Eton very different from my own rather academic and Philistine memories. Indeed it makes me feel very old and out of date while reading it—though I am delighted too that the torch should be carried on so brightly. You as Editor naturally deserve the chief congratulations, but as a defunct Editor[4] myself may I send a special token of respect to your advertisement canvasser—of such is the real Kingdom of journalism . . . With all good wishes for future candles, torches, flares and bonfires.'

Edmund Gosse, the poet and literary critic, thought it more than held its own with the old *Oxford Sausage*, 'your essays and poems in it make me sure that I shall follow your work in the future with great interest, though I will not go so far as to say always with agreement . . . P.S. Swinburne would have been much touched and pleased by your dedication.'

Sir Shane Leslie's letter began charmingly: 'My dear Brian Howard—drop all Mistery with me—I must congratulate you on the *Eton Candle*. It is unlike all Eton journalism that I ever read and a permanent literary possession. Whatever the Cloisters and the Eton Society and the School Office think you have given Eton a real literary distinction. Your poem to the slain artists I can only read over and over again for its solemn sardonic truth. 'Murdered magnificently' is a phrase we shall all have to borrow from you. Acton's *Still life by Cézanne* ('the cork seems restless' is mighty good) and Beardsley-ish *Hansom Cab* I like too—but the whole production with its spirited defence of *vers libre* pleases me beyond words—and from Eton!! . . . I gather with great approbation that Clutton-Brock and the Sitwells are Old Etonians. And you have skimmed Maurice Baring[5] at his best and his best is a little subtler than Max Beerbohm and a little cleverer than Belloc. I had no idea that I would not see my poem wedged in between a list of House Fives Competitions and the Annual Meeting for the Eton Mission. With best wishes for your brilliant venture!'

Even the Vice-Provost of Eton and classics tutor, Hugh Macnaghten, succumbed: 'Dear Howard' [he wrote], 'I am too old to love the modern poetry,

---

[3] Sir Charles would probably have been amused to know that Brian had had the *Eton Candle* advertised with the help of Latimer's famous words of encouragement to his fellow martyr, Ridley: '. . . we shall this day light such a candle by God's grace in England as I trust shall never be put out', but the reaction to such a liberty by the somewhat formidable Eton Master, H. E. Luxmoore, was reported to have been the equivocal comment, 'Out, out, brief scandal!'

[4] He was Managing Director and joint Editor of the *Burlington* magazine from 1904–1909, successfully extricating it from its difficult days, as recounted in his *Self and Partners*, published by Constable, 1936.

[5] Maurice Baring's clerihew: Sir John Simon
    Was unlike Timon;
    Timon hated Mankind;
    Simon didn't mind.

but not too old to admire some of it. One of your poems. *We haven't forgotten you! We haven't forgotten* I liked and admired greatly. It is full of force and fire. Do come and see me next half if you care to do so. *No answer.*'

The *Eton Candle* definitely set Brian a few rungs up on the ladder of fame and it is no wonder he had self confidence of a kind at this stage—and for the next few years. There are not many boys of barely seventeen who could create an 'Eton Candle' and produce such reaction to their first published literary efforts. The best school magazines of today are ones of experiment and protest, but singularly lacking in any evidence of literary erudition.

5. Signs of promise, with Tunisian interlude

It would be quite wrong to assume that the *Candle* aftermath would leave Brian in a state of anticlimax; he continued his illuminating correspondence with Harold Acton from April to July 1922, giving a graphic account of his life and times, including a schoolboyishly spiteful description of his first visit to his poet patron, Edith Sitwell:

. . . Yesterday was the private view of the International. I had a most amusing time showing 'The Lady with the Flag' (my sketch for a fancy dress—which was accepted) to Lady Lavery, Kelly, Ernest Thesiger, Lady Juliet Trevor (the great friend of Bakst, Stravinsky and Diaghilev) and all the rest. Dulac, Lady Cunard, Lowinsky, Ranken, Brockhurst, Aldous Huxley were a few of the people who were there. There are some excellent pictures by Orpen, Pryde, Ranken, Birley, Lavery, Millais, Sandys, Procter, Brockhurst, seventy *superb* water colours (of the 'Sleeping Princess' mostly) and four oils by Bakst; things by Philpot, Munnings, Sargent, de Glehn, Domergue, (de) Laszlo(!), sculptures by Watts, Bourdelle, and some most amusing 'negro' things by Zadkine. There is also an enormous and inexpressively appalling painting of the Dowager Lady Michelham by Boldini. I never knew how bad he was until I saw this great, grinning, vulgar, flashy portrait. It's a monstrosity—but then, Boldini *is* monstrous . . . Well, I went to see Edie (Sitwell) and was very disappointed indeed. I arrived at Moscow Road—an uninviting Bayswater slum—and toiled up flights and flights of bare Victorian stairs (very narrow stairs). From outside, Pembridge Mansions looked like an inexpensive and dirty hospital. I arrived at a nasty green door, which was opened by Edie herself. She has a very long thin expressive face with a pale but good complexion. She looks rather like a refined Dutch medieval madonna. She had on an enlarged *poilu* hat of grey fur, an apple green sheep's wool jacket, and an uninteresting 'old gold' brocade dress. Her hair is thin, but of a pleasant pale gold colour, bobbed at the sides and bunned at the hind. I do not care for the people she usually has around her—to Saturday teas, for example, at all. They are common little nobodies. Also I don't like her teas—*as teas* at all. Tell William I got *one penny bun, and three-quarters of a cup of rancid tea in a dirty cottage mug.* Also I don't like her apartments, or, rather, room. It is small, dark, and I suspect, dirty. The only interesting things in the room are an etching by (Augustus) John, and her library, which is most entertaining. The remainder seems to consist of one lustre ball and a quantity of bad draperies. Miss Helen Rootham, whom she lives with, is one of those terrifyingly forceful women—she proffered me a picture by Kandinsky—an incoherent smudge of colour and murmured with great vim into my ear,

56

'Isn't that *pure* beauty?' I replied in the affirmative. I always do that when I meet muscle.

Edie told me that she thought the *Candle* was very good indeed, although she disagreed with some of my article. Especially about Sachie (of course) and, curiously enough about Aldous—whom she admires most reservedly. She likes your prose much better than your poems which *she* says are a trifle immature and too '1890-ish'. I don't agree at all ... I admire your latest work—beginning with your splendid *Town Typing Office* more than your earlier work. Oh my dear Harold—continue to write like that and you will be *great*. Don't slip back into Verlainesques. Let *Town Typing Office* be the foundation stone of your literary career. It is so good.

She has made me the virtual business editor of *Wheels*. A most damnably unpleasant position. There will be no 1922 *Wheels* unless I can get advertisements for it, and I am finding it very much more difficult than getting them for the *Candle*, which is going to be sold in London in about three or four days. I have apparently risked all the profits by having a second edition, but I have taken the liberty of having one as I know both you and Roger [Spence—the Business Editor] would rather have it sold in London than scrape up a few pounds. Of course I'll see that Roger loses nothing. As it is I've had to put the price of the second edition up to five shillings, as apparently each copy *costs* that to make, and the only reason that I was able to sell it at all at half a crown was that the advertisements paid for it. As they won't pay again for the second edition I have had to put the price up.

... I can foresee myself resigning from the Eton Society of Arts as clearly as anything. If I do it, I shall do it in the grand manner (as I always do everything, my dear!) and of course William will come with me—if he has any sense. No Ruskin for me! I'm sick and tired of *arty Eton*. It's like a rather faded flannel flower in a bowl of Gladstonian soup. The *Candle* has had a great success in London, you'll be faintly pleased to hear ... I think I shall write something or other for both (Burnett) Hitchcock and Clutton-Brock [who were producing two new Eton magazines], and shall sign my name. It is just as well to keep in the 'lime-light'. I advise you to do the same. (Insist on the signature.)

... I return ch: 2 of your *Hansom Cab*. As you know, I don't *very* much like it, excepting the dwarf dancers and their mistress—all of which part is excellent ... I think you have done some ill work over the food. After all, it is a great opportunity—food. I love the last line in your *Diary of the Future*—'Houp-la, the world is gay'. It is so characteristic of the Harold I love! Do tell me how the *Candle* is selling at Oxford. I am terrified that this second edition is a failure. I am having Edie down here to lecture soon. You *must* come. I am in a House Four and am having myself (especially my behind) torn to pieces. I am altogether depressed. P.S. In the leading article of Clutton-Brock's magazine he has burlesqued you and me—amalgamated into one person, bearing my name. The article is called the *Aspidistra*,[1] or something like that. God gall his guts!

---

[1] I cannot trace this article.

... I also have begun a novel, which I am pouring all my knowledge of nuance into. You will appreciate it if no one else does. I enclose my *Impertinent Improvisation* which is going into Hitchcock's paper (the *Latest*).[2] I pray to God that the bits about McNeile and Sheepshanks [two masters unpopular with Brian, Colonel Sheepshanks being Corps Commanding Officer as well] will get through the censor. It is the best satire I have ever done. *How* it will madden them if it gets through ... No. I shouldn't send any serious work to Clutton-Brock. It isn't dignified ... To tell you the truth—I am in the last stages of depression. I am doing *no* work for the Certificate, and if I fail in it for the third time I shall be disgraced and shall have months of misery as the result. Also I am becoming a self-indulgent, egotistical, selfish old boor. God help me! I am writing *nothing*—I am being killed here. I hate it. Love—Claiborne.

After a certain amount of self-censoring Brian's *An Impertinent Improvisation* appeared in the *Latest*, sub-titled, 'being a short conversation upon the subject of Art, between Queen Victoria, Mr. Wyndham Lewis, Alfred Lord Tennyson, Oscar Wilde, Mr. Clutton-Brock of *The Times*, Mr. Augustus John, Whistler, Mr. J. C. Squire of the *London Mercury*'.

AN IMPERTINENT IMPROVISATION

Clutton-Brock: Of course, what is wrong with contemporary art is that people will not look at things from a sane, utilitarian point of view. Now all art should be based on everyday life, and have its origin in use. Take all the horrible stuff produced in France in the Louis Quinze period. It was all so artificial.

Whistler: Amazing! Amazing, that anyone could be so entirely lacking in aesthetic sense. Don't you think so, Oscar?

Wilde: Yes, James. And apparently the dear man can't have the least understanding of that so subtle and beautiful a thing—the exquisitely unnecessary.

Squire: Clutton-Brock, I quite agree with you. Now take a Rugby football match. What a fine subject for a poem!

Tennyson: Are you mad, sir? Have you no feeling for romance?

Wyndham Lewis: Bogey! Bogey!

Tennyson (purple): What the devil do you mean, sir, by saying that to me?

Wyndham Lewis: Do you really believe in your own sloppy sentimentalities?

Tennyson (purple *foncé*): Do you mean my poems, you popinjay, you?

Wyndham Lewis: Yes, I do—you rude old man, you!

Queen Victoria (pacifically): You know, dear Albert always liked a dog and some moral uplift in a picture.

Augustus John (roaring with laughter): Nothing matters in art but to paint life—life, as an artist sees it.

[2] Published by Spottiswoode, Ballantyne, 1922.

Wilde: Yes, but do you see it like an artist? Have you the scarlet embroideries in your paintings that I have in my prose?

Augustus John: No! Grace be to God!

Wyndham Lewis (to Queen Victoria): There is nothing more beautiful than a Vorticist building.

Queen Victoria: Haven't you seen Lincoln Cathedral?

Wyndham Lewis: Bogey! Bogey!

Whistler: Ah, but listen! Have you known—any of you—as I have known, the delicate aloofness of art? Art is Art. Art is alone—a shy, fragile goddess who visits only the minds of artists—people like me . . .

Wilde: Art is Art. Art knows neither good nor evil!

Queen Victoria (to Wilde): I must say I think that's a very unsettling statement.

Wilde (sweetly): Ah, dear lady—you must not reject art for her rouge!

Clutton-Brock: What an unhealthy thing to say! I do dislike epigrammatical conversation. It isn't useful.

Squire (fervently): So do I, Clutton-Brock; I prefer healthy, sane statements. No artificiality and almost no subtlety.

Wilde (curiously to Squire): And you are the editor of the largest literary periodical at present in England?

Squire: I am.

Whistler (to Clutton-Brock): And you are the art critic of *The Times*?

Clutton-Brock: I am.

Whistler: (to Wilde): Amazing!

Wilde (to Whistler): You see, James, England is England. Still!

Continuing letters to Harold:

I'm afraid poor C-B has descended to doing a poorish imitation of the *Candle*. However, we shall see what the genius from Heal's has done when it comes out. Hitchcock's was very bad. [Even so, Brian contributed largely to it] . . . The 4th of June was really quite enjoyable. By far the best clothes I have seen this year, *and* from a totally unbiased point of view I think my mother was the best dressed of all. She had a large blue hat and a straight, slim, low-waisted dress of the most exquisite appearance I have ever seen. She was marvellous! It sounds silly of *me* to rave like this, but I've never seen anything quite so perfect.

Danielson's magazine is perfectly extraordinary. It seems full of unknown writers all crazy about sexuality between white men and black women, or the other way round. I've never seen one theme used so much in a single number of a periodical. Edie is coming down next Sunday: it is going to be 'somewhat of an ordeal' for me—especially if she comes in her fur cap and green wool coat! It will be amusing, though.

Who is this Proust? Huxley was talking about him. Perhaps I ought to read him? I don't much like your *Pensile Gardens of Babylon*. Occasionally you seem to descend to intimidatory verbiage. It seems to be a trifle heavy and lengthy, too. Seven or eight lines are *excellent*.

We have decided to put off our trip to Canada until next year—so I have to go to CAMP! [It would seem that he had not, after all, resigned from the Corps.] . . . I spoke to William very severely about not writing you—I expect he will. I don't know what's the matter with him. Since you've left he seems to do nothing—*especially* mentally—but trot around and drawl remarks for all the world like a third rate character in the *Green Carnation*. He's a dear sweet thing but I wonder whether he'll ever accomplish anything. I like your note-paper, me dear, but do put sufficient stamps on, as your letters always arrive 'with 3d. to pay'.

. . . Edie came down here looking like one of her own poems, and lectured for an hour to a tiny audience (in the Queen's School Lecture Room) containing all the bloody Eton intellectuals—(Gow, Lyttelton, Butterwick, Lubbock, Whitworth, the Vice-Provost etc. etc.) She whispered her speech into a table, and as a result it was horribly difficult to hear anything at all. Ostensibly lecturing on Modern Poetry, she went on for hours about Stravinsky. What people *could* hear of her speech astounded them so much that they sat there smiling, with their mouths open, and tittered every once and a while—genteely, of course. I heard that Gow and Lyttelton—Lord God damn and shrive their smelly souls!—kept nudging one another and grinning. If I ever speak to either of them again I shall say—'Oh, I was so surprised you liked Miss Sitwell's lecture, I should have thought it would have been rather too hard for you to understand.' After the lecture—it was an excellent lecture ('Squire's poems exude the odour of wet mackintoshes') and quite a success—William and I drove up to Tull's in a barouche, and damme if the whole audience, including Gow, Lyttelton etc. didn't stand and gaze at us as if we were crazed. I had to make a speech at the beginning and introduce her—*and* at the end, and just when I'd finished 'thanking the audience for listening with such courteous attention' the beastly old Vice-Provost—Macnaghten—got up and advised Edie to *speak louder in future!* Eton is a queer place, isn't it? I nearly smacked his face.

Your *Orangerie* poem is one of the very best—in my opinion—you have ever written. There is an admirable subtlety in the choice of words, and the phrases: *Clotted leaves—smart electric globes—topaz books—like drunkards in a tudor farce—* . . . *brains, for ever shunting railway trains—hard hearts melt like liquorice*—all these are *supremely good.* Excellent, my dear, EXCELLENT. Write more of that type. That poem is *subtler* than Edith.

Now, let me tell you a wee bit about my *chef d'oeuvre.* It is a habit—as you know—of mine to say that my newest work is my best, but it generally *is*, and in the case of my novel *Emerald Park* it is by leagues the best thing I've done. I have the whole thing mapped out now. It is to have four, very long, chapters, or divisions. I have nearly finished the first. I am longing for your opinion on it. If any one ever appreciates it, you—my dear friend—will. Oh, the labour that has *already* gone into it. The jewelling—the *mots justes.* However, I must not surfeit you with such adulatory chatter, else you will tire of it before you read it. I read it to Edith, and she raved over it. Please, God, let it be appreciated! I can think of *nothing else*, and here is the Certificate in three weeks!

I have seen some of the contents of Clutton-Brock's rag, and it is going to be definitely worse than the *Latest* (Hitchcock's). What I have read is *appalling*. Last meeting of the Eton Society of Arts [Anthony] Powell 'forgot' to come!!!

Alan Clutton-Brock accepts Brian's scorn with graceful modesty:

Brian was quite right to say that I had produced a 'rag'. This was a magazine which came out at irregular intervals and its real point was the advertisements. Because of the magic name of Eton a large number of firms were willing to advertise in its pages; we circularised many such, from gun-makers to Horlicks, and could make as much as £100 out of each issue. We made some attempt to provide interesting editorial as well, but this was, I fear, a secondary consideration.

Brian continued to Harold:

C-B's wretched little paper is so bad that it has been an *utter* failure. Simply *no one* bought it. How are you getting on with your novel? Certainly submit it to a publisher. You say you hate being out of touch with modern English literature. There isn't any. I'm so bored I don't know what to do. Edie says that Aldous is going to go into *Georgian Poetry* (the new one just coming). He really is a disloyal turn-coat if it's true. (He *struck* me as being out for fame at any price. He's writing worse all the time.) P.S. I am longing for your criticism of my book (*Emerald Park*). It has been polished to a degree. There are things in it which, as far as I know, only you will appreciate. But I don't wish to point out *any* special bits really. It's all—in your humble servant's opinion *decidedly* good! [But alas not good enough for all eight thousand words of it to be reprinted here. It was a highly mannered essay with supernatural overtones, and full of *fin de siècle* imagery.]
. . . I am so glad you like *Emerald Park*. C-B.'s father came down and gave a mediocre, Ruskin-esque middle-class lecture full of very common sense. So silly . . . When William and I walked up the platform to go to Henley we were cheered and clapped (on account of our clothes) all the way up in the train. It was something in the nature of a triumphal progress. What will happen to us when we go to Lord's in braided coats and large Victorian sticks (William has a black satin waistcoat and I have white slips)—I *don't* know. My new brown suit is cut exactly from a 1900 pattern and was a huge success at Henley.

To his mother Brian wrote in one of his depressed moods:

. . . I think I shall do rather well (in the Certificate) in English, altogether. Maths and Latin Prose are what I'm worrying about. You know I sometimes wonder whether I'll ever do any good—I let myself go so terribly. You're such a comfort—a 'very pillar of strength unto those that are weak'. May I be some day worthy of you! I must be such a puzzle to you with my colossal selfishness. Heavens above, I am the most odious of creatures. Anything good I ever, in the future, do, say, or write will be entirely due to you, and can *never* make up for my callous, wicked cruelties in the past.

... I didn't have a chance to really 'see' you on Sunday; for some reason I now am never quite at my ease with the 'family' around—or Daddy, for that matter. I can hear you saying—'Why? there's no reason why you should not be.' I know ... but I'm not. It's embarrassing. At lunch I couldn't think of anything to say. It's queer—all my fault, I'm sure. *In a way* I shall not be glad to leave Eton, and in another way I shall. I am sure I have got what I can out of it, and it is time I subjected myself to new influences. Curiously enough I feel as if I want to soak myself in natural scenery. Mother dear, I hope that if anything dreadful ever happens to me you will always remember that *sometimes* I had something in me. You know, I suppose it is morbid and silly, but I have often wondered whether for some reason it was impossible for me to escape misfortune of one kind or another. Somehow I don't seem to be intended for *continual* happiness. I never seem to be allowed (or to allow myself) to be 'all right' for any *length* of time. Something invariably goes wrong. I can't *quite* believe that this is *all* my fault. If it is I don't think I can ever conquer it, whatever it is. I wonder if you realise how lucky you are. You control yourself. I don't. I *can't*. But I *must*. How? Some great systematic daily change must be made in my life when I've left Eton. I am determined to discipline myself. It is my ONE hope. The alternative is insanity.

One does not know whether Brian was largely referring to his aversion to serious study, masturbation, or his emergent homosexual proclivities, and although he had written as if he were leaving Eton at the end of the summer 1922 half everything depended on his passing the required subjects in the School Certificate, and his report for that half was dubious:

> ... he has plenty of talent and ability, though perhaps more for other things than history—but a facile pen alone will not see him through the Certificate ... A very nice person to deal with ... he can write fluent English and, even if it is inclined to be too florid, his style shows promise ...

Mr. Blakiston's end of half letter to Mrs. Howard 'showed improvement', but:

Brian's reports are not very clear indications of how he will do in the School Certificate examination ... I sincerely hope he has passed and will be able to take up work more congenial to him next half. If he fails he must go in for the same examination in December: and if he fails then, he must try for Responsions in March and the Christ Church entrance later. He has worked well this half, and with some concentration: and has learnt how to compel himself to set aside some part of each day to voluntary study.

He has been particularly well conducted this half, and not given me any anxiety or cause for complaint—his attitude to discipline and school routine has completely changed for the better, and in all his dealings with me he has been thoughtful and considerate. In the house he has got on well, has enjoyed his summer on the river, and deserves a good report.

His 'facile pen' was put to many uses at this time. In a long, sophisticated paper on *The Application of Colour* that he read to the Eton Society of Arts he stated some early home truths:

> ... An unreasonable, elderly-minded prejudice exists among the more beefy of English people that good taste consists in decorating with dull, meaningless colours. Colours that the directors of Waring & Gillow would possibly describe as 'mellow'. ... or they proceed to devastate one by the use of bright cretonnes, fresh from the sleek inferno of Harrod's Decorating Departments ... the demand (for Jazz patterns) being supplied with a desolating efficiency by ... that hive of criminal aesthetics, the Omega Workshops ...

Much of the long summer holiday of 1922 seems to have been spent in keeping up his correspondence with Harold and William Acton who were at their home in Florence. Brian wrote to Harold from Henley:

> Last weekend—Thursday to Monday—we spent at the Monds, where I enjoyed myself immensely. The guests were Sir Frank and Lady Newnes, Sir Frederick and Lady Keble (Lillah McCarthy), the Belgian Attaché and his wife, and Condamine [Robin de la Condamine, who used the stage name of Robert Farquharson]. During the evenings Lillah McCarthy recited beautifully—she is a wonderful personality—and Condamine sang like some inspired devil. He is the greatest *diseur* I have heard. Apart from singing he struck me as a *most* charming, witty, good-natured, well-mannered person. He dresses badly, however. I must say I can't quite understand why you consider him so scandalously odd and outrageous. I think he is most delightful and sweet and have made great friends with him. I adore talking to him: he is a *superb* talker.
>
> Norah Mond is very clever, and a deep intellectual thinker. It is an interesting fact that Shaw wrote love letters to Lady (Violet) Mond. 'If only I had come upon the scene before another man had carried off the prize'—a quotation. She must have been lovely in her youth. She is an impressive wreck now ... The whole house is typical of the *best* kind of 'nouveaux riches'. When one goes in the front door one feels that one is going into a very expensive 'tasteful' hotel—Claridges. ... While I was there I went over to see (Lord) Herbert—that nice boy at Lubbock's—at Wilton, *which is my favourite house in all the world* ... Supreme. Superb. Exquisite. Paradise. Nothing can *ever* be greater.
>
> My Papa and Mamma have taken this little place right on the Thames in a very beautiful stretch of the river just above Henley. We have a tennis court, two boats, and lead a peaceful, rural, American, charming life. P.S. Camp nearly killed me ... My God, the rain! (Staying with Roger Spence

at Wroxton Banbury): . . . I am leading a charmingly rural existence with dear Podge. He doesn't like *Aaron's Rod* so far, but he has only just begun it. I never did like Lawrence, although he is considered wonderful. My novel is slowly progressing—I find that I have to fight a tendency to become a social moralist *à la Shaw* all the time on such subjects as war—religion etc. etc. However it is progressing. I am going to give it to Chatto & Windus. I have decided to have a separate American publisher (not an American edition) by name of Knopf. He is the best, I believe.

There are some beautiful old Tudor-Elizabethan houses around here, each one containing something like a lavatory used by Charles when fleeing from Cromwell. . . . I am reading George Moore's *Confessions of a Young Man* and I find them infinitely entertaining. I have been reading *Prejudices* by H. L. Mencken. Although it is all raucous, *destructive* criticism it *is* amusing—but . . . so American! *Unicorns* volume of criticism by James Huneker—an American critic also) is much better, in fact excellent. One thing about both these books that I notice is the wide vocabulary. Americans seem to use more words than we. I put lots of them down. I have also read *The Symbolist Movement in Literature* by Symons. What a book! Read it, and read the others too. I HAVE JUST DISCOVERED OUR CATEGORY. I have just found out to what school we belong, whose work *we* are developing. We are the New Symbolists.

Incidentally I think James Joyce and Proust are bad writers. *Good writing does not consist in details.* I, in my novel, am going more and more in the direction of choice; selection—putting in nothing but the least possible. A few, *superb* things—is the best way to write. A welter of minute and appallingly tedious or shocking detail is WRONG. Don't you agree? That's all that Proust and Joyce are.

I so long to talk to you about my latest ideas for my book and for Oxford. I think that we, at Oxford, ought to remain *exclusive*. Harold! Remember that you *know* more, *write* better, and do everything else to do with the Arts better than any of the arty people at Oxford and for that reason you ought to go there (apart from your studies, I mean) as a *conqueror* not a novice. *Don't* go and join any societies *please*. Keep clear of all that damned nonsense. When I go to Oxford I am going to continue the *Eton Candle* as the *Oxford Candle*, AND I am going to have a replica of the Rhymers' Club in a Candle Club to which no one shall belong except very, very few. The really elect. You see, Harold, if you start at Oxford on the definite plan of being *exclusive* you will (i) avoid being bored, (ii) avoid being patronised, (iii) make a name for yourself. If you take up an attitude—not an offensive attitude—of calm, conscious superiority and aloofness— security in superior attainments and knowledge, you will get an enormous reputation as an intellectual.

Do you realise, Harold—please pay attention to this—that you and I are going to have rather a famous career at Oxford? Already we have got to a stage *way beyond* the Oxford intellectuals. We are genuinely gifted people, we are comparatively mature. They are NOT. When you go to Oxford next term, I pray you to keep yourself free from the *canaille* of arty and vicious people. Make discoveries, for Heaven's sake—if you happen to find friends who seem to you to know as much as yourself—keep them, and, if you wish to, group yourself with them . . . but—you must not expect me, when I come a year later, to follow suit. At present I am looking forward, Harold, to an Oxford which, on its artistic side, shall be ruled by you and I together—as we ruled Eton.

It was to William Acton that Brian recounted his Algerian Prince hoax at Sulgrave Manor in September 1922:

I enclose a photograph of the Mond party. My father bet me £10 that that large white woman was Mamma (it was Lady Newnes). I won (hurray, I shall buy the Ballet book that the *Commedia Illustré* have just brought out). . . . There is a tennis tournament (big one) at Phyllis Court in which Lady Wavertree and my Papa (who is in the semi-finals) are playing. Last night we dined with her there, and Iris Ford (who had on the most ravishing brick-red dress—£40 at Ospovat)—she and I danced a great deal and very well! The food was very mediocre.

This morning I was halfway through my American cereal when I had *the* most awful row with my father over whether the English *Patrician* had the same contents as the American *Vanity Fair*. Of course it HAS. He said it hadn't, and then flew into a rage and threatened to box my ears, and give me the damndest thrashing anyone ever had. I am so furious that I can't trust myself to speak. My Mamma is allying with him against me! I loathe this silly domestic boredom and bickering.

The day before I left Roger's [Spence] we went to Sulgrave Manor—(the birthplace of the Washingtons and Mecca of all good Americans) and to a tennis and tea party of about twelve people. I went in Arab shoes, long white stockings, Arab baggy trousers, a white silk shirt, black satin bow tie, Arab waistcoat (green embroidery) and Arab cape (white). I was introduced as Prince Mohamed Chebbah, and talked with a heavy, thick foreign accent. They all believed it. I said it was my first visit to England, and that I had learnt English in Strasbourg with 'Podge'. It was the finest and most sustained piece of acting, I have ever done. The nearest I came to exposure was when I said—'Oh, I find that Europeans put such an enormous value on human life. When I was young a man stepped on my toe in the street and he was executed at once!' Podge's sister, Peggy, laughed at this and nearly gave me away. However, they *still* believe they were visited by an Algerian Prince!

. . . Has your family bought *Ulysses* by James Joyce? You must! We can't afford it, and I won't be able to read it if you don't get it. By the way I HAVE PASSED THE CERTIFICATE only I have to take Latin, Divinity and Maths again. Anyway, I've *got* a Certificate (with credits in English, History and French).

Well, I went for the first time in my life to Oxford. It is a huge town with about eight lovely buildings. I think it is an interesting place, if the tiniest bit in the world disappointing. It is so Gothic. However, it seems a bottomless well of interests—literary and artistic, and full of *violently interesting* clothes and bookshops. We will have a *violently interesting* time there. I am *violently interested in* it all. I am going to have £400 a year when I go there, I think; it isn't enough, but it will *just* do, so everyone at Oxford tells me. How much is Harold having? I'm told Oxford is a mass of hypocritical, gossiping, back-biting cliques. However, you and I and Harold will rule it, when the time comes, just as we ruled Eton, on the artistic side I mean. THEY KNOW NOTHING about Art at Oxford. The aesthetic lot there are *known* to be *immoral* charlatans.

Brian's relationship with his Eton Housemaster had by now become positively companionable, Mr. Blakiston even giving him an article to read in the *Quarterly Review* on James Joyce's *Ulysses*. 'It's a mediocre book', was Brian's comment. Mr. Blakiston wrote to Lura Howard about Brian's future, suggesting he went to Paris to learn French for a while, adding: 'He has come on most wonderfully, and I am very well pleased with his development not only in intellect but in character: and I do feel he has rewarded our venture of faith.

Brian's last letters from Eton to his mother (in December 1922) speak for themselves:

I am somehow having a splendid, glorious, happy, time here. At Eton! I wouldn't have believed it a year or so ago. I positively *adore* the football—and everything. It is so hard to suddenly love it all when you are leaving. However, I shall see that *my* son starts here with the right ideas about it well knocked into his head—knowledge which only an Etonian can know. It is much easier to like it when you are in the 'Library' and know the people and the ropes like I do! Thank you, thank you, thank you for making me see straight. I shall do the other things you hope I will even yet, just as I have 'made good' here.
  . . . Is the arrangement that I come with you this winter if I pass the remainder of the Certificate? I certainly hope so. I couldn't bear you to go to Algeria again without me. However, I quite realise that it may not be convenient, or desirable, that I should go. . . . Troubles are fast disappearing and there is everything to be done and seen yet. We ought to be very happy soon, you and I, Mum.

So, examinations were taken but results not yet known when Brian went on another winter trip with his mother and grandfather, this time to Tunisia via Paris, Rome, Naples, Capri, Taormina and Palermo. As usual, the Acton brothers were kept up to date with his news during January and February 1923. He wrote first to Harold while en route for Tunisia:

I was really heart-broken at leaving Eton. I may have been unhappy a good part of my time there, but it has been the scene of such a large and varied part of my life that it hurts to cut myself off from it . . . All Paris is covered with Domergue's posters. He has an enchanting 'chic'. By the way, have you seen the really wonderful Christmas number of *Femina*: the Drians in it are masterpieces of their kind. He draws the modern woman's clothes with the greatest insight of any artist I know. As well as *Judith* we saw *Oh! quel nu!!!* and *Ta bouche*. I was a trifle disappointed in the acting of *Judith* but was amply compensated by Soudeikine's scenery—rich and barbaric— Holofernes' tent was superb, the most marvellous archaic designs in the most brilliantly perfect and subtle colours. *Oh! quel nu!!!* is said to be the most scandalous thing ever produced in Paris, and I can well believe it. You will never believe how licentious it was: practically no one had *anything* on. There were dozens of entirely nude women (except for two square inches where it is absolutely necessary) and the things said were incredible. 'The Parfum de Vice' actually came on to the stage with a whip, and the leading man was a nightmare of Wilde's. Seeing this has permanently prejudiced me against the female figure—'*nu*'. *Ta bouche* was dullish, except for the music, which was, at times, quite gay. The Théâtre Daunou itself is very interesting and amusing, being decorated by Lanvin in white and gold. (Lanvin are decorators as well as dressmakers). It is done in this new contemporary French adaptation of the pre-war Austro-German Secessionist art. But this theatre is really quite amusing in a kind of *Vogue*-esque way.

One night I was trotting down the B. des Capucines when a lady of easy virtue clasped my arm informed me that I was *so* good-looking. '*Pardon, madame, pas ce soir*', I said. But it was in vain. She continued to clasp me. I was seized with a brilliant idea. I said, theatrically, '*Madame! Je suis fiancé*'. She left me at once ... But then, coming back from my walk she found me again, and seizing me firmly round the waist, propelled me down a side alley (every word of this is God's truth) and told me that she would suppress her generous inclinations and merely embrace me—if only I would '*venez avec moi!*' I said NO. 'But,' said she, 'I have preventatives.' 'Madame', I reply, 'I am convinced you have preventatives and are really *tres gentille* but I must go home.' '*Non, non, écoutez-moi* ... etc. etc.' After an interminable argument I persuaded her to leave go of me—with the assistance of five francs—and I fled. A nice experience for such a proper young man as your Bri-Bri!!

You will, be amused to hear that I have taken to writing sonnets. I enclose two, and I think they will astonish you, the heretofore monopoliser of the verse medium. I really do think they are rather good, and I have tried, in them, to purge myself of our mutual disease of adjectives— richness, precious-ness, local colour ... 'And in the court a monolith, of pure translucent amethyst, stands sculpted with a ravelled myth, concealed within a purple mist ...' Austerity—simplicity is my new note. Enough of *Salomé!* I beg you, too, Harold to abandon the purple mists for a while. Let us sharpen our creative wits by being a little simple, a little direct, a little W. H. Davies—M. Angelo—R. Brooke—Shakespeare-esque—don't you think? A little less Mallarmé, a little more Blake?—don't you think? I would like to discuss all this with you. But then—you may not like my sonnets; I hope you do. In them I have regarded rather the emotional than the aesthetic values. (One is reprinted below.)

IMAGINATION

I find the greater beauty in this street,
And, having it, I can forget myself,
And, lacking it, myself is incomplete.
My single candle on my empty shelf
Burns, for these eyes, the clearest flame of all,
Showing me rarer richness in my room
Than I could think to see in Heaven's hall,
And I will swear that these plain walls assume,
When they enclose me, a new power to move,
A dearer splendour given me alone:
They hold a spirit that compels my love,
That I have borne, that here with me has grown,
And my own soul gives this my room a glory
Fairer than ever found in fairy story.

P.S. Lanvin has named one of their children's models after my little cousin, Carley, who bought the first one.

[From Naples] ... You ask me what I have been reading. Well—I began (St. Loe) Strachey's *Autobiography* but, taxed beyond my capacity for endurance, I soon stopped. I had a similar experience with *Babbit* by Sinclair Lewis—which is exactly like a Ford car being cranked up. The only things that have given me pleasure lately have been Davies' new poems, Rupert Brooke's memoir and poems, which I have been re-reading, and, curiously enough, the new *Last Poems* of A. E. Housman. I am well aware of the fact that, being on Edith's visiting list, I should abhor him as out-Georgianing the Georgians—but I find it is not so. On the contrary I discover a deep, fine pleasure in his melancholy little poems. However, I hesitate to commend him to you, lest you should dismiss him as cursorily as you have my sonnets, in which case you would give me real cause to be a little surprised ... doubtless, you are quite right to be as brusque as I found you about them, but am I wrong when I say I notice something a little queer about your criticism? Is it perhaps a little lack of understanding? ... and your conclusions a trifle over-emphatic ...? Nevertheless—and, of course—I am always delighted to have your opinion on my work ... next time, however, I beg of you—as courteously as I know how—to criticise me with the thought, insight, and sympathy that you are never without— when you are in a good humour. P.S. the head waiter here is the LIVING SPITTING (isn't that the word?) IMAGE of David Cecil ...

From Taormina Brian wrote to William Acton:

What do you mean by having the impertinence to tell me that this lovely place wasn't respectable! I swear to you that nowhere have I seen such streams of utterly respectable people—all English. I might be in Kensington. All the ladies wear elastic-sided boots and read Baedeker all the evening, and *all* the men are Old Etonians who remember Queen Victoria's coronation *vividly*. I search the roads eagerly for wicked-looking people and find nothing but hideous children and English school masters. It's tragic ... *But*, what an adorable place! Our hotel is perched up over two bays, high up on the great cliffs, over the vasty sea. Just under the hotel are two romantic little promontories enclosing a small bay in which I bathe. This is heaven, this place. I could just live here for ever and ever and ever—never writing, never talking, simply living ... it is so wonderful to sit on a hot cliff-top and watch the mountains—Etna—and the sea. And the sun ... makes me feel so happy.

Well, I wish you were here, too, you and your brother. I was given a large Kodak for Christmas, so I photograph everything, and quite well, too.

While I was at Naples I went to Capri, which delighted me, and yet did not. I do not think it comparable to this place. The blue grotto, besides being green, was rather disappointing, but an interesting experience. Getting in there is rather disagreeable: my mother and I had to *lie down in the bottom of a wet, smelly rowboat* and then get barged in on the crest of a wave!! Monstrous. Capri is most certainly not a chaste spot. Two women lunched next to us ... they had gaunt faces, terribly good figures, and they eyed one another hungrily ...

In February 1923 Brian wrote, from Marseille, a monumental letter to William who had by that time returned to Eton. Brief extracts follow:

I have failed in the Certificate examination, and, as a result we are returning to England and not visiting Florence. It is a fiendish bore, but it can't be helped. I have to take Responsions now. We arrived in Marseille today after an appalling journey from Tunis. I am flying from Paris to London, probably tomorrow. I hope it will be comfortable—I have never been in an aeroplane before. I hear they are rather smelly and noisy. However ...

Well, my dear, you need a long letter, down there all alone, and so now I'm going to write you one ... Leo d'Erlanger gave me an introduction to Baron d'Erlanger, his father; so one lovely day we all motored out to his beautiful little Arab town—Sidi-bou-Saïd—which hangs over the bay of Tunis like a white pearl over a plate of jade. William! I *wish* you and Harold could have been there. You would have gone mad with interest. About twelve or thirteen years ago the Baron came to live in Sidi-bou-Saïd for his health, and, for his residence he bought an old palace overlooking the sea from the Bay of Tunis. He tore this down, and spent *three years* building the most exquisite building you could possibly imagine. For a building of one particular type and style (Moorish-Arabic) it is PERFECT ... There were no pictures in the house; instead—he would hang the most ravishing, *ravishing* faded old Persian carpets on the wall—carpets fit for some national museum ... As you know, I do not approve of any kind of specialised decoration, any decoration devoted to one period or style, but as far as a stylistic house can be made supreme, this was. *There was not one bad or cheap thing in it.* It was a marvellous flower constructed of silk and marble. Empty, delicate, troubling, rich, exquisite . . . and think of the aesthetic dandy who made it all for himself. How subtle of him, how strange . . .

In Tunis I met some delightful Americans—a mother and two daughters. One night I was sitting with these two American girls—who are quite charming, have a Pekingese called Johnny, and dress very well—in an Arab dancing café. It was quite a big café, with a *purely* Arab audience. An Arab girl was dancing to this wild tuneless music—music that expresses the soul of Africa, and presently she stopped. Suddenly I turned round to the girls, and told them that I was going to dance. NEVER has anyone looked so surprised as they did. I was astonished at their astonishment. They hadn't realised before, I suppose, that I am a genius of a rather unusual kind . . .!! What is more natural, William, than that I should do something like that? Anyway, I went to the proprietress and told her to ask the Arab dancing girls if it was convenient that I should give an exhibition dance, and that I was a famous English dancer. Everything was stopped, and the audience became excited. At once I stepped on to the small square wooden stage. I said one word to the wild little orchestra—'*Vivement!*' They began—*très vivement*. I began to dance—slowly, like a snake. Then I quickened, and then abandoned myself to an amazing fury. Oh—that music—if you can imagine *Schéhérazade* stripped of all subtlety, all beauty, and left, sullen, rhythmic, primeval, savage . . . it was that . . . you know how we have danced together, William, to the little gramophone at Eton. Well . . . I did that, only better, more madly. Once during the dance I suddenly fell down—on purpose—flat on my back, fell down in all the dirt, and lay there for several seconds, and once I looked at my two American girl friends, and do you know, they were looking at me with the fixed hypnotised stare of a rabbit at a snake? Can't you see me, writhing over them . . . at length I stopped, exhausted, amid a roar of applause—a roar of Arabian applause, and, what do you think? The Arab dancing girl asked me if they danced like that in England!!! I replied—'*Non—on danse comme ça parmi les Bolshévistes, madam*'. She believed me, the dear. Think! I have altered the opinions towards English dancing of a whole Arab town. Sousse was the name of the town, on the coast, east of Tunis.

Well, I've been writing this letter most of the day, it seems, and so I will end. If I come down on Thursday to Eton I will ask Henry Yorke to arrange a special meeting of the [Eton Society of] Arts—just for fun—for which I will stay.

6. Old Etonians look back

'Those who have never had the pleasure of listening to Mr. Brian Howard, for instance, can catch here a notion of his pyrotechnics, so wayward, so personal, so spontaneous even when they seem most affected.' That was Raymond Mortimer reviewing Harold Acton's *Memoirs of an Aesthete*[1] in the *New Statesman*, when it was first published in 1948. No one else has quite caught, let alone sustained so well, the essence of Brian. Here is a brief extract from these reminiscences:

'I am said to be the image of Max Beerbohm when he was beautiful as well as brilliant,' my new friend Brian confided to me, and he did bear a close resemblance to Sir William Rothenstein's early lithograph of Sir Max. At the age of thirteen he was definitely a dandy.

During a walk to the Copper Horse I proposed that we should sit under an oak tree, but he demurred with a quotation from *Intentions*, which he must have known by heart. 'Nature is so uncomfortable,' he sighed. 'Grass is hard and lumpy and damp, and full of dreadful black insects.' Our friendship was an endless series of bickerings, but his company was so stimulating that it soon became a necessity to both of us. Brian could be very old and very young at the same time and his mischievousness was far more than the ebullience of youth. When one got the better of him in argument he would resort to crude mockery and personal invective, which often turned to violence. Once I had to push him into a shop window in self-defence. He had an intuitive gift for the malice that could stab and fester beneath the skin. Scarcely anybody was spared the shafts of his ridicule . . .

But, Harold Acton goes on, Brian could also detect talent in the most unlikely people:

'My dear,' he would say, 'I've discovered a person who has something, just something a little bit unusual, under a pimply and rather catastrophic exterior. Of course I may be mistaken and there is a faint risk that he may develop into a bore, but what do you think, my dear, he has a passion for campanology.'

'Really, Brian. And is that interesting?'

'Why, it is the art of ringing bells, my dear. He knows everything, simply everything there is to know about it. I'm trying to persuade him to write a causerie on the subject. It could be extremely suggestive. I think I shall send it with a covering letter to the *Eton Chronicle*, explaining to the editor why

[1] Published by Methuen, 1948.

I think it so very important. It struck me that every house should build its own belfry, then it could be distinguished both musically and architecturally. I'm afraid m'tutor is bound to choose Lutyens; I suppose it can't be helped, though one hears that he has made some tolerable designs for New Delhi. You, of course, will want to erect, a Florentine campanile over Keate's House. Having originated the scheme, I shall insist on being Chairman of the Bell Committee. I shall choose m'tutor's bells . . .'

'At Cartier's I suppose. And of platinum inlaid with cabochon rubies.' Brian frowned and flickered his eyelashes. 'Now don't be facetious dear, it doesn't happen to suit you. I am in earnest. I was thinking of something rather less obvious. I should see to it, of course, that the bells had elegant shapes, but it is the tunes more than the shapes that matter. The carillons, my dear. I should commission Rimsky-Korsakoff . . .'

'But he's with the angels, Brian.'

'Will you stop interrupting! It impedes the flow of my ideas. I can see that you're getting into one of your mosquito moods. Of course Rimsky's dead, we all know that. I meant Granados.[2] It would be nice to have a Malaguena or a Seguedilla to soothe one at lock-up time with memories of Spain, bullfights and matadors with enormous shoulders and no hips—I can't think why hips were invented—and sunlit patios with Moorish fountains'—(Brian had never been out of England).[3] 'There again I can see an endless argument with m'tutor, even'though he is a trifle more cultured than the average beak. He's bound to plump for Elgar or Vaughan-Williams. And when the belfries are completed, there are bound to be bats, symbolically speaking . . .'

As lower boys of different houses were not allowed to visit each other's rooms, most of the discussions on which we built a foundation for our flexible friendships were evolved in the open air. Brian and I spent much precious leisure at Dyson's the jewellers, where one could hire a gramophone in a back room and play one's own records . . . Many of these were from the Russian ballet, and Brian and I would leap into riotous dances there. Far more than football was this an outlet for our animal spirits, and whoever burst in upon us would think we were mad as March hares. Without having seen Massine's performance of the miller's dance in *The Three-Cornered Hat* Brian would stamp his heels and snap his fingers to de Falla's rhythm and produce a creditable equivalent.

Cyril Connolly also recalled Brian's Eton in his *Enemies of Promise*[4] in 1938, a good decade before Harold had committed his *Memoirs* to paper, and yet another graphic picture is distilled from those times:

One day Teddy Jessel introduced me to the editor (of the *Eton Candle*), a boy in his house with a distinguished impertinent face, a sensual mouth and

---

[2] Incidentally also dead—in 1916!
[3] Except to America as a small child.
[4] Published by George Routledge, 1938; Penguin Books, 1961.

dark eyes with long lashes. He wrote to ask me to tea. I accepted, on Pop writing paper, and went round one summer afternoon to find *foie gras* sandwiches, strawberries and cream, and my postcard of acceptance prominently displayed on the mantelpiece. Seeing it up there for the world to know that Brian Howard had had a Pop to tea with him, I was miserable. I felt that once again I had let the Eton Society down. It was natural for Teddy Jessel to know Brian who was in the same house. The question was, *Who else did?* I swallowed down my tea like a lady who is offered a swig by a madman in a railway tunnel and bolted.

Afterwards when I saw Brian alone I would talk to him; when I was with other Pops I avoided him, as in the Dark Ages Wilfrid had avoided me. I need not have worried for he soon became the most fashionable boy in the school but, as it was; though I grew to know him better, his politeness overwhelmed me. He belonged to a set of boys who were literary and artistic but too lazy to gargle quotations and become inoculated with the virus of good taste latent in Eton teaching and too disorderly and bad at games to be overburdened with responsibility and who in fact gained most from Eton because of the little they gave ... They were the most vigorous group at Eton for they lived within their strength, yet my moral cowardice and academic outlook debarred me from making friends with them.

The late Robert Byron commemorated the impact of the Eton Society of Arts as long ago as 1926 in a discursive review of Henry 'Green' Yorke's first novel, *Blindness*,[5] in the Oxford magazine, *Cherwell*, under the title of *Henry Yorke and the Eton Society of Arts*. In this review (signed 'B.G.' because the character of those initials in *Blindness* was largely based on himself) he quotes an account of the 'Noad Art Society' continuing with:

... The E.S.A. was founded jointly by Brian Howard, late of Christ Church, who himself hopes to publish a volume of poems this winter, and Alan Clutton-Brock, who alone of his contemporaries has elected to make tremble with his brush and pen the stucco spires of the lesser University. The opposition of 'a great public school' to the project was unanimous; the attitude of the masters resembled that of someone discovering the first symptoms of leprosy in his mother. ... These suspicions were eventually quietened; though naturally not eradicated—the Society would have lost its incentive to existence if they had been. And the whole brunt of these initial difficulties fell on Henry Yorke. He, however, born with a mature view of human nature, received them with equanimity—with actual pleasure it might be said, since we were now a compact body and could all laugh together at the angry football fodder outside ...

Henry Yorke, who first met Brian at Eton, talks of him with affection:

[5] By Henry Green, published by Dent, 1926.

I think he was quite the most handsome boy I'd ever seen—and remained so as a man up till the war. He was not well off, in fact poor compared to what we were, and I wasn't rich. He was a brilliant conversationalist, even as a boy, and was able to dominate people by his conversation. But he was also a terrible poseur and a wild snob, always making up to everyone in Pop. He became a great social success at Eton. Boys are easily ignored, but with Brian everything flowered there. He knew a lot about painting and carried it all off—he hated Rembrandt and was all in favour of the Post-Impressionists . . .

He had tremendous charm—and could put it on when he wanted to. Harold Acton and Brian, who were great rivals, started the Eton Society of Arts, which met once a week for two years, and I was the Secretary. I was always running after them.

Lapse of time does not make the recollection grow any fonder as far as Anthony Powell is concerned:

I don't quite know what to say about Brian Howard. I never liked him, nor thought, even at Eton, that he had a vestige of real talent in any of the arts. All he seemed to me interested in was self-advertisement and forms of exhibitionism that brought him into disrepute, though I suppose one must admit that it was partly his energy that produced the *Eton Candle*.

Another member of the group, Sir Colin Anderson, remembers an Eton Society of Arts puppet show:

. . . a strange amalgam based on the story of *Hansel and Gretel*, put into verse by Alan Clutton-Brock, the scenery designed arid created by myself, the actors created by Mark Ogilvie-Grant, the music by Tchaikovsky (the *Nutcracker Suite*) and electric lighting effects by Henry Yorke. I cannot remember who declaimed the words. Brian was the impresario . . .

Jim Knapp-Fisher, one of Brian's oldest friends, gives the finishing touch to this Eton era:

I knew Brian from the age of thirteen, I suppose. We arrived at Eton the same half (Summer 1918) and were in the same class, or 'Divs' as we called them, on numerous occasions . We knew each other's minds intimately and tended to copy each other.

Brian was terribly naughty while at Eton, going into the sock (tuck) shop and causing chaos by hurling a cream whisk about so that the whole place was bespattered with cream, but he used to get away with a great deal. He took the whole of school to be a fearful bore, and was frightfully funny to sit next to. He would talk all through class, and with particularly stupid masters would get away with murder. I think it was Harold [Acton] who said one day, 'Might we do the lesson *weewa wocky*, Sir?', Brian promptly following with 'I second that, Sir.' The answer was a furious no, and a tittering class.

He and Harold were very jealous of each other although great friends, for they were both out for the same sort of thing—determined to be creative in some way. Where the average schoolboy would go to the latest Dorothy Dickson show, for instance, they would go to the latest ballet at the Alhambra. One time I happened to be with my family at the Alhambra when Brian and Harold walked into the stalls, in full evening dress, with long white gloves draped over one arm, and carrying silver-topped canes and top hats, looking perhaps like a pair of Oscar Wildes. My step-mother was astonished at the sight of them, and thought they must be foreigners. I was much too nervous, at about fifteen, to say they were two of my great friends from Eton. I was very relieved that we were safely installed out of sight in the dress circle!

Brian, who had tremendous feeling for music and poetry, used to spend hours playing records. He especially adored the 'Liebestod' from *Tristan*, and the *Kreutzer Sonata*. It was at Eton that he really discovered and absolutely worshipped the 'Liebestod' with Nordica singing on a Columbia record. At the same time he had this enormous interest in early jazz. I can remember him buying all the records of people like 'The Virginians', and really having great feeling for them.

I once went to the Howard's Warwick Square house (where they lived until 1921 when they moved to Bryanston Square) when Brian was drawing in the Bakst manner. He called one of his efforts 'Odalisque' to which Mrs. Howard took exception. 'Brian,' she said, 'I think that word means something horrible, and you must not call it that.' 'Oh . . . ohh,' said Brian, in that wonderful way he had. But he was awfully frightened of his mother then, so he changed the name. I remember Warwick Square as being very, very opulent. I was too young to judge whether it was good taste or not, but there were some lovely things in the house, rather in the flamboyant taste of the early 'twenties—silver witch balls everywhere. I was most impressed, finding it to be a very grand, rich house. My father being Receiver General for Westminster, we had an official residence in Dean's Yard, a sort of Gothic doll's house really, with some lovely things in it, but by the standards of the rich it was a poky house. The Howards, being American, seemed to have everything *new*. The whole idea of luxury had penetrated England very little. Even the aristocracy had little comfort and less heating.

In spite of Brian's very good brain he was extremely idle, a thoroughly lazy person who, with all his genius, only wanted to use it for what *he* wanted to do, never what would be of any use. One of those unfortunate people born to do what he did from the moment he came into this world. Whether it was due to Papa or Mamma it is hard to say. She was a very stupid woman, I think, and the father certainly a brilliant art dealer. Brian was saddled with this ridiculous false name—Howard. If people wanted to be difficult and unkind to him at Eton they would say, 'And how is the Duke of Norfolk today?' It did have an effect on him, but he would try and shrug it off, saying, 'Well, I'm American. I don't understand these silly English ways.' Once he was beaten at Eton for peeing in the bath. How anybody knew this, I don't know (but the bathrooms didn't lock), and he would tell everyone about being punished for it by the 'Library', remonstrating that he had 'never heard anything so ridiculous—why in Baltimore people are constantly peeing in their bath—Americans are always doing it—how idiotic the English are, how intolerable the hearties in the Library are . . .' and so on.

About the 'snob' tag, he always felt he hadn't the right background, and this mattered much more, I think, in the 'twenties than it does today. Brian certainly wanted to know the right people, the grand ones, whether in the literary or the social world. And he had this feeling he couldn't succeed, firstly because he was lazy (which he knew himself to be), secondly that his other friends were cleverer than he was, and thirdly because deep down somebody of his origins never could succeed. Something like that. He was frightfully vulnerable. He really hated the jokes about his name and his Jewishness. People were unkind about Brian's surname (Gassaway) all his life. Roger Hinks used to call him, *'Die geborene Gassaway'* (after the German style of identifying the maiden name of married women)!

He never quite believed in anything, not even in his friends' successes. The Birkenheads (who were always upheld to him by his parents) were at least visibly successful. He always thought people were blaming him *personally* for misdemeanours, never that he was only punished for the acts committed. He had to write about these episodes and think about them for years afterwards. He went sour on himself because he felt himself to be the victim of his own background. Had he been average upper-middle class, instead of consciously Jewish-American, he might have turned out very differently. But society was very racially conscious in the 'twenties and 'thirties—Indian Princes were accepted, but not 'common' people, and Jews were sometimes thought to be common. Knowing Jews, however rich, was doing them a favour. People are only just beginning to realise this, and thank goodness the times are changing.

Brian also hated himself, oddly enough, and if you can't like yourself you can't really like anybody. Even so, I would adore to see him now, if he were to walk into the room. He was one of the most amusing people in the world, wonderful company. You could never be bored by him, you could only be maddened if he suddenly decided to become satanically destructive. He would love to have gone in for black magic—perhaps it's just as well he didn't!

7. Oxford, the happiest days

1923–1925

With the prospect of 'Responsions' before him Brian was packed off to a crammer near Salisbury as soon as he returned from his Tunisian trip. He did not take kindly to the place, complaining to Harold Acton that he was 'studying in an odour of sanctity for Responsions—with the Rev. X'. To his mother he wrote, 'Since I *am* here I must make *quite* certain of Oxford for the sake of appearances *at least* . . . we aren't idle, but we do not get on . . .' To Harold, safely at Oxford, went the bad news in June:

> The impending tragedy was fulfilled, and I have failed for the House! [Christ Church] *Ave et Vale!* I shall try, now, for Balliol. [From a different crammer, near Tonbridge]: Thank God I have only two more weeks of this spewing place. My mother says she saw you at *Façade*. I was kept here, of course, God blotch the place! Oxford is certainly making me suffer for her sake, and I can only hope I pass after all this intolerable restriction. . . . I *am* sorry about those blasted boys breaking your windows. Oh! I wish I had been there—I had cast missiles upon them, and scotched them soundly. A woman who sat next to my mother at *Façade* said, 'My son smashed a Bolshevist's windows at the House the other day'—If I'd been there I'd have unloosed her corsets on the spot.

Brian kept Harold's reply to this letter:

> Dearest Brian, Delighted to get your letter and your poem, which I admire *immensely*. It shows the strong influence of Sacheverell though, doesn't it? However it is a good one (I mean influence). 'The birds peppering the angelic legions with their droppings' is brilliant, and I am really flattered that you should dedicate it to me. Evidently the Bolshevist to whom the lady referred was myself, for no one else has had such a smash-up as I had in the House. I, tucked up in bed and contemplating the reflection of Luna on my walls, was immersed under showers of myriad particles of split glass, my head powdered with glass-dust and my possessions vitrified. A band consisting of nearly thirty big ruff animal louts tried to break in my 'oak'—but I remained adamant and their force was wasted. Yet I had never before received a poker through my window and hope that I shall never experience it again.
>
> I enjoyed Edith's recital (*Façade*)—it was beautifully done, and Willy Walton's music blends marvellously with the various subtleties of rhythm. The backcloth by Dobson was very good too; simple but effective—two

masks, one large and one small, through whose mouths issued terrifyingly human megaphones . . . Love from Harold.

Brian was piqued at hearing through a friend of his mother's that Harold had published a book of verse, 'Why wasn't I told?' he grumbled to William, yet he managed to congratulate Harold:

I think your poems (*Aquarium*)[1] most diverting and extremely clever—I much like 'her bustle panics peacocks in the park'—charming, charming it is. Here and there are really fine lines, too—I do hope you are well noticed. If you have time do go to the Leicester (Galleries), I would like you to see my portrait by McEvoy,[2] and if you have time do come to the tableaux at the Queen's Theatre—I am in a 'Lancret' picture—and there will be an amusing audience and entertainment.

  . . . A rather tragic thing has just happened to me. 'X' and I—like everyone else in the room during Matriculation—did our Latin and French papers largely *ensemble*: this has been discovered and there is a possibility of our being disqualified for the House. However—I hope that we may only have to do the papers again. My dear, you may think it foolish of me to have collaborated in an examination—but *who* would not do so when some fifty other people were engaged in doing so? I must have been especially stupid about it to have been discovered. However it is most annoying and upsetting, isn't it? It would be kind of you, I think on the whole, to let this remain *entre nous*. Am I not unlucky?

Despite his earlier *cri du cœur* of having failed for the House, and this last disaster, Brian finally succeeded in getting into Christ Church for the Michaelmas Term, 1923. His cribbing *confrère* remembers the awful occasion, and how self-righteously they complained about being singled out for disgrace in their collaboration—when practically everyone else was equally guilty. This 'Let's get into Oxford somehow' attitude was characteristic of Brian and part of the strength and the weakness of his type. 'I can go where I like—do what I please—get what I want' might have been his tripartite motto at this time.

Lura Howard kept few of Brian's letters from his Oxford days or, possibly she received but few to keep? His undergraduate life can still be followed through extracts from his revealing letters to the Acton brothers, from his infrequent contributions to the Oxford weekly magazine, *Cherwell* (now a pale newspaper ghost of itself), and the more recent reminiscences of his fellow graduates. The *Cherwell* editorial staff of the early 'twenties were unashamed in their production of elaborate, parochial in-jokes, often intelligible only to their own select cliques. Whereas Brian might well have developed his journalist flair

---

[1] Published by Duckworth, 1923.

[2] At a dinner-party to celebrate the forthcoming appearance of Harold Acton's second book of poems, *An Indian Ass*, Brian dedicated a photograph of this portrait to: 'Harold, the poet of my generation—Brian 1924', but after a row he took it back and it was found amongst his personal papers, after his death. The use of the personal pronoun before 'generation' was something of a back-handed compliment.

in the editorial seat there, he favoured the outdoor life (or the choice was thrust on him by his parents) and he did not in fact become a contributor until 1925—however popular a target he was for their gossip columns.

His first letters from Oxford to his mother, in October 1923, were guarded:

. . . I am trying to join the O.U.D.S. [Oxford Union Dramatic Society]—it's a good club. Mother, if I am unhappy for the remainder of my life these eight weeks will be a sufficient memory to live on—'these I have loved . . .'

It was decided last night that I could do History. Oxford seems a very charming place, I must say, as long as one does one's work and doesn't overspend. (I've joined the Tennis Club here, so there will be as much tennis as I want.) I've managed the social part rather well, so far . . .

Too well, as can be seen from his letters to the Actons in the winter vacation of 1923–1924:

[To William] I am more depressed than I can say. One reason that you have not heard from me lately is because these last three or four weeks have been so hysterical . . . you see, about half way through the term I let work—money—everything—just go. My God! I am miserable, though, as a result. I spent about £180 in two months—which, on an income of £450 a year, is idiotic. Last night—it is *awful* I can't stop spending—I spent £5 simply taking a friend to dine at the Berkeley—theatre, and on to the Cabaret Club (which I loathe). You may complain about Eton, but at least one is protected from oneself, there. I told you that Oxford was nothing from the point of view of wit, intellectual enterprise and artistic interests generally, and it isn't—but on the other hand one lives an extraordinarily marvellous life there—a sort of passionate party all the time—one rushes from one amusement to another until all one's sense of proportion and self-control gradually vanishes, and one becomes careless, mad, happy, hysterical, miserable, brilliant, ill—anything . . . then—I come back to London, burnt out and bankrupt.

I wonder if you can gather from all this what I mean. I hated leaving Oxford. At Oxford one is at least oneself. Here one is one's family, and I can't talk to any of them as I should. In my family we are terrified of sincerity, of frankness. I do so long to burst out to someone with all the ideas, despairs, sillinesses, hopes and other things which make my life and its happiness or misery—but I can't.

[To Harold] William tells me that his newest diversion is taking strychnine—an amusement which does not seem to lack a certain element of hazard! I travelled up on the train (from Oxford) with John Sutro—whom I think quite delightful. I have decided that even if (J. B.) Fagan[3] does offer me the part in *Hamlet*—I have not yet seen him—I shall not take it, purely because I shall not be able to do that and *pass* my examination at the end

---

[3] The theatrical director, who was producing some of the O.U.D.S. plays at this time.

of next term. As a result of idling last term I have more work than I know how to deal with.

... Every time I read *The Waste Land* I find something ... It is a great poem. I am not sure it isn't the challenge of the new movement in poetry that has been imminent for some twenty years. It is certainly the most important poem since the war. I think it will have enormous—and probably very beneficial—influence. It shows such an erudite intellect and such a finely *modern* mind. There you have the *genuine* modern. The poetry that is coming ...

T. S. Eliot's *The Waste Land* was originally published in this country in October 1922 in the first issue of the quarterly review, *Criterion*, which Eliot edited. (Tom Driberg remembers introducing the poem to Auden in 1926 when they were both at Oxford, 'we read it together and were staggered by it, uncertain whether to be swept in by it or to laugh at it or both.') Brian continued to pass on all the news fit to write to William:

My Schölte suit is almost wholly admirable, except that it makes me a shade too thick in the torso: being a country-ish suit I did not have it too shaped, and I have had to have the coat altered *three times* before I was moderately satisfied ... As for my news, the Chelsea Arts Ball was the event of these holidays. Without any exception it was the most striking thing I have ever seen. Kreisler told my uncle that he had never seen such a wonderful ball. It was extraordinary. Four thousand people and a blazing, amusingly decorated Albert Hall. We stayed from 10.30 until five in the morning, and the costumes never came to an end. The principal costume there—in a way—was Mrs. George Belcher in a black and silver Velásquez costume, a perfect copy exquisitely done. Our box were all Orientals—turbaned by my mother. We were rather good really—a mixture of Drian, de Meyer and Bakst. During dinner my father told Duveen's brother, who had no costume on, to cut his finger and go as a bloody fool—which annoyed him exceedingly! It was meant as a joke, of course.

... Last night we saw *Hassan*—it is an expensive production—well worth seeing for the occasional beauty of the actual play, but the scenery, all except the first scene—a perfect reproduction of a piece of Tunis—is abortive. The music by Delius—instrumental flatulence, and Henry Ainley altogether too offhand and blasé—there are a few good costumes, copies of old Persian pictures, and excellent dancing staged by Fokine. There are moments of real dramatic intensity, also. The *Little Revue* I have seen twice and it amuses me. Jack Hulbert is witty and a genius in the 'City Blues'. By the way, the new dancing place is over the Leicester Square Tube and is called the 'Lambs'—Harry Melville runs it.

... Harrington Mann[4] has just gone to America, having completed my father's portrait—which is exactly like him. At this very moment he is

---

[4] According to Mona Macdonnell (née Mann) Tudie Howard was a wonderful friend and patron of her father's, never taking any commission on works sold through his connections.

sitting in a chair in the drawing-room saying how beautiful he thinks it is, and I can hear Mother shrieking with laughter at him.

The new white evening waistcoats have a very much rolled, protruding lapel—curling low down. The new evening collar has a *very* wide opening—and Hawes & Curtis are beginning to sell batik handkerchiefs . . . P.S. This letter [only brief extracts included here] took two hours and ten minutes to write, and while I wrote London has turned from black to white—the snow. P.P.S. The lavatories in the Queen's Doll's House which Lutyens built with seats the size of a sixpence—actually work. The Queen admired my aunt's flowers.

It was Aldous Huxley who named these concoctions 'sculptured flowers'. Grace Robinson had begun making miniature flowers in 1921, first out of parchment paper, then turning to thin tin or brass sheets, usually painted to reproduce real flower colours. She later started dipping the metal ones in acid and heating them so that they took on soft metallic tones of pink, green and blue. They were highly decorative but still authentic flower reproductions. The work was so fine that she had to use an eye surgeon's magnifying glass, and the larger bouquets took six months to complete.

As 'Mrs. Avery Robinson' she held a successful exhibition at the Leicester Galleries in 1921, at which Queen Mary bought two of the exhibits, 'a white and a pink May, done in the Chinese manner in fine Chinese porcelain cups.' The bouquets done for the Queen's Doll's House were a bunch of mixed flowers, standing two and a half inches high overall, and a thumb-nail size bunch of sixty violets.

A light-hearted letter to his mother in February, forewarning disaster in his Prelims,[5] was soon followed by an extenuating one:

If I do fail in this exam, please don't pull a long face. Most people, e.g. Teddy Jessel—have a couple of goes at it. The first exam is meant in a way as a trial . . . Oxford is *not* a city of grey cloistral study and quiet, full of Birkenheads working three hundred hours a day. Life's hard, hard business comes soon enough. Merciful heavens, I'm only eighteen or nineteen rather. I'm not 'busy having a good time'—I'm busy LIVING, *for the first time in my life*. I have come into the popularity and companionship that I have always yearned after so, don't you see?

(But) I am sent here at far too great a relative expense to complete my education and retrieve something perilously *like* a failure . . . the moment you become really regretful at having sent me here I shall be ready to leave. You must know where you stand, and until you and Daddy have got it firmly fixed in your heads—which it is going to take years to do—that I am not going to be the traditional great man, the 'brain', the public character, you must realise that it is for you to tell me what your wishes are . . . I'm afraid I see tragedy ahead in the kind of ideas which are solidifying in yours and my father's heads about my future. Must there always be war before peace? Your loving and anxious Son . . .

---

[5] The exam that all undergraduates have to pass by the end of their first year.

[Later] Today I beagled, and am dog-tired as a result. I am enjoying myself here as I have never enjoyed myself before. It *is* such a marvellous life—even the work is agreeable. It really is comic—the set I am drifting into. Of course I am now certain that if I had the money it would be a mere question of time before I ruled Oxford. P.S. Please tell Carley that all my friends *keep on* asking me who this lovely young girl is in my photograph. They really do.

Not too surprisingly Brian failed his History Prelim (*In rudimentis historiae modernae*) in his second term. There are no notes or letters from this period at all, so it would seem that he must have neglected his letter-writing for fear of being sent down, as he wrote briefly to Harold, 'I am utterly bankrupt and my London existence is *ruinous—ruinous*—and also, if I don't pass at the end of next term I get sent down—so I *must* do some work. It will be so difficult, too, during term.' Much to the relief of himself and his family he managed to pass his exam in Trinity Term 1924, and so was able to enjoy his summer vacation at Maidenhead (where his parents had rented a house), from where he wrote to William Acton:

This place—Cannon Hill—is a large white nudity of a house—comfortable, with two tennis courts, a little lake on which we have a silly little motor boat, and a large vegetable garden with hundreds of very nearly ripe peaches. People are continually coming and going. I am fairly well amused with it. I have been staying in Derbyshire with Ian Walker. Hell's Bells, what a house! That part of England is dotted with terrible palaces built by the northern industrial potentates in the early 19th century—huge, grey, stoney, pseudo-Gothic, filled, filled, filled with stuffed bears and stuffed people—'Turkey' carpets—darkness—1904 comfort—and yet no vulgarity, gentlemanly withal (in this particular house) and full of amusing things like swimming baths. For a large house-party I enjoyed myself. I am going up to stay with Barty Clowes (the Oxford roulette king) in September. It interested me so much when I saw his house. One could use it for copy—easily. Forty to lunch—that sort of thing. The other night I and Eleanor Smith [Lord Birkenhead's daughter] burgled the Jungmans in the middle of the night and they aren't quite sure whether it was, or wasn't burglars even now!

Allanah Harper, one of Brian's life-long friends, fills in here with an eye-witness account of these times which discredits Brian's last words:

I think it was at Charlton, the Birkenhead's house near Oxford, that I first met Brian—in the early 'twenties. Lura and Francis Howard were staying for the weekend and Brian came over for luncheon on Sunday. He was very handsome, tall and slim, with enormous black eyes curtained by long, thick eyelashes. There was something oriental about his fine nose and black hair; he would have looked magnificent wearing a tarboosh. He had great elegance and a rather 'Yellow Book' affectation. He appeared to be

82

maliciously amused by what people said, but even the youthful Brian would not have dared be rude in the late Lord Birkenhead's presence. He would have received what he gave tenfold.

I remember on that occasion Brian and my friend Eleanor Smith locking me up in a loose-box with a beautiful Arab horse who was famous for biting people's buttocks—if given the chance. He was given every chance at such close quarters. He turned his neck into an arch and was about to nip me with huge, rather yellow teeth. I thought love was the only way and flinging my arms round his neck I kissed his velvet muzzle. It was a risk but it worked. The horse was perfectly docile for the remainder of the time—it seemed very long—that I was in the box. I heard Eleanor's voice saying, 'I'm rather worried by the silence, do you think he has devoured Allanah? We must look.' 'Not yet,' said Brian, 'we must torture her a little longer. After all we are only teasing.' I was eventually let out. I had quite enjoyed my privacy with the horse.

This kind of teasing and worse, was inflicted upon me by Brian during the thirty years of our friendship. Sometimes, however, we persecuted other people. Soon after I met Brian his mother asked Eleanor Smith and myself to stay at a house she had taken near Ascot. We thought it would be fun to burgle the house of friends living a few miles away. Brian, Eleanor and I put on old trousers, scarves, check caps, masks, and tennis shoes for silence, taking nips of brandy to give us courage. We got into my tiny Citroën car that looked like a yellow chicken and drove to a lane near the Richard Guinness' house. We crept into the garden and were greeted by growls from Saki, the black chow dog who was sitting by the front door. 'Saki, Saki,' we whispered, and he wagged his tail. He knew us well because we were frequent visitors to the Guinness' house in London. We looked through an opening in the curtains of the drawing-room window, and there were the whole of the house-party playing mah-jong—Richard and Beatrice Guinness, Lady Oxford (then Mrs. Asquith), the daughters of the house (our friends, Zita and Theresa Jungman), and several young men whose names I have forgotten. Nothing could have been easier for burglars than the family and guests closeted in one room, the servants in a separate wing.

We climbed up a drain-pipe and found ourselves in Theresa's bedroom; there we rummaged about in her chest of drawers, rolled on the bed and generally untidied the room. In the next bedroom, laid out on the bed were a flannel nightdress with lace round the collar and a pair of woolly bedsocks. 'It can't be true,' Brian said, 'that anyone could wear such a garment, in bed too. Brevity is the soul of lingerie: into the fireplace with it.' We heard later that Mrs. Asquith had brought only one nightdress with her, and had to wear one of Beatrice's transparent flowing ones that night. Then to Dick Guinness' room. There we put his knife-thin Cartier cigarette case inside an armchair. The adjoining room was Beatrice Guinness', and her famous three rows of pearls lay on the dressing-table. Brian pocketed these.

We then became fearless and rash, dancing down the stairs into the dining-room, to devour peaches and other fruits. Then, out of the window we flew—no one had seen us. Once in the car again we decided to play the same joke on Dick and Gladys Pinto, old friends of mine who lived not far away. However, just as we were climbing through the window of a small cloakroom, Dick Pinto appeared in the doorway. We told him who we were before he had time to get his revolver. Dick was rather a pompous Guardsman, not the kind of man to find unconventional behaviour funny. He looked shocked by our appearance; nevertheless he asked us to come into the drawing-room where his pretty wife, Gladys, introduced us to the house-party, who were bejewelled and in long evening dresses. I think our presence gave them more discomfort than pleasure. It was several years before we were known as 'The Bright Young People', and 'Baby' and Zita Jungman became leading members of the company. We were then still regarded as débutantes, and a certain circumspection was expected of us.

The pearls were still in Brian's pocket. The next day rumours were heard that Mrs. Guinness' pearls were missing, the police had been called, and the search begun. We confessed to Lura Howard, who telephoned to the Guinness'. We returned the necklace and were severely reprimanded by Mrs. Benjamin Guinness (Beatrice having retired to bed with a nervous collapse). She told us how dangerous it was to creep about in the dark, and that a relation of hers had been shot at and wounded in New York while climbing into someone's window. There were many other adventures of this kind which I could tell, but they seem rather childish now.

A diet of practical jokes wears thin, and Brian became despondent (except on the subject of fashion) in his last letters of the summer vacation to the Actons:

[To William] If you have the time in Paris, please call in at Charvet and select me one or two very restrained (I can see you smile. But then I prefer Chanel to Poiret)—in tone—things ... but remember—my tastes are a little more, how shall I say, *foncé* than yours, and Charvet *can* be so like Queen Victoria at Monte Carlo, if you know what I mean.

[To Harold] Do come and stay, for Heaven's sake, before you go back to that rowdy pothole of sterility—Oxford. You are such a comfort to me, you know. I am sorry to overwhelm you with a gushing of rather ill-expressed admiration, such as this, but you seem the only genuine person I know. Oh! all these snobs, these bitches, these stupids, they fill me with contempt. God! can't they see one only lives ONCE. Time so wasted in the sillinesses of adolescence can never be re-lived. They have no ambition, no 'drive'—these contemporaries of ours. We two are, in truth, voices crying in the wilderness—and I cry so very intermittently ...

Harold, dear, you and I—we must get together again. Too long have I dallied with dullards. I am stunting my talent with laziness, and cheap successes at bad parties. Am I so *very* surprising in these last few letters? I feel so strongly just now, that there are things to be thought and written by such as us, that I am not, though you are, doing. How are you? Tell me about Paris, and these new young writers (Radiguet?) that I hear such a pother going on over. What a bloody generation ours is in England! P.S. Let's go to Cambridge. Or is that worse?

[To William] I am being bitten with a disease peculiar to this blasted generation, which I thought could never touch me—'Failure'. I cannot think or write a thought that does not seem to have been done better before. My guests—of my own age—here are fools, lovely fools some, maybe, but fools. I am of the sort that can be brilliant among the brilliant (what conceit!) but grow duller than the dull if I am with them. My brain, my creative instincts are growing feeble, feeble, feeble. At Oxford what ascendancy I have is because of the cut of my clothes—not my tongue. I have no money. I know nothing about politics; am rusty over literature; prejudiced over art, and hysterical about myself. [Later] . . . my irritation at my present literary incompetence is aggravated by the fact that I have stomach-aches and headaches continually lately. Also, my mother has discovered that I am living at double what I can afford, and I am going back to Oxford in a state of utter penury without a ha'pence to betake myself to the movies with. Literally.

What an asinine article on clothes that was you sent me. 'Galluses' indeed. God! *what rot.* As if Schölte made 'scallop-topped' trousers!!!—and objecting to suède shoes—'outside the cake-eater set it would never be possible to popularise such footgear in this country.' Good Heavens, who cares anyway? . . . In clothes the double-breasted coat is being made vulgar by the Prince of Wales, and the famous Hawes & Curtis woven silk tie that I always wear is beginning—only beginning—to die. A new shop from New York—a sort of American Charvet—has appeared in Bond Street, called Sulka & Co. With skill and brilliance as its keynote. The newest record is *Oh Baby—don't say no, say maybe* . . .

[To Harold] I have written to a firm called Shakespeare & Co. in Paris for a copy of *Ulysses* and they *won't* send it. It's infuriating. Harold, I am still sad at myself. I am an unsuccessful type and I will never get any further. If there is one thing more tragic than being a type it is remaining true to it—as I do.

. . . *Is it too late to stop that silly thing* going into *Oxford Poetry* and substitute something else? I *do* hope not. I have been mad for a year. I have wasted, wasted my mind and my time. I intend to begin writing again seriously. It may be unsatisfactory at first—but I must—that is my only real interest at bottom. I must give up this silly frittering away of time at Oxford. There is work for me, in myself. Can you see about that bad derivative thing coming out of *Oxford Poetry?* I think I will have something really much more vital and better for you—please.

Harold remembers that this edition of the annual *Oxford Poetry* was already in print, so that he was unable to substitute a new poem of Brian's. The same image (likening music to 'the rubbing together of biscuits') appeared in both of his poems that were accepted—which amused Harold at the time. Yet John Betjeman remembers to this day only the singularity of this musical analogy,

'Brian wrote some immortal lines, e.g. *Four lips make a mouth* . . . and *A little furtive music like the rubbing together of biscuits* . . .

Oxford Poetry (1924)[6] duly appeared and was refreshingly reviewed in the *Cherwell*:

> The Editors of this year's *Oxford Poetry* (Harold Acton and Peter Quennell) have fulfilled their difficult task with a somewhat surprising result; they have not taken the icing off the top of the cake, they have given us a complete cross-section of it . . . their selection has been admirably catholic. It has embraced almost everything from real poetry through the varying grades of good, mediocre, dull or disgusting to real nonsense. Of real poetry it would be exacting to expect more than a little, but a little there is, and the editors themselves supply a fair proportion of it . . . Mr. Howard was very funny and: some may think him vulgar . . .
>
> After so many anthologies in which the poems are all good, it is a relief to meet one in which some are downright bad. It is unhealthy always to be a spectator and never to take any exercise.

The selection was considered controversial, and a few months later Terence Greenidge slipped a neat comment into the *Cherwell*: 'Harold Acton's magnificent reply to the stupid critics of *Oxford Poetry* does not represent what Oxford thinks poetically, rather what Oxford poets think.'

The 'Oxford Poets' even got themselves on to the air (in January 1925), but did not impress the *Sunday Express* 'Londoner's Log' columnist, 'The Dilettante':

> . . . the maddening part of wireless is, of course, that you cannot heckle, however much you want to. The 'Poets' Symposium' showed the remarkable variations of which the Oxford manner is capable. First we had Mr. Harold Acton, who recited, lispingly, a poem about people bringing 'their bananas and sandwiches to munch on battlefields', and charabancs which tooted . . . Mr. Howard then drawled with a careful precision and asked himself a number of questions. The next poet spoke with remarkable unction and found his r's difficult . . . There was an interval of one minute. It was not enough.

Brian's two poems in question follow:

PANORAMA SEEN BY THE YOUNG AMERICAN WOMAN SLEEPING

The shining queens have run away over the mountains
   carrying their stone dolls wrapped in white lace,
and they have left their soldiers behind to maltreat me
a company who have no legs, but only a curling fish's tail
like a leaf of tarnished metal, which they flay thunderously

---

[6] Published by Blackwell.

in the inky interstices of these secret rocks, while their
   single eyes
shoot beams of coloured light, now up into the celestial
   fires to seek me out
and now in amongst this cold shrubbery
   where I am hiding with such difficulty.

(I wish I was back home in Philadelphia).
Why did the small queens all run so hurriedly?
just because I play Satie on my musical box
a little furtive music like the rubbing together of biscuits
coming from behind a laurel bush in the vegetable garden
   made them all go running away . . .

The Prince de la Fine Fleur said I look very approachable
   when he stepped back and looked at me
after putting that peony in my corsage
so why did all those charming ladies—sleep well, ladies!—
   abandon me without so much as saying, 'See you soon,
   my dear?'

SCENIC RAILWAY

   For a harp, an oboe, and three glockenspiels.

I sit in a truck painted a shiny vermilion and chocolate,
   Grinding along—clanking along a little black iron track
     poised
Way up here on a sparse framework of overgrown needles,
   in the hot
Blue powder of the sky—the shrilly vibrating sky—
Silky blue powder. Ooh, I *am* hot . . .
Out of its metal shutters the blue powder sky showers bursts
   of granulated lights
Which twinkle, slowly, and flash in the white sun . . . pink,
   blue, mauve, and iridescent orange . . .

Here's a tunnel in the sky—covered with swiss chalets . . .
   What a strong smell of caramels! *Bang bang*
Merciful sakes alive . . . what was that? . . .
Ooh, here are the panoramas . . . see the fern rockery? and,
   ooh look! a grotto with a glass bead waterfall—and
   there, a wedding cake, with coloured icings and silvery
   seraphim—and over there, a tin mermaid with coral
   eardrops—and a fairy queen in brown poplin with fur
   cuffs . . . isn't *it pretty? Bang*
Ooh! now we're in the open again. How the sun crashes
and sparkles
On the viridian sponge-cake of the trees . . .
Look at the flags! pink and yellow . . . green and magenta . . .

Listen to the roundabout music! like electric bulbs bursting
    on asphalt, or the rubbing together of biscuits . . .
Bang
We get out here.

Brian never achieved membership of the exclusive Bullingdon Club at Oxford, but he was a guest at their dinner in November, of which two versions are on record, the first as given to William Acton:

I got extremely tipsy, and broke several windows in Peck. 256 panes of glass were smashed altogether—which amounts to £60 at 3s. 9d. each; not counting all the lamps in Peck also. After the Bullingdon dinner I had a tumultuous sleep with someone who remained extremely chilly until we actually got 'between the sheets' . . .

Parents are rarely on the receiving end for truth; to his mother he showed only the brave face:

I went to the Bullingdon dinner, and got filled with a lot of champagne. The visitors were toasted—my toast was 'Brian Howard—that rare combination, the intellectual and the horseman'. Nice, I think. I enjoyed myself immensely, although I broke a shop window and rushed about on bicycles, in cars, and a hansom cab! . . . I had a day's hunting on a sweet, sensible and quite fast horse and enjoyed myself VASTLY—with the Bicester. I flew along like anything.

This 'tumultuous sleep' is the first overt reference to Brian's homosexual promiscuity. The freedom of Oxford (where he was known as the Black How) went to his head and for the next few years he indulged in an extravagantly frenetic round of sex, parties and drink, surprisingly punctuated by forays into the heartier pastimes of huntin' and shootin'. Although ostensibly 'in love' with one of his male fellow undergraduates (a passion that Brian was later to claim besotted him for nearly seven years) this did not prevent him from revelling 'between the sheets' with many other contenders of the same sex.

By complying with his parents' wishes—to exchange his more intellectual friends and aesthetic interests for the titled set and their physically energetic sports—he dug his own academic grave, achieving neither scholarly distinctions nor the sublimation of his sexual desires in outdoor activities. There is a lesson here for all parents, although it is doubtful whether any authority could have effectively changed Brian's inclinations towards more normal spheres at that time. He combined superficial maturity with a curiously adolescent approach to pleasures of the moment, and what no one will ever know is whether his homosexuality directly resulted from his mother complex, or whether he fostered this complex to bolster his immediate tastes. There is certainly no evidence that Lura Howard wanted to keep him as a 'mother's boy', and in Brian's *Spanish Diary* that follows he takes it for granted that he will marry when he is 'older, and sane'.

8. Spanish Diary

1925

Whenever Brian found himself abroad he would start writing an introspective diary. During the Easter vacation of 1925 he visited Madrid and kept: '. . . an extraordinary sort of autobiographical diary, full of lies and wanderings off into stories or descriptions. *It has cheered me up a very great deal.* At last I am doing something, I say . . .' [Brief extracts follow.]

THE SPANISH DIARY OF IAN WARD (Br)Ian (Ho)Ward
(April 1925) Gran Café de Puerto Rico.

It is Good Friday, or was, three-quarters of an hour ago, and everyone is leaving the Café. But I do not feel inclined to go, and I won't yet. I came here hoping to be able to write, and I can't. And just for that reason, tonight, I will go on writing. I will give up all ideas of form, or economy, of reason, even—and write. Three dark men are laughing at me because I am writing, with a pencil, in a book. I don't care. But the real catastrophe is that I don't particularly care what I write down . . . It is so terrible to come to a city where one has never been before, and be so incapable. This is a new city. Noisy, and parvenu, and opposed to subtleties, the qualities of life that inspire, but still *one should be able to force something even from such a situation as this.* Especially if one knows, and execrates, one's laziness—if one is weeping inside, frantic to get something done. If one is so sure one has it to say. But how pathetic that surety is. How is it possible to be sure? . . .

I can imagine myself talking now, to a friend. There would be no brilliance. But there would be life, if he was here. This place would become, mysteriously, entirely alive. I think I become mentally awry when alone. Which is devastating, if true. The fact that I am sitting here, doing this, is an insufferable artificiality. It is too like taking drugs. A friend would clarify. But a friend can't just sit, like the people that melted in Madame Tussaud's, and watch me write . . .

A woman has just come in, with a lovely face. A skin that I can see, at once, is admirable. The pink and white resolving into one another with most certainly the right restraint. Soft, tender hair with the subtle, negative lights in it that, also, are right. Features that combine character and what might easily be called beauty. She wears a good dress, black with enough white. She would consider that I should be moved by her, undoubtedly. She is thinking so, now.

Has she, I wonder, ever felt everything dissolve into a kind of blazing, painful happiness merely because of an unconscious intonation in someone's voice? A careless note that breaks one into little bits? Or the hard agony that sometimes descends just because someone hasn't happened to hear something that one has taken too much trouble to say? But why this? Indirect introspection, and totally unnecessary.

> April is the cruellest month, breeding
> lilacs out of the dead land, mixing
> memory and desire . . .

God! how applicable that is. But one is so apt to be like that, at a quarter to two in the morning, with a band . . .

*   *   *

Last night I went to a music hall, and so was let, liturgically speaking, from writing. It is a most beautiful morning, and fills me with regrets at having to go back to England in a few days. What a dull frowsy place it seems, when one is half awake, in this sun, vaguely recalling it, from the south. Awful men in bowler hats and bad tempers trotting up and down the wet pavements—wherever it is, the same. London or Leeds. Oxford. Cambridge. Bexhill-on-Sea. Onward Christian Soldiers. *To do something.* Always just setting out, firmly laughing at nothing, like destroyer boats, *to do something.* Golf. A walk. Missing the grain of life with grotesque precision, missing every nuance that their eyes and ears could possibly ignore. Trundling along, like stupid trains, using churches as stations if they are serious, and whiskeys-and-sodas as stations if they are not. 'So you've been abroad?' (How they hate abroad). 'That must have been rather fun.' What they feel like saying is 'rather funny.'

*   *   *

So odd, how one dashes from Eliot to 1880. The cruellest month breeds, or seems to, not lilacs for me, but a desire for drooping silk cravats, and seventeen-year-oldish fascinations of that kind. That's my splendid youth coming back to me, that never went away, I suppose. Back by way of the music. It recalls to me how I sat in an hotel bedroom in Naples reading Brooke's *Grantchester* to my family, and finishing the last lines with the tears running down my face . . . or, earlier, when football was rendered impossible because I had become 'des Esseintes'.

And now, when ones' friends think one has read it all, that one has got there, so to speak . . . *what* a miserable business. *I know nothing.* This is such a fabulous period of existence. People think one has more or less formed opinions. They argue. Ignorant really, one argues back, settling oneself into frames of mind about everything. Taking a stand on one's views. Decided. This seems to me such a hindrance. If they would only agree, how quickly would one begin, with anxiety, to review one's position. Examine again, the values. Begin the ever-needed reformation . . . I have aroused the kindliness of two of the waiters here by my regular appearance. They talk at me with gusto, and I do so wish I could have back at them with a rush of appreciatory language.

*   *   *

When I am older, and sane, I shall bring my wife to Spain, and, if I remember, I shall persuade her to dress like Raquel Meller[1] (surely she is going to be something vaguely like that to look at) and conduct her to this Café. Having electrified the clientele, we will sit and eat *leche merengada*, and talk about myself, and she will say how charming I must have been, sitting here—the young, earnest writer, writing . . . and then, quite suddenly, I shall probably dislike her, and, for the moment, dislike everything else, except the memory of now.

Oh Lord! Rupert Brooke at the *Café des Westerns*. Pining for his 'little room'. Why couldn't he look round him at that moment and *see?* But—'when you were there, and you, and and you . . .' He is so insidious, all the same, in that sort of mood. He couldn't write, but he was so clever about finding one's sentimentalities. We, of this generation, should never allow our sentimentalities to be so found, if we can help it.

I have had a triumph. Forgive me, please, for continually talking about what happens to me in this Café. But I have had a triumph. What do you think? At the end of the last number, *all* the waiters, *all* the three musicians established themselves here, at my table, and talked at me. One of the orchestra talked French and acted as interpreter. Their curiosity is now satisfied, and my popularity is confirmed. *Olé!* And now they are playing a special tango for me—*Don Quintin el Amargao.*[2] They nodded before they did it. I never felt happier in my life.

---

[1] The Catalan dancer and *diseuse.*

[2] He chose this as the title to his poem, *Don Quintin el Amargao, or Conversation to Music in Madrid*, finally published as *Young* in *First Poems* (see Appendix I).

9. In and out of Oxford

1925–1927

Spanish dreams were soon forgotten and Oxford life continued as before, but no documentation remains to cover this Trinity Term 1925, only a few letters from the summer vacation. The first was written from Longleat, staying with Henry Weymouth (now Lord Bath), who knew Brian very well at Oxford: 'He was a great friend of mine. To my Father's amazement he actually came and stayed once at Longleat . . .'

Brian wrote to his mother from Longleat in August:

> I am having Heaven's own time here. Riding in the morning through the lovely, lovely park. Today we went along the ridge which some nice person called 'Heaven's Gate'. Shooting in the afternoon. Duck, mostly, and I'm getting a good shot, you know. I can shoot *running* rabbits while in a moving car. Henry drives along the rides in the woods, and I shoot out of the car as he goes along. Marvellous practice. Daphne was here during most of the week. I do like her *so* much. She really is the sweetest of all these people . . .

Daphne Vivian (first married to Lord Bath, now Mrs. Xan Fielding) described the same visit in her book, *Mercury Presides*,[1] and included a faintly incriminating anecdote that Brian did not pass on to his mother:

> Henry invited me to Longleat for a weekend party . . . Cocktails were unheard of there, so Henry made them secretly in his rooms at the top of the house, where we all met at six o'clock. We had arranged a plan in case of an interruption, and this was successfully put into operation when Lord Bath made an unexpected appearance. Henry had a bastard Sealyham which was a wicked fighter: its arch enemy was Charlie Brocklehurst's shaggy mongrel. As Lord Bath opened the door Henry kicked the two dogs together, and, in the hullabaloo that ensued, whisked away the cocktail paraphernalia while we all hid our glasses.
>
> During this visit Brian, with unusually good intentions, stirred up a scandal for me. During some game which entailed creeping about in the dark, I had given him my shoes and ear-rings to look after. He had taken them to his bedroom, and to avoid the discovery of my belongings there, had slept with them under his pillow, where they were found by the housemaid next morning. The housemaid took them to the housekeeper; the housekeeper took them to Lady Bath; and Lady Bath sent for Henry

[1] Published by Eyre & Spottiswood, 1954.

and asked him to identify the earrings. Henry only just succeeded in vindicating me to his mother ...

A marathon letter to William Acton told of Brian's other holiday visits, from which I quote an extract. It was written from Cullen, Banffshire, while staying with Lady Seafield:

The conditions of my life, conducted for the most part as they have been in other people's houses, have not been favourable to the writing of any letters at all. But, being the most good-natured person in the world I am sure you will forgive me. After the end of term I remained in London for some time dancing and scandal-mongering generally. I then went to Ireland—to stay with Michael [Rosse, at Birr Castle]. There were one or two older people, Michael himself, his sister Bridget, and his younger brother Desmond. His mother is one of those quietly nice Englishwomen, and really very likeable in the muted way one likes that subdued type. Bridget has the best 'shingle' I know, clipped short and mannish in the way that it grows. Heavy, thick and undulant, like a Kennington pastel. I have never been to Ireland before, and I enjoyed it, especially my glimpse of Dublin, which seemed a very charming, grey, 16th century city in the early morning light. At Birr I rode in the mornings. In the afternoons we walked and sometimes I shot. I shot my first snipe there ...

In London I went to the first night of (J. R. Ackerley's) *Prisoners of War*—a dreary homosexual play (the first yet produced in London) and then came up to this damned Scottish mansion belonging to Nina Seafield. My dear, I travelled third—nearly six hundred miles—since I am now suddenly so poor (something has happened in America, and I shall not be able to hunt this winter) and there were three frightful men in the carriage with me, who insisted on my sharing their disgusting beer—I hate beer—and who talked, or, rather, bellowed until 4 o'clock in the morning. I nearly died of cold, fatigue and dirt, and arrived at this gaunt, baronial house—so like a Victorian setting for *Hamlet*—very discouraged and apprehensive. It was pouring and blowing when I came on Saturday, and it is pouring and blowing still. The house is filled with tittering young fools whom you do not know—boobies from whom I have been flying for months. Mark (Ogilvie-Grant) is here, however, which is a comfort(?) and Bryan (Guinness) arrives tomorrow.

However I am here for at least ten days and how I shall be able to stand the perpetual storm of giggling that convulses this ridiculous household, I don't know. You know Nina by sight? She is like a slimmer Queen Victoria, with marvellous orange-coloured hair. She has a very fine skin, like white jade, and startlingly green eyes. The conversation in this ménage is completely confined to 'young' jokes of a coy, or lavatory-ish nature, and fragmentary sentences like—'Well—*I* find the *Green Hat* so difficult to understand, don't you? Bosh, anyway, I think.' God in Heaven! And the servants are impudent. This morning I was a trifle late for breakfast and the butler sternly admonished me that breakfast was from 9.15 until 10 SHARP. I loathe Scotland ...

Mark Ogilvie-Grant, reminiscing about Brian, emphasises that half the fun of being with him was hearing the crack come out absolutely pat. He remembers the Scottish visit at his cousin, Nina Seafield's, when Brian became exasperated with a certain young man who was in love with Nina. Finally Brian could not stand the boy moping around the house any more and turned on him, 'My dear X, I feel that your fly buttons will burst open any minute and a large pink dirigible emerge, dripping ballast at intervals'. This was neither the language nor the humour of even remotely conventional twenty-year olds, so one can imagine the misfit rôle on which Brian was already modelling himself.

From Scotland he went to stay with the Ernest Guinnesses at Luggala, in Co. Wicklow, from where he wrote to his mother, expanding on the healthy life he was leading:

This is one of Ernest Guinness' shooting lodges, twenty miles from Dublin, and really the *most beautiful place I've ever seen*. A tiny little house on the edge of a great lake with huge feathery mountains towering all around. We're out all day. Yesterday *we rode* fifteen miles to a haunted lake and wished three wishes each in a little cave where a saint called St. Kevin used to live. I wished that, from now, you should be happy for the rest of your life, and then that I should be, and that Daddy should be. This morning we sun-bathed, and this afternoon climbed a real mountain ... this evening we're going out to tell ghost stories in a cave in the woods, and tomorrow we go grouse shooting. It's all too lovely ...

The other day we climbed the famous Powerscourt waterfall—Henry, Daphne and I, and at the Powerscourts' they told us that some people had *once attempted it before* but had to be rescued with ropes! While we were climbing we suddenly saw a *whole* rainbow beneath us in the valley—brilliant and complete. I've never felt quite so well in my life. We're out all day—riding, rowing, and climbing. I write 'po'try' in my spare time. (I've written five sonnets since I have been away, which are really rather good, and different from my usual kind of stuff.) What a life to lead—so perfect. Meals when you like. Everything when and where you like. Plain nursery food, which I love, and the nicest play fellows in the world. We draw one another, photograph one another, write things about one another, and adore one another, realising the indisputable fact that WE are the nicest young things in the world! P.S. It's like a Barrie play here. The scenery ... *Mary Rose*, EXACTLY.

Daphne Fielding detailed their activities a little more succinctly in her book, *Mercury Presides*:

Soon after the Longleat party Henry, Brian and I met once more in Ireland, at Luggala, Ernest Guinness' house. The eldest of his three daughters, Aileen, was a friend of mine. I confided to Brian that I was in love with Henry, and from then on he excelled himself in weaving Machiavellian schemes to further or frustrate the romance, according to his whim ... There was something about the atmosphere of the place which produced high tension, emotion and episodes. Brian was in his element here; he only needed a cauldron and a blasted heath to complete him as one of the three witches from *Macbeth*.

. . . High up in the craggy rocks surrounding the house was a cave where, after creeping out of the girls' dormitory and meeting the others at midnight, we would spend the rest of the night telling ghost stories round a fire in which we baked potatoes. Most of the day we spent by the lake in dressing-gowns and pyjamas, fancying that we looked like the photographs we had seen in *The Tatler* of smart people at the Lido. In the evening we rode and, in order to make things more exciting, pretended to be highwaymen. Wearing scarlet jerseys and slouch hats, we reined our horses across the road and refused to let pedestrians pass until they had given us a coin. These rites were very unorthodox. Sometimes we rode two-up on a horse, standing in the saddle or back to front; often our mounts returned to the stables riderless. There could not be a more romantic and exciting place than Luggala, and it was here that Henry asked me to marry him. We decided to keep our engagement secret until his twenty-first birthday.

Later that summer Aileen invited Henry, Brian and me to join her father's yacht, *Fantôme*, for a cruise along the west coast of Ireland. This was my first experience of yachting . . . Henry was always climbing and swinging about in the rigging; and when the boat sailed he sat astride the bowsprit playing his ukelele. Showing off to him, I climbed up to the crow's nest, where I got stuck like a panic-stricken cat in a tree, unable to move either forwards or backwards. I remained there for hours with my face turned to the mast until we reached Limerick harbour, where I was ignominiously lowered in the bosun's chair before a gaping crowd . . .

Brian described the *Fantôme* to his mother:

The yacht is just too wonderful. Black and white outside, with three masts with square-rigged sails. It used to be a French trading barque and then belonged to the Duke of Westminster, and is one of the biggest yachts on Lloyd's register—700 tons. Marvellous food, twenty sailors or so— bathrooms, electric piano, electric heaters, and three motor boats on board, one big launch, one racing one, and a small one. The cabins are lovely. Daphne, Henry and I are the only ones besides two old men and the crew who aren't Guinnesses. The cars in which we go motoring inland follow us on land. It's a most exciting life . . .

Brian was apparently warned off the turf while at Oxford because he could not pay his bookie, his father being glad of this ruthless expedient which prevented him from doing any more betting. This may account for more literary interests, including writing for the *Cherwell*, starting to figure in his life during 1925–1926. Having been represented in *Oxford Poetry* (1924), Brian was approached by the new editor, Patrick Monkhouse:

Dear Brian Howard, It has fallen to my lot to take over the orts and abjects of *Oxford Poetry*, the which, without your potent stimulus, languishes not a little. Won't you liven us up a bit? Or have you sworn the oath of an eremite? Yours in all humility of spirits, Patrick Monkhouse.

Patrick Monkhouse is pretty confident that he did not reject anything sent in by Brian, 'We would have been glad of it. We had Acton in the book, of course; it wouldn't have been *Oxford Poetry* without him'. Possibly in connection with this business, he recalls getting a letter from Brian which ran, 'Dear Monkhouse, let us dine together and discuss our mutual antipathy'. 'We did dine, and got on very pleasantly, but nothing much came of it. We weren't built to be intimates.'

Brian let off his esoteric steam in several *Cherwell* essays. The Union did not often tempt him into speaking, although of one debate, *That this House calls upon the United States to renew their allegiance to the British Crown* (ultimately lost by 39 votes) it was reported: 'Mr. Brian Howard (Christ Church) was, Oh! so cultured, and with a deliciously languorous self-composure entered into the history of the affair. Having charmed the House with his picture of Americans as prodigal sons conspiring with savages to surprise English generals at dinner—still with the utmost grace—he faded away, giving place to . . .'

Another type of 'Debate', part of a series published in the *Cherwell*) caught his interest. The subject was *A Man owes more to his University than to his Public School*. It was 'proposed' by Aubrey Herbert, replied to in the following weeks by Patrick Monkhouse and others, Brian's 1,500-word contribution to the series (on 13th February 1926) preceding ones by Bryan Guinness and Frank Pakenham. His piece was largely serious, and with one more term to go Brian must have written with conscious subjectivity. It was as good a condemnation of the likely outcome of his own way of life at Oxford as any of the critics could have conjured up. Due to lack of space only a brief extract follows.

. . . For some reason, discipline, the parent of happiness and achievement, is considered unnecessary to a man as regards his education, after the age of eighteen.

. . . As regards Oxford itself, there has never been a place where work of any kind was made difficult more systematically. Meals, motor cars, *mésalliances*—everything combines, like the sequent notes of some over-whelming lullaby, to ignore the educative idea. No, to kill it. Unencouraged to apply oneself to one's studies, one is not even noticeably advantaged if one does. One is forgotten, the charm of which thing appeals to few.

. . . It is believed that the Earl of Birkenhead is about to bring forward a Bill proposing compulsory hours of study for undergraduates. Now, when I give this, as I do, my sincerest support, I will be indicted, doubtless, as a lazy fellow. I am: and so, I believe, are a great many others at this University. It is a source of continual fret to me that I cannot accomplish a sufficient amount of work from day to day, and, while compulsory hours of study would be profoundly exasperating, it would interfere, in practice, tolerably little with other activities, and constitute the one source of present and eventual content . . .

Already in the Easter vacation Lura Howard was predicting failure for Brian in a letter to her great friend, Edith Olivier: 'Brian cannot possibly take a Law degree!! He hasn't worked and now is in despair: well deserved—it may help his outlook. I'm waiting to hear what the Tutors are going to allow him to do . . .' She was writing to thank Edith Olivier for sending her one of the 112 privately printed copies of a symposium[2] in memory of her sister, Mildred Olivier. It contained thirteen vignettes by friends and relations, with a portrait drawing by Stephen Tennant and decorations by their great family friend, Rex Whistler. Brian concocted the graceful introduction to the book:

YOU

WHO SHALL TAKE UP THIS BOOK

DURING THE PROGRESS OF THE YEARS

THINK THAT YOU HOLD IN YOUR HANDS

A WREATH

MADE FORM EACH TREE AND PLANT

IN A LADY'S GARDEN

FOR

AS SHE LOVED HER FLOWERS

SHE LOVED HER FRIENDS

AND NOW

HER FLOWERS AND HER FRIENDS

ARE HER BIOGRAPHERS

B.H.

He also contributed his memories of 'Mildred at the Daye House'. He was just twenty-one, and young to be included in such company.

In her own essay Edith Olivier wrote: '. . . At the Daye House Mildred found herself in the world of youth, making friends on absolutely equal terms with the rising generation . . . (amongst them) Brian Howard, so terribly modern, whom Mildred used to tease and to argue with . . .'

Laurence Whistler, Rex's younger brother, produced this extract from Edith Olivier's Journal of the *following* year (as yet unpublished). It gives a vivid pen picture of Brian, the spoilt boy blessed with charm, but still remarkably juvenile in character.

27 *August* 1927. Brian and I drove to Romsey to see John Hill in the Nursing Home there, after an operation. Lunched at a teashop. Brian very rowdy and noisy and funny. Other customers father shocked. . . . Rex (Whistler) arrived at tea-time bringing his brother Laurie, rather a dear little boy of fifteen, with white face, dark eyes, and a nose.

(After tea.) Brian was wild to make the others bathe, and furious when they wouldn't. At last he said *he* would—so we went to watch. He was terrified at the cold water and wouldn't get in for ages, but shivered, screaming on the bank.

---

[2] *Mildred*, published at the High House Press, Shaftesbury, 1926.

28 *August* 1927. Brian left after luncheon. He is in much better mood and health. Didn't want to go, but I had to make him—three boys, one being the exhausting wilful tremendous Brian are too much for my strength, my household, and my baby Austin. When he had gone we were marvellously still and peaceful.

Laurence Whistler remembers all this 'fairly well'.

Brian was rather formidable to me, in his extravagant and uninhibited way, though kindly enough. I had no bathing suit, and he wanted me to borrow a pair of Edith Olivier's knickers: this I would have done, with some embarrassment, but my brother prevented it; and that no doubt was why Rex didn't swim that day, since we both loved bathing as a rule. He also disposed of a pressing invitation from Brian that I should go to stay with him alone. I was more or less aware of a certain quality in his kindliness towards me!

He spent a good deal of time abusing the pretty servant girls as 'skivvies', and 'sluts', I think, and chasing them in and out of the kitchen with much screaming. His boisterous rudeness was amusing to me, though rather boring to E.O. and Rex after a while. 'Filthy food!' he would cry, as he helped himself to more at the side table. Then he would kneel in adulation beside Edith's chair, his hands weaving up and down, saying, 'Needle-eedle-eedle' and a great deal of soothing and affected nonsense.

He and Rex composed impressionistic portraits of each other in free verse, of which I remember little, except that Brian's portrait of Rex had these rather felicitous lines:

> Laughter in the bathroom,
> in the bar-room
> in the ballroom—
> But the laughter is an urn.

I don't think I ever saw him again.

Re-reading this it strikes me as more censorious than I had intended. He *was* a most amusing companion, and a great personality, and at a rather childish fifteen I was excited by him but of course it was a very brief encounter.

Brian was obviously unhappy at his lack of evident success at Oxford, as well as going through a generally bleak period of failure and rejection. He thought himself to be in love with Daphne Vivian, and the fact that she became engaged to (and then secretly married) Henry Weymouth did not help to raise his spirits. He must have confided in her early that summer because he kept her sweet letter in reply amongst his most personal possessions.

Dearest Brian, I have never thanked you properly for the lovely ear-rings—enough to say I love them. I have had the screws put on. I simply *couldn't* summon up courage to have my ears pierced. I never answered your telegram about acting in the cinema—I would as long as it wouldn't be likely to come to Daddy's ears. It would mean hell's bells for me. It wouldn't *appear* anywhere, would it? As long as it is amateur I should think I could do it—you see he hates me acting because my mother went on the stage, and it would be just like a red rag to a bull ... Ask Henry if he wouldn't do a little teeny weeny part in it (from me). Tell him he must be a crowd or a butler! But I think he would hate doing it, poor darling! Although the cinema has proved that he has got an ideal film face. Lord Digby took one at Minterne and Bobby (Digby) tells me that Henry can out-Rudolph Rudolph Valentino—I would love to do it if he could be persuaded too.

... Brian, I hope you are not still finding life a grim burden—I am so glad you cleared the air by your volcanic outburst. It is much better to know these things definitely. But I don't want you to think you ought to go away—don't let's be tragic over it, although it *is* very sad. Surely we can still be friends—unless you really feel miserable when you see me. I know I am thoughtless in talking so much about Henry to you—but it is difficult not to when he is my whole existence. And you used to be the one person that I felt I could talk about him to ... Brian dear, I do hate hurting people, so please don't be unhappy over me. I may be a rebel but I am only rebellious in spots, and I am being tamed, and I glory in it! I *want* to be tamed. I have got the slave instinct good and strong.

My dear, I believe you are in love with a wraith—a Daphne who doesn't exist, and it isn't worth while suffering heart-aches over an ideal—please realise *I have got enormous and solid feet of clay* ... I am very unhappy for you to love and be made sad through it—because I am so terribly in love I understand all the more. I want you to promise me to let me shut your love away in our box, and let's start over again at being friends, and I refuse to let you think about going away. You've jolly well not got to lie heavy on my conscience by being miserable. You have told me now, so we mustn't talk about it any more, and you can tell me when it finally dies—having been crushed by my great clod-hopping feet of clay. [*Continued later from Sledmere, while staying with the Sykes family*]: ... I do understand and I know that us two, your mother and Méraud (Guinness) are the only people who really count with you—and the sad thing is that we all hurt you in different ways. I hurt you because I belong to Henry, and Henry hurts because he doesn't understand and is shy with you, and yet you feel you can't do without any of us. But Henry has got to go away, and it will be less for you to bear than for me ... the hell of having no Henry to fly to in all my petty little everyday hurts, that count so much ... of course we must try and manage to see each other lots, and what with that and the glory you are going to win in the paths of fame, couldn't you try to be happy? I do want you to be less miserable, and I know you do suffer hell at times. I am so selfish and it's only when I am away from you that I begin to realise what a lot you have got to make you kick against the pricks. I flatter myself that I really and truly understand you. You see we are far too alike to be peaceful together, don't you realise that? And yet, if you were taken away, it would make a tremendous gap in my life . . . Best love, Daphne.

He was still smouldering in a depressed fashion when he wrote to Daphne just after his family had moved into their new country house, Nore, at Hascombe, Surrey.

It's 9.30 p.m. and I've been trudging round our enormous and magnificent estate after stray rabbits and pigeons and things, with small success, and wondering most of the time whether or not you would come to Cannes . . . I KNOW that once you're there you'll adore it as you've never adored anything before. Irish fairylands and Scotch mists are all very well—but they're nothing to an autumn in the South. There you have all the romance of the North, but in a decent temperature, with casinos, cocktails and Callot, thrown in. And other things!

[Later] I've taken to thinking rather too much about you lately, I shall have to do something about it, though what I don't know. I so want you to see this place. Although it's tiny,[3] and ugly outside, and rather Victorian and perched and dishevelled, it's acquiring rather a 'good atmosphere'. And although I should have done it very austerely inside—to suit the white walls and beamed ceilings—my papa and mamma are making it extremely entertaining by the mixture of things they have put in it. And nothing is really wrong, exactly, about the mixture. You'd think that Chinese lacquer and pots—Italian candlesticks, and Renaissance pictures would look awful jumbled together inside a minute Gothic farm (it's Gothic inside and Victorian out), but they don't. They give it an extraordinary character.

Daphne Fielding writes from her home in France:

I was *very, very* fond of Brian and extremely touched that he should have kept that letter of mine all these years. I don't think that he would have been happy if he had married and had children, although he might have succeeded more in literary fields because of a family life keeping him from 'questing', but then he wouldn't have been Brian.

He didn't really like children[4] and was not at all interested in my small step-brother and step-sister, whom I adored. In those early, Oxford days Brian thought that he could be married happily, and to me, but looking back on it all I think he only wanted this because it was impossible, and he must have known that I wouldn't when he asked me. I can't think how it would have turned out . . .

[3] When Nore was to be let, furnished, a few years later, the agents described it as a 60-acre property, the house with 14/15 bedrooms, 6 bathrooms, a 'Stone Hall', drawing-room, dining-room, panelled sitting-room, cottage for menservants, garage for 2/3 cars, hard tennis court, 60-foot long studio in garden, etc.
[4] Brian's attitude to children must have changed through the years as Heywood Hill says he was marvellous with his small daughters (after the war) and knew exactly how to talk to them.

Brian had a tremendous influence on me, and I think it was a good one which opened my eyes to beauty. He was always incredibly sweet, never turning his terrifying Mr. Hyde face on me.

It felt very strange when I was staying some time ago with Dirk Bogarde at Nore, from where Brian had written to me so often describing it (although I never saw it when he lived there). One was conscious of Brian all the time, and his own very particular atmosphere seemed to dominate even Dirk's.

This romantic set-back did not prevent Brian from recounting all the gossip of the season, from London and Nore, to William Acton:

I've been doing very little. A healthy week at Harry's (Stavordale), riding, chasing dogs and listening to 'Kitsch' on his wireless. Before that there was London, as there is London again. I have to be here as I have two distracted barristers in the Middle Temple trying to teach me law, and visit them—for my sins—daily.

The other night I dined at the Benjamin Guinnesses to find Mrs. Patrick Campbell threatening to bob her hair. I believe she's done it by now. She'll look like some nonconformist cook who's stayed too long in the kitchen. *Dreadful.* Marvellous hair, it was. Another night I went to the *most* horrible party given by Evan Morgan, which began at the Eiffel Tower and ended at somebody's bedroom at Prince's Hotel in Jermyn Street. I rushed out, clutching my remaining bits of virtue—bundled them into a taxi, and trundled home. I've never seen anything so stupendously naughty, even in Oxford! Never again—as I value my reputation.

The best play I've seen was the *Three Sisters* by Tchekov, produced by Komisarjevsky, with John Gielgud in it. It was really great. The best stage management I've ever seen. The lighting and decorations were productions of genius. I also went to see Tom's [Douglas] play, *The Snow Man.* Admitted that I arrived at the commencement of the third act—it was appalling. Jeanne de Casalis was good. I consider her a very fine actress indeed. But the play was so bad. From the third act alone—which is the best I hear—I could see that. Tom, I am told, burst into tears after that particular performance (the second night). Perhaps he saw my face in the second row. Other things were queer that night. There were no people to show one to one's seat. And the audience gobbled peanuts *all* the time—laughing, in dulcet Jewish at private jokes. A fiasco.

... One very terrible thing is that my grandfather is dying of cancer which hangs like a tragic cloud over the house. Money and work are dreadful.

... I am writing from our new country house. This harassed little farm is perched, like some dishevelled little Victorian lady, on a spur of the southernmost Surrey hills, commanding a very lovely view of Sussex. Situate upon a modest precipice, one gardens in spiked shoes, hanging on to the cabbages with one hand, so to speak, while pruning the roses with the other. Having been a farm since the 16th century (it was builded on the site of a Roman camp) it would have been perfect in its miniature way, if it had not been renovated seventy-five years ago. This has ruined it, largely, outside, for ever, but a persistent pick-axe inside has restored something of its Tudor appeal. We have left the interior mostly white, with the original beamed ceilings. Lest, however, you should visualise it as a mansion, I must tell you that there are about two rooms and a chilly lavatory in the entire ménage, in which congested space my extraordinary Papa is piling a variety of objets d'art such as Russian sledges—blanc-de-Chine vases—gothic chests—lacquer cabinets—Venetian candelabra—Battersea candlesticks—Austrian glass—French 18th-century chairs, and God doesn't know what besides, until what should have been an austere and early Spanish atmosphere, has become a combination of a Drury Lane pantomime and the Baroness d'Erlanger's bedroom. One trips over coffins to brain oneself on a bronze. However I comfort myself with writing poems and epistles, and my nice little collection of new books.

You will find a photograph of me in the English *Vogue* in 'my old black', standing with Evan Morgan at the Guinness mediaeval ball. The ravishing beauty of my face and my figure render my proximity to this old starfish most suspicious to the ignorant. However . . . Willy, that ball was the most effective party I have ever seen in London. People took such *immense* trouble over their costumes. Even the half-dozen royalties were in the period. That, and the fancy dress party that the Americans (who have all returned to America) and I gave in Ned Murray's Tite Street studio—Sargent's—were the two parties I enjoyed most. For the latter I discovered a genius. An impudent Jewish-American pianist from the '45', who played Jazz like the Virgin Mary. I never heard anyone to touch him. Everyone came on from Mrs. Corrigan's and Mrs. Harry Brown's [two notable American party hostesses at that time]. Let me describe my toilette. I was dressed (this costume, I may truthfully say, was the best thing I have EVER done anywhere) as a Duchess of 1905. Poised on the largest nut-brown wig in the world I wore a colossal grey velvet hat, embellished with a cascade of grey ostrich plumes, and seven magenta cabbage roses. Round my neck there was a diamond and pearl dog collar; a lorgnette on the end of a black ribbon, and a narrow black boa. The dress of grey gauze, tight at the waist, and with a slight train; the corsage was decorated in front with a fichu of lace, and upon this I pinned two monstrous cameos, and a butterfly made of diamonds. On the long, trailing skirt there were oblong insertions of lace. Besides this I wore black gloves which went above the elbows; black silk stockings, gartered in pink, and extremely high-heeled patent leather shoes.

When I arrived, earlier in the evening, with Zita and Baby Jungman and Alfred Beit at the Harry Browns I created such a furore that I was compelled to leave. No one in London had ever had a fancy dress of this period before, and also there was the question of my face. I have not told you about my face . . . Willie Clarkson took an hour to make me up. My dear, in his hands my face suddenly became that of some bastard daughter with a dozen mothers. One mother lent me the aspect of a drug-fiend nun; another the quality of an early Sargent; another mother made me look a little like Mrs. Asquith. I was astounding. When I looked at myself in the glass I laughed so much that I blew all the champagne in my glass into my face. A mixture, *au fin*, of Lady Tree and an Eton dame. You can imagine me, thumping, rather top-heavy, up those stairs at Grosvenor Square. Statuesque, terrific. People waiting on the landing above recoiled. Never have I created such a sensation. Unfortunately, it got into the papers, but the notice was quite complimentary.

[Later] I can't tell you how I wish you were here. It's odd, but whenever I'm really lonely I miss you more than most people. You know you have an interest in life—which you are able to communicate—which is very remarkable.

Yes—my old letters. I'm glad you've kept them. They will become souvenirs *de jadis* one of these days, and we will smile over them a little tearfully perhaps ... I've decided, after much argument, to try and spend until next June doing my law exam: because I think it's better if one has gone to Oxford to be able to say one has a degree. Don't you? It will be hell doing it. But my mother says I can go somewhere and hunt while I do it. I shall probably go to Harry's (Stavordale) old crammer near Oxford.

When you come home I'll give you *the most* amazing book called *L'Ersatz d'Amour* by Willy et Menalkas. It is 'it', from beginning to end, and one of the most touching romances I've ever read. How long are you going to be at Venice? Have you had any adventures? I am peculiarly adventureless. This place (Nore) grows more like a mixture between Marie Antoinette's cottage and the antique section in a Fifth Avenue department store every day. I read and write all day, and have collected enough poems for a book. My cousin Bordie Harriman is coming to Oxford next term and I want you to give a nice party with aphrodisiacs on toast as a savoury.

(Anton) Dolin has asked me to do a ballet for Charlot's new revue—scenery, costumes, and story, and choose the music. I've done it—but I don't know if it will come to anything, and anyway, don't tell anyone yet. *My* name isn't going to be on the programme if I can help it. [As usual, to avoid parental disapproval]. I've chosen a 15th-century fairy story. He climbs up a tower on the stage, by means of the princess' hair, and then jumps off the top. If it comes off, which it probably will, it will create a great sensation.

Enclosed with the letter was a sketch of the set and chief costume for Dolin. The ballet was to be called *l'Escalier d'Or* and danced to the *Cortège* of Debussy. The scene was to have a white tower and coral and dark red clouds against a black sky, with greeny-blue trees. Dolin's costume combined blue velvet and soft white leather with black and silver tights.

'Pat' Dolin remembers talking to Brian about the ballet:

It was his idea and it was danced by Jessie Matthews and me in the *Charlot Show of 1926*. I choreographed the ballet (finally called *The Golden Key—a medieval episode*) and did use at Brian's suggestion, I think successfully, the Debussy *Cortège*, but his costume design I wore for another solo in the show. I knew Brian pretty well and first met him at Oxford with Rowland Leigh who was writing for Charlot, lyrics mostly. Although Brian and I were the same age I remember, and rather marvelled at—as it seemed to me then—his utter sophistication and tremendous charm.

Whether as a result of his essay into the world of ballet or not, a frisson of social ostracism is felt when Brian unburdened himself to Bryan Guinness, while staying with Edith Olivier at the Daye House at Wilton, and at Nore:

Being, as Palmerston's Princess Lieven put it—*un peu vulgaire* I was not asked ... [to a Drury-Lowe party at Locko Park]. I am supposed to start working for my degree, which is fiendish. I'm thinking of changing from Law to History as I simply cannot do Law, and did a lot of History at Eton, and during my first year at Oxford.

I have been writing a vast amount of rather better stuff lately, and expect to get out a book of poetry in the winter. ... I suppose you've seen Henry Yorke's book? (*Blindness*). I think it's rather good, and the Eton part about us all is amusing ... I haven't been tipsy for so long, I positively ache for the bottle ... At the same time as banging my way through my God-damned law, I'm writing a novel, and actually getting on with it. Only a couple of chapters so far, though, but for once, I enjoy writing prose, and have every idea of finishing it. I must do something anyway in order to get my eye in for revising my poems.

... Talking of books, if you have not yet read Geoffrey Scott's *Portrait of Zélide* you must send for it instantly. It is less obvious than Guedalla, and infinitely better written than Strachey. As an historical biography it is little short of perfect. Nevertheless, Guedalla's *Independence Day* is *most* amusing. *Concerning the Eccentricities of Cardinal Pirelli* by Ronald Firbank you *must* read. I think, on the whole, it is the wittiest book ever written. A triumph of indecent sophistication.

Although Brian had 'come down' without a degree at the end of the summer of 1926 he spent much of his time during the next year or so in and out of Oxford, and continued to figure in the *Cherwell*, however vicariously, as he kept well in with what their editorial once referred to as 'those who claim to be called the intelligent upper scum'.

Before becoming editor (Sir) Edward Hulton used to review films for the *Cherwell*, and it appears that one double feature programme he reviewed in December 1926 particularly appealed to Brian and his friends:

The Midnight Sun at the Queen Street Cinema is not original in portraying the so-called gilded life of pre-war Russia without any attempt at accuracy or fairness. But ... it is huge fun ... The other big film—of nature life supposedly—was not such fun. We saw groups of weird creatures sitting about on the floor. Perhaps it was all filmed at the Moorish Café. In the last scene a decadent-looking young man lies helpless on the ground like an aesthete after a blind. Whilst what appears to be a good portrayal of an

Oxford landlady covers him with a cloth. The picture is no doubt an allegorical description of modern 'Varsity life.

Published in the same issue was the following *Letter to the Editor.*

Dear Sirs, Upon attempting to enter the Queen Street Cinema at 9 o'clock exactly this evening, we were refused seats, although they were available, by two extraordinary little men, who, we feel, must have been impersonating the manager and the commissionaire. Their rudeness was only equalled by their tiny, tiny size. The good manners of our address were only equalled by our sobriety. The fact that a belated member of our party secured admission by a fee of one shilling, not paid to the box office, which was shut, lends us to suppose that, while the management is losing what we believe is termed 'good money' somebody else is reaping a rich, though reprehensible harvest. We remain, sir, yours etc. H. H. Rogers, Rosse, T. E. W. Waddington, M. C. H. Bull, Brian Howard.

The incident seems to have been forgotten by most of the signatories, but Lord Rosse feels that the letter has Brian's hallmark quite clearly 'their tiny, tiny size' being especially typical.

A few months later, Oxford distractions notwithstanding, Brian was writing in despair to Bryan Guinness: '. . . my infernal Law examination will be over by the end of June [1927], and I shall be a public instead of a private failure. I can't pass—I know it. I have tried to do two years work in four months, and whereas a brain could have done it, I could not. However . . .'

10. Oxford in retrospect

Brian's most ambitious *Cherwell* essay appeared on 25th June 1927, a wonderfully microcosmic piece of nostalgia for the Oxford of his time, the people and the place, illustrated by Mark Ogilvie-Grant's pen portrait of him. A long extract follows:

A POSTSCRIPT by Brian Howard

One day last year I was talking to an elderly dandy who had been at Oxford in the 'nineties. Speaking with that particular, and, to me, always fascinating manner of those who rolled through their youth in a hansom, he said, among other things: 'Yes, London may lose her charm, but Oxford *never* will. You see, Oxford has moods. These moods, I believe, change every five years or so. Her moods change as her inhabitants change. People in London overlive their welcome. Like myself. But in Oxford that is not allowed. So Oxford has her moods, which is, of course, her charm . . .'

An indoor memory is considered . . . a little *unpleasant.* No really nice young Englishman, no *sahib* who can be called truthfully *pukka*, is expected to have anything worth remembering that happened indoors. He should have not *been* indoors when it occurred, unless it was at night, and then it certainly ought not to have happened in any case.

However, there are some of us, rakes though we may be, whose remembrances of Oxford take a less draughty shape. Not that I myself have not many visions left, and dear they are to me, which are quite roofless. For instance, at a steeplechase, the vision of Mr. William Acton, in racing colours, of, I think, plum, attempting to cajole his horse over a hedge at the same time as Mr. Robert Coe. It was an epic contest, the New World against the Old. Mr. Coe's steed was white as Pegasus, but lacked his wings, Mr. Acton's horse lacked everything. As far as I can remember, they both achieved their object in the end, with the terrified and involuntary assistance of the combined competitors in the next race . . .

Another memory of the same time that remains as lucid as any, is that of a breakfast party given by the Earl of Rosse at Christ Church. It was rather the form which the party took than the events which occurred at it by which we all remember it. The guests, to begin with, arrived in every kind of vehicle from all over Oxford. For half-an-hour Canterbury Gate consumed a carnival of dressing-gowns, masks, pyjamas (beneath which, in one case, two huge *papier mâché* feet clapped the cobbles), high neck jumpers (that was the day when Mr. Hugh Grosvenor set his first fashion), and genuine fancy dress. We entered our host's room to find the candles glittering over a Christmas tea-table. June, and the sun, were gone. Instead, there were crackers, and sugared fruit, and, I believe, a bottle or two of cherry brandy. Lest such a party be criticised for an extravaganza, a putting of the times and seasons awry for silliness' sake, let me remind you that if you enjoy a Christmas tea-party at Christmas, there is no reason why the element of surprise should make it any the less a piece of fun. By adding December to June, you add—you do not subtract . . .

During the whole of this period, and half-way down St. Aldate's, flourished a club. In spite of a tendency towards beeriness and elderly Sussex bards, it was, at the time, the one club which had entirely freed itself from the jejune snobberies, various and vapid, which constricted the life of every other. Hypocrites in name, they left hypocrisy to the rest. Nightly, Mr. Peter Rufer extracted beauty from the most unwilling of pianos, while Mr. Robert Byron, looking like some possessed Hungarian prince, added the gimlet of his voice. Mr. Hugh Lygon, for those were the days before he dressed himself in sackcloth and put ashes—in a City ash tray, wandered sympathetically about with that vague, slightly surprised look of intense spirituality, which always, in a young Englishman, marks the future public benefactor. Mr. Harold Acton, who had not yet remembered his age, presided over us all, of course, like some cosmopolitan Pickwick. Others there were, and the pity is that I cannot remember them all. Mr. Evelyn Waugh, the best of all our artists of that time, and Mr. David Rice, who now unearths forgotten cities in Asia Minor. The beginning of the following year saw the return of the Mayflower. This time it was not a ship, though it bore the name Berengaria, but the largest motorcar it has ever been my privilege to see. It must have been one of those ordinary, greyish Oxford afternoons, bicycled and bored, when the first sauntering under-graduate was transfixed by the sight of a green mountain grumbling its miraculous way down the High Street. Inside, ensconced cosily behind an embankment of glass, there was a small, dark, cheerful person, looking, behind tortoise-shell spectacles, like a determined bee. Mr. Robert Coe, and his Renault . . .

Shortly before, Mr. Coe had visited the French Automobile Exhibition with a friend. Exploratory, the friend discovered that the whole Exhibition seemed to centre around one car. A car, shall, we say, that had been made just to show what France could do. Nothing, of course, had been seen like it before, as was remarked, long afterwards, by the assembled drivers of a fleet of lorries which had been requisitioned to remove it from one of the ditches in between Eton and Maidenhead. The friend suggested, waggishly, to Mr. Coe, that he buy it. Mr. Coe, cursorily, bought it. However, the observer of this historical entry into Oxford would not have been able to see the other occupants of this leviathan, since the chauffeur was beside Mr. Coe, and the others, the crew, were locked into the poop. This poop, in shape like an enlarged Cartier cigarette box, contained Mr. Edward Murray with his bundle of charcoal, Mr. Eugene Reynal, and Mr. Benjamin Kittredge. It had been my intention to construct some felicity, some succinct phrase, with which to conjure up Mr. Kittredge. But the vision I have of him, that ample, that infinitely benign, vision, is inexpressible. A Bourbon, but with pep. A Johnson, but without a temper. I continue to see him, seated, the Sultan of South Carolina, upon that divan that made safe a corner of No. 50 High Street, holding, with one expressive hand, a cocktail, and, with the other, our admiratory attention.

Each day, as the bells of Magdalen tolled six vesperal notes, a silver vessel, relatively as vast as the Renault, now shook a small reply. This vessel began its illustrious career in a room whose windows disclosed the grace of deer, where it provided for the thirsts of so many, including Sir Ian Walker, who, I believe, was the first to wrest the ballroom of the Randolph Hotel from the clutches of anxious bishops in search of a place to entertain children to breakfast, and who gave there, unassisted, and with the preparation of a few days, a dinner of the kind which the Bullingdon Club can hardly sustain once a year.

Later, however, this most imposing of cocktail shakers was set up in the High Street, and it is with perhaps the most vivid pleasure of all that I recall those long evenings in its company before a dinner at the George. A bottle of gin would be inserted into the broad mouth of the receptacle. It would empty. One would peer, as into some well, and descry, remotely, a dampness. Another bottle. And another. Eventually, it would be filled. Sometimes the mixture was excellent, and sometimes (the mixer always forgot before he had finished what he had put in at first, some ten minutes before) strange. Lord Stavordale, recumbent, as good as dressed, and in a collection of clothes which would be gradually recognised by their owners during the course of the evening, would receive his glass with that absent-minded, but devastating, smile which has made him famous from Alexandra Park to Leopardstown. Mr. Charles Brocklehurst, perched nearby, with one thin, mousey lock a-dangle, and his inevitably blue tie hanging outside a restrained riding-coat, would contribute to all the noise that silence which only he knows how to make so vivacious. Anon, he would caper a little. In the corner. Alone. Then he would stoop down to caress, and, in a flash, entirely disappear behind, an improvidence of hair called Beezbag. Only a moderately sized dog ...

As regards that Oxonian rarity, silence, nothing, that I knew, could defeat Mr. Hugh Grosvenor. Mr. Grosvenor, possibly the finest rider that Oxford has known for a decade, once, to my knowledge, spoke. He had taken me, unawares, for a sail in a little yacht. We had been bound for Godstow. I was wearing a new suit that day, an event which is always with me, as fatal as it is unusual. I was admiring the continuous Constable of the shore, when the boat, in a trice, turned upside down. It was in the intervals of my cries, standing up to my waist in water with my feet on the submerged keel, that I thought I heard him imprecate.

Others would be there as well for their evening cocktail, like Mr. James Phillipps and Mr. Peter Thursby. I remember that on the days when I was feeling particularly tired, and more than ever plain, I used suddenly to catch sight of Mr. Thursby, and feel less tired, but far, far plainer.

As likely as not, before setting out for dinner, the door would open in a rather conspiratorial way to admit Mr. Rowland Leigh. Amidst several quite determined American accents, you would soon hear the improbable voice of Oxford's Peter Pan, relating some new and amusing tid-bit of London gossip. I can hear an echo at this moment. 'Well, Brian? ... No-o-o. I haven't been doing much lately. Of course there's all that about this kid ... etc.' It was Rowley, as he is called, that kept us in touch with London.

Mr. John Drury Lowe would also have appeared, immaculately. A few days ago a London journalist was commenting in one of the daily papers on the cleavage between what he chose to call the Oxford Set and the young officers of the Guards. Of course, there is no real cleavage, just as there is none between the young man at any university and the young men at any public school. However, Mr. Drury Lowe is the one person I know who has successfully bridged this gap, if gap there be. Beginning his career as one of our most popular and sprightly Oxonians, he has now disguised himself with the most irreproachably military of moustachios, thus achieving an unique combination, rather than transformation, of *métier*. I saw him, only a night or so ago, at Mr. Edward Tatham's night club. A symphony in starch, I thought he shuddered a little at the asymmetry of my cravat. Besides, it was black. Creeping to my corner, I pondered disconsolately on an earlier evening. An evening when a figure, just as slim, but sartorially less correct, had pranced the can-can, his neck encircled with nothing more soldierly than can be produced by the knitting needles of Mr. Turnbull and Mr. Asser. I wondered whether, on any of these more modern evenings, when the port has achieved its complement of orbits round the mess-room, Mr. Drury Lowe does not sometimes a little regret ...

Eventually, we would all descend, in Mr. Coe's favourite phrase (a phrase which has now become a club), like locusts, upon the George. Arrived, Mr. and Mrs. Ehrsham would usher us to that long table in the corner, and provide us with glasses of aerated golden syrup, appetisers which, while they served to while away the time during which we waited for dinner, served also to remind one that it is a far cry from the Cornmarket to the champagne cocktails of the Ritz Bar in Paris. As we supped this viscous confection, we would recognise about us such faces as that of Mr. Harold Acton, who would, mayhap, be dining with Mr. Peter Quennell, a poet who is now, I hear, the young laureate of Bloomsbury. Mr. Acton would be drinking red wine, and, as he leaned slightly forward, his mouth would engender such conversational jewels as made the princely fragment of amber that lay beside his plate seem a nothing. For was not Harold's the voice of Oxford herself? Was he not, indeed, the high priest of our Temple?

It was on the night of a certain party of Mr. David Ponsonby's, given some five years ago, that a new star rose upon the Oxford heavens. A little crowd of expectant people had gathered in his rooms in Tom Quad to meet a young poet from Eton. Perhaps you yourself were there? You will remember the tall room containing, at first sight, little but a great piano and the shadowed silence of a winter evening. Gradually, by the light of one tall candle, you discovered a tense figure or two. Sequestered in some far corner of the room, enshrouded in discretion, crouched a cleric. Already, he had an anticipatory back against the wall. Suddenly, as if the night had spoken, a great star mounted the sky without. A portent, it blazed in the aperture of a high, latticed window. The cleric made as if he would flee, but he had lingered over-long, for already there was a rich rat-tat upon the door. It opened, and young Mr. Harold Acton swayed in, Charvet's longest scarf afloat behind him, and the sceptre of his Muse, a megaphone, in his hand. The cleric prepared, instinctively, for death. In that sculptured voice, the apotheosis of style, Mr. Harold Acton began to convey a poem. A passionately Roman Catholic, he instantly detected that slightly acrid savour that pursues the Church of England. Setting the orifice of his megaphone, as if it had been some engine of siege, at the clergyman, whose face was now one of the blank pages in his own prayer book, he recited a terrible poem that told of his desire for the moon.

Later that night, while his desperate wife, as a final medicine, read him aloud a poem of Mr. Alfred Noyes' [Lord David Cecil was the name in Brian's original MSS], the clergyman, so I am told, died. After the funeral, none in Oxford read Mr. Alfred Noyes' poems again, as it was considered, thenceforward, unlucky.

Thus Joshua had sounded his trumpet, and the walls were down. The town was taken in a night, and we had a new king.

Often, and just as the ice began to shake out its evening music in the house of Mr. Coe, a drowsy little company could be observed debouching into the severity of Beaumont Street. This would be the finale of one of Mr. John Sutro's luncheon parties. Many is the delicious time I have sat down at that generous board to rise again but with little space to prepare for dinner. They were unique, those endless, loquacious luncheons. It was in this house more than in any other, except perhaps that of Mr. Romney Summers, that wine was felt to be of importance. I recall a hock. Not the usual hock that is possible, if there is drought and soda-water, but a hock that spoke of Rhenish hillsides, a hock redolent of sun, and informed with the South. Again, I once found it necessary to climb many and formidable walls in order to return a glass of champagne that I had been given in this house. This champagne had been sent especially from Paris, and was, I remember, Pommery & Greno, Nature, 1915. I have since tasted it elsewhere, and I now understand why Mr. Sutro had those particular bottles sent from Paris. But I have wandered, as is natural with Uncle Julius, from luncheon to dinner, and must return. A representative party would include Mr. Maurice Bowra. Mr. Bowra occupies one of the most enviable positions in Oxford. He is a don, but he is also an undergraduate. He is an Olympian, but he is also a man. No plethora of essays to correct has desiccated him. He continues to be able to laugh without convincing you that you yourself are the joke. Unlike some of his kind, he has not been made wry by the ineptitudes of youth. The fact that a young man is a scholar does not in itself inflame him. Neither, and not even if they be blues, does he approve the inarticulate. Approached in his gay white rooms at Wadham, where his library and his collection of modern pictures are a continual temptation to the intelligent, he does not greet the visitor with a dreadful explosion of synthetic good nature. You are not welcomed as if both your soul and your hand were of iron. You do not sit bolt upright upon one of hell's forgotten chairs, your alternately red and white face gasping in an atmosphere pervaded with embarrassment and tobacco. In fact, you are, when you visit him, at home. Provided with a glass of sherry and an equally excellent cigarette, you stretch yourself in every way. Unwilling, from the first, to go, you recount, leisurely, the things that you think he will like to hear. Always they are the things that you will like to recount. Presently, his words will begin to flash between yours, and you will be rewarded. For the Dean of Wadham can crowd more wit into an hour than all the High Tables of Oxford can accomplish, with their auxiliary decanters, in a term.

Mr. Hugh Lygon, and Mr. Robert Byron would be at luncheon as well, both of whom I have spoken of previously as members of the Hypocrites. Mr. Byron, our Voltaire, lived on the ground floor of the same house, conducting his existence with all the vigour that a great talent for irritation and writing can give. Enshrined in a storm of Victorian whatnots, he eventually turned the *Cherwell* from an Oxford, into a good, paper. Of the *Cherwell*, Mr. Robert Byron was more than fortunate in his editorial successor—Mr. Bryan Guinness possesses all the virtues, and more than his share of talents.

At luncheon, after regarding us with acidulated frustration for several minutes, Mr. Byron would enliven the entire afternoon with the happiness of his hatreds. Blessing my ears, as I played with one of Mr. Sutro's giant matches, I would lean back while Mr. Bowra and he destroyed something odious with the battery of their tongues. Perhaps it would be Mr. B— M—. The attack, to begin with, would be manoeuvre. Mr. Bowra would collect himself. Builded for war, his compactly constructed form would no longer offer a perch to any propitiatory dove. One watched the guns swinging out over his sides. One visualised the stokers working inside him, preparing for even more knots. Robert would have already expressed the general annoyance of the table for Mr. B— M—. Suddenly Mr. Bowra's guns would deliver the preliminary broadside. Of all men the most *boastful*, the most inexplicably *vain*, and *wicked* . . . etc.' At the end, as you can guess, Mr. B— M— was done for indeed.

It was generally at a later hour even than that at which his luncheons were used to end, that Mr. Sutro enchanted us with his now celebrated imitations. So many dying parties have been revivified, so many dwindling ones swiftly re-populated, by his sleight of tongue. These imitations are almost frightening in their subtle accuracy. Often and often when Mr. Drury-Lowe has been at the other end of Oxford, ruminating over a drill manual, his stutter has been heard in Beaumont Street. Frequently, when Mr. William Acton has been doing Heaven can never know what nor where, that room has been electrified with the contralto enthusiasm of his laughter.

Mr. William Acton . . . If it was Harold who was our high priest, it was William who was the master of our ceremonies. The astonished sunlight of his first Oxford summer was illuminating the somehow eastern architecture of his form as he once cruised across the gravel of Peckwater. Compelled by Mr. Schölte into a double-breasted suit of bottle-green, his physique cannot have been apparent to the truculent athlete who approached. The athlete, exacerbated by the suit, but more by a crêpe-de-Chine shirt of the colour of crushed raspberries, made, with an oath, an hostile gesture. Mr. William, wheeling upon him with a brilliant smile, knocked him, as they say, out. Then, with a low titter, flicking his fist with an handkerchief upon the hem of which Callot Soeurs had lavished their most intimate stitching, and in the heart of which Chanel had dropped tears of fragrant admiration, Mr. William trotted off to the splendour of his apartments.

Thereafter, Mr. William reminded Oxford, the home of hosts, of how to entertain. Before his advent, it had been either quality or quantity. With him, it was always both. Only one other in our period, Mr. Gavin Henderson, ever equalled him. Larger parties, more expensive parties, were given at the same time. But they were not, somehow, Oxford parties. Perhaps it was the conversation that made the difference. At such parties as Mr. William gave, one was not bored by technique. The children of Nimrod were kept in their place. Pink youth did not make itself magenta with the blowing of horns. One was not wearied by the triumphs or tragedies of the tee. On the other hand, the Muses were not insisted upon. Diana held equal sway with Apollo. From the soup, agog with every condiment (that extraordinary, blood-like soup heavy with eggs, and, sometimes, magical potions) to the cigars, one could ask for no more splendid entertainment. Linens embroidered in Russia clothed the table, over which marched an army of glasses, of every size, shape, and colour. On the bursting sideboard a hundred bottles displayed their invitations in as many languages. The fainting scout, supported by half-a-dozen distracted boys, tottered in and out with flagon after platter. Once, I remember, the company was so great that the Lobster Newburg had to be conveyed to us in a dustbin. At another time, a small hipbath was utilised as a punch-bowl. In a brocaded corner, a gramophone would be singing a blues. Deployed over the walls in painted lanterns, electricity would supplement the light of day, since the number of guests would often shut out the sun ... but I cannot go on. Soon I must make an end of all the tiny histories. Let me hurry, while there is yet time.

During this period there was a house in Holywell, to which no memoirs of the time must be without a reference. Here, with the diamond background of his exquisite collection of old English glass, reigned Romney. Mr. Romney Summers possessed an inestimable advantage in Oxford. A private house. To call on him at noon, was to come in upon a little eighteenth-century *levée*. He received you like some *grand seigneur* of 1780 who, fatigued by the follies of Versailles, had taken to reading Rousseau—there was the dignity, but there was the dressing-gown. Enthroned at the head of the table, he would pour you out a vast cup of tea. If you preferred it, of wine. However, you would soon be provided for, whatever your taste, and you would find yourself listening to the seemingly rather bored recital by your host of how yesterday he had acquired a

Jacobean goblet for twopence-halfpenny, or to a diatribe against the inefficiency of hired aeroplanes. As he talked, a wolfhound would amble hither and thither, delicately . . .

Of all the times that Mr. Robert Coe entertained Oxford, there are three supreme examples, and with these, though unwilling, I can only deal with two. The first, which I enjoyed the most of all, was a *fête champêtre*. In punts, we took the Thames. A mile or so above Magdalen, we disembarked into a field. There, like some snowy hedge, stretched our riparian feast. The college servants had transported the tables earlier in the evening, and, as we seated ourselves in sunset, we knew that they had not transported tables alone. I remember that it had something strange about it, that feast by the water. Something of another country, and something of another period. After the night had come, and we were wrapped in shadows of violet and lilac, when the simple smells of clover and wet grass had changed, suddenly, into a fragrance that suggested the proximity of *parterres*, I thought that I saw a figure leaning against one of the willows. A figure that might have wandered out of a Watteau, in crumpled white silk, and holding a ribboned guitar . . . but then, I think it must have been merely Mr. X, with his coat off, playing his ukelele, seen through a glass of wine . . .

The second party was held in a barn, some several miles outside the town. A band, which had conveyed itself from London in a motor car of the most refined mauve, supplied us with music, from a dais, during dinner. The vast walls had been made merry with posters, in which the characteristics of some of the guests had been made the subject of quips. After dinner, and out of half-a-dozen laundry baskets, were produced smocks and large, curving hats. We were soon clothed with suitable reference to our surroundings. All this time, as I subsequently discovered, flying squads of infuriated elders, hot for our hiding place, rent the welkin of all Oxfordshire with the noise of their Fords. I believe that it is still remembered, still whispered of in the county, that strange night when, peeping from behind barred casements, the rustics watched taxi after taxi bang by on its be-bowlered way. And I like to think of the spirit of Mr. Peter Quennell, like some will o' the wisp designed by Burne-Jones, capering ahead of them, ensorcelling them on, and on, to the bogs of frustration.

I have not the space to describe one last festivity that I should have liked to include. A party that was given to hearten the departure of someone who, than of all those I have known, liked leaving Oxford less. A party that was most ludicrously in the tradition. Beginning with the bathos of lilies, it ended in a midnight bathe at Bablock Hythe, and it was not until close upon the dawn when, as we all waited impatiently for his return, Mr. Martin Wilson emerged heavily from a field of turnips, where the long night alone had been privy to his nakedness and the startled fieldmice his only companions.

But the moment has come for me to cease this ephemeral chatter. A truce upon these garish little memories that, if they interest a single soul, will interest so few! Nevertheless, before I quite shut up, I must disclose the weakness of my position by a protest. An ignorant reader of my postscript will, as likely as not, as he closes this journal with as much of a snap as he can manage, exclaim 'Fie upon this vulgar biographer of vulgarities! To think that these young creatures had nothing better to do with their heyday than waste it, with their pence, upon folly! Were they so blind to duty and beauty that they could do no more than rush about, like so many devils, desecrating the countryside with bottles as empty as their heads? What virtue did they discover in champagne, what elixir did they hold it to be, that they made it the companion both of their days and of their nights? Did they find happiness in extravagance, and the fulfilment of youth in gold? Did they never know peace, nor solitude, nor a cup of philosophic tea? Did they consider study so far beneath their parvenu notice that they would do nothing but play, not games, but the fool? Good Heavens, to think that I have read through this diary of moral disaster, and even, at times, felt a suspicion of interest, when I should rather have burned it at once for one of the minor documents of the devil!'

Well ... if one of you tell us all this, you will be something right. We were not, we are not, model. But then, I have not told you all. In spite of your disgust, you are really quite human and if I had related the things which you pretend would have been more suitable, you would only have been bored. If I had edified you with the ordinary stories of university life, you would have known them all too well before, and called me dullard. Again, if I had exposed for your greedy, beady little eyes, the sentimental— if I had romanced upon the conversations that began at sunset, and ended on the river, at daybreak, in laughter, you would have twitted me for a silly. Thus it is that I have told you what I have. You may arraign us as vulgar if you will. But stay! I swear that you too, austere and spectacled though you may be now, you poor creature, were thus vulgar once. At least I, hope so. No ... perhaps you were never vulgar enough to be young?

An unpleasant inspiration has suddenly taken me. If one asks where, as I have done at the cost of so many words, are the poses of yesteryear, there is an all too obvious and horrid answer. *Plus ça change, plus c'est le même pose.* So, when I walk, as I now do, hungrily the High, in pursuit of faces that I will no longer find there, I may comfort myself, I suppose, with the thought that all I have told you, all these adventures, whose virtue, if they had one, was that they were ours and ours alone, are going on still, and that only the host and his guests are new. Well, if this be true, I, for one, prefer to lie. I prefer to forget this. I will forget it! Beside (to use a phrase employed by a young man nearly thirty years ago under much the same provocation) I already feel myself a trifle outmoded. I belong to the Acton period, and, indeed, it pleases me. Perambulating upon my crutches I need little persuading that Oxford is gone dead. I am almost sure that these unfamiliar military, red-faced striplings can never do what we did. A moment more, and I shall have utterly convinced myself that these new boys will never waste their time ... so well.

As with Brian's essay, an account of the Oxford of his times cannot be contemplated apart from the other members of his 'Oxford Set' and the following evocative extracts from books and comments are by some of these contemporaries. The obvious first source was again Harold Acton, whose response to my original enquiry was characteristically generous: 'Your letter sent me rummaging among old papers and I was surprised to discover a considerable pile of Brian's letters to my brother William and myself, dating chiefly from his and our Eton and Oxford days [already extensively quoted]. . . . Brian was exceptionally brilliant in his youth, though his talent was apt to be more destructive than creative. He excelled in ridicule and his mastery of language was precocious, but he lacked staying power and, of course, discipline. Under all his panache and posturing there was a sad, lost, bitter child. Towards the end it seemed to me that he must have been possessed by devils . . .'

The following extracts are taken from Harold's *Memoirs of an Aesthete*. (After Brian had successfully matriculated, Harold recounts that Mrs. Howard was worried about his mixing with 'the wrong set', which resulted in Brian solemnly declaring that 'the thing to do at Oxford' was to ride.)

. . . That poem of his in *Wheels* had been a mistake. Determined to live it down and distinguish himself as a horseman, he began to cultivate the riding set. From a distance I was tickled to see how quickly he swayed these simple souls: very soon he was organising their dinner-parties and their wardrobes, a despotic arbiter of taste to whom they listened with naïve deference. Now and then, very casually, he tossed off a few *vers libres*, but the sporting life claimed the better part of his time. Ezra Pound and the American Imagists were now replaced by Surtees and Peter Beckford on his shelves and prints of cantering stallions adorned his walls. His attitude to me became quite patronising. I put up with it for old time's sake, wondering what the next phase would be. With his talent for dramatisation there were many turns by which he could still astonish his old cronies.

. . . Brian's facility of invention had not left him but his impulse to write had diminished in his round of Bullingdon parties. Now and then he set off a squib in the *Cherwell*, but there were moments when he was aware that he was wasting his dramatic talents and he looked back wistfully to the *Eton Candle*.

It was Edith Sitwell who introduced the famous Gertrude Stein to Oxford. When she told Harold Acton that Gertrude Stein was in England—'If Picasso was part of our Zeitgeist, so was she'—he immediately invited her to address the 'Ordinary' at Oxford:

. . . Curiosity about her was rife in Oxford . . . If Gertrude Stein led a school of disorganisation ('her work was supposed to be connected with insanity') let us hasten it, I thought. We had no such school at Oxford . . . Nobody was prepared for what followed—(her) placid reading of *Composition as Explanation* and several word portraits, including one of Edith Sitwell, who sat so near that the portrait could be compared with the original . . .

Gertrude left everybody in an excellent humour after a solid two hours' session. The proof of the pudding had been in the eating. Those who had come to scoff were disarmed and charmed. When the lecture was published[5] one missed the medium of her voice. As Maurice Bowra had said, it had sounded like Kant's *Critique of Pure Reason*. I wish I had kept the accounts in the Oxford papers: not one of them was dull, and parodies of her portraits continued to appear for some time afterwards, the wittiest by Brian Howard, testifying to the sensation Gertrude Stein had created.

These parodies appeared in the *Cherwell* as 'By one who feels it wiser to remain anonymous' and under the title of *Oxford Portraits of 1925–6 in the Manner of Miss Gertrude Stein*. The subjects—victims—were suggested by a few letters and asterisks, most of them easily identifiable as Robert Byron, Harold Acton, John Sutro, Bryan Guinness, and Lord Stavordale, the indeterminate two being called 'Prince Charming' and 'A Don'. These were apparently well received, a signed follow-up appearing two weeks later as *Continuation of Oxford Oxford Portraits Portraits of* 1925–6 *and also and Christmas* (*sic*) by Brian Howard. The second instalment covered Lord Herbert, William Acton, Mark Ogilvie-Grant, René Crevel, Lord Weymouth and Charles Plumb. I have selected three to reproduce here.

J*HN S***O

Mature can be younger than mere youth I mean the pink kind. If you understand me youth is merely pink unless it is also old because real youth is an immortal thing and therefore is old in that it is immortal and youth isn't youth it is a spirit and a spirit that is an experienced spirit spiritually and wonderful which mere pink isn't and it is a rarity.

B**AN G****ESS

It is extremely remote to think that good is not good because it may produce an impression of remoteness. Because shy is not spry it is not therefore sly a lack of loudness or rather quietness does not mean no sound but generally something louder in a better way than just loudness and because industry is courteous and because industry does not hiccup that does not say that it means nothing because it is so courteous it is curious that so many people insist on the hiccup but the fact remains that industry is courteous.

L*RD WE****TH

The best eagles never have eerie eyries. Eerie eyries are unnecessary to really good eagles really good eagles are silent and real eagles are efficiently silent too whats more and a really good sword doesn't have to have a sheathe sheathes are shields in a way and dark eagles dark swords don't need eyries or sheathes they just do without they just act without they just are an eagle and a sword and extremely dangerously safe too.

---

[5] In the Hogarth Essay series, after Tom Driberg had written to Virginia Woolf about it.

The present Lord Birkenhead (who was so often held up to Brian as a model) considers that Harold Acton and the other aesthetes, including Brian, made a real contribution to Oxford life during this 'most civilised' period:

Harold, in particular, brought to it a maturity which it greatly needed, a Florentine culture which was previously unknown, and an authentic whiff of the great world beyond the University. I always thought Brian unfortunate in his parents. His father detested him, and his mother ruined him with her folly and indulgence. I remember the father describing with disgust how he had seen Brian at a party 'smacking his great blubber lips'.

I see Brian as a fascinating period piece, and it is a period on which it is delightful to dwell. What I liked about him was that he had real artistic integrity which was never strangled completely by the bindweed of snobbery and social yearning. Also I believe that he had genuine ability although this was always denied by Evelyn Waugh who disliked and despised him almost as much as did Brian's father. He was a definite, if minor figure of his period, and it is right that he should be remembered.

For a change of viewpoint I wrote to another successful contemporary—Emlyn Williams. He replied: 'For me Brian Howard was in another world, infinitely remote, aristocratically languorous and unassailable in his poise . . . I only saw him across a crowded room.' Brian was briefly glimpsed in Emlyn Williams' autobiography,[6] at a party: ' "My dear", he was saying, "I've only ever seen one passable undergraduette and *she* looked like a vain boy scout", (which last simile Brian later managed to fit into one of his *Cherwell* essays).

In reviewing Evelyn Waugh's first autobiographical volume, *A Little Learning,*[7] V. S. Pritchett commented in the *New Statesman*: '. . . of Robert Byron and Brian Howard . . . we have striking, not to say pungent, preliminary sketches. Brian Howard, particularly, was one of those dangerous, brilliant and seminal nuisances, a plaguing character of wasted talent who begins to barge about in the corridors of Mr. Waugh's early fancy . . .'

I had been re-reading with pleasure some of Evelyn Waugh's early novels, and wrote to ask for his permission to quote 'Ambrose Silk' (from *Put out more Flags*) and 'Anthony Blanche' (from *Brideshead Revisited*) where the remarks seemed to be particularly characteristic of Brian. He replied that it would be misleading to quote from the novels as although the characters I mentioned were suggested by Brian they were wholly fictitious in that nothing they did or said was actually true of Brian, but that I was welcome to quote the following extract from his autobiography:

To give a picture of my generation I must name three whom I did not greatly like but whom, in my innocence, I was proud to know. [Basil Murray, Peter Rodd, and Brian Howard.]

---

[6] *George*, an early autobiography, published by Hamish Hamilton, 1961.
[7] Published by Chapman & Hall, 1964.

... The third man was someone very different and it is true that the characters in my novels often wrongly identified with Harold Acton were to a great extent drawn from him. He was called Brian Howard, the patronymic being the capricious choice of his father, who was reputedly born Gassaway. I have no doubt that before we are dead someone, not I, will write a memoir of Brian. He is a rich source of anecdote. All that has appeared so far is Cyril Connolly's *From Oscar to Stalin* (represented under the title *Where Engels fears to tread*),[8] a brilliant pasquinade of 1937 which, incidentally, provides a leper's squint into Cyril's own life as an undergraduate.

Brian, when he came up, determined to eschew the arts and to pose as a sportsman. He never got into the Bullingdon, but he charged gallantly at the fences in the Grind. More than this, in the intensely snobbish era which immediately succeeded my own, he contrived to make himself more than the entertainer, the animator, almost the arbiter, of the easy-going aristrocrats whom he set himself to reform in his romantic model, like the youthful D'Israeli inspiring 'Young England'. *Put your trust in the Lords* was the motto on the banner in his rooms on his birthday and there are many placid peers today who may ascribe most of their youthful fun to Brian. Sometimes he embarrassed them as, when Trinity hearties broke up a party he was at and impelled the guests to the gate, he threatened: 'We shall tell our fathers to raise your rents and evict you.' At such moments I think he really believed that Gassaway was a Whig magnate.

... At the age of nineteen he had dash and insolence, a gift of invective and repartee far more brilliant than Robert's [Byron], a kind of ferocity of elegance that belonged to the romantic era of a century before our own. Mad, bad and dangerous to know.

The reference to Cyril Connolly's 'pasquinade' led me to pursue that elusive parody. Before I could obtain a copy of the book, *Press Gang*,[9] in which it first appeared, I came across an earlier and less glowing review of it by Evelyn Waugh himself (in 1937) in that ill-fated magazine *Night and Day*, inspired by the *New Yorker*, expired by a costly libel suit:.

Press Gang—a successor to *Parody Party*, which had a deserved success last year. The notable contribution to that volume was Mr. Cyril Connolly's completely silencing parody of Mr. Aldous Huxley—a criticism so penetrating and so savage that in a gentler age its victim would have despaired and pined or perhaps disembowelled himself on Mr. Connolly's doorstep. This year the editors have chosen a more general topic—the British Press. For most of the contributors it has proved too easy a target ... It is left for Mr. Connolly again to lift the book from the level of paper games to art. Unfortunately for most readers he has chosen to devote his prodigious talent to a private joke (*Where Engels fears to tread*). The object

---

[8] Reprinted in full as Appendix II.
[9] Edited by Leonard Russell, published by Hutchinson, 1937.

of his satire has for some years been a figure of fun to a tiny circle, but he is totally unknown to those whose adolescence does not happen to have co-incided with his. A dozen readers in London, one in China, one in Gloucestershire, and possibly a handful in Spain, will revel in Mr. Connolly's laying of this pathetic ghost . . .

To jump forward in time, Maurice Richardson remembers meeting Brian in Sloane Square, just after Cyril Connolly's *The Condemned Playground*[10] had been published—in 1945:

I had the book in my hand. This contained a reprint of *Where Engels fears to tread*, extracts from an imaginary autobiography by Brian, a marvellous evocation of his personality, and the most brilliant piece of creative pastiche I have ever read. Brian was a bit downcast. 'So he has put that in. Oh Lord!'

I said, 'Don't worry, Brian. It's a wonderful bit of writing and it's obvious to anyone with any sense that only a genius could have been the model for it.' He said he didn't mind in the least so far as he was concerned but there were just one or two little things, that business of the names, which might faintly upset his mother . . .

Brian was mortified when *Engels* first came out in 1937, but when Cyril Connolly warned him of its imminent reappearance in 1945 he took the news in good part:

Dear Brian, Prepare for a blow. I have reprinted *Where Engels fears to tread* and without altering a word of it, as I couldn't bring myself to read it all again—but it is sandwiched in between a lot of other parodies and I don't think it looks in the least personal. I still think it is essentially *kindly* and admiring and quite unlike Waugh's stuff . . . though I realise how tiresome it must be for you to be a constant source of imitation to your contemporaries.

Needless to say much of the piece is *not* about you, and Christian's mother and father have no relation to yours, and the whole thing is soaked in Firbankitis, which I had at the time . . . Do let's meet again soon and please forgive me. Yours ever, Cyril.

To this Brian replied:

. . . it is not without faint trepidation that I look forward to it. I admit, C, to hoping that, if Christian de Clavering is to appear, he will do so under a less resoundingly hintful name. I don't, I suppose, *really* mind, but now that Evelyn has almost stopped, after all these years, the approach of obscurity was so very delicious. On the other hand . . . perhaps a sufficient degree of obscurity is already here?

---

[10] *The Condemned Playground—Essays* 1927–1944, published by Routledge, 1945.

Not only did Brian accept its republication with grace but he even went so far as to include praise of it in a lengthy *New Statesman* review of *The Condemned Playground* as a whole: '... There is one review, re-published here where Mr. Connolly's considerable comic inventiveness is employed to perfection. *Where Engels fears to tread* deals with the imaginary autobiography of an Oxford aesthete of the 'twenties, and still makes me laugh almost aloud ...'

Maurice Richardson takes up the portrait again with memories of his first encounters with Brian:

With most people it is the first time you meet them ... with Brian it was the first time you saw him. October 1925. My first term at New College. A fine misty blue morning; on the south side of the High at the Carfax end. He was dressed like the typical undergraduate in a brown tweed coat, grey flannel trousers, brown suède bootees from Flack & Smith, but his clothes looked very expensive, and beautifully made. He looked so tall and dark and distinguished with his large brown eyes and long lashes, I thought he must be foreign. He was smoking an exceptionally fat Turkish cigarette. Two black spaniel puppies were padding along at his heels. This was the height of his sporting peer-chasing phase.

Back in the snug recesses of New College, where I was too much the romantic would-be Bohemian to feel really at home, I described him to David Nicoll (killed in North Africa). He identified him at once.

'French?' he said mildly, raising his pale sandy eyebrows. 'Oh no. He's er English—or rather American, Jewish as well. A pretty awful man, really, I suppose. Clever? Oh yes! I suppose so, very.' He agreed that Brian was the arch-aesthete, the King Vampire. Compared with him Harold Acton, whose reputation had spread beyond Oxford, was as homely as plum pudding.

One evening in the next Summer term, term of the 1926 General Strike, I was dining at the Spreadeagle at Thame with David Nicoll and John Duguid, equally nice but even quieter and mousier. We were at a table in the small room at the side. It was a fine warm evening and the window on the garden was wide open. Suddenly a very tall young man with a pink face and a rather small head, climbed over the window-sill into the room. 'Er, I'm terribly sorry,' he said, 'but do you mind if I, er, go through ... If a rather awful man called Howard asks if anybody went this way would you mind saying they didn't? I'm trying to escape. Thanks awfully.' He rushed out. We heard from the garden outside a high authoritative voice calling: 'Henry! Henry! Silly little creature, where are you, Henry? Come here at once!' Then Brian stepped into the room.

'Has a rather tall peer with a head the size of a walnut passed this way? I see from your faces he has. Go on with your dinner. Don't let me disturb you.'

Later that same term I met him for the first time in Maurice Bowra's rooms in Wadham. Maurice was having his infallibly stimulating effect. I launched into an elaborate comparison of Patrick Monkhouse to the coxswain of a moral lifeboat, always ready to put out to sea and rescue distressed souls. Brian, looking at me quizzically, was amused. I felt I was being a success.

I never knew him intimately, but by the end of the Summer term of 1926 I seemed to know him, and of him, well. I remember Maurice Bowra describing a farewell party by the river and giving an imitation of Brian's voice in the night: 'Martin! Martin! It's Brian calling!' And Kolkhorst, Betjeman's beloved 'Gug', commenting too acidly on the article Brian had written in the *Cherwell*: 'Silly young man, he's been gilding our dreaming spires'.

Sir Maurice Bowra's book of reminiscences, *Memories 1898–1939*,[11] has a memorable chapter on 'The Next Generation', the new arrivals of 1922 'who set out unashamedly to be aesthetes and to revive some glories of the 'nineties':

By common consent the two leading aesthetes were Harold Acton and Brian Howard ... If Harold was welcoming, Brian was aloof and self-contained. He spoke with marked mannerisms, emphasising each point as he made it and choosing his words for their unusual flavour, often with a hint of inverted commas when he dropped into colloquialisms. He addressed one frequently as 'my dear' and sought more to dominate than to please. He suffered from social ambitions. At Eton he had cultivated the sons of noble houses, and he kept up with them at Oxford. They could not quite make him out, but accepted him as a bird of paradise, and recognised that he knew much of which they were ignorant. With them he assumed a pedagogic, even moralistic tone. He would chide them for their stupidity, their dull opinions, their flat vocabulary, their young women ...

He once asked me to a dinner at which every guest except myself was a peer and made a speech beginning, 'My Lords and gentleman', with a strong stress on the final syllable of the last word. When the *Surréalistes* first appeared on the horizon, he gave a party for them and during it led me aside and said, 'My dear, all that they are trying to do is to write without any *effort*, and we all know what that leads to.' ...

He had a striking, if disturbing, personality, and might have been an artist if he had not been brought up among pictures by his father in what he called 'that mausoleum, my home' and come in the end to dislike them because of this association.

For his Oxford farewell party invitation Brian excelled himself. A thick cream-coloured card, measuring at least fourteen inches wide and ten deep, was heavily printed in gold:

'PARTIR, C'EST SOURIR UN PEU'
'LE JARDIN DE MON FRERE'

CHEZ

M. BRIAN CHRISTIAN DE CLAIBORNE HOWARD

ROBES DE FANTAISIE.   CE SOIR, A NEUF HEURES.

---

[11] Published by Weidenfeld and Nicolson, 1966.

A select twenty-two guests were invited—Harold and Willie Acton, Patrick Balfour (Lord Kinross), Maurice Bowra, Charles Brocklehurst, Bob Coe, (Lord) Claud Hamilton, Ben Kittredge, Rowley Leigh, Oliver Messel, Ned Murray, Mark Ogilvie-Grant, John Philipps, Eugene Reynal, Ian Sinclair, Harry (Lord) Stavordale, Romney Summers, John Sutro, Eddie Tatham, Peter Thursby, Henry Weymouth (Lord Bath), Martin Wilson. Sad to relate, of the party itself nostalgic memories appear to be non-existent, although Lord Kinross still has his outsize invitation.

It was his 'snobbery' that alienated many of Brian's contemporaries—Anthony Powell in particular, whose reply to my request for recollections was as uncomplimentary of those times as of the earlier Eton days:

At Oxford Brian was snobbish in the least attractive use of that often abused term ... and any later journalism of his I read appeared to be bad-mannered and intellectually flabby, the former probably to conceal the latter. Do believe me that it was not all the things he represented that I object to, but his total lack of the gifts of a contemporary French scallywag like Maurice Sachs, with whom he might perhaps be compared.

John Sutro, the begetter of the famous Railway Club, was affectionately described by Brian in his inscription of a book given to John 'on the occasion of the most riotous, glamorous, vinous meeting of the Railway Club—to Brighton.'—*To John, dearest John, the Engine Driver, the Ticket Collector, the Porter, and the Guard of our Youth.* John Sutro, in retrospective mood, talks about those days:

It was at the Hypocrites that I met the 'Oxford Set', during my first term up in the winter of 1921—Harold Acton, Clonmore, Elmley, Mark Ogilvie-Grant—and Robert Byron was the pivot. Even senior members of the University went there, like Sidney Gordon Roberts (known as 'Camels and Telegraphs' because he was Professor of Tamil and Telegu). It was originally rather a hearty place, but when lots of people like ourselves joined we soon swamped it and went there every night. We drank enormously ... and talked. ἄριστον μεν ὕδωρ (water is best) was our motto, hence Hypocrites. The club became more and more disorderly and the Proctors wanted to close it because 'biting' went on there! It was finally closed down for a more prosaic reason, because of the noise we all made in the street on leaving.

It is John Sutro who puts the snob tag into perspective:

Brian was not exactly a snob, but being in Christ Church he was with the most amusing people, the better looking—the ones who led the best life, and many of them happened to be 'Lords', and mostly ones he knew from his Eton days. He became a member of this heartier set by force of character. He influenced them towards aestheticism, Stavordale, Weymouth, Grosvenor, Brocklehurst. It was really a waste of his time, but it was what he wanted *at the time*. He had a very strong character and could influence these people. He was a mixture of ferocity and fear, he was afraid and yet not afraid. He was very courageous at Oxford, making himself ride in steeplechases. He had a great affection for one of this group, and it was probably this attraction, rather than any form of snobbishness, that made him want to become its leader. He was far more intelligent than any of them, yet he did not wish to excel in the literary arts at Oxford—only at the things in which he really had no part.

He started to drift away from Harold Acton at Oxford, and they had sharp differences. The contrast was noticeable, Harold always very industrious and about to make a serious literary career through hard work, Brian contributing to the undergraduate magazines but not much else. Although he had such a keen intelligence he hardly wrote anything during this time. Although at Eton Brian apparently seemed years older than the normal boy in knowledge and ability, he didn't develop much at Oxford. Possibly through lack of any kind of *industry*.

Henry Yorke also talks nostalgically of those days:

I can't think of Brian ever *giving* a party—he had no money, but he was accepted for himself, and used to be seen in the George every night. At Oxford he really came into the sun. He adored the life of ease and luxury and never had a job—he wouldn't dirty his hands with regular work. He was absolutely commanding in looks and conversation at Oxford, and tried to put his conversation into writing. We were lucky. In those days there was something to go for—excitement. Now there's nothing but slog . . .

Bryan Guinness (now Lord Moyne) also knew Brian quite well at Oxford:

He seemed to many of us 'the glass of fashion and the mould of form', but like Hamlet also to be haunted by some inward discontent. He was a brilliant conversationalist. He moved, however, increasingly into Anglo-American hunting circles, though never shedding his aesthetic interests. He was famous for his verbal duels with Harold Acton, to whom I remember he once sent a lemon on a plate in the George restaurant as a gesture of defiance. After he went down I remained in touch and became a friend of his mother's and of her niece, Carley Robinson.

In the original hand-written copy of Brian's long *Cherwell* essay that opened this chapter there was the following reference to Roy Harrod, but for some reason or other it did not appear in the published version:

. . . Beside Mr. Bowra one would find, quite possibly, Mr. Roy Harrod. Of Mr. Harrod I cannot write, as I do not feel that I know him quite well enough to say much without presumption. Suffice it that he, also, commands our affections.

It is a nice reversal of rôle to end this retrospective collection of the Oxford times remembered with Sir Roy Harrod's most graceful, up-to-date reminiscences of Brian and his 'Oxford Set':

It was the morning after I had arrived at Christ Church. It was my first function as a tutor of that college. The occasion was the oral examination for admissions. Quite a number of my colleagues-to-be were present and we sat in a long row. Before each of us was a pad of paper of foolscap size and a well sharpened pencil. Candidates appeared in succession and were asked questions about their age, the number of credits they had obtained in the School Certificate, what they intended to study at Oxford, what they thought of doing afterwards etc. The Dean had a habit of asking, 'What of after life?' This sometimes puzzled the candidates, because they thought it was a theological question. My colleagues made notes on the paper before them about these various points, but I did not do so. I was not involved in the process of admission, and thought it better to sit at my ease and gain a general impression of how things were done.

After some twenty candidates had appeared, one came in and, having been confronted with the 'after life' question, drew himself up and looked very serious indeed. In a studied and precisely articulated voice, which I was to get to know so well later, he replied, 'I should like to write'. I took up my pencil and wrote on the large sheet of paper before me, *Howard, B. 'I should like to write'*. The colleague sitting next to me, who was considerably my senior, looked over my shoulder to see what I had at last written down, and, seeing, gave the most scornful sneer. From that moment I did not dare write again. The morning passed, and the afternoon also, and, at the end of the day my great sheet of paper had nothing on it except only the words *Howard, B. 'I should like to write'*.

It turned out that the matter was not quite over; in the evening I was, after all, involved in the question of admission. I was summoned by Mr. Dundas, who was then Senior Censor and, as such, had the control over admissions. He wanted my advice. There had been a case of cribbing. The persons in question were 'Howard, B.' and X. My heart sank. My fear at once was that my poor, pathetic aesthete had not only incurred the scorn of my colleague, but was a cheat into the bargain. X's father held a position of unimpeachable respectability in the upper-middle walk of life.

It was a question of textual criticism. The men had sat next to one another. The evidence for cribbing was the occurrence of identical mistakes of an out of the way character in both papers. By examining these and other mistakes and the texts as a whole, it became quite evident that it was X who had cribbed and Howard, B. who had been cribbed against. My heart rose again. Howard, B's papers had been in general quite good, and he was admitted. X was not admitted, but later gained a place in another college, whether by similar methods I do not know.

When Brian later came up, I got to know him very well. Actually there were links between us, but I did not think of them, or perhaps did not even know about them, at the time. His father, Francis Howard, commonly known as Toody (later 'Tudie'), had in times long past been a great friend of my mother's. She called a yellow cat which she owned for many years Toody after him. I do not know if that was a compliment. (Incidentally in her English translation of a work by Pierre Loti, with a preface by Henry James, my mother referred to Loti's cat as 'Toody' without any authority from the French text.) Toody's mother was a woman of great brilliance, who married *en secondes noces* the then doyen of British journalism and an Irish M.P., T. P. O'Connor, who happened to be my godfather.

It was not for this reason that I got to know him, but because he was a member of a certain set of undergraduates, with whom in due course I became an intimate friend, being then myself a very young don.

It was what might be called a very close set. Doubtless they knew and saw something of other people, but they were in the company of each other most of the time. In that respect they were rather like the Bloomsbury set. In the old days a favourite subject of conversation was the question, is so and so *really* Bloomsbury? It may be of historic interest if I put on record who, according to the best of my recollection, belonged to that Oxford set. I lunched and dined with them frequently, and the same faces almost invariably re-appeared. I do not include Evelyn Waugh, the finest prose writer of his particular generation, in the list, although perhaps he ought to be there. I do not know. I knew him at Oxford but do not associate him in my mind particularly with that circle. He was a little senior to them and I only got to know them really well during the latter part of their time at Oxford, and he had probably gone down by that time. Brian was constantly in their company. Although he was a man of quite original genius, I think that he was also much influenced by what he absorbed through being in this group of friends.

The unquestioned leader was Harold Acton. He was an endless fount of brilliant and witty talk, with a quite unusual range of knowledge for an undergraduate. The principal topics of conversation, apart from perennial gossip and comment on the characters of friends, were in the field of art and letters. It was doubtless Harold's famous home in Florence that gave his learning in these matters a cosmopolitan character. He seemed to know of everything of importance that was happening in Europe in contemporary writing, painting and music. He had a very special voice, with an undertone that was perhaps not quite English; he spoke with great emphasis and with very exact articulation. He kept us laughing endlessly. His humour was entirely personal, original, quite unlike anything that one has heard before or since. It was daring and highly imaginative.

To us it seemed obvious that he would be the literary leader of his generation, rather as Lytton Strachey had been in an earlier decade. Although he has written a number of interesting books, he has not achieved quite that position, perhaps because of being too heavily anchored to his parental home in Italy.

Brian was a sort of foil. He too had a very special voice, low toned, but emphatic. He did not talk so much as Harold, but what he said was always witty and to the point, sometimes a little barbed. He would come in quietly, 'But, my dear Harold, do you not think . . .?' One of Harold's bubbles might then be pricked in a rather devastating fashion. Harold was not incapable of being nettled by these counter thrusts.

John Sutro was at the centre of the set. Throughout life he has been known to his friends for being a wonderful mimic. The word 'mimic' is only provisional and not the *mot juste*. His main medium in life has been the portrayal of types, rather than of particular people. I recall him coming to lunch one day—this was long after the undergraduate period—and assuming the rôle of a visiting American professor. He started at the lunch table and his observations were still going on when we adjourned for dinner at the Randolph Hotel. John Betjeman was there, for part of the time at least, to act as interlocutor in the parts of commercial traveller, colonel, schoolmaster, clergyman etc. John Sutro's performance was a great Homeric saga; every aspect of life was touched on by the American professor, and in depth too, all the nooks and crannies and waywardnesses of human nature being explored. It was a classic piece, unmatched in my experience; alas, it was not recorded, but dissipated into thin air. I have never read anything better in the pages of famous essayists, whose works are re-printed from generation to generation for our benefit.

John also took on particular people sometimes, and one of his finest subjects was a dialogue between Harold and Brian. This was also a great classic. It was not a set piece; I heard him do it many times, and each time the matter was quite different; it was a spontaneous outflow. He caught their two very special voices to perfection, both emphatic, highly articulated and unusual. Some people might describe their voices as affected, but I am sure that that would be quite wrong. To me they always seemed perfectly natural, being the mode of self-expression of two very special and rather strange individuals. But it was not only the voices that John caught, but their turns of mind and the ways in which they would approach certain topics. The topics were themselves esoteric, discussions maybe about artistic matters. John succeeded in entering into their separate points of view, which were special and unusual and always fascinating. One thinks back ruefully to those days, with their richness and variety.

Robert Byron was of the circle. He too had a very special voice, low toned, a little nasal, and also, although quiet, very emphatic. His words seemed to be forced out with some effort from some deep recess of body or soul. He often spoke with lowered eyelids, but then relented and revealed his beautiful eyes. He had already published many volumes, when he was sunk at sea in the first year of the war. Some were excellent. He was hard up and had to work correspondingly hard. His work was mainly on artistic subjects, but he also had political ideas. All his friends felt that his thought was continually deepening, and that one day he would write a magnum opus of great moment. He was certainly deep, but also had the utmost gaiety, and was very funny, daring and mischievous. Christopher Sykes, who belonged to a later generation, wrote an excellent account of him in his *Four Studies in Loyalty*.

Billy Clonmore was a valued member of the party. I do not recall his ever being called 'Cracky' in those days, a nickname for him popularised, and perhaps invented, by John Betjeman at a later period. We always called him Billy; Robert sometimes even referred to him as Cecil.

Then there was Henry Yorke, who has published under the name of Henry Green. His novels are very distinguished, and gained a great réclame in America also. He did not talk very much in those days. Handsome, pale and with dark hair, he would sit quietly at the table. When he did utter, it was always something very good, a little mordant.

Then there was the infinitely charming and gay Mark Ogilvie-Grant, who has lived much of his life in Greece. He also had a very special voice. I would not mind it if we all had to sit in heaven in uniform white sheets, provided that we had the authentic voices. Harold, Brian, Robert and Mark—what a wealth of meaning, what a joyful experience was to be found in those four voices.

Michael Rosse also had a very special voice. Pink and very youthful, he sat there, mainly listening. He did not do much academic work at Oxford, but in later life has been one of the hardest of workers, on behalf of museums and galleries, of Trinity College, Dublin (Vice-Chancellor) and of his own park, unique from an arboricultural point of view, at Birr. I have sometimes felt that, as he sat there listening to the talk of those extraordinarily brilliant people, there may have formed in him a pool of interest and enthusiasm, which provided the force that has since driven him onwards in his heavy labours on behalf of art and culture. My colleagues at Christ Church are always insisting that we must make our undergraduates work harder at their studies. That is against older tradition. How much would have been lost, both to themselves and to the nation, if those particular people had devoted more time to working for their tutors. That does not mean that their own thoughts were not being continually enriched by their life in Oxford. It is surely too pessimistic to hold that no such circle could again come into existence in these days, or in the future.

A much loved member of the group was Hugh Lygon ('Sebastian Flyte' in *Brideshead Revisited*) who died rather early in life.

Then there was Roger Spence, very exquisite, who, for some reason obscure to me, was Harold's godfather. By a paradox, he became a professional soldier.

Coming along a little later, as I recall, was Bryan Guinness, an accomplished writer of novels and poetry.

The subjects of the conversation, which was dominated by Harold Acton, were mainly personal and artistic. I do not recall any talk of politics, or of the more formal kind of philosophy. This is not to say that it was without its philosophic implications. It was very light, gay, varied and quick moving. Alas, it was a long time ago now, and I cannot specify the such and such. I remember the delight and joy of going in among it, so far above and beyond, as it was, the normal discourse of Oxford High Tables. There was a tremendous sense of power in it, and sureness of touch. Nothing banal could ever possibly be uttered.

The natural group with which to compare this Oxford set was that of Bloomsbury, my principal contact with which was being a regular diner at the Cranium Club. There too, as I have tried to explain elsewhere, there was a continuing stream of wit and fun, doubtless under the influence of Lytton Strachey himself. One felt, however, that the Bloomsbury group was rooted in some specific point of view, perhaps stemming back to the philosopher, G. E. Moore, and one might criticise the Oxford group as being without roots. There are advantages on both sides. One was sometimes inwardly prompted in Bloomsbury, but I never dared to yield to such prompting, to say, 'We know that you are all supposed to think like that, but can't you forget about it for a moment?' But perhaps Brian would have had a more purposeful life if he had acquired at Oxford that almost religious sense of principle that seems to have been instilled into the Bloomsbury set, when at Cambridge, by 'the Society' (the Apostles).

It cannot, I think, be denied that there was a touch of self-importance in the Bloomsbury group, or, shall we say, that they took themselves a little seriously. These Oxford men never for a moment took themselves seriously, and that was their crowning glory, if we think of them as a social circle. They found intense joy in commenting on life and things; they were entirely unselfconscious. They wandered along the paths of thought, being led into strange countries by their own vivid imaginations.

There was at that time a recently founded Railway Club, of which this group in due course became the principal members. I do not think that any of them, except John Sutro, was particularly interested in railways, but it seemed a convenient way to spend an evening from time to time. We put on our dinner jackets and had a dining car reserved on the train from Oxford to Leicester. We dined on the journey out; at Leicester we caught a return train and there followed speeches. Harold again dominated the scene. The motion of the train seemed to inspire him to embroider his utterances even more richly than usual.

There was one occasion when, for some reason, we journeyed to London instead of Leicester. Brian had not appeared, and the train was already beginning to move. Then suddenly he was seen beyond the barrier, clad in a jockey cap and colours. He had been riding in a point-to-point. The ticket collector had vexatiously closed the gate, when the train began to move, so that all seemed lost. But Brian rushed at the rather high barrier and leapt over it, perhaps inspired by the horse that he had recently been riding. There must still have been a touch of the schoolboy in Robert (Byron), because I regret to have to record that at the Paddington Station Hotel he rushed along the corridors changing the places of the shoes that had been put outside the doors.

There was a revival meeting of this Club, although not entirely composed of its old members, on a journey from London to Brighton, a few years ago. Once again Harold dominated the scene with marvellous flights of *ex tempore* imagination. It was a strange experience after forty years. Of course at times since those old days one has had doubts about whether one had not been looking at the past through rose-tinted spectacles. But not at all; I am now of fairly mature years, having had much experience since the nineteen 'twenties and Harold seemed to be just as brilliant as ever. Alas, Brian was not there.

2 1927–1940
Years of Waste

11. A taste of the 'twenties

The scene is set for what, according to Peter Quennell's commentary in *Time Exposure*,[1] was one of the most extraordinary periods of human history, 'a period as remarkable in its way, and perhaps as catastrophic, as the epoch that preceded the fall of the Roman Empire'. He was referring to the time-span 1923–1940, 'an age conspicuous alike for its solemnity and its frivolity, its desire to escape from a dilemma it is bound to recognise and an inability to resolve that dilemma into component causes'.

Brian, one of the few chosen for sure-fire success, had begun to make a cult out of failure. He scrawled a note that could have been the title of this book, *The Work of Art—History of Myself as the Failure*. Erstwhile admirers tended to become critical: 'I have always admired Mr. Brian Howard's writings, from the days of the *Eton Candle* downwards, but I hope he will forgive me for thinking that he has recently reached a stage of slight decadence. His manner is still magnificent, his matter is failing . . .' This was Terence Greenidge in the *Cherwell* as early as February 1925 (after Brian had denigrated the O.U.D.S., of which society he was a member for only a short time).

The manner never left him, but what was acceptable at Oxford to aesthetes and Lordly hearties was not necessarily tolerated in London or the grander country houses. Lord Kinross remembers Brian as a slightly lost figure at this time. He would not dissimulate and the full force of his homosexual circumstance came to light in this post-Oxford period. Had he taken a job, or appeared more regularly in print, his private life might have been less noticeable. As it was he shouted despair from the house-tops, and to a large degree it was only the greater friends who stayed the course, and as most of them were committed Bright Young People or rich young married couples his more serious talents were not overworked. He had neither the money to keep up with this social life, nor the willpower to ration his concomitant drinking. Scenes were the order of the day—whether with friends, or his mother after the inevitable requests for money which had already been spent twice over.

Was Brian's failure therefore all of his own making, or did the times conspire against him? Peter Quennell recounts (in 1941) that the between-war period was prolific of talent and produced a heavy crop of eminent or intelligent men and women (who possessed sometimes both qualifications at one and the same time), but looking back on it he found there was a strange absence of heroic and commanding figures amongst his contemporaries: 'It had been an age not of personages but of personalities. Who, for example, could be more of a personality than Miss Gertrude Stein, a kind of Biblical prophetess crossed with American business man?' But by comparison he felt her literary impact to have

---

[1] *Time Exposure* by Cecil Beaton and Peter Quennell, published by Batsford 1941.

been slight and passing: 'She has collected and encouraged, annoyed and stimulated. But the rockets she has shot skyward have always come down again.' Brian's potential rockets, one has to admit, rarely left the launching pad. Miss Stein admitted to being much influenced by street sounds and the movement of cars. She liked to 'set a sentence for herself as a sort of tuning fork and metronome and then write to that time and tune.' Brian was intoxicated by sights and sounds, but the beat of the metronome was not amongst his choice. He preferred free-falling into the landscape, drunk with the natural ambience of the great outdoors. Much of his writing, especially in the diaries, is redolent of adolescence seen through the eyes of an *ancien terrible*.

Brian became a man to whom the only state of grace was that of being 'in love', with or without sexual connotations, a state that for him unfortunately precluded work in any form. His way of life took on the pattern of perpetual sightseeing combined with pleasure-seeking, all the while fraught with hours of letter-writing. European tours were seen to be planned (if not always undertaken), itineraries confirmed, people, places and things described minutely in the constant stream of letters to his mother who became his armchair-travelling lover *par excellence*, as well as receptacle for his *idées recues*. Oh, the lecture tours he could have done, the audiences he could have hypnotised into ecstatic convolutions—had he needed the money more (as did Dylan Thomas), or alcohol less.

As it was, the days would idle by with more than the statutory working hours taken up by reading, letter-writing, travelling, eating and drinking, more drinking and still more reading ... His early mentor, Aldous Huxley, had also suffered from this book mania while teaching at Eton. In 1918 he wrote to his sister-in-law, Juliette, 'there is too much to read: and it so easily becomes a mere indulgence, a vice of the mind quite as deplorable as any other bad habit.' Brian knew this too, but had not got Huxley's driving conscience which insisted: 'I never really feel I am performing a wholly moral action except when I am writing. Then and only then is one not wasting time.'

The artist, John Banting, enlarges the portrait here with an impression of the many-sided Brian that he first knew in the late 'twenties:

Let's face it, Brian was a Failure and a Waster according to the outlook of the Philistines, the Lick-Spittles, the Go-Getters, the Knee-benders and the smug Play-Safe Sheep-People. 'Brindle' (Peter Watson's nickname for Brian) was brindled in that his moods and friends covered a wide range, however chaotically but inevitably he retained his own individuality. Such 'universality' was hard to appreciate: established scholars, layabouts, beautiful women, wild men, tame men of all classes—and others and others—were his friends. He was an 'outsider'. He 'belonged' nowhere, nor wished to.

I first spoke to Brian—it must have been about 1927 or 1928—because I suddenly saw him as through the eyes of Matisse. I wasn't a great admirer of that painter at the time, for I thought he repeated his glorious canvases too monotonously and too gloriously. But Brian was almost a 'ready-made' with his dark arched eyebrows, heavy brown eyes, and regular oval face. So

I asked him to sit for a portrait. He looked rather surprised, but consented, and came to my studio. After a few sittings I painted a caricature of him, his head balanced on his lapels. I didn't much like it then or now, and only photographs of it survive.

Although Brian's creative powers took this apparently frivolous form for a few years he was also quietly writing poems and making drawings. As life became more grim people 'took sides', but Brian's views never really drew him into any movement—political or artistic. He was of course Left in sympathies, not hugely anti-religious—perhaps one might say non-religious, and with the years more and more *au dessus de la mêlée*. Nor was he a member of the Surrealists as I was (although it now seems part of the Establishment). Those who disagreed with his not very extreme views will slyly represent him in a bad light. Of course there was a lot of roistering, but no 'frivolity' or mediocrity, as his imagination saved him from that. Raymond Mortimer admired Brian's lively wit (and his brightening up in the 'thirties and 'forties of the 'New Staggers'). In those days the words 'success' or 'failure' were never heard, and Brian worked for the pleasure of it. Maybe a very unworthy and unprofitable condition, but the disinterested pleasure used to burst through all the virtuosity of his professional craftsmanship.

At times he could hold varied types of people in fits of laughter, either by his satirical wit or by fantastic nonsense of the Lear or Goon type, accompanied sometimes by a few grotesque yet also dignified movements. These were his most popular, enjoyable and endearing moods. Yet Brian was not the dashing prankster or 'Merry Andrew' that some preferred to dub him (a sly way of treating those in disagreement with oneself). He was often filled with *Weltschmerz*. No melancholic, he acutely realised the suffering, swindling injustices and hypocrisy of the human condition. To breed can be a cruelty or a vanity or more often an accident—*tous lasse, tous passe, tous casse* has a double meaning. He was a serious and individual person, not a 'Fascinating Eccentric', and I suppose that made him quite unique and suspect to the Bowler Hat Brigade. And there were sparks of spite amongst his literary contemporaries. I think that some envied his lavishly thrown away brilliance and his tragi-comic twist and irony, for he could be both a bitter and a gentle satirist. He threw himself away deliberately in conversation rather than writing.

Brian was a keen appreciator of the beauties and faults of women. Nancy Cunard and he adored each other and admired each other's looks. In some ways they were very much alike in character—determination, frankness and hatred of compromise. There were long affectionate friendships and brief affaires with women, even to beddings, but he once told me that although he might get one of the special ones to marry him, for her sake he would not try to do so as he felt he would make a terrible husband. But he would have made a considerate father—neither smothering nor neglecting.

He could appear to adjust himself, if he wished, to dull or unsympathetic company, and assume a featureless and conventional façade of a temporary kind. But with the fatigue of any drink (sometimes used as a shield against boredom) the façade would crumple and he would deliver a violent stream of argument and abuse at the hearty philistine, or the bore, in whose company he had accidentally fallen. He never attacked those unable to defend themselves, and never gossipped behind people's backs. Instead they received it full in the face. Whenever I was present at those scenes I longed to melt into the floor, but failing this I kept my mouth zipped up, for Dissuasion would have become Persuasion and made the row far worse. I would afterwards tell him he had wasted his energy upon Snots who should be ignored. With an easy laugh he would reply, 'Can't, won't, shan't, don't'. Write it down instead, I would urge, and he sometimes did.

During the 'twenties Brian still spent occasional weekends with his parents at Nore, their country house, where certain friends of his were welcome. Jimmy Stern, the writer, recalls an occasion with Robert Byron, Brian and Brian's father after dinner while the men were sitting round the fire:

That night must be close on forty years ago, but the scene and the atmosphere are still vivid. Brian sat in the shadows, while the glow from the room's one lighted lamp fell on the father's black velvet dinner jacket, and on his hair, which was turning silver. Suddenly he began to talk, or rather to relate, in a voice that never faltered. Soon he was telling a story, about something strange, something uncanny, that had happened to him, on a winter's night, during a great storm, somewhere in the Scottish highlands . . .

Robert and I were sitting on a sofa, in the gloom. We stared spellbound, at the older man, as the story unfolded, as we slowly began to realise that on that night in Scotland, in the howling wind, Francis Howard had actually *seen a ghost . . .!*

Was it possible that Brian, motionless in the shadows, was listening to this eerie adventure, tonight, for the first time? Finally, and on a note as frightening as it was convincing, the story came to an end. In the stunned silence Francis Howard lifted a finger to his full lower lip, and raised his eyes, to where the fire was throwing nickering shadows on the ceiling.

'Well?' he said at last, glancing at each of us in turn. 'Well?'

But none of us could utter.

'Ha!' exclaimed the father, rising triumphant from his chair. 'You don't seem to know your Stevenson very well!'

Brian's cousin, Carley, remembers that Brian was very wild during the late 'twenties and early 'thirties:

But his acts were, to me, acts of rebellion and desperation. He was against the Establishment long before this attitude became popular. It was sometimes hard to distinguish acts that were intended to shock and jar stuffy people out of their usual pattern, and some of which narrowly skirted mental aberration. For example, I remember one holiday Whit Sunday at Nore. Brian was bored. I was still in my teens and Brian in his early twenties. It was hot. He suggested that we put on bathing suits and go down near the main road, hiding in the wheat, and jump up making faces and waving wildly at the passers-by. This we did, but Brian began doing it too well, and I soon saw that startled drivers thought a maniac was loose. When a car stopped and the driver began walking back to investigate, I fled.

Another 'shocker' which today would seem very tame, was done from the same point of view, *pour épater les bourgeois*. During May Week at Oxford Brian waited until all the respectable girls and their 'county' mothers were assembled at dusk, on the tops of the house-boats along the river. Then he sent floating down a large chamber pot on a small raft, with a lighted candle inside. He then joined one of the groups who at first, to his delight, peered into the dusk, saying, 'What *is* that little light?', and then fell sharply into a horrified silence as what the little light was *in* came into clear view. In this type of thing it was impossible not to be on Brian's side.

Carley believes this post-Oxford period could have been a turning point in Brian's life, but having failed to get his degree at Oxford and given up studying law in the Middle Temple, he now fell into the trap of the times—the Party.

Vogue's social diarist commented on this glut of parties, particularly fancy dress: 'At Hampden House there was more lip-rouge than I have ever before seen. Lord Portarlington and his son Lord Carlow, as Victorian mother and débutante daughter respectively, were smothered in it ...' This behaviour apparently caused less unfavourable comment in 1927 than it would today.

Cecil Beaton (who goes on record for saying there was a time when it was quite usual for him never to put on ordinary clothes for a week or ten days at a stretch, his life consisting of a whirl of fancy dress party-going) knew Brian at this period:

He was extremely urbane, svelte and sophisticated. Very much at home in the grand world of London, or what I thought was the grand world. I was introduced to him by the Guinness sisters, Tanis and Méraud. He had a great charm, style and an 18th-century manner—which in those early days was not exaggerated, as it was later when he became a caricature of himself.

I thought he was delightful, gay and funny. Nice looking in a slightly effete way. He knew what he was talking about—and the effect was mellifluous, honeyed. The whole atmosphere around him was very congenial, whereas later it became so waspish, wicked and malicious that one's hackles were always up. Although he was then easier to accommodate in everyday conversation, it was sometimes rather too much of a set-piece.

I was clearing out my old negatives the other day and came across some photographs very typical of the 'twenties period. When I was beginning to take in an amateur way what I liked then to call 'camera portraits', Brian came to be photographed. I remember enjoying the experience very much. He came with a young man called Paddy Brodie and the two of them really made a meal of it! They brought all sorts of outrageous sailor clothes with them. There was something rather marvellous about the audacity of it. It took a long time to take each pose—I was not so quick in those days—and

PORTRAIT OF A FAILURE

I had to change the lights between each shot. We went on long after the point of attrition had been reached. I'm surprised that he wasn't drawn and photographed more by people like Curtis Moffat, Man Ray, and Tchelichev. He was so vain.

Barbara Ker-Seymer (who was then also a highly original photographer) was one of the few of Brian's friends and contemporaries genuinely liked, and approved of—to a degree—by Lura Howard. Barbara's mother had been at art school with Tudie, and she herself had known Brian since they were children:

I remember Mrs. Howard coming to call on me once, begging us all to put a curb on our activities, and reminding me that we were all middle-aged, so it was time we slowed down and behaved in a more circumspect manner. We were then twenty-five!

Brian at one time announced that he was going to be my partner, as being a professional photographer was an excellent way of introducing himself to the more 'difficult' people, as failing all else they always succumbed to having themselves photographed. In fact it all started with a boy in the swimming pool who was being tiresome, and as a last resort Brian said he was a photographer, and then had to come flying to me to confess and ask me to stand by him. It ended up by Brian making a tremendous business of posing, arranging the lighting etc. and his 'assistant' (me) taking the actual photographs! Unfortunately he got fired with the bug, and decided to become very modern, hence the metal tubing, chicken wire and rope etc. that he insisted on wrapping all the clients in. He really got the devil in him, as the more 'twin set and pearls' type of customer, the more they got wrapped in the tubing. I was allowed to take my more normal portraits, but Brian invariably turned up for the proof showing, and intimidated the wretched clients into at least taking some of the horrors.

In those days Brian loved to go to what he called 'Grand Parties', and Allanah Harper writes:

I remember one dance (we called dances 'balls' then) in Carlton House Terrace when he was whirling me round and round at breathless speed, to the strains of an enchanting waltz. I must have said something to Brian which made him think I wanted to marry him. He looked at me with his charmingly ironical smile and said, 'Don't you think I'm going to marry you, my dear, I'm going to marry a Peeress in her own right—she's an heiress, too'. I thought at the time that I was in love with Brian, and felt hurt and crushed.

The *Weekly Dispatch*, whose social half-page was edited by Lady Eleanor Smith under the heading of 'From my Window in Vanity Fair', described the dance Lura Howard gave for Carley in May 1927:

... Many London dances are dull, pompous, and lifeless, which is slightly depressing when you think of the hundreds of pounds spent on these

136

entertainments. I went, however, to one on Friday night which I enjoyed enormously. It was given by Mrs. Francis Howard for her niece, Miss (Carley) Robinson in surely one of Bryanston Square's most beautiful houses. We danced in Mr. Howard's enormous studio, which had been cleared completely, much to the owner's strongly expressed disapproval. The evening was considerably enlivened by some of the best cabaret turns I have seen for a long time. Roland Hayes, the coloured performer, sang and played delightfully, while a sleek young man danced the Black Bottom most energetically.

Daphne Fielding wrote of the Charleston and the Black Bottom having just been introduced into England in her book, *Mercury Presides*:

Brian decided that we should all become proficient in the steps of these dances, and encouraged us all to take lessons in London from Barbara Back, the wife of a Harley Street surgeon. Michael Rosse became an expert, and he and his sister, Bridget Parsons, caused surprise and envy in London ballrooms as together they danced a furious Charleston, both with a look of earnest concentration. When Michael was at home at Birr Castle, he used to lock himself up in his room for hours, turn on the gramophone and practise his dancing. If he was in a bad mood he would Charleston so frantically to drive out the evil humour that the ceiling in the sitting-room below shook and quivered.

Daphne Fielding also gave a glimpse of what happened when Oxford friends came to London:

... I often went with them to the Fun Fair at Wembley. There was a side-show called 'The River Caves', where little boats floated through dark, subterranean caverns past illuminated troglodyte scenes, including one of Dante's Inferno, where papier mâché figures chained to cardboard rocks writhed in paper flames and an enormous scarlet Mephistopheles poked his pitch-fork into victims. As our boats drifted past, we would jump out and land among the lost souls in Hades and play our ukeleles, while Brian Howard, looking like a sinister Spielmann, defied the Devil, who seemed insignificant beside him. Meanwhile our boats, one after the other, floated back empty; and we would have to take off our shoes and stockings and paddle to the entrance, where we made a barefoot getaway from the angry attendants.

At other times, led by Brian, we played follow-my-leader through Selfridges, up and down in the lifts, in and out of the departments, and even over the counters.

As Lord Bath now writes, 'a game which would not be tolerated in these days, but the management took it extraordinarily well. There must have been two dozen of us at least, jumping on the counters and doing everything which Brian did at the head of the game.'

Setting the Thames on fire at Henley was another exploit. Gavin Henderson (now Lord Faringdon) gave a bachelor's dinner party for thirty friends on the eve of his marriage in June 1927. This party took place at the Phyllis Court Club near Henley. After dinner some of his friends got hold of eight two-gallon tins of petrol which they proceeded to pour into the river—and then someone 'set the Thames on fire'. Brian was always considered the culprit here.

One of the first of the memorable parties was given this same year by Captain Neil McEachern. It was called the Impersonation Party and everyone had to go dressed as someone else—preferably living. Tom Driberg who was as thin, dark and saturnine as Brian in those days, impersonated him:

I simply had to make up my face, giving one of my eyebrows much more of an exaggerated twist. One of Brian's was always raised in that mocking, satirical twist. I wore the same sort of suit he usually wore—plain, loose, dark blue, and carried a package of twenty Gold Flake cigarettes in my hand. Brian would never put one in his jacket pocket in case it spoilt the line. He was staggered when I confronted him—the near-mirror image. I remember Martin Wilson being superbly dressed as Queen Mary in yachting costume—about 1910 period—white moiré silk, stiff skirt, and an enormous powdered wig and toque to top it all.

Sir Martin Wilson vaguely remembers this party, and going in yachting costume, but not as Queen Mary! But these were still early 'Bright Young People' days, and the more notorious parties were yet to be 'thrown'. Even so, Lura Howard feared the effects of these hectic times on Brian and by the autumn of 1927 she decided to have him discreetly psycho-analysed in Frankfurt by the renowned young Dr. Prinzhorn. (Enquiring friends were told he was going to have his 'lungs' examined.) One assumes that she hoped for his sexual tastes to be steered towards a normal marriage, as she would have enjoyed family life with grandchildren.

Brian had really wanted to go to 'Greece—America or somewhere' with Bryan Guinness and Robert Byron, but for some reason Bryan G. wished to elude him as travelling companion at that time and slipped off on his own to Germany, leaving his mother to explain his sudden flight to an unknown destination. She wrote to her son, Bryan: 'I have had a most unpleasant amount of lying on account of B.H. I'm not sure that I don't like him very much, and think you have behaved very badly to him!! . . . I did not give away your address but he will certainly get the whole truth from his cousin, and we shall be in the soup, and as I am the innocent one, I am bound to get the worst blame . . .' Needless to say Brian did descend on her and he wrote to Bryan G. the day before leaving for Germany himself: 'What an extraordinary person, Y., you are. Incalculable. Suddenly bolting off to Germany, like this. Most unlike you . . . I thought that only the irresponsibles of this world, like myself, did these things . . .' (These two namesakes used to write to each other as 'I' and 'Y'.)

Brian felt the need for friendships now more than ever, and he wrote a revealing letter to Harold Acton after one of their major rows:

... I am unable to resist writing to you and telling you that I think it is silly for us to quarrel. You mutter—'Well, I don't care. You began it. You're so disloyal. Anyway, *I* don't care whether we see one another or not.' I can't help it if you *do* mutter this. Shortly, the 'trouble' is this. You think of me as a *flâneur*—a dilettante with an uncontrollable tongue, addicted to boring friends on the count of snobbishness. A dangerous, superficial creature. Presumably you think this. You may have an older, more perceptive thought or two about me, somewhere. I think of you as much the same—uncontrollable and irresponsible—but with *inverted* snobbery ... All this is such a pity. You see, you are right about my being a snob. But you are wrong about the people I choose to be snobbish about. I am snobbish about my old friends only. I have a sense of 'We'—if you understand me—about them. 'We' must not be divided against ourselves. There are too many of 'they' who would be delighted ... If you are prepared to obliterate this last fracas, you will never hear of an unpleasant thing I have said about you again. Unless it is fabricated ... I go to Frankfurt tomorrow to see a doctor about my lungs ...

12. German Journal

1927

This hand-written journal was conceived with an eye to later publication. From time to time Brian would append tart little criticisms to certain pages, neatly initialled and dated, but apart from a few paragraphs that he typed out he never seriously edited any of it. The Journal as a whole (only brief extracts are included here) gives an idea of the range of arts, entertainments and books ready for tasting by a young man in 1927—in the middle of the Roaring 'Twenties, but before the slump, and a good few years before political oppression was to change the face of Germany. These last three months of 1927 were also to set the pattern for Brian's future: he acquired a taste for travel, the knowledge that he could live more freely and economically abroad, and a life-long affection for Germany.

German Journal (September–November 1927):

Unsentimental Journey—to Frankfurt

I left England yesterday willingly and unwillingly. I wonder why I can never leave a place without mixed emotions. It would have been so much more complete if I could have been entirely happy or entirely miserable. And one must be complete to live.

The train to Harwich was wonderful. The chimney of the engine must have been stuffed with soot, because we travelled in a cage of fire. Large, strong sparks screamed past in the night on both sides. They lasted so long that they made taut cables of fire, the straight bars of a cage. On the boat I ran into one of those boring, universal young Englishmen. He was carrying the *Tatler* and wore a black Homburg hat with a sneering brim. The type that is convinced of its charm ... I tiptoed away from him, and safe on the upper deck watched England's lights fading. The clouds were thin bands of white silk, torn everywhere and stretched vertically across the sky.

I got my first taste of Germany from the advertisements in the dining-car. The Zeiss one is good. A man wearing spectacles. He looks like a poet or a professor. The sort of man who would wear Zeiss spectacles. In England he would have looked like a second lieutenant in the Guards, with a touch of hermaphrodite, and the spectacles would have been almost invisible.

I have brought with me as reading matter D. H. Lawrence's *Women in Love*, Gibbon's *Decline and Fall of the Roman Empire*, Goethe's *Wilhelm Meister*. The Gibbon, I know, will make me cheerful again if ever I get depressed.

140

When I get homesick I have only to read some sentence like this—Gibbon is writing of the early Christians: *It was their favourite opinion, that if Adam had preserved his obedience to the Creator, he would have lived for ever in a state of virgin purity, and that some harmless mode of vegetation might have peopled paradise with a race of innocent and immortal beings.* If that isn't English I don't know what is.

Flight

This afternoon I went to a Flying Exhibition just outside Frankfurt ... Rattling little aeroplanes thundered and danced round on the short grass in front of us, swinging their tails like hard little birds getting ready to leave the nest. One of the airmen, an Englishman, did extraordinary things. He roared up and down a few feet above our heads, flying backwards and forwards along the line of spectators. Occasionally he veered round with a rush, and spun away over the roof behind, his wings quite vertical. Each *time* everyone thought he had come to a bad end out of sight. Each time he snored round the corner of the roof again, and continued his smoky patrol.

Presently there was parachute jumping. Holding off the sun with my fingers, I watched the little black protuberance flick off the aeroplane, very high, so that it seemed that the pilot had swatted a fly on the fuselage and it had dropped off, dead. Almost at the same moment, but not quite, the beautiful parachute opened, with a kind of swaying, gracious generosity, over it, pulling it back, holding up the little, silly corpse. A white, female flower opening quickly, with an extraordinary gaiety. A sunlit woman laughingly holding a child back who is trying to fall over something. Then the long, lilting descent. Vague. And the arrival. The fly had been kicking and twisting, saved and alive, long before. On reaching the ground it seemed to kneel and pray, a minute's thanks, and then stood up a man. The flower became a dead flower as the man stood up. A dead parachute.

Saturday Night in Berlin

Last night, as often happens in Germany, I was compelled, through overcrowding, to sit at the same table as someone else. This person looked exactly like our family doctor. Fifty, silvery, rather rich-looking, with a dark blue bow tie spotted with white, a dark blue suit, with a sparkling white shirt. He saw I was English and spoke to me. Being at the moment lonely I was rather pleased. He seemed cultivated and agreeable, and had been in England. He really seemed very charming in a slightly upper-middle class sort of way, and when he suggested that we should go somewhere else, I readily agreed. He said that he thought it would be amusing for me if we went to the American Dance Palace, as it was typical of modern Berlin night life. Off we went in a taxi. Our coats were taken at the door by a young man in Bavarian national costume. We passed through a chypre-impregnated and scarlet outer room into an enormous, pillared hall, in the centre of which a cabaret performance was taking place on the vast dancing floor. We watched it, over a hundred heads, and it was really very entertaining. Two Bavarian peasants dancing some kind of folk-dance. One, an elderly man, and the other, the largest lady I have ever seen. Huge, rippling with fat, like St. Sophia. I was astonished when he turned to me in an interval and told me that she was a man. I laughed. It seemed to me rather amusing. The whole place seemed to me rather amusing, at that moment.

Presently, the cabaret finished, and we secured a table by the dancing floor. I remember quite distinctly the precise moment at which I became sensible of the true nature of my companion and surroundings. My mouth had just met the grateful chill of my beer—it was exceedingly hot, with the heat of a perfumery department in a great shop—when the band commenced. Instantly this enormous floor was convulsed with movement, and I hiccoughed with astonishment to see only men dancing together. The women, of whom, I now realised, there had been few, had apparently been pushed under the tables, or something. No—presently, an ordinary couple came jigging past us. I pointed them out to my companion, and said that she seemed to be the only girl dancing. 'Yes,' my companion said, rather absent-mindedly, 'They say she is a sailor from Hamburg, but she looks too slight. Personally, I—what did you say?' He turned to me, enquiringly. 'Oh, nothing—really.' 'No, but what *did* you say?' he repeated. I had to tell him. 'I said, it's a long way to Tipperary, but you won't understand. It's just an English joke . . .'

After a short time I left. He wanted to come with me, out of politeness, but I persuaded him to remain. On my way I looked at the men carefully. They nearly all had had their eyebrows practically removed. My own are particularly luxuriant this month, and I felt embarrassed, and rather top-heavy. However, I threaded my way out firmly, and gained the street unwithered by fifty glances of elegant contempt. In the street, I stopped to breathe, angrily, a breath of ordinary, unpainted air. I felt suddenly extremely masculine, and unaccountably angry. Suddenly, I felt a thin touch on my squaring shoulders. As if my shoulder had been pressed with a pencil. I twisted my head and looked. It was a long, white finger. Reversing myself completely I found myself facing the ingratiatory smile of a creature such as would have intimidated Dempsey. All that I can say is that it was male, neither to any intent nor purpose, but male. And thin, thin as some worn, flexible piece of black rope. Bent and black, with a face like the tail of a rabbit that retreats into the evening. It said, suddenly, '*Bitte* . . .' 'Please,' it said. 'Bitter,' it said. Bitter, I suddenly felt, the whole world was. Rancid, and cancerous, and crawling. I struck out at it, not blindly, but with a purpose, because I knew I must destroy this thing. It sifted down into a little evil of black rope at my feet. Like a knot of black rope that has suddenly been undone, loosened. People began to gather. I ran, and got away . . .

P.S. It has struck me that my account of 'Saturday Night' suggests an attitude of puritanical protest, of virtue astonished and at bay. As if I had been 'shocked'. I was not shocked. I am quite familiar with the existence of such phenomena in the modern city life. I find it as significant, and as interesting, as a museum. But I was overcome with a certain disgust. Prostitution is disgusting. Male prostitution most disgusting of all. It is the full, the final human disaster.

Cocaine, at first sight

Last night I saw a drug fiend, for the first time in my life. There is a little café in one of the largest and most central streets in Berlin which is extremely respectable, the prices are, as they call it here, *zivile*, and it possesses a passable quorum of musicians. I have been there several times, and have become acquainted with the proprietor, who conveys himself and his cargo of stomach among the tables with great charm and a pair of crutches. He speaks a sort of English, and smiles when he sees me, both of which things I value.

The café is in the shape of the letter L. As a result, one can only survey half of it at one time. The proprietor and I were hammering away towards a mutual exchange of ideas yesterday evening, at about eleven o'clock, when a man who looked as if he might be a retired Prussian General, certainly an Herr Ober-something, advanced with great deliberation round the corner from the other half of the café and proceeded to closet himself in the embrasure of a nearby window, where, scantily shielded from my astonished observation by an extremely open-work curtain of what I think was Nottingham lace, he began to do his deep breathing exercises. A great gold ship's cable of a watch chain clinked and clinked at the violence of his respirations. The other patrons of the café took no notice of him whatsoever. 'What is he doing?' I said. '*Warum—wass iss?*' I faltered. Leaning his generous face towards me over a metre of waistcoat, with a paternal smile, the proprietor said, not too quietly, 'He smellss hiss coke.' 'What?' I said. 'Hiss coke—he brithss it in.' 'What?' I said, 'is he eating coke? What for?' Presuming that I must be hard of hearing, if not downright dense, the proprietor now bellowed at me, with some asperity, 'CORK-HA-EEN!' He began to illustrate his meaning by going through a process which looked as if he was taking snuff. 'Oh', I answered, hurriedly, 'I see, I see—cocaine, yes.' 'His vife ant chilrrun iss rround de korrner. Dey tink he hass nid of larva-tory,' my companion continued. At this moment the drug fiend emerged, wiping his face with majesty and a large silk handkerchief. Importantly, he walked off to his table. I rose. I felt that I must see whether it was true that he was here in the bosom of his family. It seemed incredible. I edged round the corner and peeped into the other part of the café. There he was embattled behind four Fürstenbraus, with a vast, blonde wife like a Zeppelin, and two little boys with shaved heads, and khaki Norfolk jackets. Herr Oberst out for the evening with his family. And to think that tucked away in one of those capacious pockets lay a little folded slip of paper, or a little bottle, containing all the sugars of hell.

It is puzzling that Brian should have been so disgusted and surprised by his visit to the transvestite club, and the sight of the cocaine-sniffing *père de famille*. Was he putting up a pretence of healthy unsophistication (he told Bryan

Guinness that he was writing this diary with an eye to publication), or did he feel that only his 'set' had the rights to deviation? It seems to me that what shocked him most was the fact that the pathetic male prostitute should have mistaken him, the twenty-two year old Bright Young Brian, for a paying customer, and that the 'Herr Oberst' should take his cocaine incognito but in public, instead of in private with birds of a feather.

After an interval of some days Brian decided temporarily to relinquish his Journal 'in favour of a treatise which I have been planning since I visited Heidelberg. It is to be a sort of philosophical speculation on the nature of the contemporary gentleman.'

Jimmy Stern, who was to become one of Brian's greatest friends, was then working all day in his family bank in Frankfurt—and half the night at a Nachtlokal, or bar. Brian meanwhile was being 'psycho-analysed' by Dr. Prinzhorn (who called him Kuno), and writing desultory notes in his Journal or, as Jimmy recalls:

> ... often spending all day in bed in a haze of tobacco smoke. Sometimes, on returning from the bank in the evening, I thought Brian's room had caught fire. The mass of black hair on the pillow was barely visible. Then, from out of the grey cloud came a stifled groan: 'Oh, all *right*, dearie. The old spider's getting up now. .... By the way, bring any nice crisp Markies?' (cash).

After Jimmy had revisited Germany in 1945 with a U.S. Army team surveying what effect aerial bombardment had had on the morale of German civilians, he wrote of those days—and Brian—in his book, *The Hidden Damage*:[1]

> Heidelberg ... recalled the years when few of my contemporaries contemplated the possibility of another World War. Was it really twenty years since the day, during that Irresponsible Era, when I had come out here from Frankfurt in a fourth-class carriage with one of London's brightest of Bright Young Men? Perched up on those wooden, right-angled, back-breaking benches, squashed between gloomy middle-aged men with long pipes and bulging shiny-faced *Frauen* with bald-headed babies, he had suddenly turned to me as the train grunted into Heidelberg: 'Christ, my dear, these *hideous* people!' and thrust something hairy into my hand. Looking down, I saw a false beard, chocolate brown and very long. By the time I'd recovered from the shock and glanced up, he had transformed his pale, Greco-like appearance into that of a furious old gentleman in pince-nez and drooping black mustaches. ... I wondered, smiling at the memory, if I were to walk into the Hotel zum Ritter after all these years, whether I should still find in its registry the entry of a guest describing himself as Dr. Whipplebottom—Profession: Murderer.

Of the famous Dr. Prinzhorn he also wrote pseudony-mously, but the image is there:

---

[1] Published by Harcourt, Brace 1947.

... at Beethoven recitals 'Dr. Wolfgang Dunkelmann', the dignified Goethe-like psychiatrist, would stand up, hypnotised, in the back of the packed auditorium and with staring eyes and outstretched arms start singing until he had to be carried out in a trance. Next day, remembering nothing about the night before, he would insist on hearing every detail.

'Very interesting. Very interesting, indeed!' he would say, and start comparing the hypnotic effect the master's music had on him with that which a certain tropical plant, used as a drug, was said to have on Mexican Indians.

... 'Dr. Dunkelmann', who worshipped and physically resembled Goethe ... whose life had been spent studying the art of the insane, interpreting dreams, living with and marrying beautiful women, and who, on being informed by 'Gisela' [the wife that Brian knew] that she was about to leave him for 'Kurt' [one of his disciples], glanced up from his desk and said: '*Meine Liebe*, I congratulate you! This is the first time I've been surprised by a human being!'—then went on with his work.

Brian can't have been as destitute, or his life as grim, as he sometimes made out in his letters to his mother. Again Jimmy Stern filled out the times in his book, when he revisited Prinzhorn's ex-wife 'Gisela' in 1945. She had already dreamed the night before of his coming.

'In my dream you weren't alone, but with Kuno [Brian] and Wolfgang and Papa—'

'Kuno!' I exclaimed, remembering that this was the name Gisela had given the friend, the Bright Young Man from London who'd stuffed the false beard into my hands in the train near Heidelberg.

'Naturally', she was saying, 'I never think of you without thinking of Kuno. That was how we met. I always thought Kuno was a genius, you know.'

'So did he,' I laughed.

'Wolfgang didn't,' she said ... 'he used to say young Englishmen like Kuno never finish anything but their visky-sodas!'

'I know of worse things to finish,' I muttered, and there flashed through my mind a vision of a crowd of depressingly earnest young men snapping at one another over the works of Schoenberg, Krenek and Hindemith, snapping away in a room with barely a seat to sit on and not a damned drop to drink. 'Christ, my dear, what *bores!*' I heard Kuno growl as we had both made for the door.

'D'you remember,' Gisela went on, 'the night Kuno invited us all to caviare and champagne in the Tanzklause?'

'Yes, indeed,' I said, 'and your mother had to pay the bill!'

'And Kuno insisted on waltzing with the waiter! I don't think I've ever laughed so much in my life!' she said ...

Brian wrote regularly to his mother from Germany, frequently repeating what he had already roughed out in his Journal:

[October–December 1927] Prinzhorn I admire, I think, more than any man I know. He is a real, *real* intellect. One of the two or three foremost in Germany, as many people have told me. And he is interested in me, and in helping me to get my 'dominion of life' as he puts it.

My Journal already contains many of the best bits of writing I have yet done—about circuses—cafés—books etc. Well—I suppose I must get to the beastly fact that I have only £2 10s. in the world now. Everything is paid, but that's all I have. I know how this last bit of news spoils everything, but just do me the favour of overlooking it.

As regards Henry (Weymouth) and Daphne's wedding present (oh, how I want to go to the wedding, but still) do try and make it something rather tremendous—I would rather give a good present on this occasion than on *any* other. Couldn't Daddy buy me a silver tea set or something, for them, and not give me a Christmas present. I wish to *sacrifice* something, remember, to give them something even better than you would normally arrange for. Because I love them both ... I have just returned from Berlin. I have done the museums—which mainly consist of the great Kaiser Friedrich Museum, which has the famous Holbeins, Dürers, Botticellis, and Cranachs of the world. Also the finest 13th, 14th, and 15th century sculptures I have ever seen, and far *earlier* embroideries. Why don't people *know* about this museum?—Even the taxi-drivers don't. The thing is, no one ever goes to Berlin. I believe it is the most unvisited city in the world. This is, of course, because there is absolutely nothing there except *music* and this *one* museum. The early Flemish school at this museum—my goodness, I never knew what early Flemish pictures could be. There are also some excellent modern masters in Germany who, of course, are utterly unknown in England. Liebermann, the doyen of them all, of course is known. Otherwise, who has heard of Corinth, Slevogt, what of Kokoschka, and the earlier 19th-century ones, Van Marées, and Feuerbach? Marées is a genius, Feuerbach is a great genius. My goodness, if I had the money I'd organise a German art exhibition at the R.A. tomorrow. 'German Art: 1827–1927'. It is an exhibition which is more needed, and would create more *interest*, than any of the possibilities now remaining.

... As regards money particularly, if you think it is beyond endurance, I'd better come home. That's all I can say. Even if I did, my German expedition would have been a success. Hans Prinzhorn has made it that for me. I admire and respect him more than any man I have ever met. He, as one might put it very shortly, KNOWS. He has made my job clear to me, and given me much heart and strength. He has also damaged my conceit considerably ... In a few things he has made me happy by confirming instinctive opinions of mine. I have always felt, most deeply—really *deeply, but blindly*, the supreme war-cry of his and the new German philosophy. Which is that nothing in this earth matters two pins but the one necessity of getting into contact with Life. The Life that there is pulsing out of the Sun and the Mountains. The Life that is the rhythm behind the great money exchanges. The Life that animates great music. It is all we have on this earth. There is only that. Once one feels it, gets into it, devotes oneself to it—one is right, to a certain extent, whatever one does. Even if one happens to devote oneself to it by committing murders—almost. Because one is doing. To do with the mind is nothing. To do with the soul, *which is Life*, is everything.

. . . Because man *thinks*, gradually, more, and *lives*, gradually, less, do you see, he becomes more and more of a tiny, separated, egotistical, plotting creature, and less of a part of Life? . . . Prinzhorn was talking to me about Beethoven. I have not got to Beethoven—yet. Now I ask you—what do you think Birkenhead's life work looks like next to Beethoven? You may say—one can't compare them. Well, one can. And the result is terribly comic. Birkenhead juggled brilliantly with facts which are neither true nor untrue—ephemeral regulations of one particular social fabric. He tinkered brilliantly with laws which were all made by somebody else. He made very witty remarks—'Well—Lord Birkenhead, and what do you think of Americans?' 'They have attempted some emendations in the matter of spelling which have not recommended themselves to my individual taste.' Very good. Very good indeed. 'Mind' at its best. Then one takes Beethoven—who interpreted the whole language of the World and made it divine—more than it was—with the help of a piano, a violin, and a 'cello.

Birkenhead and modern Christianity and Cézanne, and Daddy and Mr. and Mrs. McGrath[2] are *Geist*. Mind. They will go, when they go, for good. You and I (hard, shrill, prejudiced, extravagant ME) are *Leben-Seele*—Life-Soul. Aren't we? All of love to you—a Chip of the old Soul . . .

A few weeks later he wrote to his Aunt Grace:

Dearest 'Virginie', . . . Am I so nasty—sometimes? I suppose I am. But, Aunt Virginie, you don't know how hard it is to go through life pretending one isn't an egoist, when one is! I fear I shall always have spasms of dictatorial conceit. Fundamentally, possibly, I realise my limitations more than most, but superficially I don't.

. . . When I heard from you that Daddy was so gay at Nore, I had hoped that, as a result of my absence, he was happy, and getting on well with Muzzy. Apparently not. What a nuisance he is! *Why* can't something happen to him. Something quick and painless—but final! As regards my coming home for Christmas—I really don't know, but somehow I feel a new person. I feel capable of dealing with the situation and God knows it's got to be dealt with one day. I can't stay abroad for ever. Also I wish to start publishing, immediately. I have material ready, and it's time.

. . . I quite agree that Muzzy ought to go to her specialist. Either that or a divorce—and in my opinion a divorce would be a less expensive and more permanent rest-cure, of the two alternatives. I can see my papa

---

[2] Rosita Forbes, the traveller and author.

roaring at Eleanor[3] [the maid] with centenarian lungs. Ugh! 'LuRA—where's the evening paper!!!' 'LuRA, I met Lady Situpon at lunch and she says that Brian was very extravagant at Oxford, and went to Tallulah Bankhead's for cocktails on Thursday. I won't *have* it!!!' 'LuRA, Mrs. Nichols has put sherry in the soup. It's disgusting.' When he eventually departs this life, we'll be sitting at Nore one evening, and from somewhere *below* the floor will come, 'LuRA, the Devil says that Brian etc.' Love 'Paul' (Brian).

Continuing letters to his mother, from Frankfurt (November 1927):

... Please let me know whether you would like me to come home for Christmas. Frankly, I would like to, if you don't mind—I'm getting a little lonely. In a way I rather want to get to work in England with Robert (Byron) on certain projects. In my opinion, as far as I can truly judge, I have *enormously* benefited by my association with Prinzhorn, and my expedition generally. He has given me ground to stand on . . . and . . . I see little of him now, because—simply—it is not necessary. And it saves money. . . . I was in a hopeless, miserable tangle when I came out. Now the air is clean and cleared. *I wish to work*. I wish to reconstitute my existence. I don't say that I will never go to another party or drink another cocktail, but I can assure you that I have altered my grip of things entirely. I was diseased with *laissez-faire*. I now am *full* of energy . . . I simply must come home and make some money.

Dr. Prinzhorn was not so convinced that Brian could do without his help, and wrote to Mrs. Howard from Frankfurt at the end of November:

Dear Mrs. Howard, I am sorry that I have got to tell you that Brian told a friend of his he did not like to come any more. He had begun to write again, and what he wrote was much better than all he had shown to me before. ... About three weeks ago I felt already the danger that his admiration for me and the philosophical studies, which I like most, could go too far for his critical mind and that he would soon fall into the contrary, because he does not like to admire . . .

He really has extraordinary gifts especially in the literary direction—but it is out of my power, to help him in finding the centre of his own personality, if he does not like to go the severe and rather cruel road that only leads to this clear aspect: the destroying of any self-deception, which would permit him, to neglect and tyrannise his friends, to alter everything in his mind just after his own wishes and humours.

Perhaps he will find his way by his own forces—I would be very glad to hear so one day. I do not think I lost my time with him—nor does my wife, who spent more time and sorrows for his interests, than she ever did for somebody else.

---

[3] One of the duties of the faithful Eleanor (who was to remain with Lura Howard for well over 40 years) was to wash out Tudie's paint brushes, and as he liked to amble about stark naked while painting she was often to be heard screaming down the hall at the sight of him unadorned.

148

With my best wishes for the further development of your son, Yours sincerely, Hans Prinzhorn.

[Continuing letters to his mother] . . . There's no doubt—none at all—that Nore is one of the most charming small houses in England. Dissociated from any family bias at all—you made it. You have often expressed a desire to write. You have. You have written with stones, a far better book, I fear, than I will ever write. Nore is your book, and the advantage of your book is that *everyone* likes to read it and *no one* ever gets tired of it. If I have, ever, a son, and he asks why you never wrote anything, like me, I shall take him to the south side of the grass tennis court, and tell him to turn round, and look at the Lodgings over the Elizabethan garden. 'Sermons in stones, books in the running brooks'—they needn't all be in ink on paper. *Then*, Muzzy dear, he may ask for tangible evidence of his grandfather—and I don't know *what* I shall say, I'm sure! Perhaps I will point out the hard tennis court!

. . . You always put people you think a certain thing about into one class. You don't realise that people can be all sorts of things at once, and that *one cannot be sweeping about them.* You simply MUST read Jung *again*, if you have before. He's better than Freud, and treats sex as it should be treated. Nowadays one has just got to realise what sex *is*—of all sorts—and *deal* with it. But not misunderstand it, or make bogeys out of it. To speak plainly—you make a bit of a bogey out of homosexuality. *Naturally—you are worried into a state of prejudice on my account.* But *don't* be prejudiced. Admit facts for facts, and we'll arrange it all together. Most of my sex instincts, anyway, take themselves out in Art etc.—the remainder I must deal with wisely. So as not to offend anyone—most of all, you. But you musn't tell untruths to me, which you are inclined to do, about your beliefs. It's NOT hopeless, if we are sincere with one another. Your insinuations of impurity, uncleanliness, perversity, evil etc. only *cloud the issue.* They are wrong, and you know it. No sex is unnatural or impure or anything else. It becomes unhealthy, physically and mentally, if *it gets out of hand*—like food or anything else. Drink. But the roots of sex, buried as they are in the very life-spring of human nature, *cannot* be impure. It is idle to say that children are the only legitimate cause for sex, and that women are the only medium. It's like saying that people should only eat bread when they're hungry. It's penning in the infinite. However—fear you will never pay any attention to me on that score. Suffice it that my sexual side is under my control—that I am *utterly* sane in that respect, and that my work will render any worldly dangers in that line improbable. *Only, at present, I don't like women.* . . . I KNOW that my sexual instincts are NEITHER wrong nor right—they merely ARE.

You don't say anything definite about Christmas. Let's economise and go to Cannes. We'd have fun and sun, and I want you to go about a little, *abroad* a little. We will go and reconstitute ourselves in the sunshine. If my father must come too—very well.

Prinzhorn is helping me very much with my new book, which is going to be the fruit of coming here. It is the story, roughly, of a young Indian

Maharajah who makes it the object of his life to become an English gentleman, and gradually comes to the conclusion that that is the last thing in the world worth becoming. It brings in everything that I want to write about. I have planned it, and nothing remains but the writing of it, which will be a question of time. At present it is called *The Cow jumps over the Moon*. The Cow symbolises the Maharajah/India plus Nietzsche plus the *élan vital*. The Moon symbolises the English gentleman/England plus Christianity plus materialism. I am very excited about it, and feel confident of writing a book that will put me at the head of *my* generation.

Brian had not completely cut himself off from news of London life, as this extract from a letter from one of his closest friends, Méraud Guinness, shows:

... I don't feel you are missing much by not being here—London seems as dreary as ever except that Tanis gets smarter and smarter and more and more social—as for me, my life merely seems to get more and more involved and revolved until I feel quite dizzy. I find it very difficult to concentrate on social news—however, briefly, the Fancy Dress Ball [given for her and her sister Tanis by their mother]—I arrived from Paris one hour before it began and dressed as *Les Biches* in blue velvet and pink tights—only to find Nini Hart the-same-only-better. Practically everyone else came as Schéhérazade with oceans of artificial pearls strung under the chin and everywhere else in every available space. Except your father who wore a costume made of the red silk walls off the Grosvenor Galleries ... David (Tennant) has bought the flashiest, most enormous, cream and brown car in the motor show and drives about London in a black leather coat, followed by a large crowd ... Write to me in Paris, Love, Méraud.

Brian was to continue leading a double life on his return to London, sometimes writing poetry and working on his projected book with Robert Byron, at other times as one of the leaders of the Bright Young People. His attitude to women was ambivalent, to say the least. He still talked of his future children as if marriage would be bestowed on him at a suitably distant time, although he was quite open about his distaste for the female sex as such. On the one hand he would be genuinely concerned ('devastated') about an impending divorce, such as the Plunket-Greenes, and its consequent unhappiness for both sides; on the other he did not lightly forgive any of his past lovers should they be rash enough to take a wife, indulging in the most repulsive practical jokes at their expense which showed distinctly psychopathic tendencies.

13. A question of 'Values'

Where to start on Brian's post-Oxford, post-Frankfurt life? There are copious draft notes on a projected 'paper' to be edited by Robert and Brian. It is impossible to tell whose ideas came first. In one of Brian's many notebooks is the following draft scheme, mostly written in late 1927:

> VALUE—*Five Conversations*—edited by Robert Byron and Brian Howard. An Enquiry into Contemporary Values.
>
> *Prologue*: There is no Truth: there is only Value.
>
> This volume has been entitled *Value* less from an unseemly over-estimation of its worth by the editors than from their conception of its immense contemporary significance as a word. Truth, during the past, has occupied the position in the general mind, as a word, that Value will occupy in the future. The reason for this can only be inadequately represented by repeating that there is no Truth, there never has been Truth, and there never will be Truth. There is only Value. . . . Man can create Value and, in fact, man's function is the continual creation of new Values, but he has never been able, and will never be able to create Truth, for, as we shall never tire of repeating, *Truth does not exist.*

Brian sent these notes, together with endless variations and extensions of his theme to Robert Byron, who then started what seemed to become a singularly one-sided correspondence concerning this *Value* project, enclosing *his* version of a draft scheme:

> My dear Brian, I don't know whether you think this any good. Last time I sent you anything of this sort I begged you not to show it to anyone and you immediately did. This time *please* don't—otherwise this will get laughed at before it is launched. Fancy, for instance, Connolly hearing in cold blood that he is to write a story called 'The Red Earth of the South' at our dictation—
>
> Will you try and get hold of Evelyn (Waugh) and explain that the fact of his omission from writing anything is due to my having tried to keep each person down to one thing—and he is one of the two artists. But he must write obviously—someone is certain to fall out so that there will be a place—if not one will have to be made. Can you try to make some arrangements with Evelyn's father about our going to see him together [at Chapman and Hall, the publishers]—all this of course is subject to your approving of the enclosed as an outline—tho' details may annoy you. Yours, Robert. (*don't lose it*).

151

Robert's outline took the project one step further, with hypothetical titles for the various contributions, and random notes. Robert and Brian were to write the *Prefatory affirmations*, then in the 'Material' part Patrick Monkhouse would provide an essay on *The Threshold of Civilisation*, Henry (Green) Yorke a story called *The Factory*, and Tom Driberg a poem—*Restaurant*. Robert Byron felt humour was needed at this point so suggested a photograph, to be composed by Brian and himself, representing *The Impression recorded by the term 'World' on the mind of an English Bourgeois*. The next part, called 'Transcendental' would include an essay by Robert Byron on *The Philosophy of History and the future of Revealed Religion*, a symbolic story by Timothy Coghlin, *The Amours of a Ritualist*—'this is perhaps too frivolous a title', and a poem by Peter Quennell. Evelyn Waugh was to supply a drawing of *God* consisting entirely of abstract form—'yet in some measure coherent and having perhaps some slight relation to the Revelations of St. John the Divine.' The third part, 'Aesthetic' was to include an essay by Brian on *The Problem of Representation*, a symbolic story by Cyril Connolly called *The Red Earth of the South*—'only a southern setting can produce that pagan atmosphere, with which I feel you will infect this section', a poem by Harold Acton called *Michel Angelo*, a *Self Portrait* by William Acton—'Willie himself embodies the whole problem of the etherealisation of the sensual through aesthetic perceptions.'

Even though Chapman and Hall seemed favourable to the idea 'as they wished to keep in touch with the younger generation', and long form letters and synopses were sent to some of the potential contributors, and many hours spent on their arduous preamble, this *Value* symposium/magazine seems to have been still-born.

14. Ups and downs with the Bright Young People

From the sparse documentation of the next few years it would seem that Brian was going through one of his worst periods, drinking too much, desperately in love with a decidedly non-reciprocal young man, not yet established as a reviewer, and bemused by his position as one of the leaders of the Bright Young People. He stayed in various flats in differing grades of discomfort, running up bills at every complaisant restaurant, his worthless cheques finally having to be redeemed at each and every last moment by his mother. She would not give him a regular allowance, and although he would certainly have failed to live within it, he would at least have known the set limitations. As it was, like Oliver Twist he went on asking for more, but like the ageing spinster with sex he usually got too little, too late.

Although Brian's parents were beginning to lead separate lives, Lura, quite rightly, was not prepared to treat Tudie's withdrawal as an excuse for Brian to make his own bed of roses. It is true that every time he misbehaved in London and overspent he would be eased abroad, to their mutual satisfaction, but in his mother's eyes this recurrent but temporary exile was apt to extend rather than diminish his non-earning tendencies.

From Nore Brian wrote to William Acton of his present predicament in April 1928:

I returned to England in love with Germany, and I am only waiting until I accumulate sufficient funds to leave England again. I am heartily sick of London and London parties—which remain exactly the same as they were five years ago. In London NOTHING changes.

One day I went to stay with Henry and Daphne in their country cottage, where they are exceedingly happy with their gramophone, their cocktails and their mutual admiration. Of all people I met 'X' there, with whom I had cut off relationships nearly a year ago, since which time I have neither written nor spoken to him. He discovered, during the weekend that I had to go to Manchester (where I was going to interview Patrick Monkhouse about Robert's and my paper, all about which you doubtless know—it appears in the autumn[1]) and he asked me to stay the night with him. (He lives nearby.) Out of curiosity I went. Prepared, I will admit, to begin the tragedy all over again. Well, X came into Manchester, met me, and we went to Cochran's new *Revue* together, which was trying itself out there. The *Revue* has been praised beyond its deserts. There are some amusing

---

[1] This was wishful thinking; it never got beyond the planning stage.

Victorian dresses designed by Doris Zinkeisen, in lime colours, magentas, pale blues and sugar pinks—but nothing much else. Oliver Messel's contributions to it are not particularly good. But the Ballet always spoilt one for these pseudo-people.

After seeing the *Revue*, X and I motored back to his grim, square, isolated, grey, sad, pretentious, small, country, little house and had an exceedingly unappetising supper consisting mostly of cold beetroot and brand-new Graves. After supper, I waited—we both waited—for the drama to begin. I didn't know what sort of drama to expect. I didn't know why he had asked me, even. Anyway, I waited. Slowly, he walked over to the gramophone and put on a record. It was a Mendelssohn organ record. I stood this as best I might. Then he produced an enormous portfolio of drawings. He had been going to art school. I looked over these dreary scribblings with him—said nice things about them—and waited. He put other records on, things like *Hark! Hark! the Lark* and *In a Monastery Garden*. I squirmed about on an extremely unyielding sofa, and suddenly realised that I was maddeningly bored. *Bored*, with the person I had adored for nearly seven years—alone with him, too. I began to regret, as I listened to that unbelievable music, the nights I had spent playing *Petrouchka* to him, I did, indeed. Eventually, I became absolutely comatose with ennui, and tottered off to bed ... One cannot fight against that English blood. It is too thick—too strong. He has lost his charm—he is, now, just a little snob—eager, usual, frightened, conceited—finished, for ever ... Anyway, that is one very devastating section of my life done with, and a good thing too.

As for my work, I have nothing much to do now until the latter part of May, and June, when the hard work on the paper—which will probably be called *Values* comes on. Meanwhile I ache to get abroad. I really haven't the space to enlarge upon the aims and objects of Robert's and my paper. Roughly, it is meant to be the first concerted move on the part of our generation. It is carrying on the spirit of the *Candle* and the Eton Arts Society, whereas, of course, it is primarily, Oxford, not Eton, people. Still, we are a collection of people full of talent, and it would be a pity not to do something of the sort. I meanwhile publish nothing. It is my plan to wait, as regards my own work, until I am certain of its worth and potential success. I watch Robert and Harold (*entre nous*, now) publishing book after book ... gaining a little notoriety, but nothing really. I write, too, steadily, but I prefer to let my juvenilia remain in my notebooks. I don't want to be handicapped, in the future, by a mass of bad early stuff. I know I have a genius, of a kind, and I prefer to let it mature slowly. Meanwhile I educate myself. I am fortunate to have the money to live like this, I know.

Cornelian[2] [Harold's book] is having a moderate success, but I don't think he should have published it, do you? Don't please, Willy, tell him I said so. But it is essentially the clever young man's first novel—the thing that no one ought ever to publish. I'm not being malicious. It is my opinion, genuinely.

[2] Published by Chatto & Windus, 1928.

Lady Birkenhead is getting up an enormous pageant at a London Theatre (Daly's) in May—directed by Oggie Lynn—entitled *Hyde Park since 1765* in which I'm going to be Disraeli and Oliver (Messel) is going to be Byron. I don't know which of us will be the more ridiculous.

The Prince of Wales intimated his desire to lease this house for the summer at fifty guineas a week (the Metcalfes stayed here and told him about it) but we have refused. He'd only break all the furniture to pieces playing Blind man's buff with Mrs. Dudley Ward. However, I don't suppose we'd get quite as much as fifty a week again if we tried to let it. It's so small. But it is becoming a very charming place.

Brian's mother must have got restive at the lack of profitable results from his projected *Values* book, for within a month he was abroad again, writing to Harold from Arles:

. . . I left England, as I always leave, in a flash. I seem to be coming to the end of my parents' patience in the matter of remaining without a tangible occupation, and whenever this happens I seem to find myself abroad. I hope to make a little money out of writing about, and photographing, the really intensely interesting gipsy ceremonies at Saintes-Maries, on the coast near here. This country—which van Gogh and Cézanne loved so much—is really delicious. Pure, vivid colour and real *warmth* . . . I find it an ideal countryside for persons such as myself—no more feeling of being in a quarrelsome, rainy cabbage patch. I shall live down here eventually, I think. I like it better than Spain or Italy, or even Germany . . . though I have yet to see Austria. It is so curious to me that more of our friends have not been here—it has been the cradle of so much—the playground of Rome, so rich, so reliable in the matter of weather, so inexpensive, so dramatic in things to be seen . . .

He stayed at Arles for several weeks and Jimmy Stern remembers, in particular:

One Sunday, during service, in that fortified church at Stes.-Maries. At this time (needless to say, it did not last very long) Brian was obsessed by photography, or rather by taking photographs. It was as though no one had ever taken a photograph before. His new camera was like a toy at Christmas to a child. At such times Brian *was* a child, and at his most lovable; and most un-self-conscious, unaware, on account of the (for him) enormous concentration required. Oblivious of his surroundings, of the Sunday solemnity, of the packed pew in which we stood, and determined to steady his camera for a time-exposure, he suddenly saw—and promptly grabbed—what he considered would be next-best-thing to an actual tripod: the top hat of a distinguished-looking gentleman in the pew in front of us. Appalled, the owner promptly snatched it back.

'Silly man!' shouted Brian. 'As if one wants a hat in church!'

Brian expatiated on this occasion to his mother during May and June from Arles:

... Please get my six rolls of photographs developed at Kodak and make a TERRIFIC fuss *beforehand* so that they take exceptional trouble over them. I'm sending my manuscripts for *The Times* and the *Daily Express* (Driberg said he wanted it) first; the *Country Life* article will follow.

... It's the only Christian celebration left—half candlelight, half day-light, with the pointed ark containing the Maries' bones slowly dropping from the roof amid cries of *Vivent les Saintes Maries* ... a sense of miracle in the air ... heat ... babies making noises ... and then, in the unbearable sun, the Archbishop clambering into the little yellow fishing smack—the Curé shooing little boys away. The incompetence. The refusal of the boat to launch. The cowboys of the Camargue riding out into the sea, to make a double line, a road for the boat. Banners and flower-crowned images lurching into the first small ripples. I myself, I may say, a startlingly conspicuous figure, ten feet out in front of the crowd, unconcernedly photographing them, up to my waist in sea, fully and rather gaily dressed—having nipped off my shoes! The Anthony Edens, who I persuaded to come, perched on a nearby boat, shouting encouragement. But really, the *interiors* should come out. I experimented so much before. ... Concerning MONEY. I have spent just over a pound per day. *This is too much.* This doesn't mean I need any money now, you know. It's just to let you know.... But you can't afford *that, can* you? ... I hope, so very, very much, that I will make a success of the Stes-Maries articles. I have a double inspiration. Firstly, to uphold you—secondly, to defeat my father, who has filled me with such a *hatred* for him by his behaviour at the table and then at the telephone that I only long to say, 'You were wrong, you see, you were WRONG'. So what with love *and* hatred what cannot be accomplished? You will never regret sending me—it was the extra bit of indulgence which shattered all the wisdom of the disciplinarians. You'll see.

The family split was becoming definitive and Brian's cousin Carley writes:

The break between Tudie and Lura finally came as the result of Tudie's finding an unfinished letter from Brian—a love-letter, I gather, to one of his homosexual friends. The letter was between the leaves of a blotter on a writing desk at Nore, and Tudie was basking in the friendship of King George of Greece at the time. The thought that the King, or some other of their 'titled' friends, might have come across this letter, was the final straw. Tudie told Lura she could choose between him and Brian. So they finally separated and Nore was later sold.

In confirmation of this break Brian himself wrote to his mother years later, 'When I took my father out on to the lawn at Nore and told him I'd never speak to him again, I meant it. And I've done it'.

Carley continues,

156

Although Brian knew that his mother loved him, he also realised that she really adored his father, and that he, Brian, had not been first in her affection and perhaps never would be. Therefore, to me, Brian always seemed someone hungrily on the outside of his own family, not wholly in dead centre of his mother's attention; excluded from his father's affection—at first, for reasons he never knew (possibly an immature jealousy on Tudie's part, and a resentment at the added responsibility. Tudie was not able to accept responsibilities), and therefore unloved.

And so Lura chose Brian. But they couldn't live *with* one another or without one another. When Brian was grown, it often seemed to me that Lura leaned toward an almost lover-like attitude, which certainly could have done nothing but further complicate their mutual feelings. I've studied Tudie, Lura and Brian all my life, and found all three of them fascinating characters, but Brian with his gifts, not only of writing but of caricature, which he could easily have broadened into something of real worth and biting power, *perhaps suffered most*. A pattern for all time of how *not* to bring up a child.

Dr. Hans Prinzhorn, who still called Brian 'Kuno', continued to take an interest in him, and it was probably following on the suggestion in his letter from Frankfurt that Brian spent some time in Paris during the later months of 1928.

Dear Kuno, Your letter does not sound so badly—its contents as well as the hand-writing. There is, on the contrary, something in it of concentration and modesty, which I find superior to the ordinary state you were in last winter. Of course I can't judge about your steadiness and real vigour or *élan*. As to the Provence-impressions and the essay you are writing, could not this really be an earnest start to get into the business you are apt for? Which at all events is the only one I could imagine you dealing with and getting on nicely. But you know as well as I do, that you can't expect your family to provide you with everything for years and that life is brutal against everybody who does not get himself at least into a certain compromise—balance with it . . . So there can be found only one alternative: either you get a success with your writing now, in the moment of the most favourable exterior situation—or agree to take some job. No doubt I would avoid London at all events. What is the matter with Paris? Couldn't you stay there? I shall live in Paris from October to January and could have a look on you. But try at all events to get some regular work—you are (at least until now) not apt to live a grand-seigneur's life without getting into absurd situations at every moment. With my best wishes, yours sincerely, H. Prinzhorn.

To his mother Brian enthused about Paris:

It is so cheap . . . and I am so enjoying it. Everyone here is ABSOLUTELY DIVINE. I never *knew* Paris before. It is a wonderful place to live. If I could I would like to stay here and work. It's perfect for working. I've been writing. Also, I think I can make arrangements for my book (*Values*). Everyone here says it would make thousands for me in Germany, and I am trying to get an introduction to a publisher in Berlin. I am terribly glad I came. It's all been very *happy*, and a great *success*. I met Marie Laurencin yesterday. Everything is perfect. I knew my 'fate was changing'.

Back in London Brian wrote to Harold Acton, 'I am disgusted to have to return to this dull, damp, devilish country'. But was it so dull and devilish? John Sutro says of those times:

> It all appears as if one did nothing but drink and go to parties. It wasn't true, but inevitably one gets that picture of the 'twenties and 'thirties. We probably drank more than the present generation, but entertaining and drink were so much cheaper. We seemed to have more money to spend and it went further. The atmosphere was more like Dublin today. We were also lucky in that there were several houses in London where we could all meet for parties. Friends were welcomed, and time seemed to go very fast . . .

Allanah Harper, one of Brian's oldest and most sympathetic of friends even in the sad, later years, turns a more caustic eye on those memorable, if meretricious times:

> So much has been written about the Parties in the 'twenties. I must admit that I enjoyed them at the time, but on looking back upon them now, they appear like a Jerome Bosch hell. There were so many parties, but two remain particularly in my mind, one because I was one of the hosts and the other because it took place in a swimming bath.
> The first was called the Sailor Party, everyone had to be dressed as a French sailor. I think the only exception was Raymond Mortimer who came as a 'sponge-bag', and Mrs. Christabel McLaren who was regal as 'Rule Britannia'. Tallulah Bankhead, dressed in wide English sailor's trousers, was the noisiest person in the room, and her cacophonous laughter made it difficult to hear the band. Lytton Strachey came resplendent as an Admiral, but being both an amateur Admiral and dancer he got his sword between his legs and fell down, from which disadvantageous position he was rescued by Brian and Clive Bell. Soon afterwards I left, but heard that poor Gerald Reitlinger (who had kindly lent his house for the party) had to throw embracing couples—still clinging to each other—out into the street at five in the morning.

Gerald Reitlinger, to whom I wrote in search of further reminiscences, replied that all he could remember was not only quite unrepeatable, but that the period itself—the 'twenties and 'thirties—seemed as remote as the Saxon Heptarchy and even less real! However, a few weeks later serendipity caught up with him and out of a book he was reading fell one of the original invitations to the famous 'swimming bath' party.

It was printed—not engraved—in a rather nasty, fanciful script type with angular, non-decorative 'rules', and showed a singular lack of design sense in its presentation. It emanated from '44 Grosvenor Square', but did not carry the usual R.S.V.P. It read as follows:

Mrs. Plunket-Greene, Miss Ponsonby,
  Mr. Edward Gathorne-Hardy and Mr. Brian
  Howard request the pleasure of your company
  at St. George's Swimming Baths, Buckingham
  Palace Road, at 11 o'clock, p.m. on Friday,
  13th July, 1928.
    Please wear a Bathing Suit and bring a
    Bath Towel and a Bottle.
    Each Guest is required to show his invitation
    on arrival.

Tom Driberg, who had started working for the *Daily Express* early that year (and initiated a more biting, style of social journalism as 'The Dragoman' of 'The Talk of London' page) was a guest, and therefore able to cover the occasion more authentically than his rivals. It was something of a scoop for him, and he had to keep rushing out to the nearest telephone kiosk to keep the editions up to the latest scandalous 'happening'. This was his eye-witness account in the next morning's *Daily Express*:

The Bath and Bottle Party organised at the St. George's Swimming Baths last night was justified, if by nothing else, at least by the weather.
  Bathing costumes of the most dazzling kinds and colours were worn by the guests. Dancing took place to the strains of a negro orchestra, and the hardy leaped later into the bath, of which the water had been slightly warmed.
  Great rubber horses and flowers floated about in the water, which was illuminated by coloured spotlights. Many of those present brought two or three bathing costumes, which they changed in the course of the night's festivities. Cocktails were served in the gallery, where the cocktail-mixers evidently found the heat intolerable for they also donned bathing costumes at the earliest possible opportunity. A special cocktail, christened the Bathwater Cocktail, was invented for the occasion.
  The Hon. Stephen Tennant . . . wore a pink vest and long blue trousers. Mr. Clive Bell was another there, and Miss Elizabeth Ponsonby looked most attractive in a silk bathing costume of which the lower part was red and the bodice rainbow-like with its stripes of blue and red.

When the party was still going strong in the not so early hours of the next morning, and the bedraggled guests were playing up to the astonished gaze of the world's workers passing by, policemen were brought in to encourage the last guests to depart. It appears that their efforts were somewhat hampered by the more rapacious ones dragging them off to the changing room cubicles—in the hope of a general disrobing.

Allanah Harper has the last word, in retrospect:

The last party I went to with Brian at that period was one given by David Tennant. It ended in a free fight, I found myself in the middle of a jealous fracas, scuffle and scrimmage, which although it had nothing to do with me, resulted in my dress being practically torn off and tufts of my hair held up as trophies. After that experience I never went to parties of this kind again.

Tom Driberg, again in the *Daily Express*, filled out on the Bright Young People, eminent amongst whom were Elizabeth Ponsonby (later Mrs. Denis Pelly), Babe Plunket-Greene (née McGluskie, step-daughter of Arthur Bendir, then married to David Plunket-Greene, later to Count di Bosdari, and subsequently to an American Hollywood magnate), Edward Gathorne-Hardy, David Tennant, and Brian.

Elizabeth Ponsonby—Eternal sophistication looks out, a little wearily, from under her heavy eyelids, and her mouth, smiling as enigmatically as that of the Gioconda, can utter all knowledge and all wisdom.

Tom Driberg's up-to-date recollections are more explicit:

She was a very emphatic and rather pathetic character at the same time, rather thin and scraggy but quite pretty—a bit older than the others. She was one of the vital sparks who got the parties going, and I liked her tremendously. Babe was much more placid, absolutely round-faced and innocent-looking, with very little expression on her face, but very beautiful in a way.

And of David Tennant the *Daily Express* noted, 'When in London he drives about in an electric brougham [which belonged to his cousin, Stephen Tennant] of the Edwardian period. He says it is like riding in a bow-window . . .' Although Eddie Gathorne-Hardy had been at Oxford at the same time as Brian they became great friends only after one of the memorable Chelsea Arts Balls of these years. Cecil Beaton described him in his 'Diary of 1922'[3] as looking like Andrew Aguecheek: 'uncommonly tall, vellum complexion, tortoise-shell glasses, long hair, a bemused expression about his eyes and mouth. He had a deep crumbling voice, out-shone his brother in lewdness as he talked about seductions and affairs . . .'

Norman Hartnell gave a tremendously elaborate Circus Party in July 1928, and he remembers Brian coming to see him with a list of guests he wanted invited—mostly of the Bright Young People set. John Sutro thinks that it was

---

[3] *The Wandering Years—Diaries: 1922–39* by Cecil Beaton, published by Weidenfeld & Nicolson, 1961.

for the Circus Party that Brian perpetrated one of his less admirable jokes, and had several invitations professionally 'forged' so that he and his uninvited friends could go. Needless to say, having got in pseudo-legitimately they left soon after, not having found the party sufficiently to their taste! They probably preferred the Boat Party from Chelsea Pier to Tilbury when the favoured few were asked to come as 'stokers, third class', the others having to make do with first.

'Corisande' of the *Evening Standard's* 'Woman's World' column heralded one of the early 1929 efforts:

> Some of the smartest and prettiest women in London have been searching wildly for a dress appropriate for a Wild West Party, and cowboy costumes are at a premium ... Fifteen bachelors will be entertaining their friends in Lancaster Gate on 1st March ...

Donald Rolph remembers going on a great expedition to the East End in search of suitable cowboy clothes. 'The great fun was getting ready for the occasion, making all the preparations, dressing up. The actual party was often a bit of an anti-climax.' The *Evening Standard* described some of the hosts: ' "Hal" Acton was "Owner of the Premises", Lord Donegall "General Bottle-Washer", and "Jumbo" Joliffe "Chief Poisoner". *No Matrimonial Hoofing* was the legend that confronted those who wanted to dance, and the rule did not need an intolerable effort on the part of such as obeyed it.

Giving a 'freak' party was definitely the smart thing to do, and it was possibly as a gesture of non-conformity that Brian devised the most ambitious party of all in authentic 'Greek' as opposed to 'freak' style. The printed invitation itself was over sixteen inches high and nearly a foot wide.[4] It was a typographical triumph, headed THE GREAT URBAN DIONYSIA, flanked by two vertical columns symmetrically ranged at the outer margins; to the left, under the generic heading *J'accuse* came the hosts' pet hates, to the right under *J'adore* the loves of the moment. The centre of this document was taken up by lengthy instructions for the honoured guests and extracts from Jean Desbordes' *J'adore* and Cocteau's preface to that work, the paragraphs decoratively divided by typographical ornaments of a wine-bibbing nymph and a spreading vine pendulous with ripe bunches of grapes. This must be the longest invitation to a party of all time, and it is worth reproducing in full, with apologies to the people temporarily penned under the *J'accuse* column. I believe Gertrude Stein never forgot or forgave her placement there.

As with so many over-prepared enterprises, the party outplayed itself. Donald Rolph was briefed by Brian to lead the procession of guests up to Olivia Wyndham, who would be enthroned as Minerva. 'You'll be dressed in something beautiful, my dear, and ride in on a bull.' Donald says it was to have been a wonderful entrance—only the bull never materialised and the party fell a *little* flat. John Banting, who went as Mercury *à la Cocteau*, with a winged, engine-driver's hat, says Brian took immense trouble over this party, doing endless research at the British Museum.

---

[4] Reproduced in the photographic section.

The next day 'Domino' of the *Evening Standard's* 'What London Tells Me' column gave a dead-pan account, at second-hand:

... Last night a number of young Society people discovered the tedium of immortality. ... 'The Great Dionysia' was what they called the party, but at moments it was definitely sub-urban in its lack of excitement. These things were told me by one of the guests, whom I met this morning. He said the party was so wonderfully well staged that *one* was almost persuaded to take one's immortality seriously, and that is fatal.

There were, in fact, some wonderful costumes; everybody had to be dressed as a character in Greek mythology. Mr. Ernest Thesiger wore menacing black robes as the Medusa. Mr. David Tennant, in a red smock, looked extremely impressive. Mrs. Plunket-Greene, the clever and versatile young woman who was the hostess, wore a beautiful blue dress copied from a vase, and a wig fashioned in the Greek style of hairdressing ...

Maurice Richardson, who had not seen Brian since their Oxford days, met him in London again at a party in 1929:

There I fell for Valerie Taylor, in a gold evening dress. (She was then playing Nina in *The Seagull*; I thought I was going to make her but got brushed off later.) There was some sort of fight at this party and Brian said to me: 'As the only boxing intellectual present it will be your duty to defend me if necessary.' I also remember in Leonard Bower's flat in the Adelphi, Brian in love with a golden-headed young naval officer, showing me a cheque he was writing—*To the Bank of Love: Pay X-Y one million pounds.*

Rumour has it that Brian was at his apogee of manic-alcoholic depression alternating with elation about this time. He even threatened suicide and jumped into the Thames, but owing to a combination of low tide and deep mud he merely ruined the effect and his clothes, and had ignominiously to be smuggled back into a nearby flat for a hot bath. He was also being particularly befriended by women, although he only very occasionally accomplished the rôle of lover.

Between parties Brian, as penniless as ever, wrote despondently to his mother:

... Whenever I feel how silly and unkind it is of you to leave me in this condition, in which, to be frank, I can scarcely eat, I immediately say to myself that, viewed from your angle, what else can you do? So there it is. I'm afraid I can't give way. You, of course, are waiting for my friends to get to the end of their tether. Well, Eddie (Gathorne-Hardy) says he never will. But then he is very nearly an ideal character. He sees your idea as clearly as I do, but he thinks, as I think, that you are going about it mistakenly. I am a person, for better for worse, who simply does not react to even the most unpleasant compulsion, and I never will. It is part of my rather obstinate, selfish nature. What I *am* going to do (because I don't like the idea of your not knowing, and worrying) is live on Eddie until I have

162

written some saleable stuff, which I really hope to be able to do at once in the rather more comfortable surroundings of David's (Tennant) flat in the Adelphi, which Babe (Greene) has taken and lent me until the end of the month.

... You ought to know that I'd starve sooner than take a job except if I liked it, and could do it well and of my own free will. As for my character, you should be able to see, too, that in an odd, rather upsetting way it's a good one. I'm a small part genius, a large part silly, a larger part lazy, but the largest part a sincere person. And you don't deal with that sort of person in this sort of way. But don't count on either Eddie giving up helping me, or on my giving way. ... Poverty *can* paralyse, as well as spur on. I only hope it'll spur me! I am not ashamed of receiving material assistance from Eddie until I no longer need it, because we always share our assets of every kind. That is one element of friendship.

... *Couldn't* you have seen that it *might* have been better or righter to trust me with a little freedom for a *few* more months, *however* much I *have* procrastinated, now that I'm *really* serious, *really* trying to get a book done? Now I have got to write a quick, bad, *succés de scandale*. If I'd had no friends (these contemptible friends of mine—these 'freaks'—these bright young persons—these 'people we can't have at Nore') and had been unable to get a job, which is perfectly conceivable, I should have literally starved rather than ask you for money.

[Later] ... Things are going well. I have not yet actually *begun* on Selfridges[5]—but then Tony Bosdari has been so extremely busy. Next week, I fancy, will see things under weigh. He is quite consistent about ultimately making me a supervisor of the settings for First International Pictures, which the new company is being called. And Selfridges is settled, as I told you. I think our troubles are nearing their end. Because, you see, I have found work that is not only work, hard work, but also hard *play*. Things I *like* doing. And that has always been my necessity. I knew, one day, it would come. That's why I couldn't and wouldn't do anything until it did. I wouldn't have been a *success*. And there's little good really doing anything unless you are—character-question or no character-question.

Brian was not one to be easily discouraged, and despite jobs that never materialised and after the suspicion of a Greek fiasco, he conceived his most ambitious project yet, of which advance information was 'leaked' to Lady Eleanor Smith for her *Sunday Dispatch* feature 'From My Window in Vanity Fair':

BRUNO HAT. What will be almost a cocktail party, is the private view of the exhibition of paintings by Bruno Hat, to be held next week. Bruno Hat is a painter of German extraction, and his work is mainly of the abstract type, seemingly derivative from Picasso and Chirico. But the queer thing is that his work is not derived from any painter—he was discovered by Mr. Bryan Guinness near Clymping. Bryan Guinness went into a village general

---

[5] Probably some kind of display work which never materialised.

store, and entering by mistake the wrong room, he found a number of very good paintings in the modern French style.

The paintings were done by the son of the old lady who keeps the store. His father was a German, and he paints quite naturally thus without ever having been to Paris. In fact, he had only been to London about twenty times in his life, being very shy and retiring. So good were the paintings that they are to be on exhibition at Mr. Bryan Guinness's house in Westminster. I have seen one or two, and they are surprisingly clever.

Alas for scoops that turn into hoaxes. The day after the show (which took place on the 23rd July 1929) the newspapers gave it the full treatment, especially the *Daily Express*. A news column was headed with a photograph of 'Mr. Bruno Hat' in a wheelchair, the headline reading:

AMAZING HOAX ON ART EXPERTS
UNKNOWN ARTIST WITH FALSE MOUSTACHE
'MR. BRUNO HAT'

Half social and artistic London were the victims yesterday of an ingenious and amusing hoax at a cocktail party given by Mr. and the Hon. Mrs. Bryan Guinness at their house in Buckingham Street, Westminster. Mr. Bryan Guinness, a rich young Oxford graduate, is a son of the Right Hon. Walter Guinness, M.P., Minister of Agriculture in the late Conservative Government.

The guests included many eminent art critics and connoisseurs (though not the *Daily Express* critic). They had been asked to see the works of a hitherto unknown artist. Their hopes had been raised high by the invitation . . . The pictures were, in fact, the *Daily Express* understands, painted by Mr. Brian Howard, son of Mr. Francis Howard, the distinguished collector and Chairman of the National Portrait Society. They were of a kind familiar to all students of ultra-modern art, though some of them bore such titles as 'Leda and the Swan', and 'Portrait of my Brother'. . . . Some of the guests knitted their brows over a leaflet[6] lying on a table. It was headed *Approach to Hat*, and was a pompous parody of a 'high-brow' artistic eulogy.

In the same issue 'The Dragoman' (Tom Driberg) of the 'Talk of London' column gave further details:

'Mr. Hat'[7] sat in a wheeled chair, a morose, taciturn figure, with a marked German accent, a moustache worthy of Harry Tate and smoked glasses. In one hand he held a thin cheroot, in the other a glass of iced coffee, and as he sipped and puffed he grumbled about the colour of the walls and about the publicity he was receiving. Admiring connoisseurs crowded about him: 'I *do* so admire your rope frames, Mr. Hat,' said one. 'Ja,' said Mr. Hat, 'it ees mine own idea.'

---

[6] Apparently written by Evelyn Waugh.
[7] Impersonated by Tom Mitford.

... Mrs. Converse, the American hostess and artist, stood in apparent rapture before some of the exhibits. And an eminent art critic murmured his appreciation of the colour values. But some of the pretty girls who stood looking at Mr. Hat or drinking Mrs. Guinness' excellent cocktails, seemed, I thought, a little overwhelmed. Nothing, however, can overwhelm Mr. Maurice Bowra, who is an extremely brilliant and exuberant young Oxford don. He approached Mr. Hat, and began talking volubly in German. Mr. Hat made a gesture of distaste. 'Ach!', he said, 'I am naturalised Englisch. I do not care to remember that I speak Cherman.'

Although it had begun as a joke and a hoax Diana Guinness (now Lady Mosley) thinks that Brian was secretly disappointed at not being hailed by the critics as a great new discovery. She remembers the pictures as being, 'lovely, amusing and decorative', Lytton Strachey even going so far as to buy one. Soon afterwards, according to the *Sunday Graphic*, Evelyn Waugh showed his latent antagonism to Brian by painting a parody of Brian's parodies 'as a skit on the sort of atrocities which all the would-be connoisseurs admired at the Bruno Hat exhibition'.

Despite the parties and the hoaxes that must have occupied so much of his time, Brian was by now seriously considering writing to be his vocation, and he would make notes for himself—for inspiration, for discipline, as a matter of principle—but never, under any circumstances, were they brought into practice. In one of his numerous, large notebooks (he loved to *start* one, rarely to finish it) is the following outline:

THE NOVEL. 45,000 words, 5,000 words per week. The descriptive-parts must be poetry, rather in the manner of Virginia Woolf. The dialogue, of which there must be a lot, very realistic. The tone of the novel must be light and humorous without being in the least satirically so, like Firbank. Serious childishness, rather. No 'wit' and, of course, no 'epigrams'. *There must be a supernatural flavour*, about ordinary incidents. It must be outspoken, conveying the impression that it could not be anything else.

The following story, *Today!*, shows his highly charged 'supernatural' imagination at work. He also translated it into French, but I can find no trace of its publication in either language.

TODAY!

Today I begin my life! Today I command myself to be re-born, at eight o'clock in the morning. Today shall be one life. The first. It is eight o'clock. I rise. The English country is outside my window. Still simple, and still old. But I am no longer twenty-three years of age. I am one year of age. Therefore I will disregard the simple English country. Time has stopped. I have stopped it. Today it shall always be the Present, every moment. You will ask why I am doing this? The answer is that I am preparing to go to Paris. I must lead new lives henceforward. Each day, a life. In Paris, I must live lives in this way. Today is a test. Today I begin. I am on my way to London, in the small motorcar of yesterday. 'Mother! it is so sad that we have only one life to live. So little time. I must run, every moment. I must run so fast that I keep level with Time. That is how I shall live one life every day. If Time gains an inch on me in the race, I die. That is death.' Trees catch fire as we pass. As we roll slowly on to London, the streets disappear in flames. They cannot run. That is because they cannot love, as men can love. If they loved, they would not burn, but live; *Today I love everything, and tomorrow I shall love even more.* I love the earth, and even the heat of the burning trees which is so sad. I love my lover. But I love the Present most of all. I love it so much that I am running to keep up with it, so fast that my heart nearly bursts. I love it so much that today I am living the first of my new lives.

We have arrived in London. I will take the lift. 'How are you, Brian? We did not expect you so soon.' 'No,' I reply 'but let us go at once.' I run round the rooms. The sun follows me, laughing. *'He knows,'* the sun chuckles, *'he knows.'* I run round and round. David begins to run with me. Hermione has only just finished her bath, but she runs with us, her bath towel flying between the fingers of the sun. It is like a game children play. As she runs, her clothes leap up from different places on the floor, and embrace her. Flap, flap, flap, flap, and *flap.* She is dressed. Her yellow, blue and white scarf is the sun's flag. 'My flag,' roars the sun, shouting with laughter, as we run out of the room and down the stairs. It is quicker than waiting for the lift.

The car is waiting in the streets. It is murmuring impatiently. The driver seems a man of another and a future age, so perfectly does he fit into my life today. Round his neck is a piece of fine fur. His cap is wrenched down on one side of his face. His face is like a mad eagle. A beam of blue light streams out of each eye. They swerve, these thin blue beams, from one side of the street to the other, like endless rapiers.

We start forward into London. The engine explodes, like a big gun firing at regular intervals. At each explosion a house slides into the Thames, causing a tidal wave which washes away corpse after corpse from those which hang eternally over its banks, looking for nothing. At once, we are travelling at fifty miles an hour. Our feet drum on the floor, we still run inside the car. The car is enormous, the bonnet is a little bit longer than Buckingham Palace. Consequently we pass Buckingham Palace before we pass it. The sun is following us! We are running level with the Present! I realise with a jolt of pleasure in my heart, that no time has elapsed since I got up this morning! The sun follows us, shouldering his way through clouds of every colour. It is October, according to yesterday, according to the Past. But now, in the Present, it is no month, it is No Time. The weather shows that it is No Time. Never has there been such peculiar weather.

The chauffeur is Von Möltke. He screams his orders to the passing traffic with the godlike authority of a future Von Möltke. Everyone makes way for us. They make way sadly, for they know they are doomed. They are slipping back. They are losing the race. They are being caught in the Past.

The blue swords that stream before us from the chauffeur's eyes fence together, but they fence *for* one another. Clearing the traffic. The chauffeur's high, steel voice directs them. Each explosion drives a thousand people, a thousand houses back into the Past.

We are in the country. The speed increases to eighty miles an hour. The chauffeur is Nietzsche. I see this plainly now. With Nietzsche as chauffeur *we may gain on the Present! We may reach the Future!* The trees and fields that we pass do not burn. They are green. The sky is quite clear. We watch the sun as it rushes along overhead. We have no shadows. We laugh, louder and louder, cheering it on. 'Sun!' we shout, 'still following us? Still following us?' The sun dips in its course. The wind that flies past becomes southern. The sun answers, 'Yes, I follow! I will keep up with you. I love you. You are the parents of the Future. I love you.'

We arrive at David's house, where we are to eat. Nietzsche jumps out of his seat, clearing the bonnet of the car in one leap. The airplane stands waiting. The propeller is already invisible with speed. Humming with impatience. We run into the house. Ah! but it is difficult to keep level with the Present now. Lunch is not ready. We run up and downstairs. We run right up into the attic, and out on the roof. We are frightened that the sun will go on without us. No. There is the sun. Dancing with impatience a few thousand feet above the roof. Whirling and bounding in great epic circles. It waits for us. We are still level! We run downstairs. The dining-room is filled with white light. We throw great pieces of bread and meat down our mouths. Outside, in the courtyard, Nietzsche is massaging the silver airplane. He does not have to eat. 'Quick,' David hisses 'we have no time for coffee.' The servant is terrified. He pours the coffee straight into our mouths from the silver coffee pot. We are scalded, but we swallow, and are happy. We have not ceased to run. We ate our food running. We run out to the airplane. I leap into the front seat, and drag Hermione in after me. She lands on my stomach, head first. There is no time for us to arrange ourselves. Who would arrange himself for the sake of comfort when, by so doing, he loses happiness? Because, to be the Present is to be happy. Already the airplane has risen. The earth, betrayed, turns over on its side and resolves to die. The sun grunts as it increases its speed. Pieces of fire shoot off its sides, so fast does it go in order to keep level with us. Now, Hermione is sitting on my lap. She is laughing uncontrollably. Sometimes she tries to say 'I live! I live!' but all that comes out of her wide red mouth is laughter. David drives us faster and faster. Below, an infinite distance below, we see Nietzsche driving back to London. The countryside splits into two pieces to let him pass. The car seems like a tiny golden bullet piercing the surface of the earth. The fields part before him, like green cloth being torn in two pieces. We seem to hear the sharp, small echo of his mad commands.

We are rising continually. Hermione and I peep ahead between the black pistons of the engine. They crash up and down like the fingers of the fastest negro pianist in the world. I have no sense of vertigo. I am in the Present. I peer down over the side. I see the Past. The clouds of London rise again to meet us. Directly in front is the largest white cloud. It is made of marble.

We will smash to pieces on it. It is made of ice. It will destroy us! It is the gate of Heaven. It will break an anti-Christian airplane to powder! But overhead the sun bellows down words of comfort to us. 'Don't be frightened. You are safe. I will protect you. I am the Sun, and I am Dionysos. I am the Earth as well as the Sun. You are my chosen children. You are the parents of the Future!'

We fly straight on. I see, I see. This cloud is the white beard of God, the old God, the God of the Past. It is made of soft, cheap, animal hair from a theatrical costumier. We meet it. We pass through it like a living needle. There is a smell of dust, that is all. We have transfixed God's beard. Now we are in Heaven. Long, thin angels with faces like white mules fly from us in every direction, their starched nightdresses crackling in the wind. They are all hermaphrodites. They were hiding behind God's beard! Away they go, like heavy fragments of newspaper, too frightened of us to scream, too frightened to do anything but make an undignified escape. Their harps fall down, moaning, to the thickly growing roofs of suburban London like stones. But they turn into rain as they fall. They were made of cold, dead ice, those harps. What cold skeletons of tunes they must have played! We have flown through Heaven, and Heaven was defeated! I scream down the speaking tube to David in the back seat. 'Oh, David! Did you see how frightened the angels were!' 'Yes,' he screams back 'we are nine thousand feet high. I thought Heaven was higher, didn't you?' 'David,' I scream 'look—look!' For we are entering the largest amphitheatre in the cosmos. The amphitheatre of Heaven. On either side clouds as large as continents form two enormous curving walls. Beneath us are clouds. The sun, whizzing along above us, has lit a white fire within each cloud. They seem incandescent. All is empty. The people of Heaven have run away. The clouds divide beneath us. I see that each cloud stands upon a pillar of rainbow. A broken, brilliant rainbow connects each cloud with the suburbs of London. 'Brian!' David screams to me 'I am the new Satan. Milton must now write *Paradise Lost* again. I conquer Paradise.'

I am growing frantic with ecstasy. Of course David is Satan. I begin to recite down the speaking tube. 'David! This is the last time Milton shall be spoken. Listen:

> At last his Sail broad Vannes
> He spreads for flight, and in the surging smoak
> Uplifted spurns the ground, thence may a League
> As in the cloudy Chair ascending rides
> Audacious . . .

'Stop!' David interrupts. 'I will continue:

> . . . but that seat soon failing, meets
> A past vacuitie: all unawares
> Fluttering his pennons vain plumb down he drops
> Ten thousand fathom deep!

Now Brian, the old Satan fell out of control. The new Satan shall fall because he wishes it. He shall not meet the vacuity of the Past. The new Satan is the Present. He leaves Heaven because he has conquered Heaven, and Heaven is empty and useless to him. He has caused Heaven to become the Past. *Now, I fall!*

The airplane stands on its head. We descend. I watch a machine which tells our speed, 100 miles an hour. 110 miles an hour. 120 miles an hour. The wires between the wings sing with triumph. The earth beneath, the houses, the fields and the aerodrome, turn over and over in agony and terror at our holy approach. The sun falls at our heels, chanting a hymn. To the new Satan, the parents of the Future, the conquerors of Heaven, Time, and the Past.

We land. We jump out. The airplane folds itself up and packs itself away in its hangar. We rush into a taxi. I get out at my house in the middle of London. I go to bed. I shut my eyes. I open them. It is eight o'clock, still. Today I begin my life! Today I command myself to be re-born, at eight o'clock in the morning. Today shall be one life. The second.

Both David Tennant and his first wife, Hermione Baddeley, confirm that *Today!* is an imaginative account of true events. She writes:

I do indeed remember taking Brian over to Paris in our Moth. He was very fond of flying with David, but on *this* occasion we touched down at Lympne aerodrome and the authorities stopped our journey as we were overweight (the Moth was an aeroplane made for two!). So we had to leave Brian at Lympne while David flew me to Paris, he then returned for Brian and we all finally teamed up in Paris and celebrated in no uncertain manner.

Brian was a dreamer as well as indefatigable organiser, his imagination sometimes taking precedence over actuality. His notebooks were filled with his 'ideal' menus, seating arrangements for little parties of seventy or more in the desolate La Napoule house he was lent one year, or complete casts of characters for elaborate fancy dress themes for Parties that Never Were, with indications not only of who was to come as who, but also with whom.

To jump forward in time, one of the last of the wild parties (as late as 1931) ended in disaster. It was called the White Party (there had been a series of 'coloured' parties) because the host, Sandy Baird, who gave it in a big barn attached to his mother's country house in Kent, insisted on an all-white theme. A band came down from London, John Banting decorated the place with all sorts of things painted white—branches, a bicycle and so on, and of course everyone came dressed all in white. There was a row towards the end of the party between some of the guests, and one young man drove off wildly with Elizabeth Pelly. The car crashed and he was killed, but she was unhurt. It made headlines in all the papers, and this accident helped to sober up the Bright Young People more than any amount of adult disapproval.

Brian missed it because he was abroad, but on hearing of the accident from his mother he promptly replied:

169

... The 'White Party' sounds as if it had been very amusing. I wish I had been there. If it still shocks you when high-spirited young people get a bit tipsy (though of course to drive a car drunk is monstrous) you must find both History and the U.S.A. very alarming indeed. You doubtless visualise that party as an unbridled orgy of stupefying dreariness conducted by brainless and worthless nobodies—or at least would seem to visualise it from your tone. I see it as an amusing, wildish party given by the only group of young people outside the Continent who—motley in social status though they may be—know genuinely how to enjoy themselves, rid as they are of most of the restraints self-imposed by their more titled fellows— restraints of social aspirations and sexual taboos. Years ago, such a group was led by Nancy (Cunard) and Iris (Tree)[8] and Diana Cooper. Daddy— and it is simply no USE denying it—would have been proud to have been at their parties (he was at one or two and was heartily disliked). Daddy's whole life is so tainted with snobbery that he is busy erecting what begins to look like a first-class tragedy out of what remains of it.

---

[8] 'Who mildly outraged the aristocracy by leading what was plainly a more or less agreeable existence', according to Brian's essay on *The Modern English Girl.*

15. Poet-critic in the balance

1929–1930

After reading of the ups and downs of those frenetic days with the Bright Young People it is surprising to realise that all except two of the eighteen poems in Brian's forthcoming collection were written at Nore or in London during 1929 and 1930, and at La Napoule where, as John Banting writes, they spent some months in a borrowed villa during the summer of 1929 and the following spring:

We decided to go to the South of France together to work in some small place on the coast, away from the hurly-burly and expense of smart places. Of course we finally veered towards Cannes, where we met several mutual friends. One of them, Peter Spencer-Churchill (now Lord Churchill), was staying at La Napoule where he knew of an empty villa. The owner agreed to let us stay there rent-free until it was sold. We hired beds and bedding from an hotel and bought plain kitchen tables and deck chairs, and a *batterie de cuisine*. The rate of exchange was then much in our favour, and we were happy on very little money.

The villa was right on the sea and larger than it appeared. There were four long rooms, two bathrooms, several small bedrooms and *five* lavatories. It had been owned by a doctor, who must have been treating resident patients. All the walls were white, and with our sparse furniture the general effect was that of a studio. There was no hampering effect of domesticity, and with such surroundings it was ideal for work. It was one of the happiest and busiest periods of my life. Brian chose a small room, three sides of which were windows, jutting out over a small boat-house, and nearest to the sea. In fact, so near that one windy night the 'tideless' Mediterranean rose up and slapped out one of the windows. During the periods of the mistral the shutters rattled continuously, but we got used to it—more or less.

Although all sorts of friends came and stayed we both got a lot of writing and painting done. Sometimes we would take the bus into Cannes to the *Boeuf sur le Toit*, and if we did not have the money for a taxi we would walk the nine kilometres back, along the coast-line road. We met Clive Bell there and Brian treated him with the respect and appreciation due to the first English art critic to recognise the genius of Picasso, Braque, and others. We three had a festive night at the *Boeuf* and Clive Bell certainly enjoyed Brian's company.[1]

---

[1] John Banting notes: 'It is sad to read of the later episode recounted by Sir Roy Harrod (on page 325), as Brian always had a regard for creators or innovators of the past.'

We were content with a fairly frugal life, relieved by sallies into the bars of the Majestic or Carlton, where the atmosphere was Firbankian. The *Continental Daily Mail* listed the names of new arrivals with strange titles and names, probably unknown to *Debrett* or the *Almanach de Gotha*. (The Riviera still has a Firbank fantasy about it, and can be very funny if one is not horrified.) Brian said that a book should be made of its crazy architecture— *Belle Epoque*, Oriental, Mock-Tudor and *Faux-Corbusier* all mixed up, whilst only a few miles away was a 'Scottish castle' with palm trees on the terrace.

This Chateau de la Napoule belonged to Henry Clews, a rich American sculptor and individualist. Taking our morning swim in the warm sea, we would see him and his wife breakfasting elegantly and graciously on their terrace, attended by a butler in black. It looked very formal from the distance, and probably enjoyable too. When Nancy Cunard was about nine or ten this Mr. Clews made a marble bust of her with an owl sitting on one shoulder. When asked by her sadistic governess, 'Why the owl?' he replied, '*Say lar mistaire dans l'arme de mademoiselle . . .*' His carvings on the large stone entrance included sympathetic dislikes with names such as 'Business Sharks', 'Social Climbers', and so on. We never met him, nor wished to.

It was there that Brian Wrote several of the poems for his book, *First Poems—God Save the King*, later published by Nancy at her Hours Press. I had two commissions for mural decorations, and a project for redecorating the Cannes *Boeuf*, which never materialised. But after several months the villa was sold, and we had to leave.

Brian wrote several letters to Alan Pryce-Jones from La Napoule, the first being particularly nostalgic for the Oxford *neiges d'antan*:

. . . How strange it is the fateful way in which Oxford has gone from bad to worse during the last three years or so. The last time I went there it was almost insupportable—nothing but Belgian butcher-boys buggering bar-maids almost in one's lap. I feel, at least for the time, that I'm well rid of it all—a deliquescent Oxford, an Alhambra that has somehow become a citadel of all one fears (I shall go there, doubtless, quite often, when I return—but more, now, for copy than copulation). It is a ludicrous, and an easily misconstrued, thing, for an old reprobate like myself suddenly to acquire standards, disdainfulnesses—but really I begin to prefer the politer forms of debauch.

. . . . A day or so ago I went to Monte Carlo. It was a disappointment. I had expected a large, wicked grandeur—an architecturally well arranged collection of poisoned wedding cakes. But there was nothing but two large Bath buns of buildings—the Casino and the Hotel de Paris, stumpily dumped down in a single acre. The vegetation was amusing, so manicured . . . But inside the Garnier Casino it was simply Harrods, without the stock, but with the people.

[Later] . . . the 'anthology' is to be of *unpublished* work. Please, if you can, give me two or three poems—if you can rake them up by the beginning of April. I *so* want as much as I can have of yours.

172

This referred to an anthology of *Post War Poets* that Leonard Woolf had commissioned Brian to edit. They had been introduced when, as literary editor of the *Nation* Mr. Woolf was trying out a lot of young people from Oxford and Cambridge for reviewing. Although a dozen or so of the best had sent in their offerings, by invitation, the book never materialised, at least not under Brian's umbrella. Some of these poets became decidedly agitated, C. Day Lewis asking for his poem *Ode to Autumn* to be left out, 'as this now seems to me an exceptionally bad poem'; Louis MacNeice, having sent his selection to Brian in longhand, hoped 'the fact that they are not typed is not criminal?' He wanted to see proofs, 'as I invariably suffer from insidious misprints.' William Plomer suggested two other suitable contributors—Douglas Garman and Roy Campbell, and modestly asked in a postscript if contributors were to be paid. Brian had already been sent original poems by Richard Church, William Empsom, Robert Gathorne-Hardy, Robert Herring, Peter Quennell (from Tokyo, tastefully typed on Japanese hotel writing paper, with blithe disregard for the guiding *vertical* lines), Edward Sackville-West, Stephen Spender, and others so confident—or the opposite—that they did not sign their manuscripts. It would have made an interesting anthology.

In the summer of 1930, unlikely as it sounds, Brian abandoned London temptations in favour of a caravan tour in Scotland, from where he wrote to his mother:

It's more beautiful than words can describe, and I feel so *well!* I cook; wash up; wash myself in icy water in little burns; rise at 8; sleep at 10. I have been writing you your birthday poem, but I'm not going to send it. It has been too much for me as usual. I'm afraid. If you only knew how many times I've had to give up doing it in my life. My only chance, about writing poetry, is to keep more or less 'calm'. *Emotion remembered in tranquility.* But whenever I start writing a poem to you for you I always get into such a *state*. My love for you is fundamentally *all* my love for *everything*. It's like trying to take a part from a whole, that won't be divided.

While travelling in Scotland Brian received a telegram from his father saying that he could not return to the London flat (where he was temporarily boarding with a mutual friend of his parents) owing to some alleged misbehaviour of his, or one of his friends. Brian was most incensed at these allegations and immediately put the matter 'in the hands of my solicitor, as slander may be involved.' His reaction to a suggested meeting with his father was promptly negative:

My dear Father, . . . I am extremely sorry that you have been worried. I hope, you will understand me when I say that on my return early next week I cannot see you. My reason is due neither to want of affection, nor of respect, but simply that I can see no reason whatsoever why you should suddenly find yourself compelled to assume a rôle which, if you had ever really wished to, you would have assumed fifteen years ago, and that since I have never had any reason to suppose that my reputation has benefited

173

more than it has lost at your hands, I can see nothing but a mutual embarrassment in our putting our heads together over anything which may affect it now.

... I hope you will not let my intended action in this case interfere with our present relationship, which, nowadays, is quite a happy one. Your affectionate son, Brian.

No more was heard of, this incident. Meanwhile the struggle for survival, after his return to London, was still being carried on by letter to his mother:

This is a begging letter—begging for money—to allow me to stay in London. I have drafted a talk on poetry for the B.B.C., and Moray McLaren is going to try and get me a job on the strength of it next week. I have finished two reviews for the *New Statesman*. Finally, I have written four thousand words of a novel which I intend to continue daily until it is done. It will produce immediate money—whereas the 'anthology' will only produce eventual money—indirectly, articles etc. Do you realise that to write *intensely*, as I do, is almost agony in itself? It is a terrible labour—a page of my book. It is poetic, concentrated—my writing—if I write any other way it is bad. It's no *good* trying to make me a journalist. I would rather kill myself. Fortunately, I am the kind of writer who will make money. It is only *now* that it is desperate. Your thoughts are these, 'You can work perfectly well at Nore and ought to be glad to have the chance, etc.' Yes, I know. I *am* glad I have a home, you and Nore. But I *can't* work there. My father—the prohibition of my friends—and the last, most important fact, that the person I love next to you is up here—don't you see I can't come? ... I call upon you to help me, probably for the last time. Not to help me for a week, a month, but to say, 'Brian, you shall be assured of your £5 a week from now until you can make it yourself—which I know and you know will be very soon.' ... Nancy (Cunard) and I did the proof of my book. Daddy has been so appalling to Lady C. about me. He's been saying amongst other things that I haven't written the poetry I propose to publish and the whole thing's a fraud on Nancy. Naturally, she's furious. ... I cannot agree with you that to deprive me of all money would be good for my character. *Success will come.* Think of when my poems appear, and all the really important people like them. Remember I love you—more than everyone *really*. Forgive me for what I have been—understand, if you can, what I am—and be happy about what I will be. We'll triumph—yet.

It is now that Brian should have reached his turning point, the crucial factor being whether he could sustain the reviewer's grind *and* produce original work of his own. He had already contributed one or two reviews to the *New Statesman and Nation* in the spring of 1930, anonymously or as 'Proteus'. His first signed article (probably thanks to Raymond Mortimer, who believed in giving by-lines to writers) appeared in November of that year, and was a long appraisal of T. S. Eliot's poetry, and specifically of his new poem, *Ash Wednesday* (Faber). Brian opened with:

174

1906 Lura Howard with Brian, whose beautiful eyes even impressed his 'supercilious' godfather, George Meredith

*910 Caught in pensive mood and immaculate
ilor suit*

1915 Playing with his first pet, Squeezle, a guinea-pig

1917 'I am homesick . . . with constant fits of moodiness'

1894 Francis (Tudie) Howard, Brian's father, aged 20

Early portrait of his wife, Lura, by Francis Howard

Grandfather William Chess, ex-Civil War Artillery Captain

Tudie: 'a beautiful figure, a bitter enemy, a warm friend'

?10 Brian's beautiful grandmother, Mrs T. P. O'Connor

b-grandfather 'Tay Pay' O'Connor, at home in Chelsea

1922 Eton school play, 'Howard showed real dramatic power'

Lura: 'most distinguished grace of appearance and manner'

Edith Sitwell to Brian '. . . you will become a very fine writer'

Christmas 1922 'I was really heart-broken at leaving Eton'

1922 Inspiration for Sulgrave Manor
'Algerian Prince' hoax

'923 In post-Eton, pre-Oxford period, by Ambrose McEvoy

1925 Harold Acton, friend and rival at Eton and Oxford

1927 Cherwell 'Postscript' impression by Mark Ogilvie-Grant

The Railway Club at Oxford, which John Sutro conceived and Harold Acton dominated. Left to right, back row: *Henry Yorke, Roy Harrod, Henry Weymouth, David Plunket-Greene, Harry Stavordale, Brian Howard;* middle row: *Michael Rosse, John Sutro, Hugh Lygon, Harold Acton, Bryan Guinness, Patrick Balfour, Mark Ogilvie-Grant, Johnnie Drury-Lowe and porters*

1927 Alone in Frankfurt, seeing life and being analysed

1928 In caricatured maturity, by 'Angus' in the Cherwell

1925 Happy days with Henry Weymouth and Daphne Vivian

In 'Bright Young People' era, John Banting's caricature

1926 Nore, the Howard's country house at Hascombe, Surrey

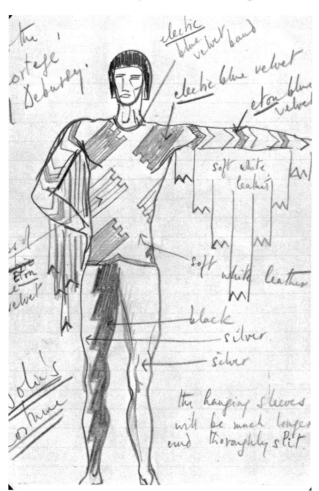

Brian's costume design for Dolin (Charlot Show of 1926)

Late 1920s, by Cecil Beaton

*Self-expression by Brian,
as aspiring art photographer*

THE GREAT URBAN DIONYSIA

J'ACCUSE

J'ADORE

J'ACCUSE

Intellect
No
Ladies and Gentlemen
Chic
Anglo-Catholics
Hicks
Public Schools
O.T.C.
Officers
Débutantes
Ascot and Lords
English " Society "
Those incredibly " Private "
Dances
The *Tatler* and the *Sketch*
The London Group
Masters Club
Orpen
Tell-tale-tits, slit-tongues,
lickspittles and all social
snippet writers
Sadist devotees of
blood-sports
Keyserling
James Douglas the Bigot
People who still think
that a title is of the
slightest importance
Gertrude Stein
Bowler hats, the
gravestones of charm
People who find
themselves out of
place in a full
third-class carriage
anywhere in the world
Missionaries
John Bull, Blunt and all the
rest of that ranting,
canting rot
Le Touquet
" Eligible bachelors "
The Spectator
The Fortnightly Review
Hodder & Stoughton
People who dislike going
to pubs
Elgar
People who say they can't meet
so-and-so because " they've got
such a bad reputation, MY DEAR"
Belloc
The sort of young men one
meets at great, boring, sprawling
tea-parties in stuck-up, moronic
country houses, who say, when-
ever anyone else says, at last,
anything worth saying: " Well,
I prefer Jorrocks " and snort
into their dung-coloured plus-
drawers
Inge
The Bright Young People
Melton
All those people with faces like
forks who roar about " bad
form "
People who confuse nakedness
with indecency
Sir Reginald Blomfield
Nationalism

THE DIONYSIA WILL OCCUR THIS YEAR
AT 1 MARYLEBONE LANE, OXFORD STREET
(BEHIND BUMPUS'S) ON THE 4TH OF APRIL 1929
AT 11 P.M., CELEBRATED BY
BABE PLUNKET GREENE
IN HONOUR OF THE TWENTY-FOURTH BIRTHDAY OF
BRIAN HOWARD
AND BECAUSE THE NEW ATHENS IS SORRY THAT
DAVID TENNANT
IS GOING TO ARCADIA

Each guest must be dressed as a *definite* character in *Greek*
mythology, and is bringing wine. Extraordinarily beautiful dresses, which are not expensive to make, may be
copied with great ease from the Greek vases in the
British Museum.

The accompanying card will admit you, and you alone.
Please do not forget to bring it with you.

" Jeunes gens glacés des villes qui portez votre intelligence
à côté de vous comme une canne, relisez cette *Lettre a
Maritain* si mal, si vite lue, que vous avez prise pour une
confession bruyante, alors que c'était un de ces cris du
coeur où les doctrines n'ont que faire. N'entendez-vous
pas crier dans les glaces? Ne voyez-vous pas cette preuve
que Dieu exige toutes vos forces et tous vos scandales ?
Aimez, aimez, aimez, comme bon vous semble et quittez
cet air fin qui paralyse les ailes et vous empêche de voler."

from " J'adore "
by
JEAN DESBORDES

" Jeunes gens qui m'écoutez, qui me regardez, qui me
croyez, jeunes gens de partout, du vieux monde et du
nouveau monde, je monte à un balcon en l'air qui
domine les murs qu'on cherche à mettre entre nous, les
mensonges et ma légende; je vous parle: ce livre
enseigne l'anarchie nouvelle qui consiste à aimer Dieu
sans limites, à perdre votre prudence et à dire tout ce
qui vous passe par le coeur."

the concluding paragraph in
the Preface by
JEAN COCTEAU
to " J'adore "

J'ADORE

Intuition
Yes
Men and Women
Elegance
Love
Plato
Charles Chaplin
Robert Bridges
The Crystal Palace
Nietzsche
Lily Morris
Picasso
Wild Flowers
Eluard
Tennyson
Acrobats
Duveen
Mathias Grünewald
Boxing
Kokoschka
American Food
Edison
Duncan Grant
Dionysos
Einstein
El Greco
Grass
Donne
Wood and Stone
Slevogt
Segrave
Germany
Stanley Spencer
Jazz
The Incas
Granville Barker
Lindbergh
Sherlock Holmes
Desbordes
Russian Films
Cocteau
The Mediterranean
Marianne Moore
Milton
Mary Wigman
Small Islands
D. H. Lawrence
Beethoven
Stravinsky
The British Museum
A Field-mouse in a Bonnet
Schubert
Diaghilev
Montaigne
Havelock Ellis
Dornier Superwal
Norman Douglas
Greek Vases
Spengler

The sort of people who enjoy
life just as much, if not more,
after they have realised that
they have not got immortal
souls, who are proud and not
distressed to feel that they are
of the earth earthy, who do not
regard their body as mortal
coils, and who are not anticipating, after death, any rubbishy
reunion, apotheosis, fulfilment,
or ANY THING

*...eek Party outsize invitation (it was 16 inches high). Patrick Balfour (who was not invited) denigrated the party in his
...aily Sketch column, pointing out that since Arcadia was spelt without an 'r' Mr Tennant's ultimate destination seemed
...be in doubt*

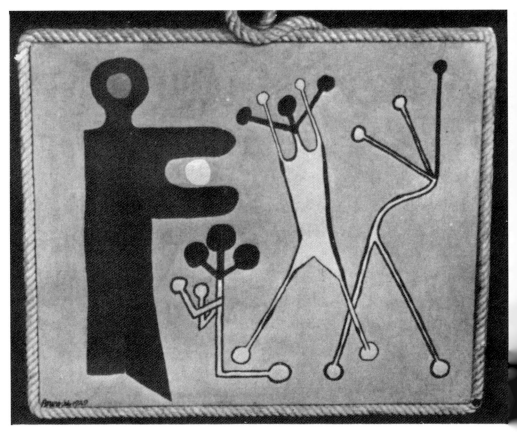

1929 'Adoration of the Magi', by Bruno Hat (Brian), 'the first English abstract painter, a pioneer of pure form'

Tom Mitford, in heavy disguise, impersonated the artist

John Banting helped Brian set up the rope framed bathmar

Lytton Strachey even bought a Bruno Hat painting, seen here with Iris Tree

Evelyn Waugh wrote 'Approach to Hat', a spoof catalogue note

Bryan and Diana Guinness promoted the Bruno Hat exhibition

Elizabeth Ponsonby, one of the first Bright Young People

Hermione Baddeley (then Mrs David Tennant)

1930 Raymond Mortimer

1929 Nancy Cunard by Cecil Beaton

Tom Driberg wrote 'The Talk of London' Daily Express *column*

1930s Brian with Toni and friends, somewhere in Europe

1931 Ski-ing like 'a concentrated panther'

931 Nancy Cunard, Henry Crowder, and friends, in Obergurgl

1942 Osbert Lancaster's 'Landscape with Figures – Café Royal'; Brian on balcony, Driberg, Quennell and Connolly, etc. below

Eddie Gathorne-Hardy, with Barbara Ker-Seymer

Mid-war, as an A.C.2 in the R.A.F.V.R.

Post-war, first trip abroad—
to W. H. Auden in Ischia

1950s Writing travel articles

1950s Lura Howard with her niece, Carley Dawson,
and Sam

Pre-war, on the eve of the Anschluss, 'this means war'

Inspiration for a book-plate—
one of Brian's Taras coins

To Lura: 'I am so happy, I wish you were here' (Ischia)

1957 The 'elderly aristocrat of Victorian vintage—very courteous and gracious', as described by Sir Roy Harrod

1956 The final home, Le Verger, near Nice. Lura 'bought this house behind my back . . . and chose an architectural design for its reconstruction which is so conventional'

It has been the delightful, but exhausting, task of the writer of this article to collect, during the past year, an anthology of verse by the younger English poets: one of the most exhausting things about it has been the numberless variations, generally in the treble, key, upon Mr. Eliot's renowned poem, *The Waste Land* . . .

Brian then placed *The Waste Land* in perfect context:

It is now some ten years since *The Waste Land* appeared, like some austere and unfamiliar flower, in that blown-up cottage garden which was English poetry immediately after the war. The Georgian poets were busy planting hardy perennials where hardy perennials grew before. Not even Mr. Siegfried Sassoon, sedulously slipping weedkiller into their watering-cans, was successful in deterring their dreary reconstruction. *Wheels* itself creaked in vain. The young poets, who, because of their age, had escaped alive, were dazedly trooping up to help. Suddenly—*The Waste Land*, and it may be said, with small exaggeration, that English poetry of the first half of the twentieth century began . . .

At the same time as his official *New Statesman* début Brian was crossing swords in the *Architectural Review* with the redoubtable critic, R. H. Wilenski, over a book called *London Promenade* (Studio), written and illustrated by William Gaunt. The *New Statesman*'s anonymous reviewer found it 'a fascinating book, the cheapness of which is almost beyond belief' (twenty-five shillings). Not so Brian. He annihilated not only poor Mr. Gaunt, but Mr. Wilenski for the latter's 'approbation' of it in a full-page review (with illustrations from the book) in the weekly *Graphic*. This slashing review of Brian's appeared in the November issue of the *Architectural Review*, and was strong stuff coming from an unknown—as he then was—twenty-five year old critic. I quote his most provocative statements:

. . . Whenever I read one of this gentleman's [Mr. Wilenski] enthusiastic articles in the newspaper, hailing, in his madcap way, yet another world genius, I feel exactly as if I were some Dartmoor farmer who hears, resigned but resolute, the baleful drone of the prison siren. It means that one more unfortunate has got to be harried back into the obscurity from which he should never have been permitted to escape. But it is at this point, with a pen for a pitchfork, that I set off in pursuit.
    That Mr. Gaunt is, plainly, young, would not, perhaps, have been interesting enough to mention for its own sake, were it not for the fact that he exhibits, to a startling degree, that chief and most melancholy fault of the young draughtsman. He simply cannot decide how he wishes to draw.
. . . As one proceeds through his book, from page to page, from Grosz to Muirhead Bone, one realises that what is important about Mr. Gaunt is less his originality than his origins. While he finds the problem of how he himself should draw quite insoluble, if not downright dull, no one could complain of his lack of interest in the technique of others. In that part

devoted to drawings of people, which has been the most highly praised portion of his work, Grosz dominates; tyrannises, one might go so far as to say. With the architectural pictures Mr. Gaunt vacillates between those of the ordinary Pennell type, suitably tinted, and imitation Muirhead Bone. There is a church, however, which might irritate Nina Hamnett. Some of the drawings, generally tail-pieces, show no discernible influence. These are the worst in the book . . .'

This was too much for Mr. Wilenski, whose expostulating letter in the December issue of the *Architectural Review* was replied to on the same page by Brian, who took every advantage of having the last word. This correspondence considerably exceeded the original review, in length, and I again quote only the most salient points:

[Mr. Wilenski's Complaint] . . . Your reviewer suggests that I have hailed Mr. Gaunt as a world genius. I have not done so. . . . Of Mr. Gaunt, as an artist, I wrote: 'Gaunt is a self-trained artist. As a social satirist, I fancy, he is likely to prove a great success because he is good-humoured; he has an eye for the grotesque but he does not see his fellow-man as a grimacing horror; and he writes and draws to amuse himself not to rid himself of spleen. . . . His drawing is quite personal, and it tells us just what he wants to say, neither more nor less.' I headed this article 'A New London Satirist'. The editor changed the heading to 'A New Rowlandson'—which was quite defensible, seeing that Mr. Gaunt's outlook and some of his technical procedures are more analogous to those of Rowlandson than to those of Herr Grosz, whom your reviewer regards as the source of his inspiration. . . . I have had the privilege of writing some hundreds of appreciations of works of artists in the last ten years. I have all the appreciations filed and I remember fairly accurately every word I have written. Your reviewer may come and look through the cuttings and I will give him sixpence for every occasion when I have hailed a living artist as a world genius or even as a genius. But I do not advise him to waste his time in this way—because he will make, in fact, exactly one shilling.

Much of Brian's published reply was taken up with the 'sixpenny' joke and objections to Mr. Gaunt being hailed as 'A New Rowlandson'. ('The Reviewer's Reply'): 'You will excuse me, I know, if I answer Mr. Wilenski's letter without a moment's delay. A sixpence in the hand is well worth the two, if he will forgive me, in Mr. Wilenski's bush. . . .'

At this distance of time the remaining protagonists of this critical triangle are of the opinion that (Wilenski): 'it seems pretty small beer, the only durable thing being William Gaunt's pleasant, witty and personal, book[2] round which the little polemic revolved', and (Gaunt): 'that it was certainly a fierce storm in a small bottle of ink!'

---

[2] A drawing from which, 'At Collins' Music Hall' is reproduced in the 1964 edition of Mr. Wilenski's *English Painting*, Faber, 1933.

Brian's book of poems was published, by Nancy Cunard's Hours Press, within a few months (January 1931, although the spine bears the year 1930), and Philip Toynbee includes all except four in his selection in Appendix I. Brian kept his original author's copy with the following hand-written dedication:

for Brian Howard
(Heart and Brain
get them together)

With the love and delight
of the publisher of these first poems

Nancy Cunard

and the admiration
of the makers of this book:
Wyn Henderson   John Sibthorpe
And John Banting to cover the lot[3]

He also seems to have acquired at some stage the copy he inscribed for Nancy Cunard:

for Nancy Cunard
Hours Press
1931—Paris
re-dedicated, ten years later,
with all the love there ever was,
all the love there ever will be. B.
London Sept 27   1942

These poems were not reviewed at all until October 1931, when Alan Pryce-Jones had managed to get hold of a copy. Brian wrote to him from Toulon: 'I am glad there is going to be at least *one* review of my poems. Nancy—with characteristic super-realism—forgot to send any review copies out. So I've had none . . .' Alan Pryce-Jones' review appeared in the *London Mercury*:

. . . I do not mean to disparage Mr. Howard's poetry when I say it is essentially of our age—as easily dated as Cowley or Monkton Milnes, or T. S. Eliot. It has the extreme sensitiveness to external impressions, the pride, and a sort of anguish at being alive at all, which are usually the springs of modern inspiration. Just as sleeplessness often attacks everyone in a house together, visions of collapse overshadow the arts. The disruption of our times has cracked the face of nature.

---

[3] The covers were designed by John Banting.

> O Life!
> bend down, bend my bow, send my arrow high, now, not
> low, below.
> I am my arrow. I have thick hearts to kill, that have killed
> me. Yet, I am.
> I, still, am. Hurl me hard, high, and I will kill, and live
> and still give life, O Life.[4]

This is the poetry of defence. Mr. Howard takes his philosophy from Germany rather than from France—it must be granted that the philosophy, the spark, of any poetic renewal comes to us from one or the other; perhaps that in all times and countries radical changes in artistic outlook have come violently in from abroad—and he is on the whole pessimistic. But the philosophy of poetry ought not to be an integral part of poetry, but a screen for poetry to play against; so it is more important to say that Mr. Howard, except when the hard brilliance of his style rarely glitters without illuminating, writes extremely well . . .

Allanah Harper writes of this period:

Brian was no scholar, he read poetry and the best contemporary writing, but he was far from erudite. I remember once sitting with him in a café in France when the name of Julien Sorel was mentioned. Brian exclaimed eagerly, 'I must meet that young man, please introduce me to him in Paris. I know you know him, Allanah.' I found out later Brian thought I was talking about Julien Green. I gave him *Le Rouge et le Noir* to read; he was equally fascinated by 'Julien Sorel'.

And so the 1930s might have marked the beginning of a serious and successful literary career for Brian (despite the above intellectual confusions). But he did not keep up the literary pace, preferring to indulge in the pleasures of several weeks' skiing in Austria, and the pains of writing his own version of the diary of a madman.

---

[4] Extract from *Up*, see Appendix I.

16. Obergurgl Journal

1931

At this period Brian was living through a stormy and characteristically unrequited love affair with a young man, 'D', and his journal is largely centred on this doomed relationship. It is a highly introspective study (only brief extracts are quoted here) which gives more than enough insight into his incipient masochism and permanently tortured state of mind.

1st January: The journey here was decidedly happy rather than not. A certain incompetence and haphazardness in travelling always gives me a warm confortable feeling. Scarfs trailing, rushing incompetence, and voices . . . It is extraordinary that even travelling, which must be an emotional strain even to the most dead people, doesn't seem to affect more than a few . . .

It was very exciting climbing all the way, with the snow changing from patchy, gritty white dust, to milk, and then to cream. Thickening. And one's ears going off like little pistols. *Whiteness* began to arrive, the whiteness that makes the whitest teeth look yellow. At Oetztal we took a charabanc to Zwieselstein. Purest moonlight. Winding always up, just fitting into wild wooden bridges over violent black and white chasms. Shaving the railings by less than an inch, which was rather frightening. But one couldn't care, on account of the really stupendous grandeur of the scene.

The next day we walked to Obergurgl, stopping for lunch at Untergurgl. In a room in which *wood* is so much present that one almost worships it. The situation at Obergurgl is incredibly stirring and lovely. It is in the very middle of a huge, swinging valley. Great breasts and limbs of snow soaring up on every side . . .

I put on skis for the first time for a lesson. I did not fall, but it was only the mildest slope. I like the crouching, slow-bouncing of skiing. A concentrated panther.

3rd January: Have finished the first book of the *Joyful Wisdom.* I read it with more interest than I have ever read Nietzsche before. Yet if only he had a little more of the 'mocking laughter' himself! He understands it, yet has it not himself. He *oppresses* a little. Still, his is the greatest of all our voices.

There must be *variety* in this journal. Real variety. The language itself must change from time to time. *No nerves.*

5th January: Yesterday D. and I went for the most enchanting walk down to Untergurgl for tea. We had tea in that stuffy little wooden room, to Tyrolean music on the gramophone. We drank some red wine and luxuriated in it. It was Brueghel. One really might have had such an experience in this part of the world at any time during the last 400 years.

We were both exquisitely happy. We almost gave off light. We walked back through the marvellous snow-dusk. After dinner we began playing some excellent German jazz records and we drank some white wine. We had a very minor squabble over a tune—and the evening ended in an appalling, savage row. I said a great many silly things. Why do I always, *always* make a fool of myself in the same way? Why do I always make myself into the tragedian—out of a kind of exhibitionism, masochism? Other people always win, in the end, emotionally, with me. I seem to force myself to be hurt more than is necessary, by exaggerating my own feelings, my own dependency. (I sometimes speak of my ideals as if they were selfish schemes.) If love, even disguised in a quarrel, really hardens D. he is, of course, worthless. Can this be? If so, it is the inner emptiness Lawrence speaks of, and I MUST FLY . . .

The point is this. *I know, now that the situation is definitely unsafe for my peace of mind* . . . All this identifying myself with abstract conceptions of love etc. must go, *and go once and for all.* I suppose it is ridiculous of me always to expect people to forgive me my extravagances on the grounds that I am an *honest* friend (or whatever it is)—what *is* this honesty that I am so proud of?

I shall now address myself:

Be less of a *pervert.* Recognise the invincibility of your own egoism. You suspect *others,* of course, of a hollow core. What about you?

A. But I know I have a *gold* core.

Q. How do you know?

A. Because I know I *could* be a good poet, even if I am not. And for this one has to have a gold core. And because they always trample on *me* with their purposeless, empty aloneness, *pretending* they need me.

Q. Do you see how *slave-ish,* how *untrue,* how *appalling* your second statement, at least, is?

A. Yes.

Q. What then?

A. I will apply *every* energy to simple, soft, interior, personal *growth. I will let all else go.*

(Later): I am now in the grip of the craziest depression.

Our present room, a tiny double one is, of course, too small, and at all events D. wants a room of his own. I suppose I do, really, and yet something weak and lonely in me is horrified at the thought. I must conquer this. I *loathe* the idea of being alone. Will ever the time come when one will find someone at whose side one could *always* be? Someone who would benefit me in every way by always being with me; and whom one would benefit in turn? I must be courageous, but the most difficult time not to be a coward is when one does not know what one is frightened of. It is oneself, of course.

Here is my book out, a successful year, a year in which I have *grown*, got *beyond* this, and yet here I am. Twenty-five. *Still wailing.* Time goes so quickly. Each year that I live passes more quickly; it is terrifying. I must begin some *work.*

7th January: I am planning, fairly confidently, a *huge* poem. *The Song of Zarathustra.* To be real attempt at a longish poem in complicated, strict metre. In the grand style. . . . I so believe in my theory of writing—that it is an attitude (the attitude of *honest* interest)—rather than a talent. The *technique* comes as it comes in skating, or anything else. All this mystic business—'born' writers etc. is all rubbish. Anyone can write who can see honestly, and this is a quality which can be learned. . . . Two skiing lessons. Am gradually improving. Long, endearing letter from Nancy (Cunard). Her mother has found out about Henry [Crowder—her negro lover]. My papa has a finger in it, I'll bet. A delicious letter. If only she can come here with Eddie (Gathorne-Hardy). I want no one else but Eddie and she. The only PERFECT people.

13th January: I told D. last night that this expedition was a coin. It had to fall on one side or the other. Heads—the flower (my romantic imaginings?), tails—a) my realising his essential 'aloneness', b) writing a book about it. I can see the notes he is filling his notebooks with—notes for poems: 'False attachments—annoyance of the soul at pity . . . the horror of pity is my only cruelty—to GET AWAY.' Out of Gide, Lawrence, Nietzsche he sucks the bad with the good, and he, unfortunately, has only to suck in that one small, but so BIG, bit of badness that they ALL share, the hate for pity, and he is done . . . Never to get beyond hating pity, *this is what is wrecking my generation.*

[Later] Look at the situation. What are my demands, needs? Sex? No. Continual companionship? No. Too much intimacy, of any sort? No. But I want him to come out to me spiritually and come out with me occasionally, to eat together the beauty of the place. In this way only, would we have done, more than come here to ski. He knows all in my mind. Yet he becomes more alone every day . . . the 'I must find myself' business. It makes the last four years ridiculous. What has it all been about, one wonders? Here we are, with him becoming a cold, cut-off whizzing piece of snow.

However, one cannot let oneself be annihilated . . . I will write a study of this thing I have discovered in him, the real loneliness. To be a writer—perhaps THAT is the REAL loneliness? *The third eye.*

. . . No more stewing, cigarettes and wine and ill health. No more dependence on others, real yet false. No more fancifying over sex. And the poems, not *one* trick, but what I FEEL only . . . I am not to stew, that above all. I am to *strive* for honesty . . .

15th January: Last night was the most terrible of my life. D. became ice slowly, as I melted. How anyone can be a Napoleon about love, I don't know. I can understand freezing (D.), melting (me), but to be a Napoleon about it—really manage—this I cannot understand. D. told me that there were three points he disliked in me which were insuperable. That 'we' were finished. Remember, now—pride is a necessity, even if it hurts love. I must suppress *egotism, conceit,* and what D. considers *insensitiveness.* If it is to him—it is.

16th January: I am utterly purposed to get him back. He is getting power, he is criticising. He is feeling superior—he is getting away. Is all this panic, already? DEFEAT already? The tragedy of being in the inferior position in an emotional struggle is that so many of one's capabilities, virtues, *weapons* become negative. Not repeating mistakes is almost all one can do. Stand-offishness won't do. Effusion—'I-am-still-the-same' won't do.

22nd January: Mrs. Guinness is dead. So awful for Daddy, Birkenhead and now she . . .

At the same time he unburdened himself in a long letter to Eddie Gathorne-Hardy, who was in London:

There is no point in trying to make out that things are all right again or ever can be all right again. Naturally, two people who know one another so well slip back into a more or less continual (with the most dizzying drops) *superficially* happy relationship. Yesterday, for instance, D's birthday, was divine. In the evening we had a lovely party in the small sand-coloured, panelled *bierstube*, with a large white cake in the shape of a heart surrounded by a huge dark green wreath of Tannenbaum, into which were stuck twenty-three candles. An enormous bowl of Steinwein and oranges and cognac cup cooled in snow . . . the first time I've seen exactly my idea of what a really BEAUTIFUL party is. We all put on fancy dress—me as a Lesbian, in silk stockings, a short black skirt, a fur jacket and padded bosies, and bracelets. I looked a dream and did an apache dance with D. that woke up the whole hotel. Then we all rushed into the big dining-room madly drunk and insulted that German woman tennis player who is here and who we don't like.

I am being pursued by the hag from Buda Pesth, so last night at the dinner-party when she told me she liked kissing 'mountainous men' (meaning the guides) I said, 'SO DO I' at the top of my voice. I then got crazily tipsy, and really horrified everyone by insisting on dancing with all the men and being more chi-chi, twitching my skirt, than I've ever been in my life.

Tonight, I am being made, in full ceremonial, a member of the Ski Club. A speech is made to say that I am the most marvellous athlete, *that I love the Fatherland* (one's actual extraction is disregarded) and everyone gets up and bawls 'SKI-HEIL!!' three times. It's tremendous and I shall cry. There has been the feeling that I must become a member as soon as possible (compatible with my skiing—now that I am at the stem-Christiana stage it's all right) because of D's being a member. (The way D. climbs is portentous—he tires the guides.) The 'friends' business is seriously regarded here, of course. So we will be joined in a kind of snowy, Theban union tonight, the real emotions connected with which will be peculiarly wrenching.

Continuing Brian's journal:

26th February: Started to write about love. I loathe the modern Christian idea of love. These young girls who have never had anything but a few gentlemanly proposals and flirtations—perhaps a slight difficulty in a taxi-cab—think that LOVE, august, dirty, terrible, pure, all exacting, all-torturing, all-transmuting—can suddenly arrive, like a telegram from God? A Zulu would be less gullible—far. Or do these people simply live in an imitation world, where such things as love are really polite visitors that arrive, punctually, for lunch, when they are expected? . . . In my *First Poems*—only a line or two of *Two in One* manages to FLY. When Love does come, silent, violent—will I then have a *quiet mind?* Oh, I hope so, more than I hope *anything.* Or will I be Marie Bashkirtseff-ing away over a glass of red wine, while my love gradually turns from a star into a stone? Am I the most boring person alive? AM I? I am more vulgar than anyone in the world this morning, because I am more interested in myself than in anything else. Oh myself, how *sick* of you I am . . . Later this morning I read over this journal thoroughly for the first time. I do not know what to think, but I *disapprove.*

I did the Waldabfahrt today in one hour. My guide said, 'Quick Tempo.' I only fell four times. I have decided that if I can SEE I can ski. I will go in for the guest race. I should so love to win. But D. will, of course. And I shall arrive five minutes after him, spitting blood, to die of rage and exhaustion—principally rage—in the ski room.

It is extraordinary what happens to me when I can't speak a language. It is always the same. PEOPLE NEVER STOP TALKING TO ME. It makes me nervous and miserable. How I hated this evening. There I was, trying to read Shelley. I was forced to join a table where there was an awful great caryatid of a Baronin, and the woman who never stops a hoarse, dim flow of banalities. Longfellow. My shirts. My non-existent talents. If she gave me *time*, I might like her—the dried up dormouse. I hate people who finger one's possessions and finger one and finger one's mind, oneself. She is a fingerer. (It is so superbly ironic that D. will quite shortly have persuaded himself, probably, that I am a fingerer.) Then the PAWING began. She squeezed me and kissed me—OH . . . HOW I HATE BEING MESSED. How repulsive nice kind women are, pawing and nuzzling— dirty filthy *beasts*. She has a heart of gold, but WHY IN GOD'S NAME MUST SHE KISS ME?

Why do they all keep on asking me if I am angry or unhappy? But *once a minute.* I laugh and joke very well and very continually considering I don't know German. The second my mouth shuts, for once, 'Are you annoyed?' More often—'You look so *serious.*' DAMN THEM. Holding my hand, patting me, peering at me. A kind of cannibal interest. I can understand them pawing D., he is good-looking. But why paw me? If I complained about it to D. he would wearily suggest to me that they are being polite, kind. THEY ARE BEING SOMETHING ELSE TOO THOUGH. There is something horrible in me which excites cannibal solicitude. It turns women into cannibal mothers and men into cannibal jokers. As if I were some extraordinary invalid. Some semiprecious, perverted, mad, curious, thing to be put in each of their show-cases.

28th January: D. told me of his intention to go to Munich. At some time in the evening I could not resist saying, 'Are you coming back?' No answer. Later we met on the landing and the following contemptibilities took place:

Brian: 'Are you coming back here?'

D.: 'Why shouldn't I?

Brian: 'Because you don't seem to be enjoying it . . .'

D.: 'I like everything here except you.'

Brian: 'You're going to dislike me a great deal more.'

D.: 'Lame Christ—Jew.' (The door slammed.)

I should imagine that it is the first time for about 1,500 to 2,000 years in Europe that Christ's name has been used as an insult by a really furious person. I got extremely drunk at the party afterwards.

20th January: I sometimes feel as if my mind might go, literally. But I must be courageous. I must be strong. But I am trembling sick with nerves. D. left for Munich, of course. I dislike him. It is finished.

[Later] Finished, indeed. After writing four pages of 'finishedness' to D. I suddenly tore them up and wrote to say that I adored him. I love him and there's an end of it. I am sick of wavering, wobbling and wibbling. I am just as miserable pretending to dislike him as I am loving him. I love him and everything can go to hell. He can do what he likes. I can't be unhappier than I am, anyway. I am honest, AT LAST. Let what comes come. The walls are down etc. and there's no more pretending. But oh—but oh—but oh. He will be kind and I shall be sad.

31st January: Looking through D's poetry notebook I found the following references to myself:

Has Vanity, Intuition, Taste, Affection, 'charming', Scheming, Meanness, Effeminacy, Language, Dishonesty, Lies, Acting, Superficially brilliant. Physically—moulting black plumes, Animal eyes, too big—more than life size. 'Carnival' figure—scarecrow body—that meagre torso. The Smell. Intolerance, which may suit really important people becomes petty criticism in someone who is not profoundly serious and sincere. Since he has the poorest knowledge of any language except English he *knows about* foreign authors by intuition.

It is written in a fury, obviously. The 'meanness' seemed a little severe after the bracelet and the Shelley presents, both of which I adored, too. The 'physical' section is only too true. (I have noticed that I really am *quite ghoulish* lately.) However, though I *do* look like an El Greco inquisitor who hasn't had lunch, I refuse to believe I *smell*. So appallingly, anyway. Really—'The Smell'. Just like that, is too terrifying. And one can't *know*, which is so awful. But I haven't got indigestion, I wash a great deal, my *batterie de toilette* is immense, I am not decomposing and am perfectly healthy and I DON'T BELIEVE IT. It makes me roar with laughter, somehow, too. Though one *may*, of course. I must ask Eddie.

The Saxon couple at my table are the most interesting people here by far. The only unique people. They are each fifty-five, short and fat, infinitely amiable. The greatest lovers, in a way, I have ever seen. Unanimous, utterly. One. One, leaning forward over the bill. One, bowing to me. One, over their grandchild. One, in conversation. They never speak but at the same time, but as they say the same thing, it's all right. I adore them. Ah, what is it that forbids intelligent people from having love affairs like that. It must be a double drink at life. It is the reward of simplicity.

This January has been WITHOUT DOUBT the most unpleasant month of my life.

Brian wrote again to Eddie Gathorne-Hardy:

. . . I really am quite ridiculous. I know it. I am simply madly, madly in love with D., I've fought it for two years—and now here it is, and I am lost. Thank GOD Nancy and Henry arrive soon.

Several times I have wondered if I am going dotty, really. I have a thick pile of letters to D.—which he will never see. Some idiocy seizes me, and I sit up all night writing them, and then start again instantly at crack of dawn. I dream of nothing but him. It seems to me that the more one is capable of love—as the Victorians understood it, at least—the more of a failure one is. Am I a sort of innately comic-tragic figure, Eddie? The sexual aspect of love I have long since been taught not to press, therefore what is it that *always* makes me repulsive, a failure? Sitting about all over Scotland, Frankfurt, London and Austria with quite genuine tears streaming down my face? With only you to turn to, to belabour with the stick of my invariable failure? I am not a bore. I do not nag with love. I am not hideous. Well, well—

. . . Our 'set' here is already considered absolutely dotty, and when Nancy and Henry come I simply cannot conceive what will happen. I have given up all attempt to look hearty. I consider, quite rightly, that my excellent skiing compensates for it, and so I simply sit about in clouds of Queer de Russie, with all my handkerchiefs knotted round my neck, the tears streaming down my face, writing impassioned letters, like any character in a Rossetti poem.

One alarming thing has occurred. The only place for Nancy and Henry that I can find for their first week is in the house of the *local priest*. I suppose they will simply insult him. I have visions of Obergurgl ending in such a storm of craziness as never was before. The priest is tremendously severe, and *I* can hear him praying all day and all night from *my* bedroom, so considering their room will be next to his I simply cannot imagine what will happen. He has an enormous beard, which he uses as a sort of cupboard for a number of large, gay crucifixes, and is always bellowing and praying about in the snow surrounded by a crowd of guides, and cooks and children . . .

Continuing Brian's Journal:

2nd February: Well, Nancy and Henry arrived, rather like the hero and heroine of a highbrow revue in 1950. Nancy with a lump of gold at her throat (me with one in mine), a little brown hat, with her white pencil face poking out of a black veil. Long stick legs in large furry 'bottines'. Henry in one of those terrible Homburgs that are rimmed in tape and turn up all round, and Sir Bache's (Cunard) coat. Great rivers of sable over his shoulders. So off we set, Nancy full of the London row and her ladyship's detectives. [Her mother had found out that she was living with the negro Henry Crowder, and threatened to cut her out of her Will.] Noailles has been turned out of the Jockey Club because of his patronage of *L'Age d'Or*, etc. At the inns on the way to Zwieselstein we were looked at, and treated, like rich, royal lunatics. It was the most fantastic progress. On the way I roughly outlined the situation with D. to Nancy. She did not get a biased account. It *isn't* his *fault*—she must see that. While seeing it isn't mine either.

5th February: The sun was shining and we had a very agreeable day. The afternoon I spent talking to Nancy in her room. I got her to see my situation here and she cried a little at the end of my recitation, but I could not. She is old enough, she knows what it means. But I was not glad she cried. I wanted no key to self pity. She talked so much, seemed unable to stop. The whispery, staccato, disjointed voice goes on and on. A kind of sober drunkenness. Drinking is now fatal to her. Particularly cognac. She has the most marvellous face. The best woman face of our time. That extraordinary, wavering, perched walk. Thinness—other people are thinner of course—reaches a sort of thing-in-itself in her. She is the only woman I know who can be *really impassioned about ideas almost continuously*. She is anything but 'right', of course. And her bickering with impassive, infinitely patient, stupid Henry is very rasping to me. She is in an extremely nervous condition, now, of course.

She wants me to write a long pamphlet for her. Blasphemy—*lèse majésté*—buggery—colour. I thought of a title, *How to cook a Gentleman*. To be *like* a cookery book. Perhaps I could get three years spleen into it. I've been writing attacks of that kind on and off for that long. It might be a good thing to get it all into one. Really outspoken. I could say anything I like if she published, of course. *I shall do it*, and really let fly and get it off my chest.

7th February: Entrancing drive down to Innsbruck in sledge with Nancy. She is rather terrifying. She is as if permanently drugged without being—which is frightening. I think she is a little in love with me—talking all the time of doing things together, 'come to Réanville—come away etc'. Divine of her, but she has gone over the *edge*, somehow. Alternating between extreme solicitude and sudden ugly unprovoked coldnesses ... Saw myself in mirrors towards the end of the Alpen Vereins Ball. So *thin* and *mad*. A hideous, wan, goggling wraith.

8th February: Understood for the first time what D. thinks of me sometimes. I am a grotesque. Of course I am a bad lover. I am like some caricature. I am *grotesque*. I saw myself—outside—as I am, and it is only just not inhuman.

I find myself unable to face putting down all I feel, plus overtones about Nancy. A) she is ill. Drink plus never drawing any line. Henry says she drinks far too much and she obviously does. Those awful snarling little yelps of self-assertion. B) before lunch today she came into my room when I was finishing dressing, lay on the bed, pulled me down beside her and did a lot of hair smoothing and kissing, and 'comforting'. Not sexily, but with sex near *enough*. She is definitely in love-ish, put it like that. It simply makes me freeze. I suppose I am a sort of Nancy to D. But I do not, or did not, anyway, repulse D. as much as she repulses me, I am certain. I sometimes shiver at the sight of that small, inefficiently eager mouth. Soft, tiny, narrow, bright, puckered, dangerous, with hard teeth so *near* behind it. I AM IN FOR A PLAGUE OF WOMEN. Oh, Christ, if only she wouldn't smooth my hair. It makes me feel bald and ill. C) her danger for D. and myself, (she) being so illy mercurial and jagged and upsetting. Such an egomaniac. D) her *divine* appearance—part of today—as an object. She can do this. The best appearance in the world. E) her *genuine* affection, concernedness for me. Her desire to *help*. F) her superiority to all other women, and *most* men, in *many* ways.

If only she was (i) *well*, (ii) I felt she would never require anything much given *emotionally*. I *could* give, *have* given, and I think *do* give, a lot in this way. *But I can't be kissed and mauled.*

14*th February:* After considerable delays Nancy goes. She said 'I love you in every way' etc. A bottle of white wine and a bottle of liqueur poking out of the sledge as they left, huddled in their furs. [Nancy later told John Banting that it had been a frightful visit and she pitied Brian and the whole thing. She also described him as 'looking like a Mexican Indian flying down the slopes'.]

D. returns with a charming German boy who plays the mouth organ. We have a terrible scene one night . . . eventually I suggested we go to Munich for a few days rest, and he added 'to start all over again'. [In Munich, where they plunged into the middle of Fasching, they spent a highly drunken, promiscuous ten days, until D. was suddenly called to England on urgent family business.]

25*th February:* Return to Obergurgl, with Bobbie Burnett and Charles Lambe. The journey up here was spent in planning a film, to be done at once, with Charles, who has brought a movie camera. He has 900 feet of film, which lasts 40 minutes. Am terrifically excited by the idea. The first English surrealist film (!) Telegram from D. saying he is returning. I am really sorry in a way that he is coming back. I feel it is all so hopeless. And I was being quite happy without him. Much happier than with him, except at rare moments.

And so Brian's journal ended, but meanwhile he kept up his usual flow of letters to his mother, and how subtly different is the atmosphere conjured up in these more circumspect outpourings. We all know from Wilde that truth is never pure and rarely simple, but in one who held 'truth' above all, can these protestations be forgiven? '. . . *ten hours* sleep every night . . . Obergurgl is an *admirable* place to write . . . apart from money I am a *lucky* person.' Lucky? Never again can letters to 'Muzzy' be read without a very liberal taste of salt.

Letters to his mother (January–March 1931):

... I think I may easily complete a prose work here. I feel myself integrating slowly, very much *more* than ever before abroad. You won't recognise the lean, brown, hearty sporting English gentleman that I shall be when you see me next. I am *very* happy, *very* well, *very* economical and *very* industrious ... I have written a long article for *Life and Letters* called *Pitiless*. It is an attack on a certain type of young person who thinks pity degrading. It is a modern disease. In it I have begun to find my prose style. I have long striven to combine force and naturalness in prose, and I had to do it before starting my novel. I am beginning to find it. 20th century prose, Lawrence—Aldington—Robert Graves—early James Joyce. That is the one to use, now—the only one for my sort of mind, anyway. It *looks* easy, of course. But in my opinion it needs years of honest thinking to arrive at. In *my* experience.

... *I am extremely worried* and cross with myself over not having written you for so long. The truth is that things have been rather tempestuous here. Now there is one thing that I want you, *seriously*, to realise. And that is that I adore and admire Nancy and I always will. She has the kind of integrity, spiritual purity and devotion to ideas that is unique. Nothing can deter her or make her dishonest. She is a marvellous woman, and if she were younger and less ill and attracted me, I'd marry her. I almost believe. But really her advent here, and Henry, was simply volcanic. She is *ill*, which I didn't realise. Her mother and Beecham having her hounded by detectives and the fact she is hiding a young *surréaliste* (Louis Aragon) in her house near Paris who is running away from his father, who is a *chef de police*—these things have made her almost distraught. She also had incipient sinus, awful catarrh, and a bad throat. Also it was too cold for her, she couldn't ski, and she was uncomfortable in the annexe (there was no room here). Well, she was all right in the daytime, but at night she simply drank. Added to this she fell quite insanely in love with me. Letters and telegrams, they never stop, even now. Well, it was AWFUL. There were fights, with poor dear coal-black Henry being so good and patient, D. being irritated and Nancy threatening to go every minute and then crying in my arms all night, having smashed all her windows with rage because I couldn't come to Vienna. It may have been Michael Arlen on the surface—to *read* of—but it was King Lear underneath all right. She made us all rather crazy. Now, mother, you must make an effort to understand. Nancy, for instance has *never* taken drugs. She is *devoted* to her art and to poor dear Henry. She drinks a *lot*, normally, but *never* like that. I KNOW her. She is a fine, noble creature. You cannot *know* how her nerves have been wrecked, fighting her mother because her lover happens to have a black face. She is ILL, now. That's why she flies to drink. Anyhow, it was BEDLAM. And it all devolved on me. Complaints from other visitors, rows over bills—all had to be smoothed over by me.

... The priest here, who has *complete* power, roars out denunciations of the visitors to the peasants every Sunday. I shudder to think what he said about Nancy and Henry. Do you know that Henry was the first negro who had ever come here? They touched his face to see if it would come off?

[Later] You say about Nancy, 'that episode is totally unlike life—it's just abnormality, which is never interesting except to doctors'. And Shakespeare, you might have added. '. . . totally unlike life'—what DO you mean? 'Unlike the sort of life you approve of? Is that what you mean? And it's just abnormality etc.' What is normal? What is abnormal? Things that interest doctors, particularly psychologically, interest and *must* interest writers, emotional struggles of any character are bound to be interesting to anyone who is interested in humanity. Haven't you YET realised the terrible dangers of Limiting, Labelling, Dismissing, Generalising? Your 'asphodel' passage seems to amount to a request that I should always get the sun to shine upon the objects upon which I look—am interested in, and write about—from the most becoming—to the object's—position. This would undoubtedly make my life, and my writings, *jollier*, but I doubt if it would result in my immortality. Remember that a good writer is a writer for whom the sun MOVES. Into unbecoming positions, sometimes.

[Later] . . . Please don't worry about the *Priest*. I daresay he didn't even *see* Nancy—I only imagined her effect on him—and oh my goodness I daresay she'd have done him a lot of good—nasty old man stuffing these poor people with lies all their lives . . . I daresay clergymen are one of the most serious menaces to progress that we have. And precisely because people will go on insisting on *respecting* and *protecting* them, like you, instead of demanding, *loudly*, what they are DOING AND MEANING. What sort of poor fish do you think I'd be now if I'd listened to the various clergymen I've known? I'd have committed suicide long ago—at the thought of how shocking it was of me to share my sexual appreciations with Bill Shakespeare, Mike Angelo and Walt Whitman . . .

17. Ten year Odyssey—with 'Toni'

1931–1940

The Obergurgl saga was over, leaving Brian to look for fresh places both to conquer and from where he could lick his wounds in peace. He managed to get himself facilities as a 'privileged correspondent' in Ragusa, and wrote to his mother during April–July:

> [From Ragusa, now Dubrovnik, Jugoslavia] I could talk about Venice for a long time—so many reinforcements of my ideas on art did I find; my main thesis being that art, however beautiful, is hollowness when it is not the expression of a *whole* attitude, the integration of an entire direction of living. 'Pure' painting, 'pure' architecture—is all bosh. Art must be *for* something—then, and not until then, does it become something-in-itself. That something-in-itself *is* what it was done *for*. That is what makes art the tangible representation of man at his highest. And man at his highest is simply man living as *fully* as he can. To some, to live fully is to be an anchorite, to others, to build a Venice. The building of a Venice today would not be allowed by Geneva. Perhaps rightly. There are no ends to these questions.
>
> Ruskin I read and admire enormously—in spite of his silliness over Christianity, he was the last of our art critics. He would never go yammering away about 'pure' art. Henry James I have been reading, too. I am inclined to think *him* the last novelist—large one. He and Proust. Miss Compton Burnett is one too. She is probably the best woman Anglo-Saxon writer. The more I hear of England—through occasional *Daily Expresses* etc.—the more I take refuge in the Victorians and *loathe* the idea of my clever young contemporaries. Beverley Nichols & Co. are, of course, the dung heap—but all these Waughs and young pseudo-serious writers—Anthony Powell—*Afternoon Men*—are worse. Alan (Pryce-Jones), Robert (Byron) and Peter Quennell (who'll probably turn into a useless don) are the best.
>
> Ragusa is a small, heavily walled, plain façaded Venice, with two or three exquisite early Venetian buildings. The weather is varied, but always very hot. Occasionally what an old Anglo-Indian lady, who 'sketches' here calls 'a sunstroke day, my dear Mr. Howard, a sunstroke day. The wrong rays, you know, come through the clouds, as in Indiah'. I don't think I shall stay here longer than it will take to collate my notes. Athens is just round the corner and I could write something there I feel, but I shall have to make enquiries about expense.

It was not Athens that he next visited but Walchensee, in Bavaria, where he stayed for some weeks, writing to his mother:

I will let you know the minute my book baulks me—until I do you may count on definite *money*. I have made a charming friend—a thing which happens so seldom. It is Klaus Mann, the son of Thomas Mann. Last week I had lunch with his father—a great experience for me—and, later, I had supper with him and André Gide. To meet at the same time at the same table the men who are considered by many (including myself) to be the two greatest living writers was an unforgettable experience. Klaus Mann is himself well known in Germany. He is extremely charming, simple and sensitive and knows Prinzhorn (who has translated Gide's *Nourritures Terrestres* into German).

Please can you find me a small, cheap, elementary manual of BOTANY and one of Natural History. I feel I do not know enough of plants and animals. I am almost literally besieged with applications for poems through Nancy (Cunard) for periodicals, but am sending none . . . collecting slowly for a new book.

[16th July 1931] The situation in Germany at the moment is more serious possibly than you imagine in England. All banks are now shut indefinitely . . . food prices are rising . . . The French newspapers are at a pitch of abuse, but of course war is impossible. On the other hand, a revolution is *not*. In Munich there is disquiet. Please find out from the Associated Allied Newspapers of North America whether they want articles on the present situation (and photographs of bank queues, police, etc., on what *may* come, in the way of riots). If trouble comes I will establish myself in Munich, photograph and write it up. I'm perfectly capable of looking after myself and the idea of a few machine guns perturbs me not a whit (Hitlerites etc.).

Much later in time (the mid-1940s) Brian wrote in one of his innumerable notebooks that it was in Munich in 1931 at a luncheon-party of Thomas Mann's that people laughed at an inadequate remark of his about Hitler:

Forthwith, I determined to fathom the German political scene. I succeeded, and I despaired of it. Worse, my pleasure in things quite removed from politics, began to dwindle—the Bavarian landscape, for example. Soon I was not only unable to enjoy it; I couldn't even see it properly. (To understand the inside of any country is to cease to observe the outside.) Austria followed. In the end, the whole of central Europe looked, to me, like a faded photographic negative.

In his autobiography, *Turning Point*,[1] Klaus Mann described their experiences of the anti-Jewish atmosphere in Munich in this summer of 1931:

---

[1] *Turning Point—thirty-five years in this country*, by Klaus Mann, published by Gollancz, 1944.

The scene: a gigantic tent on the Theresia Meadow, a vast field situated at the periphery of the city. The tent is jammed with people, twenty thousand, thirty thousand of them. It is dark; only the platform glares, singled out by the spotlight. And from there, from the illuminated rostrum, comes the voice, a ghastly howl of a mad dog.

'The Jews!' hurls the barking voice, in a monotonous paroxysm of fury. 'Those filthy Jews have done it, who else?'

A young chap not far from our place screams abruptly, as if bitten by a snake and unable to repress his outcry: 'Hang the Jews!' Whereupon the voice, with slimy banter: 'Patience! Patience, my friend! They'll hang, all right.'

The crowd snickers and guffaws.

'Dear me!' whispers our English friend who was so eager to attend this lurid affair. 'He is a paranoiac.'

'Who dominates this so-called Republic?' bellows the voice. And the chorus responds: 'The Jews!'

'How extraordinary!' whispers the English friend. 'He is positively demented. Don't they notice it? Or are they crazy themselves?' He looks aghast with surprise.

The voice, panting now, breathless with hatred: 'Who dominates the so-called League of Nations? The international trusts? The newspapers? The Kremlin? The so-called Catholic Church?' And, following each question, the stereotypic roar: 'The Jews! the Jewish rats! Hang the Jews!'

'Are they mad? Or what?' our friend keeps asking. He repeats his question in various idioms, finally in German. '*Sind Sie toll, mein Fraulein?*' he inquires politely of a buxom Hitler maiden sitting next to him.

Happily she is too excited even to hear his question. She flutters, trembles, perspires, all beside herself, in a quasi-sexual trance. But the British observer insists, with merciless courtesy: 'I beg your pardon, Madam. Did you ever consult a really good psychiatrist?'

How much like him that is! That's the way Brian is, Brian Howard, a young writer from London, with whom we spend the summer in a funny little hotel on the Walchensee. He doesn't care a straw about people hissing him and piercing him with their looks. One of those husky fellows might rise and knock him out with his little finger. Brian doesn't care. Frail but plucky, he wouldn't mind a scrap with great big Goering himself.

'We may as well beat it,' I suggest. 'He's a bore, that's all there is to it. Nobody takes him seriously, anyhow.'

The murmur of indignation around us grows ominously as we withdraw from our seats. 'They must be foreigners,' I hear one Hitler youth whisper. And another, rather angrily, 'To hell with them. They've made dirty cracks about our Fuehrer.' Whereupon a third one, with a superior grin: 'Never mind. They're nuts.'

While we struggle our way towards the exit, the hideous voice, dispersed and amplified by the microphones, follows us throughout the hall. 'Versailles ...' hoots the voice. '... disgrace of our nation ... I promise you, German mothers! ... heads will roll ... the Bolshevists ... I promise you, German peasants! . . . the national upheaval . . . the Nordic race, those exorbitant milk prices . . . And who profits by it? Our arch enemy, those parasites and scoundrels—those swarthy, greasy, hook-nosed, stinking . . .'

Where to escape from this hideous voice?

In Klaus Mann's diary he had already noted under 25th May 1931: 'Serious talk about the necessity of leaving Germany. Appalling triumph of madness.' And the next day, 'Again long conversation [with his mother] concerning exile. Is it inevitable?' Bavaria still defied the new masters, and after the Reichstag Fire he noted that 'many a liberal journalist or cautious Jew thought it wiser to move from the banks of the Spree to the Iser River.' His sister, Erika Mann, had started her *Peppermill* satirical cabaret venture, where she did a bit of everything as well as being master of ceremonies. Surprisingly enough, the Nazi theatre critics were in the habit of praising her as 'the embodiment of sturdy Germanic humour, ignoring the fact that she was passionately anti-Fascist to boot.'

Erika Mann writes about Brian in retrospect:

We were very young when we first met him, my brother Klaus and I, and we struck up a friendship as only very young people can, instantly and for ever. On that first evening we realised that he was enchanting, with his thirst for life, his wit, quick warmth, curiosity, intelligence and high talent. But we soon realised that dark shadows lay over all this brilliance and that he was in danger, not only from the world about him, whose harsh features had already appalled him even in the late 'twenties, but from dangers within himself, *de profundis*. Suddenly, in the middle of a gay conversation, he would turn deadly serious as though overcome by some awful dread, or he would provoke an instant quarrel, become violent, indeed menacing. Then he said the ghastliest things and no longer seemed to be the same lost lovable creature whom he had been a few minutes before. Even then there was in him a streak of violence which would have stunned us, had we not been quick to realise that his wild malice had nothing to do with evil but that it was deeply rooted in unfathomable despair.

Like every decent person he was, of course, an anti-Fascist, but he was probably the first Englishman to recognise the full immensity of the Nazi peril and to foresee, with shuddering horror, what was to come. While people like Klaus and myself could still laugh disdainfully at the Nazis, any mention of them put an end to gaiety as far as Brian was concerned.

Since their virtually separate existence, Tudie and Lura Howard's country house, Nore, was proving too expensive and they were thinking of selling it. Brian sent his suggestion for a *modus vivendi* to his mother from Walchensee:

I suggest a cottage, rented, of course, where Daddy *could* come but won't—where there's *a* room extra and Daddy will not feel inclined to get that owner feeling and come rushing down all the time with his friends etc. When my book is finished, and when I begin to make a little. I want very much to go East, or somewhere, with you. I think if you had a garden again you could do, in a cottage, what you always wanted to do—but *Daddy and Size* got in the way of your doing at Nore. Daddy *is* impossible. I have seen it for years. Of course he is the companion you are most used to, and, I imagine, prefer on many occasions—but ought you not to seek some mode of life at once not in dis-union but more apart from him, in a way? Daddy's influence nearly caused you to distrust me—his influence coupled, of course, with long follies on my part. Homosexuality, for instance. Daddy, plus a determination to turn a resolute back on modern psychology, inclined you, at one time, to think of me quite seriously as a sort of demon. Whether you ever really thought that: Alexander the Great * Michael Angelo * Botticelli * Lord Byron * Catullus * Cocteau * David * Diaghilev * Norman Douglas * Edward II of England * Von Eulenburg * Francis II of France * Frederick the Great * Stefan George (Germany's greatest living poet) * André Gide (France's greatest living writer) * X (one of England's greatest living painters) * the Guards * the Homeric heroes * Jonathan * the Knights Templars * the Mahommedan races * Von Möltke * half the Navy * Eddie Marsh * partridges * Peter the Great * Petronius * Plato * Charles Ricketts * the Romans * William Rufus * Shakespeare * Charles Shannon * the Siamese * Socrates * the Spartans * Lytton Strachey * Tuke * Virgil * Hugh Walpole * Oscar Wilde * Walt Whitman * William III* and dear old Wagner (½)—were all demons too, I don't know dear.

Please write me fully, and speaking of fullness I forgot: Verlaine * Rimbaud * the 1st Duke of Portland * Tchaikowsky * Oscar Browning * Beardsley * half the schoolmasters in England * and Proust—

P.S. Anyway, I shall marry one day.

In alphabetical, yet surprising, juxtaposition about thirty more names were listed, of living—or lately living—people who might not relish commemoration in this particular roll-call. The next letter to his mother digressed on the subject of 'barebones metaphysical poetry', a new pre-occupation of Brian's:

I will give you a tiny resumé of *why* one writes poetry like this nowadays. In order, nowadays, to sing, it is necessary to *speak*. Beauty and Truth never go naked. And their clothes change. So do *they*. If Shakespeare wrote today he would not only be unrecognisable to most of his admirers, but his poetry would not be considered *good*, as being by *anyone*, by most of them. Whether I am a bad or a good poet is beside the point. For me, in reality, as a *person*, the point is that I am on the right *spring board* ... To be, nowadays, melodious, rhythmic, *satisfying* in the sense that the great Victorians satisfy *musically*—is simply to be out of touch with reality. Poetry is never really of any ultimate value unless it concerns itself with philosophical truths (as they develop). When such truths (which continually change) have been agreed upon for some time, poets have breathing space in which to grow confident, e.g. *melodious*. When a time of flux comes (e.g. now), one *hasn't time*, breathing space. One has to be *barebones*.

The rest of the year 1931, from September onwards, Brian spent in Toulon, from where he wrote to his mother, especially concerning the present economic situation:

Your saying that Bandol is now more fashionable than Cannes is over-fashionable of you, I think. If one or two rich amateur artists do genteelise fragments of the vicinity, I can avoid them or go and have tea with Duncan Grant or Huxley. I am now established in a very cheap hotel here. Fortunately Cocteau was here and he has got me the most charming little flat high over the harbour belonging to a woman friend of his. The flat is in Toulon and not at Bandol, admittedly . . .

My book is progressing very, very, *very* well. Please let me know what you are doing and what you have found in London. And how Daddy is, now: it has been such a dreadful year for him. I am going to do a new book of poems shortly, *Splendours and Decorations of Bavaria* is the title.

Well, this is a business about the pound. Apparently, it hasn't fallen yet (22nd September). It seems difficult to believe anything serious will happen, though God knows we've never had such a stupid government. One longs for the Victorians again. I move in a practically exclusively literary world over here, wherever I am, but ne'ertheless I pick up scraps of information, and it seems to me that if I had money I'd invest it *nowhere* nowadays save in *Holland* or *Switzerland*. America may crash just as well as England, France or Germany. *All* these belligerent, vast army-navy nations are unstable in the modern world.

The whole capitalist system is beginning its death throes, anyone who isn't prejudiced can see it. Every responsible authority, psychological, sociological, economic, prophesies that the whole social fabric has got to be reorganised in the next ten years. It has been admitted for years now that Church, State and Finance are spiritual shams. But the thing is that they're material shams too. The psyche of the race is changing and will and can not support them longer. The whole *business* is wrong—*finished*. From the silly sex laws to the money systems. I don't pretend to know what ought to be done. One just sees that it is the old order changing, giving place to new. I think I'd probably be miserable in Russia, for instance, though it is the only enlightened state.

I hope the money system lasts out our time, for purely selfish reasons. It will, perhaps. After all, I was born, as well as you, in the old system—I don't want to work at soviet propaganda poems, or in a factory, for a pittance. But the truth, the spirit of the world is against capital. One must try and progress. The spirit of Man and its advancement. To be intellectually conscientious.

[A few weeks later] . . . Well, I have never taken much interest in politics. I have always felt intuitively that Russia was the one beacon of progress, and now that I am beginning to read official documents I see I was right. Nothing can be done under capitalism because the very germ and heart of it is wrong. A State which permits an individual to acquire the vast mass of power represented by, say, a million pounds must be reformed or destroyed. *Because* his surplus profits should have been either (a) taken by the State to ameliorate general conditions, or (b) taken at first hand in the form of higher wages for the men. There's no way OUT. (Don't answer, 'we live on capital'. I know we do.)

[Mrs. T. P. O'Connor, Brian's paternal grandmother—of whom he was very fond—had just died.]

... Well—I didn't know 'Damma' had so much money, to tell you the truth. Wear the diamond, for her. I am touched and proud she has left me her manuscripts. I would rather have them than anything else—FAR. Now that Daddy has, with what he had previously, almost as large an income, if not quite, as you, he will of course help you to live at Nore again. If he does *not*, by any chance, offer to do it, it will be *the last closing of the last door* between he and I. Because it will be the *uncontrovertible* proof of what I fear of him.

My £50 legacy I, of course, give to you. Please keep for me any funny little things of Damma's—you know how much *letters and books* mean to me. *I have a terrific feeling for family things.* When one's family consists of one person—Heaven knows who Daddy *really* is, still less his father—one is rather apt to feel as I do, not for snobbish, but for deeper, reasons.

... This is to say I am illish. I have long suspected these *stumblings* that my heart makes in bed at night. The best doctor in Toulon says that I have no organic disease of the heart or lungs but my heart is the *size* of a child's heart.[2] My blood rate is nearly a third too low. The nerve which makes the heart go slow, with me, is out of control. It is continually stopping and decelerating my heart When I am nervous this automatically gets worse. One terrible thing (for me) is that I have been forbidden more than 12–14 cigarettes a day. I smoke between 25 and 30. I have been given Adrenaline and two other medicines to take. At the present I am like an engine, as he said, running on two cylinders instead of three. This business explains a *great deal* to me. You will deny it, but it explains my small output of work to a very important degree, and also why I get up late. He tells me that the whole thing began and has its origin in *nerves*. Nerves turning themselves into physical phenomena.

... I see that my hesitation in telling you of my *single* and rather amusing adventure with opium was to a certain extent justified. I can make not very much of parts of your letter—frankly. 'Your body is being poisoned with tobacco, wine etc. and you add opium ... you can't like anything that is the opposite of being in control and being master of your own body.' I quite agree, yet narcotics (which include wine and tobacco) have vast uses. Who shall name the exact degree?

But was the opium adventure singular *in* any sense of the word? Brian wrote at this time to Alan Pryce-Jones, who had become a great friend of his:

At the moment I am racked with rheumatism as the result of smoking too much with 'Cocktoe', who is *a dear, agreeable creature of whom I am very fond.*

---

[2] A too small heart was also diagnosed in 1927 in Frankfurt.

Desbordes is so much the cross little hearty that I am convinced Cocteau wrote *J'adore* for him. There was a funnyish incident with a terrible old *cantatrice* who complained to the manager of the smell of opium. She stood in the passage half invisible on account of the whirling mists of it, raging. The manager told her she was a disgraceful liar and must leave, which she did. I puffed a last volley at her as she thundered away down the stairs . . .

Half my problems are solved by 'Toni' being with me—what I spend on him I save on shoe-leather really—since one no longer traipses through the sewers of Europe searching for love. And it is such a comfort being permanently with a really sweet *stupid* person. The trouble with the South of France is that one cannot avoid the smarties and the mistral at the same time. The moment the mistral ends—at about St. Tropez—the smarties begin. I've chosen the mistral . . .

I have a book to finish—a sort of travel-diary-novel—and may take a flat which Klaus Mann may come and share with me. I hope so, as he is my find of the year—*delicious* person.

P.S. Gerald Heard's two books are the most important that have ever been written since the Ice Age.[3]

[Later] . . . You should be envious of me, Alan. I am become shriven, pure, translated, free of the chains at last. *Never*—am I coming back. At *last*, I am beginning to glimpse what I *want*, and London has no place in it. Opium has no place in it either. For example, before Cocteau *got* typhoid I smoked every night and *enjoyed* it. In a rather fast literary way. Now that he's in hospital I only smoke twice a week, or less, with a friend of his, and don't miss it at all. But it's very agreeable—I do so *hope* it doesn't affect the heart—*does it?*—that heavy, floating feeling, as if one was some immense Einsteiny Ganymede resting in the arms of some far more immense hard beautiful Zeus. Saying vast, architectural witticisms. And Toni is so funny, guzzling it down and roaring about sausages and Hitler and being the perfect great swinging captain-of-the-eleven contrast. And then I think of people I dislike, like . . . and a huge cold glow of Piero della Francesca-like omnipotent contempt and superiority flows over me. Quite extraordinary—how great one feels. Very comforting to totally unsuccessful minor poets.

. . . Russia is all right except that they are Fascists. Which is so dispiriting to realise. And it's all very fine about the death of individualism, etc. It's all quite true and quite right, I dare say, but I AM one, and I don't want to be shoved forward into a psychological condition I'm not ready for. But I'd like to go there, with you and Eddie, say. We might consider it one day. (Later): . . . Would the *Mercury* consider three prose poems of mine? And an article, and some translation of Ducasse?[4] Cocteau is staying on here, thank goodness—what with Toni to be silent with and he to talk to, it is really idealish here.

---

[3] Probably *The Emergence of Man* (Cape), and *Social Substance of Religion—essay of evolution of religion* (Allen & Unwin), both published in 1931.

[4] A pioneer of surrealism in literature who wrote under the pseudonym 'Comte de Lautréamont'.

The reaction of the *London Mercury* must have been favourable because Brian wrote again a few weeks later to Alan Pryce-Jones, saying: 'I shall be delighted to contribute', but as usual the spirit lost out to the flesh.

Although there had been, as yet, no references to him in Brian's letters to his mother, he had taken on as permanent companion this young German boy, Toni, whom he had originally discovered in Munich. For the next ten years or so Toni, a young 'dumb chum' type, was to be Brian's net joy and gross liability, if such a calculating metaphor can be accepted. Friends are divided in their opinions of him, but basically he was a bisexual good-time boy, blond and exceptionally handsome, silent and simple, with an instinctive weakness for alcohol. Some of his later letters to Lura Howard, illiterate as they were (and, of course, in fractured English), have considerable natural charm.

Barbara Ker-Seymer, who was staying in Toulon during that summer of 1931, describes her first encounter with Toni:

> I well remember us all sitting at the Café de la Rade in Toulon—Cocteau, Desbordes, Bérard, etc.—waiting for this glorious creature to appear for the first time. He was eventually seen making his way down the Rade and oh, horror of horrors! He had been back to the hotel and got himself up in what he thought were his best clothes, a most unbecoming, very cheap business suit, and his golden locks were smarmed down to his head with some sort of glue-like substance. I have never forgotten Brian's face at the sight of this apparition. He leapt from the table and forcibly dragged him off down the Rade. For the rest of his stay he was not allowed to be seen except covered from top to toe in a black leather bicycling suit, or full Tyrolean regalia. Very odd in Toulon, in the blazing Mediterranean sun!

Brian was reputed to be merciless once he started to castigate Toni for his clothes, or snub him for his attempts at conversation. At all events he did not figure in Brian's correspondence with his mother, which took on a decidedly 'highbrow' turn:

> I think Virginia Woolf is a genius, and will live because she has true originality, new-ness, in writing—not in 'how', but in 'what', not in technique (though she has originality there too) but in content—her beauty is seen with *her* eyes. Some of her flower descriptions, for instance, make one see them in a *new* way, and that is the important thing.
>
> Don't be too sniffy about highbrows—Bloomsbury. They have a disconcerting way of remaining on library shelves after the jolly, and the popular, have somehow vanished. You say 'There is a tremendous reaction against highbrows'. This is like saying there is a tremendous reaction against blondes. Anyway, you can thank your stars there are such people. 'By the way, V. Woolf is in and out of asylums etc.' I hold no brief for V. Woolf as a *person*. Because she is pompous, however—not because she may be dotty. I am interested in her as an *artist*, as you should be, as I am interested in van Gogh and Nietzsche, who both went mad. And Blake. And Clare, the pastoral poet. And what is madness, anyway? Do you know? And,

'V. Sackville West said the other day that Heard and Julian Huxley were literature these days, as they gave what she called the *larger* view, the scientific view as opposed to the personal view.' V.S.W. is, then, a fool. Literature proper, is 'creation', not 'comment'. Heard *could write* his sociological-philosophy in such a way that it would be literature, but he doesn't. Few, if any, sociological-philosophers do, or have done, for some reason. Julian Huxley *could* write science in such a way, but he, also, for the same reason, doesn't. . . . If you prefer science to literature you are at liberty to do so. Many intelligent scientists do. But as for science *being*, or becoming, the new literature—it is simply a confusion of ideas.

. . . Do tell me more about your *club*. Evelyn Waugh I'm not very fond of. Remember that no matter *who* it is there—seeming sympathetic or not—you must talk to no one with the same *kind* of freedom that you talk to Barbara (Ker-Seymer). I know those sort of clubs—they are very agreeable, but people have STONY CORES in them. And you are always too trusting. It is, too, the sort of place that you will, inevitably, hear that I have been seen, dressed as Louis XIV, kissing a crippled postman in Warsaw. Upon which, you *may* believe it, and start an indignant correspondence with the Polish postmaster-general!

It was during this Toulon period that Brian scribbled the following note in one of his many notebooks: 'I am dominated, to a degree in which few men alive are, by the Intellectual Conscience, and at the same time must prevent myself—because I am purely a poet—from writing criticism. It is very tiring.' Of his projected travel-diary-novel there is no trace except for this fictionalised piece on his attitudes 'About Writing':

'You've just seen me drink a glass of brandy' said Russell, leaning his thin, chocolate arms on the table. 'Do you know why?'

'No,' I replied.

'Because of the terror of trying to write. You can have no idea how terrifying it is. Rimbaud has given it to me, partly. Everything drives me to write a book. Money. The consciousness of not keeping up my position as a clever young man. The necessity of not disappointing one's father too long. Yet—what? A travel book? Every young man I know writes a travel book. Each one becomes more *personal*—more full of small, clever, personal observations. Yesterday it was observing how beautiful beauty spots are—today it is observing how ugly beauty spots are. That travel book! The clever young man's travel book. A list of his irritations.'

'But couldn't you write a better one. Stand opposite the Pyramids etc. and *deal* with them?'

'No . . . I am haunted by a preference for trying to make a work of art. Not a Bright Young Baedeker. My travel book—I am afraid it would be like the others . . . I so sympathise with them, too. The past is so vile.' He paused. 'I said, a moment ago, my position as a clever young man. I haven't any. I could have had. Sometimes I want it. Sometimes, you know,' he smiled sideways, 'I want to give a dance. In Carlton House Terrace. And have the Prince of Wales. Sometimes—always, really—I don't want it. I have done well to be lazy, to fly them all, poisoners—idiots.'

'Why not try a novel?'

'A novel! Heavens. A novel is a story. I can't make up a story. I can't live other people's lives. I can't live my own. Besides, I am not a novel-writing person—yet, anyway. I don't belong to a novel-writing generation. Story-writing. One can't write stories, now. One can't do anything. *Alix, noch ein cognac!*' he continued. 'I'm being silly, I know. I only met you for the first time five minutes ago, and here I am ranting and raving. I'm in that hopeless mood. An appalling bullying ghost—that's what art is. One is too shamed to compromise, so nothing gets done. I'd *write* a travel book, full of the tippiest remarks—go back, or on, a step, for that's all that's needed—admire just the opposite things in just the right way etc.—if I weren't too ashamed. So nothing—*nothing* get's done.'

He became involved once more with Nancy Cunard, now in Toulon, while she was preparing her famous pamphlet protest against her mother, and wrote to his mother:

I was only thinking last night, as I was reading the pamphlet that Nancy has written about her mother and Beecham etc. and which she is sending out broadcast, how different and lucky you and I were—and how the same pamphlet is sent out, but invisibly, by *most* children about their parents.

You've no idea what it's like. Her mother behaved with the utmost folly and narrow-mindedness and has, of course, brought it on herself. I should regret to write such of you! I may say. But I quite understand Nancy. Her mother has been 'asking for it' from Nancy, by behaving *vilely* to her and her friends, for years. I am having you sent a copy—and I had *great* pleasure in addressing Daddy's copy. The description of the luncheons in Grosvenor Square, 'for sixteen', are *admirable.* 'Her Ladyship: "Now what's this I hear about *fairies*—what do men *mean* by such things? I don't *understand.* What does it *mean?*" The homosexuals present grin.' ETC. You'll see. I think it is going to create an explosion such as has never been known, and will very likely be her end 'socially'. (It is going to everyone, and is being printed here—I am helping. Take heart, *because I'm not mentioned* in any way, *indirect* or *direct*).

The 11-page pamphlet (privately printed in Toulon) was called *Black Man and White Ladyship—an anniversary,* by Nancy Cunard, 1931. The 'anniversary' was of the moment a year before when the Colour Question really affected her personally. Shortly after arriving in London on one of her several visits with her negro friend, Henry Crowder, Nancy learnt of the following remark that had recently been made at one of her mother's ('Her Ladyship's') lunch-parties by Margot Asquith, Lady Oxford: 'Hello Maud, what is it now—drink, drugs or niggers?' Half of London was immediately telephoned to: 'Is it *true* my daughter knows a Negro?' etc. etc. Sir Thomas Beecham, as a 'family friend', took it upon himself to advise Nancy not to come to England with a gentleman of

American-African extraction ... her mother cut her allowance by half, and threatened to cut her out of her Will. All this is documented in the *White Ladyship* half of the pamphlet, but it was not only Lady Cunard's attitude to the negro that was exploded, but her refusal to accept or discuss the existence of 'pederasty' ('too *un*pleasant'), her horror of Communists—'you can't *know* people like that', her losses in the Art game or Picture racket, and her nonchalant statements to the press on why she spent a fortune on clothes: '. . . I do not have to bother about money.'

Black Man, the second half of the pamphlet, consisted of a reasoned exposition of the plight of the negro, George Moore (of whom, incidentally, Nancy Cunard was very fond) being quoted for his strangely reactionary replies to questions on colour prejudice:

Self: 'Have you ever known any people of colour?'
G.M.: 'No.'
Self: 'What, not even an Indian?'
G.M.: 'No—though my books are translated into Chinese.'
Self: 'Not even an Indian ... such as might have happened had you met, shall we say, an Indian student. Don't you think you'd like to talk to an intelligent Indian or Negro?'
G.M.: (calmly) 'No. I do not think so. I do not think I should get on with a black man or a brown man.' *(Then warmly, opening the stops):* 'I think the best I could do is a yellow man!'

Brian continued to his mother:

I see Nancy about twice a week. She is compiling a vast reference book on the Colour Question[5]—of great erudition and interest. The present Scottsboro case in Alabama is iniquitous—do you know eight negro *boys* are being killed by the State because they are suspected of having had affairs with two white *prostitutes* who *deny* it? That they have been lashed on the *throat with rubber pipes* to make them say they did? The whole negro press of America is *aflame*, and rightly. And do you know there are over six *lynchings* a month? The position of the American negro is one of the *greater* wrongs of the world.

A slight *froideur* grew up between them, according to Brian's letter a few weeks later to Alan Pryce-Jones, 'Nancy is here, with her tiny, frighteningly 'intelligent' *surréaliste* (Aragon), but I don't see her often, as she has begun to be Calvin in some curious way . . .' Allanah Harper fills in with a brief sketch of these two friends:

Nancy Cunard and Brian resembled each other in many ways. They were both idealists and romantics, both were true to their own vision, and they often expressed their opinions with violence, causing scandal—which more

[5] *Negro*, anthology made by Nancy Cunard, 1931–1933, published by Lawrence & Wishart, 1934.

often than not was detrimental to the cause they wished to advocate. They never followed the middle way. Nancy Cunard's manner of fighting for equal rights for coloured people was certainly not that of *Uncle Tom's Cabin*. They both had lovable personalities, they both looked distinguished and very elegant, however drunk or violent they were; the other people looked vulgar beside them.

I remember being taken by Brian to her flat in Paris. She lay on a tiger skin rug, her arms encased in huge African ivory bracelets, with a necklace made from equally large lumps of ivory. Her great green eyes were quite the most fascinating I had seen. Brian said in a loud voice, 'Nancy is the only type of woman a man like me could fall in love with, in fact I was, my dears, and reciprocated too.'

At the turn of the year Brian wrote that he had had an offer of a series of articles in *Everyman* (a twopenny!)[6] 'I'm going to make some money if I DIE at it in London. I can't retail my ideas *here*. I shall come at once to you. I wish to have a place, room or what not, of my *own*, to begin with. Be cheerful about 1932 please. It's going to be *good*.'

Whether 1932 turned out to be as good as Brian expected one does not know. He annihilated Reinhardt's production of the *Miracle* in the *New Statesman*, and eulogised Cocteau's film *Sang d'un Poéte* in the American *Harper's Bazaar*—of which I quote one characteristically perceptive extract:

... One of the reasons why this film is often so beautiful is because of its successful presentation of *magic*. Cocteau's incessant discovery of beauty in the natural objects of everyday life is one of his most important qualities. While most artists seem only to be able to convey their messages by means of customary media, Cocteau will contrive beauty with such things as a part of a bicycle, or with pipe-cleaning wire. His eyes are so pure that the curtains which familiarity hangs between almost everyone and the simple objects that surround them—the beauty of blood, for instance—do not exist for him. He really *sees* ordinary things. They reward him. Substances, forms, elemental things, give him, in return, the secret of their mysteries, and enable him to re-present them to an astonished world with all their continual newness, their reality, blazing forth ...

The greatest advantage that the cinema has over the stage is its power to dominate matter, its relative freedom from physical laws. It is able to move as fast, or as slow, as a dream. It is able to present the poetic imagination visually, as it flies ...

Of the *Miracle* he took a very different view (in the *New Statesman*) under the title 'Miracles never cease; or dommage à Diaghilev'. I quote a few extracts:

It is as the derisive and gangsterish funeral service of the Russian ballet, not an inspired blast of propaganda, that I view this remorseless

---

[6] He wrote an interesting appreciation of Lytton Strachey in a January 1932 issue.

production, the Lyceum *Miracle*, since, when we are not staring at processions of what seem gleaming débutantes disguised as nuns, supporting electric fixtures, and intoning they know not what, the stage is chiefly occupied with a series of ballets . . .

The chief pretensions of the production, naturally, are to be found in the scenery, costumes and choreography. Half the auditorium has been transformed into Hollywood Perpendicular, while the cathedral on the stage is more a triumph, possibly, of the parrot, than the Paramount, mind. The Forest scene, opening the second act, is conceived with that nice admiration of the natural and formal most detrimental to both, and succeeds in resembling an effeminate vegetable garden . . .

As regards the dresses, there are two pages and some negroes in the coronation scene whose clothes are as beautiful as their *provenance* is suspect. For the rest I would like to remind Herr Reinhardt and Mr. Cochran, that if they find Picasso or Chirico too highbrow, there are designers in this country who, although they might not be able to compete with Mr. Oliver Messel on his own ground, might be accorded preference when there is apparent need for serious and original work. We can all remember Bakst for ourselves. The choreography is, with the exception of one dance, disgraceful . . .

This attack so incensed the ballet dancer, Lydia Lopokova, that she rushed off a letter of protest to the *New Statesman*, which was backed up the following week by a reasoned justification from Cochran himself.

Oliver Messel remembers being called in at the last moment to re-design the costumes for the *Miracle* as Reinhardt did not like the original production ones. About Brian's scathing comments, he recalls no reason for such animosity—in fact Brian and he had been good friends ever since they were at Eton together. 'Brian was often capricious, and you never knew how he would take things—or write about them. He probably thought I needed taking down!' (Brian later commissioned him to do a painting of his great friend 'Sam', so his work was acceptable in the end.)

To telescope time, some thirteen years later, in the same place (*New Statesman*) Brian contributed a very mellow, and flattering review of Cochran's autobiography, *Showman looks on.*[7] The critical extrovert in his late twenties had given way to the forty-year-old analytical critic, as the following extracts show:

. . . As one reads, one realises again the enormous boon which the author has conferred upon the English theatre-going public during his lifetime. It was he who brought Duse and Bernhardt on their final visits, and he who suggested the *Miracle* to Reinhardt, and produced it in 1911 at Olympia. This was probably the most significant event, as regards Spectacle, in modern theatrical history. He revived it at the Lyceum in 1932 . . .

English revue, in the inter-war period, was largely his personal creation. Few who watched those sumptuous, judicious, exhilarating displays at the

[7] Published by Dent, 1945.

old London Pavilion will have forgotten them. In theatrical decoration he gave Christopher Wood and Bérard their first commissions, and to him is due much of the early stage success of such brilliant designers as Messel, Beaton and the late Rex Whistler . . .

Brian's first published political feature was something of a *coup*. He obtained an interview with Hitler's press chief and social secretary, Dr. Hanfstaengl (which the *New Statesman* published in April 1933). The actual interview had taken place the previous summer, and Brian was already writing to his mother from Munich in August 1932 about seeing Hitler himself:

> I have been struggling with Hitler's secretary and expect to see him tomorrow. If so, it means £30 or £40 from the paper because they promised a bonus as well. I shall leave here the *minute* I've seen Hitler. He lives in a sort of marble house like a Turkish bath—the ceilings moulded into swastikas—surrounded by hideous young athletes in fancy dress who clicked their heels at me and growled 'Heil!', raising their arms. I thought it only diplomatic to do it back, and dropped my umbrella . . .

According to Alan Clutton-Brock he never achieved this meeting with Hitler owing to some last minute row with Unity Mitford ('Just for that, Brian, I won't introduce you to the Fuehrer'.) The appearance of the Dr. Hanfstaengl interview in print, quoted in full below, led to the German Embassy in London telling Brian he would have to stop criticising Germany or he would no longer be a welcome visitor there. In fact he became officially 'unwelcome' in 1936. From then on he had to use a pseudonym for his more outspoken political articles (which were to appear in the *News Chronicle)*, choosing 'Ian Ward', a beheaded version of his own name, and 'Edward Kent'.

THE NAZI LOOKS AT ART (reprinted from the *New Statesman*)

(Mr. Brian Howard guarantees the following conversation as an accurate record of an interview which took place during August of last year at the Brown House, Munich, between himself and Dr. Hanfstaengl, press chief and social secretary to Hitler. Our own correspondent in Berlin reports a very similar conversation with Dr. Hanfstaengl. Our correspondent asked, 'Can you give me an indication of Hitler's economic policy?' Dr. Hanfstaengl replied, 'Oh, it is all quite simple. Everything will be all right when we have turned the Jews out of Europe and the niggers out of France. If the French won't do it for themselves we shall have to do it for them.'—ED., *N.S. & N.*)

Myself: Now, Herr Doktor, to speak frankly, you realise that Herr Hitler is considered abroad, at least, as principally a military figure. It is hard for us to think of him as taking any real interest in Germany as regards art, for example.

Dr. H.: I, Mr. Howard, have been with Hitler for ten years. Do you suppose I could live as long as that with a stupid man? Why, I play him the

Gretchen am Spinnrad of Schubert on the piano—frequently. Almost every day, And he enjoys it very much.

Myself: But does he talk about these things?

Dr. H.: No. He refuses to talk about anything. Particularly at the moment.

Myself: Never talks?

Dr. H.: Well, sometimes he talks about music and architecture. He is not literary, only artistic.

Myself: What?

Dr. H.: He is interested in a great many things that mere army officers are not. Remember that. Do you know the Guinnesses?

Myself: Yes, I like some of them. Dr. Hanfstaegl, what modern literary work do you consider embodies the Nazi ideal most representatively?

Dr. H.: *Peer Gynt.* It is the greatest thing written since *Faust*. It is blond. Spengler knows. Houston Chamberlain knew. Germanic.

Myself: I see. I want to ask you rather a delicate question, now. Why this hatred of Jews?

Dr. H.: Jews? Jews! Because they've never produced anything at all. Because they made the English and American theatres into sewers. Ours, too. All women and nakedness. Look at Reinhardt. Muck [where I put the word 'muck' Dr. Hanfstaegl must be understood to have used the word '*scheiss*']. *Moissi*, muck. Martin Luther said that the Jews were all right so long as they were frightened. Frightened. It's true. Besides, they aren't blond. Not Germanic. They are not *Germans*. They have never produced anything except *muck*.

Myself: Well, Herr Doktor, what is the Nazi opinion of Thomas Mann? He's not a Jew.

Dr. H.: Muck. Darling of the Jews. I'm delighted he wrote during the last fourteen years in Germany. It just shows.

Myself: But he is considered—

Dr. H.: Possibly. The little great man. Always feels it his duty to churn out a new masterpiece every so often in order to be a greater little man. I myself, you know, Mr. Howard, agree with that hero of Huysmans. I read anything. One astonishing word a page is enough for me, even if it's a misprint.

Myself: Really? What about Bruno Frank?

Dr.H.: Superficial.

Myself: German films?

Dr. H.: Conscienceless.

Myself: Freud?

Dr. H.: I daresay he's not as bad as his supporters.

Myself: Einstein?

Dr. H.: Jewish propaganda.

Silence.

Dr. H.: And I've grown rather to dislike Nietzsche. *Which* Guinnesses do you like?

The usual money troubles made Brian look to cheaper ways of living, and this interview achieved he thought of Greece, where Leonard Bower (who was an attaché) had asked him to stay in Athens. As he told his mother, 'I am to have an interview with Venizelos, and there are the 19th-century palaces which Robert (Byron) has neglected to be done for the *Architectural Review*. I give you my word of honour also, to return with a complete and publishable and unalarming book.' This plea was re-inforced, unknown to him, by Robert Byron who wrote to Lura Howard from Athens:

Dear Mrs. Howard, I must add one exiguous prayer to his many that Brian may be allowed to come out here. It is a cure that I have been advocating for a year. 'Cure' perhaps is scarcely the word—but I think, and perhaps you will agree with me, that the life that he leads—and we all of the younger generation lead in England, especially in London, is too artificial— a horrid platitude—but what I mean is that from the writing point of view it is apt to rob one of the very grammar of life, to conceal the cardinal elements of human character—without which no character can be described—and to obscure the proper comparisons beneath a veil of very delightful, but for real creative art, too sophisticated humour and appreciation . . .

I do honestly think that before he starts serious writing, and after the appalling exhaustion of last summer, his mind *must* be refreshed. . . . You know I am devoted to Brian and would not write all this if I didn't feel it really—so I hope you will forgive me, as it is rather impertinent I am afraid. Yours very sincerely, Robert Byron.

The answer was obviously yes, as Brian's next letters to his mother (from September 1932 to March 1933) were written from Athens:

. . . The elections passed off very quietly after all—I fly to excitements only less quickly than they fly me. My new plan at the moment is neither essays nor a novel, but a kind of travel book. Simple, but original. Mrs. Sikelianos, who does the Delphi festival every few years, is a friend of mine. *Aeschylus* etc. is done in the ancient theatre with the army, who volunteer for it, dressed in clothes she weaves. She wants me to be 'Orpheus' in the next one, in May 1934.

. . . Damma's grave sounds to me simply dreadful. All those 'Honour- ables' are so characteristic and such a pity. I'm sure that even real Honourables don't have it put on their graves except in operettas. It's very pathetic how Daddy has so swamped his good qualities with pretentious- ness and snobbery.

I am very glad to see you are at Nore. I may be English, but, pretty soon, someone really must confide in me about my paternal grandfather. I get twinges of real tiredness, at intervals, of not knowing anything about him. . . . I have come to my last decision about Daddy. His attitude is impossible—not seeing you on account of me. He is a *stupid* man, of course, primarily. Secondly, insensitive and unbalanced. A pretentious vulgarian, with his silly, snobbish dreams and his rotten pictures . . . You despise 'words' as you call them, but what do you mean by phrases like, 'Daddy has, of course, triumphed over you'. What does it *mean*? Perhaps he feels it incumbent upon him to work himself up into some sort of emotion about me, knowing that I have none at all for him. He 'triumphed' over me, come to think of it, quite successfully from the day I was born, in presenting me with an obviously false and pretentious name—not even adding the slight support of deed of poll. Why didn't he choose 'Jones'? People might not have found out.

[He commented on his mother's disapproval of a recent homosexual scandal that had received considerable newspaper publicity.]

. . . People should be left alone, dear. As long as children are protected, it really doesn't matter going to bed with a lamp-post. Napoleon and Lenin thought so; Rome and Greece thought so; the modern pschyologists think so—and so do I. Certainly it isn't a virtue to be homosexual. As society is now constituted it is excessively inconvenient. But it certainly isn't a vice. I myself am not, completely. I shall marry some day. But even if I have twenty children, no one will ever catch me sneering. I know—to boast—too much. Do you?

. . . My one dream, as you know, is a cottage in England—or, and it is an important or, to be able to live at Nore with you. But then I am twenty-eight—and you don't want me to live as I want to. I really believe that the very idea of a visit to Nore on Toni's part, or on the part of many of my friends, would 'defile' it for you. Strange. And stranger still when one thinks you produced me! Perhaps you haven't found out enough about Daddy's father? I certainly haven't. But it strikes me as odd that you should feel that I am so reprehensible (having Toni as a friend) on my *own*, so to speak. You can't just go and *have* children, you know, and then sit back and watch them become Chancellors and members of White's. Sometimes they turn out odd. . . . My life is rather turbulent at the moment as I am making a stand with Toni about various things—nothing is so illuminating for me as to see what you have had to go through with, with me, than this. However, that is my business, and I see to it quite successfully.

This was a slight mis-statement, as can be gathered from the following reminiscences of that era by Cyril Connolly, which he sent to me under the title 'Brummell at Calais'.

In February 1933 I took my wife Jean to Greece, to recuperate from an illness, and settled into the Grande Bretagne. It was in Athens that we ran into Brian who with his friend Toni was recovering from a visit to Francis Turville-Petre (the 'where's Francis' of *The Dog beneath the Skin*[8]) on his island near Euboea. This terrifying place is described at length in Isherwood's novel *Down there on a Visit*.[9]

---

[8] By W. H. Auden and Christopher Isherwood, published by Faber, 1935.
[9] By Christopher Isherwood, published by Methuen, 1962, Four Square, 1964.

Most guests came back very worried whether they had contracted syphilis from their host, who made it a point of honour to ignore his condition. We were bored with official Athens to which we had one or two introductions and also rather bored with ourselves. I have described this feeling in a piece, 'Spring Revolution', originally published in the *New Statesman* and reprinted in *The Condemned Playground*, but it is not on record that Brian and Toni were the friends who were out on the street with us when we were fired on during the abortive coup of General Plastiras.[10]

We soon became constant companions, as Brian and I had sometimes been in the past, at our O.T.C. Camp, or in Oxford, or London, but only then for very short times. Jean, being a Paris Baltimorean, both witty and affectionate, adolescent and maternal, was an ideal catalyst. Brian's Athens proved very different from ours. Every night he and Toni would set off from the Hotel Mistra for the Pangion, a *louche* café on the way to Piraeus which played the same rôle as the Mabbot street entrance to nighttown in *Ulysses*. Here adventure started. Here were bars and taverns where hashish was smoked and sold, where sailors and lonely young men wove about in the intricate local dances to semi-Turkish music, or sang the laments of the Greeks of Ionia. It was before Bouzouki was famous and there were hardly any tourists. Brian depended on Nico Kalamaris ('Kalas'), a young surrealist of good family, as general mentor and interpreter. He was always calling Brian's behaviour 'really quite intolerable' but turned up regularly the next evening. For me it was a substitute for Flamenco and for similar evenings among Andalusian gipsies of which I was passionately fond. The mystique of 'low life' is the same everywhere.

Then we took longer trips: voyages over rough winter seas in small rough steamers. We spent an arctic week on Mytilene and returned via Salonika and Mount Athos where we were not able to land at Daphni, viewing the forested capes with their monasteries across the angry water. A boat brought out a sick monk who was hauled screaming on board, roped up like a donkey. He was to be taken to Salonika for treatment. In fact he had gone mad and at a late moment that night he jumped overboard and, though the ship turned about, nobody saw him. The incident depressed us all profoundly. We made another trip to the Peloponnese and occupied a fine suite in the inn at Nauplia where our meals were served round a 'brasero' in the sitting-room for a few shillings a day. (Many years later I found Brian had written 'Shit. Prig' against a Greek quotation I had left in the visitor's book at Mycenae. But perhaps it wasn't him.)

By now we were tired of the long Athenian winter and decided that we must have greenness at all costs; green fields, trees, the south-west wind, butter. This developed into a longing for Portugal, in many ways, we

---

[10] Referring to that 'Dictatorship of a day' in a letter to his mother, Brian wrote: 'I and Cyril Connolly and his wife were walking in the streets looking at processions and commotions, when suddenly the army came out and started shooting down the streets with machine guns. I have never been under fire and was rather alarmed. However, we crouched in doorways and eventually ran into an hotel. Out of the windows we saw them shoot down a man on the steps of the university ... It was terrific for a few hours. Airplanes showering leaflets; armoured tanks etc. ....'

decided, the antithesis of Greece, where fountains and the Baroque are absent. But how to get there? I discovered that the American Export Line ran a passenger-carrying cargo service from Piraeus to Seville and we four took the next one, the only passengers. The American crew accepted us as part of their job, as we accepted their extraordinary meal times and their fondness for dishes like Jello. We bought the tickets and there was an agreement that Jean and I would carry Toni; Brian keeping an account of what he owed us himself. Brian recorded his share very faithfully and, when he could, paid it up. But he was under the terrible strain of sharing a bank-account with his mother so that every cheque he cashed became known to her and, if too large, forced her to do without something, which she quickly rubbed in. They were like two prisoners manacled together: the classic Baudelairean situation. It was part of Brian's tragedy that he should have been so like Baudelaire—it was all there; the dandyism, the wit, the father-hatred, precocious sensibility, mother-fixation—all except the poetry or rather the ability to get the poetry out. 'I know I'm a genius,' he would say, 'but I don't yet know what at.'

He suffered agonies of sterility, envy, frustration and remorse; he was in fact in constant pain from the cancer of the soul which eventually killed him, which drove him to outrage and humiliate all who might help him. Drink released his demon as if what he really wanted was for someone to put him out cold and bring oblivion. Toni would have made him happier if he had recognised the 'punch line', as did in later years the young officers whom he called queers or traitors, the waiters, taxi-drivers and hotel managers who he accused of cheating or being police spies. 'Why did I do it? What is the matter with me?' he would wail after one of these nights of insult. An irresistible death-wish was at work in someone who was resolutely determined not to die.

At this period Brian's fortunes were at a very low ebb, but he was still under thirty and there was time for almost anything to happen. He was Brummell at Calais, not yet relegated to Caen. He looked deliciously handsome and distinguished, and dressed with negligent charm in Mrs. Stewart-Richardson's shaggy Greek silk suits and tweeds, with a handkerchief knotted round his long neck. He played his voice like a guitar. I remember two characteristic poses: the head thrown back, the large mocking eyes sparkling with malicious glee; the finger outstretched as he began to tease someone about their appearance—a Club tie or a handkerchief in the cuff—'What is that extraordinary object . . .' and the voice revved up: then, the next morning, the fallen *Fürst*, the *Desdichado*, unshaven, fingers ruffling his hair, the voice a pitch higher, full of infinite weariness. 'It's no good, my dear. I shall always like you (him) more than you (he) like(s) me—it can't be helped. That's how it is.'

Both Jean and I were rather infatuated with Brian and Toni also was still unravaged by time; he looked like a nice conventional English schoolboy, not a prefect but certainly in the Eleven—Wodehouse's 'Mike', or some handsome blood out of *Sinister Street* or the *Loom of Youth*. He was good-tempered as well as good-looking but stupid and rather obstinate.

I can't remember anything he said except '*Aber* Prian!' in permanent expostulation. One day, on the green cloth of the cabin table, I read part of a letter of Brian's to Eddie Gathorne-Hardy, who has unearthed the following postcard of the time: *What does A do when he sees the phrase 'much too much of fortune's darling and sometimes almost common' over B's shoulder. (Just after his offer to pay T's fare to Lisbon had been accepted)? I suppose blister in silence like Gray and Walpole. Much love from yours rather pompously, Cyril.* But one cannot remain angry for long on a tramp steamer.

March became balmy April. We called at Palermo and drove up to Segesta, then on to Naples and crossed over to Capri, with a visit to Count Fersen's old villa with the inscription 'Amori et dolori sacrum' and his collection of opium pipes, and finally steamed up the Guadalquivir in time for the fair at Seville. We entered Portugal by the ferry over the Guadiana at Vila Real and spent a week at Praia da Rocha, which was everything we had pined for—air and sun and huge breakers which crept up to demolish his sandcastles, with the owner's flag flying from the turret, which Brian spent hours in constructing and repairing to the last final engulfment. And there were green hills and white roofs, flagons of green wine, excursions to Faro and Loulé and Monchique with its perfect climate. (The quest for the perfect climate was to become an obsession of his.) Finally we went north and settled at Cintra, searching for the ideal quinta (going, of course, for a song) and re-living Beckford's letters. We took elaborate steps to make evenings as agreeable as possible, each acting as host in turn in the little pension, brewing special cups and cocktails, wearing our best clothes, planning distractions.

Brian, like many whose long-term vistas all ended in despair, was a master of the Bagatelle, a Pierrot of the minute, a captivating companion and commentator on the passing scene. He would pretend to be a speechless scarecrow of a schoolmaster whom I baited and taunted till he would go berserk and chase us through the quintas. Our favourites were Beckford, Ramalhao and Seteais, now a hotel. Or he would dress up as an ancient crone from a Goya etching, a Madame Sesostris, and tell fortunes. Always there was a dignity which we were lured to destroy, to everyone's secret satisfaction. He was also a specialist in practical jokes; one night we were woken by the rattling of the lid of the big hot water jug. Broken by strange intervals the rattling came and went—a rat? A cat? A burglar? Two invisible black threads had been attached to it and taken under the door and along to his room far down the corridor. We called him various names according to his role, like 'Brindle' ('dear Andrew with the brindled hair' from Stevenson's poem to Andrew Lang). One evening two dear old ladies in the restaurant stopped me after he had gone out and asked me if that was his real name. I told them, 'Oh—*we* call him Mr. Beautiful.' But the spring idyll was ending. Brian and Toni had discovered the Casino at Estoril and an expensive taxi would take them off there after dinner. The dollar had just been devalued. We were all by now rather broke and the financing of Toni had become a burden. One morning Brian did not appear until after lunch. He had played high, he said, to win back some of the money he owed us, had lost and lost again and made out a huge cheque on his mother's joint account. A terrible letter followed, listing all that Mrs. Howard had had to give up, including her summer hat and other appurtenances of a London season. Brian shut himself up, his long tragic face enclosed in his even longer hands, got drunk and returned to the Casino.

Through some Dutch painters, the Leydens, he had met one or two grand Portuguese whom he pointedly kept from us. The afternoon before we left by sea (Brian and Toni were staying on) there was an incident in our favourite bar in Lisbon. One lady in our party, a teetotaller, was charged for several gin fizzes; we refused to pay the extra; the porter barred Jean's exit and Brian hit him, whereupon a fight started and we were all of us taken to prison and fingerprinted. Fortunately the Embassy lawyer was reached and the porter was compensated all round to the point of withdrawing the charges. In this case Brian was not really to blame since he was championing the two ladies and was perfectly sober. We did not see him again till he came to stay with us near Rottingdean later in the summer, where Alan Pryce-Jones took some photographs.

Brian's trouble—as with so many aesthetes of his generation—was a basic ignorance due to having failed to learn anything or to have learned how to learn when at school and university. This vagueness had the effect of casting suspicion on the things he actually had learnt—except for matters of clothes, deportment and behaviour, in which for a few years he reigned supreme. He should have been a Prince Genji composing epigrams and perfumes, despatching footmen with love-letters, judging flower-arrangements. But he was too poor and too intelligent. He was also extremely ambitious and determined to be famous and to dominate the company he found himself in. This he could only manage to do through mockery of those who were stupider or commoner than himself. A Dante to the frivolous, a dandy with the stuffy. When he did acknowledge a superior, like Auden or Cocteau, he was happy while they lasted, his ambition abated. That spring of 1933 we saw him at his best, not yet the professional anti-fascist but a prince of fantasy—in constant motion, enjoying the shifting scene and enhancing it for others. Too often he was bogged down among the bottles and magazines in his hotel bedroom, waiting for the money to pay his bill, by which time he had run up another . . .

Brian and Toni returned to London after this Portuguese interlude and rented a cottage in Hampstead. There was more talk of having to sell Nore owing to the critical dollar situation (most of Lura Howard's income coming from the States). Brian contributed a lengthy review of Herbert Read's *Art Now* to the *New Statesman* supplement in October 1933, and admitted to it being the most difficult article he had ever done, 'hours and hours of coffee-supported misery it cost me'. He realised that his income from the *New Statesman* reviews was not going to be enough, and considered trying to get a job on the *Referee*, but his heart was not in it and his life went on much as before.

It was during this period that Maurice Richardson remembers meeting Brian after a gap of several years:

Leonard Bower had asked my first wife, Jocelyn (who afterwards married the Hungarian historian, the late Bela Ivanyi), and me to stay with him for the weekend at the King's Head at Aylesbury, where he was living for the time being.

We arrived in the afternoon and found Brian and his German boy-friend, Toni. Relations between Brian and Leonard seemed quite cosy. At one time they had been at daggers drawn. Somehow it was characteristic that Brian should have provided Leonard with the target for his *mot*, if you can call it a *mot*: 'Jumpers by Reville, foreskin by Clarkson!' Leonard's friends used to say that this had exhausted his brain for the next three years.

After tea we set out on one of the pub crawls that Leonard loved. Drank Colne Spring Ale, which had to have a red hot poker stabbed into it. Toni was sharply told to attend: 'try to learn something of our English customs.' Brian was in high spirits, giving out a delightful glittering harlequin charm. Once the cloven hoof appeared. Jocelyn, my wife, said that she made hats. 'And where do you make them? Hardly Mayfair, I should think. I wouldn't be altogether surprised if it wasn't Kensington.' Jocelyn, being a good-natured, easy-tempered girl, didn't mind. A hypersensitive person might have been hurt. Brian's habit of bullying women was one of his few really unpleasant traits. I've been told that at deb dances in the late 'twenties he sometimes reduced girls to tears. Goodness knows what lay behind this symptomatic misbehaviour. He bullied men, too, but rather differently. Even some of his more outrageous performances seemed to be prompted by a satirical purpose. Like most paranoid characters he had an infallible eye for the weak spot.

In the market square we got the *Evening Standard* which had the story—I think—of Hitler's withdrawing Germany from the League of Nations. Brian became intensely serious. 'This means war is certain, and very much sooner than you think.' Leonard, who hated any mention of politics except as a joke, made fussy head- and hand-shaking movements to express his embarrassment. We were walking back to the King's Head when somebody let off a firework close behind us. 'This,' said Brian, 'is very sinister indeed. We are being followed.' All the way back to the hotel mysterious fireworks kept exploding all round us. Back in Leonard's sitting-room a squib was tossed through the window. We rushed round and caught Brian climbing back into his bedroom. We knew by this time that it must somehow have been him all along, but he had been giving a performance, with perfectly timed distractions, that was well up to the standard of any professional conjuror.

On Sunday morning he made elaborate paper cut-outs with a pair of nail scissors. 'How do you like my heavenly ladder, my dear?' I tried to do a drawing of him. 'Rather more like Queen Nefertiti, but not terribly like her either, I'm afraid.'

He must have stayed in England for the winter of 1933–1934, and the next one hears of him is during the summer of 1934 when he was visiting Germany, some of the time as travelling companion to a rich friend of his, John Davidson. He saw the young Manns again in Walchensee, and Erika Mann reminisces:

Brian ... that enchanted summer which we spent with him on the Walchensee in Bavaria, in Munich or in Salzburg where he shared with Toni a princely apartment (it actually belonged to an Austrian prince), which, like so many other things, was far beyond his modest means. He earned virtually nothing, but his charm and his casual, self-assured manner never failed to put his creditors to flight, and, at the last resort, it was always his hard-working mother who footed the bill for his irresponsible extravagances.

What was the point of Brian's having that lovely suite of baroque rooms in the Old Town if he was never to give parties—or at least one absolutely splendid party, the party to end all parties, to which we invited anybody who took our fancy, dozens of people, close friends and distant acquaintances? Everything was planned on the most sumptuous lines—the whole elaborate menu, dish by dish and course by course, the music which the little orchestra would play, the elegant button-holes which every guest would receive, male and female alike. We issued invitations indiscriminately, by word of mouth or on little scribbled cards. Only in one single instance were we at pains to describe the projected party in careful detail. We made a list of our guests-of-honour (apart from a crowd of unknown young people, many glittering celebrities figured on our guest-list). We enumerated the menu and the wines, spirits and liqueurs which we proposed to serve. We even added that beer and sausages would be brought forth at dawn. In close collaboration, on the finest paper we wrote a most seductive account of our party, which was to be one of the high points of the Festival season. We disliked the arrogant young man for whose benefit we had gone to all this trouble, and so our 'invitation' ended with the words, *This is just to ask you NOT to come* ...

Brian introduced a strangely flippant note into a letter to his mother from Walchensee, that same summer: 'Well—it has been sunshiney, and full of old friends ... full of my favourite scenery. Which reminds me—gracious, how MUCH more countries and people mean to me than politics. Politics are really death. Yet you may see by recent events how right one's dislikes are, in that quarter. Mercy! Or, rather No Mercy . . .' Was this really the same Brian who wrote a factual account of a concentration camp under the title, *The New German 'Sport'*, about the experiences of a friend of his at Lichtenburg? It makes familiar reading in the light of post World War II knowledge, but would have been a revelation in the mid-thirties. I can find no trace of its ever having been published. Or the following warning note which he even got around to ill-typing:

SCHLAGT SIE ZU BREI

Though Germany, from England, has seemed much more alarming than she really is, all the forebodings and dangers of the last two years crowded themselves, yesterday evening, into one slow minute of the purest horror. I was sitting with an English friend and two German ones in a little café in the suburbs of Munich. One of the two Germans was a man of about forty, an ex-member of the Communist party, his vivacious, intelligent face long ago made wry and quiet from conflicts with Authority. It was him that I had just been telling of the anxieties I had experienced in leaving for Germany at such a time, particularly in view of certain articles I had written. Half-jokingly, I concluded thus, 'I'm sure I shall be beaten into a jelly yet.'

In the earnestness, and straining discretion of our conversation, we had not noticed a large and jovial group of assorted uniforms in the opposite corner. Just as my murmurings ceased, however, a constellation of huge, simple faces wheeled in our direction. They regarded us exactly as not-quite-surfeited bears will eye another bun. Then, in perfect accord, they suddenly broke into a deafening song. *Schla-a-agt Sie zu BREI* ... Deeply uneasy already, I turned to the ex-Communist and told him that I could not quite catch the meaning of the words. 'The meaning is,' he whispered, paying the bill and reaching for his hat with the minimum of ostentation, 'the meaning is—*Beat them to a jelly.*'

Brian's main problem was to get Toni a job—any job, as much for occupation as income, and they decided on his training as a sports teacher. Brian was continually having to ask his mother for more money, ostensibly to pay for frequent medical treatment, first for a swollen kidney, then for stomach trouble *ad nauseam*. One suspects it was drink and God knows what else that provided both the cause and the effect. Toni then returned briefly to the Hampstead cottage, on the chance of some 'film extra' work while Brian continued 'writing' in Germany. Owing to the landlord complaining of drunken orgies Toni had to rejoin Brian in Munich for the winter. Meanwhile the Howards' country house, Nore, was finally being auctioned, Lura having found a smaller substitute nearby, 'Gorebridge'. She wanted Brian to help with the planning of this new home but he preferred to remain in Germany where he was free of family restrictions. By February 1935 he was in one of his desperate moods, and wrote to his mother:

> I started writing yesterday—but the scratchy poverty of the *practically constant terror*, of the *horror* of becoming thirty without having achieved just that tiny, tiny modicum of self-discipline and control which will, and *must* alter my life from now on.
>
> I stay in three evenings, and then suddenly rush out with Unity (Mitford) to a ball, spend too much, and go through agony the next day. My conscience grows, if anything, but my will is so weak. I'm nearly thirty and you've done about all that anyone can. And really, if I can't succeed in getting a little Order into my life at such a time as this, it has its dangerous side. I am trying to force myself up by day and in by night, force myself to stop taking refuge in reading ... but I've learnt so many tricks of self-indulgence, so many reasons for being unreasonable—alas. This horror of regularity—it's too extraordinary. *Outwardly*, I'm behaving admirably—it's only *inwardly* that I haven't won ...

For an unbiased view of the outward aspect the following vignette reproduces Brian to perfection. Mary Moss (now Mrs. Humphrey Cameron) was in Germany at this time:

I knew Brian in Munich in 1934–1935. I never expected to know him really well, and believe me, swimming into his orbit gave me a feeling of taking a part in *The Cabinet of Dr. Caligari*, which was exciting, unreal, melodramatic, and, in the end, rather melancholy.

My mother finally and somewhat glumly arrived in Munich to take me home, but just before, I can remember Brian sitting back in his chair and muttering:

'Small TOWN, small-MINDED, half-baked, half-cultivated, SATINETTE (then a favourite opprobrium of his)
American CLUBwomen . . . (pause) . . .
Who live in a Colonial house they've only just BOUGHT.'

The whole rhythm of that paragraph fascinated me so, I've never forgotten it . . . it sounded almost like *In Xanadu did Khubla Khan*. I must add, as a defensive footnote, that mother is a Vassar graduate and quite sharp, I thought, and the house in Kentucky was a perfect gem, designed by Thomas Jefferson, that my family were very lucky to get hold of. Anyway, it wasn't till we got on the *Coronia*, sailing back to America, that I once more began to feel like a 'Satinette American Clubwoman', and it felt quite nice after the *Dr. Caligari* scene.

By the summer of 1935 the search for somewhere to live (where visas were not necessary and they could remain indefinitely) had started in all seriousness. Toni was a displaced alien before his time. They visited the Brussels Exhibition, where his visa ran out; the sports teacher job fell through; they failed to get a French visa in Zurich, and on trying to fly back to England from Amsterdam Toni was refused permission to land and forcibly returned to Holland. They discovered (apparently via the Mayor of Antwerp) that this refusal was due to a report that Toni had had a 'morphinist' friend to stay at the Hampstead cottage. The situation got on top of Brian, 'I cannot stand any more of it. I've work to do, and it upsets me. I could simply dump Toni on his family, but I just can't do it.'

After these set-backs they then picked on Ireland as a haven for Toni, so he occupied himself practising his English by doing translations for Klaus Mann and Christopher Isherwood, who were both living in the same pension in Amsterdam. Here Brian started a highly disconnected 'Amsterdam Diary':

[September 1935] . . . Lazed in bed until four reading Sheean's (*In Search of*) *History*. Very entertaining, perfect money-maker. Gives me heart-searchings as to Communism, oughtn't one to go to Russia etc.? Even the social experiment has been made and *won* in Russia. Now adaptation only. Nobody knows where they are in politics. All intellectuals crippled by the inability to deal with action. Every intellectual under thirty, and many of them over it, are playing, with a greater or lesser degree of seriousness, with Communism. Lenin is the new Luther. (I have every sympathy with them.) But it is going to result, sooner or later, in such an explosion of individualism as the Renaissance never saw. And I intend to be among the first to explode.

215

The objections to Communism are that: it is a religion; it is an expedient; it is a bore.

... Had a good roar over a story of a friend of mine about his mother who belongs to one of those Guilds, or whatever they are, in Kensington. Shepherding prostitutes off the streets into homes and places where they go mad, and are tortured to death, and taught needlework. One day, after reading a lot of old copies of the *Daily Herald* and *Daily Worker* that she found lying about her son's room, she experienced a conversion and made the most astonishing speech to the assembled guild. 'Girls, we're on the wrong tack. It's all wrong. They've a life to lead as well as us. All Power to the Soviets . . .'

... Felt curiously well, calm and sensible for such feckless and expensive malingering as I am doing here in Holland. Have started this diary because ... it may, with its remorseless record of chances missed and days wasted, goad me into the tiniest effort. It may help as a painful substitute for an apparently total lack of what is called moral fibre.

... This diary was not kept owing to my experiencing a week of complete moral paralysis. In the face of a really very difficult situation (with Toni) I simply gave up, still further seduced by some cocaine and heroin sold me by an acquaintance.

Christopher Isherwood fills in here:

In September 1935 Brian and Toni and I were together in Amsterdam. I remember how, on the last day of August, there were celebrations of the Queen's birthday which became loud and rough and ugly after nightfall. Gangs of young toughs forced the girls to take part in street dancing, which ought to have been fun, but was somehow ill-natured and brutal. Brian brilliantly described their behaviour as 'Bruegeling'.

On another occasion, in the lounge of a hotel in Amsterdam, Brian produced from his pocket a twist of paper containing some white powder. 'This,' he declared *very loudly*, for the benefit of the other guests, 'is cocaine.' Not good cocaine, however, he explained, 'good cocaine is so dazzling that you can't look at it.' He took the powder with ostentatious sniffs, telling me that *cocaine* gathered in a knot in the chest and was like ozone, while *heroin* 'spreads like a stone-flower from the stomach to the legs and arms', whereas *hashish* was like toffee and made you feel 'like the gateway to Hell'. After a pause I asked him about his present sensations, what were they? He answered, 'imagine yourself partly a wonderful calm Venetian palace in the sunshine . . . and partly Joan of Arc.'

Ireland as the haven of rest remained a mirage, for by October Brian had rented a house in Portugal, at Cintra, and wrote to Alan Pryce-Jones:

... The Stracheys (John and Isobel) share it with Toni at the moment—I am sub-tenant for three years. It is frightfully cheap, 18th century, looking over the Atlantic, with fountains and an untouched formal garden. Really

216

heavenly. You ought to come and stay. I am gradually going to try and make the unanchored, nice people I know settle in Portugal, if I can. It's ideal in every way, as you know, and on the boat routes in case of war, which grows more certain *hourly*, in my opinion . . .

To his mother he described a party of the local grandees: 'We put on evening clothes. It was so very diplomat-Minister-Countessy and yet "gay" and rather tipsy-smart, if you know what I mean. A lot of shrill French *Les sales nègres en Afriques* all the time, madly pro-Italian, and Fascist. I really could hardly keep my temper. I growled a little, once or twice, but I liked our hostess so it was bearable.' When Toni was left behind with the Stracheys and their baby, instead of being companionable he either got drunk or gambled away his share of the rent, so that the situation became impossible. At all events, the plan to live in Portugal went the way of all others, and only partly due to Toni's inability to obtain a permanent visa. Back in London John Strachey painted a portrait of Brian, which he now describes:

Although somewhat caricatured it really had something of Brian and was amusing in other ways. The Victorian chimney-piece in the background was in the living-room of our house in Charlotte Street and I thought it a good idea to fill it in with a romantic landscape, in accordance with the sheet Brian insisted upon draping over himself. Naturally it led to a row between us because Brian—I rather think—objected to the Byzantine appearance he had been given and I further put my foot in it by showing it under the title of 'Brian Howard in the character of a Sibyl' (duly reported by Tom Driberg in the press) which improved matters not one whit. Brian considered himself not only the arbiter *elegantorum* but of everything else and did not care for *lèse majésté* in any form. I imagine he thought I was exposing him as a queer, than which nothing was further from my mind. I merely wished to make fun of his oracular tendencies!

There are no letters charting Brian's life in 1936 until the summer when he was back near Salzburg, staying once again with John Davidson. As always he was beset with financial troubles of his own making, his earnings having been virtually nil (only ten reviews in the *New Statesman* in two years, and five topical political articles in the *News Chronicle*). During August–October 1936 he wrote to his mother from Salzburg:

Last night I dressed up and went to the opening night of the Season—very exciting indeed. Toscanini doing *Fidelio*, Beethoven's only opera. Lotte Lehmann was marvellous, such a good actress too. In a curious way the story is very anti-Nazi—there is a chorus of political prisoners singing about *Freiheit*, and there were tears in our eyes. The applause in the intervals started each time like a lightning-crack, quite amazing. After the 'Leonore' overture in the second act the theatre seemed to be filled with thousands of incredibly rapid, ceaseless pistol shots—I've never heard such clapping, and there was stamping and shouting too. I think many people feel that the end is coming soon, and are determined to usher in what may be the last great European cultural festivity with all their hearts.

I am starting my article for the *News Chronicle* at once. My line is going to be what you will imagine—that Austria will be Nazi by next year, and that Toscanini won't come again, etc. . . .

You say, 'Toni will stay in Austria, etc.' How can he, when his passport runs out in November? I'd let Toni go back and even do his military service were it not that I am convinced that he'd probably be arrested, that he'd never be allowed out again, that he'd never get another passport. Everyone says that. Your remarks about my not behaving like a weak undergraduate, or words to that effect, may be true. Perhaps I am. Perhaps I always will be. . . . There is this horrible problem of Toni, who I am afraid to say still means more to me than anyone else excepting yourself, looming over me. After your life with Daddy you deserve something better, something more successful, more disciplined, more reliable and more *happy*. I sometimes think that Daddy was right, second-rate spirit that he is.

Well, well—it's no good going on like this. All I need is self-discipline, as Huxley so persuasively says. Yet to conquer the weaknesses of half a lifetime is no small matter, particularly with no leeway at all financially, and the Toni problem grinning like a devil night and day. It is essential to find Toni something definite to *do*, even if it's only keeping chickens. When I first took it all on, or rather when it first took me on, I thought I could blunder through somehow, as I so often succeed in doing with other things. So many problems do solve themselves for the clever-weak. I knew I had to do it, for fear, partly, of worse things. There are worse types of my type. But then you may not see what I mean. It saddens you too much for you to see that side of life clearly, I feel.

But it is a very real problem for me. Love is no less love, and need is no less need, and quarrels are no less quarrels—however firmly one may qualify them with the adjective 'perverted'.

To have left Toni in Austria would almost certainly have meant his repatriation to Germany, so, ever in search of passports and permits they went off by car to Marseille, via Zurich, with Poppet John who, Brian told his mother, 'very much wants to have a go at doing Aunt Grace's scent shop with me'.

This referred to the new London branch of the American perfumers, Mary Chess, the brain-child of his Aunt Grace Robinson (née *Mary* Grace *Chess*). In 1932 she had sent out for some toilet water and finding it to be almost odourless thought she could do better herself. She started with making cold cream (which she had already done in the First World War), then developed her Roman bath oils, friction lotions, and finally perfumes. She was thought to be out of her mind when she declared during the Depression, 'This won't last—it never does. And what people are going to long for is a little luxury'. She was right, and from experiments in her New York kitchen the firm of Mary Chess became an assured success.

Grace Robinson had always been a great gardener, and a lover of flowers (having started her 'sculptured flower' bouquets as early as 1921). No doubt she was also encouraged by her father, who was an amateur horticulturist, growing many varieties of grapes, and even inventing, I am told, the present type of wheelbarrow—with a wheel that turns—but he sold the idea for a pittance. Brian's cousin Carley, and her first husband Dick Hawkins, ran the London shop until the outbreak of war in 1939[11], and it became a favourite place for friends to stop by and order special presents from the Mary Chess selection. This was renowned, not only for its quality, but for its 'taste' in presentation. Where other firms went in for brash vulgarity or blatant opulence, Mary Chess packages were deceptively simple and well designed.

Brian appears not to have returned to England, being tempted by the offer of a farmhouse in the Engadine, 'what with the immediate prospect of a European war . . . as an asylum for both you and me if there is conscription in England'. He added a P.S. to his letter to his mother: 'The usual richochets about my name. Lord Melchett told Erika Mann that he knew quite well that it was something like Horowitz. Too boring. I'm thinking of writing Daddy about it. I don't see why we should be subjected to this immortal gossip. Do you?'

1937 started not in the Engadine but in Paris, which proved to be one of the worst places for Brian. Too many temptations. Toni became ill, complaining of his heart, and suffered from 'a sort of chronic melancholia, partly the result of having no object in life and no work'. Although Brian started reviewing new novels regularly for the *New Statesman* (having reviewed several books, mostly of political interest, during the last two years or so), alcohol was becoming the great problem and sometimes drugs, this lust for kicks more than as a permanent antidote to life as he insisted on living it.

Despite these problems he did manage to contribute a weighty and authoritative review of Stephen Spender's *Forward from Liberalism* to the *New Statesman* in January, and the *News Chronicle* (which had already run his much publicised five-day serial *Life Story of a Merchant of Death—Zaharoff!* in November) published a frighteningly detailed article on the way of life for children in Germany, under the title *Born to Die for Germany*—by 'Ian Ward'. It fell on singularly deaf ears in February 1937. Early that year he wrote his mother from Paris:

I have just seen Auden off to Spain, and he liked my poem. He is, to my mind, our best poet. I was elated, too, today, Isherwood and he both joined in praising me, my reviews, my poems (of all things!)—messages came from Stephen Spender, too, who is also in Spain. Apparently, from one book of poems and a few reviews, I have a name. I didn't know. It's nice to be reassured. One feels oneself such a poor creature.

I am worried about Toni. He has heart and is *good.* (He is lazy, too, which you despise—so do I.) But has he spirit? Have I? Failure has its successes—*you don't see them.* By this I mean *myself.* . . . I have always known I was going to be a 'great man'. It is only that I was told so. Again. Today. By people I BELIEVE. So perhaps I will be—who knows? Praise, from the right quarter, goes to my head. But I get so little of it. Only from you,

---

[11] Lura Howard then managed it until 1950.

who I *love*. And one never quite trusts people one loves ... Don't be frightened. I have been doing something I never do—drinking Pernod alone. Which is why my handwriting is so sloppy ... I want to go to Spain. But I shall come to you first. P.S. I haven't even begun to write. Not even BEGUN ... This is the first time I have 'drunk' alone ... Well, off this goes and you must make the best of it.

As far as personal participation in the Spanish Civil War was concerned Brian's feelings were decidedly subjective, and as he would not abandon Toni they both stayed on in Paris. (It is not clear why Toni could not also fight in Spain.) Klaus Mann, who was still editing the literary review *Die Sammlung* from Amsterdam, wrote to Brian in February: 'I like the idea of going to Spain, and I had, myself, a long time the firm intention to do so—but I can't. I have to work, and I feel it is better for me, in this moment to stay in a place which is less exciting and a little more peaceful. ... I wonder if you would be able to manage it, yourself, to go to Spain. It seems to become more and more difficult. And, of course, it is dangerous; but that wouldn't disturb me, I think. I feel, IF somebody is going to Spain, today, he most certainly *has* to FIGHT. Otherwise it *is* a little shameful ...' In his autobiography, *Turning Point*, he disarmingly put into words his own attitude or predicament:

When any one among my listeners got up to bother me with cumbersome questions, I presently turned lyrical and elusive. 'My dear friend,' I said, irritated but gentle, 'the minor technicalities are really none of my business. After all, I am not a politician, but a poet: which means that my foremost interest is in the mysterious essence of life, not in its practical organisation ...

[But he knew he could not get away with that]:
Life is indivisible: you cannot split it into various departments, with limited responsibilities. The full stake is required, whatever you try to do. The price you have to pay for every valid thought or constructive deed is invariably the same: it is suffering and unflagging endeavour, a long tedious effort, and suffering again.

A writer who wants to integrate political subjects into the scope of his work must have suffered from politics, just as he must have suffered from love in order to write about it. He must have cruelly suffered: nothing less will do.

It is this last paragraph that is so applicable to Brian. He did suffer, but from his own 'sprain in the spirit' rather than from direct, let alone dire, political consequences at this stage. That spring he continued writing to his mother from Paris:

I am doing my best to accept Gollancz's job—it starts at £400 a year. ... Have just got a letter from Gollancz[12] saying that *although* he has decided

---

[12] Sir Victor Gollancz could not remember meeting Brian or, '*a fortiori* offering him a job'.

that it is absolutely essential to have someone as sub-editor who has had previous experience inside a newspaper office (alas!) he is going to make me an offer of a *permanent* 'feature' in the new weekly paper. Either a page or two to edit, or write myself.

... Did I tell you that Wystan Auden asked me to collaborate on a book with him? I consider this a great feather in my cap, from the most famous young poet of England. He is simply *charming*. He upset me a great deal by saying that he got up every day (he lives in Birmingham) at 8.15, breakfasted and answered letters until ten, worked until lunch, then again from two to four, and then never worked a stroke after that—read, talked. He said that he couldn't allow himself to read after ten or eleven (!) at night, and that unless one had a physical rhythm it was all quite impossible. I said 'you talk like my mother!'

[From Chapelle-Réanville, Eure, staying with Nancy Cunard] This is an old farm. Full of lovely African sculptures and books. We have no servant but there is hot water. John (Banting) cooks, Nancy prints. I am trying to write poetry. Auden is encouraging me to try and make a 'come back' as a poet! There are great plans brewing, in fact. Nancy is publishing a poem of mine on Spain, which is to be sold for the benefit of the Government—printing it herself, with others by various people here and in England. Some of the leading Spanish writers are now in Paris. ... Nancy has been sweet. The pillar that she always is and I respect her increasingly. I think she's the only intimate I have for whom I have never sensed the least faint trace of any kind of second-rateness.

Nancy Cunard's series of leaflets was called *Les Poètes du monde défendent le Peuple Espagnol*, and Brian's poem, *For those with investments in Spain: 1937*, appeared in No. 6, with four others by Nicolas Guillen, Robin Wilson, Randall Swingler and Hans Gebser. This poem (included in Philip Toynbee's selection in Appendix I) was later reprinted in *Poems for Spain*, edited by Stephen Spender and John Lehmann in 1939, when Brian wrote to his mother that, 'Stephen Spender has written me an extraordinarily complimentary letter saying that it is one of the few things that makes the anthology worth printing. I'm pleased.'

The indefatigable Nancy Cunard also helped to canvas writers and poets for their support over the Spanish 'question'. In June of 1937 she sent out a broadsheet—over a foot in length, and strikingly printed in red and black—headed, *SPAIN—The Question*, addressed to—*WRITERS and POETS of ENGLAND, SCOTLAND, IRELAND and WALES*, and signed by Aragon, W. H. Auden, José Bergamin, Jean Richard Bloch, Nancy Cunard, Brian Howard, Heinrich Mann, Ivor Montagu, Pablo Neruda, Ramón Sender, Stephen Spender, and Tristan Tzara. The question, in short, was: *Are you for, or against, the legal Government and the People of Republican Spain? Are you for, or against, Franco and Fascism? For it is impossible any longer to take no side.* Six-line messages were invited, the collection of answers to be published 'forthwith'.

I found no further trace of this project until I came across a brief reference to it as being in the *Left Review*, in Hugh Thomas' formidable history of the *Spanish Civil War*,[13] where he also referred to Brian in a footnote: 'For those

British persons who worried about their investments in Spain, that genius *manqué* of the epoch, Brian Howard (often regarded as the original of Anthony Blanche in Evelyn Waugh's *Brideshead Revisited*) wrote a poem, urging them to . . . *Spare a thought, a thought for all these Spanish tombs, etc.*'

An autumn issue of the periodical *Left Review* advertised the following: '*Authors take sides*—on Fascism—on the Spanish War. A most revealing document. To be published in November (6d.). A *Left Review Pamphlet.*'[14] The pamphlet itself, not unlike a monthly edition of the parent review, had a 'hard-selling' cover listing over forty names of well known contributors, and the rider 148 *contributors*—10,000 *words*—6d. 126 of these intellectuals were for the Spanish Government, 5 against, 16 neutral? (the query included), with one Stop Press Unclassified—George Bernard Shaw. Nancy Cunard's original broadsheet was re-printed, and the contributions—necessarily short—followed on alphabetically. An arbitrary selection of four 'messages' follows:

Nancy Cunard: It is as unthinkable for any honest intellectual to be pro-Fascist as it is degenerate to be for Franco, the assassin of the Spanish and Arab people. Spain is not 'politics' but life; its immediate future will affect every human who has a sense of what life and its facts mean, who has respect for himself and humanity. Above all others, the writer, the intellectual, must take sides. His place is with the people against Fascism; his duty, to protest against the present degeneration of the democracies.

Evelyn Waugh: I know Spain only as a tourist and a reader of the newspapers. I am no more impressed by the 'legality' of the Valencia Government than are English Communists by the legality of the Crown, Lords and Commons. I believe it was a bad Government, rapidly deteriorating. If I were a Spaniard I should be fighting for General Franco. As an Englishman I am not in the predicament of choosing between two evils. I am not a Fascist nor shall I become one unless it were the only alternative to Marxism. It is mischievous to suggest that such a choice is imminent.

George Bernard Shaw: In Spain both the Right and the Left so thoroughly disgraced themselves in the turns they took in trying to govern their country before the Right revolted, that it is impossible to say which of them is the more incompetent. Spain must choose for itself: it is really not our business, though of course our Capitalist Government has done everything it possibly could to help General Franco. I as a Communist am generally on the Left; but that does not commit me to support the British Party Parliament system, and its continual imitations, of which I have the lowest opinion. At present the Capitalist powers seem to have secured a victory over the General by what they call their non-interference, meaning their very active interference on his side, but it is unlikely that the last word will be with him. Meanwhile I shall not shout about it.

---

[13] Published by Eyre & Spottiswoode, 1961.
[14] This idea was adapted by Cecil Woolf and John Bagguley, who edited *Authors take sides in Vietnam* (with some of the same contributors), published by Peter Owen, 1967.

Brian Howard: A people, nearly half of whom has been denied the opportunity to learn to read, is struggling for bread, liberty and life against the most unscrupulous and reactionary plutocracy left in existence. Utterly unable to crush this people alone, their enemies have hired foreign mercenaries, whose governments self-confessedly covet Spain's raw materials, to butcher whole civilian communities. With all my anger and love, I am for the People of Republican Spain.

Unfortunately the names of the 124 other people who underwrote *for* the Government would take up too much space to repeat here, but it is interesting to see who voted *neutral?* and *against:*

Neutral?: Ruby M. Ayres, Vera Brittain, Robert Byron, Rhys J. Davies, M.P., Norman Douglas, T. S. Eliot ('I still feel convinced that it is best that at least a few men of letters should remain isolated and take no part in these collective activities . . .'), Vyvyan Holland, Charles Morgan, Sean O'Faolain, Ezra Pound, W. J .Turner, Derek Verschoyle, Alec Waugh, H. G. Wells, Vita Sackville West, Malachi Whitaker.

Against the Government: Edmund Blunden, Arthur Machen, Geoffrey Moss, Eleanor Smith, Evelyn Waugh.

To return to Paris in the early summer, life went on as before, Brian being very much taken up with his idea to start a 'bar' which Toni would manage. Mrs. Monck, an American, was contributing £400 towards it but the preliminaries were never-ending. 'Business is not my Thing, and makes me quite nervous, sometimes, with the way people "go on".' He and Mrs. Monck lived in a whirl of lawyers, going to look at places, and interviewing prospective waiters. Brian wrote to his mother about it:

I have got Jean Cocteau to do the decorations free, and give the whole thing his backing. (He has chosen the decorations—quite inexpensive, but lovely—already). From a Paris point of view this is as important as it well could be—he made the *Boeuf sur le Toit,* the most famous night-club since the war. He is helping me in every way, simply out of friendship.

The idea is this—a perfectly ordinary small cocktail bar, not night-club, without music, of a kind which Paris specialises in. Half highbrow, half chic. Opening at five, closing at two. Toni will be 'host'. I know it is hard, rather awful sort of work, but I can't go on supporting him unless I make, rapidly, a great deal more money.

. . . Every day there are new complications about the bar. It isn't going to be the one that Cocteau did the décor for, and I've now got to get him to do it all over again. Cocteau's sending me to his lawyer (for Toni's contract to be looked at).

Cocteau's charmingly phrased letter of introduction, written on hand-made paper, seems never to have been presented. It started off: *Mon ami Brian Howard, grand poète anglais, veut acheter à Paris une sorte de bistro pour que ses amis se reunissent* . . . But of course the bar did not materialise, and one wonders how much apathy was caused by alcohol, or even drugs. Although Brian had toyed by now with drugs for several years (as did many of his companions), and took them more seriously during his friendship with Cocteau, John Banting clarifies Brian's basic attitude to the subject at this time:

> During the 'thirties drugs were very easily obtained in Paris (and posted to London). Brian never *sought* them, but if someone had a little packet of 'uppies' (cocaine) he would accept—and enjoy—a few sniffs. No one was instantly 'hooked' (as the newspapers declare)—that is the danger, as people can sample drugs for a time and feel safe, but they are *not*. The danger is in that very fact, for what one enjoys one will repeat (and concoct all sorts of alibis to oneself for doing so). Since people cannot be 'on their toes' all the time with stimulants they later on seek the peace of soporifics, such as morphine, or heroin (three times as strong and carrying the bait of a stimulant too).
>
> Eventually several friends, after perhaps two or three years of occasional drug-flirting, became addicted, but after the miseries of deprivations and cures they no longer offer a dose to anyone. Talented and attractive people became unproductive hermits and hypochondriacs, only interested in swapping ailments or doses with their doomed 'playmates'. Brian was very sensible in not joining them, although he had every opportunity, but he was too interested in life, and having seen the results of addiction had no wish to become a sexless invalid.

There were moments of pathos—and bathos—in these Paris days. An old friend, who wishes to remain anonymous, recollects:

> There was one thing one liked particularly about Brian, his ability, one could perhaps say flair (after, it is true, much storming and angry words which, laying on his charm with a spade, he apologised for afterwards), of coping with the difficult situations of his own creating in which he found himself, with great panache and good humour. I remember once in Paris, after a long night of drinking in night-clubs, he found himself in a *maison de passe*. When he woke in the late morning he found that everything he had had with him had been stolen except his shoes, from which the thief had thoughtfully removed the laces. Using a sheet as a toga he asked the proprietor of the hotel if he could use the telephone and ring up his hotel behind the *Deux Magots* and arrange for clothes and money to be sent to him. The proprietor refused. He said he would have been bankrupt years ago if he had helped his clients in their predicaments. He was impervious to Brian's charm. Not so, however, an elderly housemaid who lent him her very small frilly apron, and in this he marched into the street and hailed a taxi.
>
> I was sitting at the *Deux Magots* when he arrived at the hotel. It was an enchanting sight, a kind of burlesque of a *Folies Bergères* number—the neat little apron in front, behind nothing but a starched bow, the laceless shoes flapping on the pavement like wooden clogs. No one at the café, I remember, showed more than mild surprise. They knew Brian well. He had

promised to return the apron but he never did. 'I cannot remember in which of these *silly* little streets is that *maison de passe* and anyway, my dear, I *like* having a souvenir so *very* inappropriate to that night's adventure.'

Constantine FitzGibbon remembers Brian being particularly bad-tempered towards Toni one day, and bullying him:

'Go and get me a copy of *The Times* . . . Go and wash your hands . . . Go and brush your hair . . .' At one point he was being particularly nasty—it was in the early evening at the *Café de Flore*—and Toni made a mild protest. Brian blew up, 'Well, if it weren't for me you would still be rotting away in Dachau.' Then, what I took to be an Englishman, totally unknown to me, got up from another table, walked over to Brian and said, 'I don't like the way you're talking to that boy, and I would like you to step outside, because I intend to knock you down, and I don't want to have a row in the café'. Brian said, without getting up, 'My weapons are words, not fists'. Whereupon the strange Englishman said, 'Well, in that case I shall tell you what I think of you,' and proceeded to do so at great length without, as they say, once repeating himself. It was one of the most impressive pieces of invective I have ever heard. It was so cruel—Brian blanched, trembled and eventually left the café, followed by the German boy.

The Englishman went back to his table and sat down. I then went up to him and said, 'That was a very impressive performance. Who *are* you?' 'It doesn't matter who I am, but I'll tell you what my job is—I'm Professor of Oratory at Trinity College, Dublin.' As I never saw the man again the story may have got somewhat exaggerated in my memory over the years. Brian, of course, never referred to this episode again.

Yet Brian usually held his own with words, often briefly and to the point. After the funeral of a somewhat millstone of a friend it was his remark that conveyed just the right mixture of mournful relief, 'Oh, the *sadness*—and the *gladness*—my dear.' Or to a pallid pianist, 'Play *louder* and *prouder*, my dear.'

Jock Jardine, who used to see Brian fairly frequently in the 'thirties, recalls one of his favourite ploys:

Brian often carried in his pocket a bottle of Mary Chess scent or toilet water given to him, presumably, by his mother (from the family firm). When he got into an argument with strangers or people he hardly knew (which he did frequently if he had been drinking a lot) and anyone began turning nasty, he would whip out the bottle, shake it, take out the stopper and dab the astonished person behind the ears, exclaiming, 'now that you smell like a tart, my dear, your arguments carry *very* little weight'.

It was the mixture of extreme frivolity, pre-occupation with intellectualism, and passionate awareness of political events that made Brian such a unique figure. Easier in retrospect than in the present person, as so many of his friends are at pains to make clear.

He must have abandoned Paris for a short spell in England to visit Wystan Auden in Colwall, near Malvern, from where he wrote to his mother: 'I have plenty of time to work (at *New Statesman* reviews) while Wystan teaches. Although this is a Quaker school, run by the Cadburys, it is quite 'ordinary', yet such an advance has been made (since I was at the same sort of place). They are all *so* happy—with their school paper full of jokes and their art school and sensible clothes. . . . I am to see Gollancz next week, so that looks as if it was settled.'

But of course it wasn't, so in July Brian and Toni were back again in France, this time to spend most of the next six months at Sanary, Var, from where he wrote to his mother:

> The people here that I am getting to know consist of Feuchtwanger, the German writer (*Jew Süss*), Professor von Gumbel, who was the man who called the late war 'the war of dishonour', and was one of Hitler's best enemies; Eva Herrmann, an old friend of mine, Jewish caricaturist, and very charming and intelligent; the Kisling family (he is about the sixth best known French painter), and finally Sybille von Schoenebeck [later Mrs. Bedford] who 'runs' the place. It is quiet, un-Cannes-like, but it suits me very well. Occupations: a lot of reading—bicycling—some bathing—no sunbathing—and picnics.
>
> [Later] Sybille turns out to be an angel. I really think that I can get a bit of writing done, that it wouldn't do me any harm to remain. I bicycled twelve miles on Saturday . . . I feel so WELL, it's really wonderful. Again, everyone likes me, and I seem, with so little work behind me, known here, in some odd way. Toni has never been nicer—and doing half the housework.
>
> . . . Toni's permanent *carte d'identité* has not been granted after all, and his papers are marked 'up to 30th October' only. The despair and expense of starting these wanderings again—where to—is too much. The *emigrés* are all being turned out of France because of the bombings—I see many *emigrés* and it is perhaps the most tragic of contemporary worlds. It is horrible what those devils in Germany and Italy have reduced the world to—it is like some terrible stagey detective story being lived in real life.
>
> . . . Tonight I dined with Raymond (Mortimer), and Clive Bell. I was very pleased with Raymond begging me to start writing again for the *Statesman* as soon as I could—'I need talent, etc.'—as I thought he might be satisfied with whom he'd got.
>
> . . . Toni's passport runs out in a month . . .

1938—and Paris again, with the situation as thorny as ever. It is difficult to reconcile some of Brian's letters of inertia and despair with the fact that he was still able to contribute, and deliver to time, lengthy political and literary book reviews to the *New Statesman*; lead a hectic round of parties with far too much to drink, ending up with spaghetti fights on the floor; and be in a position to receive the following St. Valentine's Day Greetings telegram from his old family maids: THE BIRDS ARE COURTING WHY NOT YOU MRS. NICHOLS

& ELEANOR. This unlikely piece of 'domestic' rhetoric was kept amongst his treasured papers, right to the end.

One of Brian's most interesting *New Statesman* book reviews, on the subject of 'race', was published in February 1938 under the title, 'The Great Psychosis', from which I quote the following brief extracts: *Race* by Jacques Barzun (Methuen); *Racism* by Magnus Hirschfeld (Gollancz):

'I am not a Jew, I am just an ordinary Briton of Aryan stock.' This remark was once made, according to Mr. Barzun, by Sir John Simon, and it is a magnificent example of what may come to be called Racism. In point of anthropological fact, of course, there is no such thing as an 'ordinary Briton' and no such thing as 'Aryan stock'. Most educated people today are aware, as an unforeseen result of Nazi propaganda, that there is something suspect about the words 'Aryan race', and many of these realise that 'Aryan' is only permissible as a purely linguistic term. But the majority of such people still believe in 'Races' as entities. How long will it take to persuade them that the comparatively parvenu word 'Race', has lost its meaning from the scientific standpoint, is a matter for conjecture, and when one considers the sociological effects of Racism, for intensely gloomy conjecture . . .

. . . Magnus Hirschfeld (who founded the famous Institute for Sexual Science in Berlin) . . . emphasises anti-Semitism, but this is not unnatural, and the superb quotations can only make one grateful. One German ethnologist, Herr Hauser, complains of Ostics, and defends Nordics, thus:

'He (the Ostic) is extremely sensual, and boasts of his potency, while being as a rule much less of a stallion than he pretends. He pays his way wherever he goes, seldom gets into difficulties, and is too shrewd to allow himself to be fleeced by blackmailers; whereas the Nordic is again and again victimised in this way, often on account of some trifling peculiarity in his sexual life.'

. . . One of Hirschfeld's most entertaining and instructive discoveries is the squabble between Mussolini and the official Nazi medical journal. It is beyond comment:

'In the *Basler National Zeitung* of October 10th, 1933, Mussolini is reported: "It is a humorous fact that hardly any of the champions of the pre-eminence of the Teutonic race were themselves Teutons. I think of Gobineau, who was a Frenchman; of Chamberlain, an Englishman; of Woltmann, a Jew; of Lapouge, another Frenchman."'

He might have added something about Hitler and Goebbels. Two weeks later, speaking in the Piazza Venezia, he said that since Fascism was spiritual, and the Nazis were materialists, the Latin race 'had no need to isolate itself from other races, from foreigners, being prepotent enough to absorb other races, and even to assimilate Jews'. On November 25th, J. von Leers, President of the Nazi Students League, replied with a long onslaught in *Deutsches Aerzteblatt*, of which this is one sentence:

'Mussolini has had to put up with Marxians, democrats and Catholics. He could not formulate a racist ideal, for the simple reason that most Italians look like Jews, and most Jews look like Italians.'

Many of Brian's reviews (including over seventy lengthy articles between the years 1930 and 1947 to the *New Statesman* alone) make for slow reading today, especially where the subject itself is no longer of topical interest. On the whole he kept his natural wit—malicious and otherwise—strongly in check, but there are pin-points here and there and felicitous phrases worth re-printing. Keeping roughly to chronological order, the following extracts are from reviews of 'New Novels': (1937) . . . *The Great and the Goods* by Ivor Brown (Hamish Hamilton).

This is Sedition Week. (Three) novels that everyone can enjoy, and all three strongly tainted with subversive opinion, which is such a comfort. It is quite extraordinary the way that Left fiction is cornering the market, turning every lending library, in spite of itself, into a Left Book Club, while the Fascists, like the Nazis, haven't a novelist to their name.

. . . Straight Socialist propaganda, like all propaganda, is like carrying Nazis to Londonderry. Capably turned out, entertaining works of fiction, such as Mr. Ivor Brown's, get at quite another audience. The great marble-bosomed men and women who stride around Harrods putting creditable purchases irrevocably down on unquestionable accounts. Home they pound, Bolshie-haters every one, settle down to *The Great and the Goods*, and before they know it, sedition is at work. For Mr. Brown's book is meant to be funny, and frequently is, but the criticism implied is as incisive as it is merited. It is a diverting satire on what Mr. Spender calls 'the politics of personal ambition', and what the late Lord Birkenhead extolled in some such scrumptious words as 'the glittering prizes still to be won by young men whose swords are sharp'.

Dr. Edgar Chirrup runs a College of Triumphant Living. Behind its exuberantly respectable and eupeptic catchwords, it is a school to teach what every young Tory knows by instinct—how by hooks, looks and crooks to get on. Only the grander professions are thought of, and several of these are minutely examined. In the Church, for example, the study of emoluments is advocated, since these vary to the point of madness. There are splendid tips for clever, despondent curates in suggested theses: 'Surrealism and the Christian Mythos', 'Freud and Faith'. . . . And the Doctor's advice to aspiring politicians seems irreproachable. A telegram is sent in answer to a young poet just down from Oxford who desired to know on which side to butter his bread, and if the mention of the poetic chances of Fascism seems absurd, it is only that the Doctor leaves no stone unturned:

'My terms as stated. No reductions possible. Cut out Anglo Catholics. That market now past the best. I am bear of Eliot but bull of Auden, Lewis & Co. Be Fascist or Communist. Perhaps big chance for Fascist poetry coming, but Marx and Spender much most promising investment at the moment.'

It isn't just that the reviews are apt in themselves, but one gains such useful nuggets of information not perhaps directly concerning the book at all, such as this 'Surrealist' vignette: *The Bells of Basel* by Louis Aragon (Lovat Dickson and Peter Davies).

'*La Revolution Surréaliste, la revue la plus scandaleuse du monde.*' In 1928, M. Aragon chose these words with which to introduce his Surrealist book, *Traité du Style*. It was a boomerang remark, because that movement (now mainly English, ten years late, as usual), was in a sense truly scandalous. It still is. Aesthetically, there are enough bones to be picked, but, politically, it is indefensible: it wastes the valuable political energies of many artists, writers, and others, in a romantic fit of studio fidgets . . .

In one review Brian took on Mann, Gorki and Faulkner in his stride, but it was Gorki's insight into the paralysis of the doomed intellectual, as it were, that particularly appealed to him: (1938) . . . *The Specter* by Maxim Gorki (Appleton-Century).

. . . So thoroughly has the author explored the whole intellectual and historical panorama, that he has created, in Samghin, an almost ideally representative intellectual of our time. He has not made another Dostoievski hero, or just another glumly incompetent Russian highbrow. Samghin can run his everyday life quite reasonably, stopping well short of dramatics. This is what makes him so universal, and so very contemporary. What Gorki intended was to expose the paralysis that attacks the majority of intellectuals when once they realise that the system in which they live is doomed, and he has succeeded so well that *The Specter* seems to include portraits of a great many people one knows. It is anything but reassuring to realise that, from 1905 on, educated political discussions in Russia were absolutely indistinguishable from those in Paris and New York, and even parts of London, today. (The talk about Tolstoy's non-resistance to evil parallels the Huxleyan pacifism of the moment, for example.) Problem for problem, the situation is derisive in its similarity, and nothing could be more instructive than Samghin's scrupulous, helpless, fatal havering. When things go obviously wrong, after 1914, he typically has the 'idea of joining a party', but doesn't. He finishes by longing for a catastrophe. 'He longed for an end to the indefinite.' . . .

On quite a different bent Brian claimed that William Saroyan's new stories, *Love, Here is my Hat* (Faber):

. . . not only prove again that he is one of the most fascinating and original short story writers alive, but also that he is turning out to be a serious artist. He seems able to play with new techniques and amusing, legible ones, as fast as others can play with punctuation. . . . There is only one way, after all, for one person to write at one period—not one style, but one *way*—and he has found his way. . . . A tipsy old liar is describing how he got out of a hotel in spite of a six-foot man with an iron claw:
'That's bad on the nerves. Kicked him in the mouth when he swung for my head with the claw. Would have lost an eye except for quick thinking. Rolled into the gutter and pulled a gun. Fired seven times, but I was back upstairs. Left the place an hour later, dressed in silk and feathers, with a

hat swung round over my face. Saw him standing on the corner, waiting. Said, 'Care for a wiggle?' Said he didn't. Went on down the street, left Town.'

To return to everyday life in Paris. On the eve of the Anschluss Klaus Mann was in Paris, and later recorded the impact of this disaster on himself and his friends:[15]

> ... While we still indulged in conjectures and calculations, Hitler's armies already moved towards the Austrian frontier. And there it was—the inevitable, incredible event. This is the night of 10th or 11th March, and this is the Boulevard St. Germain in Paris. Our table at the *Café de Flore* is piled with newspapers. I am with a crowd of English friends—Brian Howard, Nancy Cunard, Sybille Bedford, James Stern, and three or four others. Brian is all flurry and agitation. He loathes Hitler much more than do most Englishmen—I mean than most Englishmen used to do at that early point. For Brian had lived in Munich and Salzburg and Vienna: he knows what it is all about. 'Now, really!' he snapped at Nancy Cunard. 'It makes me rather nervous, my dear, to watch you eat this horrible welsh rarebit, while our friends in Vienna ...' And, as if suddenly struck by a weird and irrefutable intuition: 'This means war, my dear!'
>
> My friend Brian was wrong. It was not yet the hour. Our hopes and shudders were premature. The fall of Austria meant bloodshed, but it did not mean war. It meant suicides, firing squads, more concentration camps, more fugitives, a hundredfold increase of anguish and distress. But peace was saved, once again.
>
> ... (But) how can the Germans endure the vulgar trickery of their present leaders, since it was unmasked in advance by Heinrich Heine's illuminated flippancies and by the hallucinatory diatribes of Friedrich Nietzsche? It was he, the most formidable intellectual energy Germany ever produced, who hurled this terrific arraignment against his compatriots.
>
> 'I feel a desire, indeed a duty, to tell the Germans for once how much they already have on their conscience. They have all the great cultural crimes of four centuries on their conscience—and all for the same reason, because of their innermost cowardice in face of reality, which is at the same time cowardice in face of truth; because of their untruthful-ness which has become distinctive; because of their "idealism"!'

In retrospect Allanah Harper considers Brian's greatest virtue to have been his political consciousness:

> He was acutely aware of the evil forces at work in the early 'thirties—a time when most people considered Nazism a joke—the local activity of a group of renegades led by a fanatical house-painter with mad ambitions.

---

[15] In his autobiography, *Turning Point*.

Brian was tortured by the knowledge that Concentration Camps existed all over Germany even by 1933–34. How few people cared enough to find out, as Brian did, or even wanted to know. I can hear Brian's voice saying, 'The knock at the door in the night, the brute in uniform, then—hurled into the darkness—the Jew, the liberal, the leftist and the artist—never to be heard of again.' Brian watched the evil monster, Nazism, rearing its horrible head. He saw only too clearly what was to come. When the inevitable came, the horror and cruelty of war broke his heart. The fact that man could inflict tortures and death on such a scale made it impossible to hold up one's head again.

Another great friend, and early protégé, of Brian's, Ivan Moffat, distils a vivid picture of the Brian of these times:

... In terms of meeting him—one would be abroad, in Central Europe, say, and Brian would suddenly be audible there, at a café table, this person with a slightly over-large head, huge brown eyes, dressed in an extraordinary version of Austrian peasant clothes, lederhosen, and velvet coat. Creating a mask to hide behind really, a mask so absurd that even when seated alone he would expose it and tear it off.

He had a tremendous element of self-mockery. Young as I was when I first met him, I felt instinctively there was a scheme of ruin there. He was always bursting with laughter at himself. 'We're failures, my dear—every night living in a world of failures—ghosts.' He often talked about ghosts. He was a 'haunter' rather than an 'inhabiter' of his world. I think of Brian as the archetypal person who was already *manqué* in a period that was only later known to have been *manqué*. He was a pioneer. One realised that the 'thirties were coming to a disastrous end in 1938–1939, but Brian had already sprung head first into the cauldron of failure, with the greatest amount of noise, and way ahead of everyone else. He wasn't really a 'twenties person at all.

Usually when a person collapses or fails he is considered representative of something else that is failing—either they, or the thing they represented, had some sway or importance; but Brian's downslide was more significant than his accomplishments. He suffered from the disease of being more famous than his work.

You ask how Brian achieved the transition from Bright Young Person to Serious Left Wing figure. I don't think he did achieve it. It was a problem the 'thirties must have imposed on many people who'd started on one thing, and then had to stop. To go on being a 'Bright Young Person'—or do a volte face into frivolous Stalinism. (Guy Burgess was an example here.) It's no criticism of Brian to say his left-wing side was mostly an aesthetic reaction against Nazism—he shared that with other poets and writers of the 'thirties; his poison was that he had by then drunk too fully of the B.Y.P. cup, and had suddenly and too late become a Left Wing figure. It didn't always fit. Yet in his own way, he earned his honourable place in those indexes of books about the Spanish War, in which you find Connolly and Kesselring, Toynbee and Goebbels, Franco and Brian Howard incongruously intermingled.

Was he always predictably temperamental? He had this sudden compulsion to turn from amiability to vile accusation. Of course he had his favourites, who were immune, but it was difficult even for the favourites. I remember when Guy Burgess, Brian and several other friends were in some Salzburg night-club in 1937, the whole party dressed up in lederhosen, with Brian lashing Guy all the way down the table with purple-paragraph whips. Brian used Guy by alternately laughing with him and then lashing out to smash him. Sitting there at the head of the table, he was like the driver of a ten-mule team, his great cracking whip lashing out all down the table, encouraging some, crushing others. To Guy, above all, Brian was unsparing, but Guy loved it ...

As against that, however, towards young people he could often be protective, generous and encouraging. He was a great, and even promiscuous, discoverer of virtue in almost everybody—finding virtue and point where it perhaps didn't exist, or wasn't easy to see. He would build up this surprised person into a pyramid of marvel and perfection, and then dynamite the whole structure, himself with it. And that would be the end of the evening.

By mid-1938 Toni was on the edge of a nervous breakdown, and they went down to Sanary again for several months. Brian wrote to his mother:

I am absolutely convinced that if I can get Toni through this year things will be all right. There is no reply about the German Army yet. With his *carte* now finally coming he can get protection to a certain degree. It's for three years and very heartening, I must say. So many have been refused.

Cyril (Connolly) has been here. His book *Enemies of Promise* is *brilliant* this time, and contains *really* complimentary things about me, for a change. You remember my review in June of Arnold Zweig's German Officer book, *The Crowning of a King* in the *New Statesman*? Well, he came here, sought me out (he lives in Palestine) and told me my review was the best in the whole press of the world. Rather nice! I am sending Toni to a photographic school this winter, I've decided. My second *Listener* review is sent off. The first was a success, I hear.

... It would take too long to tell you all the rumours and counter-rumours to which we here have naturally been subjected (during September–October). The Italians may try to bomb Toulon, which is about five or six miles away, but the defences are the strongest in France, and they certainly won't bomb us. Toni has been officially asked if he wanted to volunteer for military service. We decided against this, hoping for an internment camp, which, as far as we know, is the alternative. It now appears that Germans in internment camps may be eventually exchanged against French prisoners in Germany. So the position is agonisingly difficult. As soon as his fate is decided and I and my friends have done what we can, I will, of course return at once.

[From Paris] I personally think there will not be war. That, however, is purely intuitive. One really can't tell. All Americans here are being evacuated, but not the English. I have expected all this for so long that now it is actually happening I feel perfectly sane and calm. I have been *intensely* frightened, but am so no longer. I simply have certain problems. First, Toni has burst his ear-drum bathing and is in definite danger of permanent deafness in one ear, and possibly mastoid. Second, although Erika Mann is helping me to try and get Toni included on an official *émigré* list, which will improve his future lot, this is difficult. Thirdly, I am most unwilling to return to England in the event of war, I don't deny for a moment that perfectly ordinary fear hasn't a lot to do with it, but, in addition, I utterly refuse to take part in *killing Germans.* It would be—it is—quite a problem as to whether one should kill Nazis. In an English civil war against English Fascists—one might. I refuse, however, to join another nationalist war, exactly similar to 1914, except that the slogan now will be 'Against Fascism' instead of 'Against Prussianism'. We, of course, will win, but the result will be as bad as before and the only people who will benefit will be the rich, the generals, the arms manufacturers, bankers, etc. etc. Hitler will fall, but he will have triumphed at the same time, because the world will be a ruin, and a ruin ruled *less* justly, probably, than before.

In short, I agree absolutely with the verdict of the English Independent Labour Party, to whom I telegraphed my adherence today, as a result of their manifesto. You may ask, 'Really, but I thought you wanted to get rid of Hitler?' Yes, but in order to get rid of an unpleasant lodger it is not only foolish, but criminal, to set fire to the boarding house. Other people live there.

You may say—'Yes, but now it's too late. One must fight. Think of the Czechs.' The answer to even that, as I see it, is that Peace *must* be maintained, because no inconvenience that any person, or nation, can suffer is worse than war. That we actually are IN this terrible position is the fault of English and French policy for twenty years.

I am sorry to go through all this, but I want to make my position clear. If war comes, England will have conscription in five minutes, and I do not intend to be 'conscribed'. I am well aware of the charges of cowardice etc. that will be levelled and they mean nothing to me. If I was not quite sure that conscientious objectors will not be tolerated this time, I would return. *But we know they will not be.* Consequently, we—I say 'we' because all my friends agree—are simply in the position of Lytton, David Garnett etc. during the last war, *except* that, this time, we are not *allowed.* I am frightened of fighting; I hate the idea of it; and I disapprove, to the bottom of my heart, of the principles on which the fighting is being engineered. And, by the way, even if there is no war *now*, I have made up my mind *absolutely* to get a job in America. War or no war, Europe is finished for the time being. ... You shouldn't have returned from America, really. The truth is that even on such a serious occasion as this my feelings of guilt (about money, etc.) are so strong that I feel it is almost impossible to put my case. Added to that, there now comes the feeling that you may think I am 'running away', 'getting out of my responsibilities', etc. etc. which is also depressing.

Well, my dearest, I will end by saying that I don't think you will be very severe about this letter, because you must, of course, realise what these days are meaning to Toni and me. We are being well punished for our sins! His broken ear came at a bad time and poor thing, he is terribly frightened. I have no time to be. More than that, I feel a strange clarity and calm. I have waited and known for so long. Earlier in this letter, I said I *was* frightened—but perhaps I am not, after all. Not in that way. I am frightened of evil, not death. I wish to protect and help, not kill and destroy. So—really, I have no plans, except to do my best for Toni and keep in touch with you. And if the worst comes, I am, at least, spiritually prepared.

The early part of 1939 was taken up with working out the idea of the book planned by Brian and Auden. The prospective publisher—Robert Hale—wanted an immediate synopsis, on receipt of which he was going to give Brian an advance of £6 a week for two months. He wrote to his mother about it from France:

> ... I haven't decided whether to take the advance or not, but I do want to do the book. I feel I suddenly can. The main part of the book will have to be done in London, of course. But the synopsis and the introduction, I'd like to do now. Allanah (Harper) has lent me this house (at Gadencourt, Eure) to do it in. The time it will take? I should say six to eight months. To write the introduction and a specimen chapter (which *sounds* little, but is *really* the whole book)—say, two months. The rest is interviewing, checking up, library work, etc. and is impossible to do anywhere but in London. ... I have not accepted the publisher's £6 a week (yet at least) because I don't yet feel quite sure of my ability to do my share at the right tempo, etc.
>
> About the book. I have had certain ideas whizzing about in my head for two or three years, and Wystan more or less showed me how a book could be made of them. He will go over it before it is published, and I think they would like him to write a preface. Anyway, about the philosophical theme of the book, which, so far, is to be called, *The Divorce of Heaven and Hell*—five, up to ten, 'Studies in English Literature and Behaviour'. (Compare Blake's *The Marriage of Heaven and Hell*.) This is the same theme which has occupied me ever since Prinzhorn, ever since I came to understand anything, really. There is, in man, one great final division. Between the Body and the Mind, to use the jargon of contemporary philosophy, Intellect and Intuition.

Brian never got further than a lengthy two-part synopsis which first expanded the above theme, and for the second part rather surprisingly exposed the dangers of popular authors who turn out books which provide a wish-fulfilment for the great British Public. Names such as Housman, Sir Arnold Wilson, Ruby M. Ayres, Buchan, Sapper, Francis Brett Young were suggested. One of Brian's chief conclusions was that unless the *general* level of education were forthwith raised—unless the necessity of self-conscious knowledge were immediately recognised—Democracy was doomed, and chaos would ensue. A little pencilled comment after this, dated 1946, consisted of the word *h'm*!.

It was not all nose-to-the-grindstone at Gadencourt, as Allanah Harper remembers Brian hiding one evening in a cupboard in her bedroom. She had undressed and was half asleep in bed when an apparition in a sheet flung itself on her. 'In my struggle not to be crushed I called for help. Sybille Bedford, who was also staying in the house, banged frantically on the locked door, thinking I was being murdered. I had locked my door for safety, but had not looked in the cupboard or under the bed.'

Brian filled in that long summer of 1939 with regular book reviewing for the *New Statesman*. Especially interesting was his long review under the title of 'The German Emigration' of the American edition of Klaus and Erica Mann's *Escape to Life* (Houghton Miflin), listing the prominent 'exiles' from Germany of that time. On the lighter front he gave a characteristically neat summary of E. Morchard Bishop's *Two for Joy* (Cape):

> ... In the end, the book is about the torments of legitimate desire. There is something peculiarly English about refusing to go to bed with people, and something still more English about refusing to go to bed with them *enough* ...

He pinpointed the English again with unfailing accuracy, this time for their subjective obtuseness as shown up by René Behaine in his novel, *The Conquest of Life* (Allen & Unwin):

> ... What is wrong (one asks oneself as one closes this admirably translated book) with the eyesight of the majority of contemporary English novelists? M. Behaine sees with exceptional efficiency, no doubt, but then most French novelists see what they look at. The English look at a teapot, for example, and they see their dear old nurse, or their school, or their overdraft, or themselves—anything but the teapot. One might say that to see is only the beginning: not to see, however, is already the end. This new English lack of objectivity inevitably breeds lack of seriousness. Without seriousness it is not only impossible to form correct intellectual judgments but it becomes impossible, eventually, to feel correctly, to entertain the emotions proper to a good novelist at the proper times. When, therefore, the average English novelist tries to create character, his creations are not only boring, but inhuman. They are not even mad. They are not there ...

Pink Danube by Arthur Pumphrey[16] (Richards Press) greatly appealed to Brian despite its 'considerable faults of construction, lack of detachment etc':

> ... *Pink Danube* lies in what, to me, is the most comforting of modern fiction countries. To the north, lies the new, industrial town of Isherwood-stadt, and to the south, the vast, old, lazy pleasure-cities of Comptonia and

---

[16] In fact, Alan Pryce-Jones.

Normanville, from which, on fine days, one may descry Firbank Island. It is somewhere on the central plateau, near the site of the old, deserted capital, Yellowbook, that we find Pumphrey Cottage. *Pink Danube* deals with the adventures of a young intellectual of eighteen who has just been sacked from Eton, and who is trying to be a university to himself in Vienna: period, the Dollfuss bombardment of the workers' flats. The minor characters consist, of course, of inquisitive, seedy *gräfins* ('Is he of your first society?'), odd, rich American ladies, and odder, less rich English gentlemen. . . . Mr. Pumphrey champions a virtue which seems to me both important and very neglected—correct Idiom. . . . In the future, when the social historian wants to write a piece about how intellectual dandies talked in the 'thirties, he will be misled by nearly all our authors, especially Coward. The 'twenties had Huxley and Compton Mackenzie, and there is Norman Douglas going back farther than that. Today (and whether it is a 'good thing' or not isn't the point) there is practically no one. This is what gives *Pink Danube* a particular value.

Of all the 'Letters to Sydney Cockerell' in the volume edited by Viola Meynell under the title *Friends of a Lifetime* (Cape, 1940), Brian found T. E. Lawrence's the least satisfying: '. . . there is something subtly wrong about them. They are not specious, nor pretentious, but they had a kind of *sprain in the spirit* . . .' The italics are mine. He had this facility for twisting just the right analogy to suit the subject. Another felicitous phrase of Brian's concerned an author he thought had made a good start but with whose every successive chapter he 'could feel her craft ebbing . . .'

A month before war was declared Brian and Toni were still in Sanary, Brian worrying about his own eventual future and the immediate—as always—need for money. He told his mother to put his name down at the Ministry of Labour as a volunteer for translation and, or, propaganda work, on the outbreak of war. If necessary he begged her to sell his library, 'ask the advice of Heywood Hill, who will help. There are quite a lot of Huxley first editions, Sitwells etc. I'd much rather, at such a time, have the money to try and help Toni than the books. Please, dear, *try and understand*'. He kept a diary, spattered with fluctuating prognostications: '*24th August—War almost inevitable; 25th August—End of everything for us; 31st August—Home from party* 3.30 *a.m.* . . .'

The same day he wrote to his mother: 'A slight war atmosphere. My intuitive feeling is that there will be no war. (I am basing this optimism on the belief that Hitler has missed his chance. Of course I may be wrong. I feel, though, that I'm not.) . . . my tooth is undoubtedly infected, and in order to keep the pain tolerable I have to take a certain amount of sleeping stuff—Allonal. The only possible dentist is mobilised . . .'

Brian concentrated all his energies on organising Toni's fate, writing again to his mother on 3rd September:

This morning England declared war, and in an hour and a half, unless a miracle occurs, France will also be at war. How and when I shall be able to get back I don't know. I am actually waiting for the authorities to take

Toni, which is inevitable—today? I am told he will probably have to fight. Technically, I suppose I am already mobilised as England is at war and all men from eighteen to forty-one are required. When Toni's fate is decided I will try somehow to get to Paris. Anyway, you can rely on my making the best of things. I won't let you down. Bless you.

... Toni has now volunteered for the Passive Defence of France—I think they may understand that he can hardly fight when his own brother is in the German Army.

... Toni is now at a camp in Toulon. The moral atmosphere of the place is not bad, and the French military authorities kind and considerate. As your 'Adopted Son' you might write him a cheering note. There are many intellectuals in the camp, and unfortunately there are also two or three real Nazis. So strange of them not to have gone back to Germany.

... Willie Maugham is at Bandol with his yacht and can't move. I see him every day. Yesterday a new ruling was made that all Germans between the ages of fifty and sixty-five have to go to the camp at Toulon—that means many people from here, including Feuchtwanger, the celebrated anti-Hitler writer.

Somerset Maugham included some recollections of his meetings with Brian at this time—but without identifying him—in his book *Strictly Personal*,[17] which was about his experiences during the first fifteen months of the war and written originally for American readers. These references were not too complimentary, implying as they did that Brian was an averred coward, and Brian wrote of them 'that was a grinding time at Bandol when I visited Willie Maugham on behalf of the refugees, and later had my conversation falsified for my pains in that rather unfortunate little book of his about escaping from France'.

Nancy Mitford remembers a few days after, or before, the war broke out Brian saying to her: 'I'm very much afraid, my dear, that when it comes to *cold steel* I shall run away ...' He chose to assume this *folie de 'peur'*, but in fact he was to prove fearless when it came to the danger point.

To return to Brian in Sanary, after interviewing the Camp Commandant he was told that it was possible Toni might be released as a political refugee, depending on the provision of certain elements which were lacking in his dossier. He kept another of his introspective diaries going during these early war months. I quote some typical extracts dated from December to February 1940:

The *Sureté* man says Toni will be out, without much doubt, before Christmas. There is nothing much to do except wait. It's been less agony, then deep, dumpish, dull, distracting misery. Increasingly despairing, though, too, what with writing to Mother and hardly knowing what one was at. The hedonist at bay, etc. But the lover at bay, I add. But the waster at bay, they add ...

I saw the document from the camp, hurriedly. What has swayed the balance is: my own letter to the *Mairie* here (supposed to be written by Toni

[17] Published by Heinemann, 1942.

himself); Klaus and Erika's attestation. Which means that the decision was made *before* my mother's letter from London, signed at the American Embassy, the Paris official's letter, the two letters from responsible English friends, and three from local French residents, including a financial guarantee. In fact, he need never have been interned, according to their own final decision. The important phrase in the document I saw was: '... that he has been judged worthy of being liberated etc. because *il peut être utilisé à la France à cause de ses hautes relations*'. (Less 'because of' than 'in view of'.) It seems then that Toni is being freed *as being useful to* France *on account of* his powerful connections. Very muddling; slightly alarming—v. funny.

... Phrase which has been in my head since the War—'Sir, there are no such things as public worries. Nobody ever lost so much as two inches of sleep over public worries.'

... How good Claud's (Cockburn) *Week* is! It contains the only real news I can get. Even the *News Chronicle* seems *gleichgeschaltet*, the *Manchester Guardian* only a little less so. I continue to see the *Observer*, the *Sunday Times*, *Reynolds* (for Brailsford), the *Statesman*, and *Picture Post* (for fun).

... My spots keep me awake scratching. I musn't get into the habit of taking Allonal, although it isn't habit forming, and one wakes perfectly fresh.

Dipping into a Cambridge history this morning, it occurs to me that the 15th-century Turkish system of constant aggression, also the religious domination of their whole social fabric makes a striking parallel with Nazism. Janissaries were trained very much like the Gestapo. But the Turks were civilised.

... early morning, after three Allonal. Idea, which might make money if one could DO it, and which might DO GOOD. A Symposium by eminent contemporary writers—200 words each, 'What shall you do, young man? etc.' ... my hands are difficult to wash with in the mornings, what with these strange bumps and lumps. Glancing into the mirror as I write I find that it is possible that I am a fiend. Heavy. Nosey. Black-browed. Under-slung-lower-lipped. Frontal—top—baldness—becoming—bald. *Enfin*, rather a horrible look. Seriously. Not 18th century. Not 'Bismarck'. Nothing, I fear, in any way, nice. Just *heavy*, and Levantine and baldish-growing. Plus, and this is very important, a curious weighty weakness.

He indulged his introspective tendencies in a long analysis of his future life with Toni and his mother, continuing with:

But, really, how long is this going to go on? Till you earn? Till she dies? Or what? ... I am selfish, lazy, tipsy. Drink has become a No. 1 problem. I am nearly thirty-five. More than half-way through what can reasonably be called Life ...

'My spots *worse*. Must not be so alcoholic and depressed. As regards the War, I prefer to go mad ... Moved to the Clinique at Bandol. The Doctor has diagnosed my spots as being a perfectly ordinary vulgar disease called *la galle*. They say they can cure it in a week with baths, ointment, etc. Wrote Toni, telling him to go *direct* to Cannes if he gets here.

[7th January] Listened to Haw-Haw for the first time on the radio. First amusing thing I've heard on the radio since the war. Not bad at all. Saw a refugee friend of Toni's who said Toni used to get up before any of them at the camp to get the coffee. He was most good, and unselfish, it seems. But he did say that the drink problem with Toni was very grave. That he needed it terribly, pathologically, and that once started he couldn't stop. Some solution of this will either have to be found, in the future, or a tragedy will be eventually absolutely inevitable. I see this now *clearly*.

[12th January] Letter from the *Prefet* arrived three days ago saying Toni was free . . .

[29th January] The last fortnight has been extremely nerve-wracking and agitating as, owing to the new law of *Prestation* (invented for the Spanish refugees) everyone requiring *droit d'asile* must join (up to the age of forty-eight) a uniformed auxiliary force—and that, as a favour. Only proven political refugees may enter. It confers the same rights as French soldiers; leave, pay etc. and I imagine French nationality at the end of it, the duration, of course. Well, there is much to be said for it. Toni's health would probably benefit and it is a solution to several problems, but if the War goes badly, what then? Combatant service? At all events, I am determined to make a final struggle to get him liberated completely.

In February he was still in Bandol, and wrote to his mother:

'All facts were to him free and equal' expresses the point of view that I have tried always to adopt. So you be a little more 'free and equal' about the *Week*. There's a lot in what it says. In fact, I couldn't keep a level head without it. Do you know what I *saw*, in a leader of the *Sunday Express* (or *Dispatch*) the other day? *The only good German is a German with a bayonet at his throat* . . .

The other day Hitler spoke on the wireless. Within two minutes I had to go back to my room. I cannot physically stand his voice—it seems to me like the voice of evil itself. And, unfortunately, it reminds me, curiously enough, of Daddy in a rage!

About Toni—I don't think he's going to get out. Anyway, he is now moved to a much nicer camp at Manosque, on the Durance. Everything is still uncertain, except that he won't have to go in the Foreign Legion, which was one of the nightmares I've had to face.

The Ministry of the Interior wrote that his liberation has been put off until the establishment officially of the '*prestataires*'. Selected refugees are to be given their freedom and allowed to go, before the end of the month.

Brian had managed to get a P.E.N. Membership card which enabled him to have journalist's privileges, and in April he wrote to Cyril Connolly asking if he could be officially appointed European, or Foreign, Editor of *Horizon*, at a nominal fee. He was seeing Heinrich Mann and André Gide and would try and persuade Gide to produce something. This request was obviously made so as to facilitate his movements, as civilians had great difficulty in obtaining permits to move about in unoccupied France. At the end of May he wrote to his mother from Le Rayol:

The morning's papers all have the headline *La Patrie en danger* and I think, at last, it is true. The whole thing is so appalling that it is very difficult to get it in proportion. There is a kind of hideous justice somewhere—the advice of the good and the wise has been rejected, for twenty years, in favour of the advice of the foolish and the wicked, and here we are—just beginning, after nine months, to get rid of the Chamberlains etc.

I'm sorry that you don't like Aldous' book—the old philosopher who lives near Hearst's 'castle' seems to me quite unanswerable. And what do you mean about Hindu philosophy 'in Hollywood language'? Oxford language, perhaps. Huxley is evolving—alone—a contemporary philosophy out of something that you have always believed in and wished me to believe in, and now that I *begin* to feel of it as true, you complain. And I think it was decidedly bold of you to assume that Aldous doesn't *understand* Hindu philosophy? Another thing—it is practically indistinguishable (though finer in its Thought) from Christ's *life*. And now, back to reality. As I foretold, Toni has been spirited away from Manosque to a place called Le Mans, near Chartres. Three days ago he was spirited from there to an unknown destination. I cannot help hoping it is not the front, and will say no more. I calculate that Hitler will have Abbeville by tomorrow morning. In which case, how will this letter reach you?

... I think only about ten per cent of the German women in England will be interned, if one can judge from the press. Here, of course, is utter despair—they are all going, all my Sanary friends. When I think that there is not a single substantiated case—not even in Holland—of a refugee in the fifth column. They were all naturalised, or 'tourists'.

My principal care—worry—is that Toni, and his two friends, have disappeared for two weeks now. And habitually Toni writes daily. And he has no money. One almost wonders—have they quite simply been killed? It is inexplicable. They are in the star organisation—Manosque was the Eton of camps—which only the absolutely perfectly dossiered people can get into, and they were about to enter the 'Pioneers', part of the English Army.

There seems nothing but bad news. It is now fairly plain that Italy is going to come in against us. In which case, this part of the world will probably—what? be rather trying. I'm sorry you think I let 'personal matters rule my life' too much in war-time. I fear it is so. Public matters, Hitler, etc. ruled a large part of my life at a time when it was considered *highly eccentric and unnecessary.* Now that what people like myself saw coming, and tried to prevent, is here, I feel a little like someone who repeatedly begged someone else not to smoke in an ammunition room. They smoked. You may find this superior, or cowardly, or heartless. I can't help it. *I feel* that way. My only interest is in the people I am interested in. My patriotism, or interest in the public welfare, or whatever one chooses to call it, is a *real* one—that is to say, it doesn't have to wait for a war to come into a hysterical and temporary existence. When war comes, it rather sinks, because there is nothing one can really *do* in a war, for people like myself. One can destroy, or heal people so that they can return to destroy others, or themselves, but what can one do *really*? So, as I say, I fear that 'personal matters' do count more with me now. And, also, I rather agree with Huxley. I am not sure that the things which finally matter *can* be defended, or imposed, by force. I'm not trying to defend my appalling laziness and lack of moral energy—I'm simply stating a general question.

You will hear more regularly now; and may expect me to begin my move home soon, because there is nothing to be done, now. All I want is to know the worst, or best, about Toni. If anything terrible has happened, I will let you know gently, and don't worry about me. Nothing can really hurt me, mentally, as long as I have you.

P.S. If this letter, in its entirety, seems to give an impression of my not being affected enough by the horrors of the war, etc. etc. 'what is really going on' etc.; 'one's responsibility towards it', etc.—it isn't really so. It's that the war started for me, a long time before September 1939, and the mind boggles, after a while.

[20th June, from Cannes] I left Le Rayol today—in a hurry. The Germans are near (or in?) Marseille, and it is now a question of getting back to England. Unfortunately, this appears difficult. For instance, the government have sent no boats, yet, for the English living on the coast. Consequently some people are trying to get away on a yacht belonging to the Ex-Khedive of Egypt. Since the alternative is to be imprisoned here, or in Germany, for goodness knows how long—as an enemy subject of military age—I have agreed to go on this yacht. It is supposed to be leaving tomorrow evening, in the direction of Gibraltar. I believe Furness, the Felloweses, Marian Cameron and others will be on board. We will be leaving without any naval escort, and it is, in fact, slightly comic opera—but that is what things have come to. It is either that, or imprisonment for the duration of the war. I prefer the risk. I don't think, on the whole, that we will either be bombed, or torpedoed, but we may well get landed, in both senses of the word, for some time and one doesn't know where. So don't worry if you don't hear from me for even as long as a month, or two, even.

I have left most of my papers and, indeed, most of my 'things' etc. at Le Rayol; I have been unable to get any money at all, so the various sums sent lately are still untouched; Toni is in the English Pioneers as a Prestataire in the B.E.F. And now I suppose I must use the traditional phrase. 'If anything happens to me' please look after Toni. After all he has given me what amounts to his life. Apart from this my love to Eddie (Gathorne-Hardy). No messages to anyone else ...

If this should prove a last letter—which I don't think it will—I have, really, nothing to say to anyone except you and Toni. My heart belongs only to you two. As you know, most of it belongs to you. To Toni, I say nothing. He knows. To you, I think also nothing. You know.

Read a poem of Alice Meynell's—a sonnet—which ends, *I run, I run, I am gathered to thy heart.* If you die before me, I shall put it on your grave. And if anything else should happen—well, it will. And you will be happy, or should, in one thing. In our case there actually was *perfect* love, *perfect* trust and *perfect* truth. Always. Your love is with me. I thank and bless you for it, my dearest one.

[27th June, from Gibraltar] I am writing this from the cargo-boat *Cydonia*[18] on which I just managed to get away from Marseille the day before the Germans entered. The worst of it is that I don't know *where* we shall go. It may be to England, but people are saying that we may have to go to Canada, or somewhere. We have been four nights getting here—quite an adventure.

Of Toni, I cannot, *dare* not, think . . .

We are only allowed off the ship for a few hours, and may sail for England at any time. There will be a convoy of warships and there will be practically no danger. I am sleeping on deck in the stern in a hammock—rather fun. In fact the dirt and discomfort are so fantastic that it seems unreal and therefore bearable.

My one worry—and hope, in a way—is that you have decided to go to America? Don't worry—we will meet soon. I have turned Toni out of my consciousness because I would crack if I didn't.

Back in England, Brian immediately wrote an extraordinarily moving account of the last few days in the south of France before 'the Fall'. This was published in three parts in the September, November and December 1940 issues of *Horizon* under the title *Notes on Civilians at Bay*.[19] It was dedicated (anonymously) to Toni, and referred to a pathetic letter from an elderly refugee friend of Brian's about his German wife being taken off to a camp:

. . . I don't know exactly where you [Toni] are, or if you will survive. If you do, you will one day know that from July onwards, I began to fight the subhumanity which is doing these things—making K. write such letters—with *all* my strength. I first began attacking Hitler, for instance, when people in England knew nothing about him. Then I attacked him through the period when they were admiringly curious about him; then, through the period when they were bored with him. Next thing they knew, he was at their throats. But never did I fight systematically; wholly. I just talked, and wrote a few articles, and helped a few refugees. I never really *fought*. I now utterly dedicate myself to this struggle. In the name of your escape to Africa, which you always longed to see. On behalf of K., on behalf of the civilians. On behalf of the innocent. That is my Dedication to you . . .

There are lighter moments, as when Brian describes the reaction of his various friends and contacts to the immediate situation. Particularly felicitous is the following:

It had been at the end of May when I went to tea with a not unintelligent Russian woman and the Baronne de V. . . . The Nazis were near Paris, and

---

[18] The name was blacked out by Censorship.
[19] Short extracts are quoted as it is too long to reprint in full.

the suspense was severe. At tea, the conversation so shocked me that I protested, but I am sure it was the *bien-pensant* conversation of all France at that moment:

They: Ce salaud! on doit le fusiller!

I: Qui?

They: Blum, cher ami. *Blum*, naturellement. Thorez aussi. J'en suis sûr que c'est lui qui donne les discours sur le radio allemand.

I: Fusiller Blum?'

They: Mais sur le champ! C'est épouvan*table*. Il a volé tout l'argent que nous avons donnés pour la ligne Maginot. Voilà pourquoi les Boches, etc. etc.

Shaking with anger, their extremely distinguished faces pinched into masks like newts, they expatiated; and my vigorous protests were simply ignored. Then, suddenly, a French doctor in uniform ran up the steps of the terrace; a devoted, charming young man who was giving up his short leave to his patients. He described the German advance:

'Three million men are advancing shoulder to shoulder with their Chicago-guns at the hip. It is indescribable.'

Next: 'Some parachutists are dressed from head to foot in pale blue, with transparent pale blue parachutes, and each one has a bomb in his hand, painted flesh-colour.'

The women: 'No!' The officer: 'Yes, they look like something by Schiaparelli.' More talk and tea. Then the officer left. He said, with a tender kind of dignity, kissing the women's hands: 'I never expect to see you again, of course.'

There was no more anger that day . . .

By the 23rd June Brian had succeeded in finding out that an English collier boat would be made available to take off British subjects from Cannes:

. . . We had been told that we must embark with at least four days' worth of provisions. It was Sunday; the shops were shut, and 'C.R.' and I decided that the only chance was to beg what we could at the *Beauvau*. After a great deal of eyebrow-raising and head-wagging—food had obviously become a matter of concern already—an amused waiter made up an extremely expensive box-full, which we discovered, during the next few days, to contain endless *jambon de Bayonne* and *Roquefort*, but very little else.

We came to a jerked stop (at the Bassin de la Joliette dock in Cannes) before a toiling, nervous mass of people each of whom was carrying about twice as much as he, or she, comfortably could. Above us, there towered the sooty side of what was in reality only a moderate-sized collier, and the way from the dock to the deck was up the rickiest and longest companion-way I have ever seen. I had left two-thirds of my luggage in Le Rayol, and my friend G.R. had abandoned most of his, but between us we still had three ponderous suit-cases, three overcoats, a rug, various parcels, and the handle-less unmanageable box of food. We got it all on board, in the end, with the help of some spectators; French boys who had got wind of our departure, and wanted to come to England as volunteers. A young

Frenchman called Alexandre Petersen, whom I was to meet in a moment or two, did not wait for permission. While we were legally lumbering forward with the rest, he had swarmed up a hawser to the poop, his enormous knapsack on his back, and he told me that he watched a mysterious lady in a fur coat follow his example.

On board, we made a hasty tour of inspection. The ship had been ordered to leave Oran, where it had discharged its cargo of coal, at three-quarter's of an hour's notice, and there had naturally been no time to clean her. A thick, soft, indelible blackness stamped itself on any part of one that touched anything. As for accommodation, there appeared to be nothing but the hold and the deck: one could choose. C.R. said he would get claustrophobia in the former, and settled down in the open air on one of the hatches. I descended thinking of rain and cold sea-winds.

The next four days have telescoped themselves somewhat in my recollections, but there is one point that I cannot resist making before I begin trying to recapture them. Mr. Somerset Maugham, who made much the same journey a few days earlier, also in a collier (his was one of the two vessels known colloquially in Cannes as 'the Hell Ships', that I missed), has said that he was much edified by the fact that although the voyage *began* with a chilly division of classes—the poor at one end of the boat, the rich at the other, etc. it *concluded* with a thoroughly democratic mix-up. My experience was the precise opposite. On the first day, the Chaplain of Marseille; the villa proprietors from St. Raphaël to Nice; the Canadian priests (one coloured) from Rome; the English Admiral and his wife; Vice-Admiral Muselier; the French theatrical manageress and her myrmidons; the Australian millionaire sisters; the Hungarian adventuress; the two English Government officials; the English painter; the nondescript French characters; the nondescript English characters; the Palestinians, the Maltese and their children, and the eccentrics, were inextricably commingled. On the last day, the poorer Maltese and their children, tended by the English woman-doctor and the Chaplain, had confined themselves to the fo'c'sle; the French theatrical troupe and the Australian millionairesses were still disputing the bridge with the amused ships' officers and some very unamused villa-proprietor English of the more elderly kind; the narrow decks between the funnel and the bridge were bristlingly staked out by the more active villa-proprietor English, including the unofficial committee which ran the boat, and had opened the Consulate; the platform beneath the funnel was given over to the loves of Alexandre and the Hungarian flibbertigibbet; the central portion of the deck was the property of the international nondescripts; part of the hold was the preserve of the well-to-do Maltese, and the refugee priests, and, lastly, the poop, over which our one gun's platform spread an iron umbrella, was inhabited by the English Admiral and his wife, an English family, and Lady E. with her two Pekingese. Thus were the social levels, at the last, so mercilessly mapped out that one was able to find any given person within a minute. And that is why Mr. Maugham's experience seems to me so very surprising.

... The last evening was almost windless; hot, limpid, and restful. After dinner, at about eight o'clock, I was sitting on the hatch beneath and behind the bridge, smoking, and watching the land, which was some three miles away. Its pastoral character had changed, and we were now following an irregular but unbroken line of cliff and rocks. It must have been near Almeria. The first colours of sunset were coming, flashes of pink in the smooth blue hollows of the sea, and a golden incandescence over the cliffs. Suddenly, I heard a patter of feet behind me, and a cry. A man and a woman were running along the deck that faced the open sea, and pointing at the water. At first, I thought that their child must have fallen overboard. Then I looked beyond them and saw a kind of lane in the sea, as if an invisible iron was smoothing out a long ribbon of water, coming towards us amidships. I realised that it was a torpedo, and I could see that it was going to strike a few feet from where I was sitting. For a second or so, I became incapable of thought or action; I simply watched it come. It met the vessel, squarely, and I waited for the explosion. Instead, there was a noise like a smothered gong; the ribbon reappeared on the other side of the ship, and the torpedo made off in the direction of the coast, which it never reached. (In discussing the affair with the English Admiral, I learned that the gong-like sound was probably made by the torpedo's passage just below the empty, resonant hold.) The Italian submarine commander had set the torpedo at the customary level for cargo-ships, but had forgotten that we carried none, and were, therefore, unusually high out of the water. At the time, everyone was convinced that a second torpedo was coming, or that the submarine, which must have been about two miles away, would rise to the surface and shell us.

I recovered from my trance, and my first thought was to observe my own behaviour with great care. The wreck of the *Birkenhead*, the *Lusitania* panic—the classic situation, here it was. In fact, there was no panic, but rather an indescribably mournful congestion of passengers on the landward decks. I found that my only problem was my legs, which vibrated in a way over which I seemed to have no control.

... I went to the poop and offered the use of my binoculars to the men on the gun-turret, who asked me to climb up and look for the submarine myself. A commotion was caused by my sitting on a case of cordite with a lighted cigarette in my hand, but soon I was settled against the rails, examining the sea as I have never examined anything before. The Captain had turned the ship, and we were making for the shore as hard as we could go; I had hopes that the ship was going to be beached, but apparently this was not in accordance with merchant navy routine. Some hundreds of yards from the coast we turned again, and began to continue our journey. When it became too dark to see, I returned to the centre of the vessel. The passengers were still crowded against the rails, desperately calculating the distance—now close enough, now too far—to the dimming rocks. The appearance of a grey-faced father with two little girls was too much for me, and I offered to take one of them in charge, should we have to swim.

... As the night deepened, a new danger appeared. Hitherto, the ship had managed to hide itself completely. Well inshore, against the black cliff, we were quite invisible. Then, out came the local fishermen, each boat with blazing flare at the bow. They were between us and the land, and during most of the night, for minutes on end, we were silhouetted again and again. At our slow rate of progress, each silhouetting gave time enough for the submarine, which could have crept up to within a quarter of a mile, to sink us.

The following afternoon, 27th June, we crept along the vast curve up to Gibraltar, and turned into the harbour. French and English soldiers waved and cheered from the troopships as we sidled to our anchorage, and flags were broken at the mastheads. They were signalling 'Congratulations'. I myself had begun to worry again. What was going to happen now? What was happening to so-and-so? I had decided, once and for all, that the gravest physical danger is as nothing compared to the smallest of one's familiar anxieties.

3 1940–1958
War and Peace

18. From M.I.5 to A.C.2, with anecdotes

1940–1942

It was not until 1940 that I actually met Brian and certainly none of his early history or background was known to me until I was given access to his private papers some twenty-five years later. He was first pointed out to me by my father in the south of France: 'Oh, there's that frightful man Gassaway—no wonder he changed his name to Howard.' I saw a hollowed out figure in a red shirt, with a Disraeli profile, standing square against the unaccustomed winter cold (it had just snowed for the first time in about ten years) and bleakly looking out to sea at Antibes. It was during the long, phoney war winter of 1939–1940, and we drove on, chattering, to the internment camp to deliver delicacies and warm clothing to our particular Austrian friend who had been caught up in the intricacies of improvised wartime regulations. Behind the barbed wire, next to him and other more moneyed companions, were the now destitute aliens whose jobs had so suddenly been taken from them, passing their camp food rations *out* to their starving, dependent families. It was not until much later that I heard about Brian's German companion of the last ten years, Toni, having been taken off to a more stringent type of camp, and of his struggle to get to America after France fell.

From time to time the name of Brian Howard would hover around, and recede into, my subconscious mind—during dimly heard conversations in bars, in *boîtes*, at dinner-parties, but the essence of the man was never there, and I felt no great compunction to wonder what became of the lone figure on the sea-shore at Antibes.

When I returned to London just before the fall of France, in the spring of 1940, I soon became an eager protégé of Willie Acton (by then a painter) whose Tite Street studio was the scene of many strange parties peopled by other artists and writers and assorted Indians of varying degrees of interest. (Willie was going through his 'Indian' period at that time.) It was there that I first met Brian face to face, and found myself deputed to accompany him to the nearest off-licence pub to buy more drink for the insatiable guests. It was dark that evening, cold, and the usual air raid was on so we walked quickly to the 'local'. Once there Brian insisted on having a few nips *à deux*, to give 'moral' courage, he said, before stepping out again under the familiar rain of shrapnel. I listened like the devout eighteen-year-old disciple I was to this thirty-five-year-old sophisticate, only briefly mystified by his oblique reference to working for the British Intelligence. I did not really know what he meant, and some few weeks later when I found myself unexpectedly sitting in a small cell in Wormwood Scrubs Prison (the 'Scrubs' having been requisitioned by the War Office), as one of the many new secretaries having passed the test to work in 'War Office Intelligence', I was even more sceptical of his claim to be *one of us*.

The next time Brian mentioned the subject in public I thought I would test him by asking if he worked in Section 'A' or 'B'—or whatever the main divisions were currently called. He made some unintelligible reply to my tiny attempt at the *agent provocateur* game, leaving me smugly convinced that he had fabricated the whole connection. Little did I know my Brian; a few minutes later he drew me aside and gave me hell for a solid five minutes—about how indiscreet I was, how could I possibly ask such stupid and dangerous questions—didn't I know that we were not supposed to talk about our work and so on—and on—until my tears were imminent. His conviction was such that I almost believed it was I who had been making mildly indiscreet references to 'Intelligence'—not Brian. He had this extraordinary capacity for turning the tables on people whereby, having started from a highly untenable position, *he* finally appeared as the righteous one. On this occasion my 'folly' merely endeared me to him. He took me out to dinner to celebrate my neo-guilt and later showered me with rare Mary Chess frivolities.

Within a few days, as I was walking down one of the endless prison corridors during an air raid, hugging the side wall so as to avoid falling glass from the central skylight roof, who should appear in a wildly improbable pepper-salt-and-*mustard* tweed suit, nonchalantly smoking a forbidden cigarette *and* ambling down the dangerous middle area of passage, but Brian?

'Hallo, sweety,' he said. 'Do take me to tea in the canteen, I'm much too scared to find my way there alone with all those steely-eyed prisoners about.' (For a time some of the civilian prisoners were kept in another part of the prison, and were visible from the corridor windows leading to the canteen.) I was appalled. It was not done for the new, junior secretaries to have tea with Officers—let alone stray 'contacts' in plain—or in Brian's case *fantaisie*—clothes. I was not sure whether it was even good for me to be seen with such a dubious character at all. However, we braved the canteen together, and so our friendship started.

My mother, Jaqueline Hope-Nicholson, was the most long-suffering of all parents during these early war years and provided an overnight refuge to any of our homeless friends in her cavernous Tite Street house in Chelsea where I was one of many transient lodgers. Mattresses and sundry bedding were laid out in rows every night in the ground floor dining-room, and no matter whose figure should be found semi-moribund after an all-night party, she would be the first to greet him, or her, with a cheery 'Good Morning' while she breakfasted off miniscule rations congealed in out-sized silver chafing dishes at the head of the family table. Brian became a frequent late night guest, but never quite took to waking up 'in public', as he called it.

In almost every man there lurks the desire to mould a person to their will, and Brian was no mean Pygmalion. He should, of course, have been an eccentric don-without-a-degree at an enchanting college for intelligent misfits. Not only was he a mentor in what I should read, look at and listen to in all the arts, but also what clothes I should wear, how I should talk and behave ('a little graveness suits your face, sweety' after too ribald a belly-laugh), the food to choose in restaurants, the moment to stop drinking ('beddy-byes for *you*, young lady'— against which there was no argument). I was, I suppose, one of his favourite pupils during our half-decade of intermittently close friendship. Had I been a young man the whole character of our relationship would, of necessity, have been different and impossible to keep at that high key for so long. As it was I loved him in a trusting, devoted, uncomplicated and undemanding way. The only way, in fact, to keep any great friend. For one whose behaviour at times could be so atrocious and inexcusable, it is quite extraordinary how he managed to reinforce in me the basic code of right and wrong in terms of everyday life that had been initially implanted by my parents, but he did. Brian was a bad exponent but a good master.

Only once was the magic link severely strained, when he suddenly faced me one night, in the street as I recollect, on the way to yet another unsavoury night-club.

'You know, sweety,' he said, in teasing, serio-mocking mood, 'you and I could get married.' I was completely taken off my guard by this side-stepping of his accepted role of detached Svengali, but knew that *how* I answered would seal or sever our very special relationship. I was tired, nervous and non-plussed, and Brian was far from my idea of the ideal husband. Words evaded me, and I could only falter:

'Well, I don't really see the point . . . we get on very well as it is.' There was an awful silence, and those eyebrows arched up to heaven while the mouth turned down.

'Get on, did you say, get *on*? Is that what you think? *Get* on, and you say you care about words. *Get on* . . .' And then the mood changed, and he started to laugh, and we danced all night. He was a good dancer in a sexy, slinky way—no jiving nonsense, but closer than close, as if you were the proverbial only one in the world. I had, it seemed, passed the test in dispassionate love with flying colours. I remained the pupil-protégée, and favoured dancing partner. In future I took care to look at my words before leaping into the late night space with them.

I was not the only girl on the scene. Pauline Tennant (now Mrs. Euan Graham) remembers her first meeting with Brian during the blitz of 1940, when she was thirteen years old and had been taken to have a drink with him by 'a charming but somewhat eccentric American friend' with whom she had been parked while her mother, Hermione Baddeley, was touring in a play:

Brian had a room on the third floor of the Berkeley. We went up the lift in a trice, he opened his door and said, 'Ruthie, you've arrived at last and with a FRIEND, a young person I see rather in need of a *brush*.' I saw a willowy person, dark, with rounded but hawk-like features, protuberant eyes with hooded lids, aggressive but somehow not threatening. He welcomed us in with expansive gestures and offered us some champagne. There were some other young men in the room and a party atmosphere with bottles and glasses everywhere. I sat in an observant daze listening to dazzling firework conversation and felt privileged to be there.

251

Brian, suddenly aware that a schoolgirl was present and wishing to include me in some way into the conversation, pointed an accusing forefinger at me and demanded, 'Which is *the rose-red city half as old as time?*' I blushed, wondered if there was a trick, and mumbled *Petra*. 'Right,' cried Brian triumphantly, 'of course she's David's daughter.' I wished he hadn't said that but felt pleased that I had not let him down. When I got to know him better I discovered that this sudden shooting of questions was a habit of Brian's, particularly if he was losing an argument. 'The date of Mohammed's birth?' he would shout to his adversary, who, if he couldn't answer, would then be considered unfit to continue a discussion on any point.

Another young friend, Theodora FitzGibbon (now Mrs. George Morrison), describes the essence of Brian's appeal to young girls; something just this side of forbidden fruit:

Brian was a genie; that is he would appear after many months, in a variety of guises, but a moment later, the great dark eyes would roll, the mellifluous, yet slightly querulous voice would speak, and it would be as if he had never left, and the conversation continued. I must have known him for some six years in such a way, and yet never, once, did I ever know where he lived, how, or what on.

I first met him with Peter Rose Pulham, when I was twenty years old; had I been told about him in advance, I might have showed off, and behaved badly, and that would have been that. As it was, I didn't, and Brian called me the 'Wicked Madonna'. What girl of spirit doesn't want to be thought both good and bad at the same time? And the way he pronounced 'wicked'. Could anyone, ever, get more out of a word than Brian when he wanted to? He rolled the word about in his mouth as a gourmet would a new and delicious sauce. Delicious sauce: that is somehow as I would describe Brian.

The curious thing is, that on looking back (a dangerous occupation), I never remember meeting Brian by appointment. That is to say, I don't think he ever telephoned to announce his arrival, and yet it is mostly over long and lingering meals, always in my own house that I remember him. As this was wartime London one wonders how they lingered so long.

But that is exactly the quality he had, to make even the simplest meal seem like an enormous banquet. You could live a lifetime during one of them; eat, drink, laugh, quarrel, make up, and still discuss ideas with gaiety and spontaneity.

When the fall of France was well under way, in mid-1940, Maurice Richardson encountered Brian once more, and he gives a one-day picture of him during that period of suspense:

In Leicester Square a bearded man in a bath-chair, some kind of street poet who used to hand out broadsheet poems, I think his name was Carveth

Wells, was addressing a little knot of people telling them that France would fight on from Algeria and it would really be a much more satisfactory arrangement all round. After dinner I found myself in Peter Quennell's flat in Rossetti Mansions. Brian was there, not long back from France. He told us to expect German parachutists in blue silk nuns' habits at any moment. I was at the height of my most sectarian communist phase and bored everybody with harsh diatribes. Peter was very polite and tolerant. Somebody played Ella Fitzgerald (was it?) singing *It was a lover and his lass.* Brian went into raptures. 'Listen to this, my dears—Shakespeare and swing . . .'

We left together and ended up in Lyons Corner House in Coventry Street. I kept lecturing him on dialectics. Hegel. You couldn't understand anything unless you were steeped in old Hegel, the original source, when stood on his feet, of Marxian wisdom. 'You may be anti-Fascist but you're not properly educated, you old gilded Bohemian flibbertigibbet,' I boomed. 'There are other philosophers, my dear, but perhaps you haven't read many. Let's see. Now, who wrote a book called *The World as Will and Idea?* Nietzsche, wasn't it?'

'Schopenhauer,' I said. 'You can't trap me.'

Erika Mann gives another view of Brian, making nonsense of his earlier premonitions of fear:

Brian and I lived through the big blitzes on London together. Every night we were out and about. Since I was a correspondent of the New York *Nation* and worked on the German service of the B.B.C., I had to know just what happened and how people reacted to it. Brian came with me on all these excursions and his crazy courage, his rebellious daring kept landing us in the most awkward situations. What was it? Bravado? Contempt for death? I think that it was despair, not 'unfathomable' any more but become tangible, despair because war had been unleashed—murder between us and the Germans—'who are mostly social-democrats, and Toni's cousins anyway.'

November 1940. It had taken Brian a scant four months to infiltrate the War Office. He knew someone who knew someone who introduced him to an impressionable officer in the Ministry of Home Security, euphemistic cover name for dear old M.I.5. At his final interview the officer had to leave the room for a moment, and Brian, never one to lose a snooping chance of this kind, managed to get a quick look at the original screening report—or so he said—and much to his satisfaction caught the words, *has compelling eyes.* Brian's mother was at last able to boast of him to her great friend in America, Yvette Andrews, 'The War Office have given Brian a *very fine job!* Well paid, so as soon as things settle down financially he will be able to do things'.

It was not surprising that the Intelligence Service wished to make use of Brian's extensive knowledge of pro- and anti-Nazi personalities, and to do them justice they did not make him a permanent staff member but engaged him as an outside 'contact' in strictest mufti, in which branch he had many colourful contenders but none perhaps quite so unpredictably indiscreet according to his alcoholic whims of state. The 'old school tie' worked for some people but not in the long run for Brian. There is a story that when he reported to his superior. officer that a certain key personage had had strong pre-war Fascist sympathies, the officer reacted to this lead with, 'Don't be ridiculous—he went to Eton with me!' Not unnaturally, Brian became disgusted with this aspect of 'Intelligence'.

There is no doubt that during this War Office period Brian was killing time and drowning sorrow until news of Toni arrived. And for this he had to wait a long, long time—until May 1941, almost a year after their final parting in France—when a cable arrived saying that Toni was leaving for New York from Tangier. This was the first he knew of Toni's survival of the fall of France. Some of Brian's most faithful friends took over the burden and responsibility of looking after Toni—Erika Mann, Wystan Auden, Sybille Bedford, Marty Mann (who found him his first job at one of her residential homes for 'Alcoholics Anonymous'). This was not without its irony because of his predilection for the hard stuff.

Toni was finally given permission to work anywhere in the States and got a night job as a truck-loader somewhere in New England. He took great pleasure on his 'payday' in sending over regular parcels of American cigarettes and magazines for Brian and his mother. Brian appeared more tortured by the separation than Toni, writing to him: 'It goes without saying that I am having an affair with no one, only very infrequent and horrible incidents that I *hate* and only do to avoid going crazy in that direction. I often *think* of forming some sort of attachment, but it is SIMPLY IMPOSSIBLE. It might be better for me, actually, but I CAN'T. There's nobody, nobody else I want ... P.S. Evelyn Waugh has made an absolutely vicious attack on me in his new novel *Put out more Flags. You* come into it, too!'

By June 1942 their correspondence had tailed off to vanishing point. They both tried to write too long letters too seldom. And then what? Toni must have saved enough money, at last, to become independent. And independence meant becoming an individual with the right to choose his own way of life. After twelve years of chequered relationship with Brian he made the final breakaway and chose marriage—to a wealthy American woman. This blow, announced to Brian, I am told, by a callous postcard, set the pace full steam ahead for alcoholism.

The writing was on the wall for Brian at the Warhouse and they parted company in June 1942, ostensibly 'owing to lack of sufficient work.' It was a case of too many indiscreet incidents, mostly of drunken intimidation in night-clubs, 'If you aren't careful, my man, I'll have you put *inside* ... I've got it all *here*' (tapping his briefcase which he would then most likely leave behind in the last night haunt). 'Call yourself a gentleman, I think I smell a *Fascist*, hmm ...?' and so on, *ad absurdum*. Some of the anecdotes are funny, others shaming, the wit is there, but oh, so often distorted.

Out of the many anecdotes recalled in varying degrees of accuracy I find the following most typical of this sadly bar-flown period. Some 'we were there' purists may cavil and carp that I have kaleidoscoped times and places, but it is atmosphere that I am after more than a Bradshaw-cum-Baedeker accuracy.

To kick off, who better than Gerald Hamilton, to whom Brian used to say, 'Why do you persist in remaining so "Right" when all your friends are "Left"?':

I knew Brian well for many years. We really got to know each other in Amsterdam in 1933 when I was there with Christopher Isherwood and others who had lived in Berlin, but had left when Hitler came to power.

Soon after Guy Burgess became front-page news I pretended to have discovered a private letter from 'Mr. Norris'[1] to Christopher Isherwood, which was published in the *Spectator* of 4th November 1955. I teased Christopher about his introducing Guy Burgess to 'Mr. Norris', and amongst other things recounted two characteristic meetings with a 'Mr. Q', alias Brian Howard, during the war:

'. . . We (Guy and I) agreed to meet for dinner—in London. The evening developed along markedly saturnalian lines . . . Guy Burgess had lost none of his tastes for the lower night haunts. After dinner he and Q. guided me to a basement club in Soho so manifestly *louche* that it reminded me, with, I confess, a slight pang of nostalgia, of the closing hours of the Weimar Republic, which you, dear Christopher, have so brilliantly portrayed. While we were there, the place was raided! The police approached our table. Q., who was by this time very drunk indeed, on being asked for his name and address, gave his name, and added: 'I live in Mayfair. No doubt you come from some dreary suburb.' I remarked to Guy Burgess that, in my experience, this was a *most* tactless way of receiving the attentions of the civil arm. Guy, however, for his part, behaved with such assured nonchalance, giving his own name, address, *and* occupation (*diplomate de carrière*), in stentorian tones, that I could only conclude that a new—and how welcome!—spirit of tolerance was prevailing in Whitehall . . .'

Clerics and 'failed gentleman' aroused Brian's animosity, but it was people in uniform for whom he had the most obsessive hatred. His great old friend Harold Acton, who was a Flight-Lieutenant in the R.A.F., never saw Brian again after he flung a cocktail at him in the Ritz Bar with the words, pronounced sarcastically, '*à Monsieur l'Officier!*' (Brian did *write* to him after the war—about settling in Italy—but they never actually met again.) An eye-witness recalls an unfortunate evening when Brian and he were alone at the bar of the Gargoyle:

It was soon after the Dunkirk period of the war and Brian was fairly tipsy, weaving about like a python. There were no other guests about except for five or six Army officers, not a particularly typical sight for the Gargoyle. Brian swayed towards this hated spectacle, his huge brown eyes wide open: 'Hmm, my dears.' The uniforms paid no attention. 'Hmm.' The victims started to become a shade uneasy. 'Hmm. Members of a rather unsuccessful profession, my dears.' Shaking a finger at them, waggishly, he went on,

---

[1] Of *Mr. Norris Changes Trains* by Christopher Isherwood, published by Methuen, 1935. Gerald Hamilton was the original model for 'Mr. Norris'.

'Dunkirky, wirky!' Brian was of equally military age as his audience. Instead of beating him up they ignored him, out of complete astonishment. In retrospect Dunkirk could perhaps be judged as one of our less successful exploits, but at that time it was a heroic act of withdrawal, and criticism would not have been popular.

There was often difficulty in being allowed into places with Brian after he had misbehaved, verbally or physically. Even the Ritz in London drew the line one New Year's Eve night—this time at young friends of Brian's who had appeared to join him at his table in palpably informal dress. 'What are you doing detaining my friends at the door?' asked Brian of the head waiter. 'We've got Royalty, Sir. They can't come in here dressed like that.' 'Royalty? What do you mean?' 'King Zog, Sir.' Brian bristled and bridled, 'King *Zog*, do you say, *King* Zog, do you mean the man who pays his bill here by chipping bits off that gold he managed to extricate from his poor country?'

Trains, hotels, restaurants, were always a stimulus to his mischievous, sometimes malicious propensities. Once he hailed as a porter a man outside the Regent Palace Hotel who was obviously a Middle-Aged-Guest. When he mildly explained that he was not a porter Brian became his most ingratiating self, 'Of course you're not, my dear. I can see that. You're a house detective, naturally. And there's nothing against that—you defend our property, after all. Tell me, do you prefer boys or girls?' The M-A-G, rather taken aback, thinking doubtless of his pigeon progeny at home, 'Well ... er ... depends on how you feel ...' 'Oh, you wicked, wicked creature!'

And to stretch time to the postwar years, the most apocryphal story of all concerned Brian's insistence on visiting a new 'queer' night-club in the south of France with great old friends of his, a married couple who were well known for their anti-Jewish convictions. Much against their will they consented to accompany him, whereupon Brian promptly asked the husband to dance (women not, apparently being encouraged to do anything so conspicuous). Rather than risk a row in public, the husband accepted, and just as they reached the dance floor Brian faced him, took him by the shoulders, looked him triumphantly in the face and said, 'And to think that *you* are one of the people who would have put *me* in a gas oven!'

Throughout the early 'forties, when I was close to Brian, he was constantly referring to his 'writing', and how he really must go back to work. For a long time I never saw any evidence of his writing at all, except for the account of his escape from France in *Horizon*, a few poems, and infrequent *New Statesman* book reviews. He was curiously modest in never referring to his Eton and Oxford exploits, his Bright Young People persona, let alone any earlier published work. He kept silent even about five B.B.C. radio propaganda scripts of his that were actually being broadcast in 1942. He seemed to want the slate wiped clean as far as his new young friends were concerned, to be liked for himself and not for what he had been, or could again be. But his will to write was never strong enough to combat the desire for drink and late nights. Occasionally I would wonder whether this writing complex was not a personally induced mirage, a misty target to get him through the war years. And yet one at least of these radio plays, *Baldur von Schirach*,[2] used surprisingly up-to-date techniques and was referred to in the *Observer* as being a brilliant script.

To return to the immediate facts of life. It was the middle of the war and Brian was in an awkward position, without job, occupation, or income (other than what his mother irregularly gave him, to pay off his incipient debts rather than as a stable allowance). So he did the unexpected and volunteered for the Royal Air Force. He was accepted as a Clerk, Special Duties, for the Voluntary Reserve in October, and hastily started the wheels grinding towards applying for a commission and an eventual job in R.A.F. Public Relations by writing to a Flight-Lieutenant contact of his in the Air Ministry.

---

[2] Reproduced in full as Appendix III.

19. Aircraftman Extraordinary

1942–1944

The day of Brian's enlistment, 10th November 1942, found him at Penarth in deepest Wales with a mixed bag of recruits. His letters to his mother (of which brief extracts follow) give a fly-on-the-wall account of what it was like for a sophisticated, pleasure-loving thirty-seven-year-old to muck in with a lot of other A.C.2s.

[From Penarth] My first letter to anyone as a member of the Forces. I started with a party of twenty-six and at Penarth (pure Victorian plus fog) we were marched up and down several wrong streets to get our tea by a poor R.A.F. man who didn't know the way—then sausages and mash. I am sleeping in blankets with only four others in an empty house. Lights out are at 10. P.S. The heaviness of my case as I marched up those wrong roads in the gloaming!!

[A week later, from: 1831951 A.C.2 Howard, B. C., R.A.F., Blackpool] As I should have to repeat more or less the same course in the O.C.T.U. I should welcome anything that can be done to get me into it *now*. A rule has been made forbidding people under forty-one to be Clerks, Special Duty, so I took the next best thing in Group IV, namely Equipment Assistant. The R.A.F. are really very modern and efficient. At Penarth we had one dinner consisting of red cabbage, cheese, watercress, celery, bread, margarine, and jam. Very un-Army.

. . . Today I drilled for the first time, and as I prophesied, it began to come back to me. I even rather *enjoyed* it—between you and me! I also had a 'service' haircut, and have achieved the perfect compromise between Claridges and Borstal. It satisfies both me and the non-commissioned officers. Tomorrow I do physical training, in vest and shorts, on the beach; tonight, I peeled a tub of potatoes in the lodging house. I use Silvo on my buttons, and Wren boot polish. You see, by expecting the worst and receiving something not quite so bad, and by living—with a certain efficiency—in a kind of dream, I am managing fairly well. In other words, it is so grotesque that it's alright. P.S. I am childishly pleased by the fact that whereas most of the people here can't have 'V.R.' sewn on their uniforms, I can.

. . . The people in my house are charming and nice, as souls, but, my goodness, I do wish they wouldn't address one another, and me, as 'Mr. So-and-so'. Here I was expecting a stream of foul language, and instead: ME: 'Would you like some potatoes?' ANY ONE OF THEM: 'No-o, thank you, Mr. Howard, Ai hev sufficient.' One of them actually said the other day, 'Well, Ai only laike macaroni with stew'. . . . Really it is a bore, living with eight, nice, stupid men in a lodging house, sleeping with them, eating with them, night and day, and NEVER ONE INTERESTING REMARK. If they poured out their private lives—if there was only one of them—if they weren't so frightened. Frightened of *everything*, R.A.F., money, life, poor dears. I understand, but it's infernally DULL.

... Today we had a lecture about the STEN CARBINE, a tommy gun which occupies, in machine gun history, the place that Ford occupies in motor-car history. The first simple, cheap, brilliant, *portable* quick-firing gun for one man. You will be glad to hear that although the lecture was delivered by a corporal who lectured with his back to me, with a cigarette in his mouth, with a cold, with an almost impenetrable Lancastrian accent—I was able to re-assemble the gun, from its component pieces, with only one mistake. And I can do the P.T. standing on my head, but it is the *drill*. I can do it, because of the O.T.C. at Eton, but there is one difficult movement so far—the 'about turn', which has something of a ballet skip about it, although it sounds simple.

[December] The training is intensifying a little. And the drill and lectures are very closely packed. . . . There are forty Musketry lectures, alone, on the course. I made six and a half pages of notes on Gases this morning. For example, R.A.F. people who are gassed by nasal gases are automatically disarmed lest they commit suicide, so depressing is the experience. Though they are not lethal gases and dispersed by DEW. On the other hand, they are tasteless, odourless, and invisible! Chloral-Picrin, however, *is* lethal, and it is usually disguised as Tear Gas. There is a 'well-being' period of twelve hours with this gas, during which one feels fine. Next thing, one just begins choking to death. This, if you please, is what Mussolini used on the Abyssinians in 1935.

It is the Nasal gases which will be used by the Germans to try and gain command of aerodromes, as it turns one for an hour or so into a coughing, spitting drunkard who can't remember orders. Remedies—hot tea with salt in it and the spitting out of all mucous into the gas-mask *without taking it off!* It arrives disguised as an incendiary bomb. I'm fairly good at drill. Have to be, because I am the corner man (height, such a nuisance) of about a hundred. The food remains burlesque English. . . . The pity is that my two bedroom companions are the most inferiority-complexy of all. They *still* say 'Mr. Jones', and 'Mr. Smith'—also 'Mr. Howard', which is so unnerving. They are also a tiny bit mean, which really poor people aren't. I eavesdropped on them a few days ago and heard this (about me): *Jones* '. . . yes, but his accent!'—*Smith* 'Of course, it's an officer's accent, but don't tell me he could lead men.' I felt rather chastened. . . . A combination of a reasonable efficiency—to drill and *never* to be reprimanded—together with a capacity to be straightforward and possibly rather mysteriously charming at the same time, will do the trick. You see, *if* I bother, I can erase my mistakes, and charm—yes, it's the only word—myself back into favour. (And so far there've been no mistakes.)

... I'm getting on all right with the labourer types, but it's ticklish sometimes with the others. I'm being fairly quick, though, and have concealed my few grandeurs (the War Office, my travels etc.) with entire success. Nothing, however, can alter my accent, and already the household are picking up words from me with the most harrowing results—using them wrongly etc. It's 'delicious', at the moment. Then this fashion I indulge in of putting 'un' in front of unlikely words—of P.T. 'it's quite unstrenuous, really'. I only mention this because it bounces back at one, one's language, suddenly. I thought I would do best by being quiet and going my own way. This, I find, created too much of an impression. So now I join in, regardless of my vocabulary. It's better on the whole, in spite of the half-fascinated, quarter-suspicious silence with which my speeches are greeted; and followed, the next day, by imitation.

. . . I have heard several N.C.Os, during lectures, say straightforwardly, 'All this drill and button-polishing is nonsense. You know it. We know it. But it must be done, because otherwise (they didn't use these words, but they made it clear) you wouldn't react quickly and *cohesively* enough if the Germans parachuted down on an aerodrome. It is pure training.' So true. On the whole it is very *intelligent* the attitude. An Aircraft Recognition lecturer, describing the Beaufighter, said, 'the way to remember this aircraft is this. A pilot once said that it resembles nothing so much as two huge engines hotly pursued by an airframe.' The *tone* of this is so enlivening, I find.

. . . My news—we did shooting, fifteen shots with a light rifle at twenty yards. They never told me the rifle had a hair-trigger, and for weeks I have been messing about with an Army rifle which has a double-pressure trigger. I got sixty-five (my first shot missing the target). The highest score among a hundred men was seventy-three. So I missed being the champion shot. Rather tiresome.

. . . This afternoon we did a route march about two miles to outside Blackpool, and had a lecture on a hill as to how to divide up a landscape and examine it for hidden enemies, followed by having to hide *in* the landscape ourselves! I became fascinated and so neatly concealed myself in an old rusty bucket that although practically under the noses of the examiners (half of us, in other words) I wasn't seen. Bayonet practice I had dreaded, naturally. The horror of it; I won't go into it—you understand. Well—it proved so difficult to do *well* that I managed to submerge its reality and do it as if it were some particularly complicated kind of knitting. Or, rather, billiards. Flicking something forward with exactness. Rather sad, all the same. The Assault Course was not so terrible. In fact, nothing like the illustrations in *Picture Post*. One did walk across water on 8-inch wide logs, and there was one 7-foot drop. But the drop was on to sand, and the water was six inches deep.

. . . My sergeant rushed through my interview with my C.O. yesterday, and within four minutes he'd promised to recommend me for a commission. But when will this be? Meanwhile I shall be busily learning to be a sort of haberdasher in Yorkshire. Rather a waste of time?

. . . Today we marched ten miles with full pack—and I feel quite alright. By the way, about getting up, which you find me so bad at. I have often wondered how you could *bear* to get up the way you do, but I see it is purely practice. (I don't mean that I, at thirty-seven, oughtn't to be ashamed—I am.) I now rise at 6.30 with only slight difficulty, really, and find that if I am asleep by 11 p.m. *regularly*, it can be done. But don't expect it on my leave!

[January 1943] Our N.C.Os are already running about between the ranks during drill like a lot of hens, tipping rifles up, or down, and generally titivating us. It's so amusing to watch. I like *all* the N.C.O.s—they're so like nannies at heart. Today I had my first, last and only public reprimand. Someone asked me for a cigarette, and I gave it and lit one myself. The Corporal arrived from nowhere and of course everyone was suddenly not smoking—except me. I kept on saying, 'I'm sorry, Corporal,' and 'Yes, Corporal,' and he didn't put me on a charge.

[From Milton] About the R.A.F. complications. I feel more depressed than I can say and *I haven't been depressed about it before*. The thing that I so dreaded seems to be beginning—namely, delay and nobody doing anything and the Machine Taking Charge, so to speak. On Friday, when I saw Willoughby de Broke (one of the two heads of Public Relations at the Air Ministry) there was no time to really talk to him. He was charming, but seemed dimly disappointed that I had no technical experience of newspaper offices—as a sub-editor or reporter. (He also said, 'Would you be prepared to fly and report battles from the air!' I said yes.) He intimated that Public Relations was very full, etc. and that with my qualifications 'Intelligence' might be a good thing. All this without finally rejecting me, at all. [The Air Ministry had written a formal letter to Brian asking him to come for an interview with Group-Captain Lord Willoughby de Broke next time he was up in London. This was sparked off by Brian's original letter to his Flight-Lieutenant contact there.]

Tonight I had a long talk with the Flight-Sergeant here, who really runs this place *for* the officers, so to speak. He says that it is plain that the process of becoming an officer has never been properly explained to me. Roughly, the rules are that one must complete one's 'course' (in my case, Equipment, which I haven't begun and don't want to do), and that people can't normally become officers before six months service. Of course I could become an officer in a week if someone asked for me—such as the Air Ministry. He also said that the three men they had sponsored from Milton for commissions had all been turned down by the Air Ministry. You see, I am trying to get a job which is only for officers and am not yet one. The Flight-Sergeant tried to comfort me by saying that the R.A.F. was full of people of talent who were forgotten, or misplaced. I have often heard this. *I refuse to be one.*

[March] Roy and Billa Harrod and Gerald Berners came over for the concert party, which went without a hitch.[1] I was a great success, I may say, and was congratulated by everyone, including officers, the Flight-Sergeant and my fellow players. The next morning early I was leaving

---

[1] See Sir Roy Harrod's account on page 325.

Milton for good (for Eastbourne) and there was quite a dramatic and moving atmosphere—people came up and shook hands—it was all very touching. One felt people's real natures coming out, everything over-shadowed by time so terribly. Life in the services is so very ephemeral—a constant saying goodbye. I was sorry to go, and I think I shall be a good deal sorrier before long.

[From Eastbourne] There was a great deal of mathematics in the preliminary 'intelligence' tests for Equipment Assistants, but in spite of leaving out two questions in the test I have been put in the first class—A—and it is really terrible. I looked down the list of civil occupations of the other men in the class and they run like this, Chief Accountant, General Manager, Chief Clerk—the cleverest business men from Blackpool. The other two Milton men only succeeded in getting into Class B—and they both have their own business. All the others are in E and F—where I *ought to be*, where I can learn *slowly*. It is a real catastrophe. Now they will expect me to keep up with these people. But what could I do? One can't deliberately do a test badly, *can* one?

[April] Whatever comes now, the R.A.F. has given my nature a shock that was needed, and the effects of which I believe will last. In a way, I really had my war before other people—mine left off when theirs began. Now the war is integrating me, instead of the opposite, which some—many people find happening to them. Don't ever despair of me because it won't be true. Try and forgive my having been so few of the things you wanted me to be. Remember that in my heart I know how disappointing I am—how wretchedly, in a way, I've failed. But I haven't entirely failed yet. The sun has gone and the instructor has come instead . . .

One of Brian's senior N.C.O.s on the Eastbourne course remembers having many interesting discussions with him, 'but he seemed to have a good many secrets and was certainly suspicious of authority. One did feel that his intellect was completely in the wrong environment at an Equipment Assistant's School, but he gave the impression that this had been deliberately planned by some bureaucratic higher authority. He never gave a hint that he might be, or might become, an alcoholic . . .'

During April Brian had managed to get his Wing-Commander to take him off the Equipment Course and docketed 'with a view to more important part in the war effort.' A month later he was, nevertheless, posted to go overseas as an Equipment A.C.H., General Duties. As a last hope—and a great favour—he was allowed to write a formal letter applying for a commission to 'Group'.

Finally, the contacts worked, but only just in time. Brian found himself at Bomber Command, High Wycombe, as a clerk in the Public Relations department, with his old Etonian contemporary (now a Squadron-Leader) Alan Clutton-Brock, who casts a nostalgic eye on those times:

I am afraid my recollection of how Brian got to Bomber Command is shaky, but he did get posted to our department, known as Public Relations, at Bomber Command headquarters. Our job was to get out communiqués and other matter for the newspapers, wireless, etc. Most of the people the Air Ministry sent us were professional journalists of a rather low order and hardly any of them could write a line of straightforward English, so it was as an educated writer that we wanted Brian. I remember particularly two of our misfits (who happened to be Roman Catholic) of whom one had religious mania and the other tried to rape a W.A.A.F.

Brian's unit had been posted to India, I think—anyway overseas—and he described the terrible sigh of envy from the others when his name was called out at the last moment as being someone to stay in England. However, Brian was not quite as useful a writer as my colleagues (John Lawrence and Hugh Massingham) and I had hoped. He was not much interested in the technicalities that really had to be more or less understood if he was going to write about bombing. But there was a lot that was useful that he could do in the way of plain writing. He also gave himself the job of making tea, and used to come along with his tea tray, from the room where he worked with our other clerk, a girl, push the door open and exclaim, 'Delicious Teazle'. He could very well have done this when we had some Air Vice Marshal or what not in the room, but I don't think this ever happened.

We wanted to get him a commission and thought we could easily do so, but when Lawrence applied to the Air Ministry a note came back to say that this airman was never to be given a commission in any of the services. There are many obvious explanations for this decision, but I gather he had blotted his copybook at M.I.5. . . .

Brian, of course, drank a great deal then, as a good many of us did after the awful boredom of the day's work. He used to come, often with a bottle, to the lodgings where I was staying with my wife near the camp and stay on much later than his pass allowed. I would then have to write a note to say that he had been detained by me to finish some work, and I used to wonder what the authorities would make of this but nobody seemed to mind. At the local pub, where it was thought rather odd that a squadron-leader and an airman should sit talking together, it came to be believed that Brian was my wife's brother. Towards the end of the evening he could get tiresome, and once when my wife was about to drive him back to his camp, long after midnight, he lay down in front of the car and said he wouldn't go. 'Very well, Brian,' my wife said, 'I'll drive over you then', so he got up and climbed peacefully into the car. We were, I may say, very glad of his company in the evenings.

Among the other airmen he became considered an important figure; one of them was anxious to have a souvenir of his time at Bomber Command and even had some sort of a wooden tray made, on which he got his officers, including the Commander in Chief (Harris)—and Brian—to sign their names.

At one time Brian decided he wanted to get out of the R.A.F., having 'fallen in love', and seemed to think I could or should help him. I had just heard that my son, by my first wife, had died in Africa, and was impatient. I said that I also had my troubles but that one had to do one's work even so. Another thing that annoyed him was when he lost his uniform on leave and his mother rang me up at Bomber Command to ask what he should do. I said he must come back anyway, or something like that, and she thought I was being unsympathetic. Brian became very cross and we weren't on good terms after that. Later on I was asked to say whether his work had been satisfactory, and I said that it had been—which infuriated Brian because he thought I was then trying to keep him *in* the R.A.F. So I'm afraid our association had rather an unhappy ending. But he was a bit difficult . . .

Jimmy Stern recounts in his book, *The Hidden Damage*, how Brian reacted to his enquiry about life in the R.A.F. '. . . I was jolly popular . . . ever since the day I lost my uniform. Seems no one'd ever done that before. People are really *too* extraordinary. I just left the silly thing in a public lavvy. Like 'Kopenick'. They simply wouldn't believe me. They called me Cracky after that!'

Christopher Sykes remembers hearing two particularly characteristic stories of Brian's attitude to R.A.F. *mores*. The first was when he was hauled up before the Station Commander for some major infringement of R.A.F. etiquette, and after suffering a thoroughly intimidating and lengthy ticking off Brian bent forward to say, 'you . . . ogre!' at the offending officer. The second was when Brian made fame at one of the Orderly Officer's regular mess inspections. The more usual *complaints* were apt to be of uncooked meat (indicating that a good cook had left some taste in the joint), or a blemished potato. Water-swilled cabbage and foul tinned gravy never seemed to bring forth comments of distaste. On this occasion, the officer having barked out 'Any complaints?' there was the usual hush until Brian, with his theatrical sense, rose, a solitary blue figure in the great mass of silent men. 'It's absolutely delicious, Sir,' he called back.

Having evaded the overseas hurdle and achieved the jump to R.A.F. Public Relations, Brian's life was not one long joke. Hardly had he arrived at Bomber Command headquarters before he penned the following 'Notes written in dejection at High Wycombe':

[June 1943] Saint-Exupéry's book, *Flight to Arras*, superb on the psychology of the French army's collapse, also on the satisfactions of doing one's duty. See the description of Hochède, the whole, simple, unintellectual. The best description of this type I have come across for years. Is it what Tonio Kroger admired, and what I admire? Is there a flaw in praising this type, though? Yes, though in *Arras* it is difficult to find the flaw.

Wrote an article on the Ruhr bombings, supposedly for the *Sunday Express*. It was accepted by my officers here with very little alteration. A note from Eastbourne, via Blackpool, that my application for a commission could not be entertained. I suppose this means in Intelligence only. I hope so. If so, it doesn't matter. But it is unpropitious.

Drink is only really important in its secondary effects. Nevertheless, it is worth remembering that there are days when five whiskies will leave you the same, and days when two glasses of beer will not.

. . . At the moment, Love. Not, luckily, the love of the most frightening of all French proverbs, 'There is always one who loves, and one who lets himself be loved.' But, at the moment, mutual love. And complete love, completely, on both sides. Good. Now. What can destroy this? Only one thing. Forgetfulness that Love—not love—cannot continue alive unless, happy or unhappy, it trusts, and builds, and if possible, creates. Firstly. Quarrels are natural, but contrary to the belief of many intelligent people, they are also harmful. Therefore, one must not quarrel.

... I, who have wasted over half my life on a few reviews and two or three poems, find myself, as enthusiastic as ever about clouds. Because the vast, living cloud is the only place I have ever seen wherein there can be no questions, no balancings. *No fault.* To go there, in the mind, is to love, to marry, to know, and, finally to be. To go there in an aeroplane would be to remain ...

To his mother he wrote the news of the day from High Wycombe:

This is just to tell you how I am getting on. My room itself now holds four people; myself, two young lady secretaries from the maps section, and a lady clerk. I either type my own work out, or telephone it direct to the Air Ministry. Sometimes we are almost overwhelmed, after a big raid, or something unexpected. The telephones go, the bell that summons us into the bosses next door—one ring for the lady clerk, two rings for me, and the three telephones next door. All going at once, then, sometimes, as now, there are lulls.

Today I've written two articles—one for the press, an account of a crippled Halifax shooting down a Nazi fighter, and one account of the same incident, treated a little differently, which will be pasted up in Halifax factories *to tell* the workers what a Halifax can go through without literally falling to pieces. It was, indeed, a remarkable incident.

Harris whirled past in his lovely long car, and I saluted. I find it rather romantic, like a movie. Must stop now as I have just been given another fifteen hundred words to do on the Ruhr, which we refer to as 'the battle' now, and so it is.

The 'lady clerk' tells me that Brian never really wrote anything much, at least during the first months when she was there. What she remembers most vividly is his making the tea and using the kettle as a hot water bottle for his permanently frozen feet.

For over a year Brian had accepted the reality of Toni's disappearance from his life for good and, subconsciously at first, had been looking for someone to take his place permanently. He had already met a young man, just down from university, 'Ian', for whom he had developed a strong affection over the past nine months. Ian was actively bisexual, and the idyll became as stormy as any relationship could be under those circumstances and within the freedoms and restrictions of wartime. But he provided another outlet for Brian's consuming need of correspondents other than his mother. 'Writing it down' was as compulsive with him as alcohol, and more rewarding psychologically. He also kept another of his introspective, self-obsessed diaries for most of the time he was at High Wycombe.

Extracts from Brian's diary, High Wycombe (July–August 1943):

Yesterday my mother told me that I 'tell everything to everyone', that I 'tell too much'. It has to do with my theory, my belief about frankness. Can a relationship approach anything like perfection without utter frankness, without telling all the truth as one knows it?

For more than nine months I have written Ian two or three times a week, at least; often more. In all this time I have concealed absolutely nothing, with the exception of two very recent, tipsy and unimportant acts of sexual self-indulgence. I am sorry for these, because they spoiled something I have never managed before—sexual fidelity to one person. Apart from this I made clear every aspect of my love, every hope, every idea, every fact about myself and my past. Everything. Have I, incidentally, very naïve ideas about the good, the true, and the beautiful human love-affair, I wonder?

Last night I visited A. C-B and his charming wife. His being here is a godsend. We haven't met since we were at Eton. It would seem that he is the only friend I have left—that I am in touch with ... After three days, when I think for the first time in my life I have been unable even to read, I have been able to interest myself in a book, *Of Human Bondage*,[2] a copy that Willie Maugham gave my mother. Being rather elementary-minded, at the moment, I was struck with the passage about the hero Philip's 'most delightful habit in the world'—reading—which provided him (unwittingly) with a refuge from worldly cares as well as creating 'an unreal world which would make the real world of every day a source of bitter disappointment'. True, indeed. It literally saves one. But what, nag I, about reading as a drug? And what about Philip's companion Hayward who saw everything in a golden mist of sentimentality, and 'honestly mistook his sensuality for romantic emotion, his vacillation for artistic temperament, and his idleness for philosophic calm?' And again when it was pointed out that he lied he said that lies were beautiful. 'He was an idealist.' H'm.

... I want to try and put down something of my amazement at how I ruined my, and Ian's leave. The truth seems to be that it was ruined by months, and years, of self-indulgence on my part. Here, for the first time, we had had time to plan. We had enough money. There was nothing to be done but be happy; nothing. Yet that very night I was sitting alone at a table in that unspeakable night-club, the Jamboree, with my own bottle of private poison, costing four pounds, while Ian and various other friends sat in worried, good-humoured puzzlement at another. And I cannot remember why, the superficial reason why. The real reason why is what I hope to have finally realised. It is impossible for me to drink spirits. It is impossible for me to be drunk. And I am a drunkard. And, somehow, I must cease to be one. *I have written it down, for the first time.*

I finally got down to Gorebridge and unburdened myself completely to my mother. As ever, she poured strength back into me. My extreme anxiety about her remained [she had just had a heart attack], producing, I hope, a

[2] Published by Heinemann, 1915.

change of behaviour in me, and the world began to come back into focus and perspective. I could not express then, and I cannot now, my love, my admiration and my gratitude. Sacrificed, and more or less betrayed, again and again, as the years go by, she is like a phoenix. On the day I was to return to High Wycombe came Peter's (Watson)[3] letter, which, as a discipline, I will copy out:

'My Dear B. I am going to write you a stinker because I am so angry with all your follies and self-deceptions. You have got to stop all this nonsense and drinking soon or you will complete your own self-destruction which is what you are aiming at. Ian did not go back wherever he was supposed to be going that night—he was around town and told a friend of mine in a Turkish bath that he couldn't stand more than three days of drinking and spending money like water and bickering with you, so he had to leave in order for a day or two's peace. So you call that love do you? For goodness' sake stop all this self-deception on your part. You spend over £50 in three days and at the end of it look such a wreck and behave as you did yesterday . . .

'I loathe and fear for your life but I don't know why I have a certain fondness for you so I am telling you all this because either you change now or it is too late to ever change. Personally I should think the latter is true.

'And then you sit back and sentimentalise about love. It's all so stupid, can't you see. Love means you wish to do someone some good not to destroy them and yourselves . . . You are a bloody nuisance to everyone and the whole thing is just inflated egotism which you have the impudence to call love . . . Love, P.'

Apart from being the sternest letter I have ever had in my life, it came from the person of whom I am fondest in England today, and whom I suppose, on reflection, I consider my best friend, Eddie having been away so long. (There is Nancy, but I see so little of her.) But the real reason why it was such a blow, is that it is, on the whole, true—there is no avoiding it. I deserve it all.

The real blow was the revelation, of course, about Ian. It is this that has been giving me these positively physical attacks of bitter despair. Has he now decided that I am really too much of a handful, that he doesn't want to have anything more to do with me? It is conceivable. My mother has always said that in reality I never have the slightest inkling of what other people are thinking about me. Am I, was I, simply an extraordinary escapade in his life, a departure from the norm? Like someone getting off a ship and visiting an Arabian bazaar? . . . Surely one can't be as tiresome as that? Surely the past nine months of mutual affection count for something? I suppose no one tests their friends as unremittingly as I do. I know this. But several survive. I don't have fewer really intimate friends than most people, on the whole. On the other hand, he is twenty-one and I am thirty-eight, a situation of which I have no experience . . .

---

[3] Peter Watson was the unflagging sponsor of that unique literary magazine, *Horizon*, and one of Brian's greatest friends.

Another letter from Peter saying, 'for goodness sake get yourself something to do, otherwise you will in your boredom just drink yourself out of everyone's life. I hate that completely false diabolism you indulge in when drunk. It's all so neurotic and nothing else . . . The war has gone on too long now without you carrying your own private war against yourself everywhere you go.'

. . . Towards the middle of August a reconciliation with Ian was effected, but he made it a condition that I do something about drinking so much. During August I have confined myself to beer, port, sherry and wine. The situation is now that Ian will be drafted abroad as a *lorry driver* unless he can be sent to a new unit and re-apply for this special O.C.T.U. course. We have just had three days leave together in London, in a Chelsea attic that Ian managed to borrow for us from friends of 'Harriet's'.

I am now sticking to two double whiskies, with beer afterwards, in the evenings. Spent another weekend with Ian in the Chelsea house. All went well until his 'meeting with Harriet' there—which was supposed to be concealed from me, but which I heard of at once. I behaved politely and nonchalantly about it, but noticed increasing impatience in Ian. I sensed the beginning of the end and began to drink a little more.

For the next eight months Brian lived in a fever of correspondence—with Harriet about Ian, with Ian about themselves. His relationship with Harriet was ambivalent, to say the least; it was part mentor-pupil (she was the same age as Ian—twenty-one), but loyalties had been tested and proven on rather desperate occasions when less charitable acquaintances accused him of using her as a decorative decoy for his own purposes.

Harriet had fallen in love with an American soldier, 'Gary', to whom she was to be married if, and when, he ever returned from service overseas. Being at an all too loose end in this interim period, she found Ian a most 'companionable companion'. Harriet's sudden intervention in the Ian-Brian *débacle* put Brian in a dilemma. He felt that his friendship with Harriet, in the final analysis, would be the longer-lasting, yet he could neither relinquish Ian nor condone what he was pleased to call in public her 'poaching' of his property. Their triangular correspondence brings out the mixture of self-obsession and selflessness that churned up so much of Brian's life; it also exposes only too clearly the complete insouciance of the young in wartime, where promiscuity masqueraded as companionship, on the assumption that 'tonight is for living it up—for tomorrow we may all be dead'.

Harriet was doing war work in the provinces; Ian, who was about to be posted overseas, suddenly got accepted for an Intelligence Course training, while Brian was still stationed at High Wycombe. They corresponded unceasingly, but their leaves coincided both inconveniently and infrequently. The following extracts from Brian's letters to Harriet are as revealing as his diary entries:

[September 1943] . . . When I went to London this last weekend there was a certain amount of 'Brian mustn't know about Ian and Harriet', which was very kind of everyone concerned, but I really am quite sincere in my attitude—all the more so where you are involved—about Ian's unsissy escapades, and didn't mind at all. Naturally one has the unavoidable flicker of pain, but my goodness, one expects it, and is perfectly able to manage it. One doesn't grow up to no purpose, I hope.

I know very well that one of these days Ian is going to marry, and naturally I shall accept it. But I know for sure that I shall never again have this opportunity—put it like that—of having a similar relationship. It is something to do with Toni having disappeared after twelve years; something to do with my age; something to do with the kind of people I like (I wish I liked the other, easy kind, but I don't) . . . at all events, I know that this is the last happy, reciprocated (for-the-time-being) affair. The last, and as far as I am concerned, the best. There will be other things, but they will be of a different kind. This you must believe. Well, over it hangs the marriage. So every month, every day, every hour counts.

Now this is where you come in. You wrote me that no one could be happier than you and your promised but far-away Gary. I think this is true, and I'm glad. You of course think that at this point I'm going to say, 'Please don't see Ian any more'. Not at all. I believe he wants to visit you on his next leave, and I've already said 'do'. He is particularly *devoted* to you, which pleases me vastly. It is so difficult, in a way, to try and get him to be discriminating. I'm all for him and women (not only because I have to be, but because I want him to be happy too) but it is sometimes rather a task coping with that cheerfully dotty catholicity of taste. No? The other day we went to the Swiss pub and he had the audacity to say that he thought 'Carla' was attractive and he'd like to go to bed with her. *Imagine.* She looked like a very, very old Pekingese that someone had forgotten to dust! However, whatever he does in that line I don't fundamentally mind (except for Carla), it's the other thing—another me—that's going, if and when it occurs, to turn me into that well known old life-like imitation of the Fiend himself. My goodness, there'll be such a FUSS!

[Later] Your letter was very sweet. No, I don't feel it really a pity that we seem to coincide often, emotionally. I think it's quite cosy, as long as real pain is staved off, and we continue to be right in trusting one another to the tremendous extent that we do. I think we are right to do so. It works. But it works with very few—only the very top. It works with Nancy Cunard and Erika Mann, but they are both older. And Méraud Guinness. Of people more or less of your age it has never come up, so to speak. So, I shall leave it completely, and even half-contentedly, in your hands . . .

The tragedy is, which I can't conceal from you (or my mamma either) that it has not only replaced the Toni thing, but far out-deepened it and outdone it. I am, in fact, lost. *Tant pis.* (I mean 'tragedy' only in the sense that it cannot be permanent.) Write me again. Cheer up, Sweety.

[October] . . . Ian has told me, in the nicest way in the world, that he is no longer in love with me. He emphasised that this had nothing to do with you. In actual fact, of course, it has. He is in love with you. My feelings are completely unchanged towards you (which the Chelsea set find inexplicable), and, unfortunately towards Ian. Harriet, the thing is that I feel that I

269

can't survive this. With Toni the end was different. It was after many years, and bound up with the collapse of a whole world. History divided us, and very slowly. With Ian, *who was Toni come true*, and articulate—I can't bear it. I told Ian he could do what he liked, as long as he allowed me to be a secondary, but permanent, feature in the background ... but he even says that I'm not to write. I really survived my present job—the last year—*entirely* because of Ian. I wrote nearly every day. Now what have I got? You see, I've never been *happily* in love, Harriet, before. I'm lost now. I'm in utter despair.

Ian has no idea of how hard I've been hit. *I don't want him to know*. It might frighten him. I am telling the whole truth to no one but you. Who else can I tell? People would say you are the last person for me to confide in. That I am being abject. They would be wrong. Our affection has already proved itself indestructible ... So you must give me your advice, even if you have none to give ...

Yesterday I sat in the pub here and simply drank my way through every known form of reaction to love-in-despair. I sat there, writing Ian mental letters. The icy letter, the ironic letter, the furious letter, the resigned letter, the cringing letter, the deceptive letter—and the short, gay note. You know the short, gay note? It's the saddest of all. I sent none, of course. I am a fool about love. I tell the truth ...

All my life I have searched for a certain kind of perfection. I thought Toni was it, because I thought I had brains for two; could think for two. It was, of course, impossible. Then, perfection arrived. And went. I have been promiscuous enough to know (and know myself well enough to know) when perfection does come. It can't, and won't again. And I'm frightened of that *kind* of perfection, now. It never can work, by the very nature of things. I think it may be the very hopelessness itself of it that attracts me. (If only I could like another type, but I can't. They repulse me.) So the minute the war is over I'm going to get analysed and see what that can do. I must change. I must, in fact, marry. Mad though you'll think me for saying so now.

Do you know Thomas Mann's story, *Tonio Kroger*? That holds the *essence* of the mental side of my problem. I wish you'd re-read it. It is the completest expression of that terrible longing for the simple, usually blond, sweet, cheerful character—so different from one's own. Mann understood *very* well.

[Later] Now, an old friend of mine that I want you to meet (not such an *old* friend) called 'Sam' is coming on leave on the 24th, and I shall stay with him two nights in London. Are you likely to be there? This will be terribly important because it will be Soporific Day. You won't find him anything out of the ordinary, but he is a charming character, and not without a certain simple sunfloweriness. Not good looking in the ordinary sense at all, and rather *tough* looking. I'd forgotten about him. His *walk* is extraordinary—a tremendous sailor roll. He is in command of an Air-Sea Rescue Launch. He couldn't be more what I need at the moment, infinitely kind and *thoughtful*. 'Iron Guard' doesn't like ladies, although he looks more as if he did than words can *describe*. He's dotty about three things, Shakespeare, sailing boats, and guess? So really I feel most restored and self-respecting again. I think the quicker I break loose the better.

Peter Wattie has written me a letter nailing down my great fault in love affairs. I make the mistake of thinking that sincerity is enough, without cleverness in managing it. Which is simply *mad*. It's ridiculous, to be a sort of Rousseau-ist idealist about love. One must be Stendhal. More, possibly than in any other department of life. One must be sincere, *and* clever.

[Later] I have much cheered up, and even feel just *faintly* malicious, which is naughty, but healthy . . . Apropos your other remarks. I quite agree with you about Carla's typically semi-adult thing about people not being good in bed. Good God. As if love had anything to do with it. Personally, I'm far more inclined to fall in love with people who aren't—they're not infrequently nicer people. The point is that if one loves one finds a log of wood paradise, and a whole troop of contortionists a bore.

[Later] I am doing my utmost to involve myself emotionally with Sam, and have only succeeded so far physically. I feel quite unsafe still. But I never intend to let Sam go—it would be unkind, and crazy too. He has a character firm as a rock (and incidentally, he can drink me under the table). Never was anyone more truthful and reliable . . . and he is prepared for permanency, and faithfulness. It is a *great* responsibility. So there it is. And you know my longing for settledness, which I had with Toni. I ache to be settled, and safe, so that I can turn my attention to the business of life. A thing I cannot do unless I have someone in my life—alone, I can't be. I can't afford to miss this chance just because of Sam's social disability, which it would be silly not to admit is a slight bore. But I don't care; I'm used to it. And time will take care of it, anyway. One usually wins races with time if the other person doesn't know one is racing. Or doesn't care . . . I have been 'unfaithful' to Sam once—but I think it will be a long, long time before I am again. It's just no good any more—it simply becomes a display of technique which irritates one as one performs it. The drive of sex, for me, is liking the person as well as the person's body. If possible, loving them . . . my heart still has its conscience.

I think these extracts from Brian's letters to Harriet are interesting in that they epitomise so much of the homosexual problem. Law or no laws, there will always be heartache for the wholly queer man in love with a bisexual one. His predicament cannot be compared to that of straightforward unfaithfulness in heterosexuals, because the homosexual has to take it for granted that this bisexual type will always want the best of both worlds. The average man (or woman) does not anticipate or accept his lover's regular unfaithfulness in the same way.

Brian continued his diary through the first six months of 1944:

[January] In December Ian, Harriet and I met several times. I broke down completely one day and rather denied Sam, I fear. Spent nearly £30 in London last time. I've *got* to get money on the same basis in my

271

consciousness as drink. It is, with me, a vice, like drink. I use it to stop thinking and to avoid responsibility.

[February] Have just got Ian's 'parting' letter, in which the phrase occurs—'Crazy drunken fools have lost their glamour for me, thank God.' Then, in a less angry vein—'At one stage I was quite under your influence, and would have done anything for you. You would have done me quite a lot of good in many ways, but I think harm would probably have predominated. I want, eventually, to get somewhere in life; with you I should always have been on the *threshold* of everything that we both consider worthwhile without ever having the moral courage to take the key from my pocket and open the door.' (I have not replied.)

... Yesterday I was walking just outside the building towards the bus, when a small blue four-seater car stopped in front of us. An officer (S/Ldr.?) jumped out. Tall, dark, good-looking in a disagreeable, public schoolboy way. 'Are you Howard?' Salute. 'Yes, Sir.' 'Well, unless you stop going about London talking the way you do, I shall see that you are court-martialled and posted. Repeating things you hear in your work, from your boss. Spreading alarm and despondency. You know what I mean, don't you?' Salute. 'Yes, Sir.' Off he went, in the car. He was far too cross, and quick, for me to say anything at all.

Upon reflection it must either be the rocket-bombs, or that story I told about an Air Marshal. It was in front of Colonel 'X', and a strange Air Vice Marshal in the Ritz, when I was on leave. It was simply, 'The Army may be able to get them there' (meaning the Second Front), 'but how are they going to get them back?' I quoted this as an Air Marshal's remark (I did not say *who* it was), and also said what curious people they were, like robber barons. Can this be Colonel 'X's' revenge for my having invented the perfect nickname for him? *Colonel 'Cutie'!* I think I will not inform my bosses, it would only cause a commotion, and the officer obviously hasn't much to go on, or he *would* have gone to the top. Still, it remains very peculiar for an officer to pop out and berate a strange A.C.2 all on his own.

This is perhaps the most famous 'Brian' story of all. So many people have told me of it, but their versions, from eyewitness to hearsay, differ somewhat from Brian's diary entry, making one wonder whether he chose to forget the details or had no true recollection of them. It appears that he was having a drink (in his A.C.2 uniform) in the downstairs bar of the Ritz, which at that time was a home from home for many of his friends and acquaintances. In that unmistakable and articulate voice of his he was deploring the state of the war, the behaviour of Churchill, the equivocal outcome of the Second Front, and so on, peppering his semi-satirical monologue with defeatist pin-pricks as only he knew how to. It was all too much for a high-ranking R.A.F. officer sitting nearby, who got up and demanded with steely authority Brian's name, number and station. Brian broke off his private conversation just long enough to say, loudly, over his shoulder 'My name is Mrs. Smith'. There was absolutely nothing the superior officer could do, except retire—without much grace.

[Continuing Brian's diary. February] I am in an absolute bog of subjectivity ... I am either telling people far too much, and demanding advice—or telling them off, when in drink. Like some intolerable middle-aged child ...

I do so hope I keep on with this diary, and that it will help me to work through this hyper-subjective period. I must get an intellectual stream going in me, as well as an emotional one. By being in the R.A.F., by having to come daily here to the office at set hours—and I like the office—I have really a unique and infinitely valuable opportunity of getting myself properly aimed and directed.

This morning when I awoke I had a sort of warning vision of one side of my predicament. I am nearly thirty-nine. Mother is sixty-seven. Am I ready to stand alone? Frankly, no. What have I for plans? None. What have I of system in my life? None. I must try and build something out of the routine here. It is essential. And don't be too analytical in this diary. Don't cry over spilt whisky. Reach out for new ideas, and put them down. And work on some of them, too.

[March] I have had ten days of pure subjectivism again, and have been extravagant, and not so good about drink as I was ... Money I have no sense of at all, after a glass or two. This is *really* dangerous, too, apart from this tipsiness. Have realised, *at last* and for the first time, that the Ian thing is finally over ...

John Lawrence—my chief here, told me he couldn't be responsible should I commit some folly that I drank too much, and was wasting an excellent brain. Too true.

The Russian film I saw, *The Battle of the Ukraine*, by Dovschenko (cut forty times by the British censors!) suggested to me the terrible lack of community feeling that cultivated Western Europeans have suffered from for a century. Lovers in Russia today, or in the 'Maquis' in France, have something besides themselves and the problem of earning money, to live for. But today in England, for example, unless one is merely ambitious, in the ordinary sense, it is impossible to feel of oneself as an enthusiastic member of society. Now that the war is being slowly 'won', all one's doubts return. (Can one trust the Government about post-war plans, for England, or Europe? No.) Only complete introverts don't need a share in communal life. Unless one wraps oneself up in some specialised work, or creative activity, wholly (which one should not be presented with the necessity of doing) one is done for. One cannot live *outwards* at all in these decaying countries, and I miss this. So often I long, when in love with someone, to share some sort of *outward* life. It seems impossible. I should not complain, as I don't organise an inward one ...

[May] I am now *really*, to tell the truth, violently in love with Sam. I have received a letter from him which made me almost cry. It had the gravity and sweetness and complete surrender of a child—the first real love letter, I am convinced, Sam has ever written. There is *no* withstanding that particular note when it is sounded. It hardly ever is.

... I am waiting to go to Halton, the head R.A.F. Hospital. I am going to see (Dr. Edward) Glover again, *not* with a definite view to getting free,

273

but I want to hear what a first-class psychiatrist has to say about my various little weaknesses and problems. The R.A.F. at Halton have agreed to this and approve. They also say I can have a complete physical and psychological overhaul. I can't say that the R.A.F. aren't being helpful.

[June] The Halton man says that I have thyroid, but not enough to be dangerous. If normal is 100, danger begins at 140, and I have 117. I am going to have several sessions with Glover, beginning next week, and see what he can tell me about myself, drink etc. I shan't ask for a release—yet anyway. I want to see if I can squeeze through this part of the war. But it depends—

In September of that year he wrote to Cyril Connolly, from High Wycombe:

... I feel I must congratulate you on the letter to 'Victor'.[4] That it is brilliantly amusing you know very well, but it also says something that no one has said before, and that I, for one, have ached to see said. One passage affected me so severely that it brought a tear to my eye, you will be surprised to hear—it ends [*You are always fighting for me in the favoured places of the world . . .*] *Oh, why can't I fight for myself?* (I consider myself, you will see, a civilian still). Parts of the letter gave me a sense of hallucination, almost, because they were so like parts of letters that I now write to people myself. *I die by inches: you live in a continuous exaltation . . . when the war is over you will be ten years younger than you were when it started, and I shall be twenty years older: past love, past lust, past exercise, and past ambition . . .* I put it, of course, in a politer way, as one does in real letters. Oh dear, yes—and [the lot of the civilian in England as] *the unpopular schoolboy in the keen, tough school whose fees are ten shillings in the pound, with no one who will take him in for the holidays.* But it is sprinkled with jewels. Cyril dear, let me tell you without further ado that you write better than anyone in England, and that it gives me pleasure to tell you so.

In a very short time now, I shall be invalided out, with a 'recommendation for promotion' as a sop to my imagined feelings . . . Love from your bald, bitter, shabby old friend and playmate, Civilian Bri. [In emulation of Cyril's sign off to 'Dear Victor'.]

His last letters from High Wycombe to his mother were largely concerned with his discharge from the R.A.F.:

... I think that Sam is being ordered to Iceland, which is very sad for me, as it settled part of my life, but there it is. The war is the war. The main thing is that I have got what I can out of, and given what I can to, this job

---

[4] *Letter from a Civilian* to 'Dear Victor', published in *Horizon* September 1944, reprinted in *Ideas and Places* by Cyril Connolly (Weidenfeld & Nicolson, 1953). This was a wonderfully pointed 'letter' comparing the excitements of active war service overseas: the stimulus of battle, the pockets of luxury living in exotic places, with the poor civilian in London who had to be content with the daily grind under blitz conditions, indifferent food, nonexistent social life—no glory, no pomp, no nothing.

of mine, and probably it will produce something in my mind that I can write about—afterwards. I'm trying to make some notes, now.

But I know now Glover's advice should be taken. I am just frittering everything away. It *could* have been something—for instance I worked until 1.30 a.m. the other night, getting the news in and out, and enjoyed it, and did it well—my suggestions were all accepted. If it could always be like that, it would be different, but it isn't. I sit in my room for hours with too little to do (unable to concentrate on work of my own, lest I be seen), and am then reproached for not producing radio plays when I am denied the material with which to write them. One cannot make bricks entirely without straw. People seem to think one can do radio plays, and articles, about highly technical subjects, out of the blue. One can't, with the best will in the world. I am put in the position of an office boy (whether it was done out of kindness, or not, isn't the point) and expected to do the work of an editor, author and specialist. It's impossible.

I didn't think Glover would take the view he did, you know. But he quite definitely thinks it's time for me to change. I was surprised. I thought he'd say 'stick it out', or something. I think he must think I am not in too good a state. I *feel* he is right, though. He said, 'I imagine you'll want to see them through the beginning of the invasion, won't you?' and I said, 'Yes'. So he said, 'All right, come and see me when you've made up your mind.' Well, now that you agree, I have. He explained that he could arrange it in such a way that not only would nothing tiresome be put down, but I would not have to *explain*.

What I want to do afterwards is have a rest. I sometimes feel as if I hadn't slept, properly, for six months, you know. And then I want to start *really* writing, and I am going to do it on the system you have advocated for so long, which is sitting at a desk for certain definite hours, and going through the month or two's agony of nothing coming, because I believe that in the end, it does come. I have had very interesting conversations here with Hugh Massingham on that point. Perhaps if I'd had my home, and wife, here, and been an officer, I could have succeeded in leading two lives. But I haven't, and I now have not even one life, really.

So I am making an appointment with Glover for next week. I will not, of course, give him the signal to go ahead until I have settled every detail; including what the Ministry of Labour are going to do, or not, with me, afterwards. And it's all got to be without *fuss*. Of any kind. I'll see to that, so don't worry. I am tired today, but not in my mind. And I think I am doing the right thing. I know it. It's taken time to decide, that's all.

Brian was finally given an honourable discharge from the R.A.F. on 1st December 1944, because of being 'below Air Force physical standard, although fit for selected employment in civil life'. His general character and conduct during service were marked as 'V.G.—Howard is a competent worker. He is well able to adapt himself to duties which call for a good standard of education'.

And so his R.A.F. career came to an end—without glory, without undue shame.

20. The wandering years— with 'Sam'

1945–1950

What did this release from the R.A.F. accomplish? Freedom, yes, but for what? Wartime restrictions were still in evidence and most of Brian's friends were committed in one way or another, so that he may well have found his vacuum existence as limiting as his previous A.C.2 way of life. But despite his lack of continuous application he did manage to throw off a masterly review of poetry (too long to quote in full) in a January 1945 *New Statesman* under the title 'Inside Information'.

> *Springboard: Poems*, 1941–1944 by Louis MacNeice (Faber); *Eros in Dogma* by George Barker (Faber).
> ... today much of the best poetry happens, besides being poetry, to be news. What is more, it is the news behind the news. There is a popular misconception that contemporary poets under—roughly—fifty are difficult to understand ... Are they more difficult to understand than, for instance, the morning newspaper? Or the radio? ... Is there anything more difficult than successfully to extract the real news from the censored, biased, policy-ridden press, and radio, of today? The best you can do is invariably to try to read, or listen, between the lines.
> Here, by Mr. MacNeice, is the news behind the news:
>
> > Patriots, dreamers, die-hards, theoreticians, all,
> > Can't we ever, my love, speak in the same language,
> > Or shall we go, still quarrelling over words, to the wall?
> > Have we no aims in common?
>
> ... Having read your morning paper, do you perhaps begin to despair of people themselves? You may find a certain reassurance in these lines from a long and magnificent poem called *The Kingdom*:
>
> > Subjects all of the Kingdom but each in himself a king.
> > These are the people who know in their bones the answer
> > To the statesman's quiz and the false reformer's crude
> > Alternatives and ultimatums. These have eyes
> > And can see each other's goodness, do not need salvation
> > By whip, brochure, sterilisation or drugs,
> > Being incurably human ...

... Mr. Barker's view of the news is more individual. It is also, as it happens, more tragical. But both are poets in their evaluation of the vital truths, and lies, of our civilisation. In the following melodious and poignant lines, there speaks the European man-of-conscience of today:

> Everywhere is our wilderness everywhere.
> I hear the scapegoat's scream wherever I go
> And not only from my throat but also
> Everyone is our scapegoat everyone.
> When by the ilex I lie in the sun
> Thinking I'm free a moment, then the crown
> Of bleeding Christian leaves comes down
> The scapegoat coronation also there.

And here is one terrible reason for those words:

> The ache at the break of the heart
>   Is nothing a pearl knows this.
> What remains eternally intolerable is always
>   The Justice, the justice.

... Mr. Barker passes on the news to us, like Mr. MacNeice, ungarbled. When he says, as he does in this volume:

> Somewhere an Austrian corporal shall be mute
> At whose word once, from Europe to the sky,
> Suddenly everyone everywhere began to die.

he does not imagine, and neither does Mr. MacNeice, that this will be the solution. The solution—I am sure that both would agree—has seldom been better set forth than in the lines below. They are by a third poet, Mr. Auden, and they also make the news behind the news quite clear. I see them as the headlines in the Final Night Extra of our time:

> All I have is a voice,
> To undo the folded lie,
> The romantic lie in the street
> And the lie of Authority
> Whose buildings grope the sky:
> There is no such thing as the State
> And no one exists alone:
> Hunger allows no choice

to the citizen or the police
We must love one another or die.[1]

If he was to keep up this level of regular reviewing he needed a pied-à-terre in London, if only to keep in touch with editors, etc. When he discovered that I was living in a Westminster backwater (having just married), Brian wrote asking me to find him a furnished room nearby:

> As you will gather, I am trying to crystallise slightly. It is time. I don't care how ugly the building is—but your district I ache for—there's you to begin with, and then there will be the relief of not being in a part of London crammed with living ghosts and one's rather rapscallion past, like Chelsea. I now possess, in Sam, someone who provides both the contentment and the inspiration necessary for a little work. I think it tremendously important for me at this juncture to free myself from past associations. I have the emotional backing—supply line—without which I have found I go to pieces, and so there is no excuse.
>
> I hesitate to embroider this theme to you—I only mention it at all because you are one of the very few people who have unfailingly understood me—because I may fail in my endeavour. But I am going to try, and *where* I try is of great importance.

There is no doubt that in many ways Sam was to become very good for Brian. He was a nice, good-looking boy from what is conveniently called 'the lower-middle classes'. He had originally been invalided out of the navy owing to foot trouble, and got himself a reasonably good job at the B.B.C. before deciding to live abroad with Brian. He was mad on sailing boats and little else, but he was astute about money and tried to curb Brian's extravagances in every direction. Unfortunately he also loved to drink, and later became an easier victim to drugs than Brian. There was one great drawback, he was a monumental snob—for titles, celebrities, money, all things material. Many of Brian's friends simply could not tolerate Sam for this reason, yet with others he managed to suppress the snobbery and become liked for himself. Rather surprisingly, he got on extremely well with Lura Howard, a genuine affection arising between them which went far beyond gratefulness on her part for Sam's protective qualities concerning Brian.

Theodora FitzGibbon recalls so well these early post-war times:

> Can Brian in these years ever be thought of or written about without mention of Sam, the 'Rose of Tralee' (Tralee having been his birthplace),

---

[1] Stanza from '1st September 1939', *Another Time* by W. H. Auden, Faber, 1940. Brian would be sad to know that according to Auden's Bibliography (Bloomfield), on re-reading this poem he came to the lines: *We must love one another or die*, and said to himself, 'that's a damned lie! We must die anyway'. So he altered it in the next edition to: *We must love one another and die*. He did not think this was right either, so cut out that particular stanza. 'Still no good. The whole poem, I realised, was infected with an incurable dishonesty and must be scrapped.' It is not included in his *Collected Shorter Poems* 1927–57, Faber, 1966.

278

as I called him? Sam was just right for Brian. Bold, in the Irish sense, and yet utterly concerned about him.

Once, when Sam and I had spent some time cutting up a very small joint of meat, and carving down small twigs of wood from a Chelsea garden to make skewers for a Shashlik, Brian said later to Sam, 'Why don't we have meals like this at home?' to which Sam replied, 'Because we don't have a home'. For once Brian had no answer. And I suppose, that subconsciously, even as a young girl, that is how I thought of him: the genie who didn't need a home.

The last time we met was in 1945, and Constantine, Desmond Ryan, Norman Douglas and I had been drinking with him for many hours in the Cross Keys pub in Chelsea. Con and I left with Norman and Brian, and Brian insisted on holding Norman's arm in the blackout. By the time we got to Upper Cheyne Row there were sounds of a conversational scuffle.

Norman: 'Do stop holding my arm, please.'

Brian: 'But the steps are very difficult to see, Norman.'

Norman: 'I had to live on nothing but carrots in Estoril for two weeks, and my eyesight is much better than yours, duckums, I'm sure.' They both went off into the darkness.

Maurice Richardson remembers meetings with Brian at the Pier Hotel in Chelsea:

Where the presence of old Norman Douglas, a bit piano, often bored, always very civil, used to draw one in. Once, after he had gone, Brian said, 'That tweed tie of Norman's, my dear. There's something faintly fusty and depressing about it. New English Art Club 1907. I wouldn't for one moment ever suggest that he's even the tiniest bit of a bore, but I don't think he's really moved with the times as much as some of his more frenzied admirers would like one to believe.'

I saw him a few times after that at the Authors' Club in Whitehall Court, that odd little Edwardian enclave, where he had become a member, one of a mob recruited by John Davenport. He complained of the rather penetrating voice of the genial Hugh Kingsmill, Malcolm Muggeridge's friend and mentor, 'A human corncrake, my dear'. I wasn't there on the occasion when he was so naughty and pulled the Bishop's nose. 'Oh, so you're one of those matey cocktail-drinking padres, are you? Don't think I didn't see you winking at that young waiter . . . What did you say? I've a good mind to pull your nose. I think I will!'

Once Brian said to me, 'You are writing very nicely, my dear, but you're getting suspiciously urbane. Rather a lot of hedging, don't you think?' I said I did some ditching as well. And once, in a sudden sententious fit, I said, 'You know, Brian, when the time comes for your biography to be written they will say, 'he did a remarkable amount of good'. His eyebrows shot up to the ceiling, 'Well, really, that I do confess I find rather surprising'.

A home from home was not forthcoming in Westminster, and Brian continued to disrupt the Palace Gate flat of his great friend Peter Watson. Peter, who had returned to his Paris flat as soon as the regulations would allow, bombarded Brian with tough letters telling him in no uncertain terms to pull himself together:

My dear Brian, Alcoholism is difficult to deal with, I know, but not so difficult as you think in your case (proved by the fact that you do not drink at Gorebridge, but only in London). Thus with you it is neurotic. Therefore it is *you*, not the next two years, which will decide the matter one way or the other ... I cannot bear to see self-destruction in friends or in anyone else, and I react violently against it. As an attitude it is quite *démodé*, and valueless today ...

W. and I lunched with X. and he brought up his anti-Semitism—so tactful as W. is half-Jewish. Why do people go so terribly wrong? They admit to neurosis and yet accept it without a struggle in a way that no catholic accepts sin—oh, dear. ... It is lively here in Paris, but quite obvious that the next thing to be forced on all of us is pro- or anti-communism. What a BORE it all is.

[Later, from Gstaad] Everyone is horror-struck at the Labour victory. They give it one year. I am amazed, delighted but apprehensive. Can they equate freedom with security? Can anyone? however, it is the most hopeful Event since the end of the war, and perhaps *more* important. Even the atmosphere of England may change subtly. Love P.

Later that year, in December, the *New Statesman* published Brian's complimentary article on Cyril Connolly, whose collection of essays, travel pieces, satires and parody (including a reprint of *Where Engels fears to tread*) had just appeared under the title of *The Condemned Playground* (Routledge), and whose authorship of *The Unquiet Grave* by 'Palinurus' (Hamish Hamilton) was revealed. Brian enjoyed his rôle of reviewer reviewing the reviewer on reviewing:

... these essays cannot be said to lack depth. It is rather their brevity which sometimes disappoints; but this was inevitable, as most of them are reviews, and very few reviewers in England are happy about the space allotted them. While I am fond of Mr. Connolly's flashes of irony, I am not so fond of his sustained satires, because I become nervous about how his 'apparatus' is going to behave. For instance, among some very entertaining pages on reviewing, one finds the following, which is not ironic: '... the early expectations one had of discovering a new writer are perhaps less keen a pleasure than one's hopes of being able to discredit an old one.'

This may not be a puncture, or even a tweak. But to adapt a phrase applied by Palinurus to Somebody Else: 'What a tone for a Reviewer!'

The reviewing sting in this article is removed by Brian's final paragraph:

Authors who write too much, too often, are apt to accuse Mr. Connolly of writing too little, too well. If I were to suggest the possibility that Mr. Connolly may become a writer of the first importance, they might tell me that this would be astonishing. I, in turn, might reply that there are less auspicious places in which to await astonishment than the vicinity of an unquiet grave.

Another of Brian's *New Statesman* reviews, of Hugh Massingham's *The Harp and the Oak* (Cresset Press) in early 1946, contained a perceptively witty description of the type of person who, by continuing to read them, 'incites the publishers to produce contemporary English novels':

... It is an association of women, or, rather of strong ladies, members of which follow or precede me all over London. As a body they have decided to join the *League for Sanity in Art*, but not until it gets a little smarter. Each member looks, dresses and behaves exactly like the rest. She wears a dark blue jockey's cap with a swollen crown (above the peak of which is poised a miniature regimental badge in diamonds), a bright brown fur coat, and a faint, courageous lady-smile. Both my quotations from her will be verbatim. At the Picasso exhibition she stood next to me, accompanied by her child, who whinnied at a picture. 'But darling,' she said in her unnecessarily calm voice, the kind of voice that can never quite lie and never quite tell the truth, 'the man has a perfect right to paint like that if he wants to. As long as you're not taken in, darling.' I cannot visit a lending library, or a large bookshop—excepting, naturally, public libraries, the London Library, or Zwemmer's—without meeting her, and as I have never seen her look at books other than novels, I am certain that it is she who is the dictatress of our fiction. It was in a lending library in Wigmore Street that I overheard her rejecting a suggestion of the assistant's. 'No, I don't really want anything *realistic*, or sort of terribly *good*. I want something ... *you* know.' Yes, we do know. A hot-water bottle for her tiny, chilly, lady-brains. And this is why, meanwhile, our novels are so terribly cosy, so terribly aloof, and so terrible.

Well, she is not going to be best pleased with Mr. Massingham's new novel, the whole of which she will find, thank God, in questionable taste. ... Not only is Mr. Massingham's theme anti-Semitism, but his background is an English village of 1942, and several of his characters are both unreassuring, and exactly the sort of people the lady is likely to know, and rather admire ...

Brian continued to correspond with Peter Watson about his predicament:

People tell me airily—'Oh, nonsense, Brian, with your gifts you could easily earn a lot of money if you took the trouble.' Idiots such as these never take into account the fact that the earning of money, in no matter *what* profession, requires a certain very definite attitude of mind, and approach to the world. I mean to earn money *successfully*, a good deal of it. I don't mean trying and failing, of course. To want to get on in the world socially and financially is *practically* identical, and I simply DON'T. What I would adore to do, is produce something creative in a literary way. I believe this might turn me back into the comparatively agreeable person I used to be, a long time ago. And am by flashes, still. But this wouldn't produce *money*, in any impressive sense of the word.

In a nutshell—to carry out my mamma's hopes and ambitions for me would be simultaneously to bring about the final tragedy of her existence. To leave her. She left my papa half because life with him was intolerable, but also half because I didn't get on with him, and she wished to devote herself to me. It is an absolutely *boringly* classical text-book case—sissy son, Oedipus, and everything. If I 'make a success', I leave her. If I continue as a failure, I naturally remain.

By 1946 Brian knew what the cards were and clearly opted for remaining the failure. Was this due to a combination of indolence and a true lack of ambition, or did he honestly believe that all success was despicable? On his own reasoning he could at least have tried to be a literary (however unprofitable) success while still tied to his mother's apron-strings. But the complications to come of living *with* her yet largely *away* from her seemed to stifle all his intellectual energies.

There was some talk of Brian writing a short biography of Norman Douglas for Home & Van Thal, but nothing came of it. Meanwhile Sam, the boat-lover, had always dreamed of having his own sailing boat one day, and Brian appears to have obtained enough money (from his mother, presumably) to buy one that he found in Teddington. After many vicissitudes the deal went wrong, through no apparent fault of theirs, but they eventually lost money on the whole transaction. Brian's news for the rest of 1946 was characteristically catholic; Louis MacNeice asked him to write a play for the B.B.C. Third Programme; John Davenport asked him to be godfather to his second son, Roger; and he fought a winning battle with Lura Howard's Gorebridge cook: 'I suppose I should try and "win and keep" the respect of the cook? Well, I'm afraid I haven't the least desire for the respect of such an unreliable and disagreeable person. I dislike respect as a thing in itself. Affection, interest, love—yes. Respect, no.'

One of Brian's tasks that must have mixed pain with pleasure at this time was to review Christopher Sykes' *Four Studies in Loyalty* (Collins) for the January 1947 issue of the *New English Review*. I quote only from the extract concerning one of the four studies, his great friend Robert Byron, whose mother was so touched when she read it that she wrote to Brian, 'I would like to thank you for the understanding review in the *New English Review* . . . It is so much the nicest and truest of all that has been written of him and it will be very precious to me'. (The other studies were of Sir Tatton Sykes, Bahram Kirmani, and various members of the French Resistance.)

> . . . Mr. Sykes, in his innermost self, is an idealist, of the best and least cloudy kind. Like the subject of his principal study, the later Mr. Robert Byron, he is observer without, but believer within. This is why I have called this review, 'Portraits in Belief'. They are portraits of it; they are also made with it.

... The third part of the book ... is devoted to memories of Robert Byron and to a just and much needed appraisal of his work. On the night of his departure for Greece on government work in 1941 we dined together. His ship was torpedoed off Africa, and a number of people besides myself sustained their greatest personal loss of the war. I regarded him not only as one of my most loved and valued friends, but also as the most original, the most intrepid, and the most stimulating of all my Oxford contemporaries. It was the immediacy of his vitality which was so unique. Anything worth doing was not only, to him, worth doing well, but worth doing immediately, and despite opposition of any kind. For lazy persons like myself, to be in his company was to be refreshed first and then renewed—to feel like an empty electric battery which has suddenly and mysteriously become re-charged.

Byron died at the age of thirty-six, but he had already completed some ten works. Among them are: *The Station*, the modern classic on the monasteries of Mount Athos; *The Byzantine Achievement*, a passionate and brilliant, if partisan, volume, which Mr. G. M. Young recommends as a corrective to Gibbon; and *The Road to Oxiana*.[2] This last is Byron's most considerable *oeuvre*, and tells of his astonishing and arduous journey (mostly in Persia, and often in the company of Mr. Sykes) in search of the origins of Islamic art. Part of its importance lies in the fact that it is the first non-technical book in English to reveal the medieval and more majestic Persia which has been obscured so long behind the illustrations to limp-leather editions of Omar Khayyàm. Byron's own illustrations, magnificent photographs which he took himself, show specimens of architecture—such as the mausoleum of King Kabus, 1007 A.D.—which are among the least known and most noble in the world.

The Road to Oxiana, moreover, is a small classic, as Mr. Sykes says, of 'humanism and travel'. Although he was far more talented than most of them, Byron was a direct descendant of the indefatigable, eccentric English traveller-writers of the late 18th and 19th centuries. He would have felt at ease with Mr. Norman Douglas: there is the same sparkling curiosity, the same observant, ironic humour, and the same affirmation and enjoyment of the variousness of life. No antiquity was too inaccessible for him, no bug-besprinkled inn too disgusting, and no official, however idiotic and hostile, unpersuadable.

In appearance Robert Byron was a shade portly, very fair, with a pale, plump, 18th-century face and a revolving, ruminant eye. I remember well his reverberating laughter, and even better his fidgeting impatience. He was impatient a great deal, and usually with justification. A lowered chin, a pursed mouth, a portentous clearing of the throat, and then, in a clear hiss: 'Oh, the irri*tation* of it!' He cherished a number of prejudices which were as fantastic as they were violent. He loathed Shakespeare, for example. But they only contrived to emphasise his ineradicable, ever-present sincerity and integrity, qualities which burned in him to the point of almost visible

---

[2] Published by Duckworth, 1928; Routledge, 1929; Macmillan, 1937 (and John Lehman, 1950) respectively.

incandescence. As regards his courage, it was not displayed to armed and thieving Oriental soldiery alone. Once in perhaps the smallest and most august of London dining clubs, where the members eat at a single table, some eminent friend of Chamberlain's began to speak in his praise. Robert Byron leaned across the table and asked him a question. The man naturally imagined that he had heard wrongly and continued to speak. Some frightful premonition must have assailed him, however, because he soon faltered and ceased. It was then, through the appalled silence, that Robert's voice came again: 'Are you in German *pay*?' Such actions on Robert Byron's part—he held it a duty to uphold one's convictions if one is a responsible individual—were particularly courageous in that his *milieu* was not an intellectual one. He had his career to further and his living to earn. Moreover, he was perfectly aware of the benefits that prudence can confer, and regarded them with gusto. Nevertheless, moral compromise was impossible to him. It was this which gave him, together with his gifts of heart and mind, the strain of greatness which he undoubtedly possessed . . .

Violet Wyndham bears witness to the fact that Robert Byron reciprocated Brian's respect and affection. She writes:

I remember being surprised when Robert told me very seriously that Brian was one of the most important people of his vintage at Oxford. I asked in what way? Robert replied vaguely that he had, for one example, started the cult for collecting Victoriana.

At that time I had thought of Brian as a slightly ridiculous figure, even embarrassing, although lovable and amusing. I realised that Robert meant more than he had said, and as I looked upon his words as gospel I began to look for qualities in Brian. He had talents, but not outstanding ones. What was it that attracted so many of his clever contemporaries to him? The answer is, in my opinion, that he was an exponent of high 'camp', a word that at the present time need no longer be derogatory. In its perfection (as, for instance, in the works of Ronald Firbank) 'camp' is an artistic expression. Like Baroque it is an exaggeration, but a delicate one. Brian in his attitude towards society expressed a controlled, deliberate and satiric exaggeration, enhanced in his youth by high spirits. All this was revealed in his idea for holding that exhibition of cubic art by a fictitious artist, 'Bruno Hat', which was written up in several papers. Then he was both witty and bold.

Had his health and tendency to drink not destroyed him, I am convinced that he would, by now, have achieved real fame. Like all eccentric artists, some would have criticised him, but the majority would have been in favour, thus endorsing the judgment of his friend, Robert Byron.

Earlier domestic fracas notwithstanding, Brian was left in charge at Gore-bridge in the summer while his mother visited her relations in America, where he wrote to her: 'I liked your phrase about the Washington rain-storms, "you couldn't poke your finger between the drops". We have had our discussions about what is "writing", and what is not, and that, curiously enough, is it!

In October 1947 Brian wrote a long, one-book review in the *New Statesman* (of which extracts follow) which is not only interesting in itself but the subsequent fan letter from Wolcott Gibbs is charming, and especially illuminating about the status of Damon Runyon on home ground.

Season in the Sun by Wolcott Gibbs (Heinemann): As the most decisive of winters approaches, as the world-twilight deepens and the West declines for the third, and probably final time, it becomes even more desirable than it was in 1938–9 to find some seriously amusing fiction to read during anxiety-hours, the flash-points of which are sunset and dawn. It is all very well in the daytime. A classical author, or Camus, or Corvo, or Compton Burnett should still see one through one's unspeakable lunch. But how to beat off the thoughts that assemble at sunset? What of the anguished aster-coloured evening, two or three minutes longer than the last? Detective stories, thrillers? No. Not since they moved in on life, some years ago. Well, what? In my considered opinion there are few more efficacious distractions than what Mr. Gibbs denies is 'The *New Yorker* school'. Namely, himself (my favourite, as it happens), James Thurber, John O'Hara, S. J. Perelman, Arthur Kober, Sally Benson, the late Clarence Day and Dorothy Parker.

Mr. Gibbs, in a strangely self-entranced preface, insists 'that there is no such thing as a typical *New Yorker* writer, and that the real secret of the magazine's success has been the amazing catholicity of its taste and the wide range of style, technique and attitude', etc. He adds, bravely, that the above-named writers are 'wildly divergent'. Now, although there is much in what Mr. Gibbs says, there is also a characteristic shared by these writers—and by others, including Bemelmans and Runyon—which undoubtedly unites them. This characteristic I lack the space to discuss, but it has something to do with the Beerbohm-Saki tradition minus snobbery, and it has more to do with a low level of stamina, a high level of objectivity, and a still higher level of purely technical skill. To put it lazily, they *write* so much better than so many better writers. It is this, incidentally, which largely explains (I believe) the relentless railing of the highbrows, who accuse them, as a group, of *chicté*, pinchbeck drama, superciliousness, unimportance and political vacuity, if not vice. Here is Mr. (William) Barrett, in the current American number of *Horizon*:

'. . . the slick, machine-tooled fiction of the *New Yorker* has produced a taste that would find Lardner too crude and would require Fitzgerald to be more tired, sophisticated and mincing.'

One dares say. But it seems to me that if a considerable proportion of young intellectuals would machine-tool away like crazy, for several years, they would be more profitably employed than in snickering at riper persons who can, and do, type rings round them ... Apart from the baffling fact that he seems to have fallen beneath the spell of Mr. Coward—I've always felt that Mr. Coward's works could have been written by some tremendously shrewd bird, especially the music—the reviews of contemporary drama are such as to make the English reader sigh with envy, they are so uproarious, just and impolite . . .

(In his stories) Mr. Gibbs is remarkably adroit at portraying people who become just a shade out of hand . . . Fugitive though his figures are, he can hold one's attention through his accuracy alone. To sum up—the entire absence of elevated pessimistic nagging, the lack of meritorious dullness, that, fundamentally, is why I recommend this book. And most, in fact, of the books written by what I may mistakenly cling to as 'The *New Yorker* School'. Well, anyway, by Mr. Gibbs' friends.

Wolcott Gibbs wrote to thank Brian for his 'very kind review', from the *New Yorker* editorial offices:

Dear Mr. Howard, (. . . Here) at the moment there is a strong resentment against all *New Yorker* writers. We are supposed to be everything that you quote Mr. Barrett as calling us, and in addition to that almost miserably supercilious in our personal behaviour. There is probably some justice in that. In addition to being a writer around here, I spent ten years as an editor and the memory of my struggles with young, virile, and politically energetic writers is still enough to make my teeth hurt. I guess they were important all right, but they were certainly hostile to the English language and their conversation was a good deal less rewarding than you might expect. A silly bunch of bastards, I used to think, and, along with my colleagues, I guess I developed a certain detachment about genius. Now they have all taken to criticism and there has been a good deal of suffering among the authors in this office, much of it quite innocent. I'm getting off the subject, though. I just wanted to thank you for a review that really pleased me very much, in spite of that quite justified remark about the 'self-entranced preface' and the statement that I am bewitched by Noel Coward, which I'm inclined to doubt.

My second reason for writing you is Damon Runyon. In, I think, four out of the seven reviews I've seen this name popped up, always as an example of an important influence in American writing. From other things I've read in the English press and from conversations with compatriots of yours, I gather that this is actually accepted as fact over there, and it amazes me. Damon Runyon was never a writer of any consequence in New York. His use of the idiom was never accurate, as Lardner's was, or O'Hara's, or Hemingway's. He lived on Broadway, but he didn't put down what he heard. He accomplished a kind of grotesque distortion (Kober does the same thing for the Bronx) that was at least as comprehensible to an Englishman as it was to the chorus girls and gamblers he wrote about, who never talked that way in their innocent lives. The stories themselves, of course, were almost incredibly bad, resurrections of O. Henry, glum imitations of Lardner. Long, long ago, when I was in school, I read a perfectly awful English writer called Ian Hay Beith and for a good many years my conception of your national character and speech was strongly based on his work. I should say that Runyon bears about the same relation to our actual life in this city. I think there is an interesting point here somewhere. A second-rate, false writer somehow gets to be accepted abroad as the only true reporter of manners and speech and the first thing you know he is the standard by which all his countrymen are judged. This is not an intellectual office, but it is an intensely literary one, and your preoccupation with Runyon is one of the things I hear discussed most. '*Runyon*, for Christ's sake!' they say. 'Why don't they dig up Artemus Ward?' I don't know why I go into this at such length, except that these international divergences in taste always fascinate me. May have something to do with the state of the world, at that. Sincerely and gratefully, Wolcott Gibbs.

The following month, in November, Brian produced another full-length review for the *New Statesman*, this time a tongue-in-cheek critique of Osbert Lancaster's Greek empathy—and erudition, under the title 'Through an Embassy Windscreen', of which I quote some pungent extracts:

Classical Landscape with Figures by Osbert Lancaster (John Murray):
This is a largish, handsomely produced book about Greece. Its author, as our perhaps most witty caricaturist, will need introduction to few, and he has illustrated it himself ... In a modest, yet decisive, preface he states his aim, which was 'not a ramble, nor a travel book, nor yet a guide, but a *description* in the 18th-century meaning of the term. ... No analysis of deep underlying causes has been attempted ... I have a very shrewd suspicion that in Greece there are no deep underlying causes ...'

Disregarding the slight rustle made by twenty-seven centuries revolving in their graves, prospective readers will, at this point, be able to guess at the kind of volume they may expect. An unusually entertaining, tasteful and intelligent one, with all the heavier stones left unturned ...

First, are you a Greek? If so, Mr. Lancaster is genuinely fond of and amused by you. He happens, however, to be entirely innocent of *humanitas*, in the Ciceronian sense, and consequently it would be wisest if you never even opened what must be the most exquisitely patronising book ever compiled about your country. A book in which every drawing of you, young or old, in or out of your national dress, makes you look exactly like an assistant head waiter with bandy legs ... a book in which your political beliefs are treated as being only one degree less droll—'party loyalty is purely a matter of temporary convenience'—than the fact that you can occasionally be observed dying for them. Note the music-hall touch at the end: '... the first Greek figure on whom I set eyes was a bearded warrior rolling in agony in the foreground ... of an empty Kolonaki street ... slugged through the stomach by a political opponent concealed behind some shuttered second-empire façade away in the wings.'

... Do you mind about spelling? If Psistrati's easy, who's Patnir? Are you fussy about geography? You will be surprised to learn that from Cape Colonna to Marathon the Attic coast faces north-west, that Missolonghi is at the southwestern extremity of Greece, and that you proceed west from Nauplia to reach Epidaurus.

... Are you one of the 'international planners, liberal intellectuals, and *New Statesman* readers generally?' You will be mortified to hear that you rejoiced, in 1922, at an incident which was—'to saddle the (Greek) state with a burden of unemployment, to create what had never existed before, an urban proletariat, and to ring around the principal cities with a girdle of slums . . .'

In other words, you, and the rest of the civilised world, acclaimed the escape of a million and a quarter Greek refugees to Greece after the most appalling pre-Hitlerian massacre of the 20th century, the sack of Smyrna by the Turks.

... You'd rather know how Mr. Lancaster deals with the antiquities? Epidaurus, for instance? '. . . Today there remains the finest Greek theatre in existence, as perfect, as functional and as unromantic as a well-designed gasometer . . .'

... You'd like to know what he says about the Acropolis, then, for God's sake? He's very good about the Propylaea . . . and he's extremely stimulating about Bassae, Kifissia, Ali Pasha of Jannina, Karytaina, the Frankish princes, the *art nouveau* quality of late Minoan, and the nastiness of the ancient Spartans . . . (whom) he calls 'a race of warped and sadistic scoutmasters'. Has Mr. Lancaster a style? Yes, very early Robert Byron, but with non-stop sentences. Does he display moments of imaginative insight? Can he evoke beauty? Almost. At Daphni, at Mycenae, and once when he came upon a row of empty chairs outside a cliff-café above the bay of Salamis, with an old gramophone playing a Turkish air into a lemon sunset.

You want to get back to Athens? . . . You say that surely he can't find much wrong with the temple of Nike Apteros, anyway? The most flawless of small Ionic buildings? Or with the Erechtheion, and its six caryatides, the finest in the world? You insist that these almost faceless statues are like six Demeters, timeless in majesty? Well, here is Mr. Lancaster on the temple of Nike. And then let's finish this off in straight dialogue:

'Supremely elegant and in perfect taste . . . nevertheless . . . a faint air of buzzards.'

Buzzards?

Buzzards. With a capital. And don't shout at me. Listen to the Erechtheion.

'. . . these elegant flower-maidens simper as unconcernedly as if they had never been called upon to balance two and a half tons of Pentelic marble on their pretty little heads.'

Simper? Pretty little *heads?*

Simper. Pretty little heads.

Brian received 'many congratulations on this *tour de force*, not least being a letter from his friend Hugh Massingham, who served with him in the R.A.F.: 'I really must write and congratulate you on your review of Osbert's book. Seldom have

I read anything so good-humoured, so devastating, and *final*. What a pity it is you don't write reviews more often.'

Raymond Mortimer, who as Literary Editor of the *New Statesman and Nation*, launched Brian on his reviewing career, wrote to him in 1947: 'I am in despair at the pomposity, illiteracy, verbosity and inhumanity of everyone under thirty. I wonder whether there is any chance of persuading you to let your Light So Shine Among Men—among young men—that they may amend their ways and try to acquire a few of your virtues? In other words can you do some novel reviews for us? The ceiling of the Common Man is proving a lot too common for me.'

Cuthbert Worsley, Raymond Mortimer's successor at the *N.S. & N.*, felt the same way when writing to Brian two years later: '. . . as for the mag. if it is getting weaker what it wants, my dear Brian, is not advice but CONTRIBUTIONS. If you all desert how can it keep up?'

It is hard to forgive his indolence in the face of such blatant encouragement. Even in retrospect Raymond Mortimer writes:

Brian had an extraordinary gift for writing, and it seems to me tragic that instead of cultivating it he preferred to idle on the delicious continent. If only he had slogged away, and taken his powers seriously. . . . Luckily I escaped ever having a serious row with him, which must have happened if I had seen him more often. I don't remember his being unreasonable as a contributor to the *New Statesman*. Probably he knew that I had a tough side, and would not stand any nonsense. Although he was never a crony of mine he amused me intensely, and I think it is right that a picture of his marvellous personality should be attempted.

Brian was in therapeutic correspondence again with Peter Watson in the winter of 1947–1948, and the following extracts are from Peter's letters:

Dear Brindle, . . . I seem to have suffered the death of feeling myself. I just can't react any more. It all seems so futile anyway, as we are under the sentence of death, I feel. If only the world contained some *hope*. Intelligence, freedom are monstrous luxuries which this world can no longer afford. If only I could take things for granted like any stupid person can. And yet if we all have duties and no rights what a humdrum prospect.

Without some money I would have acted worse than you. I can't do anything. I hate *doing* things. Like you I am only interested in life if it reaches a certain standard, and now that standard has gone for ever and there is no pleasure left which is not ersatz.

It is so paradoxical that those with least right to complain do complain but every day and in every way my sensibilities are attacked and OUTRAGED in London. What is so maddening is that no one *seems* to notice as much as I do. Do they possess the secret of the stiff upper lip or what? Do they have access to secret *jouissances* of which I know nothing? It's just scandalous to me. So I answer complaints with complaints . . .

How terrible it is to grow old. One loses so many tastes one had and seems to get no new ones at all. Wisdom doesn't settle anything—it only removes one from old friends and prevents one from making any new ones. Then it is so humiliating to have all one's old beliefs and enthusiasms turned inside out. The only thing is to be young as it makes egotism elegant.

[Later] . . . It is really difficult for people who like success to spend time over what isn't considered a success. The inverse is true with failure, I believe, too. *Real* success is what is most difficult to hold out for. [This was apropos Brian's lack of encouragement from certain quarters.]

[Later] . . . Surely the thing about Guy (Burgess) is that he has an imperative need to impress. I met him at the Reform yesterday, and he told two long and funny stories (political of course—one about Churchill), and then said he had invented them! All this militant atheism exhausts. As if it was theism that was causing present-day troubles. Just wait ten years or so to see the boredom and sterility militant atheism will bring. Love, P.

Brian had a recurrence of the alcoholic London blues and for some reason went off to 'recuperate' in Jersey, from where he wrote to his mother:

I am sorry to have to say that I have had rather a collapse during these last few days. I am all right at Gorebridge, and am all right when with Sam, but apparently not when in London alone. I am glad not to be at home for my birthday. Perhaps forty-three will be the year when I turn inland from this unnecessary precipice. I promise you that I am fighting hard about spirits, and about living within my income. I think I could win alone, without a psychiatrist, but I don't think I have any right to go on giving myself second chances. The strain on your credulity, and faith, is too severe. So whatever Glover says, I'll do.

Glover once said that my guilt at not being a literary success and making you happy—also Sam—also myself—is so enormous that it is paralysing me. Vicious circle, etc. This may be true. He says, 'But why *feel* so guilty?' All I can answer is that I DO. And, if I may say so, brisk advice about 'making an effort', etc. (from you) doesn't quite fit the bill. No one would *willingly* be as miserable and self-thwarting as I am. I love you so much, and I am such a frightful disappointment to you . . .

On being told at one of these psychiatric sessions that 'alcoholism was a symptom of unconscious homosexuality', Brian produced the ingenious solution that he must be an unconscious heterosexual.

Then, after eight years of 'continental' starvation, he arrived in Ischia, to spend a few weeks with Wystan Auden, from where he wrote some of his happiest letters to his mother, in May and June 1948:

I am so overcome with the beauty of Italy that I haven't yet got my ideas into order—Ischia is all I thought, and makes Capri ridiculous. We live in a rambling hotel, with huge *domed* rooms, white-washed, with blue and lime cornices, entirely alone. Right on the sea. There is a courtyard in the middle, with a vine-trellised roof. It is what I have always dreamed about—as a

THE WANDERING YEARS—WITH 'SAM'

hotel. My bath water is heated on a charcoal fire, and we eat octopi, eels, fish, veal, rice, eggs. Forio has *nobody in it* but us. I am so happy. I wish you were here, that's all.

[Later] If I can manage I'll stay a little longer. Wystan has written a long poem—*Ischia—For Brian Howard*,[3] which so deeply pleases and honours me. Though I should like to have achieved immortality on my own! I enclose a copy. He is more a moral than a visual poet, but if you pay attention to the *punctuation*, it turns out not to be so quiet as it at first seems. He wrote it because I told him I thought he couldn't be visual.

Auden later replied to Brian about this, 'Never think that I don't know that your criticisms of my lack of visual attention are just ... nearly all my closest friends are visual types. At the same time, as a poet, one of the most important lessons one has to learn is to recognise and accept one's limitations and, if possible turn them into advantages ...'

[Continuing letters to his mother] ... I walked miles through the Piano di Sorrento in a religious procession, with fireworks bursting among the mountain tops all around, and priests discoursing from a jeep! It was for the Madonna, and little girls, dressed up as Madonnas, stood absolutely still, in wayside shrines, as we passed. Very made-up, they were. Eventually the jeep broke down, of course, and Sam and I had to push it the last yards to the church! With others, naturally. As I disapprove of Catholicism, I was rather annoyed, but it was all so ridiculous and touching that I had tears in my eyes. Everyone sang hymns as they walked, but *gaily*, and all the houses had hideous rayon counterpanes hung out over the balconies. The reason Sam and I were *in* the procession was that we were going across the peninsula, from Sorrento to Amalfi, in a 'bus, and suddenly ran into it, whereupon a pale young priest came running down the road, like Christ attacking the moneylenders in the Temple, and commanded the 'bus to stop and wait till the whole procession was over. It lasted one and a half hours! Imagine that happening in England. The 'bus was full, and full of very busy, rather irreligious, middle-class Italians, who began to hum like bees. The driver actually *screamed* with rage and frustration, but Mother Church had her way. I adored it all. The fireworks were worse than the blitz, and much louder.

[Later] ... Wystan's influence is *really* good for me. I breakfast at 8; go to bed at 10.30—and have slowly succeeded in doing a little daily writing. I now know that I must eventually live here—I am the kind of plant that grows in real sun, and just doesn't otherwise. I always suspected it. And then there's the wine business.

By the way, Wystan is as perceptive a man as I've ever met. He is quite undeceivable, and he never flatters, lies or exaggerates. Well, last night, he said, to a group of people, that I was 'the least cynical person' he had ever met (he was using cynical to denote lack of love and disinterested

[3] Published in *Nones* by W. H. Auden, Faber, 1952.

enthusiasm). I was so pleased. He is an exceedingly *good* man, in the most serious sense, and his standards are ruthlessly high.

Brian returned to England via Naples and Rome, where he revelled in sight-seeing and noted in his diary:

I live too much by my senses. I like beautiful buildings, melodious sounds, flowering trees, coloured shadows, women with faces (in England they haven't faces), liveliness, taste, good weather . . . I prefer seeing to smelling, touching, tasting, or hearing. I pay too much—in the coinage of *ennui*, and even anguish—for my eyes, I'm afraid. One should digest existence, or manufacture one's own, or arrange to think—or whatever one chooses to say—through a coalition of one's senses. To allow a single sense to dominate, to begin to tell one more than the others, is to begin to pay a kind of income tax, which I can imagine gradually increasing until it bankrupts one . . .

I was sick twice—and there was blood[4] . . . how odd I am physically. It is having to leave places that does it, that and going to banks—

For almost a year there is no news, and no letters to chart the months. But the signs are bad. He walked out on his mother at Gorebridge after the servants confiscated his small stock of drink:

Ever since I have had no allowance but have had to beg for every penny I have felt, from time to time, imprisoned . . . I have come to the Priory at Corsham to think, and for advice. Will you please write to me here and tell me what, in your opinion, is the best thing now to be done? If I had any money I would relieve Gorebridge of what is now the scandal of my presence—but I haven't. I can't come back . . .

If I ever write a novel it's going to be about how it's not the wicked who make people miserable, but the good. I'm half-good and half-wicked, so I know. I know, too, of course, that what really happened was that I suddenly grew too heavy for you as a burden.

Lura's idea of what was to be done was predictable, and by the summer of 1949 Brian and Sam found themselves, not unwillingly, once more abroad. This time they began seriously looking for a house to buy, somewhere in the south of France, starting off at Grasse 'because it was unfashionable—and not HARSH, like the rest of the S. of France'. But they could not find what they wanted, and in any event were never sure that Lura would, in fact, produce the sale price when it came to the point, so they took a furnished flat in Nice for a while, as it was 'cheap, unfashionable, charming, and a CITY'. From there they gravitated towards Aix-en-Provence where Brian got jaundice and Lura's sympathy was distinctly tinged with relief in her letters 'I must say I am thankful . . . because I know you will stay off alcohol and it will be the joy of my life to

---

[4] Tuberculosis was not diagnosed for another six years.

see how you will develop—even to writing—I feel so confident somehow, with you not drinking'. Brian's forty-fifth birthday was spent at Méraud Guinness' country place outside Aix, from where he wrote to his mother:

I deeply feel that this birthday is going to be one of the major turning-points in my life. I mean from the point of view of control and energy. It is now a month since I have touched alcohol of any kind, and I feel a different person, and I have *no desire* for it. I eat all day and all night, literally. People think me crazy. I think it's a proof of what I've always said—that drink with me is absolutely and wholly a signal of psychological distress.

Lura obviously agreed about this abstemious period in Brian's forty-sixth year, and wrote him one of her highly emotional letters:

Dear Brian, This keeps coming up in my mind—*There is a tide in the affairs of man, which, taken at the flood, leads on to fortune; Omitted, at the voyage of their life, Is bound in shallows and in miseries. On such a full sea are we now afloat; and we must take the current where it serves.* I am afraid that I have been wrong in my 'mothering'. You have escaped the consequences of your actions through your own charm or my protection. But—at forty-five—charm grows thin and mothers grow old. And life which gave you great talent calls for its return—Only one thing stands in the way—the lethargy which has you in its evil sway—Somehow my love has failed you—I cannot make you see the real happiness which is yours over the hill. *The little more and how much it is—and the little less and what worlds away.* Oh dear, even Browning and Shakespeare fail me—and I have no words ever—Prayers are better anyway—and love—Muv.

The search for the right house in the right place at the right price was proving virtually hopeless. Brian wrote despairingly: 'It is impossible to convey, really, how *complicated* finding a place is. However hard one works at it. Please remember that things are quite, *quite* otherwise than what one would expect, here. One never can tell, also, what owners will eventually take. It's not like England where owners and house agents say what they *mean*. One has to look at places costing £300 with as much interest and expectation as those costing £3,000.'

The eternal financial problem was looming, and Sam wrote to Lura: 'About MONEY—this is always a difficult subject to talk about with Brian. He *knows* the position very well and yet in a way refuses to face up to it until the last minute. Then he realises, when money is short, that he is not perhaps as rich as he would like. But he does know, and any pretence of ignorance of the situation is just either laziness or acting. Both these qualities are slowly disappearing fortunately, and the bursts of the rich 16th-century host-like behaviour are becoming rarer and rarer.'

In June Brian wrote from a rented flat in Menton to his mother:

I could NEVER live here, I'm afraid. There is something so inert, so soggy, so damp-warm, so too-still, so unsharp, that it would do me harm. It would have the same effect as living in some charming comfy hothouse. My selfishness, which harms me most, is now, I fear, incurable. The only thing is that I have a few poems left *in* me, and they must come *out*.

I want to quote something by Cyril (Connolly) in the last issue of *Horizon*.[5] I know well that you think me too much of a pessimist always, and no doubt the meaning of the following passage will appear to you to be absurdly pessimistic. But do try and remember that you belong to a generation which at least began by having every reason to be more buoyant than mine. After all you did grow up, and love, and choose, and marry, and have me *before* 1914. I see no way out of it:

'One can perceive the inner trend of the Forties as maintaining this desperate struggle of the modern movement, between man, betrayed by science, bereft of religion, deserted by the pleasant imaginings of humanism against the blind fate of which he is now so expertly conscious that if we were to close this last "Comment" with the suggestion that everyone who is now reading it may in ten years' time, or even five, look back to this moment as the happiest in their lives, there would be few who would gainsay us. "Nothing dreadful is ever done with, no bad thing gets any better; you can't be too serious." This is the message of the Forties from which, alas, there seems no escape, for it is closing time in the gardens of the West, and from now on an artist will be judged only by the resonance of his solitude or the quality of his despair.'

Your answer to this would probably be that life is what the individual, in any epoch or any given case, makes it. That true happiness does not depend upon outward circumstances. I find this an odd attitude, really, because it assumes such a godlike independence of environment. For myself, I am not independent of my environment—either in Vedantist or in the material sense.

... When I think of my own generation, of the men, I mean, it is so terrifying to think that *only*, among the gifted ones, the second-rate have succeeded, in the sense of becoming fulfilled. Apart from the rather forbidding nature of my epoch, and far more formidable, is my own abiding guilt. The way I've never made you proud of me, given you the smallest weapon with which to combat the gossip. The way that my nature has prevented me marrying and having a family, which would have pleased you most of all. The way I've never earned any money, but spent yours instead, till now you are poor. The way I, still, intend to get a house out of you, here. A charming story. Every tiresome tale that my Father, or an enemy, tells about me, I either justify or appear to justify. It is true that two people love me, and that four or five people are genuinely devoted to me, but *all* of them continue to be so and do so by the skin of their teeth, and through thick and thin. Yes, I have grave doubts about myself. And the nastiness when I get tipsy is a very bad sign: 'I may be a failure, and I may know it,

[5] 1 December 1949/January 1950 issue.

but I'm a bloody sight more intelligent than you ALL the same.' So pathetic and silly; and such deplorable manners.

At last Brian found a suitable house at Le Rouret, just below Grasse, and offered £2,000 in anticipation of his mother producing the dollars from her American investments. He couldn't wait to settle down, as he wrote to his mother:

> ... I know quite well that there is an American market for me—the letters I have received in the past eighteen months from magazines like *Harper's* and the *New Yorker* are not letters which they vouchsafe—to use a rather nice word—to everyone ... Lazy as I have been, I have at least kept my literary name clean. It is all there, ready. Untouched. Stephen Spender, who doesn't know me well, said something in Paris which was nevertheless very encouraging. He said, quite simply, 'How wise you were to wait'. Well, he didn't know that it was less shrewdness than sloth. All the same, I'm ready now. I've never blotted my copybook, as they say, and within three years, or less, my literary name could be not only clean, but shall we say, well known?

But this pattern of success eluded Brian, and all was not well set for the future, as Lura seemed unable, or unwilling, to produce the necessary dollars to buy the house. Her letters contradicted each other by alternate posts: 'Le Rouret is off ... I *can* obtain 3,000 dollars ... dollars *can't* be made available ...'

In times of crises it was always Sam who wrote the calm, soothing letters to Lura. In July he wrote to explain about Brian's 'breakdown': 'I understand completely about Le Rouret and fully agree that any monies that *you* hold in the U.S. should remain there ... it is a great pity, mainly because that particular house was the result of two years expense and experience. And now we are back where we started. Brian did, in fact have a breakdown recently—but in the eight years I have known him he has never had such a bombardment of disasters, one after another.'

They decided to return to England, via Salzburg, to discuss the future, and Lura Howard suggested sending Brian £250 with which to buy a camera, in the hope that he would write—and photograph—material on the way home for either *Harper's Bazaar* or *Harper's Magazine*. He was tempted to accept but finally declined:

> I don't really want to write for *H. Bazaar*, or any of the 'glossy' papers. I would never re-publish, in book form, the kind of article they would want me to write for them. But I could, and would, re-publish an *H. Magazine* article. In which I can be nasty about the Riviera where nastiness is deserved. And for which no photographs, of course, are needed. So that's that ... but, so sweet of you, the £250.
>
> [Later] ... I think I must make an effort to bring some saleable writing back from this expedition to Austria, and since my non-glossy magazine articles will probably take me some time, I feel I should concentrate on

photographing the trip back and writing *ordinary* stuff to go with the photographs. So I *will* buy a Rolleiflex in Austria. With it I intend to produce travel articles not only now, but in the future. It is silly not to make money out of what small, but definite, talent I have for photographing. I shall certainly write about my favourite places that I will be seeing again AFTER Hitler, and *before* Russia comes, so to speak.

Our next address will be Genoa.

21. Exile *ad infinitum*

1950–1957

Although their next address was indeed in Italy it was not Genoa, nor by reason of their own free choice. The following year, August 1950 to August 1951, was to prove the worst yet. Out of the blue the Monaco police expelled Brian from the Principality, saying that the French *Sureté* considered him an 'undesirable person', and that he was not to enter France or her possessions again—even though a mere fortnight earlier the Menton Police had promised him his long-awaited *carte d'identité* within a few weeks. To leave Monaco inconspicuously, with grace and without any incriminating stamp on his passport, necessitated a good deal of bribing, so that he and Sam arrived in Bordighera with the car (half-repaired), their luggage, and just forty dollars in hand.

The projected trip home, through Switzerland, Germany and Austria (and now to Ostend) which was, a few days before, a charming idea, had become the only way of avoiding arrest. Brian wrote in reasonably good spirits to his mother:

> ... why should it not prove a way of earning some of this expenditure back? Why can't I *still* photograph and write? No reason at all. At present I am so shocked, and worried, that I can't think. But, if I can get out of this damned Mediterranean, I'll surprise you with the material I'll bring. I am DETERMINED to earn some of this back. In fact, France's disapproval of me has cancelled my disapproval of myself.
>
> ... It will be found that whatever 'the trouble' is it has nothing to do with my emotional preferences, because the French don't care about that. My solicitor laughed at the idea. My two sponsors were Méraud, and Nancy Mitford. The former had not yet been approached by the authorities when I last saw her—although Chile, her husband, *was* on behalf of Sam, whose papers are going through perfectly normally, incidentally—but Nancy was, and testified very much in my favour.

Nancy Mitford had written to Brian as early as February 1950 to say: 'I have already done the necessary and sworn by nine Gods that you are blissikins personified. Several policemen who looked as if about to twist my arm asked if it was true that you are coming to live with me. I said well quite likely since you are my oldest and greatest friend but you hadn't actually mentioned it so far, but my husband is in England and you may have fixed something with him!' When I asked her permission to quote from this letter, Nancy Mitford replied: 'I am so glad you are doing a book on Brian. It would be too dreadful if that wild, original, funny person were to be forgotten. Nobody who knew him ever could forget ... I remember Brian and Sam in Guerlain's shop just after the war when scent was £100 a drop. Sam picked up the bottle with which the vendeuse doled out little samples and began to spray himself, to the visible horror of everybody in the shop. Brian said, "Now, my dear, you're not putting out a *fire*, you know!"'

They finally extricated themselves from Italy and arrived in Salzburg, where Brian wrote to his mother that Sam had left him after a terrible quarrel:

> ... In order to survive such strains and bothers as Sam has had—he has nothing to call upon, as I have—one must not only have a good heart and nature, but one must have *brains*. Whether you think he has brains, or not, he hasn't. He is an ordinary, practical person whom such things worry MORE, really, than they worry me. It's one of the few penalties of being simple and good. He is, superficially, an optimist; just as I, superficially, am a pessimist. But when it comes to the proprietors of hotels being rude, and pawning things, there is something rock-like in me which there is not in him.

The quarrel was not too long-lasting, and they went off together to Walchensee, where Brian had first gone some nineteen years before, and for almost every year up till 1935. On this return journey through Germany Brian started probing:

> I am gradually gathering information about Germany, but it is ALL so unreservedly sad, ominous and futile that it is a little dispiriting. Of course, I only meet anti-Nazis and aristocrats, but if I met the rest it would not be dispiriting, but awful. It is impossible to explain. I used to think that the public conduct of a nation—Hitler, etc.—was the combined fault of that nation. Now, I see that it is neither one's friends, nor the workers, who are to blame. (And also not the silly princes, lazy as they are.) It is simply history working its horrible way out. The Russians *could* be right, but they aren't, because one must not force things, or torture people.
>
> In Germany there is utter apathy. I wish I could say spiritual despair, which would be better. They say, and with reason—'Whatever we have done, we are, now, supposed to be your bastion against Russia. What are we to *do*? You dismantle our factories; you refuse us an army; you don't furnish us with the means of defence. We will have to be your front line. What are you going to fill it with? Unarmed, underfed, cannon-fodder?'
>
> You see? What is the answer? I have had university professors almost on their knees, begging me to explain. What can I say? There is only one answer. 'You were wicked under Hitler; you must perish now.' How silly. Unless the West does something about Germany, and the Rhine frontier, all will, inevitably, be lost. France is as rotten as it was before.
>
> ... We came up to Frankfurt through Ulm, Stuttgart, Heidelberg and Darmstadt. Never have I seen such effective bombing of totally unrewarding targets. This was a rather rich, residential town where Heidelberg professors of the grander kind had houses, and where Stefan George, the poet lived. It was not bombed as English towns were bombed—even Southampton. Apart from the outskirts, it was *destroyed*, utterly. I was never a one for the Nazis, but I am shocked, beyond measure, at the wanton spite

of the Anglo-American bombing of Germany. And it was all done in 1945—when the war was over, as everyone knew. I could have taken photographs of ruins stretching as far as the eye can see—ruins which make the bombing of London look like a *joke*. It is simply horrible. And disgusting. And *pointless*, at the time it was done.

He might have made a comeback as a political journalist, but he did not have the stamina or will-power, or even desire, to make use of his talents in that direction. While they were still in Germany Lura Howard was very upset as she was suddenly 'retired' from her job of managing the Mary Chess shop in London, and worried over losing her salary. She wrote in irritation to Brian: 'You two can get jobs at your ages. I am too old.' Up to this period Brian had become increasingly desperate over her see-saw attitude which prevented him from ever knowing his true financial position, and her vacillation over whether she would or would not produce the purchase money for a house in France. But when she told him of set-backs concerning her American investments together with this loss of earned income, he became temporarily contrite:

It was the greatest shock I have had about our finances that I can remember . . . I must unload every publishable thing I possess to America, and unless this produces something like a contract, or a financial miracle, I must *very* shortly get a job. Sam will have to go back to the B.B.C. if he can. Sam and I, obviously, should never have set out on this journey. Don't lose heart about me—or us—because we are coming to *help*. You have tried to be too generous, and now it's our turn.

So for three months they returned to England but had to leave again in March 1951, to comply with their foreign resident status. In Belgium they parted company again, after another row, Brian telling his mother that Sam had tried to knock him out while he was driving:

Don't think too hardly of Sam. I know it was an unforgivable thing to do, even if he had an excuse. But I am a maddening person, and he means *well*.

[Two days later] I think it conceivable that Sam considers our relationship to have come to its final end. If so, I must face it, because I myself cannot make a move. I feel that if I did, he might take it as tacit permission to do the same thing again, one day. It's very surprising that we weren't both killed. . . . Temporarily I feel like a stone, like someone who has died.

Sam wrote to Lura Howard from Zurich, where he had rejoined Brian a week or so later: 'Brian behaved badly and I reacted in a way for which I am now sorry . . . although I sometimes do a wrong thing, fundamentally we are very happy together—and things are really all right. In any case, you know I would do anything for you, or for Brian. I am extremely sorry that I, who owe you so much, should contribute to your worries.' And, later from Ehrwald in the Tyrol: 'Things are going much better than I expected. After the initial fuss (which I had under control the whole time), there is now only beer. So it was worth it. I have a mission in life, and I shall not be happy until we are all happy. I shall *never* let Brian down, but if necessary I shall *shock* him with *sense*. . . . I am a little worried about us and France—do you think everything is going all right? . . . Brian has written a brilliant poem about Klaus Mann'. This poem brings back poignant memories to Klaus Mann's sister, Erika:

> Brian—the poem you wrote for Klaus has an optimistic ring, all sorrow notwithstanding, and is full of conviction that a future lies ahead in which men may live together in peace and in brotherly unity. Did you ever really believe that? I am sure that such a mirage swam before your eyes, like a *Fata Morgana* when, during those brief moments on Germany's highest mountain, you thought of your dead friend, Klaus, your 'German brother', and of all the dreams which you dreamt with him. Years later, in Zurich, you recited the poem, just for me, and you were shaken by sobs. Was it 'only' for Klaus? Ah, no! You were weeping for this world of ours, weeping for it and for yourself. Because long ago, decades ago, before they had begun once again 'to pin medals on the loudest and the least', you, life's desperate darling, received 'the only one one pins through the breast'.

While staying in Zurich Brian started collecting his best poems to form an anthology. Several of these were written during or after the war, amongst them *Gone to Report* (published in *Horizon* in 1940), *Two it takes to make a flower* (1943), *The Dust* (published in *Horizon* and *Harper's Magazine* in 1949), *Instantaneous Time Exposure—for Wystan Auden* (published in *Harper's Magazine* in 1949), *Today* (1952), and the revised version of his 1938 *Late Night Final* (published in *Harper's Magazine* in 1952). All of these are included in Philip Toynbee's selection in Appendix I. *The Dust* is particularly beautiful and drew letters of admiration from many of his friends. Cyril Connolly, then Editor of *Horizon*, to whom it was originally sent, replied '. . . I like the "Dust" poem immensely and would like to use it. I am not quite so sure about the other one. I think your gift lies in the production of the utterly simple statement, which is not so simple as it seems, and in the general coating of lyrical feeling which you give your mind. This is a most difficult thing to do and sometimes it works like a conjuring trick, at others one sees a faint whisk of the handkerchief sticking out from the conjuror's sleeve . . .'

Christopher Isherwood also liked *The Dust*, and the one for Wystan Auden: '. . . Just a brief mad wave of my fan in salute to your two poems—God they are beautiful! More! More! Are there? Have I missed them? They are exactly how I would like to write, if I were a poet. . .'

Brian wrote to his mother that he was feeling daily more sensible while working on the anthology, but it was Sam who informed her that Brian was, in fact, taking a new cure 'for his condition'. 'It is the drug which I tried so hard to get in London last year, and is reported to be permanent. As the poison is leaving, Brian's whole features are changing, and all the lines on his face are disappearing. It is making all the difference to both of us, and the future looks *much* more healthy. We went skiing yesterday—Brian doesn't seem to have forgotten how to do what I think is a most difficult thing . . . This is not a real letter, but just a word to say that the sun is beginning to shine . . .' Brian then confirmed this information:

> I, at last, agree with you that this business is affecting my mind, which terrifies me. Also, I cannot continue spoiling your life—and poor Sam's—though I do not much mind about my own. I have been such a disappointment to you—and myself—that I no longer care for myself, particularly. But obviously something must be done. If it can be, at forty-six. I said to the doctor here that the desire to drink springs from psychological sources, and he admitted this. He said that this new medicine makes drink chemically hateful to the body in such a way that the psychological situation, after some time, heals itself. But I can't take pills for the rest of my life. Or can I?

The tragedy was that Brian did, of course, become addicted to *pills* (some of them of doubtful worth), partly through undergoing cure after cure for alcoholism (and later T.B.), and partly from his growing dependence on 'sedatives' of all kinds. While Brian was finishing this cure in Zurich, Sam went off to Paris to sound out the atmosphere concerning Brian's expulsion. Without speaking much French he apparently managed to storm his way right up to the 'Chief of the French Special Foreign Service' who told him that Brian could return to France and stay there as soon as he liked and for as long as he liked. When asked for an explanation of all the trouble, the Head replied, 'Oh, times change, you know'. So they made for Nice, staying on the way at Sirmio, where Brian was announced as a distinguished visitor on the Italian radio network, and saw Stephen Spender who 'was so nice about my poems'. But, alas, just before they got to Nice the house that they had so longed to buy, 'Le Rouret', was sold. While they were recovering from this disappointment and considering whether to stay on and search for another house or return to England, their pattern of ill luck repeated itself. Brian wrote the bad news to his mother in early August, from Paris:

> On Friday morning I was arrested in Nice. Three hours of questioning, Sam with me. They said my interdiction had *not* been cancelled. I didn't believe them. So they gave me a few days' grace to go to Paris to investigate. I went to the Ministry of the Interior yesterday—and it has *not* been cancelled. Who played that cruel joke on Sam we'll never know. I asked the man if the thing against me was '*grave*'. He said, '*Non, pas grave*'. It has been the greatest shock and disappointment I have ever known. When people speak to me I start weeping. I must leave France at the latest in two or three days, and I have thirty shillings left . . . On the little green interdiction card at Nice it simply said '*moralité douteux*'. And then, as my lawyer said, one thinks of the foreigners that *are* permitted to live in France. In the *end* I can see this interdiction will be removed, but where to find the confidence, or money, to go on? And if anyone speaks politely to me I have great difficulty in not crying. You have never known the horror of arrest;

301

of having to defend oneself against stony-faced men, *in a foreign language.* And the eternal waiting in corridors. And I had made up my mind that all was well again. Never mind. I'll get through. Already, I feel tiny little pieces of you and Dampa [his grandfather Chess] edging their way back into my breast. Courage, in fact.

And so they spent another three months in England, re-planning the future once more. This time they set their sights on Italy, and Brian wrote to his old friend Harold Acton for advice:

... Within a few years, I shall be living permanently in Italy, and you are the only person I know who understands Italy, and therefore the only person I can turn to for serious advice. I want to buy a small house or villa—at least four bedrooms and an acre of land, not necessarily on the sea. My principal consideration is climate, but the sea is rather important for Sam, as he loves sailing, and the garden, preferably flat and not terraced is important to me, as I only wish to read, write and garden.

Do you ever see anything of Max Beerbohm? He was a great friend of my grandmother's, and I might consult him—and there is Norman Douglas, of course, but Beerbohm is a little ancient for me to bother him, and Norman almost too old to talk to ...

I am publishing poems in America, at too long intervals, because I am so lazy. Do please, Harold, tell me about yourself a little ... (Later) ... Thank you so very much for your letter which was more than helpful. At all events my search can now be spread over a longish time because I have suddenly taken a furnished house in Italy for what may be a year. This house is at Asolo, and is the one in which Browning wrote his last volume, *Asolando.* It is next door to Freya Stark, whom I don't know. I am taking her new book, *Beyond Euphrates,* out with me—I hear it is very good.

About Asolo, where they arrived in December 1951, Brian enthused to his mother:

Asolo, as far as I can see, is an Italian town so perfect as to be incredible—not one ugly building—like one supremely good stage set after another. A southern Rothenburg, only untouched by (Allied) bombing. This house—La Mura—is quite a shock, too. Sam describes it as 'palatial'—no other word can do. It, also, does not contain a single ugly thing ... excellent antique furniture, settees, taffeta hangings, porcelain, and done in a way which, fussy as I am, I would hardly alter at all.

... Please don't think I am depressed about the *New Yorker.* When a poem is re-written after two years, it gets out of focus permanently, and one can't 'see' it any more. It gets less good, namely. I am not surprised at its rejection. It is too long for that paper anyway, and the other poem is too savage for them. The 'Grandfather' poem will be published by someone else, as you will see. A few rejections will do me good. I have so few. It is a spur.

302

This 'Grandfather' poem, called *The Lost Street*, is an intensely personal view of his Gassaway[1] and Chess grandfathers:

> ... the young Washington poet
> and the young Artillery captain
> My grandfathers, long dead. And my envy.
>
> The poet wrote 'The Dandy Fifth'—
> > *Their uniforms were by tailors cut,*
> > *They brought hampers of good wine;*
> > *And every squad had a nigger, too,*
> > *To keep their boots in shine;*
> > *They'd nought to say to us dusty 'vets',*
> > *And through the whale brigade*
> > *We called them the kid-gloved Dandy Fifth*
> > *When we passed them on parade ...*

Brian had the feeling that work was going to come easier to him, but far from settling down, within a few months he had decided to look elsewhere in Italy for a permanent *asile*. As he wrote to Heywood Hill: 'I shall stay at Asolo, naturally, for a considerable time, but have decided against it—and the whole Veneto—as a place to live permanently. One doesn't leave England to enjoy an English climate. Fogs and snow, and astronomical fuel bills. I am now having a look round Lerici, south of the smart places like Rapallo and Porto Fino. It is unspoiled and "scenically" and architecturally rewarding. From a literary point of view it is the *Barren Leaves* district. The Shelley-Byron house is, now, lost in a welter of Victorian nonsense—though charming as a house. And D. H. Lawrence's cottage here, was, and is, terrible. A HIDEAWAY for a LIMPET ...'

Brian and Sam must have deserted the wintry imperfections of Asolo in March for the distractions of Venice, as Walter Rilla (who produced Brian's B.B.C. radio plays in 1942) remembers meeting them there:

It was a curious meeting. I was in Venice making a film, and one evening I was having dinner in Harry's Bar when a stranger, a young man who introduced himself as 'Sam', came up to my table and said he was a writer and a friend of Brian Howard's. He knew from Brian all about me, even about the long novel I was working on—*Seeds of Time*. He said he and Brian were living in a little house in Asolo and they had come to Venice to celebrate Brian's birthday, which was the following day. We sat and talked, had a lot of drinks, left Harry's Bar and had some more drinks at another bar, and at half past one in the morning Sam suggested I should come with him to the Hotel Regina, where he was staying with Brian, and wish him many happy returns, the birthday now having dawned. When we came to the hotel all the carpets had been taken up in the hall and the charladies

---

[1] The first and only reference in Brian's papers to the identity of his Gassaway grandfather.

were busy with mops and buckets and the night porter glared at us with a suspicious eye. We went up in the lift, and when we entered their apartment we found Brian in the bathroom, sitting in his pyjama jacket on the lavatory seat, with writing pad and pencil, composing a poem. He was not at all surprised at seeing me, not in the least embarrassed presenting himself like that on the 'clo', and didn't leave his seat for some time. Sam found some whisky and we drank Brian's health, I wished him many happy returns and he read to us the poem he had begun to write. It was all a little spooky and macabre, and after about ten minutes I left, Brian still sitting on his 'inspiratorial' seat!

The following day we met for dinner at Harry's Bar, and I remember we got into a heated argument about the problem of the novel which Brian considered to be only a second rate form of literature, poetry being the only really creative form of writing. We parted long after midnight, having had again a lot of drinks—too many drinks. When I finally left I promised to visit him in Asolo—but I was too busy and couldn't get away from Venice. I never saw Brian again.

He was a fine artist and writer and, but for his unfortunate disposition which brought him much unhappiness, *was likely, had he been put on, to have proved most royally.*

Throughout the spring of 1952 Brian kept up his correspondence with Harold Acton, from Asolo: 'In February I visited the Ligurian coast in the fashion you recommended—starting north from Lerici. This coast did not really appeal to me—the chic part, I mean. Too precipitous, scrub-covered, etc. Inland, especially near, and north of, Lerici I liked better. . . . I saw Max Beerbohm, and my hotel proprietor seemed to think I'd been accorded a great honour; talked of people who'd come in cars all the way from Paris only to be politely turned away etc. So I felt enhanced in his eyes—the hotelier's. I wrote down what M.B. told me, of my grandmother especially, immediately after seeing him. He was simply *enchanting*, though astonishingly acidulated about D. H. Lawrence, whom he referred to, flatly, as having 'laboured under the disadvantage of being mad'. A very competent, very polite, but slightly formidable German lady now looks after Max. She has that highly educated German quality, which I know so well, of being unable to relax, as Americans say. So, every moment, her eyes were popping out of her head at the way the 'Master' kept extending his usual 'Visiting period', and seemed to enjoy himself notwithstanding. But she eventually shoo-ed me away—very nicely.

Brian kept his rough notes of this meeting with Max Beerbohm in Rapallo in February. Beerbohm was talking of Mrs. T. P. O'Connor (Brian's grandmother—'Damma'):

The neatest woman he has ever known—so entertaining. He stayed with her and T.P. at Black Rock. Sometimes breakfast was at 9 a.m. (Max hungry)—sometimes at 10.30 when Damma arrived 'punctually—at 10.30—as neat as a new pin—every hair in place'. T.P. was 'jolly looking but never said an optimistic thing'.

[Of the 'Dieppe incident'] T.P. was lunching on the Casino terrace with Miss Evy Green (celebrated actress and beauty), introduced Max, asking him not to tell Damma. Shortly afterwards, in London, Damma says to him, 'So you were in Dieppe?' Max: 'No.'—D: 'Nonsense. I hear Miss Green sang on behalf of the life-boatmen of Dieppe. Did T.P. hand round the plate?'

[On D. H. Lawrence and Norman Douglas] 'Lawrence laboured under the disadvantage of being mad, of course.' Couldn't write. Those 'endless sentences—otiose.' When he, Max, read Magnus' book, with Lawrence's preface, he thought that possibly the rest of the book was a disguised Lawrence autobiography. Then, that Norman's attack made 'mincemeat' of Lawrence. Which is what happens when 'a real writer' comes into play, etc. . . . Max seemed faintly jealous of Norman. Deprecated his 'geological' side, slightly.

[Of Brian's parents] Told me to be sure to give his love to my mother. 'Still beautiful.' (Had shown him a photograph.) He remembered 'Tudie Howard' well—and Warwick Square—with the mirror that turned into a window over the fireplace.

Max talks slowly but with perfect enunciation, and completely on the spot. Pauses, naturally. No repetitiveness whatsoever. Wonderful to hear someone of eighty—or whatever—tell a complete story. Beginning, middle, and end. Choosing his words much better than most of the young men of today. Exquisite manners, yet natural. Wore a scarab ring, with a gold band, on the 'ring finger'. Turquoise cuff-links. Brilliant blue-violet walls of the small study. Encircled by one row of books. Above them, one row of photographs and drawings—some by him: a demoniacal photograph of Shaw; a photograph of Beardsley sitting in a room with a huge tent of a mosquito net, gazing down at a desk above which were pinned a block of what looked like French or Italian 17th or 18th century drawings (reproductions); a caricature of Whistler; a ditto of William Rothenstein as a young man, by Max; a Daumier print—many others.

Will possibly live three years more, but I think two (he had pneumonia last year). Has completely given up 'the world' and doesn't care any more. Although the dandy and writer in him make him find this necessity a pity. And a *little* irritating. But wise enough to be resigned. About as UNsecond-rate as anyone one could meet today. Emanates the distinction that they practically all now lack . . .

Brian continued his correspondence with Harold Acton:

. . . Your letters are inestimably profitable to me, as well as pleasurable. Now that Norman is dead—how miserably sad—I know *no* one who combines an expert knowledge of Italy with tastes *like my own*. You are deciding me, finally, against Florence. I shall always have (I hope) a not too miserable income—with the help of certain scraps of investments which still remain in America, but my difficulty is the inability to lay my hands on more than £2,000 to £2,500 to buy the property in the first place.

I am more and more inclined to believe that your prescription of Rome or Naples (the environs thereof, because I must have a garden) in the winter, and, if one can run to it, Venice in the summer, is the answer to my problem.

[Later] I think Lucca—where I went to see Lionel Fielden—ravishing, with a curious kind of mobile calm, like a series of animated early Chiricos, if he had been a greater artist.

There remains one further possibility—Sicily. Would you, *if you were completely free*, ever consider settling there yourself? Say at Taormina, or Bagheria. (I may add—to my confusion, and I hope not to yours—that I am *not* indifferent to certain amenities which I find a little dangerous, and difficult, in the North of Italy, but which, if my memory serves me, are both easy and unremarked at, shall we say, Taormina. Which, indeed, is noted historically for its *douceur de vivre* in this connection.)

It was during this summer that Brian figured in the farcical newspaper hunt there for the missing diplomat, Guy Burgess. Asolo had hit the front page headlines in June with a *Sunday Chronicle* exclusive story by their Rome reporter: 'Police I have spoken to in Asolo have no doubt that the Englishman at the Villa La Mura was Guy Burgess'. This newspaper claimed that a former member of the British Intelligence overheard a conversation in a bar in London to the effect that Burgess was hiding in Asolo. They flashed this news to their Rome reporter who pursued the unrewarding trail. 'I missed Burgess by seventy-two hours. He disappeared suddenly after a mysterious telephone call to the local police had warned them of his presence in the vicinity.' The local police entered into the spirit of the search with misplaced zeal, 'We did have such an Englishman here, . . . he was thick-set, about 5 ft. 8 in. high. He had a strong beard, and always wore a panama hat . . . he stayed with English people who for the past six months have been living here in the Villa La Mura, the Browning house.'

Sam was duly interviewed, and on being questioned about the man with the beard, 'looked taken aback. "That was a friend from home," was his explanation.' This particular red herring evaporated, except for a brief re-appearance in August when a Mr. J. L. Mellor wrote a letter to the *Observer*, as 'Father of Kemsley House Sunday Papers Sub-Chapel of the National Union of Journalists,' complaining of the *Observer's* holier-than-thou attitude towards 'The Maclean Case'. (The *Observer* had accused the press—especially the *Daily Express*—of intrusion, persecution and misrepresentation concerning Donald Maclean's wife's departure to Switzerland.) It was unfortunate that the accusing Mr. Mellor was also News Editor of the *Sunday Chronicle*, which fact prompted Philip Toynbee to write to the *Observer* (for whom he was Foreign Correspondent) that although the *Sunday Chronicle* correspondent had been clearly told that *he* was the man in the beard mistaken for Guy Burgess, the paper published a front page story headlined, 'Guy Burgess seen in Italy'.

This in turn led 'Critic' in the *New Statesman and Nation* to clear the air (if not the motives of the *Sunday Chronicle*) with the following explanation:

Some day a successor to Kipling will write a grand short story on how the village of Asolo became famous in 1952. It all began last May when an old friend of mine who was motoring in Italy fell into conversation with an Englishman in a café in this little mountain village. She was looking for somewhere for herself and her family to stay, and finding that they had mutual acquaintances, including various writers on this journal, she went back and had a yarn with him and his friend in the villa where they were living. It suddenly struck her that these two resembled Burgess and Maclean, and when she got back to England she compared photographs and found, she thought, a strong resemblance. She rang up to relate her discovery to this journal and also to a daily newspaper. A few minutes enquiry in this office were enough to show that one of her hosts had been Brian Howard, who used to write book reviews in the *New Statesman and Nation*. We informed the daily paper, which had put a reporter on the job; the editor thanked us for saving him further trouble. Oddly enough, that is not the end of the story. The *Sunday Chronicle* later published a front-page story on the subject . . .

The whole 'Burgess' episode ruffled, more than rattled, Brian, according to his letters to Benedict Nicolson (Editor of the *Burlington* magazine).

As soon as I can muster the necessary subscription I intend to take in the *Burlington*. It will be a great comfort out here, where one has so often to read about Art in these dago languages which I can't understand.

You will have heard about the absurd uproar here about Burgess. The horrid little reporter came *back* again to Asolo, and two London papers have rung Sam up. (Luckily the reporter did not come here to see me or Sam specifically: it was just a general rumour about Asolo.) But it is quietening down, I hope, now. As it is, I don't think that this fuss will have done me and Sam any good as people who are asking for permanent *cartes d'identités*. What a tedious, idiotic imbroglio. [Later] . . . My last letter seems, in recollection, too fussy, worried and worldly. It was only that I became alarmed at the notion of having a 'Communist' scandal added to my usual burdens of unpopularity—caused by *having* been tipsy too often for too long, and *being* an unrepentant sissy. Brazen, in fact. Since the 'twenties, and even the 'thirties indeed—the world seems to have become so retrograde that I am told people are refused permanent 'residence' in foreign countries at the drop of a hat. Still more speedily, at the flick of a *scented* red handkerchief.

About my living in Italy. England, except for country house life, has become so congested and melancholy. And I don't mean by that what anti-Labour Party people mean. There is no vitality, or fun, or affection, except of the most purely private kind, in England. I find it rather like some sort of inclement concentration camp. And there are too many ugly things to look at, and too little *open air*. Lastly, of course, even an *un*agreeable existence—economically—is getting so expensive in England.

At present, I am hot on the track of Norman Douglas' old house at Posilippo—and a monastery opposite the waterfalls at Tivoli. I am staying here till the end of July, and then I am going to Chianciano for a liver cure—which I'm told by Freya Stark's doctor I badly need . . .

Asolo's view of Brian was, I am told, far from idyllic. His neatly phrased reference to hoping to find certain 'amenities' in Sicily that were 'a little dangerous and difficult' in the North, was nothing but the truth. His diaries and correspondence give little away, but he still had an eye for the lively young 'Donatellos' of the locality and was continually in bad odour—not only with his neighbours but also with the indignant families of the complaisant boys, who took it upon themselves to show their disapproval in the most straightforward of physical ways.

Brian had always announced his particular nirvana to be a state of living with another man, equating perfect marriage, although realistic enough to know that there would be deficiencies on both sides. Yet he not only indulged in indiscriminate promiscuity but also encouraged Sam to follow suit, even going so far as to offer him on a plate to visiting friends and acquaintances with, 'Would you like to go to bed with Sam—I only allow him to sleep with old Etonians!' It is difficult to rationalise his avowed high standards of honesty, truth, faithfulness and values in general with his overt, one could almost say extrovert, sexual behaviour. In the face of Sam's continuing love and compassion Brian's compulsive promiscuity must be largely attributed to his highly developed aesthetic senses demanding that his cup of happiness be kept filled by newer and younger Ganymedes. (He professed to disapprove of sex without love.)

It seems impossible for most homosexuals to keep within faithful limits, in the way that many husbands and wives do despite equal temptations, and people tend to be more censorious of homosexual than heterosexual promiscuity, though why this should be is not clear unless the Victorian idea of 'married' women not enjoying sex still prevails. Brian was certainly to come in for his share of national disapproval on this score.

Joyce Murchie, who was living in one of the prettiest of the Asolo houses, remembers stimulating as well as horrific occasions. One day the late Archie Colquhoun was reading Manzoni out loud when Sam got bored but was quickly subdued by Brian's admonition: 'Be quiet, my dear, literature is my first enthusiasm—my second is you.' Another time it was Brian who had been reading out loud, Shakespeare's sonnets this time, when he outstayed his welcome and insulted a guest. His parting shot was pertinent and prophetic, as Joyce admits, she being invariably over-spent. 'Very well, dear. Since you insist, I'll leave now. It's a dear little house, I *do* hope you'll always have the money to keep it up.'

Despite his impossible behaviour on many occasions she still remembers with pleasure the excellent rose catalogue—a privately produced catalogue for one—that he prepared for her, giving the varieties, placing and times of planting to make the perfect rose garden.

How Lura Howard, who was living with them at this time (and looking the epitome of 'Mary Chess'—all pink and white) survived the Asolo era remains a mystery. Her niece, Carley, had visited them that summer, and fills in with her version of the times:

Most of the time at Asolo Brian was unspeakable. There was one terrible incident when we were driving back to Asolo from Venice. Brian said he had to stop at an inn on the way. He was a long time gone and when he came back Lura prudently put him on the front seat with Sam, next to the driver, leaving Lura and me in the back. Brian had either had a 'fix' or liquor. He began upbraiding Sam in various languages, and most expertly. Sam went whiter and whiter, but said nothing, except that every now and then he would hit Brian over the head, and Brian would lunge back. Lura loved every moment of it, but I was terrified. As Lura breathlessly said to Sam, 'This is madness, pure and simple.' How she loved a scene!

I once asked Sam why he put up with Brian, who was often so terrible to him, and he replied, 'one has to love. It is the only way.' [Other people have emphasised that Sam's life was enriched by Brian in many ways, despite the monumental rows, and that Sam had come to think of his rôle as a true vocation.]

It was about this time that Brian asked me to be the go-between with Tudie, as he longed to be reconciled with his father. But Tudie would have none of it. At this outcome Brian seemed sad but not angry, and genuinely and deeply regretful.

He had no idea quite how badly he had behaved during Carley's visit, and wrote to her (admittedly apologising for occasional misbehaviour) while doing his cure at Chianciano:

> ... I think that our fondness for one another has revived in all its old strength—if it ever, indeed, disappeared ... The doctor frightened me very much at first, because I misunderstood his *awful* French, and thought I had a very serious disease of the liver indeed. But it turned out to be something the nature of which I've already outlined. This functional disability, incidentally, helps to produce these outbursts of disgraceful and semi-insane irritation when I have a drop taken. '*Molto caratteristica*' he called it, of my particular complaint. I am not putting forward this condition of mine as a complete excuse—particularly when I think of how it probably originated—but I do think it lends understanding to the less pleasant side of my character ...

As for Brian's domiciliary status in Italy, it was not to prove as permanent as he hoped. The cure over, he stayed with Auden in Ischia and then went on to Rome, where the authorities told him he would now have to leave Italy for the statutory three days (having been resident for a year), and it seemed likely that he might have to do this three-day stint 'abroad' every three months. He decided to go back to England to see his mother who had returned there, but not to stay in London: 'I am not happy about London's effect on me. My hatred of it is now pathological.'

By early 1953 they were back in Italy, looking for a villa in Sicily, from where he wrote to his mother:

... I feel deeply that there must be an immediate 'digging-in'. You are not well, and I am frankly, mentally exhausted. I have used up too much on a selfish search for perfection plus economy.

You know, I sometimes really begin to suspect that I spent the age of eighteen to about thirty-two in pure selfishness, and thirty-two to forty-seven in an effort to forget it by means of alcohol. It is a distasteful thought. But the fact remains that I am OLD now—really old. I shall be fifty in three little years, and I've done NOTHING. The fact that I feel about thirty has nothing, alas, to do with it! I simply must get down to it, and NOT poetry. As usual, Wystan has given me, with all the tact in the world, a considerable reprimand. His words to Sam were less diplomatic. I am going to buy a big thick book, tomorrow morning and start, at least, keeping a daily journal. Baba has got to stop being Baba and start being Brian. Really.

[Later] ... We moved in to the Villa Valguarnera, Bagheria (near Palermo) yesterday. The house is on an eminence, and below, in every direction are lemon orchards. Beyond these, the sea (in two directions) and the lovely, very Greek, hazy-blue mountains. And always, just above my head the exquisite white marble statues on the Villa roof, gesticulating in the pure sapphire sky. It is a landscape-seascape in which ancient Greece and the 17th–18th century seems to join without any gap between.

My thoughts dwell more and more on writing, and even drawing and painting. Sam is more content, too, than he's been for ages. I think that just as our position, now, is at the end of the trail geographically, it is at the end of the trail of drama and my laziness. I really do believe that I feel a sort of peace, and common-sense, prevailing in me at last. My day-dreams, which are a great test with me, are no longer desperate refuges, but are concerned with *how* to *express* things. Perhaps, after all, it will prove advantageous to have 'wasted' so many years. Perhaps the reservoir has been filling, unbeknownst to us all. Because I KNOW I am a real artist, in the way that my father is not. I don't know if I'm a good one; I know I am a *real* one.

Brian must have been in contact with Stephen Spender again, for he received a letter from him at this time: '... I am very thrilled to hear that you are writing about Sicily for us. I do look forward to having some real writing in the magazine (*Encounter*). Do you think you could also write us an article about German Expressionist painting? I think this was a great and neglected movement, and I know you share my feelings—and have more than my knowledge—about it ...' But again no results came of this encouragement. In July they were going 'off' Sicily and temporarily 'on' to Mallorca because of its cheapness and climate, a welcome change from the heat, flies, and midges that they were suffering in Bagheria. But they were still hoping to live permanently in Italy. Lura Howard must have presaged trouble as Brian wrote:

... With that instinct of yours which, in the middle ages, would have made you into some sort of seer or prophetess—you were right about the failure to get a visa here (and poor Sam, too). The Prefect of Police of Palermo has been warned by Rome *not* to grant me a visa—as the British Embassy had told them that we were 'undesirable' people. When asked in what way, the answer was, 'Nothing specific. No special complaint. Simply undesirable.' If I do not leave by the 20th July I shall be arrested. To be chased out of Italy as well as France is really as much as I can take . . .

We sail for Barcelona, and from there to Mallorca . . .

The rest of the summer was spent in Mallorca, but Brian decided to rent a house in Torremolinos for the winter and following spring. Hardly was he installed before he suffered his third expulsion. As he wrote to John Banting:

We had a lovely early 18th-century house in Torremolinos, near Malaga— the best climate in Europe—cotton, sugarcane, and all the things that just fail to grow in the S. of France—when I was thrown out—in December. A message arrived from Madrid that I had been heard criticising the regime in a Malaga café. Perfectly true. A police spy was sitting behind me. Served me right, in a way, for going there. But I'd never been in a Fascist country before and hadn't got used to the necessity of whispering ordinary statements. This left poor mamma in charge of the house, and has been terribly worrying and inconvenient. Especially now that I am not well . . .

He had gone for a medical check-up in Gibraltar, and thence to Tangier with Sam, from where he wrote to his mother in March 1954:

We have now settled down here, and I am eating like a horse. Don't worry about drink. I am on my 'way out' of that particular danger. A horror of it is growing in me. No news about our French permits, and no letter about my being treated as a foreign resident. I don't understand why this last as I am ill and have completed my four years' probation . . .

His subsequent letters to John Banting show only too well the danger signs ahead:

No—I am not *very* ill, but I have got a touch of T.B. I am not a hospital case, but I have to take so many milligrams of these new pills, and every fourth day I have an intra-muscular injection of Streptomycin. This is to go on for two months and then I must have a second photograph taken by the Tomograph, which is a new-ish kind of X-ray. It takes photographs of the lesion, or spot, in depth—three-dimensionally, as it were. The actual lesion is at the top of the right lung, and consists of a five or six year old scar, which was 'dead', but which suddenly came to life. I went to the head of the Gibraltar Chest Hospital—a European expert, and he said it could be cured in from three to six months by what he calls 'conventional' methods (meaning no surgery) if I rested a *great* deal during the day, and cut down my smoking and drinking to one glass of wine with meals, and ten cigarettes a day. Curiously enough, I have very nearly succeeded in doing this, with the help of certain sedatives. A great thing is to put on weight, because I have become quite a skeleton during these last six months. The resting during the day is no change for *me*!

There is only one disagreeable aspect. They tell me that at my age (nearly forty-nine), I cannot take this same *pillule-piqûre* cure ever again, if I fail to make it work this time. I shall have to have an operation to collapse the lung. Tiresome, to say the least.

[Later] I am writing you in odd and charming surroundings. Namely, a café in the wickedest town in the world—and in the wickedest place in the town. I am in the Socco Chico, or Little Market, which is really a small square of shops and cafés, where the naughtiest and most shameless of the male whores (not all Arabs), bootblacks, peanut-sellers, tourists, money-changers and beggars all gather, of a late afternoon, to show off their various wares. Everyone within sight, from the tiny children to the elderly, fat waiters in tarbooshes, is for sale. And the hubbub is appalling. The lights are just coming on in MANGHARAN'S CELEBRATED SHIRTS opposite me, and the smell of Kief cigarettes is asphyxiating. (I've tried it, no effect, but I'm told one ought to eat it, in the form of tiny hot cross buns.) Sam, at the same table, is flirting with his shoe-shine boy, who is a blackamoor, squodgy nose, but good teeth and a charming smile: seventeen I guess. The other person at the table is a nice, if slightly long-winded, ex-Harvard creature of forty who is endeavouring to cure himself of morphinomania by taking this new medicine which the Germans invented during the war. There are several trade names for it. He uses two. Eukodal and Heptanal. Unfortunately, the effects are so much stronger, and more delicious than morphine *itself* that he now spends his whole time running from chemist to chemist buying it—and spends all his money on it, too. I, myself, have experimented with it (with the excuse that it *is*, genuinely, used, among other things, for suppressing the tubercular cough—and really, it is quite *extraordinary*. Especially, I find, Heptanal. One loses all desire for alcohol (excellent, for me) and I walk around in a benign dream. Also, it has *none* of the injurious effects of morphine. The only lie that its makers tell about it is that it does not produce euphoria (e.g. *pleasure*), but, of course, it *does*. However, since it cannot do me harm of any sort, I *do* take it. Here, it can be got without a prescription. (Nothing is easier to get than the drugs themselves here, of course.) I take two to four tablets, and then have to wait one and a half to two hours, because it takes that long to get going. I do *not* drink with it.

At the risk of seeming redundant—I repeat that since it is a *medicine*, employed by doctors to replace morphine, and is employed in tuberculous cases to suppress coughing, I cannot see that it can be physically harmful, in any way. And since, at the same time, it is quite heavenly—I think it rather a find.

If one keeps out of the bars, which I *have* to, Tangier is not expensive. And it is certainly extremely amusing. *Anything* goes, as they say . . .

Anyway, nothing is going to get ME down. Neither Franco, nor the tubercular bacillus. To hell with the whole lot!

But this was, of course, the beginning of the end. The end of his addiction to alcohol: the start of his dependence on drugs.

At last other things began to move in the right direction. The Bank of England Exchange Control finally agreed to Brian becoming a foreign resident, and soon after—in early June—the long-awaited letter arrived from Paris telling him that he could now come back to France whenever he wanted to, at least for three months. Then he would have to ask for an extension for three or six months more, and after that he should apply for a *carte de séjour* for a year. The only stipulation from his Paris contact was that he should be discreet about his 'sympathies' while living on the *côte* during this period.

Brian wasted no time in getting back to France, and by mid-June 1954 he was installed in a rented villa at Beaulieu, near Villefranche, from where he wrote to Benedict Nicolson, asking him to be an executor (together with Peter Watson) of his Will:

... I contracted a touch of T.B. in Spain, where we had this lovely early 18th-century house in Torremolinos, near Malaga. I thought it was the best climate in Europe till I realised about the constant wind—also there was nothing to do but exchange drinks with David (Tennant) and fight unending verbal duels with him, the normal weapons being a copy each of Milton. Also there is something horribly sad and isolated about Spain and a sort of mixed arrogance and ignorance. Most numbing. And I got into hot water through talking quite normal politics in a Malaga café ...

Luckily, my mamma found this lovely little house here (to rent)—La Bastide—and oh, the peace, the good weather, the roses, nightingales, milk, frogs, fireflies and butter!

[Later] I should have answered long since, thanking you for consenting to administer, one day, my titanic fortune. We are struggling to buy an old Provençal farm behind Nice (L'Oli). Theoretically and ideally, I should far prefer, of course, to live in Italy. There is a terrible dearth of architecture and museums in the S. of France. But other and unworthy considerations, such as climate, and accessibility have finally swayed me. If I was rich, I would plump for a large mansion between Florence and Rome—as Palladian as possible, although Palladio, alas, seems to have restricted himself to the Veneto, largely. His pupils, too. Anyway, all that is a dream; and this little farm is charming, and only four miles inland from Nice, the only town down here which remains alive in the winter.

I agree with you, Ben, that Sam deserves sanctification, but I suspect that you have little idea of how testing it can sometimes be, dear, to live with a saint. They are inclined, for example, to monopolise one, rather. And behind every saint—except the indubitably tip-top ones—there stands, arms akimbo, a nanny, and behind every nanny there lurks an Iron Maiden of Nuremberg, albeit minus spikes. However, I am sensible of how complimentary and inestimably precious it is for an old rascal like myself to—somehow—retain the affections of someone so much younger, and I know I don't deserve it.

... I read Mr. (John) Berger regularly and esteem his knowledge and candour, but oh dear! How I disagree. If *art engagé* is what he is after I can't have mine *dégagé* enough.

Brian and Sam were busy planning the re-decoration of 'L'Oli', or 'Olive Pavilion', as Brian called the farm house behind Nice, when the news came of his father's death, in October 1954. His Will turned out to be a great surprise to everyone in that he left half his personal estate (apart from specified legacies) to Lura and half to the woman who had remained his faithful companion throughout the years since his separation. After their death the British estate (or the capital from its disposal) was to pass to Brian. This completely altered his financial situation in theory, but as will be seen, not with much immediate or eventual benefit. Most of Tudie's estate consisted of his collection of pictures, but there was unexpected capital in America which his brother-in-law, Avery Robinson, had considerably increased over the years by clever investing. Tudie had intended bequeathing some of his pictures to the Tate Gallery but changed his mind as he was not 'in sympathy with its modernistic development of recent years'.

Brian's reaction to this news was somewhat surprising. He wrote to Lura, who was in London, from Villefranche:

> ... I cannot share *anyone's* pleasure at our having received more from Daddy than we expected. I find I am *only* glad for your sake. Sam is amazed, but there it is. I feel nothing but a profound unhappiness, and an even more profound sense of having 'left undone those things which I ought to have done'. That last letter of his—I recognised it at the time, and I more or less *told you so*—was a cry of despair, an appeal for help. I am sorry, but I cannot see it otherwise. 'A cottage in your vicinity,' or whatever it was he said. Oh, what have we DONE, Mother? He loved *you*. And, perhaps, he could have learned again to love me. It is quite true that an actual meeting—with you, or with me, or with both—might have been a failure. On the other hand, it might have made such a difference to the last weeks of his life. And, at least, we would have the knowledge that we had done our best.
>
> We did not do our best. I am sorry, but this is what I shall ALWAYS feel. Thank you for telling me about the flowers, and the Bach, and the hymn. I should have been there ...

Allanah Harper, who still lives in France, reminisces about Brian at this, and other, times in the south of France:

> What a strange mixture was Brian. For instance, he disliked his father and said the most unflattering things about him, had refused to speak to him after he had deserted his mother. Yet, when he heard the news of his father's death he was terribly upset. He arrived at my house in the south of France, saying that he must sleep in my room, he was lonely and broken

314

by his father's death. 'He left me his collection of paintings, this has touched me and I am full of remorse.' Brian was in tears. 'I will sleep on the mat if you turn me away, you are my oldest friend, you cannot turn me away.' I regret to say that I did not let him stay because I was leaving early the next morning for London. I had closed the house and I knew that if he stayed the night he would not leave the following morning. And what would I not find on my return?

The front door would be unlocked, the wine drunk, the bed unmade, and the cat in the refrigerator. Had he not put a cat in the ice-box one night during the Phoney War, in a house in Sanary in which I was staying? Brian had refused to leave after dinner, had settled himself in the kitchen and continued to drink until he was incapable of moving. As we left him to go to bed, he was saying to the cat who was scratching the ice-box, hoping to be given some *friture du pays*, 'You naughty puss, if you want to get in I will put you in'. It did not enter our heads that Brian would carry out his threat. For some reason Sybille Bedford felt hungry at about three o'clock in the morning—and she found the cat frozen in the ice-box. It was stiff but still alive. When I came to her room after breakfast she was still in bed with the cat lying on her, with a constantly renewed hot-water bottle on top of it. Sybille had saved its life, and what was the more admirable, she did not like cats.

Brian was horrified when he heard what he had done. 'The cat was too irritating,' he said, 'it wanted to go in, so I put it in. I must have gone to sleep and have forgotten about it.' Brian laughed his slightly diabolical laugh, his humour covering a multitude of sins. One loved his malicious smile so full of amazement, that people could do, or say the things they did.

I was a constant target for Brian's teasing; in fact during the last ten years I was apprehensive of our meetings. One never knew what he was going to say or do. When I married a Frenchman, Brian said, looking down from his height, 'Allanah, how could you marry a tiny Frog?' I thought my husband was going to punch him, but he refrained. My godchild (a pretty spoiled girl whom he had asked me to bring for a drink in a bar in Cannes), on observing that Brian seemed unwilling to pay for the drinks, had the courage to tell him to do so. Brian turned on her with disdain and said, 'You must have been brought up in the gutter, a lady does not mention money'. She burst into tears and said, 'If Mummy could hear that, she would call you a lounge lizard'. On another occasion I had asked a Catholic lady to luncheon and she had the misfortune to mention the dogma of the Assumption. Brian gave her a look of astonished amusement—'You can't believe that a Jewish lady went up to heaven in a balloon!'

I wish my memory was not so poor, that I could remember more of the very funny, witty, but often hurting remarks made by Brian to people he considered middlebrow or middle class. He refused to see the pathetic and sometimes touching side of people who pretended to be what they were not and were making an unsuccessful effort to live up to those they thought to be 'the cat's whiskers'. But had Brian been more charitable what wit we would have lost, of what laughter been deprived.

Despite obvious signs of ill health in Brian, his mother was unwilling to believe that he did, at any time, suffer from tuberculosis, and when he asked her to find out about a new anti-T.B. medicine called Pas when she was in London she went instead to a doctor for advice. Brian replied to her news:

> You go to all the trouble, darling, and expense of going to a Harley Street doctor—who writes about my 'alleged' tubercular spot. No less than *four* specialists have not alleged, but stated, that it is there. Your doctor categorically states—without laying eyes on me—that what is the matter with me is neurasthenia. Now not only is neurasthenia a Victorian word which is hardly ever used now, but it has scarcely any meaning left to it. In so far as it has meaning it means 'nervous debility', or 'weakness'. My nerves are not in a particularly robust state, but I am not having a nervous breakdown.
>
> . . . I feel almost wholly responsible for the acquisition of L'Oli, as I have a terrible feeling that, especially since Daddy's death, you would far rather settle in England? You say, 'Our luck (I do not call it that) has swung around the entire circle'. I disagree with you entirely. We have not suddenly become rich, because this is what you imply, you know. What HAS happened is, that we can now make a place like L'Oli the pretty, comfortable, enviable place it could easily be. And that's ALL.

The final buying of L'Oli was complicated by the fact that Brian's permission to live in France was not yet free of strings. There was a real threat that he might have to leave France every three months, not just the Alpes Maritimes department. He visited Paris in November to try and sort out the problem, but was despondent about the result when he wrote to his mother: 'There's always the old horror of not having money, and, still worse, not being able to *prove* I have any. I still can't really. It's at the bottom of the whole thing, as my permit contact here hinted.'

Despite the seemingly endless complications Brian was sure in his own mind that L'Oli—at last—was going to be his permanent home, and on this assumption asked John Banting to design his book-plate, based on the Greek coins of Taras—a boy riding on a dolphin, with somewhere in the design his initial 'B' (shaped like a fallen heart) containing the two words he had finally chosen as his definitive motto: 'They are, curiously enough, Sarah Bernhardt's— *QUAND MEME* . . . They seem to me to be the perfect crystallisation IN TWO WORDS of the non-"believing", humanist, optimist-cum-pessimist that I have become. Also, it is a quiet way of saying "And boo to you, too".

Of the Taras series of coins he wrote: 'They are really too wonderful, and I have a "thing" about them. A violent thing.' He did not start collecting these coins for another two years, when he spent some £1,000 at Spinks on thirty-five or so which he kept in a special box monogrammed 'B.H.'. (They were all resold through Spinks after his death.)

Virtually Brian's last vestige of political activity was recounted in a letter to John Banting in November 1954, while he was undergoing yet another T.B. cure in Zurich. He was already suffering from alcoholism, and drug addiction—

316

largely due to the anti-T.B. pills and sedatives given to him earlier in the year in Tangier—as well as the recurring T.B. It makes a sad, if characteristic, end to his political efforts:

I am having myself *competently* examined here—because T.B. must be got rid of. The signs, they say, are hopeful. Such a pity, just when we were getting down to work on the Nice place. But it couldn't be helped. I have become terribly nervous, in a deep way—and what makes it so ridiculous is that all I have fought for, for ten years, has suddenly arrived. But it is ten years too late, in a way. Unless I can shrug it all off—which of course I WILL. I have great reserves of strength, mainly spiritual and mental. Thank heavens. But they have been severely tried.

Erika Mann is here with her papa, and he is unexpectedly enthusiastic about my idea of having a last appeal made, in the form of a letter to *The Times*, against the re-armament of western Germany. In other words, to get Russia to agree to the total disarmament of *all* Germany, which there is still just a chance of getting through. Otherwise, of course, we are done for. Bevan is right. Because Germany, which is once more the most powerful (astounding, but true) country in Europe, is determined upon a war of revenge, to recover her lost territories (the East part).

The letter, which will be formulated in English by me—though, of course, not signed by me—will be signed by Mann, Einstein, Albert Schweitzer (these are certain), and, then, we *hope*, Forster, Russell and Toynbee (Philip's pa). And Faulkner to represent America. For various reasons Malraux, Mauriac, and the Italians won't do. Because it must be neither pro- nor anti-Communist, but it must be, covertly anti-American, and anti-Churchill-Eden. I think, if I get this done, I will have accomplished my 'mission'.

Anonymously, but truly. Of course, nobody will pay any attention—I mean THOSE IN POWER—but what else can one do? What more? What less? In a phrase, the letter will say: *Either you stop, NOW, or . . .*

Erika Mann writes in retrospect:

Brian chose to ignore his illness, though there were plenty of doctors whose advice he sought, only to continue a sort of life which would have turned the healthiest man into a wreck. And while all this was happening, when he knew that his legacy had come too late and that he was doomed, there were many occasions on which he seemed to be quite his old self, radiant, witty, full of delicate tenderness, at one with all mankind, furiously angry at all the stupid and evil things of this world, passionately on the side of everything good, and especially of peace. It was as though he felt certain of a long life ahead or as though he had a beloved son who was threatened by nuclear annihilation. Passionately he sought ways and means whereby mankind's destruction could be avoided, and he wept bitterly when it was borne in upon him that nobody—no individual, no group of Nobel prize-winners, no Pope, no God even, could avert the final catastrophe unless the misguided, obstinately insane human race itself took a hand and made an end of the lunacy.

It is difficult to judge how seriously ill Brian was at that time. From Zurich he went to Vienna, from where he wrote to his mother: 'My youth is returning to me both physically and mentally.' Then something went wrong with the plans for buying L'Oli, and although they were still in a position to look for an alternative from their rented villa at Beaulieu, it must have added to their worries as yet another setback. On top of that Sam had to have an emergency operation to remove his appendix, which resulted in the doctors saying that he had adhesions, scars and traces of a long illness. Brian's teeth were also giving him trouble, and they both had to spend a depressing Christmas in Vienna, with Sam still convalescing. During this uneasy period Brian wrote to his mother:

If, in one month from now Sam had not been able to have an instant operation, he might have died. You see—I live under the shadow of two dreadful things. The most important is your death. For which I must simply 'go into training' from now on. Because, if it hits me at a bad moment, I am not sure that I can stand it. The other dreadful thing is Sam's death. For heaven's sake, let us all get into a HOME, where we can entrench ourselves, as against bombs during the war.

The following note to his mother, probably written at this time, shows the almost unbelievably strong ties still binding them—for better or for worse.

End lines to a Poem—*I have betrayed myself, but never you*
And never therefore Love.

One thing at *least*—becomes the *must*. One thing I fought for, cheated for, threw up everything for. It would have been *far better* if I'd worked at the same time as doing this, would have made you and myself happier, but *short of* working, I allowed NOTHING to come between us, to equal, to attack, to rival, to destroy, to do anything. This utterly came first with me.

I made you proof against my lies, my truths, my desires, my failures and successes. Recognising in you, as I did, bottomless invincible truth, loyalty and goodness. Timeless, forever, I responded and *wholly*.

NOW I can call on, if necessary, Love to Save me, even to RE-MAKE me. I have *earned* this—(a), and (b) it is the *only* thing I have earned, ever. I *relied* on Love; I gave it everything, and it is now *re-paying* me with my particular SALVATION. It *equates* religion with me.

I could use as images of what 'you' are things such as the ruler pointing on the blackboard, *plus* the blackboard. The sum that comes out right, *plus* the figures. For example, all that bystanders see in you is a sum. I see the answer. And the sum happens to be my life.

Also—the eldorados one dreams of, the dream islands, the riches, the masterpiece hanging (for example) on the wall, I have no need of them any more. They are You.

The Eggs in One Basket DANGER. This I must risk. Your death. I do risk it. It is my great risk. But it kills the fear of death in *me* while *you* are alive. Here lies my one great sin and selfishness towards you. I hope as I never hoped anything to die before you, since to die simultaneously is too much to hope. This is wrong, because it will hurt you. GO INTO THIS, THINK. It is the unresolved part of the poem. *Very* difficult.

(This was written with no alcoholic or medical influence and is the nearest I have yet got to the moral and spiritual basis of you and self.)

A New Year letter sounded more cheerful: '1955 is going to be Our Special Year. We are going to have our house. So many times you and I have written, or telegraphed one another "All is well". Well, it IS well, at last, I know it. And when word comes from France, I'll be on my way.'

But two weeks later he took yet another new notebook, with an expensive leather cover, and started once more:

THE FIRST DIARY—Munich—21st January 1955.

In a month I shall be fifty. What has kept me from writing, hitherto, was—first—too much self-criticism, perfectionism. Secondly, a swelling guilt, I have it as others have elephantiasis.

I must, it seems, return to the scene of my first, innocent crimes. Like a newspaper murderer. (I murder myself, year after year.) Here I am again in Munich, where it all began. Once, I had not only talent, but what English people call 'character'. By which, they mean the power to refrain. Now, I have neither. Will has left me, and the capacity truthfully to imagine— vision is leaving. I consider myself damned . . .

This mood did not last as he was soon writing to Heywood Hill:

Thank you for your sweet *and* entertaining letter. Yours and Nancy's (Mitford) are unfailing. Nancy told me two stories which I liked . . . she was sitting next to Cocteau at a dinner, and he told her that he had become worried at having forgotten the birthdays of a godson of his for some time. So he bought a very, very expensive pink velvet rabbit, about three feet tall, and sent it. He received a courteous, but chilly, reply. His remark was, '*Il parait que mon filleul est Colonel*'. The other, which I adore, is as follows: in November last, Diana Cooper got a telegram from a dear friend of hers connected with the house of Dior, saying, '*Je t'offre Cecil Beaton*'. Alarmed, she stayed indoors, and made extensive and indiscreet enquiries by telephone. It turned out that Dior had paid Cecil the compliment of naming one of his new dresses after him . . .

In February Brian heard the bad news that he had permission to live anywhere in France *except in the Alpes Maritimes and the Var*; he could only visit those areas for ten days at a time. Eventually permission would be given—but not yet. He was terribly discouraged and could not think of a solution to the problem. There seemed no point in buying a house in an area from which he was disbarred as a resident. Meanwhile he and Sam went to Arosa for the mountain air, and to see his old friend, Erika Mann, who was making a film nearby. There Brian had himself X-rayed again, this time by Thomas Mann's doctor, and found his T.B. no worse.

He went briefly to Paris to settle some financial problems arising out of Tudie's Will with his mother, but the meeting was disastrous. Lura was trying to set up a Trust from the American investments left outright to *her* by Tudie, from which it seemed obvious to Brian that he was not going to be able to anticipate what he had naturally assumed to be his eventual capital, let alone advise on the present investments from which he and his mother depended for income. The family conference was not a success, and Brian apologised to his mother for his behaviour.

Sam persuaded him to take a cure at Vichy, explaining to Lura that he had had another complete mental collapse, was also having serious trouble with his liver, and his teeth were poisoning him as well. The fact that Lura had still not produced the money to buy a house must have been partly responsible for this last breakdown. One piece of good news came in the form of a letter from the Nice Consulate to the effect that the original complaints against Brian in 1950 had been lodged at Menton 'by a number of English people who he had insulted in the street'. Nothing worse. It seemed that the ban might be going to be lifted after five long years. Brian's letter to his mother after her birthday visit to him in Berne during March explained the reasons for his Paris outburst over finance:

... On the plea of my irresponsibility and my 'mind not working' etc. you are not being straightforward with me. Your decision to put half Daddy's American money on trust for Stephen [her great-nephew]—which you have a perfect *legal* right to do—was such a tremendous shock to me—because I think it a morally unjustifiable action—that I reacted with inexcusable rudeness ... there is something frighteningly disingenuous about the whole way that our financial affairs are being presented to *me*. Why was my power of attorney needed to facilitate the implementation of my father's American Will? I was left nothing, by entail or otherwise, in that Will. You can reasonably anticipate inheriting a large sum in America, also from the sale of the pictures, the Bayham Place freehold, and from certain investments of your own—yet despite all this you say it is impossible for you to borrow on interest a few thousand pounds to buy the house you have found. I find this very, very strange.

Last night you agreed with a ridiculous suggestion of Sam's that I should get on a boat and go to India, or somewhere equally remote. I have been a sort of outcast long enough, and this endless flight and exile is making me increasingly ill and miserable. I have been a 'displaced person' too long. The fundamental idea behind all our actions has been to establish a *home*. For us all. A home large enough, just, to contain us all three without sitting in one another's laps.

Even though the sale of Brian's father's pictures at Christies (in November 1955) brought Lura Howard some £20,000 and she was now receiving just under

£1,000 a year from the Howard estate as well, there seemed no great change in the pattern of Brian's life. However, she did soon afterwards buy a house near Nice 'behind my [Brian's] back'—Le Verger, Col de Bast, Vallon Obscur. John Banting remembers her looking magnificent there, imperially directing with a walking stick the pruning of the orange trees from the balcony, with her long hair and negligee flowing. She lacked close friends by now (many having died) and seemed to depend on her varied servants for loyalty and affection. She was interested in food but never ordered meals, or even commented on them to the cook. She once said, 'If you praise a dish you keep on having it too often'. Of course she thrived on intrigue, could never be direct—and this got worse as she became older. She could not sort out the truth from the fantasy, and then suddenly she would be completely on the spot when any question of money was in the air. When Brian and Sam went to help her with the new house Brian found his mother, as he wrote to Sybille Bedford, 'too overwhelming, too bossy, *sweet* as she is . . .'

The death in 1956 of Peter Watson moved Brian deeply. To John Banting he wrote, 'Of Peter I can't yet speak. He was my greatest friend, and *The Times* obituary, splendid and full of praise as it was, didn't do him justice. He was an angel, and never said or did a mean or ignoble thing his whole life long. His criticisms of me, lately, were earned, alas. I could make a list of present-day, celebrated painters and writers who owe their *all* to him. He wouldn't even tell me their names—I knew through other sources. Enough.'

It was not until a few weeks later that Brian heard of his legacy from Peter, about which he wrote to Nancy Mitford in Paris:

Peter, *angel* that he was, has left me £2,000 and I feel that I will be happier if I simply give it all in the form of presents—the kind one can *never* afford, usually—to Sam and my mamma. So I'm giving Sam half of it, for a small sailing yacht, and half I am going to FORCE my mamma to allow me to spend on her . . . What I want you to do, darling, is to take her out to look at a fur coat and clothes when she comes to Paris. Mamma is now eighty, but looks and 'is' scarcely seventy. I want her to have a good fur coat costing, say £500. I don't want her to have that horrid old-lady black Persian lamb. Those tight curls. Awful. What about summer ermine, pale caramel—rather delicious? Next, I want her to have two good dresses . . .

While Brian was writing about Sam's dream-boat, and the clothes for his mamma, Sam was reporting progress from Vienna (where Brian was being 'built up' for a T.B. operation) to his 'Aunt Lura'. He was taking over more and more responsibility for organising Brian's life. His 'vocation' was being well and truly fulfilled, even though it must have been hard going and despairing on many occasions. He wrote:

Another slight problem is the Eubine. Although Brian gets an allowance of it daily, it is *not* considered a good thing, and in any case it has to stop some time. (The French authorities would prefer it to stop too, I imagine . . .) It means a sort of disintoxication cure, possibly sleep for three or four days, and then the nervousness will disappear, and he will manage without it. Apart from its possible ill effects, it costs about fifteen shillings a day. Alcohol has ceased to become a problem, thank God, and there have been no slip-ups since we have been away. It makes the whole difference between happiness and despair ... so I think we are on the straight road at last.[2]

As for Brian himself he wrote in comparatively good spirits from his Viennese clinic to Cyril Connolly:

... I want to ask your advice about a publisher for my autobiography—or memoirs, with which I have been fiddling for a year.[3] I seem to have got really started on them now, though they won't be finished for another year and then it will only be Vol. I, because I digress a great deal. I feel, Cyril—even if I 'say it myself'—that I shall probably be able to choose my own publishers without fear of refusal, so which publishers shall it be? Whose are yours? I feel Murrays are the most reassuring. Yet who pays most? And then what about American rights? Because it just MIGHT turn out to be a good seller ...

For convenience's sake when next in London Brian was hoping to be proposed as a temporary member of White's Club, as he told Cyril: 'I'm sure I'm far too much—still—of a notorious, old sissy to get in, but I thought a pardon might be granted to such a staid and chastened invalid as I seem now to have become.'

Brian did not, after all, have the T.B. operation but returned to London in the autumn for further tests, taking a flat in Curzon Place (White's obviously not having afforded him 'a place to sit down'). It was now Sam's turn for bad luck, and he was suddenly refused a permanent visa to live in France, ostensibly owing to his lack of proof of financial resources. But there could have been other reasons. It appeared that Sam was also in need of 'sedatives', and although Brian was entitled to regular amounts (and indeed bought far more than his proper 'dose'), Sam had no such prescription. And with 'sedatives' I fear one must by now include 'hard drugs'.

From London Brian wrote to his mother, who had stayed in France, on New Year's Eve (1956):

... I am very shaken by Sam's not getting a visa and alarmed that they may not grant me one. It was obviously the Eubine Court case (in Paris) that went against Sam—therefore it will go against me, which would be

---

[2] In the mid-1950s, it was probably acceptable that addiction to 'sedatives' was preferable to straight alcoholism. The drug problem some ten years later would seem to give reason to question this supposition.

[3] Cyril jokingly suggested *Nights* (or *Knight*) *of Insult* as an apt title (from 'Nights of insult let you pass' in Auden's poem *Lay your sleeping head, my love*). Brian's papers showed no evidence of an autobiography, although the *Eton Candle* correspondence was carefully packeted, together with a few complimentary letters about his later poems, and one or two of his innumerable half-finished notebooks had pencilled comments—largely unfavourable—written in at a later date.

disastrous. I think the wisest thing to do is to return as a tourist. If I were the owner of Le Verger and could send in my application with papers proving this, I don't think the Eubine case serious enough to stop my getting a permanent visa. But I can't. The police said at the time that possibly nothing would happen—in any case to me, since Eubine had been prescribed for me—but that Sam might get fined a little. And now here we are fined £45 each—and the case reported in the papers. It's terrible, really. With hints of 'trafficking' and prison. I should have attended the case, or at least sent in the medical certificates asked for by the French lawyer—but by the time his letter was forwarded to me here it was too late . . .

This is the last letter of the old year. 1957 is going to be OUR great year, *yours and mine*—the year we start out in OUR creation—Le Verger. I can't imagine a year more fraught with importance, for us, and with potential happiness and satisfaction.

. . . About my coming back, there is the question of my visa. If France refuses me a visa for the SECOND TIME in my life it will be virtually impossible to get anything done about it. And NOTHING, now, will induce me to consent to the sale of Le Verger. I already FEEL of it as ours, don't you? I am perfectly content to live in it on a renewable, temporary *carte de séjour* for years—if needs be. I already *love* it.

Lastly, the question of Sam's boat. Well, it seems that if you have a boat built which is accepted by, and printed in, Lloyds as A1, it retains its value (unlike a motor car) for about from ten to twenty years. But it must be designed and built by a tip-top yacht yard. Of teak. So I have decided to ask my friend Jack Jones to build a small sailing boat, plus engine, to the most modern design, of teak, with every possible labour-saving gadget on it. And nylon sails. It will have berths for four, a shower, a kitchen, refrigerator, electric light, radio—and everything imaginable. It will cost, £3,800. £2,000 of this is Peter's, £1,800 I am going to ask you to let me have out of the English capital. The solicitor agrees about this. *Taras II*, as it will be called, will not only be the one thing Sam has always wanted, but also a transportable house. If the French remain tiresome, all Sam has to do—at no expense—is sail calmly down the coast to Italy. And back again. Best of all, Jack and a friend of his are going to sail it down to Villefranche from Suffolk in July, *free*.

Sam found out that they could hire out the boat during the season for a minimum of £150 a month, so that in this way it would prove an investment. He wrote to tell Lura of this, and to say that Brian rested most of the time in London, only rarely going out. They could think of nothing but the beautiful boat and all its furnishings, which Brian described untiringly to his mother:

The cabin beds are going to be proper beds, with coloured linen sheets and blankets and pillows. We have ship-to-shore radio-telephone, and a fascinating apparatus called a Depth Sounder which means we can nose into little unknown bays and inlets and be absolutely safe. There's going to be automatic hot water in the shower, the little fridge has one tray for ice cubes, and there's the most beautiful compass imaginable, cradled in such a way that its face is always horizontal, no matter at what angle the yacht is. Inside the cabin it's all shining polished mahogany—very Edwardian in the best sense. And we shall fly the flag of the Royal Harwich Yacht Club. Although the lists have long been closed the Admiralty are going to GIVE Sam a lovely bronze ship's bell—such a compliment. . . . Very soon, now, we'll have our hands full doing the most delightful thing in the *world*, which is creating a garden. Moreover, in creating the human atmosphere of Le Verger, which is going to be full of LOVE, happiness and CALM. Because we are safe, now. No one can hurt us up there. And even if, as I think, our income turns out to be smaller than we anticipated, it will be enough. The very thought of Le Verger fills me with a sense of PEACE. There is nothing on this earth that can get you and I and Sam 'down'. We—us three—are *invincible*, believe me. And inseparable.

. . . Now about doctors. Anne Hill has got fussed about me, and took the trouble to find out the name (she is a real angel to me) of *the* greatest lung specialist in England, who is Sir Geoffrey Marshall. I am having new X-rays made—then his opinion will be definitive.

Brian and Sam spent a few days with the Tom Dribergs, Brian writing in their Visitors' Book: '. . . a week-end so gay, so comfortable and so happy that it has made me (B) seriously doubt the wisdom of having built a house in France.' About the same time Brian went to Oxford for the night, with John Sutro to dine with the Roy Harrods, whom he had not seen for some fourteen years. He wrote of it as 'a wonderful "homecoming", if you know what I mean'. John Sutro remembers:

I kept in touch with Brian right to the end. He was still very funny and a sympathetic personage. My wife, who only met him after the war, found him fascinating. The last time I saw him was when he suggested spending a weekend in Oxford. We went down in my car, and he was then very ill-looking and emaciated. He had to have a drug injection as soon as we arrived at the Randolph, for which a doctor had to be brought in. We had dinner with Roy Harrod and recalled the past.

The next day he insisted on walking about in Canterbury Quad, where his old rooms had been, and after lunch with Roy at the Randolph he said he wanted to go to Skindles for tea. I can't think why.[4] It was utterly deserted and very *triste*, so we drove back to London. Brian was charming and kept talking about the past. He had a photographic memory, and said he was going to write his memoirs. He then went back to France, and I never saw him again. Now the book that Brian would have written has had to be written about him.

Sir Roy Harrod also fills out this occasion with his last recollections of Brian:

[4] Probably nostalgia for those illicit bicycle rides from Eton.

324

I did not see him much following his Oxford years, and his group did not keep together like the Bloomsbury group. I remember Brian visiting me at Oxford after the Nazis had got into power. He was just back from Germany. He had a very deep and passionate sense of disgust at the Nazi ideology. His sensitive and sharp intuition enabled him to understand the true inwardness of the situation much more quickly than most Englishmen seemed able to do at that time. He sat there telling me the horror story, drip, drip, drip, in that quiet, emphatic voice of his. He carried absolute conviction, as against the more complacent reports given by other travellers in Germany.

Our visitors' book shows that he came and stayed twice in the year before the war, shortly after I had married. I recall that there was a beautiful young lady for whom he had some affection, whom we thought he ought to marry. We proposed this idea for his benefit. For some reason I went up to his bedroom next day before he appeared for breakfast, and renewed the suggestion. He lay there in bed and said with emphasis very solemnly, 'Do you realise that it is a very wicked thing to do to try to persuade someone?'

And then we were to see him soon again dressed in the uniform of an aircraftman. He had some very lowly job in an R.A.F. stores depot at Didcot, from where he used to come and see us. Then later we went over to a sing-song organised at Didcot. There was a vast hangar, which must have held some 2,000 people, the men of the depot. First Brian acted the part of a clergyman in an old-fashioned little one-act comedy. Later he appeared as the prim ballerina of a troop of chorus girls. As he danced about, flapping his naked arms, he shot a glance at us, as much as to say, 'Yes, this is I, Brian; this is what I am doing now'.

After that we did not see him often. There was one painful episode. I was going to dine with Clive Bell at the Gargoyle. I found Brian at the bar, somewhat the worse for wear. I used to him some such words as, 'What are you working on now?' or even, more frightful, something like 'I do not seem to have seen anything from your pen lately'. He flew into a towering rage. I thought that he was going to hit me. Of course, I realised at once what a brutal thing I had said. It was partly the result of donnish habit. 'What are you working on now?' is the most frequent thing one says in academic circles. And there was a further point. When an undergraduate goes down one is apt to telescope time. One does not count the years. One has slightly the same feeling whether it is a year or two or a much longer lapse. In fact, more than twenty years had elapsed since Brian's great days at Oxford, and he had very little achievement to show for it. It was my implicit rebuke or reproach for not having done more that so enraged him and of course it was exceedingly callous of me so to address a man, who was bound to have some inner sense of failure.

And then I made matters worse. I said I was just about to have dinner with Clive Bell. Brian grew still more enraged. He made motions as much as to say, 'Show me where Clive Bell is and I will give him a slosh'. The trouble was, he was quite capable of doing that. He rebuked me violently.

325

'Why the devil did I waste my time by dining with such a worthless old fossil as Clive Bell?' It came to me at once: first I implicitly rebuke Brian for not having done enough in his life, and then I refer to a man who, when Brian was still an undergraduate, was greatly esteemed and widely read. I was, so to speak, pointing the contrast between Clive Bell's successful life and Brian's unsuccessful one. I was quite frightened. By chance I saw a friend, known to both of us, sprawled out on a sofa in a side room. 'Oh,' I said, 'there's X; let's go and talk to him.' So I led him in and, leaving the two drunks together, I found my way to my own party.

I know that there was a period when Brian drank too much and could be violent. Even his friends sometimes said 'Brian has become *impossible*'. And therefore I like to recall this episode. It was I who was entirely in the wrong. My remarks had been unfeeling and brutal. Of course, I suppose, one ought not to get into a rage and be violent, but I think it does make a difference if one has justice on one's side. Brian had very strong, and also unusual, values. One had to know him. I suspect that on some of these other occasions complained of by his friends, some deep inner sense of value had been violated. I did not see him often enough to judge authoritatively on this point; but I suspect that my view is the true one.

He came and saw us at Oxford, quite towards the end of his life. He stayed at the Randolph Hotel, but spent most of the days in our house. He looked withered and ill. Even his voice was somewhat enfeebled, but still characteristic. He was perfectly charming and still entertaining. He seemed to be an old man. He had with him a box of Greek coins, which he showed us. I felt that he had become like an elderly aristocrat of Victorian vintage—very courteous and gracious. Dear Brian.

During the first four months of 1957 Brian kept a rough engagement diary, sadly dotted with references to the amount of ampoules obtained from various doctors—*had to have eight extra ... bad night in spite of nembutal and equanil ... additional four ding-dongs ... Dexedrine is bad for appetite and heart—Drinamyl is half-stimulant, half-sedative and much better.* Sam noted in this diary, *Brian saw Sir Geoffrey Marshall—has been reprieved from the lung operation. We both thank God.*

In February Sir Geoffrey Marshall had written to Lura Howard, in France, to tell her of Brian's condition. He confirmed that there was an old-standing disease of the upper half of his right lung in which there was considerable damage and that the condition could easily become very serious without care and regular treatment. He thought Brian had a common-sense appreciation of this condition and knew how to look after himself—but that he should not be encouraged to over-exert himself. As for surgical operation, he did not think it advisable at the present time, although it could be necessary in the future. So now she knew the full T.B. picture. (Lura had told John Banting that she did not believe Brian really had T.B.) Of Sir Geoffrey, Brian wrote 'I shall do everything he says, to the last letter. He is a wonderful man ...'

The next set-back was of a different kind. Having found a suitable fur-coat—'Canadian ermine, with a deep, rich, brown-black lustre—the fur really gleams' Brian was much incensed by his mother's refusal to accept it, 'About your fur coat I prefer not to speak. A woman slips on a good fur coat, over anything, practically, and there she is Dressed, with a big D. But you have defeated me at last. Just THINK of the tens of thousands of pounds gone, and you, of all people, without a very moderately priced fur coat. . .'

Throughout early 1957 Lura was continually begging Brian and Sam to return to Nice, but as Le Verger was not yet ready they did not relish 'sitting in each other's laps' all over again in the small rented villa, and in any event Brian was waiting to know the result of a ten weeks' culture of his sputum. He was still losing weight badly, and the doctor wanted him to go abroad and be built up for several weeks before starting on the 'very tiring and powerful new anti-T.B. medicine'. Their rôles were somewhat reversed in that it was Lura who was now repeatedly asking for money to be sent over from England. Brian wrote to her: 'You will have had £3,000 and 10,000 dollars in the last ten weeks (and the rate of expenditure wasn't much less during the months before). Well, I know it's Le Verger, but it cannot continue. We shall now have only about £2,000 a year income in future—from England and America combined. I think it is the wages—Rose, Simone, Pierre and Pince—as much in a way as Le Verger. The house has been financially catastrophic—there is no other word.' (Lura had always been extravagant over staff, paying too many people too well, but they usually gave her devoted service in return.)

Brian could not leave England without paying off commitments of some £2,000, the Swiss clinic he was planning to go to would cost up to £100 a week, 'and I am buying clothes for myself and Sam for the next ten years—it's only sensible and then there are all the things you need for the garden, linen, furniture etc'. Financial worries notwithstanding Brian gave his last 'party' in March, for Eddie Gathorne-Hardy who had just retired from the Foreign Office, and a long spell in the Middle East. The Heywood Hills lent their house in Warwick Avenue for it. Maurice Richardson was there and remembers it was the last time he saw Brian: 'the copper-haired Sam was in attendance. Brian was looking terribly ill, thin and wasted and bird-like. He laid a long thin hand on my forearm. I said, "Put both claws on and hop up and perch there". He smiled.'

Brian wrote of the occasion to his mother: 'It is the only party in the true sense of one I've given for thirty years, so don't think me extravagant. I got nine letters of appreciation; it was a real success, and it was time I "got back" where I belong, if you see what I mean. It might be amusing to send a clipping of the account in the *Queen* to my American cousins, who, of course, conceive of me as a social outcast . . .' The *Queen* gave a characteristically snob veneer to their account of this 'Supper Party', listing the guests as, 'Lord Kinross, the Duchess of Buccleuch, Mr. and Mrs. Sacheverell Sitwell and Mr. and Mrs. Christopher Sykes, Oonagh, Lady Oranmore and Browne, the Hon. Mrs. Rayner, the Hon. Mrs. Lees Mayall (whose brother, the Hon. David Ormsby-Gore, is now Under-Secretary at the Foreign Office), Miss Sybille Bedford, the author, and Mr. Tom Driberg, who was talking to Sir Robert Boothby over a bowl of rum punch at the bar!'

This gathering may have done worlds of good to Brian's *amour propre* but it did not get him any nearer leaving London. He was scared to arrive in France without knowing whether he could get all his pills. 'I have had fourteen a day for six months and cannot be cut off. Dilandid, which I have here, and Eubine, which I have in France, are only stronger forms of the American anti-tension pills . . .' But I am told that both Brian and Sam had taken to heroin on the side during these last months, and that even Sam was never to be fully cured of this addiction. With Brian's T.B. condition a quick drug cure would, of course, have been very dangerous.

They moved to a cheaper flat, in Charles Street, but still could not clear up all their business, let alone finish paying for the yacht, until Lura produced £2,000 in dollars. Brian was also understandably anxious to be acknowledged as 'owner' of Le Verger, which would do much to help him get his French visa. He wrote a very serious letter to Lura about the financial situation in general, and showed it to Sam, who commented: 'It may make her cross, and won't have any effect at all . . . it is too late now for her to change her opinion of you as being a child, and, completely impractical.' Brian pointed out that it represented the lawyer's opinion as well. 'That makes no difference, you'll see.' It seemed that Lura was under the delusion that her American income had dried up—even though Brian assured her she still had about 100,000 dollars capital there.

The 'financial' letter must have made her change her mind, for she promised to send the dollars, and Brian and Sam planned to leave for Switzerland at the end of June. But before then they spent a weekend at Boughton, which he could not resist describing in great detail to his mother (too long to include in full here):

> . . . only now under this Duchess (Mollie Buccleuch) has this marvellously magical place come into its own again. She has restored it as nearly as possible to what it was in the mid-17th century, when it was built . . .
>
> I have never been in such a magical place, so full of beautiful things. Incidentally my bed linen had a little strawberry-leafed crown, with 'B. 1888' embroidered on the sheets. And do you know what they use against the moth? The housekeeper told me, the dried leaves of the Bitter Apple plant, which comes from Persia. Sam was given seeds of it, so we'll grow it . . .

Plans were changed once more, and Brian wrote next from Ireland, where he went to stay with Oonagh, Lady Oranmore and Browne, at Luggala, in Co. Wicklow:

> I am trying to do my cure independently here because the clinic at Lausanne is very expensive. I adore this place and the change of environment may just tip the scales. The psychological factors play so much greater a rôle in my life than the physical factors. Anyway, I'm going to try my damnedest.
>
> At Boughton it was the house which 'made' it. Here it is nature. . . . I have been asked to stay for as long as I like (it seems that, when Oonagh first came out in London I was the only person who really paid attention to her, and got her out of all sorts of scrapes—instead of getting her into them—as I slightly did with Tanis) which she has never forgotten. Also,

she says she was in love with me! So I am going to stay here for two weeks at least. Providence has really put within my grasp the chance of conducting a self-cure from the Eubine-like stuff in ideal circumstances. The fact that meals simply appear, at regular intervals, without my having either to help cook them, or go out to a restaurant, and pay for them, has the result of making me eat enormously. Food helps me not to need sedatives more than anything. As soon as I am CONFIDENT that I can do without them I shall go back to London, finish what has still to be done, and come to you. I am assuming that you have done something, of course, about ascertaining what kind of official reception I and Sam are going to get in France?

I believe the self-cure was sadly unsuccessful, Brian leaving behind him at Luggala a vast legacy of broken hypodermic needles. His problem was not so much Eubine as heroin.

To stop the draining away of all capital, their London solicitor suggested to Lura Howard that she make a trust for Brian out of £16,000 of her American money (from which she would, of course, receive the interest during her life), but Brian confused the issue by suddenly wanting to invest £4,000 in a British ready-made men's wear firm which had decided to branch out in France. Brian would then, as a Director, get a permanent *carte de séjour* without difficulty, and a much needed telephone for Le Verger. Needless to say, nothing came of this last idea. Even so, Brian was still writing about putting in a small swimming pool and three or four substantial trees to get the 'naked' look of Le Verger disguised, and quick-climbing plants wherever possible.

However, it was the yacht that was still considered to be the most likely source of extra income, potentially bringing in £100 a week at high-season chartering. The *Yachting World* published a complimentary paragraph about it: 'The *Taras II*, being built for Mr. Brian Howard, to the design of Mr. Jack Jones, would seem to be about the best equipped small yacht turned out by a British Yard since the War. It has "everything" from a depth sounder to forced electrical ventilation. It is pleasant to think that the Riviera ... will have a chance of seeing what British workmanship (Cardnell Brothers) can do with a sloop of only thirty-three feet overall, and a nine-foot six inches beam.'

By August it seemed as if Brian and Sam were going to be able to leave England, complete with Studebaker car, en route for Nice via Geneva. But Brian had almost outplayed himself, as he wrote to his mother:

I must warn you that I have become the prey of such depression that I feel I haven't the physical strength left to do the endless, but necessary, clearing-up. I am filled, day and night, with the most torturing, guilt-feelings. I have stayed too long away from you—my teeth aren't finished *yet*, neither are my clothes—moreover, I think they have 'got it in for me' in France, whatever you say. All these things, plus a strong inclination to resume relationships with my oldest friends when they ask me (Michael Rosse in Ireland—Harry Stavordale in Dorset) have caused delay after delay, and now the full force of self-reproach is besieging me so that I can't sleep. I am working my way out of the use of sedatives, and the purely physical result of this is quite terrible. I feel paralysed. And now the business of getting what I have accumulated here out to Le Verger seems an almost insuperable problem. Sam will manage it, somehow, bless him. The sedatives made me lazy and optimistic in the wrong way. But whatever happens—we are together. And Sam loves you—remember. Hold out till I get there, and then we'll face it all together. P.S. The National Portrait Gallery have suddenly rejected the Eves of Daddy. This means I must take charge of yet another picture. [The remaining Tudie Howard pictures had now been given conditionally to Brian, to be finally left to a gallery, or to an heir if one existed.]

The next letter came from Geneva in November:

What I am principally worried about is not my own health—BUT YOUR LEG. You must have it looked at by a first-class man. The south of France is the refuge of *malades imaginaires*, of course, but the terrible result is that most of the doctors are *médécins imaginaires!* I don't want you to become crippled through lack of proper attention. And it's no good your telling me it's age. It isn't. Why, Ava Ribblesdale has just been conducting a vigorous law-suit in New York to get her tiara back. And won. And she is ninety-two . . .

I am bringing back a sweet little wife for Teazle. Her pedigree is of an inconceivable grandeur (to make up for Teazle's), and they will have the prettiest children in the world. I don't want Teazle condemned to an unnatural bachelor life, like Schnupi and Bubi. It is WRONG. [These were their dachshund and corgi dogs.]

[Later] I really do expect to be home within two weeks. I have had an attack of pleurisy again. As soon as a certain short series of injections can be done, much the best places for me in all Europe would be either somewhere like Mürren (after Christmas when the weather 'crystallises'), or somewhere soft and sunny like Nice. So I'm ordered to my own home. So nice.

. . . About our tiny capital in America. I'm afraid I agree that we must invest as heavily as we can in what are evasively called 'Missile Emphasis Companies'. Did you ever hear of anything so hypocritical? How terrible that you and I should consent to having our money in such devilish contraptions. But, alas, these are the stocks which are going to ascend almost as fast as the beastly rockets they manufacture.

I am bringing little prezzies for now, and better ones for Christmas. Three ancient Greek coins are being sold in Paris today, which would have crowned my little collection, but I wrote to my friend from Spinks not to buy them as you and Le Verger come first henceforth, on all counts.

At last they arrived at Le Verger, the long-awaited 'home', having survived ten years of delays, disappointments and disasters of one kind or another. Did they like it? Could they live there happily *à trois* with Lura? Was Brian—and indeed Sam too—really cured of taking drugs? And did they find their dream house more mirage than reality? Reading between the lines I would say that from the

330

moment Brian realised the finality of his choice he knew it to be the beginning of the end.

The erstwhile chicken farm had been transformed into a Palladian villa, the long façade topped by a pediment, with walls the colour of warm, dry sand, and white pilasters. The two-acre garden was steeply terraced, with rows of orange and lemon, cherry, fig and datura trees, and a large *toile d'Hollande* espalier rose, with hundreds of big, deep red blooms. One view faced terraces of carnations, the other looked south towards a strip of blue sea lying between two small hills, with a few rooftops visible in the 'Col de Bast'. There were traces of Brian's taste, but it was far more his mother's creation, except for the large library room below the paved terrace. This was almost a gallery—about seventy feet long by twenty wide, with large windows on the long side, curtained outside by spectacular fifteen-foot high mimosa trees. Allanah Harper confirms that this library was to have been Brian's haven:

Brian had long wanted a home of his own. He was tired of wandering from one hotel bedroom to another in Paris or in the south of France, Italy or Sicily. 'At last,' he said, when he bought the old Mas above Nice which he transformed into a Palladian Villa, 'I shall be able to write in my own library. I shall have Lords to stay, Peers, my dear, you will see.' *Good resolutions,* Oscar Wilde wrote, *are simply cheques that men draw on a bank where they have no account.* This concern for visiting Peers was typical of Brian's half tongue-in-cheek attitude towards snobbishness. I remember years ago one of his friends leaving a fancy dress party, disguised in a poke bonnet. When a policeman chivvied him with, 'Hurry up, Aunt Gertrude,' he answered back, 'Lady Gertrude to you!' This half-snobbish, half-joking type of remark is representative of their generation. It would be impossible coming from young people today to whom, rightly, titles are a disadvantage and a bore.

Even had the horrible tragedy not happened—within a fortnight of their arrival 'home'—Brian was too ill to have lived very long. I would like to quote from his poem *God Save the King,* that was written in 1928 but which is rather prophetic of his own end—

. . . My brother has lain down to rest a moment
   to blow a tired, red bubble in the mud.
I have lived. I am now dead before I am dead.

Where is my eagle, who was to perch, at last, on my shoulder?
   Where is my serpent, the eagle's lover
who was to coil about the eagle, and guide his beak?

I came here that I should not sleep before evening
   that I should awake once, in the holy strength of the eagle
and that I should wake a second time, in the holy wisdom of the
                               serpent

and now I am dead before I am dead.

22. Finale

1958

The tragic news reached England in the form of a letter from Brian to Heywood Hill, written on Sunday, 12th January 1958:

> Dear Heywood, This place consists of a house and a sort of cottage, connected by outdoor stairs. The cottage roof is being re-built. The bathroom in it is very small, and the hot water comes by means of a geyser worked by a gas which has no smell. Yesterday morning, early, the workman removed the exhaust pipe which takes away the used and poisonous gas. Sam went in to have a bath, shut the door, and was found dead two hours later.
>
> He had taken the dogs for a walk, and written his mother a happy letter. The same morning. There's nothing more to say.
>
> My love to Anne, and Eddie if he's in England, and to you. Brian.

Brian had immediately telegraphed John Banting asking him to come out to Le Verger and stay awhile, but John did not get the telegram for three days as he was out of London. He went, of course, bringing comfort and sympathy as only he would know how—the oldest, most loyal and faithful of all Brian's friends. By the time he arrived Brian and his mother were too stunned or frozen for any show of emotion. They were kept busy attending to the necessary details, choosing the place for Sam's grave in the overcrowded cemetery, ordering flowers, and finding a priest. (Sam was contemplating becoming a Roman Catholic and so his coffin was to be blessed by a priest.)

Brian had not eaten anything for the four days since Sam's death, and although John put forward every argument against suicide in the bare two days they had together, Brian's mind was already made up. In any event, as his T.B. was never cured—because he would not stay long enough in a sanatorium—he knew that he did not have long to live. He was, in fact, a semi-invalid being consoled by drugs which in the end would only serve to make him a total invalid.

Earlier in the day he had played some early jazz, saying, when his mother objected, that Sam would have liked it. Later he put on the 'Liebestod' from *Tristan*, with a comment that it was music 'for a farewell'. All this time he was quietly weighing his continuation of life in the balance and finding it wanting. Without self-pity, but with dignity and alone he quickly took the inevitable overdose which, after the days without food, the violent shock, and his longing to die, eased him very swiftly away from misery into death. The doctor was called and, after efforts to revive him, confirmed his death. Brian's face was 'happy and serene, as if in death he had triumphed over life' as he lay finally at rest upon the bed in which he had been born.

Mona Macdonell came to give help and sympathy to Lura Howard at the double funeral which took place amongst the flowers and in the bright January sunshine at the Caucade de Nice cemetery. The dark green marble tombstone, to be laid flat over the grave, was chosen by Brian himself, also the simple inscription:

BRIAN HOWARD
and his friend
SAM ———

| March 13 1905 | January 15 1958 |
| May 2 1925 | January 11 1958 |

His mother was not to join Brian there until some seven years later. John Banting writes a last word about his friend:

A disgust of the world overtook Brian towards 1939. He was 'bad news' to the conventional or the reactionary people, and a prophet of the last World War. How he hated all its muddled aimlessness and inevitable self-protectiveness, and the Guilty Men who let it happen. He was not a defeatist about it, but simply realistic. It overcame him, in several ways, and was the cause of his final ruin. First the loss of Toni, then the post-war peace-time of vacuity—and finally Sam's death. One can't ignore his love of individualism and iconoclast inclinations. He hardly ever spoke of other people as he was really more interested in ideas, and he never reminisced or held a post mortem on the doings of yesterday. The Present was for him—let the Past die and the Future come. (His mother had the same virtue, even in her eighties.) I feel this way too . . . *je ne regrette rien, rien de rien, ni le mal, ni le bien* . . . And yet I do have regrets that the past is not the present. Both Brian and Nancy (Cunard) are now dead, but the fact that it is liberation for both of them—they had been ill and unhappy too long—is some consolation for the gap they leave.

And so Brian's line ends in confusions and disputes, but in the long library of Le Verger, where he would have spent most of his time, it is his lively, balanced and happy presence that remains very tangible, and up the little *colline*, in confirmation of his final choice, I sometimes hear a few reassuring bars from the 'Liebestod' of *Tristan*, the last record he ever played. Comforting and reassuring that everything ends . . .

I cannot write *to* Brian any more and he is the only one of my (now several) dead friends with whom I have ever wanted to try to 'get in touch' through a spiritualist medium. Writing *about* Brian no longer seems like burying him—rather more a sort of resurrection.

It was Alan Pryce-Jones who wrote the final, affectionate tribute in *The Times*:

In the small world of Eton and Oxford during the 1920s, it seemed inevitable that Brian Howard would emerge as one of the eminent figures of his generation. Exotically handsome, after the manner of a Disraeli hero, rich, brilliant in conversation, and endowed with great physical courage, he only needed the right spur to set him on the ladder of fame. Instead, he reached a degree of notoriety, as a leader of the antics of the Bright Young People, an exponent of the life depicted by Mr. Evelyn Waugh in *Vile Bodies*.

And yet his gift, though it always lay dormant, never died. It was displayed in the pages of the *New Statesman* and *Horizon*, and it showed that, had he cared, he might have become an English Jean Cocteau. He published one book of verse, but in the main he was content to talk himself out, with a verve and pungency which will not be forgotten. One celebrated practical joke, in particular, has been recorded. Under the name of Bruno Hat, a penniless, if imaginary, artist from Lübeck, he painted a number of pictures in the most 'advanced' style of the late 1920s, and contrived to have them taken seriously at an exhibition organised in the house of the present Lord Moyne. It can be deduced that he was a difficult, if often a dazzling, friend. And if his premature end has been like that of Oscar Wilde's rocket, he fell from his zenith without a trace of vanity or self-pity.

Appendix I.
Brian as a poet

A critical assessment, with a selection of poetry by Philip Toynbee

Few of his friends can have thought of Brian Howard primarily as a poet. Few who read his poems as they appeared can have thought that many of them quite succeeded in matching, or reflecting, his astonishing personality. In life he was an absolute original, though this is easily forgotten by those who never knew him and have known only his epigones or the many sub-Brians who have appeared in fiction. On the other hand it cannot be said that he was a notably original poet, or that he very often succeeded in finding his own individual tone and vocabulary. Any reasonably well-instructed reader will be able to detect the successive poetic influences to which Brian submitted himself during the forty years in which he was writing verse. The touching patriotic thunder of the 1914–18 war poem is quickly supplanted by the audible proximity of the Sitwells; then, among others, of Sassoon, of surrealism, of the Imagists, of Pound, Eliot and finally, and quite unmistakably, of Auden.

Yet Brian Howard was a conscientious and persistent writer of verse, whose faith in his own talent never entirely waned even during those terrible last years when he was able to find little faith in anything else. He published only one volume of poems, a beautiful hand-printed edition of a hundred and fifty copies, printed in 1930 by the Hours Press in Paris, with elegant covers designed by Brian's closest friend, the artist John Banting. This was called *God Save the King and Other Poems*[1] and it certainly contained the best that he had written up to that date. I have included all of that volume in the present selection, except for three short poems which seemed less successful than the others, and one of the longer poems.

Both before and after that unique occasion of a published volume Brian was publishing his verse in every kind of English and American magazine. In fact he was a prolific versifier—a good deal more abundant than most of his more distinguished contemporaries. And if that was all there was to Brian Howard as a poet—a voluble *pasticheur*, a diligent collector of other men's flowers—then the only interest this collection could hold for a modern reader would be the melancholy one of tracing each waxing and waning influence in turn. Nothing more could be expected than a nostalgic comment on the changes in poetic fashion between the first war and the middle 'fifties. I think more *can* be expected, and will be found, than this. I believe that Brian was a genuine minor poet, even though he was a wayward one who was easily blown from his true course by the winds of fashion. From a total of available verse at least five times

---

[1] Finally called *First Poems* owing to a misunderstanding, and published in 1931.

as large as the total printed here I have tried to choose the poems which seem to me to represent Brian most completely. This means that I have included a fair number of poems simply to illustrate the degree to which he could be influenced by greater powers than his own. One of the interests of this selection must lie in the art of perceiving just how, and on what occasions, Brian managed to add to the verse of his changing times that individual tone or flavour which alone makes poetry worth preserving.

I would not claim much for the poems which appeared before *God Save the King*. Their interest must largely lie in following the uneasy but enthusiastic progress of a brilliant boy and young man, trying to write verse of his own during a brilliant and captivating decade. But after 1930 I believe Brian was far more successful in imposing his own special stamp on the verse-forms of the time. The essence of his personality was romantic melancholy fortified by a watchful irony and an outrageous wit. As a man he was a dangerous dandy, charming but often deadly, the central figure of a perpetual drama which he composed and acted simultaneously. He was not affected, for the apparent and staggering affectation of his voice and manner had grown over him like a natural, and gleaming carapace. Once, when he was on his best and most apologetic behaviour, I witnessed the sudden and very disturbing abandonment of this well-known manner. He sat in solicitous gravity before his hostess; he made no gestures; his voice was deep and quite free of the usual glissandos.

But it would be absurd to suppose that this momentary apparition was, in some sense, the 'real' Brian. The real Brian was the one we knew—a man to admire and to pity and to accept on his own strange terms. So it is that I find that the poem I like best of those I've chosen here is *Gone to Report*, published in *Horizon* during the retributive month of May 1940. If any friend of Brian's were to read this poem aloud he would find his voice inevitably sliding into the familiar imitation of that inimitable voice, a dangerous drawl, curvetting up and down, implanting unexpected emphasis on words which immediately assume an inexplicable significance. I don't know whether this is the best poem here, but it is, I'm sure, the one which Brian's friends will fix upon with most affection.

But the hope, in any case, is that this collection of verse will give pleasure as well to those who never knew their author, or even heard of him. It is my own belief that there is enough genuine originality here, and enough achievement, to outweigh the admittedly large amount of promise and of imitation.

POEMS BY BRIAN HOWARD

BALLOONS
FEAR IN THE LABORATORY

EXPRESSION OF THE SEA
BAROUCHES NOIRES

From the *Eton Candle*:

LONDON NIGHT-PIECE
THE COMING
TO THE YOUNG WRITERS AND ARTISTS KILLED IN THE WAR 1914–1918

IGNIS FATUUS
PICASSO
HEAD TO TOE

From *First Poems*:

Comments by Brian Howard
YOUNG
GOD SAVE THE KING
THE LISTENING CHILD
I REMEMBER, I REMEMBER
BRANCH
SELF, with comment
SHE
HOMAGE TO TENNYSON
THE FIGURE
ALWAYS
TWO IN ONE
SAYING GOOD-BYE TO A PHOENIX
ENTENDS LA DOUCE NUIT QUI MARCHE
UP

THE SOUND OF LOVE
FOR THOSE WITH INVESTMENTS IN SPAIN: 1937
A PRAYER FOR THE FUEHRER
GONE TO REPORT
THE HIRED MAN
TO MY MOTHER, with comment
LONGLEAT: 1948, with comment
INSTANTANEOUS TIME EXPOSURE—for Wystan Auden
TWO IT TAKES TO MAKE A FLOWER
THE DUST
GARDA—for Stephen Spender
LATE NIGHT FINAL
TO-DAY

337

BALLOONS

Up, up they go—up,
Luminous sides ... rotund ... of candied veneer,
Flouting their painted sheens:
Tawny, viridian, like macaws
Acrily tottering, screaming for some anodyne,
To make equipoise ...
To stem the dizzy staggering on the Wind,
Always—for an immeasurable eternity
to totter thus; parabolically leering—

             *   *   *

Balloons—damned Balloons.

(Published in the *New Age*, 1920, under the pseudonym Jasper Proude)

FEAR IN THE LABORATORY

I am sitting on a form, making notes about the solubility of salt,
And electric light wires line the walls ... curse them ...

In front of me is a glass bottle full of sulphuric add dilution and
     twenty one test tubes in a wooden rack,
And there's a white china mortar ... desolate of motif ... with a
     background of filtering papers,
Over there, guileful gritty powders in crucibles ... and all the Devils
     usual pottles ...
Over there, five black iron cheostates—nailed up sideways.

See the compensated pendulums! and terrible tins ... each
     maelstroming internally with repugnant odours—
What does it all mean? and why was I frightened?
Why do I grimace at the Professor?

Because the bunsen burner is incinerating my soul in the name of
     Science.

                 .   .   .   .

Nine shiny brass electric switches all the same distance from one
     another ...

                 .   .   .   .

'Professor Murgatroyd, I'm dying from fright'
'Crystallisation. Fractional crystallisation of two nitrogenous
     substances. Solubility ...'

                                                      (*Eton*, 1920)

EXPRESSION OF THE SEA

expression of the sea and beach from the pier buffet,
(to be shouted in monotone by a fat, respectably dressed person,
to the accompaniment of breaking glass, with two electric bells
and two typewriters in agitation)

'. . . the green ocean . . . the green ocean . . . like a towel-horse . . .
    painted in half. alternatively rounded and peaked upsurgings
    of greenness with white feather fingers . . . all in dancing
    lines. lines. lines.
a clear-cut splotch of brown-white has fallen on the green lines . . . it
    goes up and down like a machine,—paperbags are significant
    of the futility of the kosmos when they bob up and down . . .
    next to it is a fawn sponge-finger bobbing up and down: it
    contains a thin, thin, viridian woman who grasps a round,
    round, red parasolette. the oars seem always up in the sky.

now the terrible 'band' is beginning to make a noise—a noise
    exhaling very old tinned fruit gravies . . . or dripping . . .
    yes, dripping. dripping and the sensation of sticking
    plaster that won't come off . . .
. . . it's Verdi (throttled with light lager) . . . like acrid little chopped
    up canary wings, falling down in jerks and bursts and jangles out of
    a blue-gilt sky.
. . . music that blows great nasty breaths filled with the dust on
    American chewing-gum. cheap sherbet.

the atmosphere is the atmosphere of an aquarium!
. . . the air is slowly congealing (as colding fat) into milk chocolate
    and wood spades . . .
and OH the awful misses . . . they trip along the long parallels of
    dry, biscuity planking (or asphalt) . . . their chemises
    flapping in the warm clockwork breezes that girlishly brush
    clots of Tuppeny Grossmith rice-powder into the eustachian
    Tubes. OH the pinky chemises. OH the jersey-
    flapping flappers . . .

observe, *ma chérie*, at the beach.
one pebble in a vast beach of pebbles.
one pebble in a colossal beach of pebbles. pebbles.
twenty bathing machines at the edge of the white creamings
    on undulating green table-cloths . . . periodically vomiting
    shapeless figures in cerise and magenta bathing suits . . .
    which lie down on the rolling, uncomfortable stones in
    the hard, irritating seaweed . . . loving it . . . shrieking
    with peculiarly shaped mouths for bananas at the
    imitation blackamoor minstrels . . . grabbing star-fish
    . . . that they will carry home to Cricklewood.
patches of pricking heat floating geometrically around in gleams
    of cream.

the 'Sans Soucie' (pleasure trips) is nosing out from my pier in equal
    jerks, with it's couple of revolving cart-wheels . . . thick yellow
    cart-wheels . . . and it's load of cakey stomachs . . . bottles . . .

the hairs of the young gentlemen on the pier ... hanging in spears,
    and crackling for more shampoos ...
    ... and there are bits of apple under my narrowish seat ... bits of
    apple on my water-wiped plate with the silly
    mauve monogram. THE WHOLE SEASHORE IS
    MADE OF BITS OF STALE APPLE, hard.
    gritty. you swallow them by mistake.

    ... there are moments when I think Mrs. Andromeda Cosway (the
    person who keeps the boarding-house) will give
    me an egg to my tea ... ah but then she
    won't ... and it makes me introspective and
    balmy to think of it ... *omelettes aux*
fines herbes ... Monet water-lilies ...

now the revolting stenches ... aromas ... aromas of burning chemist
    shops ... sea-aromas of the perspiration of blondes and
    brunettes ... that of the stout *gourmandise* to one
    side of me being like the bass notes of an
    organ—while that of the Polish Jew waitress being like the more nasal
    notes of an oboe ...
    ... aromas of pale piles of shrimps—blouses—winkles—bicycles—
        hotels
    —vanilla ice wafer sandwiches—
    warm road—magazines—

... the rows of buildings ... uninteresting tinted cardboard ...
    so hard and bright,
the Metropole (made of marzipan and cigarette smoke) glazes up at the
    respectable sun. the sun that crinkles down
    in orange planes ... the respectable, fruity
    sun that smiles down on buns—chemises
    —shouts—pebbles—bad and good odours—bits
    of apple ...

to-morrow, dammit, I'll go home,—lunch at the Carlton Grill,
    and hear some Debussy in the afternoon.

au revoir.'

(Third version, as revised on advice of Edith Sitwell, 1921)

BAROUCHES NOIRES

It was when I was sitting by the side of the lake,
    By the side of a lake where the great trees
        come to the water's edge,
    And when, beneath the glittering leaves, I

was watching the gleaming, mobile
water; the water that was like a
thousand living mirrors in the sunlight, that I turned my head . . .
I turned my head, amidst the green
warmth to the road,
And I saw a procession of old, frayed
barouches filing by;
Old, broken-down barouches that followed
their soundless horses soundlessly,
And contained loads of young dead people,
propped up in outrageous positions;
Dressed in the clothes of many periods.
I saw four couples sitting in a row . . .
embracing one another . . .
One couple had exchanged hats . . .
The last barouche that passed had a
placard tied on with string—
'We are the lovers that drowned them-
selves in this lake.'

(Published under the pseudonym Charles Orange in *Wheels*, 1931,
edited by Edith Sitwell)

LONDON NIGHT-PIECE

Silence . . . and a row of lamps reflected on the wet
   black street.
Over the roof-line of the surrounding houses, a brown glare . . .
The square railings are cold . . . tiny leaves and twigs
   stretch out between them—dirty and wet.
Inside; the long bed of bushes, smelling of damp earth and soot.
The sycamore trees . . . bare and glistening . . . with
   little dangling balls.
Opposite; the grey side of a house . . . half lit by a street lamp.
A trickle in the gutter, and a broken match-box floating . . .

(First published in *Wheels*, reprinted in the *Eton Candle*, 1922)

THE COMING

Taken from the French of Stéphane Mallarmé

The moon grew tragic. Weeping seraphs dreamt,
Their bows in hand, amongst the tranquil flowers
So pale, touching from half-dead violins
White sobs that kissed the fragile foliage—
It was the magic moment of your first caress.
By wonder, loving so to torture me,
Drugged its own self with Sorrow's silver breath,

341

And then, without the shade of a regret
Left to the heart the harvest of the dream.
Thus did I wander, watching the old road,
Then you, the whole sun's glory in your hair,
Came to me, with a smile, and in the evening;
And I believed the fairy had returned,
The one fire-crowned I dreamt of when a child,
Who from her opened fingers always showered
White, trailing clusters of the perfumed stars.

(Published in the *Eton Candle*, 1922)

TO THE YOUNG WRITERS AND ARTISTS KILLED
IN THE WAR: 1914–18

We haven't forgotten you! We haven't forgotten!
You were the first generation of the world's greatest century,
And you were doing, and were going to do, fine things ...
You were a great Young Generation ...

And then you went out and got murdered—magnificently—
Went out and got murdered ... because a parcel of
    damned old men
Wanted some fun, or some power, or something.
   Something so despicable in comparison to your young lives ...

Anyhow, you were glorious ...
And we will do our best to do what you would have done.
Oh, we will fight for your ideals—we, who were too
    young to be murdered with you ...

And—we haven't forgotten you! We haven't forgotten!

(Published in the *Eton Candle*, 1922)

IGNIS FATUUS
to M.E.

The hot trees mutter, and lean away
Bland July has broken down.
High over these gathered buildings
The summer lightning spins so quickly
little wires of pink fire.
Like a far drum that beats until it breaks
the stammering thunder ...

Let us stand, you and I, and look at this view
Let us stare at the running sky, and catch
the pink wires in our fingers, twisting
bright crowns for Folly out of a London storm.

PICASSO

On the other side of the air
a long bird exercises his joints.
A jointed bird a little longer than a life
swings his striped joints.

A square sky turns upon its four poles, the nest,
A railway rocks a red ball, the egg.
Inside the egg is a pyramid containing a flower,
an aeroplane which sings.

[Marginal note by Brian: *substitute next lines for above four*].

The square sky, his nest, turns slowly on its four poles, rocking
a red pyramid, his egg, while the aeroplanes kiss one another,
marry in flight, and sing a loud anthem. The words of the
anthem are the words of the bird's secret, and the words become
        naked,
future men as they issue from the happy, open mouths of the
aeroplanes. They walk towards the pyramid. The pyramid
opens to disclose a flower, which is the last flower, the result
of the last secret, and which will last always.

HEAD TO TOE

This is the ghost
The first and the last
the past, and the only one
never together, always alone.

Climb the stairs of Europe, catch them unawares
mobilise the army, stand still at fairs
wear your shoes and eyes out, spend a whole life
use your million or use your knife
use your experience, use your despair
never say die, never try and share
earn, deserve, pray, laugh, hope, brush your hair
nothing will bring you the ghost.

The ghost is a photograph, the ghost is a fool
the ghost is God, and the ghost is a Rule
The womb gave something, the school gave another
so did the father, the mother, and the brother
The ghost is the truth that you can't find out
He is that he is.

The hair is a torn sail
the eye has no iris, is transparent, is blind
is broken blue, black and blue, open.

The neck is wider in the middle, the neck is wide open
    the eye is all pupil
    the ghost is pupil.
The breast is high, the breast is cold, the breast is flat
    the breast is thick, the breast
    is curved, the breast
is brown agate, is hard, is a looking-glass for an ass.
    The stomach has a shadow
    vertical, blue, deep, soft
held, shaking, in the deep shadow-horns of the shining loins.
    The legs are longer
    than a life, twisted
    polished, fair stone.
  The shoulders are caped with heavy
    power. The stomach
    has cold domes
    of power, among caves
        of silk.

The ghost is over there, and over here, and never moves
the ghost knows, the ghost never comes, the ghost goes
You have met, you have never met, it's all the same
only you know him, he doesn't know you, and you're to blame
He is the poor ghost that you will never let alone
who is the dog, who is the bone?
And when you do find him, he's never the same
And you never do find him. It's only a game.

(*Editor's note*)

Brian gave a copy of his *First Poems* to a young friend of his in 1943, together
with an explanatory letter:

'. . . Herewith my early poems, they aren't terribly good, but there are bits.
The trouble is, they are far too egocentric. Another trouble is, that the last poem,
which is possibly the best, was written when you were eight years old. A rather
solemn thought—'I append the only explanatory list I've ever made, for your
amusement:

'*Young* was about a conversation I had with Harold Acton. I began the
conversation.

'*God Save the King.* This begins about my private school—goes on about the
last War, with me in it (imaginatively) and dying spiritually before reaching
fulfilment. (This War will do just as well.)

'*The Listening Child.* Me thinking of Ma and Pa.

'*I Remember.* About being torn between England and the South, which I still
am.

344

'*Branch*. Thirty-eight, and ditto. But it's quite sweet, I think, don't you?

'*Self*. Loneliness in the south of France.

'*She*. My mamma.

'*Tennyson*—I don't believe I ever quite knew *what* this was about.

'*The Figure*. This would have been good if it hadn't been so vague. And too ambitious.

'*Always*. Quite a nice poem. Explains itself.

'*Two in One*. This was intended as the chief love poem of the book. It has pretty things in it?

'*Saying Good-bye*. The key to this is the frightful pun in the seventh line.

'*Entends la douce nuit*. This is a double love poem which I'll explain another time.

'*Up*. Explains itself.'

The following fourteen poems were all published in *First Poems*, (or *God Save the King and other poems*), by Nancy Cunard at The Hours Press, 1930–1931.

YOUNG

Loops of red gauze, the music swoops down
    the glass passage in the wall.
Black, rolling hats on a gold rack:
    'The moon is fallen? Not at all.

Lightning's only marble. Frightening?
    Only the moon's white marble hair.'
'Stammering thunder's wicked hammer!'
    'Night's pasodoble in the air.

Tell me about it.' 'I'm in hell,
    I've lost my love, and my religion.'
'So has your friend, but then, you know
    the Holy Ghost's a carrier pigeon.

He'll fly to you, he flew to me,
    flew back again, Faith in his beak.
He also brought my love to tea.
    We laughed until we couldn't speak.'

'Bring more chartreuse! You've everything,
    I've nothing, and I hate the storm.
Fate bids me go.' 'It isn't late.
    Goya's musicians still perform.

Pains of your youth, and Spanish rains
    don't last, and hearts heal in the South.'
'I am betrayed. So stop this lie!
    These fountains merely herald drouth.

Dry death will follow quick, and I
    will burn, my tears will turn to steam.
I'll burst in bitter fire . . . you sigh?
    Thin sighing, like a vulture's scream!'

'Please write your book, and do not tease
    your pleasant present with your past.
But now, enough. They're going to shut.'
    The ruby tango dies at last.

Loud, flying flowers, odours proud,
    die in the mirrors as they go.
Don Quintin's children have gone on.
    Don Quintin el Amargao.[2]

(Madrid, 1925)

GOD SAVE THE KING

I

The conversation of a bell
striking across the afternoon
this is what we remember of our early youth.
A torch in the bedclothes is soon put out
by a morning that comes before its time
closing the book before the end of the page.

Charon rings his doorbell all day long, it seems.
The ceaseless anger of a bell
running across a foggy teatime
this is what we remember of our early youth.

Amo. Amas. Amat. Does he really? How wonderful.
A kiss translated from the Greek
we received it in the bootroom, and we prayed
prayed until our heads were cold with a pure sweat
a simple dew, and ignorant.
Not knowing the tomb when it touched us, not seeing
the small, immediate burial of a child
taking this first warning as a gift, which was only
the last tap of an old woodpecker.

---

[2] This name was inspired by a tango he heard in Spain, see Chapter 8.

Across the harsh field the bell comes like a stone
killing him who was telling us our first story.
He, the lustful elder, the dead woodpecker, is silent, so distressed
to be left alone again by youth, to be so abandoned
perched on the fence alone, in a pair of gold spectacles
with a few red feathers round a broken beak.

In an aseptic chapel, singing for Sunday supper
our voices fail at the high note, the most holy.
In the chapel sits the false eagle, the convert
armoured in Christian brass, sprawling
in a lean nest of Easter lilies.
Here, the only eagle is brass
and the saints have long since expelled the serpent
leaving the lilies, virgins in a vase, open in death
flowers of white soap, washed well, like the dead
starched, like the white cowls of the dead, waxed, smelling of
                                        an immortal Sunday.

The last word of the daily bell is said
over a cup of cocoa in the dark.
Ice, coming by night, closes the ewer with a click.
The frosted sponge stiffens against a premature cockcrow.
The cock waits patiently until we're all asleep
and then, before there's been a minute's quiet in which to wake
                                        and weep
and go to sleep again, he springs in one leap
straight from the farmyard to the top of the steeple
rattles the cross with his claws, stretches back his head, and
                                        screams to all the people
screaming and screaming that dawn is late
that the night is done which is not yet begun
lying, while his crown shakes on his head, his crown of red lead
telling the lie, screaming a false dawn and an unwanted
                        resurrection to the scarcely dead.

We rise, blind
with something that resembled sleep, a brief prostration
blind with torch, dream, or book, a few minutes of these.
A little horizontal straining, a burden born upon the back.
Rise, and shudder forward to split the ice, pour a libation
crush the sponge, and scrub the teeth, in between a sneeze.
A little vertical straining, quotidian harness, assumption of
                                        an upright rack.
                        We rise, blind.

Between the first walls of the day
my friend, it is so difficult to wait for youth
so hard to become young

To be young only in years is to be old and mad
to wear a false beard, to be a small green peach bearded with snow
its back against the wall, in a February without an end.

We, being too young, are old, and wait
at the bottom of a winter garden, for the sun
and, when the sun comes, we find no strength to grow
being green peaches, small and cold
but only the exchange of light for darkness
of nothing for nothing
only the illumination of a familiar disaster
unseen at night, but long learned by heart.
To hide tears in other tears
for no reason, save that early youth is madness
to hide laughter in counterfeit laughter
this is what we know of our early youth.

II

To smell autumn is to be seventeen.
C'est un amateur
il est toujours l'élève.
I fall with each wicked leaf
seventeen.

Ego is triumphant in this lowest time
ego in the evening season
the evening that is too sweet, too rich.
To-day there is only a banjo in tears
to-day it is yesterday.

To-morrow, spring will come, a small unicorn bringing a birthday
but I cannot be born again
I cannot give birth to myself again
Instead, I, an inferior Werther, have permitted the world to bear
                                                me a bastard
an old alien baby, and dead.
The narrow hips of my soul
shall engender me nothing. I am a silly Hamlet.

Even now I should be naked, leaning against the light
holding myself, a newborn baby, in my arms.
I should be standing in daylight, with the serpent and the eagle
sitting in consort upon a burning bush, my head.

Instead my bones are a basket of silly sorrows.

III

Under the sailing cedar tree, in a heavy August
the elders say on the lawn, eating a little tea.

The sun was in the silver, and the blue cuckoo, the bird Ophelia
spoke her pure word, down in the field
spoke and spoke again, words of virginal madness.
Mother dwindled towards the vegetables
and grew back to us again, leaning through the afternoon
a daisy on a tide
a bottle of milk in a green afternoon.

But, as dirt gets between the teeth, and sweat creeps between the
                                                    piano keys
worms into everyone, nails into a cross
so Mars, the loud newspaper boy, rode across our roses
and trampled our teacups into the lawn.
No storm destroyed our pastoral symphony, no grand tempest,
                                                but instead
as dirt gets into the teeth, the newspaper got in at the garden gate
and we were all filled with hate.
It wasn't for want of washing, of waiting and watching . . . ah, no
we were always awfully careful, even at Oddenino.
Black dirt, white dirt, all on a printed page, we didn't be*lieve* you
because of Cambridge, Cornwall, vows in a punt
because we were being *young* so *beau*tifully.

Mother returned from the vegetables, on the run
through the ruins of the minute
sat on a garden chair, and thrust her roots down among the daisies
in search of an older strength.
Father cursed, and Ophelia fell from the bough
snapping a Flanders poppy where she fell.
Father's age, too old, made itself into a monument beside Mother
an evening monument, and the eyelids were a little weary.
We went. We left by the last summer train, never again.

The Thames trembled in its bed, and Big Ben boomed
the Abbey crouched like a beast, growling 'All my boys are
                                             doomed!'
Straw hats, as hot as butterflies, like butterflies rose on the roar
that met the long, grey princes at the Brandenburger Tor.
'Splendid, splendid' cried Burlington Bertie
all the knuts were so excited
'It doesn't matter now, having empty pockets'
too excited to think of the empty eye-sockets.

Father and Mother stood at home, in the mortal sunrise
that shook on the horizon and refused to move.
They stood, dumb gardeners in a forsaken greenhouse
England, my green house, England, my green thought
in my green shade, yellow sand, emerald isle, silver sea, hearts
                                             of oak

white walls, rule Britannia, Britannia rules the waves, never
                                        waives the rules, but
the thunder's got into the milk, my darling, and the shorthorn's
                                                got T.B.
and what, we soon began to say, is going to become of me?

IV

Explosion.
There is no air. Only a blue vacuum, the hollow flame of a
                                        blow-lamp
a blue, droning flame. An open mouth
a blue, toothless mouth, kissing the young face, and droning.

There is no air, but again and again
explosion, in an exhausted Sunshine.
There is a little air, now. It comes with the rain.
Souls, dropped under dust, stir gently, and soon float
between their owners' feet
pieces of bread in a stopped drain.
My brother has lain down to rest a moment
to blow a tired, red bubble in the mud.
I have lived. I am now dead before I am dead.

Where is my eagle, who was to perch, at last, on my shoulder?
Where is my serpent, the eagle's lover
who was to coil about the eagle, and guide his beak?

I came here that I should not sleep before evening
that I should awake once, in the holy strength of the eagle
and that I should awake a second time, in the holy wisdom of the
                                                serpent
and now I am dead before I am dead.

                                        (*Nore*, 1928)

THE LISTENING CHILD

The sound of England from abroad
the echo of our parents' wedding march
reaches us. Like a gramophone in the next house
we hear our father singing in the drawing room, the past.
Beside a hot and silent sea
we listen to the noises of the past.

With mosquitoes for our foreign rain
dropping in long ropes out of these blue clouds
a rope of mosquitoes meets the sea, and spreads out
like treacle pouring upon the floor. A sigh, and the marble
day slides away.

The echo of London, London's country, comes
between the coffee and the smile
(sing, cicada, shine, phosphorous)
the slow-travelling echo has arrived.
A manly voice. A marriage bell.

(*La Napoule*, 1929)

I REMEMBER I REMEMBER

The light of lemons, a child's light.
Open the history book in the silent north
and it shines like a child.

And yet I see each bough's a finger
scratching the thin wind's skin
each finger has a nail, each knot of fingers
holds a small knife I used to know.

Ah, the war in the south is ever hateful
the islands of light in the sky, travelling fast
and for me, whose big head's always cracked with thirst
my English house is a sweet glass of water.

But must I always remember my soldier childhood
the knives in the trees?

(*Nore*, 1929)

BRANCH

Branch that flew on the hill this morning
spire of pity, rest in this cold glass.

Branch, fold your wild hands, and pray for me
I am twenty-four. Twenty four, and purity still flies before.

(*La Napoule*, 1929)

(*Editor's note*)

Brian sent an early version of the following poem, *Self*, to Eddie Gathorne-Hardy in 1929, with this note: 'Well, I send you, with *much* misgiving, my newest poem—partly because I wrote it, all except five lines in the middle, this morning. As you can imagine, I haven't *genuinely* the faintest idea whether it's good, bad, or indifferent. I take ages to reach my conclusions about a poem and then am probably wrong. Well—here you are—I'm risking a *lot* in sending it to you—*you terrify me* . . .'

SELF

What is this time when the sun stops
and stands on our little mountain like a street lamp?
A light, white ball that stops at the height of its flight
a frozen game
over violet, winter water.

In the middle of our beginning
there is a temporary death.
I see a strange Mediterranean made of a variety of violets
I have never seen before. Sown by the moon, perhaps.
All is gone from me this morning save life itself.

My hottest tear
is one with the frozen stream
my purest laughter shall reappear
in the peacock's scream.

If this should last, good-bye, my friends.
There is only myself left, and that
is the equivalent of nothing.
When I was with you I was many.

The wind has become still, has become
a large, new flower, made of air.

There is only the world itself left
the world that was in the world.
There is only myself left
myself that was in myself.

Wait, you whom I love, if you will
until the sunset picks the last rose, slowly, and goes.
It will leave, now, only black and white
and I shall be the stranger on this rock.

There is this transparent time when the world stops
and it is then, only, that I am.

(La Napoule, 1929)

SHE

Across each Rhodes, beside each sea
the maddened statue of maternity.
The two smooth moons that are her eyes
are not allowed to show surprise.
She is the pelican that broke her breast
to feed the treason in her nest.

O red, returning tide!
She was once a bride.

Blown blind, with huge, sad hands blown hollow
she leans, she leans by the salt, sombre shore.
A silent stone beside a silent harbour
she waits, she waits, nor ever knows them more.

(La Napoule, 1929)

HOMAGE TO TENNYSON

'Between the shadows of the vine bunches
Floated the glowing sunlights as she moved.'
But all my sins return. Alone I pace
the graveyard of myselves.

Oh for an old, night wood!
I would lie down upon a bank, and watch
the stars bathe in the slowly folding stream
a little stream, caught in its own cold curtains
the permanent curtains of my final sadness.
All those young ghosts that were me, stretched around
half in the ground, heads propt in moss, and wreathed
with shining strings of dew, my own old tears.
I would not look at them, having forgiven
having forgotten all the wrongs I've done
and I've been done. Only your red flower
shakes on the opposite bank like a cup of blood.
Where is this stream, the crystal of my sadness
the luminous, fallen statue of despair?
The stream, the purest portrait of my madness
and the ruby blossom, above all my dead, burning the
deep, dark air?

(London, 1929)

THE FIGURE

Believe in the body in the landscape!
The wind on the rock is a flowing flower.

A gun fires on the mountain, the great sound
flies, like another world, over my hollow past.
The flowers flow across the rock.

The figure stands. A cross, a brown star in the scaffolding
of the half built house. The heart.
The sun bounds out of the mountain

while the gun fires again and again. It is the spring.
The gun fires. And a new sun whistles straight up into the
centre of the sky
to hang and throb and flash and shudder.
White flowers and animals pour across the rocks.

The figure stands between the fingers of the coming heart
the slim beams of the heart, the veins
the scaffolding of the house. The heart.

Legs wide, and arms wide. The widest light. The man, the
spreading angel.
Cross. Star.

The worlds are one. It is the spring. The landscape are one.
The mountain is all the mountains. The stream
has swept all the world's water into one. The one rock rises.

The wind lies shining on the rock.

Stand, figure! Stand upon the future, while the past
and the present drop, nails
from your high hands and feet.
Stand, figure, and live, and live! While the future
swings and blazes upon the only landscape.
The new sun roars above. It is all the birds.
Stand, figure! All the flowers burst and roll upon the rocks.
It is the end. The heart is building. It is the beginning.

Stand, figure, brown star, in the heart!

(London, 1930)

ALWAYS

I will never give up asking, where are the days?
Still the hero dwindles upon the marble, chained with bones.

Where is the headland, where are the larger clouds?
Where is the place where there are men and women?

We have been insulted by all islands, all voices and times.
Yet I shall ask always, when will the lovers come, where are
the days?

(London, 1930)

TWO IN ONE

Parfois il parle et dit, 'Je suis belle, et
j'ordonne
Que pour l'amour de moi vous
n'aimiez que le Beau;
Je suis l'Ange gardien, la Muse, et
la Madone!'
Baudelaire

Among wagging leaves, green pots and red
I wrote you a letter when I was dead.
To-day our tears are telegrams. The rain
on the wires is made of tears. Look at those drops again.
How could I speak or eat alone in the south?
It takes four lips to make a mouth.

During a year's fear I heard a voice say
'Cease to pray, and on a last Friday
at sunrise, stand at the white mouth of the sea
up to your cold loins in water and light, and look for me.
I am the thing, the meaning, and the prize
that stands within the balls of your dumb eyes.
Come, when I fit the sun's ring on the day's hand, come
at sunrise.'

Summer and winter came together.
Statues of summer stood along the morning
and walked across the sea with hot, white feet.
Light poured from them upon the ships and flowers
till all the ships were flowers, and blinding flowers the fleet.
From the extreme birth-pain at the sea's electric lips
whence the Guardian Angel came, to the clouds of ice
the blessing statues stretched. As we entered the sky, the
Muse
in blowing fire flew murmuring by, towards the sacrifice.

As we left summer, our two isles took flight
to new, blue stations high above the sea
as 'twixt vast, chanting statues we four rose
the islands rose on the wind, and smiled at the sight.

It was to be all, all, all in a single day
all summer, morning, and all winter, noon
all love to love, all pain to love away
from the white hot sun, all love, to the cold white moon.

So love, which had broken its golden nests on the golden
                                                    sea floor
and burst into ships and flowers by the soft sea shore
            met us upon the mountain.

It seemed the sun spun round the place
and rose and set at our hearts' pace
yet, springing from each other's mouths
love left time instantly, and won the race.

From side to side, the swinging seasons flow
the green May valley flashes into snow
while we, firm founded on each other's mouths
form the world's centre, to love's centre go.

Those misers' bags, our breasts, were first undone
so did our gold each to the other run
then all our blood ran to each other's mouths.
Can two be two, when two have thus been one?

O branching blood, O twin red tree!
You have so kissed, and mixed with me
with blood for food, and wine for bed
our heart-shaped root on wine was fed
with rock for clock, for leaves the snow
how can we wither, or the woodman know?
What can we do but to new glories grow?

The cross was made, the bread was laid
        upon the bleeding stone
the cross was mine, the right was mine
        to spurn the cross, alone.
The moment nears, the heart appears
        the mountain sings and turns
our two heads change to one, a strange
        and blessèd thing, that burns.

What are the stars, poor lonely lights
that hang their cold, chaste chains across the nights?
They wink for tears, who can only aspire
to fuse themselves, as we have done, into one star, one fire.

(*La Napoule*, 1929–1930)

SAYING GOOD-BYE TO A PHOENIX

I am so proud of my rebellious phoenix
he rises, and his wings are blinding gongs.
Over our small, cold London, our dead mother
pour the grey flowers of his ash. Above them I hear huge,
                                            solar songs.

356

I cry good-bye to my free phoenix
with a sandy throat, and my heart is bared.
But I am a poet, and I can make wings, I shall make wings
and though you have flown alone to roost on the sun
the sun's nest shall to-morrow be shared.

(*London*, 1930)

ENTENDS LA DOUCE NUIT QUI MARGHE

I love the day, the yellow phoenix, but I love the terrible night.

I have two loves, and one is the day, the peace, the brother-lover,
the phoenix
he is covered with folding veils of silent fire
he sits and swells within a scroll of strong, harmless fire
that can fill the world, and that feeds me, so that I am the world.
This is the day, the gold food, my truth.

I have two loves, and one is the terrible night
the cannibal carnation, the soft storm
beautiful, blind and black, invisible, alive and dead
the carnation face, the lullaby, the kindest poison, the prison.
Oh loud, loud is the night, the flower made of mouths
louder than the day, louder than my heart.
The sun falls, and at once there swings up from the ground,
in at the window
the night, the drooping thunder, the carnation.
It is a burst flower, its blood has burst it, the petals
are waving fans of soft blood.

It is the mounting night.

(*London*, 1930)

UP

All a large black summer's death dies in this one moment
(this nought)
one afternoon. The sky, pearl in the shut shell, leans,
sick asleep
down the slum to the slum. The rain's chains, without one
sound sung
thin still chains, hang, hardly seen, locking London unlit.
Tearless, I prepare the leap up, newest, longest, most far
I crouch, one, struck, windless, fireless, heavy, heavy the wound
hoping not, speaking not, I knot the nameless muscle. O Life!
bend down, bend my bow, send my arrow high, now, not
low, below.

357

I am my arrow. I have thick hearts to kill, that have killed
                                me. Yet, I am.
I, still, am. Hurl me hard, high, and I will kill, and live,
                        and still give life, O Life.

(*London*, 10*th August*, 1930)

End of *First Poems* Selection.

THE SOUND OF LOVE

To kiss you is to fall, slowly, through a rose the size of a room
Past the noise of happiness, and the noise of pain,
Well-known echoes that I leave behind and above—
As one hears, in a house, rain.
The sound of happiness, and the sound of pain,
Are tourist echoes in the heart's mountains.
It is out of the deepest dark of the heart, where no one goes,
That no man knows, we make the sound of love.

FOR THOSE WITH INVESTMENTS IN SPAIN: 1937

I ask your patience, half of them cannot read,
Your forbearance if, for a while, they cannot pay,
Forgive them, it is disgusting to watch them bleed,
I beg you to excuse, they have not time to pray.
Here is a people, you know it as well as he does,
Franco, you can see it as plain as they do,
Who are forced to fight, for the simplest rights, foes
Richer, stupider, stronger than you, or I, or they, too.
So, while the German bombs burst in their wombs,
And poor Moors are loosed on the unhappy,
And Italian bayonets go through their towns like combs,
Spare a thought, a thought for all these Spanish tombs,
And for a people in danger, shooting from breaking rooms,
For a people in danger, grieving in falling homes.

(First published in 1937 in No. 6 of a series of poetry leaflets *Les Poètes du monde défendent le peuple espagnol* (initiated by Nancy Cunard).
    Reprinted in *Poems for Spain*, edited by Stephen Spender and John Lehmann, Hogarth Press 1939, with the ends of the last two lines reversed—grieving in breaking rooms,/For a people in danger, shooting from falling homes.)

A PRAYER FOR THE FUEHRER

In happy America, on the useless roads of Europe, in
        thousands of small, far streets,
In ditches, in prisons, in hundreds of thousands of furnished
        rooms,

358

There lives a silent, separated people, with a few pennies,
    and no plan.
A father without a child, say, or a lost sister,
Or a soldier, or just an unknown, furious old man.
Their two hands grind together every night, and again in
    the warring morning
As they kneel on the carpet, grass, stone; as they've knelt
    since it all began,
And their fingers crack like the prophecy of shooting.
Their eyes burst with tears, and liquid sounds burst through
    their breath.
They are saying their prayers. Their prayers are for your
    death.

(Published in the *New Statesman and Nation*, June 1939)

GONE TO REPORT

For twenty-one years he remained, faithful and lounging
There, under the last tree, at the end of the charming
    evening street,
His flask was always full for the unhappy, rich, or bold;
He could always tell you where you wanted to go, what you
    wanted to be told,
And during all the dear twenty-one years he remained
    exactly twenty-one years old.
His eyes were the most honest of all, his smile the most
    naturally sweet.

Many, many trusted him who trusted no one. Many
    extremely clever
Persons will kill themselves unless they find him. They
    search
Sparkling with fear, through the whole quarter. They even
    enter the Church.
Crowds, across all Europe, are beginning to feel they've
    been left in the lurch.
But it's worse than that. It's something they couldn't tell
    anyone, ever.

He's abandoned his post because he was the greatest of all
    informers,
And now he's gone to report. He never had a moment's
    leisure.
He was paid by so many powers that one shakes with shame
To think of them. Time, the Army and Navy, Pain and
    Blame,

The Police, the Family, and Death. No one will escape. He
    got every name.
And he wasn't at all what he said he was. Mr. Pleasure.

(Published in Horizon, May 1940)

THE HIRED MAN

The hired man, dressed (as always) in civvies, furred with dirt
Stirs in a corner of the deep, black room. There's a piece of light
Under the shutter. What does it mean?
A car storms in the courtyard. People go down the stairs.
What does it mean? The hired man stares, and hears.

In a room full of sleeping soldiers, have you noticed
The softest boot-scrape causes a general sigh
Like the sound of despair itself, I don't know why.
But the hired man doesn't care who he wakes this morning,
Because if this is a mistake it is the last mistake.

And now his terrible beds begin to whisper,
And a bandage snaps, and a white mouth
Hisses, 'What does it mean?' He opens the shutter.

(*Editor's note*)

Around the original handwritten manuscript of the next poem Brian had included the following notes. (The poem was sent to his mother from Le Rayol and dated 23rd May, 1940.)

'Wishing you as Happy a Birthday as possible—with all my love, for ever, my dear one. When I think of what I owe you, in every conceivable kind of way—well, it's so much that there's nothing to be said. Never mind. We'll manage. Our spirits are one.

'. . . How good this poem actually is, I have no means, yet, of knowing. But I *feel* it is *good*, and I think, perhaps, one of the *best* that I have written for you. (Many of which you have never seen.) . . . You see, poems can't be written about great historic dramas *at the time*—so they get written about smaller, but, perhaps, more important things, if one thinks about it . . . The third verse might have been written by Emily Dickinson, oddly enough. Curious how influences crop up?'

TO MY MOTHER

Here's your letter. You sigh—
'Your burning blue
Not my soft English Sky'
I like mine best. It's true.

Yet who told a child
   Of Florida, Mexico?
Murmured 'Perhaps one day
   That's where, my child, you'll go?'

Who spoke of fish like fireworks?
   Of boats more glass than wood?
Gave me magnolias first to smell,
   And turned my head for good?

Who speaking, seems to have the sun
   Oh yes, the sunlight on her mouth
Always? And in whose huge eyes
   Did I first see the South?

(*Editor's note*)

Daphne Fielding wrote in her book, *Mercury Presides*: 'Heaven's Gate or Prospect Hill, where Bishop Ken used to spend the long summer evenings waiting for the guidance of divine inspiration to compose his hymns, is now thronged with courting couples. By the side of the road that winds through the beech trees planted there by Capability Brown there is a notice-board bearing the ambiguous sign: *Heaven's Gate—No Coaches*.

'For me this hill was heavy with nostalgia, evoking memories of old friends who had so often come here to picnic with us when Longleat was still a home and not a monument—a period of time recaptured in this poem that Brian Howard sent me just before the transformation took place . . .'

LONGLEAT: 1948 (for D. and H.)

Twenty years. The curtains drawn,
Windows sleeping, door shut;
Here, the wasted, noble lawn,
There, trees cut
Hymns to murder have been sung,
Robert, Rex have gone away.
Wandering these woods among,
Have we any right to May?
Yes, Remembering well these things;
What it was they cherished,
Why they met the torture kings
Fought and won and perished.
Come, then. Stand on Heaven's Gate,
Lake below and leaves above—
This is why they found their fate.
Here is where we feel their love.

361

INSTANTANEOUS TIME EXPOSURE

(for Wystan Auden)

Not really a picture, and not even a map
And not wholly in focus; its message slight, even
For those photographed. People who happened to be
Walking about on a rock, having bathed in a sea.

It's true that this scrap of shadowed paper
Contains a face which, afterward, may
Spur someone to say: 'That one, the nearest
Made poetry mean things again. For us. In his day.'

In fact, there's a second poet. And even a hero, there
With a hand missing. But he who caught
This ordinary moment, sees, in the furling print
Proof that what might be, is in a summer world.

There, on a timeless coast famous for friendship
I see the timelessness of friends. I hear
As if my curled paper were an Ischian conch
That noon-dark echo which can silence fear.

A little behind the rest, with calm, loose arms
And hair which, though gray here
Is like a hustling harvest, stands the youngest
Of all. Sea-polished. Love is also there.

Under the limestone cliff, breathing their own air
That smells of salt and figs; with crinkled eyes
They turn to face the sun, and my machine.
Where they have always been. They always will be there.

(Published in *Harper's Magazine*, 1949)

TWO IT TAKES TO MAKE A FLOWER

Two it takes to make a flower
   two it takes to make our homes;
The lonely one, who hour by hour
   Plants, and builds. And one who roams.

Roams, returns, and sees his meaning,
   In one flower, in one place;
On one heart, and on one face,
   And, though loving, leaves still leaning.

Two it takes to make a flower,
   two it takes to make a life.
Think, then, of the child's terror,
   the silly child without a wife.

Think, then, of his only garden
 when the gardener is gone.
Who, I ask, will give him pardon,
 when the time for pardon's done?

THE DUST

No soap can wash away this sundust
And no scrubbing, this salt dust of the sea.
What is this powder with which you are covered
When the sun lies on your skin, slantingly?

Something like pollen, yet finer, lighter
And more of a mineral thing. It glows
A St. Elmo's fire, a quicksilver wire
Which grows with the sun and with the sun goes.

Is it the true state of being clean? It smells
like an approaching island, or a shipload of hay.
Made of seadust, sunsalt and flesh, is it the true sign
Of being well and whole? It cannot be washed away

All I know is, this thing is not a substance
Found on the ill or ugly, or on those
Whose favourite word is 'No'. It is very often
Worn by the beautiful instead of clothes.

All I know is, the desperate have washed you
Using their holy water, for two thousand years
And still the dust I speak of burns upon you
As bright as Love. Brighter than all their tears.

(Published in *Horizon*, and *Harper's Magazine*, 1949)

GARDA

(for Stephen Spender)

To-day, when the round and growing heart of man
Has shrunk into the violence of an arrow-head
When change has got out of control, grumbling
And stumbling faster and nastier every minute
And taking the names of those who protest—
In this least agreeable of historical moments
(when those who don't stalk to war, limp to church)
What a miracle can one perform
Merely by coming to Garda's lake, especially Torri.
Man-sized Torri, set beside the Brenner road
The most august of all roads, the double gate, where Rome
Went North, carrying the sun and the idea.

Here, the gods do not interfere
With one another, or you.
The violence and the change inhabit only
The water, the winds and the exhaustless sky
Which, balanced on mountains, is Europe's fullest
Holding.
Clouds with different names, pearl searchlights, rocks
And storms which slide between the sunlight and the sun
Hiding neither. A sky which, seeming simply southern
Moves faster than the clock.

The great ghost of Catallus
Stands on Sirmio still
Hopeful, observing change and violence still translated
Into what we can love.
But intercede, if you can, for us, Catallus
And you, later familiars of Garda, intercede
If you are able, Goethe, Tennyson, d'Annunzio, Gide.

The living can watch the opposite shore
(which, as regards other lakes, is always a shore)
Be often transformed, so odd is the weather
Into the islands you need.
Can watch the hair-fine fish-nets on the harbour wall
Change to huge ribbons of star-sapphire smoke
Can hear
The world's guns change their song to long heart swinging
          thunder
(whole minutes of thunder)
Can see the bombs exchanged for the fume of descending
          light-shafts
And invasions changed into quicksilver waves. And many
          questions
Into answers.
All, in Torri, may watch the past alive, and blessing
The present, which lives only on the lake. In beauty.
And some may glimpse the great ghosts intervening
And some may hear, through beauty's wonderful noise
Some of her meaning.

LATE NIGHT FINAL

Poets, write your final poems
   Lovers, play your game—
The leaves will fall for different reasons
One of these autumns, and none of the seasons
   Will ever be quite the same.

364

Sparkling soldiers now prepare
  What they were born to do—
The death for which they live their lives
They wish to share it, with their wives
  Their children, and with you.

(Published in Harper's Magazine, March 1952)

TO-DAY

The suicides will never cease
To sweep the peaks in fighter-planes
Informers, or the rich, will keep
The valley for their patriot pains.

The epoch of the second finest
Killing for the second best
Hangs like a ticket round our journey—
A welcome, then, to unsuccess.

Madness-in-action on the height
The spirit's death below—
There's only left the timber line
Where the pine meets the snow.

Where the last of Europe's eagles
Starve, and watch the mountain road
With the ibex for their sentry
And the wind for their abode.

(Published in Harper's Magazine, 1952)

Appendix II.
Where Engels fears to tread

by Cyril Connolly

Press Gang! Crazy World Chronicle, edited by Leonard Russell, was published by Hutchinson in 1937 and consisted of a series of spoof newspaper articles written by the following select band: Hilaire Belloc, John Betjeman, Cyril Connolly, E. M. Delafield, Francis Iles, Ronald Knox, D. B. Wyndham Lewis, A. G. Macdonnell, J. B. Morton, L. A. Pavey, Dilys Powell, Peter Quennell, Leonard Russell, Edward Shanks, Timothy Shy, and Douglas Woodruff. These articles were said to have been gleaned from the scrapbooks of one Dr. J. Albert Glump, a fervent collector of newspaper cuttings, and reproduced in volume form to give, the editor hoped, 'some slight picture of the contemporary world . . .' Dr. Glump's notes introduced each cutting, and in the case of Cyril Connolly's contribution (which was later reprinted in his collection of essays, *The Condemned Playground*, published by Routledge in 1945) they ran as follows:

What a curious young man the author of this autobiography must be! But one thing is clear from this review, which, unless my cuttings have been wrongly indexed, occupied the whole of the New Statesman *Autumn Books Supplement. His is a spirit which has been through no ordinary travail. J.A.G.*

WHERE ENGELS FEARS TO TREAD

[1]*From Oscar to Stalin. A progress.* By Christian de Clavering (The Clay Press, 12s. 6d).

Reviewed by Cyril Connolly.

At last the authentic voice of a generation: 'You are all a lost generation!' remarked Gertrude Stein of us post-war age-groups, and now, thanks to Mr. Christian de Clavering, we know who lost us. Let me try and tell you all about this book while I am still full of it. First thing you know you have opened it, and there is the dedication:

'TO THE BALD YOUNG PEOPLE'

Then comes a page of fashionable quotations all in German. The middle part by Kafka, the fringes by Rilke and Hölderlin. The rest by Marx. Impeccable. And the introduction.

'Why am I doing this, my dears? Because I happen to be the one person who can do it. My dears, I'm on your side! I've come to get you out of the wretched tangle of individualism that you've made for yourselves and show you just how

---

[1] Book Society choice; Left Book Club choice; recommended by the Right Book Club.

you can be of some use in the world. Stop worrying whether he loves you or not; stop wondering how you will ever make any money. Never mind whether the trousers of your new suit turn up at the bottom; leave off trying to annoy Pa. We're on to something rather big. The Workers' Revolution for the Classless Society through the Dictatorship of the Proletariat! Yes! It's a bit of a mouthful, isn't it! We're used to words of one syllable, words like Freud, Death, War, Peace, Love, Sex, Glands, and, above all, to Damn, Damn, Damn! Well, all that's going to be changed. Morning's at seven, and you've got a new matron.

'I'm told Mr. Isherwood is writing a book about the 'twenties. Mr. Isherwood is a Cambridge man, and we who made the 'twenties do not wish them looked at through the wrong end of a cocoa-tin. Through either end. My precious 'twenties! He shan't have them! Avaunt. Avanti!'

(And so the autobiography starts. I will quote a few of the dazzling vignettes. For the reasons with which the author concludes, I have refrained from comment.)

Home. Background. Mother.

'Mother, who is that horrible old obesity with the black chin? I believe he's following us.'

'Hush, that's Daddy.'

And so dawned my second birthday.

Home.

'Mother, where is home this time. Heliopolis? Hammamet? Ragusa? Yalta?'

'Guess again.'

'I know. Prinkipo.'

'Warm.'

'Monte Carlo.'

'Very warm.'

'Has it got a clever coastline? I know! Cannes!'

And home for the next two months it was.

'Mother—what does Father do?'

'He has his business, boy o' mine.'

'And what is that?'

'He's a sort of accountant.'

'On 'Change?'

'On the Turf!'

'Poor Mother, poor darling Mother—but we needn't see him, need we?'

'Of course not, precious, but I thought you were old enough to know.'

I pulled the hood down and for a moment it was very stuffy inside the pram . . .

Children's Party.

'What is your father, Christian?'

'He's interested in racing—my mother is the Honourable. What is *your* father, Edelweiss?'

'A mediatized prince. What sort of racing?'

'Oh, never mind now—let's ask Mother to play some *Rimsky*.'

But I realised I couldn't stay on in Montreux Territet.

My mother an angel. My father a bookie!

'And don't forget, my boy, a tenner for every little nob you bring home with a handle to his name.'

Eton. Henry's holy shade. An impression, above all, of arches, my dears, each with its handsome couple, and study fireplaces always full of stubs of Balkan Sobranie. And the naughtiest elms! While the battle of Waterloo was being fought all round me, I just sat still and watched my eyelashes grow. There were books, of course. Pater, Alma Pater, with his worried paragraphs. His prose reminded me of stale privet—and Petronius, who made me long to know more Latin. (I only learned two words, *curculio* and *vespertilio*, a bat and a weevil, but they got me everywhere, afterwards, on Mount Athos.) And Compton Mackenzie as he then was, and Huxley, before he had acquired his Pope and Bradley manner, and Verlaine of course; Rimbaud, Mallarmé, Baudelaire.

'What is that book, de Clavering?'

'*Les Chansons de Bilitis*, sir.'

'And what is this lesson?'

'You have the advantage, sir.'

'What do you mean, boy?'

'Ah, sir, fair's fair. I told you what my book was. You must tell me what's your lesson.'

'Elementary geometry.'

'But it sounds fascinating! Then this delicious piece of celluloid nonsense is—I know sir, don't tell me—a set-square?'

'I have been teaching it for twenty years, and never met with such impertinence.'

'Twenty years, and still at Elementary! Oh, sir, what a confession.' And it was a very purple face one glimpsed behind the blackboard. Ah, those Eton masters! I wish I could remember any of their names, for I was really sorry for them. What tragedies went on under their mortar-boards! Some of them were quite young, and one often got the impression that they were trying, inarticulately, to communicate; would have liked, in fact to share in the rich creative life that already was centring round me. They used to teeter round my Baksts, and once I caught my housemaster sniffing at a very special bottle made up for me by Max of Delhez, and gingerly rubbing some on his poor old pate. Worldlings, yet deprived of all worldly grace, of our rich sex-life how pathetically inquisitive! They are all there still, I suppose, and I often wonder, when I motor through Switzerland in summer, if one will not find a bunch of them spawning round some mouldy *arête*, in their Norfolk jackets, like eels in the Sargasso Sea.

The boys of course took up most of my time. I soon found that it was easy to get on with them by giving them presents, and making them laugh. A dozen of claret here, a humidor of Coronas there, a well-timed repartee, and persecution was made impossible. It was easy to find the butts and make rather more skilful fun of them than anybody else. In fact, I give this advice to those of my readers who are still at school. In every group there are boys whom it is the fashion to tease and bully; if you quickly spot them and join in, it will never occur to anyone to tease and bully you. Foxes do not hunt stoats. But always defer to the original teasers, and hand your prey over to them for the *coup de grâce*. And boys like expensive presents, though they are genuinely embarrassed by them. All the same, they were a provincial lot. I never felt very safe unless I had several of them round me, in coloured caps and gaudy blazers, puffing away at my cigarettes and looking for dirty jokes in the *Vie Parisienne*. By cultivating all the Captains of Games in this way I found my afternoons were left free. I would watch them troop away with their shinpads to some mysterious district on the way to Slough, then saunter up to Windsor with a book—on the bridge I would wave to any who seemed to be pushing a particularly big boat underneath it. Happy river of Eton-Windsor! I have always been very vague about its name, but I often pictured it winding away past Reading Gaol and into the great world somewhere—the world of the Ballet and the Sitwells, of Cocteau and the Café Royal.

'Hello, Faun, what a way to spend your *Après-midi.*'

It was Hubert, my most uneasy disciple.

'I was just thinking that summer made a noise like the rubbing together of biscuits.'

'Yes, it is hot,' he replied. 'If it goes on like this I shall have to buy some FLANNELS.'

'And be mistaken for Peter Fleming?'

'Oh, you're cruel. But seriously, what *shall* we do?'

'Well, there's Tull's, and I haven't eaten a lobster patty since this morning—or one might buy a gramophone record—or a very cool Braque or half a dozen ash-blonde oysters—then there's that place one goes to London from.'

'You mean the G.W.R.?'

'Thank you—and by now the school library will probably have heard of William Morris—or one might try the arches and see what one could pick up.'

'Or the Castle.'

'I'm bored with bearskins—but, my dear, that man—he's touched his cap—so familiar.'

'You mean the headmaster?'

It seemed an evil omen.

Then there was the Corps. I quickly joined the signal section. You didn't have to carry rifles. It was there that I first met intellectuals, dowdy fellows mostly, who went in for Medici prints and had never heard of Picasso. I realised for the first time what a gap separated cultured and cosmopolitan art lovers like myself, people who cared equally for music, painting and literature, from those whose one idea was to pass examinations; literature is a very different thing to a poet and to someone who has to make a living out of it. 'What do you think of Apollinaire?' I asked one of them. 'Good God, we won't get a question on that—he's well outside the period.' 'On the contrary, he's very much of it. His book on Sade is vital.' 'I thought you meant Sidonius Apollinaris.' I could make no contact with them. But signalling was delightful. One sat for hours beside a field-telephone while little figures receded into the distance with the wire. 'Can you hear me?' 'No.' 'Can you hear me now?' 'No.' 'Well, try this.' 'This' was the morse-code machine, and nimbler fingers than mine would fill the air with a drowsy song. Iddy iddy umpty umpty iddy umpty iddy . . . However, all things come to an end, and there were tiresome scenes—long waits in red-brick classrooms looking at huge sheets of paper—'write only on one side of the paper.' But which side? and the precious minutes were wasted. Suddenly a lot of people I had always been willing to avoid seemed to have no object in life but to want to meet one. They would cluster round some old cannon outside New Schools, gowns fluttering and tassels wagging. One afternoon, when the place was looking more Raphael Tuck than ever, I went upstairs, and unforgivable things were said. It seemed one was suspected of all the alluvial vices, in fact one was not getting the best out of the curriculum. For the last time I crossed the bridge over the mysterious river, past Tom Browne's, where rather a good pair of 'sponge bags' were being created for me for Ascot, past Hills and Saunders, who had turned out some passable groups of my tea-parties. 'These people are my friends,' I would implore the photographer, 'I want them to look fresh and good-looking and aristocratic and rich.' 'But, sir.' 'Remember, they are not the Shooting Eight, or Mr. Crace's Old Boys, and I don't want to sit in the middle with folded arms and a football. I shall stand rather over to the side and at the back, and the only way you will know I am the host is by this enormous cocktail shaker.'

*   *   *

'Oh, my boy, my boy, 'ere am I sweating away on the Turf to edicate you, and just when I 'ope you'll bring the nobs in you go and get sacked. Sacked from Eton!'

'Not sacked, Pater—supered.'

But my father could never appreciate an academic distinction.

*   *   *

Before one can understand Oxford one must have lived in Capri, and it was there that I spent the next few months, cramming. Mother had taken a quiet villa with a view of the funicular. At seventeen it was rather odd to figure recognizably in five novels in three languages. But Monty and Norman were insatiable. 'No one would think it absurd if you sat to five painters,' they remonstrated, and I retorted that I had a jolly good mind to—but I was too busy at that time, sitting for Fersen.[2] It was my first introduction to *les paradis artificiels* (not counting Tidworth), and with all a boy's healthy craving for novelty I flung myself down on the Count's couches and sampled poppy after poppy through his amusing collection of Chinese pipes. When the time came for my Oxford vivâ, I was older than the rocks and my eyelids were definitely a little weary. I could not decide. Magdalen and *Sinister Street*, Merton and Max, Balliol and Gumbril? or the House—Peers and Peckwater? Max had praised my eyelashes. Harold said Balliol was perfect for case-histories like mine, but I realised I should find it madly ungay. That Buttery! Finally it was the House I chose, two vast eighteenth-century rooms which I did up in pewter and cinnamon. Harold supplied wax fruit, and antimacassars for the Chinese Chippendale chairs, I added incense, brass trays and buddhas, and Robert a carpet from the Victoria and Albert (the Yacht, not the Museum).

My father had become reconciled to me. ' 'Appiest days of your life my boy, and don't forget, a pony for every youngster you bring 'ome with a 'andle to his name. Good for the business.' I was worried about my father. 'Mother,' I said,

---

[2] The Marsac of *Vestal Fires.*

370

'don't you think Daddy is looking definitely *blafard*?' Is he?' she replied. 'You're sitting on the Continental Bradshaw.'

Most of my Eton friends had also come up to the House, and, as my father had taken a flat in Bicester, 'ponies' and 'monkeys' came rolling in. I spent them on clothes and parties, on entertaining and on looking entertaining. Parties! 'Are you going to de Clavering's to-night?' and woe betide the wretch who had to say no. Nothing much happened at the time, but he soon felt he was living on an ice-floe, drifting farther and farther from land, and every moment watching it melt away. De Clavering's to-night! The candles burn in their sconces. The incense glows. Yquem and Avocado pears—a simple meal—but lots and lots of both, with whisky for the hearties and champagne for the dons. 'Have a brick of caviare, Alvanley? More birds' nest, Gleneagles? There's nothing coming, I'm afraid, only Avacado pear and hot-pot.' 'Hot-pot!' 'Christian, you're magnificent!' 'Caviare and hot-pot—Prendy will be blue with envy!' And then dancing, while canons go home across the quad, and David stomps at the piano. I took care at these parties to have a word and piece of advice for everyone.

There was an alert young man in a corner, looking rather shy. 'I know—don't tell me,' I said to him, 'it's your first party.' 'Yes.' I pinched his cheek. 'Si jeunesse savait!' I laughed. It was Evelyn Waugh.

Another little fellow asked me if I could suggest a hobby. 'Architecture,' I gave in a flash. 'Thank you.' It was John Betjeman.

'And for me?'

'Afghanistan.'

It was Robert Byron.

'And me?'

'Byron,' I laughed back—it was Peter Quennell.[3]

And Alvanley, Gleneagles, Prince Harmatviz, Graf Slivovitz, the Ballygalley of Ballygalley, Sarsaparilla, the Due de Dingy, the Conde de Coca y Cola—for them, my peers, I kept *my* serious warnings.

'These bedroom slippers, Dingy? I flew them over from my *bottier*.'

'You ought to look a little more like a public school prefect, Alvanley. The front cover of *The Captain*, it's rather more your *genre*. There! Wash out the 'honey and flowers', and try a fringe effect. I want to see a pillar of the second eleven.'

'Good jazz, Gleneagles, is meant to be played just a little bit too slow.'

'Graf Slivovitz, this isn't the *Herrenclub* in Carpathian Ruthenia, you must take off your hat. Yes—that green growth with the feudal feathers.'

'Sarsaparilla, only the King rouges his knees when he wears a kilt, and then only at a Court ball.'

'Harmatviz, I can smell that Harris a mile away. What on earth is that terrifying harpoon in the lapel?'

'That, de Clavering, is a Fogas[4] fly.'

'More Yquem, Ballygalley?'

'What's that?'

---

[3] All of whom, I am told (autumn 1937), still keep afloat.
[4] An amusing fish from the Balaton.

'That—if you mean the thing under your elbow—is how I look to Brancusi; the other is a kind of wine. Stand him up, will you Ava?'

'Before the war we heard very little of the Sarsaparillas—he would not dare wear that tartan in Madrid.'

'Before the war I hadn't heard of you, Coca y Cola, either; Count, this is a democratic country.'

'I am democrats, we are all democrats. *Vive le roi.*'

'Thank you, Dingy, you must have been reading *Some People*. Now I want all the Guinnesses and Astors to go into the next room and get a charade ready. Alvanley, Gleneagles, Harmatviz, and Slivovitz—you will drive quickly over with me for a few minutes to Bicester to say good-night to father.'

'No I don't think.'—'My price is ten guineas.'—'Jolly well not unless we go halves.'—'Where is my hat and gotha?'—and madcap youth was served.

My crowning moment. The Summerville Grind. Peers and their mothers and sisters in mackintoshes and shooting-sticks. My mount. A huge animal whose teeth need cleaning. For the first time in my life I wear a bowler hat. And my racing colours. White silk shirt with a broad blue stripe—but zigzag! Alvanley and Gleneagles on each side of me—off! I was petrified, my dears; the first fence was enormous and my animal seemed hours getting over it. There was time for me to get down, and I rolled over. On it thundered, its great ugly stirrups banging together. A man leant over me. 'Not hurt, are you?' he said. And then, *plus fort que lui*, 'Where *did* you get that shirt?' It was on a sigh that I answered, as I lost consciousness, 'Sire, at Charvet's.' It was the Prince.

And there was talk—all kinds—the banter of my friends.

'Ah, de Clavering, if you were only of the nobility. I would ask you to stay at Dingy. What a pity you are not a real goodfellow.'

'Apfelstrüdel! He is coming to Schloss Slivovitz with Pryce-Jones, is not that good enough for you?'

'Slivovitz—how picturesque it must be. But at Dingy we have to consider the *convenances*, my aunt Doudeauville, my Uncle Sagan . . .'

'She 'appens to be *my* aunt Doudeauville too.'[5] Her mother was of the German branch.'

'I can find no Harmatviz on Madame Sacher's tablecloth.'

'Rosa Lewis says the Claverings are an old Scotch family.'

'Sarsaparilla would know that.'

'Before the war we heard very little of the Sarsaparillas, now it appears . . .'

'Ah, bonjour, Coca y Cola, how is the Alvis?'

'Very well, would you like to look under the bonnet?'

'Haw, haw, haw, what a suggestion.'

'But seriously, de Clavering—you are rich, you are intelligent, why have you no titles? Have you spoken to the King?'

'He may have no title, but I would trust him with my waistcoats.'

'And I shake him by the hand—and say—'Well, what the hell, who cares?'

'Bravo, Harmatviz, it's a democratic country, *Vive le roi!*'

---

[5] By the marriage of Graf Hubertus Mary von and zu Slivovitz-Slivovitz with Katarina Auburn-Cord.

Then there was brilliant conversation at Balliol, where the food makes long journeys to the dowdy sitting-rooms, under tins.

'We were discussing, de Clavering, whether it was more correct to say Theophylactus Simocattes or Simocatta—'

'You should consider yourself very lucky, Sparrow, to be able to say either.'

'And what the collective noun is for a group of pelicans; there is a gaggle of geese, of course, and a pride of lions.'

'A piety of pelicans, I suggest.'

'Thank you—how delightfully Thomas Browne. I shall repeat that.'

'I don't know which I dislike most, people who repeat my epigrams or people who copy my ties—and, by the way, I hope you don't mind. I've brought Raymond Radiguet.'

'Where's he up?'

'He's not up. He lives in Paris.'

'Paris! If I get an All Sogger I am determined to go there. It's right on the way to the British School.'

'I know a very nice little hotel near the *Bibliothèque Mazarine*.'

'I can't see why they don't build an arcade from Brick Top's[6] to the Ritz.' Nobody laughs. As usual, one can find no contact with them.

My twenty-firster. Fifty people in fancy dress. The orchestra from the *Grand Ecart*. A large silver waste-paper basket. 'To Christian de Clavering, the Great Commoner—Alvanley, Alba, Ava, Abercorn, Andrassy, Aberconway, Argyll, Auersperg'—you can imagine the signatures. As the college barge, which I had taken for the occasion, glided up the Cher, life's goblet seemed full to brimming. But Nemesis pursued me. The dons descended. I suppose they hadn't had enough invitations. It appears that those afternoons which I spent under some hot towels in Germers were full of goings-on, lectures, tutorials, Heaven knows what. Divinity seemed a prominent element in the City of Lost Causes. I went down. Oxford, like Eton, had never really 'given'.

London at last.[7] The 'twenties. Parties. Parties. Parties. And behind them all an aching feeling.—Was it worth it? What is it all for? Futility . . .

'Christian—you must dine with me tonight!'

'Gawain—I can't—I've engaged myself to the '*Derries*.'

*   *   *

'Are you the manager?'

'Yes, sir.'

'My name is de Clavering. I should like to say I have never eaten such a disgusting meal. Même à la Cour. But haven't I seen you before?'

'Oui, monsieur, je vous connais depuis l'Eldorado.'

*   *   *

'Es usted el cuadro flamenco?'

'Si.'

'Si.'

---

[6] Always my favourite nightbox.

[7] A London then where everybody knew everybody and we all squeezed into one telephone book!

'Si.'
'Si.'

*   *   *

'Beverley, my dear, such a gaffe! I've just gone up to the old Dowager of Buck-and-Chan and mistaken her for the old Dowager of Ham-and-Bran!'
'*Christian!*'

*   *   *

'She's got what the Americans call "that".'
'What?'
'What the Americans call "that".'
'What's that?'
' "That"—that's what she's got.'
'But what the Americans call what? I don't even know that.'
'Oh, my dear Duchess!'
For it was sometimes my privilege to give instruction to a very great lady.

*   *   *

'M. Picasso—Mr. Hemingway, M. Hemingway—Señor Belmonte. Mr. Nicolson—Mr. Firbank—and now shall we begin without Miss Stein? I'm starving.'

*   *   *

'I can't decide whether to stay with Lorenzo in Taos or Crowley in Cefalu—where *does* one go in August?'

*   *   *

'Dear Evelyn, *of course*, put me into it!'

*   *   *

'Voulez-vous téléphoner à Mr. Proust de venir me trouver dans les bains de la rue de Lappe?'

*   *   *

'Herr Reinhardt ist zuschloss?'

*   *   *

'You know Diaghilev, of course, Dingy?'

*   *   *

'I've found the title for you, Breton—*Surréalisme.*'

*   *   *

'And for this rather brusque poem, Osbert, I shall need the "meg".'[8]

*   *   *

Parties. Futility. You can read of most of them in old gossip columns. I still remember my tropical party, when a punkah was heard for the first time in Egerton Crescent. Palms and bananas decorated the rooms. The central heating (it was in July) provided the atmosphere. Some stewards from the P. & O. worked away at the punkahs, or at distributing *reistafel* and planters' punch. The guests wore shorts, sarongs, stingah shifters, or nothing at all.

'But this is *me*,' I remember saying, holding up a slim volume. 'Why haven't I been told about this before, Dadie? Who is this T. S. Eliot?'
'He works in a bank, I believe.'

---

[8] A megaphone, and such small ability as I may have acquired with it, now constitute my 'platform manner'.

'Works in a bank—and writes *The Waste Land*! But he should be here, at my Tropical Party! Go and fetch him.'

But there is a new disturbance, and Bolitho, our butler, is at my elbow.

'Some young people, sir.'

'Their names?'

'The *Blackbirds*.'

'Ask them to come up. We shall want some more room, Patrick, help me spread Elizabeth somewhere else. Ronald, come out from under the sofa, you're hunching the springs.[9] Fallen out of the window, you say, with Brenda? Never mind, for the moment. I want to be alone. I want to read this book.'

And then the blow fell. A summons, next day, to the Royal Automobile Club. 'I'm ruined, my boy. I'm ruined. 'Aven't got a penny left. Those pals of yours, Alvanley and Gleneagles. They've skinned me. You'll 'ave to earn your own living from now on. Oh, your poor mother!' 'It's poor me, you old banana. I've no intention of earning my own living, thank you.'—'Ow, wot a boy, wot a boy.' And I flung out. Tears. Consultations.

'I can always sell my Gris.' 'But what will you do then?'

'Oh, write—paint—don't fluster me.'

'And we were to have gone to the Londonderry del Vals!'

'Poor mother.'

One thing stood out with terrible clarity in those dark days. The old life was over. I could never associate any longer with these friends who had been used to look to me for advice, loans, old clothes, and entertainment. They would see to that. The Ritz, the Blue Lantern, must know me no more.

Exile. A few months in Paris—but Montparnasse, now, my dears, *Montparnasse*; a few offers for my memoirs; then Berlin, Munich—and finally, Greece. There, 'in the worst inn's worst room,' I existed, miserably, on fried goat and raki. To write or to paint—to work—but how? Write only on one side of the paper. But which side? It was the old dilemma. A wandering exile, the quays of the Piraeus knew me, the noisy bars of Terreno, the Dôme and the Deux Magots, Bohème and Silhouette, and that place in the Marokaner Gasse. I ate rose-leaf jam with the good monks of Holy Luke, and fried locusts with the dervishes of Moulay Idris. And one crazy 4th of June, lobster salad with my housemaster! My slim figure lingered, winterbound, in dim cathedrals, and there were beaches where summer licked me with its great rough tongue. Ah, summer! There's a crypto-fascist for you! The spring I never cared for. It held nothing but a promise, and I, too, was promising. The autumns I adored; they smelt of cassia. But poverty was crippling. To whom life once had been a bed of roses—no, of *Strawberry leaves*, there remained only the 'Welcome' at Villefranche, the old Boeuf in the Boissy D'Anglas, the Pangion. It was not good enough. I came back to live with my mother.

It was then that I saw the light. One day I wandered into a little bookshop near Red Lion Square. It was full of slim volumes by unfamiliar names—who were Stephen, Wystan, Cecil, and Christopher? Madge? Bates? Dutt? These blunt monosyllables spoke a new kind of language to me. I looked at the books. Not

---

[9] Firbank's shyness was proverbial.

at all bad, and some of these young poets, I realized, had even attended my university! One quatrain in particular haunted me.

> M is for Marx
> and Movement of Masses
> and Massing of Arses
> and Clashing of Classes.

It was new. It was vigorous. It was real. It was chic!

> Come on Percy, my pillion-proud,
>   be camber-conscious
> Cleave to the crown of the road

and

> It was late last night when my lord came home
> enquiring for his lady O
> The servants cried on every side
> She's gone with the Left Book
>   Study Circle O!

And everyone was called by their Christian names! So cosy! From that moment I've never looked back. It's been pylons all the way. Of course they didn't want me, at first. The meetings behind the Geisha Café—they suspected me of all sorts of things, I'm afraid—I said quite frankly: 'I realise I shall never understand eclectic materialism but I'm terribly terribly Left!' And I showed them one or two things I'd written for the weekly reviews, all among the waffle-receipts and the guest-house advertisements.[10] And I called myself Cris Clay. Then—on a drizzling February morning—came my first Procession! It was for me a veritable *Via Crucis*, for we had to march up St. James's Street—past Locks, and Lobbs, and Briggs, and Boodles. All my past was spread out before me. There weren't very many of us, and it was difficult to cheer and shout our slogans

> One, two, three, four,
> Pacifism means War.

I raised my eyes to White's bow-window.

Yes, there they were—Alvanley and Gleneagles, with their soiled city faces and little moustaches, their bowlers and rolled umbrellas—and, good heavens, there were Peter, and Robert, and Evelyn! I never felt more ridiculous. When suddenly something made me look round. 'De Clavering, old horse!' 'Well, I'm spifflicated.' 'You old *finocchio!*' '*Spinaten!*' It was too good to be true.

'But, Harmatviz—I see you don't know the first thing about the cut of a corduroy.'

---

[10] Soon to be published under the title of *I Told You So.*

'Not a red shirt, Slivovitz—a red tie if you must.'

'And you, Coca y Cola—you look like a scarecrow.'

'These are good workmen's pants, de Clavering, real dungaree!'

We gave a boo to the bow-window that made the *Tatlers* rattle in their holders.

'But how did you get here?'

'I was expelled for plotting against the Regent in favour of the traitor Otto.'

'I was turned out for lack of enthusiasm for the present regime and communicating with the traitor Wilhelm.'

'I wanted to annoy Sarsaparilla.'

'Anyhow, we're all good anti-Fascists,' cried Comrade Graf Slivovitz.

I wanted to say something more—that I had even been told by the Party that I should be more useful outside it, but I couldn't speak. Old friends had met, travelling a stony road, coming to the same hard conclusions, and together.

* * *

And that's about all. There are one or two things I've left out, the war, the slump, the general strike, and my conversion to Catholicism, because I'm so vague about dates. But I think this will remain—A Modern Pilgrimage. And now for the reviewers. I think they'd better be careful. They'd better be very careful indeed. A line is being drawn. I'm going to say it again, and very slowly. A line is being drawn. Quite quietly at present—just a few names jotted down in a notebook—one or two with a question mark after them. They have another chance. And the rest don't. Those lines mean something. Tatatat! Yes, my dears, bullets—real bullets, the kind of bullets they keep for reviewers who step across the party line. One day you're going to see something rather hostile. It will make you feel, perhaps, a little uneasy. It's heavy—and stubby—and rather pointed. Guess? Yes. A machine-gun. POINTED AT YOU. And behind it, with his hand on the trigger, Comrade—no, COMMISSAR—Cris Clay. Did you write such and such an article? Yes (No). It doesn't matter which. Tatatat. It's no good then bleating about how you voted in the last election, or where your sympathies have always been. We don't want your sympathy. We don't want you at all.

You subscribed to the *News-Chronicle*, did you? I am afraid you will be under no necessity to renew that subscription.

You wrote for the *New Statesman*? What did you write about? 'Gramophone records.'

'To sit on the fence is to be on the wrong side of it—line him up, Gollancz.'

'Yes, Commissar.'

'And you—what were you?'

'Turf-Accountant.'

'Your face seems vaguely familiar—but that doesn't make it more pleasant—line him up, Stephen.'

'It was no accident, Pryce-Jones, that you have lived near three royal palaces.'

'But—'

But I am anticipating. There are two ways to review a book like mine, a right and a wrong. The wrong way is to find fault with it, for then you find fault with the book clubs behind it, in fact, with your advertisers. And if I seem too clever it's because you're too stupid. Think it over. The right way is to praise it, and to quote from it in such a way that you can all learn my lesson. I stand no nonsense. Remember, my dears, a line is being drawn. Tatatat. See you at the Mass Observatory.

> Something is going to go, baby,
> And it won't be your stamp-collection.
> Boom!

And that I think could particularly be meditated by the Fascist Connolly.

Cris Clay.

Paris—Budapest—Panton St.
1936–1937.

Appendix III.
Baldur von Schirach

Script of radio play by Brian Howard

BALDUR VON SCHIRACH—corruptor of German youth. Second in the Black Gallery series broadcast by the B.B.C. Home Service on 21st May, 1942, 6.30–6.45 p.m. Written by Brian Howard, produced by Walter Rilla.

Characters

1st Narrator	Dr. Necker
2nd Narrator	Sharp voice (Goebbels')
Baldur von Schirach	Boy (2)
Nazi voice	Boy (3)
Woman teacher	Boy (4)
Little boy (1)	Girl
Children's chorus	German father

BLACK GALLERY (2)

ANNOUNCER: Black Gallery!
> (*F/U Signature, hold and to background for:*)

ANNOUNCER: Parents of Great Britain. This portrait of a Nazi is dedicated to you. During the course of the story, which is also the story of the perversion of a nation's Youth, you will hear quotations—names and addresses. Incidents will be reconstructed. The quotations are accurate. The incidents happened. It all happened. It is still happening. The man responsible for it is Baldur von Schirach.
> (*Signature tune up and out*)

1ST NARRATOR: When Hitler was fighting for power, power to establish his tyranny over the German people, he spoke, once, of his enemies as follows: he said—'These old fools who struggle against us don't matter in the least. What matters is the Youth of Germany. And we'll take the Youth.'
He took the Youth.
> (*Up marching feet, then down to background*)

1ST NARRATOR: He took them, all of them, and gave them into the care of a young man called Baldur von Schirach. Twelve days ago, Schirach was thirty-five. Twelve years ago, when he was twenty-three, Schirach was given supreme command of the Nazi Youth, boys and girls. He had nine years to do his work in—1930 to 1939. Nine years in which to turn the boy of ten into the soldier of nineteen—to turn the free happy children of Germany into the fanatical, slave army that was, in its turn, to enslave half Europe—

2ND NARRATOR: How did he do it? Like this. Listen to his own words—

(Fade out marching for.)

BALDUR VON SCHIRACH: Conscience is a Jewish invention. Like circumcision, it mutilates man. *(Pause)* We want fearless, vigorous, commanding, *cruel* young men—young men with the strength and beauty of *young beasts of prey!*

(Up marching, and down to background)

2ND NARRATOR: Those are his words. What else did he do?

The girls he dealt with easily enough. He sent them to schools in which five, and only five, subjects were taught. Geography and History—that is to say How and Why the Nordic Race is superior to all others. Singing—that is to say, songs about the same thing. And lastly, Eugenics and Domestic Science—that is to say, how to bear children and how to cook and shop. A year or two of this, and they were ready for their only real duty—to have babies, future soldiers. Marriage didn't matter. Unmarried mothers were to be honoured with the name of Hitler Brides. As for the boys, he taught them that any kind of school was a waste of time; that religion was ridiculous, and that the family counted so little in comparison with the State that they were to report their own parents to the Gestapo if the parents diaspproved of the new ideas. And then he set them marching—marching—

(Up marching, and down to background)

2ND NARRATOR: We know, now, towards what goal. Marching. Boys. Firstly, the Pimpfe, the little ones. Aged six to ten. In black uniforms ...

(A rough, deep military voice interrupts: slight foreign accent)

VOICE: Heil Hitler! Attention please. All Pimpfe attending the Young People's initiation ceremony at Castle Marksburg today week will march the last fifty miles. Each boy's Efficiency Record Book must be fully up-to-date. Especially important are records concerning Map-reading, Marching, Spy-Work, Shooting—both Bull's Eye and with the Stuffed Dummy—and Hand-Grenade Throwing.

2ND NARRATOR *(continuing)*: ... the Pimpfe marched on, at ten, into the Jungvolk, the Young People. The Young People marched on, at fourteen, into the Hitlerjugend, the Hitler Youth ...

VOICE *(interrupting)*: Heil Hitler! Attention please. Instructions for the preservation of the dignity of the Hitler Youth Uniform! From the age of six to eighteen no Hitler Youth is allowed to play any civilian game in uniform. No Hitler Youth is allowed to give any sign of recognition should he meet his parents while on duty.

2ND NARRATOR: ... the Hitler Youth marched on, at eighteen, and nineteen, into—what? Into civil life? No, Civil life had become a thing of the past, a thing for old people only. They marched into the Labour Camps; into the S.S., the Black-shirts, the Gestapo—

(At this point, the marching cross fades into the mutter of heavy gun-fire, which reaches its climax after the word 'Poland')

... into the Army—into 1939—into Poland!

(Guns out and slight pause)

1ST NARRATOR: I wonder if you are listening, Baldur von Schirach? If I know you, you are. Who am I, you ask? I am the Voice of the World, the World outside Nazi Germany, and her increasingly unhappy allies. I am the Voice of

Freedom, too, and that also is outside Germany. But don't think I shall always remain outside Germany. Today, I speak to you through the air, from a free country, in English. Tomorrow, sure as Fate, I will speak to you through your own windows, from a thousand angry throats . . .

You've managed to get hold of four rather expensive houses during these last few years, Baldur von Schirach. Which would you choose to be in, I wonder, when you first hear me speak to you in German? In the house in Crown Prince Street, Berlin? Difficult to get away unrecognised. In No. 2, Ballhausplatz, your palace as ruler of Vienna? It was an unlucky house for Dollfuss. In your villa on the Wannsee lake, near Berlin? Possibly, I think, though, you'd better choose your Bavarian country house, Urfuldam, near that much more beautiful lake, Walchensee. It's safer, closer to Switzerland. And, heaven knows, you've got a fast enough car to reach the frontier in one night . . .

2ND NARRATOR: . . . By the way, your Walchensee house used to be a monastery, didn't it? You never did like priests much, did you? Do you remember that verse in the poem you used to teach the other students at Munich University, when you were converting them for Hitler?

BALDUR VON SCHIRAGH: (*in chanting voice*): Sharpen the long knives on the pavement. Plunge the knives in the parson's body, and when the hour of retribution comes, we'll be ready for any massacre.

2ND NARRATOR: And then do you remember that lesson that you had taught in the schools? It was called 'Twenty Questions in Religion.' The Teacher asks the questions. Here are two of them—

WOMAN TEACHER: Who, children, is it that most reminds us of Jesus? Through his love of humble people and his readiness for self-sacrifice?

LITTLE BOY: The Fuehrer!

CHILDREN'S CHORUS: The Fuehrer!

WOMAN TEACHER: And who most reminds us of the disciples, because of their loyal attachment to the Fuehrer?

LITTLE BOY: General Goering, Doctor Goebbels, and Captain Roehm!

CHILDREN'S CHORUS: General Goering, Doctor Goebbels, and Captain Roehm!

1ST NARRATOR: Of course, Roehm had to be left out after 1934. You yourself got into trouble about that time, I remember. You had to disappear for a while, and Lauterbacher took over. Even the Generals began to accuse you of turning the children into soulless little barbarians. Which is what you were doing, of course. All sorts of other insinuations were made about you, too. But you got back into favour with Hitler all right. You set the Hitler Youth to burning the synagogues, and knocking down Jews in the street . . . but let's see how your career began. You joined the Nazis when you were seventeen, in Weimar. Goethe's town, of all places. It is said that you met Hitler first when you were a Brown Shirt, on guard outside the Elephant Hotel. He liked you because he is a snob, and you were a gentleman, and gentleman Nazis have always been difficult to find. That's how you began. But listen to another Weimar incident. Do you remember Dr. Necker?

DR. NECKER: I remember you, Baldur von Schirach. I and two friends went to a Nazi meeting in Weimar, in February, 1925. No discussion was allowed. Even then you didn't want to hear the other person's point-of-view. At the end of the meeting, I and my friends refused to join in singing your Nazi songs. You waited outside with eight men, armed with sticks. I gave you one blow, and you and your eight friends ran for your lives. Remember?

1ST NARRATOR: And then, in 1927, you went to Munich University, in order to be near your idol Hitler. You were supposed to study German art and literature there, but you'd long given up learning anything except how to persuade or threaten more of your student companions into the Nazi Party. You organised them into a jack-booted, whip-cracking gang who burnt books, instead of reading them. Next, you went to Universities all over Germany, wheedling and bullying. And you were rewarded. In 1930 you became State Youth Leader for the Nazis. During the next two years, you did two very shrewd things. You married Henny Hoffmann, and you organised the March Past of the Hitler Youth, at Potsdam—

(*Up sound of marching, with high-pitched cheering, and to background for*)

... Goebbels was there, too. He wrote in his diary—

GOEBBELS' SHARP VOICE: For six hours German Youth marches past the Leader. They are our pride and our joy. Always the same boys, with the same faces. The movement (*proudly*) has already fashioned a uniform type!

2ND NARRATOR: 'The same boys, with the same faces—A uniform type.' That was what you wanted, of course. You were getting it already. Same boys—same faces—same minds—same loves—same hates. A uniform type, with the strength and beauty of a young beast of prey. Potsdam was a great success, and so was your marriage. You married Henny Hoffmann, daughter of Hitler's privileged photographer. Hitler always had a kindly eye for Miss Hoffmann. But you and she knew that nothing would come of *that*. Also, there were reasons why it was time for you to marry, and what better than to marry into Hitler's immediate circle, to marry the daughter of perhaps his best friend? Incidentally, of course, you were marrying into the richest publishing monopoly in Europe—they publish *Mein Kampf*. Their books look very well on the drawing-room table if one isn't quite certain, for instance, of what the Gestapo think of one. They look so respectable. There's one book called 'Hitler as No One Knows Him.' Photographs by Hoffmann. Text by Baldur von Schirach. That one made a lot of money. Helped to buy one of your houses, no doubt. More than poets usually make. Every poem you write, by the way, is the same poem. Here is the last verse of one of them.

BALDUR VON SCHIRACH: Woe to the sons who, e'er their father's fame
        The great price paid, their duty plain ignore!
        The meaning of our lives let us proclaim:
        The war preserved us for the coming war.

1ST NARRATOR: And perhaps you wrote the Official Carol, that all the children of Germany have been made to sing since 1937?

BOY'S VOICE (*speaking*): With the bells in the tower
        Let us arise
        And fan the fires
        Which to Heaven shall rise,
        And bear our weapons—for the Year is new:
        War is the watchword! Make the watchword true!

382

1ST NARRATOR: You have made German Youth say, and sing, and shout, many things. You have taught them many things, you who have always been too busy educating others to remember to educate yourself. I am going to let one or two of your pupils speak to *you*—
(Fade up roll of muffled drums)
One or two out of hundreds, out of thousands. They would all tell the same story. Thousands, think of them—listen . . .
(Up muffled drums, and to background for:)
LITTLE BOY *(close on mike)*: I am dead. I was one of your small boys, your Pimpfe. I lived near the Wilmersdorferstrasse, Berlin, and I started to march to Leuchtenburg, where you had promised me a wonderful ceremony, and promotion to the Young People. My mother said I wasn't well when I started, but I was made to go, and was glad. I caught pneumonia, but I knew what my duty was. The Doctor tried to save me, but I fought him, and beat him. I shouted at him—'Let me die! Let me die for Hitler!'
I died. Just like a soldier, wasn't it. For Hitler. For you.
(Up very short muffled roll of drums, and to background for:)
GIRL: I am alive. I am one of the young women who was sterilised by the State because I was colour-blind, and might have born a colour-blind son, an inefficient soldier. It happened in the City Hospital for Women, Ziegelstrasse, Berlin. My child died before it was even conceived. For Hitler. For you.
(Up very short muffled roll, etc.)
BOY: I am dead. I was one of the weak-minded boys who are killed off in Germany now. I wasn't mad—I was just no good at anything much, not even marching and singing your songs. A State Doctor killed me in a little shed. The shed is part of a lovely estate on the Duebener Heath, near Leipzig. It's painted white, the shed is, and they told me it was called the Hitler Room. I don't think he can know about it. Do you, Herr State Youth Leader?
(Up very short muffled roll, etc.)
MAN: I am not quite alive, and not quite dead. I was never one of your Hitler Youth. And now I'm no longer anyone. I am one of the fathers of Germany who disappeared. I wanted my son to go to school more, and do less drilling and rifle-practice. I wanted him to grow up into an honourable, tolerant, and, if possible, wise man. I tried to counter your teaching with mine. My son betrayed me to the Gestapo. For Hitler. For you.
(Drums fade out)
1ST NARRATOR: You heard them, Baldur von Schirach. Think of them a little. And think, finally, of this. In 1941, in Breslau, you made a speech to the Hitler Youth. In order to give them the impression that it was a European gathering, you sent for a few boys—strangers—from the countries that Nazi Germany has occupied. You greeted these boys as brothers, brothers in what you called the new, the great, the coming Europe. You told them that their and your ideals were the same, and urged them to organise themselves in the same way. It wasn't a great success, that speech, was it? The only organising that's been done has been done by their fathers, and you've had to shoot them for it. And perhaps these boys felt that their and your ideals are *not* the same.

(Fade in gradually, the Reveille, on a trumpet, so that the last note lingers, quite loud, a few seconds after the Narrator's final word, the trumpet gaining in volume, but never drowning the Narrator's words.)

Perhaps they feel that their ideals are closer to the ideals of another group of young people which you seem to have forgotten. Infinitely larger in number, freer in spirit, happier in heart. The Youth of the new, the great, the coming World: from the Catskill Mountains in the United States, where your mother was born, to the mountains of China—*this* Youth *is* organising itself. Not for you, Baldur von Schirach. Against you, and against everything you stand for. You've seen some of them. You'll be seeing more. *Auf wiedersehen.*

Acknowledgments

As a party depends for success on its guests, so this book owes much to die generous help given by all the people implicated by way of new contributions, old letters, and extracts from published works referring to Brian Howard. First in the list must come the late Lura Howard who originally gave me permission to start this biography in 1964, making available the family papers, and her executors (who by Chain of Executorship are also Brian's), Mona Macdonell and Fay Blacket Gill, without whose subsequent permission I could not have completed the work. Mona Macdonell was particularly helpful in bringing back the larger part of the original material after her last Christmas visit to France, a few months before Mrs. Howard's death. Brian's first cousin, Carley Dawson, gave me unstinting help with details of family history and background as well as providing her valuable reminiscences.

Of all Brian's close friends I am most indebted to Harold Acton and John Banting. From the earliest days Harold Acton gave me much needed encouragement as well as permission to quote liberally from his *Memoirs of an Aesthete*. His fascinating collection of letters from Brian to himself and his brother, Willie, during their Eton and Oxford days (to my regret too many to be included *in toto*) provided the basis on which so much of this biography was built, and gave me an inside view of Brian's reaction to his early life and times. John Banting was the first person to start enlisting support for a biography, and as well as contributing his recollections of times past and many photographs he filled in innumerable missing details from the early days.

Of other close friends of Brian's I owe much to Heywood Hill, Benedict Nicolson, Cyril Connolly, and the late John Davenport. Heywood Hill introduced me to essential contacts and kindly advised on my first long draft MSS, while Ben Nicolson (whom Brian had wished to appoint with the late Peter Watson as his literary executor) did the same for the revised MSS. Cyril Connolly, apart from his evocative contribution to the 'thirties period ('Brummell at Calais' © by Cyril Connolly 1967) has kindly allowed me to quote from various letters, extracts from *Horizon* magazine, and *Porcupine* (an Eton ephemeral), from his *Enemies of Promise*, and to reproduce his complete essay *Where Engels fears to tread*. My old friend the late John Davenport was a constant source of information, although not always of the strictest veracity, but his help did much to smooth my path of research. He told me once with perspicacity that 'Brian's inside information was always rather outside—he laboured the wrong point', extenuating with 'We all have our private wars within, but so much of Brian's war was without'. John Davenport had promised to write a special piece assessing Brian's position as a creative writer, but regrettably never did put pen to paper other than to reply most promptly to my queries 'courtesy of the John Davenstein bureau!', or he would appear in person even more swiftly, if unexpectedly, to regale me with his inimitable stories of the long-lost golden days.

Maurice Richardson has been unsparing with his time and advice, while Philip Toynbee tirelessly read more than five times the amount of Brian's poetic output than is reproduced here in order to make his necessarily limited selection.

In my quest for family history I would like to acknowledge the help of the late Dr. Pierre Lansel who put me in contact with Brian's third cousin in America, Franklin Houston, whose mother's unpublished memoirs provided the key both to Brian's Gassaway grandfather's identity and his grandmother's changes of surname; and Professor Leonard W. Labaree, Editor of *The Papers of Benjamin Franklin* at Yale University Library, who went into great detail to investigate (with sadly negative results) Francis 'Tudie' Howard's claim to be a great-grandson of Benjamin Franklin. Both Dr. Edward Glover and Sir Geoffrey Marshall were kind enough to confirm references to their diagnoses of Brian's state of health during 1944/1948 and 1957 respectively.

I am greatly indebted to the following people for their contributions, confirmations, permission to quote from letters or published books, to reproduce photographs, or help over my numerous queries: Sir Colin Anderson (to whom Brian remains 'a perfect example of a 'twenties' figure, encased in rather clouded amber'); W. H. Auden for his kindness in confirming various references; Hermione Baddeley; Sandy Baird; the Trustees of the estate of the late Maurice Baring for his clerihew (1922); the Marquess of Bath; Cecil Beaton; Sybille Bedford for her background information and constant encouragement; John Betjeman for his suggested list of contacts to pursue; the Earl of Birkenhead; Messrs. Baker, Freeman for letters and Eton reports from the late G. H. Blakiston; Sir Maurice Bowra; Lord Bridges for the postcard from his father, the late Robert Bridges; Messrs. C. & T. Publications for letters from the late Sir Winston Churchill to the late Francis Howard; Alan Clutton-Brock; Claud Cockburn for his wonderfully funny stories about Brian (alas, too ephemeral for *me* to catch in print, and I was unable to prevail upon *him* to do so); Reginald Colby for producing his original copy of the *Cherwell* containing Brian's famous *Postscript* essay (this issue being missing from the bound copy in the British Museum newspaper library); the Administratrix of the estate of the late Nancy Cunard for extracts from *Black Man and White Ladyship* (1931), Spanish War poetry leaflet, *Authors take sides* Left Review pamphlet (1937), and Brian's *First Poems* published by her Hours Press (1930/1931); G. Day Lewis; the late Robin de la Condamine, Anton (Pat) Dolin; Tom Driberg, MP, for information, especially about the 'twenties; Lord Faringdon; Hon. Mrs. Xan Fielding; Constantine FitzGibbon; Theodora FitzGibbon (now Mrs. George Morrison); Hon. Edward Gathorne-Hardy; William Gaunt; Wolcott Gibbs Jr. for the letter from his father, the late Wolcott Gibbs; the late Sir Victor Gollancz; Messrs. Heinemann for the letter from the late Sir Edmund Gosse; Graphic Display Unit for lending their early gramophone for photography; Terence Greenidge; Méraud Guevara; Gerald Hamilton; Allanah Harper, Sir Roy Harrod; Norman Hartnell; Wyn Henderson; Hon. David Herbert; Lady Anne Hill; John Hill; Martin R. Holmes for the letter from his father, the late Sir C. J. Holmes; Christopher Isherwood; John B. S. (Jock) Jardine; Lord Jessel; J. Francis (Jack)

Jones for his *Taras II* yacht plans; Sir Gerald Kelly; Barbara Ker-Seymer; Lord Kinross for information about the 'twenties and the loan of his book, *Society Racket—a critical survey of modern social life* (published by John Long in 1933), which so succinctly put the period into perspective for me; Jim Knapp-Fisher; Osbert Lancaster for his cartoon; Basil Leng; Sir Shane Leslie; Erika Mann; Kingsley Martin; Hugh Massingham; Oliver Messel; Hon. Nancy Mitford; Ivan Moffat; Patrick Monkhouse; Raymond Mortimer; Hon. Lady Mosley; Mary Moss (Mrs. Humphrey Cameron); Lord Moyne; Joyce Murchie; Michael Nelson; Mrs. Ernest Newman for the letter from her husband, the late Ernest Newman; Mark Ogilvie-Grant; Rosemary Olivier for extracts from the late Edith Olivier's unpublished journals, and *Mildred*, a symposium privately printed by the High House Press, Shaftesbury (1926); Mrs. Ralph (Frances) Partridge for the loan of photographs from Lytton Strachey's and her husband's albums; William Plomer; Anthony Powell; V. S. Pritchett; Alan Pryce-Jones; Peter Quennell for so rightly advising me against my original idea of a symposium and towards a more *Quest for Corvo* treatment; the Radio Times Hulton Picture Library for photographs of the late Edith Sitwell, Evelyn Waugh and Elizabeth Ponsonby, also of Hermione Baddeley and Tom Driberg; Hon. Mrs. Joan Rayner for her sympathetic help. She was one of Brian's favourite companions and I would like to pay tribute to her unfailing friendship with Brian throughout the bad as well as the good times; Gerald Reitlinger; Walter Rilla; Donald Rolph for the loan of his original Greek Party invitation; the Earle of Rosse; John Russell; the late Lord Sackville, who wrote from Ireland only two months before his death that he would give me his impressions and memories of Brian 'for what they are worth' when next in London . . .; the Executors of the late Dame Edith Sitwell © 1967 for her letters; Sir Osbert Sitwell; G. E. Muller of Spink & Son for the Taras coin photograph; Stephen Spender; James Stern; John Strachey; the late Romney Summers; John Sutro; Christopher Sykes; Hon. David Tennant; Pauline Tennant (Mrs. Euan Graham); Transacphot of Malbosc, Grasse for the photograph of Le Verger; Simon Ward-Jackson for the loan of his ephemeral, *Porcupine* (1963); Annette Watney; Sir Norman Watson Bt. for letters from his brother, the late Peter Watson; the late Evelyn Waugh; Laurence Whistler; W. D. (Bill) Wickson; R. H. Wilenski; Emlyn Williams; Sir Martin Wilson; Leonard Woolf; T. C. (Cuthbert) Worsley; Violet Wyndham; Henry 'Green' Yorke.

The following have kindly given permission for me to quote from published copyright material: Messrs. Alden & Blackwell (*Eton College Chronicle*, 1922); the Editor of the *Architectural Review* (extracts, 1930); Messrs. Batsford (Peter Quennell's commentary in *Time Exposure*, 1941); Oxford University Student Publications (extracts from *Cherwell*, 1924–1927); Beaverbrook Newspapers (extracts from the *Daily Express*, *Evening Standard*, *Sunday Dispatch*, *Sunday Express* and *Weekly Dispatch*, 1925–1929); Messrs. Chapman & Hall (Evelyn Waugh's *A Little Learning*, 1964); Messrs. Eyre & Spottiswoode (Daphne Fielding's *Mercury Presides*, 1954); Messrs. Gollancz (Klaus Mann's *Turning Point—thirty-five years in this century*, 1944); Messrs. Harcourt, Brace & World (James Stern's *Hidden Damage*, © 1947 James Stern); the Editor of *Harper's Bazaar*, U.S. edition (extract, 1932); Messrs. Methuen (Harold Acton's *Memoirs of an Aesthete*, 1948); the Editor of the *New Statesman* (numerous extracts, 1930–1947); Times

Newspapers (Alan Pryce-Jones' obituary tribute in *The Times*, 1958); Messrs. A. D. Peters (Evelyn Waugh's review in *Night & Day* magazine, published by Chatto & Windus, 1937); Messrs. Weidenfeld & Nicolson (Sir Maurice Bowra's *Memories 1898–1939*, 1966). I would also like to thank the staff of the Westminster Central Reference Library for their assistance at all times.

Finally my grateful thanks are due to my secretary, Anne Carswell, who gave up so much of her time to typing out the early extracts, and most of all to my long-suffering husband, Maurice, who never once complained of the paraphernalia of overflowing file boxes engendered by all biographers, or of my neglect of his comfort while burying myself in what has inevitably been a time-consuming labour of love.

London, 1964–1967   Marie-Jaqueline Lancaster

Index

Ducasse, Isidore (Comte de Lautreamont), 197
Duguid, John, 120
Dulac, Edmund, 8, 56
Dundas, R. H., 124
Duse, Eleonora, 203
Duveen (a brother of late Lord Duveen), 80

Eden, Sir Anthony (Earl of Avon), 156, 317
Edison, Thomas, 7
Einstein, Albert, 197, 205, 317
Eliot, T. S., xv, 36, 53, 80, 90, 174–5, 177, 223, 228, 335
Elmley, Viscount (8th Earl Beauchamp), 122
Empson, William, 173
Encounter, 310
Enemies of Promise, xi, 72, 232
Epstein, Sir Jacob, 37, 39
Eton Candle, The, xiv, 3–4, 19, 21, 24, 31–4, Chapter 4 *passim*, 64, 72, 74, 115, 131, 322, 337, 341–2
Eton College, Chapters 3, 4, 5 and 6 *passim*, 109, 115, 121–2, 132, 203, 236, 240, 254, 256, 259, 266, 324, 333
Eton College Chronicle, 33, 35, 53
Evans, Sidney, 25
Evening Standard, 161–2, 212
Everyman, 202

Façade, 36, 44, 47
Fagan, J. B., 79
Faringdon, Lord (Gavin Henderson), 112, 138
Faulkner, William, 229, 317
Femina, 66
Feuchtwanger, Lion, 226, 237
Feuerbach, Anselme, 146
Fielden, Lionel, 306
Fielding, Hon. Mrs. Xan (née Daphne Vivian, 1st m. Viscount Weymouth), x, 92, 94–5, 98–100, 137, 146, 153, 361
Firbank, Ronald, xiii, 37, 104, 119, 165, 172, 236, 284
First Poems (or *God Save the King arid other poems*), by B.H., 4, 91, 172, 183, 335, Appendix I
Fitzgerald, F. Scott, 285
FitzGibbon, Constantine, 225
FitzGibbon, Theodora (Mrs. George Morrison), 252, 278
Flecker, James Elroy, 36
Flint, F. S., 36, 39, 42

Fokine, Michel, 80
Forbes, Rosita (Mrs. A. T. McGrath), 147
Ford, Iris, 65
Forster, E. M., 317
Franco, General, 221–2, 232, 313, 358
Frank, Bruno, 205
Franklin, Benjamin, 5
Freud, Sigmund, 149, 205, 228

Garman, Douglas, 173
Garnett, David, 233
Gassaway, Francis Harrison 'Tudie', see F. H. G. Howard
Gassaway, Frank Harrison (Brian's grandfather), xi, xiv, 5, 6, 303f
Gathorne-Hardy, Hon. Edward, 4, 159–60, 162, 181–2, 185, 210, 241, 327
Gathorne-Hardy, Hon. Robert, 173
Gaunt, William, 175–6
Gebser, Hans, 221
George II, King of Greece, 156
George, Stefan, 194, 298
Gibbon, Edward, 140–1, 283
Gibbs, Wolcott, 285–7
Gide, André, 181, 191, 194, 239, 364
Gielgud, Sir John, 101
Glover, Dr. Edward, 273–5, 290
Gobineau, Comte (Joseph-Arthur de), 227
God save the King poem by B.H., xv, 4, 172, 331, 335–6, 344–5
God save the King and other poems, see *First Poems*
Goebbels, Dr. Paul, 227, 232
Goering, Field-Marshal Herman, 192
Goethe, Wolfgang, 140, 145, 364
Golden Key (ballet), 103
Gollancz, Sir Victor, 220, 226
Gorki, Maxim, 229
Gosse, Sir Edmund, 3, 31, 54
Gow, A. S. F., 32–3
Graham, Mrs. Euan (née Pauline Tennant), 251–2
Grant, General, 6
Grant, Duncan, 195
Graphic weekly, 175
Graves, Robert, 40, 154, 188
Green, Evy, 305
Green, Henry (Henry Yorke), 73–4, 127, 152, 178
Green, Julien, 178
Grosvenor, Hugh (4th Duke of Westminster), 106, 108, 122
Grosz, George, 175–6
Guedalla, Philip, 104